The Other God

YURI STOYANOV

THE OTHER GOD

DUALIST RELIGIONS FROM ANTIQUITY TO THE CATHAR HERESY

YALE NOTA BENE
YALE UNIVERSITY PRESS
NEW HAVEN AND LONDON

To my parents

На моите родитепи

First published as a Yale Nota Bene book in 2000
Copyright © 2000 by Yuri Stoyanov
First published as *The Hidden Tradition in Europe: the Secret History of Medieval Christian Heresy* in 1994 by the Penguin Group

For information about this and other Yale Univesity Press publications, please contact:
U.S. office: sales.press@yale.edu
Europe office: sales@yaleup.co.uk

Set in 10/12 pt Adobe Garamond by Northern Phototypesetting Co. Ltd, Bolton
Printed in the United States of America

Library of Congress Cataloging-in-Publication Data
Stoyanov, Yuri, 1961–
The other God : dualist religions from antiquity to the Cathar heresy / Yuri Stoyanov.
p. cm.
Rev. ed. of: The hidden tradition in Europe. 1994.
Includes bibliographical references and index.
ISBN 0-300-08253-3 (pbk.)
1. Heresies, Christian—History. I. Stoyanov, Yuri, 1961– . The hidden tradition in Europe. II. Title.
BT1315.2 S76 2000   273'.6—dc21   00-042833 CIP

A catalogue record is available from the British Library.

ISBN 0-300-08253-3 (pbk.)

2 4 6 8 19 9 7 5 3

Contents

CONTENTS

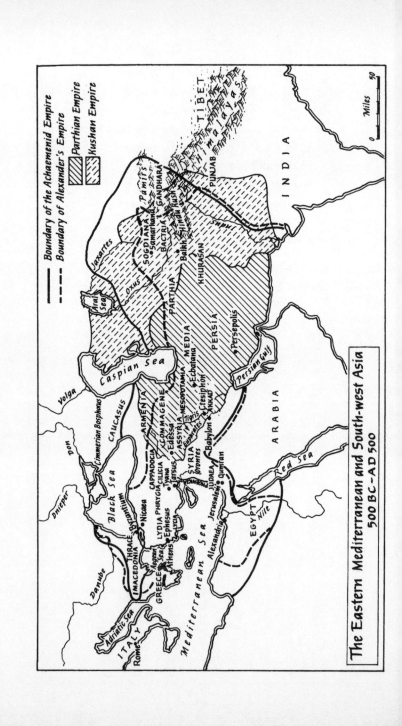

The Eastern Mediterranean and South-west Asia
500 BC – AD 500

Boundary of the Achaemenid Empire
Boundary of Alexander's Empire
Parthian Empire
Kushan Empire

0   50
Miles

ITALY
Rome
Adriatic Sea
Danube
Dnieper
Don
Volga
Cimmerian Bosphorus
CAUCASUS
Black Sea
Byzantium
Nicaea
THRACE
MACEDONIA
Aegean Sea
GREECE
Athens
Ephesus
LYDIA PHRYGIA
LYCIA
CAPPADOCIA
CILICIA
Tarsus
ARMENIA
COMMAGENE
Edessa
ASSYRIA
SYRIA
Orontes
Euphrates
Tigris
MESOPOTAMIA
Babylon
AKKAD
Ctesiphon
MEDIA
Ecbatana
PERSIA
Persepolis
Persian Gulf
Caspian Sea
Aral Sea
Jaxartes
Oxus
SOGDIANA
Samarkand
Pamirs
BACTRIA
Balkh
Hindu Kush
GANDHARA
KHURASAN
PARTHIA
TIBET
HIMALAYAS
PUNJAB
Indus
INDIA
ARABIA
Red Sea
Nile
EGYPT
Alexandria
JUDAEA
Jerusalem
Qumran
Mediterranean Sea

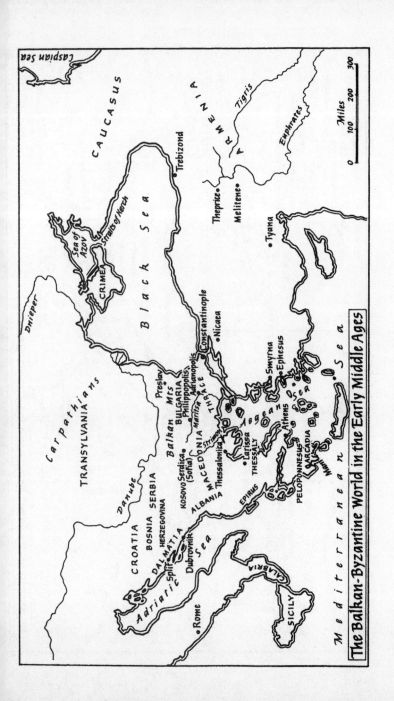

The Balkan-Byzantine World in the Early Middle Ages

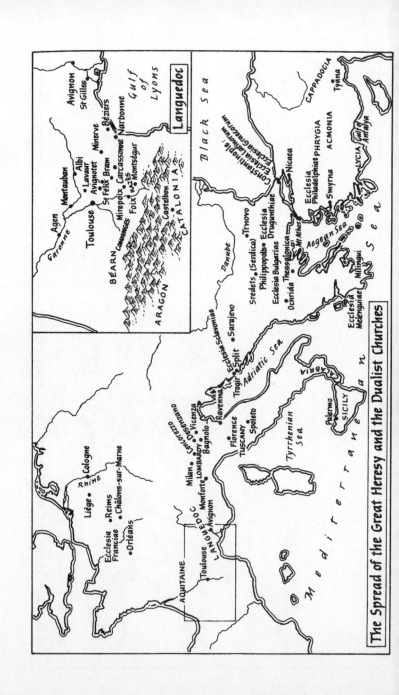

The Spread of the Great Heresy and the Dualist Churches

Languedoc

Preface

The title of the first edition of this book alluded to a medieval heretical and inquisitorial notion that European dualist heresy derived from a tradition that was 'hidden' or 'concealed' and transmitted in secrecy from late antiquity onwards. In the Catholic/Orthodox view this tradition was mostly recognized as Manichaeism, occasionally in combination with other ancient heresies, whereas according to the dualist heretics it was the tradition of the early Christian apostles before it became corrupted by the Church. Hence, in some contexts the recovery of this 'hidden' tradition can be seen as the revealing of a kind of 'secret history', an attempt to reconstruct suppressed or concealed undercurrents of religious development from meagre or hostile sources and allusions.

However, my earlier book explored not only the posited chain of transmission of Gnostic-Manichaean doctrines from late antiquity to the Middle Ages, postulated as early as the emergence of medieval anti-heretical literature, but offered further an investigation of the important dualist religious currents in antiquity, given their potential, if contested, role in the emergence of dualist trends in early Judaism and early Christianity. Therefore, the new title and sub-title of this expanded, revised and updated edition (which now includes, among other material, treatments of the movement towards dualism in ancient Egyptian religion and of the growing association between magic and heresy in late antiquity) better reflect its contents, time-scale and scope of enquiry.

Dualist religions in antiquity sought to redefine, often radically, the interrelationships between the divine, human and natural worlds, commonly by identifying the source of evil in a force or forces in the divine and supernatural sphere. An ambiguous deity or one associated with death and the underworld was an obvious choice to be singled out and enthroned as an entirely evil agency or else an altogether new deity was conceptualized to fill the place of this 'other' god. Religions that were monist and henotheistic in orientation could develop the tendency to view this 'other' god as the main adversary of the creator god, effectively as an anti-god, but this process was to be accomplished in some of the systems of religious dualism. While during late antiquity Christianity and Judaism naturally strove to deny an actual godly status to the 'other god', heretical teachings ventured to identify his functions with that of the creator god, stating that above him, the public, normative god, there existed another, hidden god, the god of the invisible world or the world to come. Such heretical doctrines were promptly condemned for rendering the evil divine, for granting a godly status to 'another' god, whether confusingly understood as the oppressive creator of this world or as the ruler of the realm above and of the future.

The cross-currents and distorted borrowings between the orthodox and heretical trends within a religion or between different religions in antiquity and the Middle Ages present a complex and bewildering picture. This is one of the reasons why the various dualist religious currents from antiquity to the Middle Ages are here considered largely chronologically – not because the book follows the diffusionist theory that seeks the source of religious dualism, for example, in a single posited dualist heartland like Iran, but because such an approach allows for a more accessible and arguably historically more balanced exposition of the development of religious ideas over a great period of time. Such an approach allows, moreover, for the arguments of the diffusionist theory to be put to the test at each stage of the enquiry, while simultaneously identifying with varying degrees of certainty what are the likely main historical and religious factors behind the emergence of a new dualist religious trend or sectarian development. Such a method of historical investigation would seem to be more rewarding than simply treating the various dualist currents in ancient and medieval religions in a religio-historical vacuum, as outcomes of a recurrently dysfunctional mental predisposition to view reality from within the framework of oppositional dualities.

This book has endeavoured to cover the present state of research and debate at each significant phase of development of dualist religious ideas in antiquity and the Middle Ages, thus encompassing as many newly opened, promising fields for further exploration in the areas covered as possible. Finally, as has been consistently shown by some new developments both in the mainstream and within sub-cultures of current living religions, the religious currents discussed in this book may shed further light on the religious and spiritual dynamism underlying the oddly fascinating and seemingly endless search for the identity of 'the other god'.

CHAPTER ONE

The Bridge of the Separator

Two Principles

With the establishment, expansion and consolidation of the monotheistic orthodoxies of Christianity, rabbinic Judaism and Islam, other religious traditions, displaying with varying intensity a dualism routinely attacked by its monistic critics as the teaching of the two principles, began to decline and even disappear from their traditional spheres of influence in Mediterranean Europe and the Near East. This process seemed to have accelerated in the early medieval period but during the High Middle Ages dualist religiosity in Europe was resurrected, mainly through the missionary efforts of the Bogomil and Cathar heresies. Centuries after orthodox Christianity had formally triumphed over its main dualist adversary, Manichaeism, the only universal religion to emerge from the great spiritual turmoil in third-century Mesopotamia, the ecclesiastical and secular elites of medieval Christendom had to pursue what they saw as a re-fight of the battle against its revived ancient foe. In Manichaeism, the traditional dualist religious vision which divided divine reality and the world into two opposed realms of good and evil was further magnified and reached extremely elaborate and influential expression. What is more, Mani, the founder of Manichaeism, proclaimed that his intricate dualist system formed the core of all religions and underlay the teachings of Zoroaster, Buddha and Christ. Before it reached this universalist phase, the dualist tradition had passed through a centuries-old evolution in Iran and the eastern Mediterranean world and its Manichaean incarnation was destined to spread from Mesopotamia to north Africa and Mediterranean Europe and further to the Far East.

Manichaeism was and is commonly invoked by its adversaries and explorers as the classical doctrine of the two principles and both within what is now recognized as religious dualist traditions and in other religious currents dualism is often defined along the same or similar lines. According to the celebrated Cathar tract *The Book of the Two Principles*, besides the good principle, as manifested in God and Jesus Christ, there is another principle, 'one of evil, who is mighty in iniquity, from whom the power of Satan and of darkness and all other powers which are inimical to the true Lord God are exclusively and essentially derived'. The tract elaborates an exhaustive theological defence of divine justice and omnipotence in the face of the presence of evil in the world. In this dualist theodicy the cosmos is viewed as the outcome and the battleground of two opposed principles, good and evil or light and darkness. Among its numerous and varied arguments for the coexistence of the principles of good and evil the tract refers to Jesus saying in Matthew (7:17–18), 'but a corrupt tree bringeth forth evil fruit. A good tree cannot bring forth evil fruit, neither can a corrupt tree bring forth good fruit' (*KJP*).

'Dualism' has a different usage in philosophical-historical and religio-historical contexts which will require some clarification. The term 'dualism' itself was introduced in 1700 by Thomas Hyde to describe religious systems such as Manichaeism that conceive of God and the devil as two coeternal principles.[1] Following Hyde's terminological innovation, however, Christian Wolff introduced the term into philo-sophical discourse to define philosophical systems like Deckart's which posit that mind and matter are two distinct substances.[2] Subsequently, the term came into use for philosophical descriptions and discussions of Cartesianism, the mind–body problem and doctrines of transcendence. In more general terms, the term dualism came to be applied also to philo-sophical systems which contained important pairs of oppositions like that of Plato, with its dualities between the mortal body and the immortal soul, or the world perceived by the senses and the world of eternal ideas, comprehended by the mind; or the Kantian distinction between the phenomenal and the noumenal world.

This use of the term 'dualism' in the framework of philosophical discourse and *vis-à-vis* the various forms of monism, as well as in broader socio-cultural contexts, has to be distinguished from its particular religio-historical significance. But even when treated within a religio-historical context religious dualism needs further terminological clarification.[3] Early attempts to define dualism as an intermediate phase of passage between polytheism and monotheism, a reaction against monotheism or 'rebellion against the world', have been superseded by a more systematic approach to the investigation of its diffusion and principal forms. Studies of individual religious traditions and in the field of comparative religion have demonstrated that dualist tendencies exist in polytheistic, monistic and monotheistic religions, whether as a pronounced characteristic, a rudimentary development or as professed by sectarian and marginal groups. However, dualist tendencies or mere ethical dualism cannot be equated with religious dualism proper.

In the case of the theology of medieval Christian dualist heresies, for example, insofar as Bogomilism and Catharism derive good and evil from two opposite principles, which are also seen as causes of the creation of the world and man, they belong to the tradition of religious dualism and are to be distinguished from religious traditions that merely accentuate the contrast between good and evil as moral opposites or that between the related traditional binary pairs of light and darkness, life and death, etc. On the other hand, the focus on the fundamental antagonism and irreducible cosmic conflict between the two supernatural agencies in Bogomil and Cathar dualism differentiates it from binary and binitarian theologies where the interaction between primary or divine polarities can be non-antagonistic and complementary.

Among the religious systems which do emphasize in various degrees what has been described as 'dual symbolic classification',[4] drawing on the polarity between primary and traditional pairs of opposites, several accentuate the complementary nature of some or most of these, while other traditions may give priority to the notion of struggle and contrariety between the opposites. But even where binary and binitarian theologies use such dual symbolic classification to accentuate the notion of contrariety and conflict between two opposing pairs, relating them respectively to two supernatural protagonists, they cannot still be defined as representative of religious dualism, unless both these principles are involved in the demiurgic acts of cosmogony and anthropogeny. Unlike binary theologies which can elaborate the notion of two supernatural principles associated with a binary system of opposites but without correlating them with the comogonic/anthropogenic process, mature Bogomil and Cathar theologies systematically develop the dualism of the two causal principles.

This dichotomy will apply not only to the 'high' religious systems such as Zoroastrianism, Judaism, Christianity and the various Gnostic

THE OTHER GOD

traditions but also to the cosmogonies of pre-literate cultures in Eurasia and North America in those cases where there emerges a second demiurgic figure, a demiurge-trickster, who moves from a position of collaboration with the first demiurge to one of active opposition to him, expressed also in his own counter-creations.[5] The dichotomy seems particularly evident when some of these cosmogonies associate a divine pair of twins or brothers with the cosmogonic process: in certain cases they are perceived as acting in a complementary relationship but in others there is a definite transition to dualism, as the twins may be seen as involved in rivalry and opposition (often manifested in the respective creations), one of them being identified as a bad twin or a type of a demiurge-trickster[6] (divine twinship mythologies are, moreover, frequently related to the system of a dual social organization of the respective peoples).[7]

The core of religious dualism usually lies in the cosmic battle between the forces of good and evil and while expounding the course of the all-embracing collision between the two principles, the different versions of religious dualism may furnish contrasting solutions to the principal theological riddles of divine reality, creation and the origins of evil. Within the manifold tradition of religious dualism Ugo Bianchi's typology of dualism,[8] which provides the most systematic treatment of the matter, defines three important lines of distinction. The first such line distinguishes radical or absolute dualism from moderate or mitigated dualism. According to absolute dualism, as developed, for example, by medieval Zoroastrianism and Manichaeism, good and evil, light and darkness derive from two independent coeternal principles, irreducibly set against each other from eternity. In moderate or 'monar-chian' dualism, represented, for example, by some of the classical Gnostic systems such as Valentinianism, one of the two principles is seen as a secondary agency stemming from the other principle which is thus recognized as a sublime first cause.

The second line of distinction concerns the temporal framework within which the two principles function in opposition to each other. In dialectic dualism they are seen as acting eternally in what is often perceived as a cyclical and repetitive process of time. In eschatological dualism, with its focus on the eschatological events and ultimate purification of the world at the end of historical time, the evil principle is destined to be vanquished in these last times and thus is not recognized

4

as an eternal agency.

The third line of distinction is related to the attitude to the physical world and matter. In cosmic dualism, as exemplified by Zoroastrianism, the physical world is treated essentially as a beneficent creation of the good principle, hence as a 'Good Creation'; although assaulted by evil, sin and death, it is designed to bring about the ultimate destruction of the evil agency. Conversely, anti-cosmic dualism equates the physical world and matter with the principle of evil and darkness which are seen as totally opposed to the spiritual world and light. Anti-cosmic dualism is usually strongly anti-somatic, relegating the body to the evil world of matter and opposing it to the soul, the latter having its origin in the realm of light and spiritual good. Anti-cosmic dualism reached its most dramatic and evocative incarnation in the mythological systems of some Gnostic schools where the rejection of a Creator-God (the Demiurge) and his universe assumed extreme and occasionally drastic forms.

The Platonic type of soul–body duality, as advanced in Plato's dialogues *Timaeus* and *Phaedo*, came to influence important Jewish and Christian traditions. A dualist spirit–matter opposition along with a rigorous asceticism was cultivated in the esoteric-initiatory trends of Orphism and Pythagoreanism in antiquity. The Orphic-Pythagorean teaching which explains the physical body as a tomb for the divine and immortal soul is shared in the Gnostic type of religiosity with its implicit focus on the rescue of the 'divine spark' in man from the bodily prison in which it was trapped by the Demiurge – a preoccupation shared by the medieval Bogomil and Cathar heresies.

In certain religious traditions diverse types of dualism could coalesce and appear in tortuous combinations with monotheistic and polytheistic conceptions. What is more, within the framework of the development of some religious traditions, there can be detected a transition from dualist tendencies or notions of duality to the dualism of the irreconcilable cosmic opposites or a reversal of this process – a neutralization of the dualist elements implicit or developed in earlier stages of the religion. A telling illustration of the first process can be discerned in ancient Egyptian religion in which earlier traditions of two-in-one polarity and equilibrium of cosmic contraries gradually were translated into a dualism of mutually exclusive principles, particularly in the case of the opposition between the gods Osiris/Horus-Seth, in the later versions of which Seth was isolated as a negative force that could not be reintegrated into the divine totality.

Two in One

Like other ancient religious systems Egyptian religion attributed a variety of mythological and symbolical meanings to the pairing and alternation of light and darkness which was also an important feature of archaic Egyptian cosmogonies. In the doctrine of creation at Hermopolis, the cult centre of Thoth, the lunar god of writing and knowledge, two of the eight primal gods, Kuk and Kauket, are associated with darkness and were depicted as swimming with the other six primeval deities 'in the darkness of father Nun', the watery abyss.[9] While all eight gods are portrayed as those who created light, the 'dark' deities, Kuk and Kauket, are given strongly beneficent roles, respectively bringing into life the light and the sunrise and making the night and calling the day into being.[10] As light is seen as coming into existence after and out of darkness, the latter indeed 'can be regarded as a necessary prerequisite for its existence'.[11]

The cosmogonic doctrine at Heliopolis, the 'city of the sun' and ancient cult centre of the sun god Re, can also depict the 'shining' creator god, Atum, as emerging not only from the primeval ocean of Nun but also from darkness.[12] To bring order into his creation, Atum's demiurgic exploits apparently include the overpowering of the serpent-dragon of chaos, Apopis, one of the serpents that emerged from the primordial darkness. This opposition and struggle in the beginning was reflected further in the daily fight between the sun god Re and the monstrous Apopis, now threatening Re's solar barque, in the mythical explication of the daily process of the 'death' and re-birth of the sun – one of the central preoccupations of Egyptian religiosity. Accordingly, in the Coffin Texts, the ways which the deceased needs to find through the darkness of the Afterworld can be likened to the paths which Atum's creative forces of light pierced through the primal darkness.[13] The deceased can also be depicted as aspiring to join the hosts of Re and to take part in his battle to 'disperse darkness'.[14] The themes of life-giving light and of light banishing darkness were understandably strong in the near-monotheistic religion of the reformer-pharaoh Akhenaten, with its exclusive focus on the solar cult and the solar disk, Aten. In the subsequent reaction against Akhenaten's religious innovations, however the overturn of his reforms and the suppression of his religion could be conveyed within the framework of the victory of light over darkness.[15]

In other Egyptian religious traditions the dichotomy of light and darkness can be used to render the oppositional pairs health/suffering or vitality/impotence (or to denounce Egypt's foreign enemies as 'children of darkness'), but still in cosmogonic terms, darkness was seen as the original form of light. The idea of the transformation of light into darkness as well as another Egyptian cosmogonic notion, which envisaged the primeval darkness as encircling the created universe, survived in some tracts of the Hermetic literature which was composed in Roman Egypt and synthesized Egyptian and Greek traditions.[16] Another cosmogonic duality that Hermetic thought seems to have inherited from Egyptian sources is the complementary pair of the creator-god, manifesting himself as a cosmic intelligence (*nous*), and the demiurge, the mediating 'divine word' (*logos*), who was also styled 'son of god' or 'second god' and sometimes identified with the sensible cosmos.[17]

This Egyptian treatment of the pairing of light and darkness generally justifies the view that early Egyptian theology was 'completely free of those logics which eliminate one of the two contradictory concepts and press religious ideas into dogmas',[18] providing further evidence for the 'deeply rooted Egyptian tendency to understand the world in dualistic terms as a series of pairs of contrasts balanced in unchanging equilibrium'.[19] In Egyptian religiosity light and darkness are seen as parts of the same cosmic totality and a pronounced tendency to retain or attain balance, symmetry or equilibrium between the two elements of other polarities or dualities has been repeatedly discerned in other spheres of Egyptian religious life. Such a worldview, that the totality has to comprise the union of opposites and be structured by their interaction, is not, of course, limited to ancient Egypt but it finds its most systematic and consistent manifestation in Egyptian theology, mythology and state ideology, with their systems of correlations and correspondences between the cosmological and political realms which extended to the organization of Egyptian state bureaucracy.

This strong tendency to apply a duality of principles active in opposition and equilibrium on the cosmological and mythological plane to the political sphere can also be observed in one of the principal cycles of Egyptian myths which recounts the violent opposition, struggle and recon-ciliations between Osiris and Horus on one side and Seth on the other. Different aspects of the myths are known from various and sometimes diverse accounts, fragments and occasional enigmatic allusions in Egyptian religious and magical texts and inscriptions on temple walls, ranging from the ancient Pyramid Texts, the Coffin Texts, the Shabaka Stone and the Chester Beatty Papyrus No 1 (containing the legend known as *The Contention of Horus and Seth*) to inscriptions on the walls of the great Horus temple at Edfu, which narrates along with the ritual priestly routine the dramatic *Legend of the Winged Disc* and *The Triumph of Horus*. Late narrative variants of the celebrated antagonism of Osiris or Horus with Seth can be found in classical literature such as Plutarch's *De Iside et Osiride*.

The reconstruction of the religious dynamism and the theological or historical reality behind the legendary cycle is made difficult by the inevitable obscurities that surround the early fortunes and evolution of the cults of Osiris, Horus and Seth in ancient Egypt. Both Osiris and Seth were members of the Great Ennead, the nine gods of the cosmogony of Heliopolis and both were sons of the earth god, Geb, and the sky goddess, Nut, who first generated Osiris and his sister-wife, Isis, and after that brought forth Seth and his sister-wife, Nephtys. Both the Pyramid Texts and Plutarch affirm that even from his birth, Seth manifested his fateful proclivity to fierceness and disorder, according to Plutarch, by suddenly breaking through his mother's side and thus affecting the order of creation – unsurprisingly, he came to be feared as the 'angry and howling god'. In general terms, the myth of Osiris' death extols him as a wise king and bringer of civilization whose fame and blissful royal marriage to his sister, Isis, earned him the undying envy and hatred of his younger brother, the violent Seth (there are mythic traditions, however, known also to Plutarch, that Osiris and Nephtys had an adulterous love affair discovered by Seth). In Plutarch's version, along with his accomplices Seth devised a devious plot to kill Osiris and take their sister Isis as his own wife. Osiris was tricked into entering a chest which Seth then sealed with molten lead and cast into the Nile (according to the earlier versions Osiris is simply killed or drowned). Eventually, Isis was able to recover the chest containing the body of Osiris but Seth again came upon the body of his brother, and this time he cut it into fourteen or sixteen pieces which he dispersed all over Egypt (or in other versions, Osiris' remains were thrown into the Nile). Assisted by her mourning sister Nephtys, the widowed Isis resumed her search for the scattered remains of Osiris, establishing traditions of Osiris worship in the temples situated in the localities where the remains were discovered. The body of Osiris was ultimately reassembled (according to Plutarch, except for his genitals), and partially resurrected: he became the first ritually embalmed being and the archetypal mummy (an act performed on some occasions by Thoth and/or the funerary jackal-headed god, Anubis). Osiris now became lord of the Afterworld and judge of the dead. Destined to inherit his patrimony in Egypt was his son and would-be avenger, Horus, whom Isis had conceived magically while journeying with Osiris' corpse and secretly reared in the swamps of the Delta (in other accounts Horus was conceived before Seth's murder of Osiris). Horus, the son of Isis, eventually coalesced with the supreme sky falcon-god, known as Horus the Elder, with all his strong links with the solar and royal cult, and in this form entered cosmological and theological traditions. The ensuing struggles between Horus and Seth, with their dramatic twists and turns, are recounted in different versions in which they can be portrayed as the celebrated pair of 'The Two Great Ones', 'The Two Gods', 'The Two Fighters', 'The Two Brothers' or 'The Doors'. When they are described as 'Two Brothers', Seth figures as the elder, thus reversing the original situation in which he was Osiris's younger brother.[20] During their encounters Seth injured Horus's weaker and 'lunar' left eye (restored to Horus by Thoth, with his sublime skills in the art of medicine), but Horus eventually overpowered Seth, applying in various degrees both heroism and cunning in a succession of trials of strength – Seth was vanquished, emasculated and decreed to be in the wrong by the tribunal of the Great Ennead. Consequently, Seth could be portrayed as being punished by having to carry Osiris on his back, or even sacrificed and carved up as a bull for the food of the gods.

This cycle of legends narrating the Osiris(or Horus)–Seth conflicts almost certainly has a composite character and the myth of the Osiris–Seth opposition seems to have been superimposed on the stories of the struggles between Seth and Horus. As an old, predynastic deity and one represented by his enigmatic, apparently hybrid, 'Seth-animal',[21] Seth had strong and early associations with Upper Egypt. Apart from elaborating a cosmogony focused on Ptah, the chief god of the ancient capital of Egypt, Memphis, the so-called 'Memphite Theology', recorded in the Shabaka Stone,[22] recounts that the earth god, Geb, acted as a judge between Horus and Seth. To end their feud, he divided Egypt into two halves, Lower Egypt belonging to Horus and Upper Egypt to Seth. This division of the 'Two Lands' was meant to bring peace but Geb's second decree was to extol Horus as single ruler over the whole of Egypt, as Horus was the son of his firstborn, Osiris. Horus thus emerged as the unifier of the Two Lands, the sole king of Upper and Lower Egypt, and could be portrayed wearing the double, white and red, crown of Egypt, Seth being now left crownless.

This legendary division of Egypt between Horus and Seth has been interpreted both in cosmological and historico-political terms. An influential line of investigation within the historico-political readings of this Horus–Seth separation seeks to explain it as reflecting an actual historic conflict which took place towards the end of the Predynastic Period (*c.* 5300–3100 BC). This posited conflict between a Seth-worshipping Upper Egypt and a Horus-worshipping Lower Egypt is deemed to have occurred before the unification of Egypt under Menes or Narmer (*c.* 3100–3050 BC) and to have been preceded by a 'predynastic union' of Egypt under an historical Osirian king.[23] The Lower Egyptian 'Followers of Horus' are sometimes seen as incomers from the Delta area; occasionally it is conjectured that Osiris was their human king who was murdered by the Upper Egyptian companions of Seth who were, however, themselves eventually overcome by the incomers from the north.

The theory of such a 'predynastic union' under the sovereignty of the falcon-god Horus and imposed on the Seth-worshipping Upper Egypt by the 'Followers of Horus' would need, however, to resolve a number of vexing problems; its failure to do so weakens the plausibility of its reconstruction. Like Seth, Horus was a predynastic god (in his earliest form he seems to have been regarded as a sky god who manifested himself in the shape of a falcon) and like Seth he had early cult centres in Upper Egypt that may or may not predate his cult sites in the north. Accordingly, the conflict between the followers of Horus and those of Seth has also been seen as taking place in predynastic times in Upper Egypt (which contained the cult strongholds of both Horus and Seth) and as predating the conquest of Lower Egypt by the 'Followers of Horus' – before this unification the kings of Upper Egypt are perceived as performing a dual role, that of Horus and Seth.[24] Such a view of a reversal of the direction of conquest by the adherents of Horus is also reinforced by evidence of both Horus and Seth affiliations to the predynastic Upper Egyptian king Scorpion who seems to have initiated an invasion of Lower Egypt. The balance of evidence appears to suggest that Horus and Seth were the patron deities of a dual Upper Egyptian alliance which at the end of the predynastic era initiated a conquest of Lower Egypt and gained supremacy over most of Egypt, however unstable this hegemony may have been.[25]

Accordingly, Menes, the unifier of Upper and Lower Egypt, may be viewed either as a rebellious Upper Egyptian king who broke up an earlier union established by conquerors from the Delta to inaugurate an Upper Egyptian ascendancy[26] or as a centralizing monarch, suppressing an attempted Lower Egyptian secession.[27]

As the cult of Seth gained particular prominence in the late Second Dynasty and one of its pharaohs, Peribsen, apparently adopted Seth as his personal god, in still another line of reconstruction of the possible historical reality behind the Horus–Seth conflict it is regarded as a mythical reflection of a supposed religious and political turbulence occurring in this period during which the followers of Horus and Seth were engaged in conflict and rivalries.[28] However, theories that postulate that the legends of the Horus–Seth antagonism reflect collisions and reconciliation between the adherents of Horus and Seth which date from predynastic times, seem to accommodate the literary and archaeological evidence in a more persuasive manner. Indeed, the existence of a sequence of conflicts and reunions between the followers of Horus and Seth, beginning in the late predynastic era, appears to offer a plausible explanation for the legendary, historical and archaeological data which in turn would account for the tradition of the separation of Egypt into two respective 'portions' under Horus and Seth, for the apparent unification of Egypt under the tutelage of the two gods (following a Lower Egyptian victory under the supreme leadership of Horus) and the amalgamation of Horus and Seth in the figure of the dual king and, finally, for the second unification of Egypt (in the wake of further strife) under the supremacy of Upper Egyptian adherents of Horus, reflected in the myth of the allocation of Seth's portion to Horus.[29]

On the other hand, the cosmological reading of the separation of Egypt and of the antagonism between Horus and Seth approaches the myth as if it belonged primarily to the 'sphere of cosmology'[30] from where it was extrapolated to political and geographical realities, as 'a part of the Egyptian concept of life, in which reality is not simple but is built up upon two principles'.[31] This marked Egyptian predilection for and systematic usage of dual symbolic classification is seen as underlying the formation of the concept and reality of the Egyptian dual monarchy, the kingship of Upper Egypt and the kingship of Lower Egypt, establishing a perfect harmony between the inherited cosmological and the new political notions, according to which totality is seen as comprising and balancing opposites, and because of which a 'state dualistically conceived must have appeared to the Egyptians the manifestation of the order of creation in human society'.[32] Correspondingly, the conflicts between Horus and Seth, during which Seth is perennially defeated by Horus but never completely destroyed, are seen as epitomizing the condition of strife and struggle in the universe, and the reconciliation at the end of the conflict re-establishes the 'static equilibrium'[33] between the opposing forces in the cosmos. This functioning of the Horus–Seth duality on the cosmological and political planes shows that in its original and early versions the opposition between the 'Two Brothers' or the 'Two Rivals' was not viewed as existing within the framework of a simple ethical dualism of good and evil,[34] although this may have been to a certain extent the case in the more popular perceptions of Seth's role in the Osirian drama of death and resurrection.

It has been argued, moreover, that most of the elements of the Osiris–Seth, Osiris–Horus and Horus–Seth stories derive from early dynastic rites related to the death of the king and the nomination of his successor and thus were linked to the ideology and ceremonies of Egyptian kingship.[35] The Osiris–Seth and Horus–Seth conflicts have also been interpreted as representing a vegetation or nature myth: Osiris (or Horus) epitomizing the fertilizing Nile waters or the fertile Nile valley and Seth the infertile desert,[36] but it is very doubtful whether these characteristics, which later came to be attached to these gods, formed part of their original associations. The conflict of Horus and Seth has also been interpreted as a clash, respectively, between the god of light and the storm-god,[37] or, in the framework of astral symbolism, as representing the alternation and struggle between light and darkness implied by the waxing and waning of the moon[38] (the left eye of Horus being associated with the moon and the right with sun), or the phenomenon of the solar or lunar eclipse,[39] or in relation to Seth's association with the northern constellation of the Great Bear *vis-à-vis* Osiris' southern constellation, Orion, and Isis' star, Sirius. The circumpolar stars were extremely important in Egyptian astronomy and beliefs in the afterlife – with their position in the sky close to the North Pole they remained visible throughout the year and appeared indestructible. The Great Bear itself, described in the Pyramid Texts as imperishable, had begun its circumpolar progress *c.* 3500 BC at the latitude of Heliopolis and proceeded towards the pole (increasing its height) for nearly 2000 years, reaching its zenith in 1650 BC and beginning to decline thereafter until AD 1050 when only its α star, Dubhe, remained circumpolar.[40] Acording to some Egyptian traditions, in one of his probably later roles, Seth leagued with the seven stars of the Great Bear to assault Horus the Elder, associated with light and the solar cult, although in earlier times Seth himself also had some sky deity characteristics and could be depicted as a giver of light.[41] A fusion of political and astral symbolism is often presumed to underlie the astronomical references to the mythical conflict, although the adherents of its historical interpretation assume that the astronomical meanings are secondary and have been imposed on the originally historic legend of the strife between Horus and Seth.[42]

Whether because of the historical legacy of the supposed dual Egyptian union under the patronage of Horus and Seth, or because of the cosmo-logical foundation of Egyptian dual kingship, the notion of the duality Horus–Seth in relation to the figure of the king retained a long-lasting impact on Egyptian royal and state ideology. The Pyramid Texts allude to the fusion of two deities in the figure of the king,[43] and Horus and Seth could be further seen as co-operating for the good of the king[44] or in the administration of the purification ceremony (the so-called 'baptism of the pharaoh').[45] As in the concept of dual Egyptian kingship, the king embodied 'The Two Lords', Horus and Seth, 'as a pair, as opposites in equilibrium',[46] indicating that he balanced and reconciled the conflicting powers.[47] Significantly, moreover, the queens of the First Dynasty bore the title 'She Who Sees Horus and Seth' and pharaohs from later dynasties such as Thutmose I (c. 1493–1481 BC) of the Eighteenth Dynasty could still declare themselves rulers of the 'portions' of Horus and Seth. The pharaoh could be portrayed as sitting upon the throne of Horus and the seat of Seth, deriving his kingship from Horus and his martial strength from Seth, who are thus sometimes diffrentiated in their functions, as in the case of another Eighteenth-Dynasty pharaoh, the celebrated Hatshepsut, with her proclamation that she ruled the country as the son of Isis (Horus) and was strong as the son of Nut (Seth). Unsurprisingly, in Egyptian theology there emerged the dual god Horus–Seth who was depicted with a double head, that of a falcon and the Seth-animal, or combining the features of both. On the level of royal ideology this new dual god may have been 'a projection of the dual divinity envisaged in the King',[48] but on a cosmo-logical level certainly represented Horus and Seth unified and reconciled in one divinity, reasserting the Egyptian tendency to view totality as a unity of two adversarial but complementary opposites.[49]

Another instance in which Seth's role in the cosmic scheme led to the emergence of a dual god derives from his crucial involvement in the cyclical struggle between Re and his greatest adversary, the serpent Apopis. Seth was portrayed as a defender of Re's solar barque, guarding it with his iron spear and all his power and ferocity from Apopis. When Apopis threatens to mesmerize the divine crew of the solar boat with his notorious evil eye, with its 'darkness', it is only Seth who can magically withstand the malevolent glance of the snake and vanquish him. With the rising of the reborn sun, Apopis is envisaged as being beheaded and hacked into bleeding pieces (to be re-assembled again with the coming sunset), after Seth has sharpened his arrows in his body, thrust his lance into his brow, and pierced his head with his spear.

On account of his formidable defence of the solar barque with 'word and deed' Seth can indulge in excessive arrogance, but he still receives titles such as 'Lord of Life', 'the Chosen of Re' and the 'Son of Re' and sometimes could even be seen as forming with Re another two-in-one god figure – Seth–Re. Indeed, according to *The Contention of Horus and Seth*, during the Horus–Seth dispute before the council of the nine gods, gathered to decide who of the two should inherit the office of Osiris, Seth gives prominence to his role as a defender of Re's solar barque and slayer of his enemies and Re himself is inclined to offer him Osiris's patrimony on account of his strength and seniority as an 'elder brother'.

Seth's fame as a dragon-slayer did not derive only from his subjugation of the chaos-serpent Apopis – apparently he was also known to have overcome a serpent monster epitomizing the sea. The battle against Apopis itself could also be described with stellar symbolism in which Osiris's constellation, Orion, chains the serpent-dragon in the southern sky, and Seth's constellation, the Great Bear, puts him in fetters in the northern sky. While in this instance the Osirian and Sethian forces are seen as cooperating against Apopis, the ambivalent attitudes to Seth and his awe-inspiring proclivity to violence are evident in the Egyptian traditions in which he was depicted as attacking Horus with the help of the seven stars of the Great Bear. In Egyptian belief the stars of the Great Bear were seen as being in the shape of a bull's foreleg (thigh) or an adze.[50] Because of his association with the Great Bear, Seth was seen as reigning in the northern sky and the Great Bear could be styled 'The Thigh of Seth'. Consequently, Seth could be envisaged as assaulting Osiris in the form of a bull and killing him with the bull's foreleg. Unsurprisingly, Horus is sometimes portrayed as cutting out the murderous foreleg of Seth (while Horus's four sons can also be depicted as guardians of the bull's foreleg (the Great Bear) in the northern sky). Accordingly, in one of the stages of the Egyptian ritual of the Opening of the Mouth, the most important part of the Egyptian burial ceremonies various elements of which are modelled on the Osirian myth, a bull is specially sacrificed and its foreleg cut off to be presented to the mummy/statue of the dead (Osiris).[51] The ritual was supposed to reanimate the mummified body for its afterlife and the officiating priest touched its mouth with a ceremonial adze (again, representing the Great Bear) to revive its senses and free its *ka* (one's vital force, seen also as a kind of spiritual or ethereal double). On the other hand, Seth is also envisaged as assuming the shape of a bull to serve his punishment of carrying Osiris on his back, and this association seems to underlie the positioning of a head of a sacrificial bull on the ship of Osiris as another indication of Seth's chastisement.

Furthermore, because of the belief that the stars of the Great Bear were shaped as an adze, the constellation was also associated with the heavenly 'adze' with which, according to the Pyramid Texts, the mouths of the gods were opened, and with which Horus opened the mouth of Osiris, its metal or iron issuing forth from Seth.[52] Correspondingly, in the ritual of the Opening of the Mouth Osiris's mouth is opened with the 'adze' and thus the Sethian constellation of the Great Bear assumes a dual significance in the Osirian drama of death and resurrection, serving both as an instrument of murdering and of raising up Osiris. This symbolism may indeed derive from a presumed conflict in the northern sky[53] and in his *De Iside et Osiride* Plutarch alludes to the apparently ancient belief that 'Arktos' (a name given early to the constellation of the Great Bear) is the 'soul Typhon (Seth)', whereas iron is the 'bone' of Typhon-Seth.[54] The so-called 'Mithras Liturgy', a revelatory text of Graeco-Egyptian provenance, describes the god as holding in his right hand 'a golden calf's shoulder which is the Great Bear'.[55]

However, it is indeed very difficult to reconstruct the mythological (and/or astral) symbolism and the various levels of meaning of the myths of the Osiris–Seth and Horus–Seth conflicts, particularly when one encounters some of the enigmatic references in the Pyramid Texts stating that Seth came forth from Osiris or that Osiris is the *ka* of Seth,[56] which have been interpreted, for example, as suggesting that by acting as a demonic initiator, Seth performed a form of sacrificial suicide – 'by killing Osiris, Seth had slain himself and given himself as a sacrifice'.[57] Moreover, the position of Thoth *vis-à-vis* Osiris, Horus and Seth is also intriguing but occasionally mystifying. In some mythic traditions Thoth provides crucial help to Isis in recovering the body of Osiris and reviving his procreational abilities; he exorcized the poison of a scorpion's sting from their divine heir, Horus, and is thus praised as the one who made Osiris 'triumph over his adversaries'. Thoth was often styled the 'son' of the solar god Re; however, in other legends he sprang from the forehead of Seth, whom Horus has cunningly made pregnant, and hence could be styled variously 'the son of the two rivals', 'the son of the two lords', or 'the son of the two lords who came from the forehead'. Thoth became involved in the 'Great Quarrel' of the two gods, in which he apparently lost, then recovered his hand, and healed Horus's injured eye. His intervention as an arbitrator and peacemaker in the two contestants' struggle to gain the office of Osiris was decisive – consequently he is represented as a reconciler, a mediator, as the one who has judged the 'Two Rival Gods' and abolished their strife. Yet some of the allusions to his role in the Osirian drama remain very recondite and difficult to decipher.

Regardless of his implicit, dangerous ambivalence, for long periods Seth maintained his beneficent characteristics (such as protector of the fertile oases) and was held in high esteem and honoured during the reign of the foreign Hyksos, 'Desert Princes', dynasts (who apparently associated him with the Semitic war and thunder god, Baal)[58] during the Second Intermediate Period (*c.* 1650–1570 BC) and the Nineteenth and Twentieth Dynasties (respectively, *c.* 1293–1185 and 1185–1070 BC). The first pharaoh of the Nineteenth Dynasty, Rameses I, was a son of a troop commander named Sety ('He of the god Seth') and later two pharaohs of this dynasty, Sety I and Sety II, took the same Seth-name; similarly the founder of the Twentieth Dynasty took the name Sethnakhte ('Victorious is Seth'). Since in the Nineteenth Dynasty Seth was apparently elevated as a state god, a division of the Egyptian army was named after the god, and such division played a crucial role in effecting the stalemate in the great Battle of Kadesh between the forces of Rameses II and the Hittites fought in 1275 BC. As far as kingship is concerned, apart from the extreme case of the late Second Dynasty pharaoh, Peribsen, who apparently identified his kingship with Seth rather than Horus, a number of other later pharaohs such as one of the great warrior pharaohs, Rameses

II (1279–1213 BC), who declared himself a 'son' of the victory-bringing Seth, manifested their personal devotions to the bellicose god and invoked his renowned strength while describing their deeds on the battlefield. As a god of war and martial prowess, Seth was occasionally portrayed as teaching the king the art of archery,

The ambivalence and potency of Seth's presence can also be detected in Egyptian magical spells in which Seth's fury, power or 'spear' could be invoked against the chosen target of the magical operation. When inducing himself into his preferred aggressive state Seth could shape-shift into a bull or a panther and was seen as possessing 'mighty magic powers', as being 'rich in magical lore'; he alone was able to resist Apopis's evil eye which could hypnotize the other defenders of Re's solar boat. The magician sought to enrol Seth on his side on account of his reputation as a ferocious 'fighter' or of his ability to send evil dreams to his victim, but the god could also appear as a skilful healer and be called upon in his role as a ritual partner of Horus.[59] These magical practices attest to the fact that the notion of the partnership between Horus and Seth was not limited to the ideology of the dual pharaonic monarchy. The two gods could be seen as joining forces even in some episodes of the Osirian myth itself and traditions shaped by it, such as the rite of Opening of the Mouth in which the two divine contestants take part side by side in its purification ceremony. What is more, the two gods may be envisaged as assisting Osiris to ascend the ladder to the heavenly realm, Seth thus asserting his dual role in the death and resurrection of Osiris.

Enemy of the Gods

Despite the long-enduring traditions of the Horus–Seth collaboration and their earlier two-in-one union in a dual god, Seth's negative associations, evident even in his early aggressive if forceful characteristics that were linked to violence, war, death, turbulence, thunderstorms, deadly winds and excessive sexuality as well as to the instigation of confusion and disorder, eventually became more pronounced. His increasing connections with the 'foreign lands', the desert (the 'red land') and the colour red (his confederates could be called the 'Red Ones'), as well as his trickster characteristics, which arguably make him comparable to Yurugu, the wicked divine twin in the ideology of the Dogon of Mali,[60] undoubtedly contributed to his demotion, which apparently began in earnest in the late Third Intermediate Period (c. 1069–656 BC), gained momentum in the Late Period (656–332 BC) and continued through the following Ptolemaic and Roman periods.

The early connection of Seth with foreign lands may originally have derived from the foreign campaigns of the Sethian pharaoh, Peribsen, himself styled 'conqueror of Asia'. It was an association that grew stronger and remained linked to later pharaonic expansions in Asia and relations with the 'Asiatics' (and Lybians), as Seth came in effect to epitomize Egyptian rule over Asian lands. The pharaoh could be portrayed slaying 'Asiatics' in front of Seth, with the god earning himself further renown as a vanquisher of the 'Asiatics'. In the Late Period when the tide was turned and Egypt suffered the traumas of Assyrian and Persian invasions, Seth's connection to foreign lands was destined to rebound on the anyway fluctuating standing of his cult in Egypt. After the dramatic battles with the Assyrian invaders, the loss and subsequent recovery of beleaguered Memphis and the brutal Assyrian plundering of Thebes and its temples, Seth's connection to foreign lands made his cult vulnerable to the Egyptian religious and nativistic reaction against the hated 'Asiatic' conquerors.[61] The Persian rule of Egypt during its first period (c. 525–404 BC) was much less turbulent and Herodotus' reports of the sacrilegious excesses of its Persian Achaemenid conqueror, Cambyses II, seem mostly apocryphal. However, even the measures of his successor, Darius the Great (521–486 BC), aimed at improving the temples and the internal administration in Egypt, could not prevent the growth of Egyptian anti-Persian and anti-'Asiatic' sentiments and successive rebellions against the Achaemenid rulers.

In the ceremonies of the purification or 'baptism' of the pharaoh, originally featuring Horus and Seth, Thoth had already begun frequently to appear alongside Horus, thus effectively replacing Seth and succeeding to his royal duties. Seth's name was also replaced in other texts in which his role may have been seen as beneficent, but the dethronement of the ancient if turbulent 'lord of Upper Egypt' was far from an immediate *coup de grâce*. As late as the Thirtieth Dynasty (380–362 BC), in the royal ceremonies described in the Brooklyn Papyrus (late fifth or early fourth century), it is still Horus and Seth who are deemed to perform the 'baptism' of the pharaoh rite.[62] From the Twentieth Dynasty onwards no more temples of Seth appear to have been built, while some of his previous temples and statues were to suffer from the iconoclastic attacks of the adversaries of his cult. However, a relief from the temple of Amon in Hibis (in the Kharga oasis, a well-known Sethian cult centre), built under the orders of Darius the Great, depicts a winged Seth (in the unexpected shape of a falcon) killing the serpent Apopis in a manner fascinatingly reminiscent of the Christian representation of St George and the Dragon.[63] Ironically, the downgrading of Seth in Ptolemaic and Roman Egypt was to lead to his virtual identification with his and Re's ancient enemy, the great serpent Apopis. Greek traditions recognized him as the Egyptian version of Typhon, the huge and vehement monster, who was defeated by Zeus's thunderbolts and buried under the volcanic Mount Aetna in Sicily.

This Seth–Typhon identification was bound to enhance the process of demonization of the ancient god in the Roman period, although some kind of Sethian festival is reported still to have taken place as late as the end of the second century AD. It is very surprising, therefore, to find in the temple of Deir el Hagar (in the oasis of Dakhle, another well-known Sethian cult centre), a depiction of the Roman Emperor Vespasian (AD 69–79), whose reign and campaigns brought about the destruction of the Jerusalem Temple and the diaspora Leontopolis Temple in the Egyptian delta, offering flowers to Seth and his sister-consort Nephtys. Despite gathering increasingly demonic qualities through his association with Typhon, in the Greek magical papyri the figure of Seth–Typhon could still be strikingly and inexplicably invoked as a solar god upon whom the magician calls when the sun is at its zenith and praises as 'ruler of the realm above' and 'god of gods'.[64] However, by the time of Vespasian's puzzling imperial offering to Seth and the god's invocation in the magical papyri, the fortunes of the latter's old-established cult were at an exceptionally low ebb. Despite frequently disturbing the natural order and his archetypal violent anatagonism to Osiris and Horus, in the past Seth had always managed to maintain his right to be reconciled in the re-establishment of the equilibrium of the divine powers. At the same time, he had been often seen as inhabiting the borderlands of Egypt and the cosmos, and inciting from there the extremes of turmoil in the natural, human and divine worlds, which could lead, for example, both to the passion and resurrection of Osiris. Now he was banished not only from the land of Egypt, becoming a god of dangerous foreigners and strangers, but also from the divine order of things – he was now styled 'that one' – and set apart as the enemy of the gods, as the other god. Thus apart from being alluded to in derogatory terms that stigmatized him as an abhorrent foreigner, he was also singled out as the one 'whose name is evil', 'the wicked one' or 'the son of evil'. Affiliated with his erstwhile adversary, the chaos-serpent Apopis (itself reviled as 'the fallen', 'the most evil' and 'the dark one'), Seth was now transposed on the negative pole of an ethical dualism, beginning increasingly to epitomize enmity, deceit and moral wickedness. As in the grim spells cast against 'the enemy' Apopis, the texts excelling in ritual curses against Seth could go beyond the verbal offensive and prescribe that a figure of Seth be made of red wax or wood, or drawn on a paper and trod upon by one's left foot; then it had to be pierced by a spear, hacked into pieces with a knife and its remains cast to perish in a fire.

This was indeed a dark and violent decline for the old and turbulent 'red god' whose power the early pharaohs had sought to integrate in their divine dual kingship. Gone were the centuries when as 'the strongest of the Divine Company', Seth could be envisaged standing at the helm of Re's 'Barque of Million Years' to smite daily Re's enemies, which no other god dared to or could do. Far back in time was the enactment of the two-in-one divinity of Horus and Seth that had not only to be incorporated in the king but to be sustained in the universe, so that the cosmic totality and the political wholeness of Egypt could endure through eternity, the era when, according to the Shabaka Stone, reed and the papyrus were situated on the double door of the house of the god Ptah in Memphis, symbolizing Seth and Horus joined and pacified, that they might act as brothers and desist from conflict, remaining united in Ptah's dwelling and in the 'Balance of the Two Lands' of Upper and Lower Egypt.[65]

Egyptian sorcerers, who both feared and ventured to invoke Seth's power, while acting as a kind of magical 'weavers', could assume the identity of the god with the formula: 'I am he who has divided that which was reunited'.[66] Paradoxically, in the late Graeco-Roman stages of Egyptian religion, an act of similar 'Sethian' separation affected the perceived union of Horus and Seth, as prescribed in the Shabaka Stone, and divided again that which was united – 'The Two Brothers' have become again 'The Two Fighters', resuming their original epic warfare. By that time a cosmic war, which was similar in some respects but very different in others, between two primordial spirits had become a focus in the Iranian religious universe in the wake of its Zoroastrian reformation. It was an all-pervading conflict in which pacts about the rules of engagement were possible but conciliation impossible, as the war intensified during the millennia, fought throughout in 'thought, word and deed'.

Twin Spirits

The early chronology of the great Iranian religious leader and reformer Zoroaster (Zarathustra) and his revealed faith, admittedly 'the only prophetic religion ever produced by the Aryan race',[67] still remains obscure and controversial. Sharply conflicting theories continue to fix the era of his prophetic mission variously at either 1700–1400 BC, or 1400–1000 BC or 1000–600 BC. If the earliest date could be verified it would make Zoroastrianism the world's oldest revealed religion; some of the cardinal Zoroastrian teachings appear to have been accepted and elaborated, whether directly or indirectly, in Judaism, Christianity and Islam. While some classical Greek traditions place Zoroaster in prehistory, 5,000 years before the Trojan war or 6,000 years before Plato, in sacred Zoroastrian chronology, as elaborated in the Zoroastrian opus, the *Greater Bundahishn*, the advent of the priest and prophet Zoroaster opens the tenth millennium, that of Capricorn, and his traditional date is 258 years before the era of Alexander the Great (336–323 BC).[68] Recent trends in research have dated Zoroaster's reformation around the beginning of the first millennium BC[69] and have indicated the central-eastern Iranian world as the cradle of original Zoroastrianism (also known as Mazdaism or the 'Good Religion of the Worshippers of Mazda'). A legendary tradition, reiterated by Eusebius and Augustine, located Zoroaster's homeland in the ancient region of Bactria, locked between the Oxus (Amu Darya) river and the western extension of the Himalayas, the Hindu Kush.[70] Praised later as the 'Jewel of Iran', Bactria certainly played a very important role in the expansion of nascent Zoroastrianism; indeed, in the religious history of Eurasia, its main city, Balkh, the 'mother of all towns', was destined to become successively a celebrated centre of Hellenism, Buddhism and Islam.

Both in Iran and outside the Iranian world, the life of Zoroaster came to be embroidered with vivid legends and parables. His alleged violent death at the age of seventy-seven also spawned prolific lore: according to one Persian tradition he was slain at the height of a Turanian invasion in a Balkh fire temple along with eighty priests, whose blood quenched his fire.[71] Outside Iran the figure of Zoroaster also reached astonishing prominence: in Greece the early enthusiasm of the Platonic Academy for Zoroaster has been described as amounting 'to intoxication, like the rediscovery of Indian philosophy through Schopenhauer'.[72] With the diffusion of Zoroasterian lore outside Iran the prophet came to be extolled in diverse religious and cultural traditions as the archetypal philosopher, magus and master of science and astronomy. Apart from magician and prophet, Zoroaster emerged in some traditions as a Magus-King of Bactria who fought the semi-mythical Assyrian queen Semiramis (Sammuramat),[73] who shared some of the features of the Babylonian goddess of love and war, Ishtar, and passed into legend as the founder of Babylon and the temple of her tutelar deity, Bel Marduk. Jewish traditions came to identify Zoroaster with Baruch, Jeremiah's scribe, while Syriac tradition associated Zoroaster, 'the diviner of the Magians', with the biblical Balaam. In Christian lore, Zoroaster can be recognized as Nimrod or else as Noah's son, Ham, and was portrayed as an arch-sorcerer who conjured up stars to be consumed ultimately by heavenly fire.[74] The tradition of Zoroaster as the arch-magician, his name being deciphered as 'living star' or 'stream of the star', persisted into the Middle Ages. In the *Historia Scholastica* of Peter Comestor (d. 1179), which charted biblical history from the Creation to the time of the Acts of the Apostles, Zoroaster appeared as the inventor of magic who inscribed the Seven Arts on seven columns.[75] In the fifteenth century, at the height of the Renaissance, the head of the new Platonic Academy in Florence, Marsilio Ficino, argued for a pagan theological tradition, descending from Zoroaster via Hermes Trismegistus to Orpheus and Pythagoras and culminating in Plato.[76] The Renaissance revived Zoroaster's fame as the archetypal Magus, hierophant and author of mystical and alchemical works, and it was in this shape that he entered the legends of Faust, who himself could be styled the 'second Zoroaster'. Four centuries later Nietzsche adopted the figure of Zoroaster as the spokesman of his new gospel in his most influential work, *Thus Spoke Zarathustra*, rendering further homage to Zoroaster and what he saw as the Persian vision of history as a 'great whole', a succession of cycles of a thousand years, each presided over by a prophet.[77] In *Ecce Homo* Nietzsche attributed to the historical Zoroaster the introduction of the notion of the struggle between good and evil as the 'very fly-wheel of existence' and the creation of 'the most portentous of errors', morality. For Nietzsche the uniqueness of the Persian prophet in history was that he was exactly 'the reverse of an immoralist' and now has to be invoked in Nietzsche's new 'Zoroastrian' gospel of the 'self-surpassing of the moralist in his opposite' – in Nietzsche himself, the self-acclaimed 'first immoralist'.

The religious message of Zoroaster was indeed underpinned by the new morality and dualist vision of the universal struggle between good and evil that confronted man with the opposing ways of Truth and Untruth. As Zoroastrianism arose and spread, initially in the eastern Iranian region, it inevitably took over and transformed the traditional beliefs and deities of the archaic religions of the Indo-Iranian branch of the Indo-European peoples. What sharply distinguishes original Zoroastrianism from the polytheism of Vedic India with its multitude of gods and semi-gods is the elevation of one supreme deity, Ahura Mazda (Wise Lord), as 'the first and the ultimate', the sole creator and upholder of the spiritual and material world, who is alone worthy of worship. Ahura Mazda was probably one of the 'lords' or *ahuras* (the Hindu *asuras*) of the Aryan pantheon but with Zoroastrian reform he overshadowed the other *ahuras* and transcended ancient Aryan deities like Mithra, the god of light and covenant. An uncreated and perfectly good god, Ahura Mazda is the Creator of everything (*Yasna* 44 : 7) and source of the lesser beneficent divinities.

The influential view of early Zoroastrianism as 'dualist monotheism' has been continuously challenged and redefined against the background of the monotheistic worlds of Judaism, Christianity and Islam. What remains undisputed is that ethical dualism and the struggle of good and evil lie at the heart of the Zoroastrian vision of divine reality: its classical formulation is found in the hymnic *Gathas* that form the oldest 'psalmic' part of the Zoroastrian scriptures, the *Avesta*,[78] and are attributed to Zoroaster himself. The *Gathas* of Zoroaster are contained in the Avestan section of *Yasna* (Acts of Worship) (28–53), and with their visionary, allusive and often abstruse verses they still appear a 'book bound with seven seals'.[79] The ambiguities and the intricacies that recur in the *Gathas* also distinguish *Yasna* 30, where Zoroaster declares the teaching of the opposing ways of the twin, primordial Spirits who are 'renowned to be in conflict'. These two Spirits are Spenta Mainyu ('Beneficent' or 'Holy Spirit') and Angra Mainyu ('Hostile' or

'Destructive' Spirit) and while they are alluded to as twins, Ahura Mazda is styled the father of the 'Holy Spirit' (*Yasna* 47:3). Both Spirits seem to proceed from Ahura Mazda but Zoroaster's utterances are difficult to interpret and laconic, forging a theological riddle that has continued to provoke arguments and differing solutions both in Zoroastrian theology and modern scholarship.[80] When the twin Spirits met in the beginning, they established life and not-life (death) and evolved into antithetical spirits of good and evil by making conflicting moral choices between *asha* (Truth) and *druj* (Untruth), the two primal principles that underlie Zoroastrian ethical dualism. Yet the position of the twin Spirits, particularly that of Angra Mainyu, prior to this split remains somewhat enigmatic. The traditional debate concerning the status of Angra Mainyu in early Zoroastrianism is whether he was regarded as evil by nature or by choice, i.e. whether his selection of 'Untruth' was predetermined by his nature or whether it was the result of his free choice.[81] The idea of free choice is fundamental to Zoroastrianism and it seems more probable that the origin of evil lies not in the innate nature of Angra Mainyu, supposedly activated by choice, but in his selection of untruth and doing the 'worst things'. What is certain is that Angra Mainyu, the evil Spirit, chose in the beginning to incarnate and to inaugurate the way of evil thoughts, words and deeds and become the great adversary of Ahura Mazda and his Good Creation. The antagonism between Ahura Mazda and the Destructive Spirit is irreconcilable and the Holy Spirit approaches his evil twin Spirit with this uncompromising formulation of the opposition: 'Neither our thoughts nor teachings nor intentions, neither our preferences nor words, neither our actions nor conceptions nor our souls are in accord' (*Yasna* 45:2).

In Zoroastrianism, Angra Mainyu's 'wrong choice' – to do the 'worst things' – was adopted by the class of the *daevas* (gods) like Indra from the traditional Indo-Iranian (Aryan) pantheon. While in India the *daevas* ultimately ousted the *asuras*, in Iranian Zoroastrianism they were forcibly relegated to demonic 'offspring stemming from evil thinking, deceit and disrespect' (*Yasna* 32:3). At the time of the primal choice the *daevas* were approached by the 'Deceiver' and accordingly chose the 'worst thought' and 'rushed into fury, with which they have afflicted the world and mankind' (*Yasna* 30:6). While the demonic *daevas* were condemned as the evil progeny of Angra Mainyu, he himself was styled *Daevanam Daeva*, the Demon of Demons.[82]

The choice of Angra Mainyu and the *daevas* and their onslaught on the world remained fundamental to the religious vision of Zoroastrianism, and a separate section of the *Avesta*, the *Vendidad* (Law against the Daevas), comprises prescriptions for ritual purification and exorcism of the *daevas*. The spiritual beings that should be entreated are the Amesha Spentas, the six 'Beneficent' or 'Holy' Immortals, who were evoked by Ahura Mazda and, together with Spenta Mainyu, became the divine 'bounteous' septet of Zoroastrianism that is mirrored in the class of the seven archangels in the later Jewish and Christian traditions. The Amesha Spentas embodied the virtues of Ahura Mazda, like Good Thought, Best Truth, Desirable Dominion, etc., and along with the Wise Lord proceeded to evoke more beneficent divinities, a process which was to recover more ancient divinities among the Zoroastrian *yazatas* ('the worshipful ones').[83]

The new system of spiritual and moral values introduced by Zoroaster provoked an epoch-making reformation of the archaic Indo-Iranian religion and cast aside some of its initiatory and sacrificial practices, like the blood sacrifice. What was strenuously rejected were the orgiastic and frantic rites which were associated with the worship of some of the demoted, warlike *daevas*, while its priests were condemned as 'whisperers and sacrificers' who evoked the violent forces of evil and deceit, the way of Angra Mainyu. Despite the break with some of the formalistic ritualism of the Indo-Iranian priestly tradition, early Zoroastrianism developed some of the concepts of Indo-Iranian or Aryan mysticism, with its focus on supernatural vision and mystical light, and preserved certain cultic traditions which could be spiritualized and reconciled with Zoroastrian ethics.[84] The cult of fire was also retained and became fundamental to Zoroastrianism, where it was seen as possessing the 'power of Truth' (*Yasna* 43 : 4) and was associated with the Holy Spirit of Ahura Mazda (*Yasna* 36 : 3).

In the Zoroastrian solution to the perennial enigma of the origin of evil, Ahura Mazda (later contracted to Ohrmazd), as an absolutely good and just Creator of the spiritual and material world, was stripped of all culpability for the presence of evil and suffering in his Creation. According to some Parsis, the modern Zoroastrians, the twin Spirits emerged as the opposing but complementary forces of maintenance and destruction, the two poles of Ahura Mazda's power,[85] but whether this view could be projected backwards on to early Zoroastrianism remains an open question. In traditional Zoroastrianism evil seems to be revealed as stemming from the free choice of Untruth by Angra Mainyu (later called Ahriman) who is, however, destined to be defeated and paralysed by Ahura Mazda at the end of historical time. The Zoroastrian sacred history came to be divided into 'Three Times': the First Time of the original perfection of Ahura Mazda's 'Good Creation' in its ideal and material side; the middle Time of Mixture, of good and evil caused by the incursion of the Destructive Spirit in the material universe; and finally the eschatological Time of Separation of the two hostile Spirits, of good and evil, and the ultimate purification of the world.[86] In the First Time, Ahura Mazda's Creation exists in two states, spiritual or ideal, *menog*, and material, *getig*, while Angra Mainyu is unable to corrupt its ideal side, being incapable of transferring his own creations from the spiritual to the material state. The physical aspect of Ahura Mazda's creation is vulnerable to the encroachment of Angra Mainyu and, following the formation of the material world, it is subjected to the onslaught of the Destructive Spirit, which marks the beginning of the second Time of Mixture, of the opposing principles of good and evil.

The Zoroastrian view of world history received considerable elaboration in later stages and, in one scheme of the cosmic process it was held to last 12,000 years, of which the first 3,000 are the period of 'ideal creation'. The remaining 9,000 years are an era of cosmic strife when, according to the scheme in the *Greater Bundahishn* (1:28), three millennia would be dominated entirely by Ohrmazd (Ahura Mazda), three millennia would pass in a mixture of and struggle between the will of both Ohrmazd and Ahriman (Angra Mainyu) and finally, in the last three millennia, Ahriman would be defeated and rendered powerless. In Zoroastrian eschatology the last era will culminate in the advent of a virgin-born World Saviour, Saoshyant, conceived from Zoroaster's seed, miraculously preserved in a lake, while some traditions refer to three posthumous sons of Zoroaster who appear as Saoshyants (saviours) at the end of each of the last three millennia. Saoshyant, the messianic leader of the Pure Ones, wages the last holy wars against the forces of evil and resurrects the bodies of the dead which are reunited with their souls. Their resurrection sets the stage for the Last Judgment and the separation of the saved from the damned, who must face a terminal ordeal by fire and pass through rivers of molten metal, the 'pure fire' and the 'molten iron', the sign of Ahura Mazda's retribution (*Yasna* 51:9). While mankind is being purified from evil and corruption, the molten metal would burn the last vestiges of 'Untruth' and would flow even into Hell to cleanse its putrescence. In the redeemed world material creation becomes immortal.

Man is confronted with the moral task of choosing freely between the two ways of good or evil in the vast cosmic drama of the unfolding warfare between the Holy and the Destructive Spirits. His use of his free will is to be judged at the immediate individual judgment of the soul at death on the so-called 'Bridge of the Separator' and at the universal judgment during the final renovation of Ahura Mazda's Good Creation. The first judgment elevates the righteous souls to the Zoroastrian Heaven, the 'House of Song', and consigns the wicked ones and the 'destroyers of this world' to the Zoroastrian Hell, the 'House of Worst Thinking' or 'House of Untruth', where they are condemned to 'a long age of misery, of darkness, ill food and the crying of woe' (*Yasna* 31 : 20). Those whose good and evil deeds appear in exact balance (*Yasna* 33 : 1) are sent to the intermediary sphere of Hamistagan (the region of the mixed). Following the resurrection of the bodies during the Last Judgment, the saved will be sent for three days in Paradise, while the damned will face another three days of punishment in Hell. In the ensuing trial by fire, as depicted vividly in the *Greater Bundahishn* (34 : 18–19), the saved will pass through the rivers of molten metal as if walking through warm milk, while for the damned the ordeal would be exactly like walking through 'pure fire' and 'molten iron', which would destroy the deceitful and save the truthful (*Yasna* 31 : 19; 51 : 19). In the *Gathas* the damned appear to be condemned to eternal perdition,[87] but in later Zoroastrian eschatology after this final crucible all human beings will be purged of sin to become one voice praising Ahura Mazda, immortalized in his renewed Good Creation (*Greater Bundahishn* 34 : 20–1). At the resurrection, Saoshyant would perform 'the sacrifice of the raising of the dead', in which the bull Hadhayans is slain and from its fat the drink of immortality is prepared, which is to be given to all men who now become immortal. The eschatological renewal of the macrocosmos epitomizes the preordained victory of Ahura Mazda over the principle of evil and destruction and the ensuing universal salvation. The Good Creation is restored to perfection and bliss prior to the assault of evil and henceforth remains incorruptible under the eternal reign of the Wise Lord. Angra Mainyu is thrown out of the sky and rendered powerless, cast into 'the darkness and gloom', where his destructive potency and weapons will be sealed up forever (*Greater Bundahishn* 34 : 30).

The Zoroastrian reformation gave apparent priority to the doctrine of the predestined final transfiguration of the world, as opposed to the archaic religious scenario of the cyclic regeneration of the cosmos. The fervent expectation of the Last Judgment and the ultimate glorification of existence is one of the dominant themes of the *Gathas*. The other texts of the *Avesta*, the greater part of which seems to have been lost, reflect later periods of the growth and expansion of the Good Religion of Ahura Mazda. Throughout its history Zoroastrianism was to undergo vicissitudes and permutations but it retained Zoroaster's dualist vision of two spiritual principles warring from the beginning of the world and the inevitable triumph of Ahura Mazda, the creator and the judge, in the last days. Zoroastrianism retained also its praise for the Good Creation of Ahura Mazda where the spiritual and material world are connected inextricably, man himself being the image of the macrocosmos and his body being the garment and the weapon of his soul.

Spirit and Flesh

Zoroastrianism remained essentially a life-affirming and active religion. The dualism of the two spirits of good and evil did not comprise an opposition between the soul and the body. The body was regarded as an essential and indispensable part of the Good Creation, an instrument of the soul, and accordingly celibacy and asceticism were renounced consistently throughout the history of Zoroastrianism. A distinct dualism between the soul and the body was to become the core of the religiosity of Orphism, an important trend in the Greek mysteries which seems to have emerged in the sixth century and, apart from the Balkans, came to exert influence in Crete, Cyprus and southern Italy.

Traditionally described as a 'drop of alien blood in the veins of the Greeks', Orphism owed its name to the pre-Homeric fabled Thracian poet and musician Orpheus to whom were ascribed many Orphic works.[88] In antiquity the mythical genealogy of Orpheus varied and he was depicted as a son of Apollo or the Thracian king Oeagres of the dynasty reputedly established by Dionysus (Bacchus) when the god invaded Europe from Asia by the Hellespont and deposed the hostile

Thracian king Lycurgus (Diodorus Siculus 3:65.4–7). According to Diodorus, the new Dionysian dynasty in Thrace was initiated into the secret rites of the Dionysian (Bacchic) mysteries and, although seemingly of Anatolian descent, Dionysus himself was seen by ancient authors as a Thracian god.[89] Various mythological stories recount the conquests of Dionysus and his cult in Thrace, Greece and even in India, which the god was said to have traversed with a great army, the 'soldiers of Dionysus', bringing to the Indians civilization and the discovery of wine (Diodorus Siculus 2:38.3–39). Ancient Orphism had strong links with the Dionysian (Bacchic) mysteries and Diodorus assigns the origins of Orphic rites to Orpheus' changes in the inherited Dionysian initiatory rites (Diodorus Siculus 3:65.6). As in Greece, the Dionysian mysteries in Thrace were intended to lead the Dionysian initiate, the *bacchus*, into 'the empire of the god', into a transformative ecstatic experience of his divinity, but were also associated with prophecy. The legendary figure of Orpheus appears closely linked with the Thracian religious sphere, with its intense spiritualist currents and renowned Thracian preoccupation with the afterlife, which was to impel some Thracians to weep at the birth of children and to rejoice at the burial of the dead (Pomponius Mela 2:2.18; Herodotus 5:4). The belief in the immortality of the soul was thought to be behind the brave Thracian conduct on the battlefield and the celebrated *appetitus mortis* (appetite for death) of the Thracians, their belief in the 'beauty' of death (Martianus Capella 6:656). The northern Thracian tribes of the Getae were known as 'the immortalizing ones' or 'those who make themselves immortal', while some Thracians were renowned for their ascetic practices and abstinence (Strabo 7:3.3–6, 11).[90] The old thesis of Erwin Rohde and W. Guthrie that the belief in the immortality and divinity of the human soul arose and entered Greece through Thracian worship of Dionysus has been consistently challenged, but ultimately Thracian religiosity is viewed as having enriched the classical world with 'a more total vision of humanity and of its destiny'[91] and seems to have left its impact on the crystallization of some concepts in Orphism.

Apart from their obvious associations with Thrace, the myths of Dionysus and Orpheus often alluded to the interaction between the rival cults of Apollo, the god of order and reason, and Dionysus, the god of wine and ecstasy. A notoriously dual deity, who was believed to drive men to a frenzy (Herodotus 4:79), the divine 'madness' (*mania*),

Dionysus could be praised as a redeemer, healer and benefactor; he could appear as a lion or a leopard, but most famously in the form of a bull, and could be revealed as the 'render of men' and the one 'who delights in the sword and bloodshed'. When Dionysus led his force from Asia into Europe he fought the Thracian king Lycurgus (Diodorus Siculus 3:65.5), who was apparently associated with the worship of Apollo and is recognized as a great adversary of the crazed Dionysus in the *Iliad* (7:130–4). In the *Iliad*, Lycurgus is blinded, in Diodorus' account he is defeated, mutilated and crucified by the invading Dionysus. In another mythical account, while hastening through Thrace, Dionysus was insulted and expelled by Lycurgus but the god drove the king mad and he slashed down his own son, whom he saw as a vine shoot (Apollodorus 3:5.1). In the wake of the murder, Thrace endured a great drought and, as was revealed by the oracle, was to be relieved only through the death of the god-fighting king. Lycurgus was accordingly tied to horses and rent apart at Mount Pangaeus, the traditional site of a famous Dionysian oracle, while Dionysus reached India and set up pillars in the land. Whereas these myths seem to allude to the antagonism of the principles of Dionysus and Apollo, the figure of Orpheus, his genealogy likewise, could appear ambiguous – he could be described as 'sent by Apollo' (Pindar, Pythian Ode, 4:176) or raised to prominence by Dionysus. What remains certain is that Orpheus was or became closely associated with worship of Apollo and, according to Aeschylus, he came to praise the sun-god, Helios, whom he recognized as Apollo, as 'the greatest of the gods', provoking the wrath and revenge of Dionysus, who sent against him his frenzied female devotees, the Bassarides (the Maenads).[92] Traditionally, Orpheus was envisioned as having been rent to pieces by the Maenads and in one mythical account of his death his severed head was said to have been buried in Lesbos, where a temple of Dionysus was erected on the site of the head's reputed burial. Orpheus' lyre was reputedly installed in the temple of Apollo and Orpheus has been seen as epitomizing the 'purely masculine', the *catharos*, as embodied in Apollo.[93] In accordance with Diodorus' testimony of Orpheus' changes in Dionysian rites and Olympiodorus' comment that, according to Orpheus, Helios has much in common with Dionysus through Apollo's medium,[94] Orpheus' mythical feats are often seen as a reformation of the Dionysian mysteries, a reconciliation and synthesis of

Apollonian or solar and Dionysian cultic traditions which were attested in both Greece and Thrace.

In Orphism, Apollo and Dionysus appear reconciled, but the supposed link between Orpheus' reputed reforms of the Dionysian cult and Orphic teachings remains controversial and bitterly debated. Concern for the hereafter certainly was or came to be one of the prominent features of the Dionysian mysteries,[95] which comprised ecstatic and orgiastic rites, including the *omophagia* (eating raw flesh), which were vividly realized in Euripides' masterpiece, *The Bacchae*. In *The Bacchae*, Dionysus comes from Asia's land, from the mountains of Phrygia and Lydia, to the 'broad highways of Hellas', along with his Maenads to establish his cult on Greek soil but it is suppressed by the king of Thebes, Pentheus, who is destined, however, to be torn asunder by the Maenads. Agave, his own mother, smitten by Dionysian madness, wrenches off and raises his head as prey, which she sees as a lion's head. The ecstatic Bacchic rites could reach extreme forms and the Bacchanalia were eventually proscribed by the Roman Senate in 186 BC. Orphism, which was associated with the Dionysian and Eleusinian mysteries and the Pythagorean movement, fostered ascetic and cathartic practices focused essentially on the afterlife and the fate and salvation of the soul. What appears to be a cardinal and originally secret myth of Orphism recounts the fate of Dionysus–Zagreus, Zeus' child from his incestuous intercourse with his daughter, Persephone, herself scion of Zeus' union with his mother, Rhea–Demeter. In Orphic cosmogony, after the first divine generation, Zeus emerged eventually as both creator and sovereign of the world; he was exalted as the beginning, the middle and the end, and upon the birth of Dionysus the divine child was enthroned as a ruler of the world and of the gods. The old race of gods, Zeus' enemies, the Titans, enticed the child Dionysus with toys and, while looking into a mirror, he was slain, dismembered and devoured by the Titans.[96] The Orphic myth of the dismemberment of Dionysus, which was represented in the rites initiated by Orpheus (Diodorus 5 : 75.4), recalls the myth of Osiris' dismemberment in Egypt and, indeed, Diodorus refers to the Greek translation of Osiris as Dionysus (1 : 11.3). Zeus avenged the horrible death of Dionysus by destroying the Titans with lightning and, while Dionysus was later revived, it was out of the ashes of the Titans that man was created. According to a widespread reading of the myth, man inherited both the Dionysian and Titanic elements and has a dual nature, his soul being of divine Dionysian descent and his body of evil Titanic material.[97] An alternative reading of Orphic soul–body dualism argues that, rather than being associated with man's bodily and mortal nature, the Titans – with their rebellious, destructive and disorderly conduct – had established models to be followed by humans and limited the human soul to within their boundaries.[98] What is certain is that, in Orphism, the soul was viewed as pre-existing and separate from the body and was held to be undergoing punishment in the 'enclosure' and the 'prison' of the body until it had paid the due penalty (Plato, *Cratylus* 400c). The equation of the human body (*soma*) with the *sema* (tomb) of the soul is traditionally associated with the Orphic–Pythagorean current in Greek religious thought; the purification of the soul was to be achieved through an ascetic life, purifications (*katharmoi*) and initiations (*teletai*). Observation of the Orphic way of life, with its initiatory, ethical and ascetic rules, was supposed to grant salvation of the soul from the Titanic nature and primordial guilt and punishment.[99] The Orphic cultivation of the divine element in man was aimed at delivering the soul from punishment in the afterlife and from the chain of transmigration of the soul through various bodies, the sorrowful wheel of rebirth. It is widely assumed that Orphic–Pythagorean concepts of the soul and its destiny influenced Plato, while Orpheus was hailed not only as the archetypal poet–enchanter who led all things by the charm of his voice (Aeschylus, *Agamemnon* 1630) but also as a founder of the Mysteries, the first to introduce initiatory rites in Greece. Evolving ultimately into 'the greatest emblematic character of the Greek mystical consciousness',[100] the figure of Orpheus was also to be subjected to numerous cultural transformations, from Virgil's *Georgics* to Cocteau's *Orphée*.

As a bringer of civilization and law, in Greek traditions Dionysus was commonly equated with Osiris and the dismemberment of the Greek god by the Titans was associated with that of Osiris at the hands of Seth-Typhon. In Orphism the body and the soul were brought together as a result of the primordial crime of the Titans – the dismembering and the devouring of Dionysus. The revived Dionysus appears to have been perceived as a saviour–god, releasing entrapped souls from a 'Titanic' prison, and Orphism is credited with introducing into European religiosity the pattern of soul–body dualism, whether in terms of distinct antithesis or mere separation.[101] In Zoroastrianism, although created after the soul, the body was regarded as being of like substance and man was described as formed of five parts – body, vital spirit, soul, form (image) and pre-existent soul (*Greater Bundahishn* 3 : 13). In alternative Zoroastrian systems man could be described as possessing four spiritual constituents – soul, vital spirit, pre-existent soul and consciousness – or being composed of three constituent powers, associated respectively with the body, the vital spirit and the soul, each of which is divided further into three parts.[102] Far from undergoing punishment in the body, in the Good Religion, the soul puts on its bodily garment of its free will as part of Ohrmazd's initial design to conquer Ahriman, his spiritual adversary in the material world. The visible world, *getig*, is the battleground of the forces of good and evil, and as the 'lord of the creation' man is at the forefront of the contest between the powers of Truth and Untruth. The cosmological dualism of the spiritual and material planes of existence does not imply opposition between the soul and the body. Rather they could be likened to a horse and horseman: the mission of the soul is to fight and vanquish the forces of Untruth as a knight mounted on his horse smites his enemies (*Denkart* 3 : 218). At death – itself introduced by Ahriman – the soul separates from the body to face its individual judgement; the 'form' of man remains with Ohrmazd and is reunited with the soul at the resurrection to face trial at the Last Judgement.

The united soul and body lead the battle against the powers of evil and accordingly Ahriman struggles to rend their union, to drive a wedge between man's essence, the soul, and its weapon and garment, the body.[103] Moreover, while Ohrmazd turned his spiritual creations into materiality, Ahriman's dark and evil spiritual essence, which has the 'substance' of death, cannot be transmuted into materiality. The spiritual evil of Ahriman does not have actual material being and can only invade the already created physical world of Ohrmazd, where it can achieve 'only a secondary kind of existence, the evil substance being clothed inside a material being, and taking on an alien shape'.[104] Ahriman's indwelling in the visible world remains in the bodies of humans, whom he tries to corrupt and to make his own; accordingly the divine and demonic coexist and fight for supremacy in man. Through adherence to the Good Religion, through good deeds, piety and righteousness, man cultivates the divine element in himself and becomes a 'Good Man', a 'friend' and 'helper' of the gods. Conversely, the wicked and sinful are possessed by the *daevas* and incarnate the spiritual evil and will of

Ahriman. The division between the righteous and the wicked is emblematic of the Time of Mixture of good and evil upon Ahriman's aggression: Ohrmazd has to appoint a fixed period of contest against him to prevent that mixture in his creation becoming eternal. The material world itself is to serve as a prison-house for the Destructive Spirit and eventually he will be banished from human beings at the Last Judgement, after which spirit and flesh will finally be wed together.

Although Zoroastrian dualism and its vision of the soul's destiny differ significantly from the soul–body dualism in Orphism and Platonism, traditions emerged in Greece that tried to associate the origins of the two forms of dualism. Some late classical authors asserted that Plato, who stated in the *Republic* (379c) that the cause of evil lay outside God, was himself introduced to the Zoroastrian dualist doctrine in Phoenicia. Within Platonism itself there emerged tendencies that sought to associate Zoroastrian and Platonic dualism and tried to make 'Zoroaster a precursor of Plato or Plato a reincarnation of Zoroaster'.[105] The placing of Zoroaster six millennia or two cycles of 3,000 years before Plato, served to link the figures as two seminal stages in the transmission of knowledge and implied 'the return of dualism'[106] with the advent of Plato. One legendary tradition, reiterated by the first antipope, Hippolytus, relates that Pythagoras went to Babylon to receive the teachings of 'Zaratas (Zoroaster) the Chaldean'.[107] Some scholars have argued for possible Iranian influences on the Pythagorean and Orphic movements but their suggestions have been consistently opposed. Affinities have also been suggested between Zoroastrianism and the specific teachings of Empedocles (*c.* 490–430 BC) of the dual and alternating action of the two forces of love and strife on the four eternal roots or elements – earth, fire, air and water.[108]

While Zoroaster's renown persisted in the pagan Greek world from the time of Plato to late antiquity, in Iran itself the original rigour of his teachings was to undergo gradual mitigation. As Zoroastrianism spread and matured it reintegrated some of the ignored deities and cultic traditions of the Aryan past, and Zoroaster's own utterances in the *Gathas* about the opposition between the twin Spirits were to receive new theological translations. With the rise of the Iranian empire of the Achaemenids as a world power in the sixth century BC and the ensuing Zoroastrian progress in its dominions, the Good Religion of Ahura Mazda was bound to encounter the rich religious world of Mesopotamia.

Creator and Destroyer

In the sixth century BC, which saw the rise of Confucianism in China, Buddhism in India and Orphism in Greece, Zoroastrianism rose to religious prominence in the first world empire, the Persian empire under the Achaemenid dynasty (550–330 BC),[109] and entered an era of expansion and transformation.

The spectacular growth of Achaemenid Persia as the new ascendant power in the Middle East was secured by the conquests of its founder, Cyrus the Great, who succeeded in uniting much of the Iranian world in what was to become the first Iranian *imperium*. The beginning of his meteoric ascent to imperial prominence can be traced to 550 BC, when he united the Medes and the Persians by taking over the Median kingdom, which had already established its control over northern Mesopotamia. In 612 BC the Median kingdom had entered into a crucial alliance with the renascent Babylon to deliver the mortal blow to the Assyrian empire, the reputed 'rod' of Yahweh's anger (Isaiah 10:5), which for centuries had dominated most of western Asia. Now it was Babylon's turn to fall to Cyrus, whose birth was reputedly foreshadowed by a dream of a vine growing from his mother's womb to cover the whole of Asia (Herodotus 1.108), while in Isaiah 45 he was recognized as the 'anointed' of Yahweh, destined to destroy Babylonian power and save Israel. Following Cyrus' conquests in Anatolia (Asia Minor) and Mesopotamia, the Persian empire began to expand to both the east and the west. Under Cyrus' successors, Achaemenid Persia consolidated its dominion over western Asia, conquered Egypt and encroached upon the Balkans, where it extended its control to the Danube delta and annexed most of Thrace and Macedonia. Around 500 BC, the boundaries of the Persian empire were already stretching from the Danube to the Indus river and from Nubian Sudan and the Nile to the Caucasus and the Caspian Sea. For the Achaemenid monarchs, Thrace apparently seemed a vital gateway for further advance into Europe and the Persian armies repeatedly burst into the southern Balkans, threatening to overrun Greece. In 481 BC Xerxes the Great (485–465 BC) ventured to bridge the Hellespont from Asia to Europe and cursed its waters when his first bridges were destroyed in a storm. Before crossing ceremonially into the Balkans, Xerxes invoked the gods of Persia to let nothing hinder his conquest of all Europe, to annex

and unite her according to the will and under the 'shadow' of Ahura
Mazda. The collision between Persia and Greece has been traditionally
seen as the first and archetypal clash of the 'monarchical, hierarchic and
priestly' east and the 'republican, egalitarian and secular' west.[110] Despite
Xerxes' occupation of Athens in 480 and the Persian burning of the
Acropolis, his invasion was repelled and the Achaemenids failed to
conquer peninsular Greece and advance further into the Balkans.
Though the Achaemenid empire was to lose its hold of its European
possessions, it continued to play an important role in the Greek world
and to interfere in Greece's affairs until, under Alexander the Great,
Macedonian troops finally led the triumphant pan-Hellenic crusade
against Persia.

The Achaemenids divided their empire into twenty satrapies and
presided over numerous satraps and vassal dynasts as sacrosanct 'Kings of
the World'. The Achaemenid royal ideology synthesized both Aryan and
Near Eastern monarchic traditions; it was the Achaemenid monarch,
Darius the Great (521–486 BC), who was the first to proclaim that he was
king by the will of Ahura Mazda, 'the greatest of the gods'. Achaemenid
Persia succeeded to the rich and varied Babylonian civilizations but,
unlike the Assyrians and Babylonians, the Achaemenid rulers recognized
and largely tolerated the native religions, customs and loyalties in their
dominions. Under their aegis the many disparate cultures and faiths of
the Persian empire were integrated and reconciled, sparking off a rich
and vibrant civilization. The Achaemenid 'Kings of the World' honoured
and even patronized the old cults of Mesopotamia. To legitimize his
succession to Babylonian kingship the founder of the empire, Cyrus the
Great, assumed the role of a benefactor and protector of Marduk's
famous temple complex, Esagila, and other main Babylonian shrines like
Ezida, the temple of the Babylonian god of wisdom, Nabu. His
successors largely continued this policy and the alleged anti-Babylonian
excesses of Xerxes, the demolition of Esagila and the melting down of
Marduk's statue – acts deemed sometimes to have virtually destroyed the
'soul' of Babylon[111] – are in all probability entirely fictitious.

Whether the first two Achaemenid rulers, Cyrus and Cambyses, were
Zoroastrian adherents remains an open question, but Darius, who
founded the spectacular ceremonial capital of the empire at Persepolis as
a sacred centre of Achaemenid kingship, was a Mazda-worshipper and
proclaimed that all his deeds were in accordance with the will of Ahura

Mazda.[112] Herodotus tells (1:209) how, in a dream, Cyrus had seen Darius with two wings on his shoulders, overshadowing Asia with one wing and Europe with the other. During his reign Darius campaigned far and wide, from the Punjab in Asia to the Balkans in Europe, where his offensive against the Scythians carried the Persian advance further to the north-east, into Ukraine. In one of his inscriptions, Darius solemnly declared: 'Ahura Mazda, when he saw this earth in commotion thereafter bestowed it upon me, made me king. By the will of Ahura Mazda I put it down in its place', and proclaimed that no one should rebel against the command of Ahura Mazda who had created earth, sky and man and had made Darius king, 'one king of many, one lord of many'.[113] The elevation of Zoroastrianism in the Achaemenid empire led to considerable growth of the Zoroastrian priesthood and changes in Zoroastrian worship, including the inauguration of temple cults and the establishment of the temple worship of fire in the so-called 'houses of fire' during the later Achaemenid era. While the Good Religion flourished and expanded under the Achaemenids, the fortunes of *daeva*-worship, castigated and proscribed earlier by Zoroaster, are extremely obscure and largely untraceable. Xerxes had apparently banned *daeva*-worship in the Achaemenid empire and proclaimed that he had destroyed a sanctuary of the *daevas* and uprooted their cult in a land where it was prevalent in order to establish the worship of Ahura Mazda 'with due order and rites'.[114] At the same time, his queen, Amestris, was reputed to have buried alive fourteen young Persians, sons of Persian notables, to propitiate the god of the underworld (Herodotus 7:114), a sacrifice which clearly did not follow the 'due order and rites' of Mazda-worship.

The consolidation and elevation of Zoroastrianism in the Achaemenid empire is commonly attributed to the Magi, the Median sacerdotal tribe or caste, which appears analogous to the Indian Brahmins or the Levites of ancient Israel and had formed the hereditary priestly class of the Median kingdom.[115] Apart from Media, the Magi were the acknowledged priesthood entrusted with the conduct of religious ceremonies in western Iran. Herodotus recounted that the Persians could not offer a sacrifice without a Magus (1:132). In antiquity the Magi were renowned for their expertise in divination by dreams, for fostering incestuous marriages and for leaving the dead to be picked clean by vultures and wild animals. Whether the Magi joined the eastern Zoroastrian priests in a single ecclesiastical body under the Achaemenids remains unknown; their earliest contacts with the Zoroastrianism of eastern Iran are enveloped in obscurity. While not all of the Magi associated themselves with Zoroastrianism, those who adopted its beliefs and practices clearly served as a vehicle for the spread of Zoroastrianism in the western Achaemenid dominions, including Asia Minor. For the Greeks, the teachings of the Magi were indeed the teachings of Zoroaster and the prophet of Ahura Mazda came to be styled 'Magus'. The Magi had certainly been exposed to Mesopotamian religious influences but since the Achaemenid era their fortunes were inextricably linked to Zoroastrianism, although at least some of them continued to participate in non-Zoroastrian rites. The religious eclecticism of the Magi was to make possible the assimilation of Near Eastern traditions within Zoroastrianism in an era when the religious policy of the Achaemenids allowed coexistence and prolonged interchange between varying religions and cults. Among the important religious developments of the Achaemenid era was the Zoroastrian rehabilitation of the Lord Covenant, Mithra 'of the broad pastures', as the supreme of the divine *yazatas* (the worshipful ones), who came to be revered as the omniscient master of the world and its wakeful guardian against the powers of evil and darkness. Another significant religious phenomenon of the period was the spread of the cult of the Iranian Great Goddess Anahita, the Immaculate Lady of the 'strong undefiled waters', which arose under strong Assyrio-Babylonian influence. The Achaemenid King of Kings Artaxerxes II (404–359 BC) is credited with erecting many statues of Anahita throughout the empire and since his reign Mithra and Anahita came to be invoked along with the supreme god Ahura Mazda as the divine protectors of the Iranian monarchy.[116]

The religious transformations of the Achaemenid era also affected the original Zoroastrian dualist scheme, which had set in absolute opposition the principles of Truth and Untruth and the related opposing modes of being of the two twin Spirits beneath Ahura Mazda, the Holy and the Destructive Spirits. While in the *Gathas* of Zoroaster Ahura Mazda is clearly above the twin Spirits, in Achaemenid Zoroastrianism the process began of the coalescence of Ahura Mazda (Ohrmazd) with Spenta Mainyu, the Holy Spirit. From 'the first and the ultimate' supreme God, Ahura Mazda was gradually equated with the holy one of the twin Spirits and came to confront what was now his symmetrical opposite, the virtual anti-God, Angra Mainyu (Ahriman). The new, Zoroastrian dualist formula, in which Ohrmazd and Ahriman were positioned as two primordial and independent principles, swiftly gained currency, even outside the Iranian world. Aristotle reported in his work *On Philosophy* (fourth century BC) that the Magi believed in the existence of two principles, the good spirit, Zeus or 'Oromasdes', and the evil spirit, Hades or 'Arimanius'. Aristotle's statement on Magian dualism is recorded in Diogenes Laertius' *Lives of Eminent Philosophers* (1 : 8), where Diogenes also attributes to Aristotle the belief that the Magi were more ancient than the Egyptians. In modern research, the Magi have indeed been credited with the hardening of early Zoroastrian dualism in the doctrine of Ohrmazd versus Ahriman and Babylonian influences are also thought to have played a role in this Magian revision of the teaching of the twin Spirits.[117] How much this fully fledged dualism affected Achaemenid Zoroastrianism may only be conjectured but it received theological elaboration and eventually emerged as the orthodoxy of the Zoroastrian state–church of the Sassanid empire in Iran (*c.* AD 224–640).

In classical Zoroastrian accounts of the new strict dualist system, Ohrmazd and Ahriman appeared as two separate prime causes existing from the beginning – two absolutely independent and diametrically opposed spirits. Ohrmazd is the Creator who is 'all goodness and all light' and dwells in the Endless Light above, while Ahriman is the Destroyer who is 'all wickedness and full of death' and dwells in the abyss of Endless Darkness below. Another dualist polarity contrasts the hot, moist, bright and light substance of Ohrmazd to the cold, dry, heavy and dark essence of Ahriman, whose abode is traditionally located in the northern realms (*Vendidad* 19 : 1). In the beginning Ohrmazd and Ahriman, Light and Darkness, are separated by the Void; Ohrmazd, who is ever in the light, is infinite in time but limited in space by Ahriman, who is slow in knowledge, possessed by the will to smite and limited in time, as he is to be vanquished in the last days (*Greater Bundahishn* 1:1–12). While originally Ahriman was unaware of the existence of Light, the omniscient Ohrmazd knew of the existence of the Destructive Spirit, with his constant desire for aggression and destruction. The unfolding conflict between the Creator and the Destroyer is recounted in the dramatic opening section of the *Greater Bundahishn*. Ohrmazd was aware that Ahriman would attack and try to merge with him. As a defence he fashioned in the Void an ideal creation which remained motionless, without thought and intangible for three thousand years. At the same time, Ahriman perceived the light of Ohrmazd and, obsessed with envy and desire for destruction, fashioned from his own darkness his destructive 'black and ashen' creation and the essence of the demons, an 'evil (disorderly) movement', designed to bring destruction to Ohrmazd's creatures. Ohrmazd offered peace to Ahriman, promising him immortality if he would abstain from battle to praise and aid Ohrmazd's creation. Ahriman forcefully rejected the offer and threatened not only to destroy Ohrmazd and his creation, but also to bring Ohrmazd's creatures to hate their creator and to love him, the Destructive Spirit (*Greater Bundahishn* 1:22).

To counter the threat of Ahriman's aggression and everlasting struggle and mixture in his creation, Ohrmazd succeeded in securing from him a pact that the conflict was to last for the finite period of nine thousand years. Mithra was seen as watching over the pact. Ahriman was then expelled from Ohrmazd's ideal creation and cast down in his abyss of darkness, where he remained powerless for three thousand years. Ohrmazd proceeded with fashioning his material creation to repulse the future attack of the Destructive Spirit, the source of the 'disorderly movement'. Following the creation of the sky, water, earth and plants, Ohrmazd fashioned the primal 'Lone-created Bull' and the radiant Gayomart, the primal 'Righteous Man'. Ohrmazd presented the pre-existent souls of men, the *fravashis*, with the free choice: either to incarnate in material form, fight the Untruth and ultimately be immortalized with their bodies, or to be sheltered in the ideal world from the onslaught and enmity of the Destroyer, Ahriman. Confronted with the menacing prospect of Ahriman's inevitable aggression and corruption of the world, but also with the vision of the final rehabilitation of the Good Creation and immortalization of man, the souls chose to descend and carry out Ohrmazd's struggle against Ahriman.

After being ejected from Ohrmazd's spiritual world, Ahriman lay in his realm of Darkness in lethargy, his fear of Righteous Man prolonging his passivity. After three millennia, however, Ahriman was finally restored to action by the 'Accursed Whore'. Seen sometimes as the first woman, she was created by Ohrmazd but defected to the Destructive Spirit, by whom she was defiled and elevated as 'the demon Whore queen of her brood'.[118] Roused by her frenzy to demolish the dignity of the 'Righteous Man' and the Bull, Ahriman rallied his demons and weapons and, rising up in the form of a serpent, burst into the visible world at the time of the vernal equinox. The beginning of Ahriman's assault seemed to justify his sinister appellation as a 'destroyer of the world' – the whole of creation was assailed, ravaged and made powerless and at noon it was invaded by darkness.

In his triumphant oration in the *Selections of Zadspram* (4:3), Ahriman claimed 'perfect victory' and recounted his feats of destruction which had despoiled the sky, waters and earth. Besides withering the plants and blending fire with darkness and smoke, Ahriman assailed the primal Bull, which died, soothed by a narcotic mercifully provided by Ohrmazd. Ahriman, moreover, let loose the 'Demon of Death', Atvihad, along with a thousand minions, upon the Righteous Man, who, though severely weakened, survived the assault of the Destroyer and lived for another thirty years.

Ahriman's offensive also set the planets against the constellations in a heavenly war in which the planets, described as 'pregnant with darkness', fought on Ahriman's side. The so-called 'dark Sun and Moon', seen as responsible for the eclipses, were bound to the 'chariot' of the true Sun and Moon and hence were incapable of harm. In the unfolding war, the leader of the constellations, the Pole Star, confronted the planets' commander, Saturn, as the Great Bear, Vega, Scorpio and Sirius fought respectively Jupiter, Mars, Venus and Mercury. Scorpio and the Great Bear, seen as the 'Chieftain of the North' and a highly beneficent force (free of any of the Sethian-like associations it had in Egypt), defeated their planetary adversaries but the 'Ahrimanic' planets also had their victories: Mars and Saturn prevailed in their contests with the Pole Star and Vega, while Mercury and Sirius proved equally matched. Feared thereafter as the planet of death, in Zoroastrian lore Saturn gained the title of 'he whose aggression reaches far', whereas Jupiter, having succumbed to the Great Bear, became the planet of life. In the Zoroastrian astrological scheme the death of the Righteous Man was caused by the predominance of Saturn, the death-bringer, placed in Libra, and 'victorious' over the life-bringer, Jupiter, weakly positioned in Capricorn.

Ahriman might have despoiled the Good Creation but his stronghold in the material world proved to be his perennial prison, as the sky was made a fortress which he could not overcome to return to his realm of darkness. After battles with Ohrmazd's spiritual forces, Ahriman was cast into the middle of the earth and firmly ensnared in the world, which itself now had to go through transformation to 'duality, opposition, combat and mingling of high and low' (*Greater Bundahishn* 4:28). On the death of the primal Bull his limbs gave rise to plant life, his seed to animal life and his blood to the fruit of the vine, while the seed of the dying Righteous Man generated the first human couple, Mashye and Mashyane, the Zoroastrian counterparts of Adam and Eve. The 'father and mother of the world' were inducted into Ohrmazd's 'righteous order', but none the less were led astray by Ahriman to proclaim him the creator of water, earth and the plants, and thus committed 'the root sin against dualism',[119] mistaking the Destroyer for the Creator. After indulging in more crimes, Mashye and Mashyane were consigned to Hell until the time of the final transfiguration and salvation.

Despite the transgressions of the first human couple, the human race, endowed as it is with free will, remained in the forefront of Ohrmazd's battle against Ahriman throughout the remaining millennia of the original pact. The demonic hosts of Ahriman are not only compelled to fight a losing battle against Ohrmazd's forces, but also the genius of 'disorderly motion' is bound finally to provoke their self-ruin. While Ahriman's infernal world was doomed to be exterminated at the hands of Ohrmazd's commanders amid demonic orgies of self-destruction, Ahriman himself was to be hurled out of the sky through the very hole he had pierced into the Good Creation. With the decimation of the calamitous potency of the Destroyer Ahriman, described sometimes as the cutting off of his head, the Creator Ohrmazd finally becomes infinite not only in time, but also in space, to reign over the transfigured world for all eternity.

The Zoroastrian account of the creation of the world and its relation to the unfolding conflict between Ohrmazd and Ahriman betrays an obvious indebtedness to archaic Indo-Iranian cosmogonic scenarios. Inevitably, some elements of this Indo-Iranian legacy have been revalorized and then integrated into Zoroastrian cosmogony, a process that cannot be reconstructed in its entirety and poses a number of riddles. For example, there are unmistakable correlations between the Zoroastrian story of creation and the all-important Zoroastrian sacrificial ritual, the *yasna*,[120] including an evident parallel between the killing of the primal Bull (one of the principal acts that ushered the second stage of 'Mixture' in Zoroastrian cosmogony) and the *yasna* priestly blood-sacrifice, with its ancient Indo-Iranian provenance. However, in the Zoroastrian scheme the killing of the Bull is one of Ahriman's most wicked acts, precipitating in the world a kind of fall from its previous perfect and motionless state, whereas in the *yasna* ritual the sacrifice is naturally viewed as a wholly beneficent act. A postulated solution to this glaring discrepancy offers strong arguments that in the archaic Indo-Iranian version of this cosmogony the transition between the first stage of creation, when the world was static and motionless, to its second, dynamic state was effected by a primeval bull-sacrifice.[121] This sacrifice was seen as a benign and necessary act and, according to some indications, was attributed to Mithra in his function as a demiurgic figure. The association between the demiurgic functions of Mithra and Indra, respectively in Indo-Iranian and Vedic cosmogony and the second stages of creation, may have led to a Zoroastrian reaction against the sacrifice myth in its original form. Due to his ambivalence and war-like aspects Indra was a particular target of the Zoroastrian demotion of the *daevas*, whereas Mithra, divorced from the act of the primeval sacrifice, retained his high position in the Zoroastrian pantheon, although traditions maintaining his original role of a demiurge-sacrificer persisted in Western Iran.[122]

Although prevalent during long phases in the history of Zoroastrianism, the strict dualism of Ohrmazd and Ahriman, the two first principles, was not the only theological solution to Zoroaster's riddle of the twin Spirits, 'renowned to be in conflict' (*Yasna* 30:3). While Aristotle alluded to the two primordial principles of the Magi 'Oromasdes' and 'Arimanius', Eudemus of Rhodes recorded another form of Magian dualism. According to Eudemus the Magi and the 'whole Aryan race' called the 'whole intelligible and unitary universe' Space or Time, from which were extracted a good god and an evil demon, light and darkness, the first ruled by Ohrmazd, the latter by Ahriman.

The Father of Light and Darkness

Besides their contribution to the transformation of the original Zoroastrian dualism in the Achaemenid era the Magi encouraged religious syncretism which prepared the ground for the assimilation of new religious concepts in Zoroastrianism. The cults of ancient Mesopotamian deities persisted in what were now the Near Eastern domains of the Achaemenid empire in the fertile climate of the encounter between the Iranian and Mesopotamian civilizations. In parallel with Iranian dualism, neo-Babylonian thought seems already to have begun to develop a dualist antagonism between the patron god of Babylon, Bel Marduk, and the Mesopotamian archetypal deity of war, death and the underworld, Nergal, the consort of the queen of underworld and darkness, Ereshkigal.[123] As a personification of the destructive power of the Sun and fire and with solar attributes, like the gryphon and the lion, Nergal is sometimes associated with the Mesopotamian Sun-god Shamash. With his underworld association, Nergal was sometimes equated with the Phoenician netherworld deity Moloch (Molech), who, besides having close connections with the cult of the dead and necromancy, was said to be worshipped with human sacrifice, the victims being 'passed through fire'. Extolled as 'Lord of the Gods' and bringer of light, Bel Marduk came to be conceived of as a deity of good, while the formidable death-god Nergal, the dreaded bringer of fever and pestilence, predictably emerged as his antipode. The rival cults of the two deities persisted into the Achaemenid era and there are indications that the worship of Nergal merged with vestiges of archaic Iranian pre-Zoroastrian traditions.[124]

In the Achaemenid period Zoroaster's Good Religion not only increased its influence and authority but also felt the impact of new religious developments in the Near East: under Babylonian influence, certain novel religious and astrological notions concerning the nature and functions of time brought about a new transmutation of the Iranian dualist scheme with the emergence of a new trend in Zoroastrianism, Zurvanism.

In Zurvanism, Ohrmazd and Ahriman were regarded as twin offspring of the higher and supreme being Zurvan, the god of Time, later identified also with Destiny. While Zurvanism has sometimes been considered an independent pre-Zoroastrian Iranian religion of a time-god, with its own teachings and ritual, the prevailing view is that Zurvanism arose as a new form of modified Zoroastrian dualism which sought the common origin of Ohrmazd and Ahriman in a deified Time–Destiny.[125] The origin and early fortunes of Zurvanism, as well as its potential links with other religious trends, such as Orphism and early Buddhism and Greek philosophical traditions, are still in dispute. What seems certain is that the Zurvanite trend in Zoroastrianism developed during the middle or late Achaemenid era in western Iran and was particularly influential throughout the Persian domains in Asia Minor.

Zurvan, as the deity of Infinite Space–Time and Destiny, was raised to the supreme status of the first principle, the boundless 'Great and Just God', who is without origin and is the source of all things. Extolled as the Lord of the Zoroastrian 'Three Times', Zurvan came to be worshipped as a quaternity, a four-fold god, associated with Light, Power and Wisdom in addition to Time. He is the primal, intelligible unitary All that has begotten both Ohrmazd and Ahriman and the related antitheses of good and evil, light and darkness, etc. As the sole ultimate *fons et origo* of all cosmic dualities, Zurvan seems essentially a coincidence of opposites, a pre-existing and eternal Being that transcends good and evil. Zurvanism came to develop its own elaborate mythology, which is preserved in fragmentary and sometimes slightly discrepant versions, expounding its central concepts of the pre-eminence of Zurvan, the primeval birth of Ohrmazd and Ahriman and their alternating rule of the world.

In Zurvanite mythology,[126] before anything existed, there was the boundless and eternal Zurvan who yearned to father a son who would create and preside over heaven and earth as a creator and cosmocrator. To provoke the birth of a creator-god, Zurvan was set to offer sacrifices for a whole millennium but eventually came to doubt their efficacy and conceived twin sons – Ohrmazd, the embodiment of his wisdom, and Ahriman, the incarnation of his doubt. In some versions of the myth, Zurvan originally appears androgynous, while other variants introduce a mother goddess figure who was brought into existence early in cosmic history and conceived Ohrmazd and Ahriman after Zurvan's plea. As Zurvan had pledged that the first-born should be consecrated king, Ahriman, the would-be Lord of darkness and evil, ventured to 'tear the womb open', and came forth to claim his right to kingship. In other versions Ahriman inaugurated Untruth and proclaimed that he was Ohrmazd, but was betrayed by his 'dark and stinking' nature. The luminous and fragrant Ohrmazd was born immediately after him but although Zurvan aspired to bestow the kingship on the younger twin son, the Lord of goodness and light, he had to cede to the first-born the kingdom of the world for the finite period of 9,000 years. While unwillingly granting the kingship to Ahriman, Zurvan conferred on Ohrmazd the priesthood with its emblem, the barsom twigs. After Zurvan offered sacrifices for his son, Ohrmazd had to offer sacrifices for his father. With divine priesthood bestowed upon him, Ohrmazd was made king over

Ahriman, apparently in the heavenly realm, and after the fixed nine millennia of Ahrimanic dominion in the world, he was to reign and order everything according to his will.

Zurvan endows his two sons with their respective weapons or 'garments', which they choose freely according to their will and which invest them with their contrasting essences. The substance of light, Ohrmazd's essence, that 'form of fire – bright, white, round and manifest afar' (*Greater Bundahishn* 1 : 44), was regarded in Zurvanism as an implement granted by his father. The weapon chosen by Ohrmazd was also associated with the robes of priesthood, the 'shining white garment' that furthered good and destroyed evil. In contrast, the ashen-coloured garment chosen by Ahriman as his essence was associated with heretical priesthood, 'evil knowledge' and the Ahrimanic planets, mostly with Saturn, the bringer of death. In *The Selections of Zadspram*, the 'black and ashen garment' that Zurvan conferred on Ahriman incorporated an implement that was like blazing fire, containing the substance of *Az*, greed or lust; the garment was also described as fashioned from the substance of darkness, 'mingled with the power of Zurvan'.[127] The investiture of Ahriman with the 'black and ashen garment' was part of a treaty centred on Ahriman's archetypal threat to bring the material creation to love him and to hate Ohrmazd, a threat defined as the belief in one principle, that 'the Increaser and the Destroyer are the same'. If at the end of his nine-millennia reign Ahriman had not fulfilled this threat, his creations would be devoured by his very own weapon of greed and lust. Unlike that of Ohrmazd, Ahriman's investiture contained the seed of self-destruction and was bound to bring about the ultimate extinguishing of the dark personification of Zurvan's doubt.

In Zurvanism both Ohrmazd and Ahriman exercised their creative potential, Ohrmazd mastering heaven, earth and all that was good and right, whereas Ahriman's counter-creations were confined to the demons and all that was evil and twisted. Yet the cosmogonic role of Ahriman appears ambiguous in some Zurvanite myths. One fable recounts that despite his beautiful creations, Ohrmazd did not know how to create light; it was Ahriman who imparted to him through the demon Mahmi the formula for the creation of the luminaries: through incest. Ohrmazd's intercourse with his mother generated the Sun, while his union with his sister gave birth to the Moon: these luminaries finally illuminated his creation.[128] Otherwise, in later Zurvanism the fortunes of man and the world were seen as being determined in the cosmic conflict between the twelve zodiacal signs, the commanders on Ohrmazd's side, and the seven planets, Ahriman's commanders, which oppress creation and inflict death and evil on it. These tendencies in Zurvanism gave rise to extreme, fatalist Zurvanite circles, whose focus on the all-pervading dominance of Time–Destiny was clearly in sharp contrast to the ethos of Zoroastrianism as a religion of free will. Apart from this fatalism, materialist trends also emerged in Zurvanism which rejected the cardinal Zoroastrian beliefs in reward and punishment, Heaven and Hell, and proclaimed all things material and that they stemmed from Infinite Time, the first principle of the world. According to another form of Zurvanism, prior to the birth of Ohrmazd and Ahriman Zurvan created fire and water, considered in Zoroastrian lore as brother and sister, the male and female principles. In this Zurvanite system both Ohrmazd and Ahriman derived from the combination of the first two principles of fire and water and it is plausible that Ohrmazd owed his essence to the heat of the fire and the moisture of water, while Ahriman inherited the coldness of water and the dryness of fire.[129]

In Zoroastrian literature Zurvanism is described as the teachings of Ohrmazd and Ahriman, as 'two brothers of one womb'. In modern scholarship Zurvanism has been evaluated variously as an intellectual–philosophical current within Zoroastrianism, as a dangerous heresy verging on materialism and fatalism, but also as the 'supreme effort of Iranian theology to transcend dualism and to postulate a single principle that will explain the world'.[130] In its search for a single unitary principle Zurvanism modified the original dualist message of Zoroaster, which had condemned evil as a force entirely separate from and alien to the supreme Wise Lord. Far from being an eternal and independent principle, evil in Zurvanism emanates from a 'doubt', a kind of divine fall or imperfection within the First Cause, the Great and Just God Zurvan. The ensuing cosmic struggle between Ohrmazd and Ahriman is virtually designed to restore the unity and integrity of the absolute Godhead. Moreover, the fixed nine millennia of strife and mixture between Ohrmazd and Ahriman in orthodox Zoroastrianism were transformed in Zurvanism into a time of Ahriman's rule in the world, fixed in a treaty with Zurvan. By enthroning Ahriman as Prince of the World for 9,000 years Zurvanism radically reshaped the traditional Zoroastrian sacred history, which had always rejected the idea of an era of Ahrimanic supremacy over the Good Creation and an Ahrimanic worldly *imperium*. None the less, in the first century AD, in his *De Iside et Osiride*, Plutarch described the notion of an aeon ruled by Ahriman as one of the tenets of the original teachings of the 'Magus Zoroaster'. In his account of Zoroastrian doctrine both 'Horomazes' (Ohrmazed) and 'Areimanius' (Ahriman) enjoy 3,000 years of supremacy and wage war for another 3,000 years. The belief that the evil principle came to preside over creation for a limited period became the crux of later religious and esoteric traditions. One of the cosmogonic systems of Bon, the pre-Buddhist religion of Tibet, which was said to have been introduced from Tazig (Iran), closely parallels Zurvanite concepts, possibly reflecting either earlier Iranian influences or the later impact of Manichaean missions in central Asia and China. In this Bon cosmogony, from the one and self-created 'Master of Being' two lights emanated, white and black, which respectively begat a white man, the radiant god of Being (The Master who loves Existence), associated with the principle of good and order, and a black man who embodied Non-Being (Black Hell), the source of the constellations, demonic forces, evil, pestilence and tribulations.[131]

Besides this Bon cosmogonic trinity, direct or indirect Zurvanite influences are often held to have underlain the New Testament allusion to the Devil as the 'Prince of this world' (John 16:11) and the 'god of this passing age' (2 Corinthians 4:4). While, however, the Iranian influences in the New Testament are still keenly debated, it is beyond doubt that the Christian concept of the Devil as the head of the realm of evil and originator of sin and death was determined by the radical transformations in Jewish notions of evil and Satan in the centuries that followed the dramatic vicissitudes that transformed and left their lasting imprint on the Jewish world in the sixth century BC – the Babylonian Captivity and the return to Zion. Apart from annexing the Judaean kingdom and deporting a great part of its population to Babylonia in 586 BC, the Babylonian king Nebuchadnezzar had destroyed Jerusalem and burned Solomon's Temple, but forty-seven years later Babylon herself was to fall to Cyrus the Great and the Persian conquest set the stage for the 'second Jewish Exodus', the restoration of Jerusalem, the rebuilding and consecration of the new Temple and the advent of the Second Temple era.

The 'Anointed' and the 'King of Babylon'

In 539 BC the short but historic war between the nascent Achaemenid and the neo-Babylonian (Chaldean) empires ended with Cyrus' bloodless capture of Babylon. Amid what the Persian imperial propaganda described as jubilant scenes of celebration he established himself in the Babylonian palace of the kings. Cyrus' manifesto, the so-called *Cyrus Cylinder*, and the *Verse Account of Nabonidus*, which was apparently composed in Babylonian priestly circles, praised Cyrus' capture of Babylon as an act of salvation for the city of Bel Marduk, which was lamented for having suffered desecration during the reign of the last king of the neo-Babylonian empire, Nabonidus. Both versions of Cyrus' collision with Nabonidus contrast the image of Cyrus as a saviour-king, chosen by Marduk to bring peace to Babylon, to that of Nabonidus as a heretical king, a royal adversary of Marduk, opposed to his priesthood and his worship in Esagila, 'the temple of heaven and the underworld'.[132]

Nabonidus may have been a son of the high priestess of the Moon-god Sin at Harran and a zealous patron of his cult extolled him in his inscriptions as the 'Divine Crescent, the king of all gods' and even 'god of gods'. Towards the end of his reign Nabonidus sought to elevate Sin to the head of the Babylonian pantheon and declared that Esagila, Ezida and other major Babylonian sanctuaries belonged to Sin and were his indwellings.[133] While the extent of the priestly and general opposition to Nabonidus' reforms has to be conjectured, the hostile testimony to his proclivities portrayed the last Chaldean king of Babylon as a self-styled visionary, guided by revelations, dreams and miracles, who had irrevocably offended the Babylonian priesthood with his eccentric endeavours to introduce the cultic image of the Moon in eclipse. Portrayed as a self-deluded and heretical ruler, Nabonidus was also accused of erecting a replica of Esagila, a type of counter-Esagila, near Marduk's old temple, interrupting the regular temple offerings, mixing up rites, uttering blasphemies at temple images and finally omitting the crucial Babylonian New Year feast. Nabonidus, who had proclaimed that all his military operations executed the will of the Divine Crescent, campaigned for ten years in northern Arabia; during his absence the New Year festival was not celebrated, while his son, the crown-prince Belshazzar, remained as co-regent in Babylon. In the dramatic scriptural version of Babylon's fall (Daniel 5) Belshazzar emerged as the last king of Babylon; warned of the imminent fall of his 'numbered' and 'divided' kingdom by the mysterious writings on the wall, he was 'weighed in the balance' and 'found wanting', doomed to be killed the very night Babylon passed to the Medes and the Persians.

Nabonidus' return to Babylon was marked by another controversial and enigmatic act: on the eve of the Persian invasion he collected in Babylon images from the traditional Mesopotamian shrines of the 'gods of the Sumer and Akkad'. During the latter part of Nabonidus' rule Babylonia was beset by plague and famine, and Cyrus' propaganda proclaimed that, with their sanctuaries in ruins, the inhabitants of Sumer and Akkad had become like the 'living dead'. The propaganda extolled Cyrus as a vehicle of Marduk's grace upon the Mesopotamian 'living dead', returning them to life, and an instrument of Marduk's judgement on the 'mad king' Nabonidus who had plunged the worship of the Babylonian tutelar god into abomination.

The account of Cyrus' ceremonial entry into Babylon eulogized him as a messianic saviour-king, chosen by Marduk, the 'king of the gods', as the 'king of the world' to re-establish Marduk's divine supremacy in god's own 'golden city', to assume the Babylonian kingship and to return the 'images of Babylonia', removed from their 'thrones' by Nabonidus, to their ancient sacred sites. Following the pattern of Babylonian kingship, Cyrus apparently ordered the immediate restoration and beautification of temple sites throughout Babylonia and as the new 'beloved' of Marduk he is heralded in the *Cyrus Cylinder* as 'King of the World, Great King, King of Babylon, King of Sumer and Akkad and of the four rims of the earth'. After the defeat of the last Chaldean king, Babylon was to pass under Achaemenid suzerainty for more than two centuries and according to the propaganda of the new rulers, despite Nabonidus' claims to hidden wisdom and revelations, his arcane exploits and creations were finally effaced and consigned to the flames in the first religious campaigns of the righteous Cyrus.

The divine judgement on Babylon and her king is among the dominant themes of Jewish prophetic literature and one of its most dramatic embroideries is the parable in Isaiah 14 where the king of Babylon is metaphorically associated with *Helel ben Shahar* (the Shining One, Son of Dawn, or, as translated in the Vulgate, Lucifer). As the 'son of the morning' the king of Babylon had boastfully wished to ascend into heaven, to exalt his throne 'above the stars of God' and to make himself equal to the Most High (Isaiah 14:12–19) but is doomed to be brought down to Sheol where he is greeted by the shades of the dead kings. Having desolated his land and slain his people, the king of Babylon, the former conqueror of nations, is destined to fall to the utmost depths of the abyss, cut out of his grave like an abominable shoot, 'a corpse trampled underfoot'.

In Isaiah 47 the unleashing of divine vengeance dethroned and cast into the shadows the 'virgin daughter of Babylon', the evil-struck 'daughter of the Chaldeans', who, with her shame finally exposed, is no longer to be called the queen of kingdoms, and who is betrayed by her own wisdom, for all her 'monstrous sorceries' and 'countless spells' (9–10). Notwithstanding the tenor of the prophetic utterances, Cyrus' treatment of defeated Babylon was famously lenient, unlike earlier conquests of the 'golden city', such as that of the Assyrian king Sennacherib, who captured and sacked rebellious Babylon in 689 BC, removed Marduk's statue to Assyria and proclaimed that he had made Babylon's destruction more complete 'than that by a flood' so that its 'temples and gods might not be remembered'. While Cyrus was to assume the Babylonian kingship and to be honoured as a builder and 'lover' of the temples of Esagila and Ezida, his triumph over Nabonidus was bound to mark the end of the 'Babylonian captivity' of the Jews that had been deported from Judaea to the 'rivers of Babylon' in several successive waves, the last of which dated from the final fall of Jerusalem to Babylon in 586 BC. Inevitably, the founder of the Achaemenid empire is extolled in the Old Testament, where it is Yahweh, the Lord God of Israel, who calls upon Cyrus, 'the ravenous bird from the east', to dethrone the 'virgin daughter of Babylon'. In the so-called Deutero-Isaiah (or Second Isaiah, composed of Chapters 40–55 of the Book of Isaiah) Yahweh unequivocally proclaims that he holds the right hand of his 'anointed', Cyrus, 'to subdue nations before him' and to 'undo the might of kings', 'before whom gates shall be opened and no doors be shut' (Isaiah 45:1). Yahweh promises Cyrus 'treasures of darkness, and hidden riches of secret places' (Isaiah 45:3, KJV) and raises him as his 'shepherd' who will fulfil all his purpose (Isaiah 44:28) and execute the divine judgement upon Babylon, which 'has been a golden cup in the Lord's hand to make all the earth drunk' (Jeremiah 51:7). As God's anointed, Cyrus emerges as a type of Gentile Messiah, a mediator of the divine grace to Israel, the prophesied 'shepherd of Yahweh', who would deliver the Jews from the 'Babylonian burden' and summon them to rebuild Jerusalem and Solomon's Temple destroyed by the Babylonian royal 'servant of Yahweh', King Nebuchadnezzar II in 586 BC.

Cyrus' historical edict of 538 BC, recounted in Ezra 1:1–4, decreed the restoration of Yahweh worship in Jerusalem and initiated the gradual return of many Babylonian Jewish deportees to Zion, which in the expression of Deutero-Isaiah had been left desolate like a widow bereaved of her children (Isaiah 49:21). The edict reflects the general religious policy of Cyrus, who, according to the *Cyrus Cylinder*, had returned Mesopotamian exiles to their homeland and had reinstated their gods to their original abodes. Cyrus had already legitimized his succession to the Babylonian kingdom: by authorizing the rebuilding of the Jerusalem Temple he apparently proclaimed his succession to the Davidic royal line in a restored and 'consoled' Jerusalem. Although for historical reasons the later rabbinic attitudes to Cyrus appear ambivalent, his renown as a pious ruler, who assisted the rebuilding of the Temple, endured and, according to some Jewish traditions, as a 'Cosmocrator' he was found worthy to ascend and sit on the throne of Solomon.[134]

The return of the Jewish exilic community to Zion under the aegis of Cyrus was perceived as a new Exodus guided by the God of Israel. The completion of the new Jerusalem Temple was presided over by Zerubbabel, a scion of the royal House of David. Its rebuilding, 'as commanded by the God of Israel and according to the decrees of Cyrus and Darius' (Ezra 6:14–15), was completed early in the reign of Darius and it was consecrated on 12 March 516 BC. The renewal of Yahweh temple-worship in Jerusalem was inevitably conceived as a re-establishment of the covenant between Yahweh, 'who chooses Jerusalem', and his chosen people. The dawning of the Second Temple era (516 BC–AD 70) was marked by fervent anticipation of the return of the divine presence and favour to a restored and redeemed Israel: 'Now, says the Lord, I have come back to Zion and I will dwell in Jerusalem' (Zechariah 8:3). Besides the restoration of the Temple the new era was expected to bring the coming of God's kingdom on earth, foretold in Isaiah 2:1–4, as well as justice, salvation and renewal to the world. The dramatic redemption of Israel was seen as the herald of the impending universal conversion of the nations to Israel's faith, when Yahweh's judgement and salvation would reach 'the end of the earth' and all men would turn to the 'Holy

One of Israel' to be saved and to 'serve him with one consent' (Zephaniah 3:9). The writings of post-exilic prophets like Zechariah and Haggai are pervaded by intense anticipation of the coming eschatological age and the cataclysmic 'Day of Yahweh' when he would 'shake heaven and earth, sea and land' along with all nations (Haggai 2:6–7) to create the 'new heavens and a new earth' where, as foretold in Isaiah 65:17, 'former things shall no more be remembered'.

These expectations were closely intertwined with prophetic hopes for the ultimate restoration of the Davidic kingdom under the rule of a messianic king of the royal line of David, the prophesied 'shoot' from the 'stock of Jesse' (Isaiah 11:1), the 'righteous Branch from David's line, a king who shall rule wisely' (Jeremiah 23:5). Besides his role of a rightful King of Israel, the Davidic Messiah was sometimes envisioned as a super-human saviour, as the ideal king of justice who would rule in 'the last days' and whose 'rule shall extend from sea to sea, from the River to the ends of the earth' (Zechariah 9:10). In the period of the Second Temple Jewish messianism received new vigour and generated traditions which were to have profound and lasting effects on Jewish, Christian and Islamic religious thought. The Book of Zechariah already distinguished two messianic figures, 'two anointed ones', the priestly Messiah and the royal Messiah, figures that are further elaborated in Jewish apocalyptic literature and the Dead Sea Scrolls. They were to be associated later with the star 'out of Jacob' and the comet 'from Israel' of Balaam's prophecy in Numbers 24:17, while in the Dead Sea Scrolls there appears also a third messianic figure, the prophet of the last days.

The expectations of the re-establishment of the Davidic kingdom were apparently centred initially on the Davidic princely 'shoot', Zerubbabel ('scion of Babylon'), governor of Jerusalem, who along with the high priest Joshua, conducted the rebuilding of the Second Temple, also known as the 'Zerubbabel Temple', as Zerubbabel was portrayed as laying the foundation of the Temple with his own hands, finishing it 'neither by force of arms nor by brute strength' but by the spirit of the Lord (Zechariah 4:6–10). In the Book of Haggai (2:20–3), on the very day of the foundation of the Second Temple, the Lord of Hosts was to shake heaven and earth, to overturn the heathen realms and to 'wear' Zerubbabel, the chosen one, as a 'signet-ring'. Apparently seen as the prophesied righteous 'Branch of David', he was expected to ascend the Davidic throne to rule as the royal Messiah alongside the priestly 'anointed', Joshua (Zechariah 6 : 12–13). However, Zerubbabel's sudden and baffling disappearance from the biblical narrative obscures his actual role in the Jewish messianic ferment during the building of the Second Temple.

Although Davidic restoration proved impossible, the ensuing two centuries of Achaemenid reign over the Jews in Palestine and Mesopotamia marked a watershed in Jewish religious and political history. Favoured by the tolerance of the Persian monarchs, the Jewish community in Judaea succeeded in establishing a theocratic state under Achaemenid authority and in completing the religious and legal reforms which had matured during the Babylonian captivity. Achaemenid monarchs like Darius I took care of the maintenance of the Jerusalem Temple (Ezra 6:1–11); later Jewish literature repeatedly acknowledges the cardinal role of the Achaemenids in the restoration of the Jewish national and religious polity. The Jewish leader Nehemiah, who rebuilt the walls of Jerusalem, was a cupbearer to the Achaemenid King of Kings Artaxerxes I, from whom he received the governorship of Judah, where he introduced wide-ranging political and religious reforms. Another celebrated Jewish reformer and religious leader, Ezra, was invested by Artaxerxes with the authority to restore and enforce the 'Law of Moses' as the imperial law in Israel. As a 'scribe versed in questions concerning the commandments and the statutes of the Lord laid upon Israel' (Ezra 7 : 11), Ezra brought from Babylon the 'Book of the Law of Moses' which was proclaimed 'in sight of all the people' of Jerusalem. The Achaemenid endorsement of the crucial missions of Nehemiah and Ezra highlights the extent to which the consolidation and codification of post-exilic Judaism depended on Persian religious policy, as inaugurated by Cyrus the Great and sustained with few exceptions until the very end of the Achaemenid empire.[135]

The Jews owed the rebuilding of Jerusalem, the Temple and their religious life to the Achaemenids' tolerant policies. Continuing Persian royal patronage of a restored and theocratic Israel undoubtedly made them more accessible to Iranian religious influences:[136] besides the apparent impact of Iranian law on Judaism, Jewish religious thought did not remain unstirred by the unravelling of new religious syntheses in the Achaemenid empire. During the ordeals of the Babylonian exile, Jewish religion had been exposed to new and alien systems of belief. During the Second Temple era it came into close contact with Iranian religious traditions and underwent a series of significant transformations. Some of the newly developed Jewish concepts and beliefs of the period betray strong affinities with Babylonian and Zoroastrian traditions and have repeatedly been attributed to direct Mesopotamian and Iranian influences on exilic and post-exilic Judaism.[137]

Despite the apparent differences between Zoroastrian and Judaic religious vision, they shared the unifying focus of the monotheistic rule of one supreme Creator-God who guides the historical process towards its climax in the final universal judgement and salvation. Both Zoroastrianism and Judaism vehemently rejected polytheism and idolatry and their prolonged intercourse in the wake of the Babylonian exile was conditioned by what is usually described as mutual religious sympathy. The seminal encounter between the Iranian and Jewish religious worlds certainly left its imprint on the evolution of post-exilic Jewish messianism and eschatology and on the rise of Jewish apocalypticism. Similarly, some important developments in the angelology and demonology of post-exilic Judaism, which elaborated and classified the parallel orders and functions of the warring angelic and demonic hosts, have been generally accepted as reflecting Babylonian and Zoroastrian influences. Moreover, it was in the Second Temple era that angels came to acquire names and individuality in contrast to the impersonal and anonymous angelic figures in pre-exilic Judaism. In the rabbinic tradition recorded in the Jerusalem Talmud the names of the angels were brought by the Jews from Babylonia and the early post-exilic Book of Zechariah, with its notion of the 'seven eyes of the Lord', was the first to acknowledge and distinguish the different angelic orders. In later Jewish angelological lore the heavenly hosts came to be classified in an intricate and carefully graded hierarchy crowned by the divine septet of the seven archangels who have entry to the presence of the glory of the Lord (Tobit 12:15). Three of the seven archangels, Michael, Gabriel and Raphael, formed the group of 'the angels of the divine Presence' together with Phanuel (later Uriel, one of the septet) and came to be envisaged as situated at the four sides of God's throne. These elaborations of Jewish angelology were at least partially motivated by the new religious ethos of post-exilic Judaism that tended to view Yahweh as a more remote and transcendent God, who acts in history through the agency of his angelic mediators. The simultaneous forging of Jewish demonology, with its demonic orders and princes, was closely related to the unfolding of new

Jewish approaches to the problem of the origin of evil and its enlarged role in cosmic history. Initially part of popular Jewish beliefs, the demons came to be seen increasingly as agents of a force that was emerging as the very personification of the spirit of evil – Satan.

Creator and Accuser

In pre-exilic biblical books the term 'satan' serves to denote generally an adversary or accuser, human or supernatural, and could be applied both in regard to David as 'satan' to the Philistines (I Samuel 29 : 4) and to the angel of God who was sent to obstruct Balaam's way in Numbers 22 : 32. However, in the Book of Zechariah and the Book of Job there already appears a distinct accusing angel, called Satan, who emerges as a type of celestial prosecutor of Yahweh's heavenly court charged with overseeing, provoking and reporting the sins of humanity. In Zechariah 3 : 1, while the high priest Joshua, the priestly 'anointed', represents Israel at the divine court, Satan stands at his right hand to accuse and resist him, being opposed by the benevolent 'angel of the Lord'. In the prologue of the Book of Job 'Satan' appears among the *bnai ha-elohim*, the 'sons of God', who are admitted into God's presence and were traditionally considered to form the divine council. In the Book of Job, Satan emerges more clearly as the allurer and accuser of the righteous, whom he subjects to ordeals, temptations and punishment. In his incessant pursuit of human wickedness and sins Satan descends to earth to test man and then ascends to the divine court to raise accusations against humanity. When asked by God whence he had come, Satan suggestively replied: 'Ranging over the earth ... from end to end' or, according to the King James Version, 'from going to and fro in the earth and walking up and down in it' (Job 1 : 7). Yet, however hostile to man, the Satan of Job and Zechariah still serves as an accusing and punishing angel under the supreme authority of Yahweh. In later Jewish thought, however, besides his ambivalent role of tester and tempter Satan came to be charged with some of the abstruse or destructive biblical exploits of the Lord of Israel.

In the so-called 'Call to Cyrus' in Deutero-Isaiah, Yahweh reveals himself to the Achaemenid monarch as the one who creates good and evil (Isaiah 45 : 7), a probable reaction to the Zoroastrian type of ethical dualism of good and evil. In earlier Jewish writings Yahweh could be portrayed variously as seeking the murder of Moses (Exodus 4:24–6), promising vengeance on his enemies in which his 'sword shall devour flesh, blood of the slain and captives, the heads of the enemy princes' (Deuteronomy 32:42), sending an evil spirit to plague Saul (1 Samuel 16:14), or putting a lying spirit in the mouth of Ahab's prophets to lure the apostate king to his death (1 Kings 22:23). In the prophetic literature Yahweh could be envisaged as teaching Isaiah his strategy of bringing desolation to Israel (Isaiah 6:8–12) or sending Jeremiah to the nations with a 'cup of fiery wine' to make them drink it 'and go mad; such is the sword which I am sending among them' (Jeremiah 25:16). The books of the prophets reinforced the image of Yahweh as an omnipotent and omniscient Creator, sovereign of the universe and inscrutable Lord of history, whose exalted judgement is responsible for both beneficial and calamitous events in Israel's history. As told in the Book of Job (36:23) the ways of Yahweh are bound to remain inimitable, unaccountable and impenetrable or in the famous words of the earliest of the Latter Prophets, Amos: 'Shall there be evil in a city, and the Lord hath not done it?' (Amos 3:5 *KJV*).

Among the biblical episodes when Yahweh's anger falls upon his 'chosen people', particularly enigmatic is the one chronicled in Chapter 24 of the Second Book of Samuel. There Yahweh, whose wrath has been kindled again by Israel, chooses to move David against Israel and prevails upon him to number her tribes, the census itself being a sin against the divine will (2 Samuel 24:1–2). David is lured into the census sin and has to choose one of the three proposed punishments: seven years of famine in the land, three months of flight before the enemy or three days' pestilence (12–14). David chooses to fall 'in the hands of the Lord, for his mercy is great', rather than into the hands of man, and Yahweh sends upon Israel three days' plague that smites 70,000 people. In the graphic scene of 2 Samuel 24:16, the avenging angel of pestilence stretches his hand even upon Jerusalem to destroy the Holy City before Yahweh 'repented of the evil'. When this 'census and punishment' story was recounted in Chapter 21 of the First Book of Chronicles, composed in the late Achaemenid era, it was Satan who set himself against Israel and incited David to number his people. Entrusted with one of the 'inimitable' deeds of Yahweh, Satan emerged as an individual and independent force and his name was no longer a mere title but was the proper name of the spirit of evil who was now opposed to the Lord of Israel and provoked man to sin against his laws. This new, magnified role of Satan heralded and paved the way for momentous transmutations in Jewish satanology – while in Job and Zechariah, Satan sought to incite Yahweh against man, in the First Book of Chronicles he had already moved man against Yahweh.

The story of David's census in the First Book of Chronicles marks the beginning of the striking transformation of the 'celestial prosecutor', who was originally subordinate to Yahweh, into the spirit of personified evil, the arch-enemy of good and righteousness, the source of all death, sin and destruction. The course of this transformation has long been a highly complicated and controversial problem and its current reading tends to seek its origins in the intensive search for new theodicies in post-exilic Judaism. With the newly developed distinctions between ethical good and evil, between the creative and destructive features of Yahweh, Satan eventually came to personify Yahweh's destructive powers, becoming an incarnation of 'the dark side of the God, that element within Yahweh which obstructs the good'.[138] Various stages and nuances of the evolution of Jewish satanology can be discerned in Jewish literature of the period that separates the last texts of the Old Testament and the earliest writings of the New Testament, the so-called intertestamental period. The crystallization of the concept of Satan as the embodiment of cosmic evil is often attributed to Iranian dualist influence on post-exilic Judaism; but still the process of personification of evil was to follow differing courses in Judaism and Zoroastrianism. Apart from the compensating monistic tendencies in Zurvanism, Zoroastrianism, on the whole, moved gradually towards radical dualism in which the King of Darkness, Ahriman, was to evolve into an anti-god, coeval if not coeternal with Ohrmazd. Although exposed to Persian religious insights, Jewish satanology resisted the lures of such dualism and the power of the Jewish Satan remained ever-restrained by the omnipotence and omniscience of Yahweh. None the less, some of the novel developments in post-exilic Jewish thought approximated dualism as Satan came to be seen as progressively independent of and hostile to Yahweh and his creation. With the increasing focus on ethical religiosity and the struggle between the forces of good and evil in the cosmos and in the soul of man, which was particularly pronounced in apocalyptic literature, trends emerged that sought and approached dualist solutions to the riddle of the origin of evil. In the apocryphal book the Wisdom of Solomon (2:24), likewise with Zoroastrian Ahriman, Satan was revealed as the superhuman agency that was opposed to God and man and had brought sin and death into the world to thwart divine purposes. Moreover, in the Wisdom of Solomon, Satan was associated with the serpent from the story of the fall in Genesis 3 and for the first time mankind appears divided into two opposing classes: the adherents of God and of Satan. The implicit association of Satan with the serpent and the bisection of humanity into men of God's and men of Satan's lot anticipated far-reaching developments of Jewish satanology which eventually set the stage for the Christian concept of the Devil. Yet, however transformed in intertestamental literature, the figure of Satan in Judaism was to retain its initial functions of a tester and accuser and in the Talmudic era one of his common appellations was still *Satan mekatreg* (Satan the Accuser).

The Prince of Light and the Angel of Darkness

The notion of a supernatural agency epitomizing the forces of evil, sin and disorder, which was introduced in the intertestamental era, came to be associated with the ambiguous biblical narrative of the union between the 'the sons of the gods', the *bnai ha-elohim*, and the 'daughters of men' (Genesis 6:2–4). In the biblical text the *bnai ha-elohim* had descended on the 'daughters of men' and their progeny was a race of giants, the 'heroes of old, men of renown'. In the intertestamental period the coming of the *bnai ha-elohim* to earth was seen increasingly as a fall from heaven and they became rebellious fallen angels who corrupted themselves with 'the daughters of men' and introduced evil and sin into the world. In Jewish apocryphal literature, and particularly in Jewish apocalyptic thought, the rebellion and fall of the angels were repeatedly assigned to the Prince of Evil, variously named Satan, Belial or Mastema. In the apocalyptic account of the downfall of the 'sons of God' or the Watchers in the early section of the Ethiopic Book of Enoch (1 Enoch),[139] the Book of the Watchers, the rebel angels were identified with fallen stars and were led by two archangels, Semyaza and Azazel, the latter being condemned as the first star to fall from heaven. Whereas Semyaza was presented as the king of the Watchers, Azazel emerged as a heavenly sage, who on his descent revealed to mankind 'the secrets of heaven' and initiated men in 'all the iniquities on earth'. However, in the later section of 1 Enoch, the Book of Parables, the Watchers were already subjects of Satan (1 Enoch 54:6), and his host of accusing 'angels of punishment' – the 'satans' – assumed a dominant position in the hierarchy of evil powers. Apart from revealing to men the 'weapons of death', one of the Watchers in the Book of Parables was already charged with leading Eve astray and the theme of the angelic–satanic seduction of Eve in some later Jewish, Christian and Gnostic readings of the biblical story of the Fall from Paradise was luridly elaborated.

In the apocryphal Book of the Jubilees the leader of the fallen angels was Prince Mastema who, in the wake of the flood, was allowed by Yahweh to retain a tenth part of his spirits to continue exercising his will among the 'children of men'. Identified with Satan (10–11), Prince Mastema was credited with some of Yahweh's biblical exploits, such as the inducement of Abraham to sacrifice Isaac, the attempt to murder Moses on his way to Egypt and the hardening of Pharaoh's heart to pursue the 'children of Israel'. Mastema–Satan was also revealed as the power that aided the Egyptian magicians against Moses and was also unleashed to smite all of the Egyptian first-born during the original Passover, the first night of the Jewish Exodus from Egypt.

In addition to such disclosures of 'satanic' intrusions in Genesis and Exodus, the apocryphal literature of the Second Temple era elaborated in greater detail the story of the sin of the Watchers – the downfall of the evil angels and their prince, a downfall variously ascribed to lust, pride or envy of Adam. In later apocryphal traditions Satan came to be identified as the main malignant agent of the fall of Adam and Eve, either by deceiving or corrupting Eve in the flesh, or through the medium of the serpent. Before tempting Eve to eat of the fruit of the Tree of Knowledge, Satan could be envisaged as pouring his evil venom upon the tree, which itself might be recognized as a satanic tool from the beginning, planted by Satan to lead Adam and Eve astray.[140]

Besides the title 'Satan', the leader of the fallen angels was often styled Belial ('worthlessness' or 'destruction'), who as the arch-enemy of God presided over a counter-hierarchy and counter-realm of evil and darkness. In the apocryphal Testaments of the Twelve Patriarchs man has to choose between the Spirit of Truth and the Spirit of Untruth, the law of the Lord and the law of Belial, as God has granted man two ways, good and evil, whereas Belial offered his adherents the sword, the 'mother of the seven evils'. The spirit of Truth and the spirit of Untruth waited upon man and in between was the 'spirit of understanding of the mind'. Belial was clearly associated with Satan, with the spirit of wrath being positioned at Satan's right hand and the spirit of hatred seen to work for the death of mankind, turning light into darkness. At the end of time a great many men would ally with Belial's 'kingdom of the enemy', which, however, would be terminated in a final war when the messianic agents of God's salvation would wrest the souls of men from Belial's captivity and with the 'judgement of truth' he would be cast into the eternal fire.

The increasing preoccupation with the riddle of the origins and power of evil in God's creation also led to the emergence of traditions that Satan–Belial was the cosmic force temporarily prevailing in the world. In the apocryphal Martyrdom and Ascension of Isaiah he was revealed as the 'angel of iniquity' who had ruled 'this world' from the beginning and in the last days would descend from his firmament as the 'king of this world', as an anti-Messiah, a type of Antichrist, seeking to enslave men with his signs and wonders.[141] The advent of Belial as the anti-Messiah and his miracles, which included the raising of the dead, was envisaged in some of the books of the Sibylline Oracles which also prophesied his destruction by divine fire.[142]

The belief that the passing age of 'tribulation and strife' was the dominion of Belial, destined to be annihilated for ever in an impending final war between the forces of good and evil, lay at the heart of the eschatology of the Dead Sea Scrolls, the writings of the Qumran sect. In the Dead Sea Scrolls the teachings of the 'Two Ways' and the 'Two Spirits' were carried to the dualist limits that Judaism could tolerate.[143] The Qumran Community Rule explicitly stated that, following his 'glorious design', God appointed for man two spirits in which to walk 'until the time of the final inquisition', the spirit of truth and the spirit of falsehood. Whereas the origin of truth was in the 'Fountain of Light', the source of deceit lay in the 'Wellspring of Darkness'. Accordingly the Prince of Light ruled over the 'sons of righteousness', who walked in the 'ways of light', while the Angel of Darkness presided over the 'sons of deceit' who walked in the 'ways of darkness'. Despite God's everlasting love for the spirit of light and his hatred of the spirit and ways of darkness, He designed 'according to his mysteries' the two spirits to stand 'in equal measure until the final age' (Community Rule 4). He also set them in eternal opposition and rivalry, which foreordained the fierce perpetual struggle between their divisions. By his 'inscrutable design' (or 'mysteries') God appointed a time of dominion for the Angel of Darkness when he would lead the righteous astray and subject the people of Israel to ordeals and terror. The sins of humanity, which was split into the opposing leagues of the 'sons of light' and the 'sons of darkness', were provoked by Belial's hegemony. The Community Rule darkly alluded to accounts of the iniquities and the sins of the children of Israel during Belial's domination, which were recited during the induction of neophytes into the sect, who themselves had to confess their sins and resist thereafter Belial's trials. The supremacy of Belial and the existence of falsehood would finally be terminated at the time of the final inquisition when every human being would be judged in accordance with his choice of the opposing ways of the two spirits. The 'sons of darkness' would suffer torment at the hands of the angels of destruction and annihilation by fire, whereas the 'sons of light' would be immortalized in eternal light.

Yet with all their apparent parallels to Zoroastrian sacred history, the dramatic accounts of the cosmic strife and war between the forces of light and darkness in the Dead Sea Scrolls do not develop religious dualism proper. The dualism between the 'Prince of Light' and the 'Angel of Darkness' remains dualism under the one God and it is God's inscrutable will that ordains a fixed era of Belial's dominion in the world. God created Belial, the angel of hostility, 'to corrupt' and with his dominion being in the darkness, Belial's purpose was to bring about 'wickedness and guilt', while the spirits associated with him were 'angels of destruction' who 'follow only the laws of darkness' (War Rule 13). Conversely, the Angel or Prince of Light had under his dominion the spirits of truth and was charged to help the people who cast their lot 'in the portion of light'. As in the Zoroastrian paradigm, the Qumran Prince of Light and Angel of Darkness were perceived as two opposite and coexistent metaphysical entities vying in the world and in the human soul, leading respectively the warring hosts of light and darkness that were marshalled in elaborate parallel lists of spirits. Other Qumran themes betray striking affinities with traditional Zoroastrian teachings but it has been shown that they were developed in a 'scrappy and incomplete fashion' and, being without apparent Jewish antecedents, suggest indebtedness to the more complete and consistent system in Zoroastrianism, indicating that the 'direction of influence was from Iran to Judaism'.[144]

While the Qumran scheme of cosmic opposition and conflict was almost certainly affected by the Zoroastrian dualist model, the doctrine of the 'dominion of Belial' – the notion that Belial presides over the current age and 'this world' – is reminiscent of the basic Zurvanite myth of Ahriman's finite reign over the world. Inevitably there have been attempts to associate Belial of Qumran with Ahriman of Zurvanism but again, apart from the obvious parallels, the myths of the Qumranite and Zurvanite 'Lords of Darkness' were formulated along differing lines.[145] Zurvanite Ahriman attained the right of kingship and finite rule over the world by violating the will and the sacrificial purpose of his primeval Father and was endowed with the 'black, ashen garment' of greed and self-destruction as part of a 'treaty' with Zurvan, whereas the Qumranite Belial held sway in the world according to God's inscrutable design and through his inborn power for corruption until the time of the final inquisition. The Qumranite Prince of Light, who was envisaged as the main defender of the 'sons of righteousness' against the reign of Belial (War Rule 13 : 10), is often identified with the archangel Michael, who came to be elevated in the post-exilic era as an *archistrategos* (commander) of the hosts, punisher of the fallen angels and heavenly protector of Israel. Following the old notion that the wars of the nations correlated to the wars of the 'host of heaven in heaven' (Isaiah 24 : 21–2), the Book of Daniel revealed Michael as Israel's angelic patron who vied with the prince–angels of Persia and Greece and was expected to arise and deliver Israel in the turmoil of the final 'time of trouble' (12 : 1). According to the Qumran War Rule (17 : 7), with the advent of the final age and the 'eternal light', Michael's dominion will be raised among the angels and Israel will be exalted 'among all flesh'.

As the guardian angel of Israel, Michael inevitably came to be extolled as the principal enemy of Israel's main accuser and opponent, Satan, and their 'war in heaven' was to assume cosmic and eschatological dimensions both in Judaism and Christianity. The Jewish opposition between the Prince of Light and the Angel of Darkness, between Michael and Satan, which emerged in the apocalyptic strands of post-exilic Judaism, has sometimes been seen either as a reflection or as a modified and tamed version of the Iranian dualism of Ohrmazd and Ahriman, whether in its traditional Zoroastrian or Zurvanite versions. The discovery and publication of the Dead Sea Scrolls have certainly deepened the problem of Irano-Jewish religious intercourse both in the Achaemenid era and in the post-Achaemenid, Hellenistic period in the Near East. Most of the already charted developments of Jewish intertestamental thought are recorded in the Hellenistic era, inaugurated by the conquests of Alexander the Great in Asia, when the meeting of east and west gave rise to novel and lasting religious currents, when religious dualism reached striking new forms and new spheres of influence in the unfolding age of syncretism.

CHAPTER TWO

The Time of Mixture

In 331 BC Alexander the Great defeated the armies of the last Achaemenid King of Kings, Darius III, for the third time in what the Macedonian king saw as a 'legitimate war for the sovereignty of Asia' (Arrian 2 : 12.5). The following year Alexander sacked and burned the ceremonial imperial capital of Persepolis, seen by the Macedonian conqueror as the most hateful of all cities of Asia (Diodorus 17 : 70.1); its devastation was to be proclaimed as retribution for Xerxes' destruction of the Athenian Acropolis. The burning of Persepolis 'violated and ended the long cycle of sacred Achaemenid kingship'[1] and despite fierce Iranian resistance in Sogdiana and Bactria, the great Persian empire fell to the Macedonian pupil of Aristotle, who proclaimed himself the new 'King of Asia', guided and protected by Zeus and Ammon. While the Achaemenids had failed to advance deeper into Europe and were eventually repelled from the Balkans, Alexander, who came to be seen as inspired by the myths of Dionysus' conquest of India, advanced through western Asia as far as the north-west extremes of the Indian subcontinent. The conquests of Alexander, reputedly crowned in Athens as the second Dionysus, signalled the end of the classical epoch in Greece and the advent of the cosmopolitan Hellenistic era (323–30 BC). Within the short space of twelve years, Alexander succeeded in unifying most of the ancient historical world into a vast empire.

For the defeated Persians the Macedonian 'son of Zeus-Ammon' was to become the 'accursed Iskander', the 'evil-destined' avatar of Ahriman, a murderer of Magi, who quenched sacred fires and brought war and devastation to Iran but was finally forced to flee from the world.[2] In the Sibylline Oracles (3 : 381–5) Alexander's conquests were portrayed as bringing suffering to Asia and Europe, while Macedonia, having captured 'fortified' Babylon and become 'mistress of every land' under the sun, was prophesied an evil fate, leaving only a name for posterity.

Notwithstanding the Persian charge that Alexander had despoiled Iran with Ahrimanic hatred and strife, his newly founded empire inherited and sought to preserve the imperial traditions of the Achaemenid *ancien régime*, encouraging further designs for Helleno-Iranian union. Alexander's empire passed its prime with his mysterious death in Babylon in 323 BC, to be split among the successor dynasties of the Antigonids, who acceded initially to its European domains, the Ptolemies, who fell heir to Egypt, and the Seleucids, whose kingdom absorbed most of the former Achaemenid domains in Asia.

With the demise of the Persian empire, Zoroastrianism inevitably seemed set to lose much of its authority and prestige secured under the Achaemenids. Following traditional Babylonian patterns, Alexander inaugurated temple-building and renovation work at Babylonian cultic sites like the old temple complex of Marduk and, according to Plutarch, it was at Babylon that Alexander was proclaimed King of Asia. Babylon may have been designed to be the eastern capital of his empire, but in Persia Alexander's reputed restoration of the tomb of Cyrus the Great failed to win renown in the Iranian world, where he was credited with burning the Zoroastrian sacred scriptures, the *Avesta*, and it is hardly surprising that in Zoroastrian eschatological traditions the unfolding era of alien rule came to be associated with the age of 'the evil sovereignty of the wicked demons' preceding the advent of the Saviour, the Saoshyant.[3] The advent of the Hellenistic era marked the beginning of the spread of Graeco-Macedonian culture in the Middle East, a far-reaching diffusion which was accelerated by the consolidation, growing influence and religious policies of the kingdoms of the Ptolemies and the Seleucids. With the advance of Hellenism in Egypt, Mesopotamia, Palestine and Iran a new syncretism developed, which blended Greek and Oriental motifs in art, architecture and literature. In the field of religion the syncretism and remarkable tolerance of the Hellenistic era were even more apparent, as the search for new religious syntheses led to the creation of composite and often exotic forms of worship. Besides the Eleusinian, Samothracian, Dionysian and Orphic mysteries, which were traditional for the classical Greek world, the late Hellenistic period saw the spread of mystery cults centred on Oriental deities like Cybele, Attis, Isis, Osiris, Sabazius and Mithra.[4] With their recondite rites of initiation and promises of secret knowledge, regeneration and salvation, the Graeco-Oriental mystery cults proved exceptionally enduring and flourished even more widely in the Roman imperial age. With the Greek political advance in the Orient, Hellenism penetrated deep into the eastern Iranian world and reached northern India, where it stimulated the rise of novel, startling forms of cultural and religious syncretism. Simultaneously, with the establishment of the Mauryan Indian empire under Chandragupta, who in 305 BC won back Punjab from the Seleucids, Indian religious influences radiated back into western Asia. When Chandragupta's grandson, the Buddhist emperor Ashoka (*c.* 273–*c.* 232 BC), inaugurated the expansion of Buddhism into a world faith, his Buddhist missions, 'the envoys of the Beloved of God', were sent to preach the Dharma not only to the Greeks in his realm but also in the Seleucid and Ptolemaic dominions and in the heartlands of the Hellenistic world – Greece and Macedonia.[5]

Three Empires

Among the Hellenistic monarchs, the Ptolemaic rulers of Egypt – who claimed descent from Heracles and Dionysus – promoted a religious policy that was perhaps the most symptomatic manifestation of the new Hellenistic *Zeitgeist* of syncretism. While Ptolemaic policy was aimed at Graeco-Egyptian religious synthesis, the convergence of Greek and Iranian traditions in the former Achaemenid domains in Asia was to breed its own cast of syncretism, particularly influential and long-lasting in Bactria, which became the easternmost outpost of Hellenism in Asia and continued to spread Hellenistic influence in India and central Asia.

The Graeco-Iranian syntheses were not confined to Anatolia and western Asia but emerged also in the large Greek diaspora in the northern Pontic-Azov (Black Sea) region, which had long been dominated by the Scythians but in the last two pre-Christian centuries had fallen under the sway of other northern Iranian tribes, the Sarmatians and the Alans. The religious climate of the region, largely determined by the strong Greek presence, was profoundly affected by the advent of the Sarmatians with their specific Iranian religious lore, which was probably influenced by Zoroastrian traditions possibly comprising a pantheon of seven gods including fire-worship. The new cosmopolitan spirit of the Hellenistic era spawned the flourishing of a rich syncretistic culture in the area of the

Cimmerian Bosphorus (the Straits of Kerch connecting the Black and Azov Seas), which was densely settled by Greek colonists in the seventh and sixth centuries. The Graeco-Iranian contacts and interplay in the Cimmerian Bosphorus, which in classical geography was regarded as the meeting point between Europe and Asia, have often been compared to those in Bactria. Under the vigorous Thracian dynasty of the Spartocids (438–110 BC) the Cimmerian Bosphorus evolved into a strong Hellenistic kingdom and later acknowledged nominal Roman sovereignty. The Bosphorus kingdom flourished in the Pontic *Pax Romana* until the fourth century AD; its culture and religion, where Greek, Sarmato-Scythian, Iranian and later Jewish elements intermingled, retained its distinct Hellenistic character into the Christian era.[6]

With its Babylonian capital and its boundaries extending initially from Asia Minor to India, the Hellenistic kingdom of the Seleucids seemed particularly suited to fostering cultural and religious fusion between expanding Hellenism and oriental traditions. Besides their Hellenizing policies the Seleucids, who claimed descent from Apollo, tolerated the varied religions in their kingdom and encouraged a revival of Babylonian learning and cults. In 199 BC the Seleucids finally won Palestine from the Ptolemies, where the growing influence of Hellenism was to bring about deep divisions within Judaism. The conflict between the Jewish Hellenizers and the Jewish traditionalists, the Hasidim, reached its climax in 167 BC when, during the infamous crusade of the Seleucid ruler Antiochus IV Epiphanes against Judaism, the Jerusalem Temple suffered the installation of alien worship, perhaps the cult of the Canaanite god Baal Shamin, sacrifices of pigs and the 'abomination of desolation' (I Maccabees 1 : 54) on the altar. In the violent Jewish backlash the militant Maccabean family restored Judaea's independence, which lasted until 64 BC when it was Rome's turn to conquer the Promised Land and eventually to destroy Jerusalem and the Temple under Titus in AD 70. Apart from its historic collisions with Judaism in Palestine the Hellenistic invasion of the Seleucid age profoundly transformed the cultural and religious make-up of Syria and Mesopotamia and made deep inroads into the Iranian world.[7]

From the mid third century BC onwards, however, the Seleucids began to lose hold of their eastern dominions. The first challenge to Seleucid authority in the east was the foundation of an independent Graeco-Bactrian kingdom, centred on Bactria and Sogdiana. In its eclectic religious climate Hellenistic and Zoroastrian traditions coexisted with a variety of cults, including what appear to have been '*daevic*' forms of worship. While Hellenism continued to thrive in the Graeco-Bactrian kingdom and also spread into the adjacent Asian region, Greek expansion in Iran itself was challenged by vigorous Iranian reaction. At the same time as the emergence of the Graeco-Bactrian kingdom the Seleucids were faced with the rise of a rival Iranian monarchy in the old Achaemenid satrapy of Parthia in north-east Iran. The driving force was Iranian semi-nomads from central Asia, the Parni, who had apparently adopted Zoroastrianism upon their invasion of Parthia. Under the rule of the aggressive Arsacid dynasty (*c.* 250 BC–AD 226), Parthia gradually extended its sway further in Iran and Mesopotamia, establishing its authority over an array of vassal kingdoms and principalities. The Seleucids were driven to the west of the Euphrates and following the Parthian conquest of Babylonia the Arsacids adopted the old Achaemenid title *Shah-an-Shah* (King of Kings) and claimed Achaemenid descent. As the Seleucid kingdom declined and contracted, the new Iranian empire expanded into a world power which came to control the crucial trade routes between Asia and the Mediterranean.

The restoration of Iranian authority over large areas of the former Achaemenid empire breathed new vitality into the Good Religion: in Zoroastrian lore the first collection and edition of the texts of the *Avesta* has been attributed to an Arsacid king. In the Arsacid era Zoroastrian worship was upheld in image sanctuaries and fire temples, while the Arsacids themselves maintained their ever-burning, dynastic fire. The Magi also continued to consolidate their spiritual hegemony in the Parthian empire. While sustaining Zoroastrian traditions, most of the Arsacid monarchs also favoured Hellenism, while in Commagene, eastern Anatolia, Graeco-Iranian syncretistic formations emerged in which Ohrmazd was identified with Zeus, Mithra with Apollo, the war-god Artagnes with Ares or Heracles, while Anahita was often associated with Artemis. These religious formulas appeared to gain some currency in Arsacid Iran, and along with other identifications, in which Heracles was also linked with Nergal, epitomized the syncretistic tenor of most religious developments in the Near East during the Hellenistic age.[8]

Parallel Graeco-Iranian patterns of symbiosis began to emerge also in the Graeco-Bactrian kingdom. In the mid second century BC it was plunged into the turmoil of a fresh and overpowering nomadic influx from China and central Asia where the rise of the aggressive Hsiung-nu, seen sometimes as ancestors of the Huns, forced massive Iranian migration to the west. While some of the Iranian migratory waves reached the Pontic steppes to fortify the Sarmatian power in the area, particularly important were the migratory route and campaigns of Iranian nomads called by the Chinese Yueh-Chih (which probably meant the Moon race or clan).[9] Around the time when the Maccabean family was establishing its rule in Judaea, these nomads overran Sogdiana and Bacteria, and the eastern Iranian world was set to become the scene of another series of convoluted political and religious transformations. The 'Moon' nomads enriched the Graeco-Iranian-Indian civilization of Bactria with new religious imports from central Asia and China and frustrated the Parthian attempts to gain firm control of the region. The Moon clan was finally unified under the Kushan dynasty, whose kings adopted the title *devaputra* (son of god), and eventually sought to 'proclaim a new imperial age in the east' [10] after the model of the Achaemenids, while their empire grew to extend its sway from northern India to Sogdiana.

The rise of the Kushan empire as a great Asian power on a par with imperial China coincided with the consolidation of the Iranian Sarmatian supremacy over large areas in eastern Europe. In the Mediterranean the Roman conquest of Greece and the Hellenistic kingdoms had already opened the way for Roman expansion in the Middle East, where it confronted the Parthian empire. However, in the first violent confrontations between Parthia and Rome in Syria and Mesopotamia the Roman forces suffered a humiliating series of setbacks and defeats, among which the most famous was at Carrhae in 53 BC, when the 40,000 strong legions of Marcus Crassus, who had already plundered the treasury of the Jerusalem Temple, were destroyed by a much smaller Parthian army. Crassus' severed head was triumphantly delivered to the Parthian king amid a performance of Euripides' *The Bacchae*, where it was raised in the Dionysian climax of the play to illuminate Agave's verse: 'I am bringing home from the mountains/A vine-branch freshly cut, /For the gods have blessed our hunting'. Later, with the consolidation of Roman mastery of the Mediterranean world under the first Roman emperor Octavian Augustus (27 BC–AD 16), Parthia came to confront the aggressive *Imperium Romanum* in the west and the expanding Kushan empire in the east. Sporadically faced with war on two fronts, the

Parthian military machine, with its renowned heavy cavalry, succeeded in halting the advance of the Roman legions towards Iran and Armenia at the Euphrates and for a time even threatened to recover Asia Minor for the new Iranian empire. For many authors of antiquity the historical world appeared virtually divided between Parthia and Rome with the Euphrates marking the new political and spiritual frontier between the Iranian and Graeco-Roman realms.

Although separated by Parthian Iran, the Kushan and Roman empires maintained close political, cultural and trading contacts. Affected to varying degrees by Hellenistic syncretism, the three great empires brought highly diverse races, religions and cultures into intimate contact and coexistence. In a cosmopolitan age when new spiritual currents and ideas were freely traversing the religious and political frontiers, the three polyglot empires served, each in its unique manner, as vehicles for new religious syntheses and creations which determined some of the most significant and far-reaching developments in the religious history of Eurasia.

Syncretism in the East

With their abundance of cults and their capacity to assimilate and transmute alien influences the Kushan and Roman religious worlds seem tantalizingly similar. Although little is known about the religious landscape of Iran under the Arsacids, the Parthian empire was also the meeting place of diverse religious traditions. In its western dominions the old Mesopotamian cultic traditions were still active; the Jewish communities, particularly influential in Babylonia, were loyal and supportive of Parthian authority, while the eastern part of the realm was exposed to Hindu and Buddhist influences. Christianity also penetrated and spread early in the Parthian realms, as the tolerant and syncretistic religious policy of the Arsacids was to continue until the very end of their rule in AD 226.

To the east of Parthia, the Kushan empire was to develop one of the most original Asian cultures, renowned for its elaborate and ingenious synthesis of Iranian, Indian and Graeco-Roman cultural and religious elements. The extended Kushan pantheon comprised Ahura Mazda,

Buddha and Heracles, while Mithra, who was increasingly assuming solar features, was identified with Apollo and Helios.[11] Some traditional Hindu forms of worship, notably the cult of Shiva, which was prevalent in north-west India, also lived on to flourish in the Kushan realm, although now Shiva was associated variously with the hero-god Heracles or Dionysus. The foundation of the Kushan empire exposed northern India to Iranian influences but eventually Indian religiosity began to gain prominence in the empire, a process that was accelerated by a radical reformation of northern Buddhism – the rise of Mahayana Buddhism.

Simultaneously with the rise of Christianity in the Roman empire the Kushan domain witnessed the crystallization of the Mahayana (Greater Vehicle) school of Buddhism with its novel gospel of 'greater', universal salvation through faith and worship. In Mahayana Buddhism the work of salvation is inaugurated through the 'Three Bodies' of the Universal Buddha: the Body of Suchness (described also as the Body of Law, pure being and absolute source of all phenomena), the Body of Bliss or Glory and finally the Body of Transformation or 'Magical Creation', as manifested by a historical line of successive Buddhas, Sakyamuni being the historical Buddha of the present world-age. Mahayana Buddhism professed the way of the high 'Beings of Enlightenment', the Bodhisattvas, devoted to bringing full enlightenment and salvation to all living beings and praised as 'the final relief of the world' and 'the guides of the world's means of salvation'. The doctrine of the threefold nature of the supreme Buddhahood and the tenfold ladder of the Bodhisattvaship engendered many diverse Buddha and Bodhisattva figures who were elaborated in Mahayana scriptures and iconography. In the Bodhisattva pantheon particularly honoured was the figure of Avalokiteshvara, Lord of Compassion, whose embodiment in Tibetan Buddhism is deemed to be its spiritual head, the Dalai Lama, with his lineage of Avalokiteshvara reincarnations. Another celebrated Bodhisattva was Maitreya (The Kind or Loving One), who was exalted as the future Buddha and with Buddhist diffusion in Asia his cult came to acquire increasingly messianic and millenarian dimensions.

In the first Christian millennium Mahayana Buddhism, with its vigorous missionary ethos, spread far and wide in Asia and became the prevalent form of Buddhism in China, Tibet, Korea and Japan, where it gave rise to new and influential Buddhist schools of thought. The great Asian expansion of Mahayana Buddhism started from the Kushan empire, which became its stronghold during the enlightened reign of the great patron and propagator of Buddhism, Kanishka I (c. 110 AD), who emerged in Buddhist tradition as a type of second Ashoka. Under the aegis of successive Kushan rulers the empire served as a vital stepping stone for the introduction of Buddhism in central Asia and China. Yet the Mahayana reformation of Buddhism did not remain unaffected by the syncretistic climate and currents bred in the Kushan empire and the Indo-Iranian borderlands. Under Kushan rule the celebrated Buddhist art school in Gandhara, to the south of the Hindu Kush, reached its zenith. The Gandhara school developed a distinctive hybrid Graeco-Buddhist art style with curious parallels to early Christian art and elaborated for the first time the images of Buddha who had never been depicted in human form in pre-Mahayana Buddhism. Moreover, it is commonly assumed that some of the early Mahayana religious themes of light and salvation may well betray Iranian influences and the very concept of the would-be-Buddha, Maitreya, is often derived from the Zoroastrian tradition of the Saviour Saoshyant. It has also been indicated that the messianic tenor of the Maitreya cult might have been kindled by assimilation of Mithra traditions in northern Buddhism during its formative period in northern India and in the Kushan empire.[12]

While Mahayana Buddhism was beginning its expansion in Greater Asia the Graeco-Oriental Mystery religions were spreading throughout the whole Mediterranean world and reaching the acme of their popularity and influence. Christianity was also gaining increasing prominence in the Roman empire and was beginning to spread in the east into Persia and Bactria. It is worth noting that certain intriguing parallels between Mahayana Buddhism and early Christianity, including its Gnostic ramifications, have long been acknowledged but never satisfactorily discussed and explained.

During the late Hellenistic period the age-old religious and cultic traditions of Mesopotamia underwent a gradual decline and the Hellenized Orient entered an age of increasing religious ferment and new syncretistic creations. Despite the political and military opposition between the Iranian and Graeco-Roman worlds, the process of religious interchange and fusion continued unabated, as cults of Saviour-gods and Gnostic syncretistic faiths spread beside Zoroastrianism, Judaism and Christianity. When, in the words of Juvenal, the waters of the Syrian Orontes emptied themselves into the River Tiber; the Roman empire seemed increasingly exposed to religious invasion from the east, which ultimately weakened the hold of traditional Greek and Roman paganism, as Roman emperors chose to become initiates and even patrons of imported oriental cults.

The mystery cults, which were vying with Christianity for prestige and supremacy in the Roman world, were often devoted to 'dying and rising' deities like Attis, Adonis and Osiris. Perhaps it is significant that the cult that posed the gravest challenge to nascent Christianity focused on the unconquered and invincible god Mithras, who represented a Roman development of the Indo-Iranian Mithra. However, unlike Mithra, the Judge and Guardian of the Zoroastrian Good Creation, Mithras emerged as a Saviour-god entrusted with the central divine act in the mythology of Roman Mithraism – the bull-sacrifice, the shedding of the 'eternal blood'.

Mithras the Mediator

In the 'Zoroastrian' Chapter 46 of his *De Iside et Osiride* (*c.* AD 70), Plutarch declared that 'Zoroaster the Magian' taught that 'votive- and thanks-offerings' should be sacrificed to the god-creator of good Horomazes, (Ohrmazd), while his rival demon-creator of evil, Areimanius (Ahriman), must be offered sinister offerings to avert evil. Plutarch even provided a vivid description of the grim offerings to Areimanius in which a herb called *omomi* had to be pounded in a mortar and, following an invocation of Hades and darkness, had to be mixed with the blood of a slain wolf and finally thrown into a sunless place. Besides dwelling on the contrasting modes of sacrifice to Horomazes and Areimanius, Plutarch recounted that, according to the Persians, between these two rival powers stood an intermediary, 'Mithras the Mediator'.

In Zoroastrian texts the Iranian Mithra could also be granted the title Mediator, but in a very different context; Plutarch's version of Zoroastrian dualism, with its prescribed parallel sacrifices to Ohrmazd and Ahriman, has understandably provoked heated controversy, as it is evidently at variance with traditional Zoroastrian values and ethics. The offerings to Ahriman have been seen as a 'conscious inversion' of Zoroastrian sacred rituals but Plutarch's account has been interpreted as representing a developed form of Zurvanism, or a mid-point between 'catholic Zoroastrianism' and the Roman Mysteries of Mithras.[13] Yet it is precisely this elusive continuity between Zoroastrianism and Roman Mithraism – between the oriental Mithra 'of the wide pastures' and the occidental Mithras the Bull-Slayer – that has proved to be one of the most notorious unsolved conundrums of the religious history of antiquity.

Roman Mithraism emerged as one of the most striking religious syntheses of antiquity: in the first four centuries of the Christian era it swept across the Roman world, becoming the favoured religion of the Roman legions and several Roman emperors. As an all-male and esoteric cult, which was diffused mainly by legionnaires, imperial officials and traders, Mithraism has often been described as a type of Roman Freemasonry. In its phenomenal spread from Syria to Britain, the cult of Mithras gained a particularly strong foothold in Italy and the Roman provinces in central and eastern Europe, while Mithras was extolled to the status of *Sol Invictus* (Invincible Sun). In his crusade to revitalize the *Imperium Romanum*, in 307, four years after launching the persecution of the Christians, Diocletian dedicated a great altar to Mithras as the protector of the empire. The elevation of Mithras in the Roman empire has been seen as a potential turning point, when Europe was confronted with the real danger of becoming Asiatic, a danger that was not matched even during the later era of sweeping Islamic expansion.[14] With all his endeavors to restore the vitality and prestige of paganism, the last pagan Roman emperor, Julian the Apostate (AD 361–3), was initiated early in the Mithraic mysteries and had a Mithraic sanctuary (*mithraeum*) erected in his palace in Constantinople. Apart from adopting Mithras as his guide and guardian god Julian also came to recognize himself as a 'human replica' of Mithras in what he saw as his redeeming religious and political mission in the Roman world. In the oft-quoted, if hyperbolic, words of Renan: 'If Christianity had been halted in its growth by some mortal illness, the world would have gone Mithraic'.[15]

However exaggerated the supposed prospects for Mithraic supremacy in Europe, the transfiguration of the ancient Iranian deity of light and war, the divine 'Judge of Iran', into a patron god of Persia's sworn enemy, the Roman empire, remains abstruse and striking. Given the renown of Zoroaster in the Greek world, inevitably there emerged traditions that the prophet of Ahura Mazda was the one who consecrated the first Mithraic cavern, but Greece proper remained largely immune to the popularity of the old and newly developing Mithraic cultic traditions. With the dawning of the Christian era, apart from eastern and western Iranian lands Mithra's worship was also active in Anatolian areas, Armenia, Commagene; apparently even in Graeco-Roman Egypt there existed residues of the Persian cult of the god dating from the era of the Achaemenid domination in Egypt. Widely differing theories have endeavoured to locate the beginnings of the Mithraic mysteries in some of the border regions between the Graeco-Roman and Iranian worlds, from Syria to the Bosphorus kingdom or the Balkans, or to associate the Roman cult with the solar cult of Mithra in the Kushan empire.[16] According to the traditional and still widespread view the mystery cult of Mithras developed in the late Hellenistic period in Asia Minor, where it seems to have been affected by some Anatolian forms of worship such as the Phrygian cult of Cybele and Attis. Formerly part of the Achaemenid empire, Asia Minor had a long-established Iranian diaspora whose Zoroastrianism seems to have been predominantly of the Zurvanite type and Magian colonies in Cappadocia are attested in the early Christian era. In the wake of Alexander's conquests Asia Minor became a fertile meeting ground of Greek, Anatolian and Persian traditions but curiously the Greek world remained particularly resistant to Mithra-worship. None the less, a questionable Latin tradition claimed that the cult of Mithra passed from the Persians to the Phrygians and from them to the Romans. In the Roman world the cult of Mithras often passed as a Phrygian cult and Mithras came to be depicted wearing a Phrygian cap and was frequently styled the 'Phrygian God' or the 'Capped One'. The role of Anatolia as the possible medium for the introduction of Mithra-worship to the Roman world is supported by Plutarch's account (Pompey 24:5) of Pompey's campaign in 67 BC against the Cilician pirates who used to perform abstruse sacrifices at the Lycian Olympus and celebrated the secret mysteries of Mithras. Despite Plutarch's evidence of transferring Cilician prisoners to Greece and Pompey's resettling of some pirates in Italy, the first steps of the Mithraic Mysteries in the Roman world still remain virtually untraceable.

What adds to the atmosphere of confusion and controversy is the obscurity surrounding the fortunes of the original Iranian cult of Mithra, which, in early Zoroastrianism at least, was largely eclipsed by the monotheistic worship of Ahura Mazda. Yet the traditional cult of Mithra did not die out and sometimes is considered to have been the prevalent form of worship among the Medes and their priesthood, the Magi, or else to have persisted in some form among the unreformed and apparently inextinguishable *daeva*-worshippers. The revived Mithra-worship of the Achaemenid era was integrated into Achaemenid Zoroastrianism but had certainly preserved some pre-Zoroastrian traditions. Some Persepolis inscriptions suggest moreover, that in Persepolis and perhaps elsewhere in the Achaemenid empire there existed in military organizations a specific cult of Mithra comparable to the Knights of Malta or Knights Templar in medieval Christendom.[17] Besides its vital role in Achaemenid Zoroastrianism and royal ideology, the cult of Mithra arguably came into contact with Babylonian astral religion and Mithra came to be associated with the old Mesopotamian solar deity, Shamash. It is also probable, as recent research has indicated, that some forms of Mithra worship, which were preserved among the Medes and were concerned with death, the underworld and the afterlife, assimilated elements from the 'underworld' cult of Nergal.[18]

In Parthian Iran, Mithra's relation to kingship, fire- and sun-worship apparently became even more pronounced, as the cult spread in the Iranian spheres of influence in the Near East, Asia Minor and Armenia. In the syncretistic climate of the late Hellenistic era, Mithra, who as a light-god was acquiring increasingly solar attributes, was identified with solar deities like Apollo and Helios and also with Hermes as a mediator between man and the gods and as a guide of souls in the afterlife. In an era when the cult of the divinized ruler was assuming marked religious dimensions and the religions of salvation were exerting growing influence Mithra was to become the focus of new syncretistic creations. However tenuous the evidence, there are theories that while evolving as a deity of salvation, Mithra was associated also with the myths of the so-called 'great Cosmocrator–Redeemer' and the messianic king–saviour.

With its spread westwards, the cult of Mithra, already modified in the Near East, was drawn deeper into the intricate and wide-ranging processes of Graeco-Oriental syncretism and was invested with new religious values. Mithra-worship received and absorbed ideas and practices derived from Greek and Anatolian mystery traditions and was also influenced by Platonism and perhaps by Orphic thought. Ultimately, the novel and composite form of Mithra-worship that

developed and became widely diffused in the Roman world was virtually
a new mystery religion, in which the old Irano-Babylonian core seems to
have been refashioned and recast into a Graeco-Roman mould tinged
with astrological lore and Platonic speculation.

Most of the ceremonies, mythology and theology of Roman
Mithraism, with their marked esoteric and initiatory character, have
been reconstructed from widely scattered archaeological remains,
inscriptions and meagre literary evidence that have generated differing
interpretations. The secret rites of the Mithraic Mysteries were celebrated
in subterranean shrines, the *mithraea*, which were supposed to mirror the
cave in which Mithra Tauroctonus (the bull-sacrificer) was believed to
have performed the central act of Mithraic ideology – the capture and
murder of the primordial Bull of Heaven. The Mithraic temple was
conceived as a 'world cave', a symbol of the cosmos, and among the cult
reliefs adorning its walls the scene of the bull sacrifice, the *tauroctonia* was
usually placed on the rear wall of the sanctuary and on the front of the
altar. The unravelling of the symbolism of the *tauroctonia* has provoked
protracted and heated controversy, since in traditional Zoroastrianism it
is Ahriman who brings death to the 'Lone-Created' bull in the violent act
of the first 'creative murder' which sparked off the cycle of being and
generation. Symmetrically, at the time of the final resurrection of the
dead the messianic saviour Saoshyant sacrifices the mystical bull
Hadhayans to obtain from his body the elixir of salvation and immortality for all men. Mithraic *tauroctonia*, inevitably, has been translated as
reflecting the Iranian paradigm of the divine act of sacrifice and
redemption which was, however, conveyed through the prism and style
of the novel Graeco-Roman syncretism. In the Mithraic version of the
divine priestly sacrifice of the bull the unleashing of the 'blood eternal'
bestows life and salvation but appears linked also to the myths of the
primordial cosmogonic sacrifice which brought about the creation of the
world.[19] Mithras' bull sacrifice, moreover, evokes unavoidable associations with Gilgamesh's slaying of the primeval heavenly bull in
Mesopotamian mythology. It is also becoming increasingly apparent that
the symbolism of the principal Mithraic cult scene and of other aspects
of the mysteries' iconography and temple structure is intricate and
polyvalent, often resisting a literal or one-dimensional reading.[20] This is
illustrated by the recent interpretations of the astral symbolism of the
tauroctonia, which while differing in their conclusions regarding the

stellar correlations of some of its elements and Mithras himself, emphasize its significance as a star map.[21] According to one of these interpretations the elements of the *tauroctonia* represent the equatorial summer constellations, as identified in the Greek and Roman periods, with Mithras denoting the constellation of Orion, which was seen as the stellar leader under whom the other constellations wheeled through the range of heaven.[22] In this view the *tauroctonia's* star chart was further related to the soul's voyage through the 'gates' of Cancer and Capricorn on the tropical circles.[23]

Another proposed reading of the astral code of the *tauroctonia* also seeks to show its link to the celestial equator, but in its position far back in time before the Hellenistic period, when the equinoxes were in Taurus and Scorpio, a situation which lasted between *c.* 4000 BC and 2000 BC.[24] In this line of argument, the *tauroctonia* thus shows awareness of the phenomenon of the precession of the equinoxes, itself believed to have been discovered *c.* 128 BC, and the movement of the spring equinox out of Taurus was symbolized in its scene by the death of the Taurus (the Bull) at the hands of Perseus, the constellation directly above it and identified consequently with Mithras.[25] Mithras, moreover, is postulated to have been conceptualized by first-century BC Stoicizing philosophers from Tarsus as the great cosmic being responsible for the precession of the equinoxes and for moving the whole universe out of the age of Taurus by symbolically killing the constellation.[26]

Still another rendition of the cosmological symbolism of the *tauroctonia* regards it as a star map of the section of the ecliptic/zodiac, insisting on the polyvalence of its symbolism, in which certain elements signify a single constellation and others more than one.[27] On one cosmological level, for example, Mithras denotes the sun, and the bull the moon and the whole scene serves as a route map for the ascent and descent of the human soul, as occasioned by the interaction of the sun and the moon, and following two celestial routes, one through the planets, and another through the fixed stars.[28]

In *The Cave of the Nymphs* (24:9–11) the neo-Platonist Porphyry extols Mithras of the Mysteries as creator and master of creation, while his carrying of the bull in the cosmic cave is apparently seen as signalling the beginning of genesis.[20] Mithras is set in the line of the equinox with north to his right and south to his left and thus he is linked with the descent of the souls into the world and their ascent to heaven through the seven planetary spheres. This seems to have been associated in the Mithraic Mysteries with the seven stages of initiation which were protected respectively by Mercury, Venus, Mars, Jupiter, the moon, the sun and Saturn. Beginning from the first initiatory grade of *corax* (raven), and via the following grades of the *nymphus* (bridegroom), *miles* (soldier), *leo* (lion), *Perses* (Persian), *heliodromus* (courier of the sun) to the final seventh degree of *pater* (father), the Mithraic initiates were subjected to a variety of ordeals and were invested with the insignia of each stage passed.[30] Among the Mithraic 'fathers', who were placed under the aegis and sickle of Saturn, particularly esteemed was the so-called 'Father of the Fathers (*Pater Patrum*) amongst the ten superiors' who is envisioned in the *Catholic Encyclopedia*, perhaps too luridly, as a 'sort of pope, who always lived at Rome'.[31]

The internal hierarchy and initiation of the cult, with its successive degrees and ordeals, pose numerous unresolved problems and the underlying Mithraic teachings appear similarly abstruse and elusive. It is still difficult to establish even the outline of the doctrines and mythology of the cult that at one stage seemed set to vie with Christianity for the soul of the Roman empire. With their focus on the labours of the invincible Mithras, from his rock-birth to the *tauroctonia*, his banquet with Sol and his final ascent, the Mithraic reliefs have generated many ingenious attempts to reconstruct the theology and central myths of Mithraism. One early and influential line of inquiry saw Mithraism largely as a Roman form of Zoroastrianism which was closely linked with the theological pursuits of Zurvanite circles in Anatolia. Accordingly, Mithraic iconography was deemed to reflect the fundamental Iranian dualism of the cosmic conflict of good and evil in which the rock-born deity of light, Mithras, led the battle against the evil Ahriman and the forces of darkness. An alternative approach to Roman Mithraism tends to assume that the mystery cult took shape under the formative influence of the Platonic tradition and reflected Platonic cosmogony and myths, the ascent of Mithras being associated with the ascent of the immortal soul in Plato's dialogue *Phaedrus*. In this line of argument Roman Mithraism is supposed to reflect not the Iranian cosmic dualism of the universal struggle between the realms of good and evil but the 'Greek polar opposition of the two realms, the cosmic and the eternal'.[32] Current Platonic decoding of the Mithraic Mysteries is sometimes taken to extremes, in which even the bull-slaying reliefs can be seen as typifying what has been described as the 'Platonic dualism of maintaining a balance between good and evil'.[33]

The dilemma whether Mithraic doctrine was underlain by Iranian or Greek forms of dualism becomes glaringly acute when one confronts the most enigmatic figure in Mithraic iconography, the winged lion-headed god. Second only to Mithras in its frequency in Mithraic iconography, it is commonly portrayed as a human figure with fearful leonine head, but it also has a human-headed counterpart who appears rather less frequently in Mithraic sanctuaries. The Mithraic lion–man was usually depicted entwined, often sevenfold, by a serpent, with the serpent's head resting on his leonine visage, which often appeared menacing if not infernal. Sometimes the zodiacal signs appeared between the coils of the serpent, and the lion–man was variously portrayed with keys, sceptres and torches or standing on the cosmic globe. It seems certain that the lion-headed god was venerated primarily in the main sites of the Mithraic Mysteries where he was revealed only to initiates of the higher grades and was honoured with offerings by the supreme Mithraic dignitaries like the *Pater Patrum* himself.[34]

Early theories concerning the nature and functions of the ambiguous snake-wrapped lion-headed god regarded him as the highest deity in the Mithraic pantheon and identified him with the time-god, Aion, and also with Kronos and the Iranian Zurvan. The apparent threatening air of the lion-headed deity was attributed to the 'menacing or devouring aspect of time'. Subsequently, it came to be recognized as the Destructive Spirit of Zoroastrianism, Ahriman himself, or as a composite figure comprising both Ahriman and Zurvan. He has also been traced to the lion-headed portrayals of the Mesopotamian underworld deity Nergal.[35] Besides Zurvan and Ahriman, the Mithraic lion–man has also been linked to Plato's Universal Soul which 'drives all things in heaven and earth' with the dualities of heat and cold, whiteness and blackness (*Laws* 10 : 896–7), as well as to his symbolic picture of the soul as 'a manifold and many-headed beast' joined with the forms of lion and man (*Republic* 9 : 588–9). In this view the Mithraic lion-headed god represented Plato's Universal Soul, with its good and evil sides, and the Platonic dualism between the 'best kind of soul' and the 'evil kind of soul' (*Laws* 10 : 897), the latter, the bad world-soul, being sometimes attributed to Zoroastrian influence on Plato.[36] Accordingly, the Mithraist worshipper of the lion-headed god is seen to have been addressing both the good and evil aspects of the

Universal Soul through Mithras' neutral dual mediation between the extremes of good and evil to reach the final purification.[37]

What seems to be the key to the riddle of the lion-man and his role in Mithraic worship is the several Latin Mithraic dedications to *Deus Arimanius*, including the one on the headless sculpture found at York, which apparently portrays the lion-headed deity. The Mithraic dedicatory statues of *Deus Arimanius* have been linked to Plutarch's testimony of the Areimanius cult with its grim wolf sacrifices but also to a late Zoroastrian testimony of the clandestine rite of the 'mystery of the sorcerers' centred on a secret worship of Ahriman, his rival revelation and his 'evil knowledge', which compels men to desert Ohrmazd's religion and turn to that of Ahriman.[38] The Mithraic *Deus Arimanius* is thus taken to show that Roman Mithraism derived from pre-Zoroastrian and later forbidden *daevic* forms of Mithra-worship which were associated with the dreaded 'mystery of the sorcerers' and which were sustained in Mesopotamia and Asia Minor. In this view the Roman *Deus Arimanius*, who was worshipped in the Mithraic sanctuaries, was radically different from the Zoroastrian Ahriman and was no less a deity than 'the Prince of this World of time and space', 'the source of power and riches', who sought to prevent the ascent of the soul to its heavenly abode and from whose sway the initiate aspired to escape.[39]

Alternative solutions to the problem of the Roman *Deus Arimanius* and his headless statue at York seek to untangle his role in the Mithraic Mysteries against the background of the 'mysteric' and esoteric trends in Graeco-Roman paganism. Rather than a Roman vestige of an aberrant Iranian dualism which opposes the 'word of sorcery' to the 'word of Ohrmazd' to worship the former or else to pay tribute to both, the Mithraic *Deus Arimanius* is considered an inferior but not evil cosmic power, associated with time and probably with the ascent of the initiate's soul.[40] Instead of a mediator between the opposing domains of good and evil, between Ohrmazd and Ahriman, Mithras has been viewed as an intermediary between the supernal realm and the material cosmos.[41] Moreover, with his position on the equinox, if Porphyry is to be relied on, Mithras was linked to the descent and the ascent of the souls. A recent synthesis of the evidence plausibly identifies the Mithraic lion-headed deity with the figure of the 'cosmocrator', the 'astrologically conditioned embodiment of the world-engendering and world-ruling Power generated by the endless revolution of all the wheels of the celestial dynamo';[42] far from being an oppressive force, it could not only embody souls but could also release the soul from its embodiment through initiation.

It is also becoming increasingly apparent that some Mithraic concepts, like the graduated cosmos through which the soul makes its ascent to salvation or the lion-headed 'cosmocrator' himself, were also shared in contemporary Gnostic schools, where, however, they were included in an entirely different soteriological and dualist framework.

Michael and Samael

The continuous search for the source of the Mithraic Mysteries and the conflicting arguments for their dualist character are indicative of the problems posed by the religious currents in late antiquity with the rise of new syncretistic forms of religious dualism and diverse approaches to the origins and reality of evil.

Following the destruction of the Temple in Jerusalem by the Romans in AD 70, Jewish rabbinic thought tended to counterbalance the dualist trends developed in some forms of apocalyptic Judaism. Rabbinic texts from the second century AD warn against the heresy of the 'Two Heavenly Powers' linked to speculation about the exalted status of an angel or viceregent of the Lord which might have influenced nascent Gnostic thought. In rabbinic Judaism the figure of Satan and the myth of the downfall of the angels lost much of the intensity which had marked some earlier apocalyptic traditions. Rather than an ultimate embodiment of evil and leader of the fallen angels, Satan appeared in rabbinic theory more as a symbol of the evil inclination within man (*yetser ha-ra*) which was opposed to the good inclination (*yetser ha-tov*).[43] Yet in the narrative section of the Talmud, the Haggadah, and in popular Jewish lore some of the traditions associated with Satan persisted and were elaborated in new legends. In the important apocryphal work *The Ascension of Isaiah*, Satan had been styled also as Samael (variously etymologized as the 'venom of God' or 'the blind god') and in the early Christian era Samael became the principal name of Satan in Judaism. Distinguished sometimes from Satan, Samael could be identified as the guardian angel of Esau, Edom and the world empire of Rome, exalted as 'the great prince of heaven', as prince of the evil angels, 'Samael the Wicked' or else prince of all Satans (Accusers). As a prosecutor Samael could be seen as standing along with the defender Michael before the *Shekhinah* (Divine Presence) during the Jewish exodus from Egypt.

Perceived as the 'venom of God' Samael was also recognized as the much-dreaded angel of death, who was believed to smite man with a drop of poison, and in later astrological lore he was regarded as the angel of Mars. The war between Satan–Samael and the guardian angel of Israel, Michael, was perceived as continuing until the last days when Samael would be finally delivered to Israel in iron fetters. Otherwise, Michael could be charged with laying the foundations of Rome, Israel's future adversary and persecutor, itself to be patronized and guarded by Samael, while the ambiguous figure of the 'Prince of the World' could be identified with either Michael or Samael.[44]

In early Christianity itself some of the concepts of Satan and his opposition to God and man, which were developed in post-exilic and particularly apocalyptic Judaism, were accepted with all their ambiguities and potential for radical new developments. The inherited opposition between Michael and Satan was reflected in Revelation, where in the 'war in heaven' Michael led his angelic hosts against the angels of the 'great dragon', the 'old serpent', that 'led the whole world astray, whose name is Satan, or the Devil' (12:7–9). Besides being the great cosmic adversary of Michael, Satan vied with the archangel for the body of Israel's lawgiver, Moses (Epistle of Jude 9). In early Christian thought the Devil was the incarnation personified and source of evil and death, a fallen angel who led the hosts of evil against the 'Kingdom of God' and Christ. He was the 'god of this world' who has blinded the minds of the unbelievers to the message of the Gospel. In Paul's dramatic light-vision on the way to Damascus the future apostle was entrusted by Jesus to go to the Gentiles and convert them from darkness to light, from the hold of Satan to God. However, Satan could also disguise himself as an angel of light and his envoys could pose as agents of good and apostles of Christ (2 Corinthians 11:13–15). Apart from being recognized as the Prince of Demons (Matthew 9:34) and 'commander of the spiritual powers of the air' (Ephesians 2:2), he was also called 'Tempter', 'Accuser' and 'Father of Lies', as he deluded and accused men and endeavoured to tempt and corrupt even the Son of God, Christ himself. Satan entered one of the twelve apostles, Judas Iscariot – according to the Fourth Gospel – during the Last Supper, to prompt the betrayal and crucifixion of the Jesus Christ. Conversely, when the apostle Peter, the Rock on which Christ's Church was to be built, tried to oppose Jesus' way to Jerusalem and to his Passion and Resurrection, he was rebuked by Jesus as Satan: 'Away with you, Satan . . . you think as men think, not as God thinks' (Mark 8 : 33).

Satan's *imperium* embraced not only the evil spirits, but also sinful and wicked men, 'Satan's synagogue', as well as 'this age' (*aion*) and this world (*kosmos*), he was the 'Prince of this World' and 'the whole world . . . lies in the power of the evil one' (1 John 5 : 19). Yet Satan's prevalence in 'this world', which began with the fall of man, was broken by the advent of Christ and his Passion: 'Now is the hour of judgement for this world; now shall the Prince of this world be driven out' (John 12 : 31). In Revelation, following his great war in heaven against the hosts of Michael, the dragon, Satan, was doomed to be cast down to earth with his angels and to be fettered in the pit for a thousand years. After being chained for a millennium Satan would be released and would win over nations from the four corners of the world for his final, satanic crusade against the city of God's people but would be consumed by heavenly fire and flung along with his disciples into the 'lake of fire', the second death (Revelation 20:7–10; 13–15). The chronology of Satan's fortunes in Revelation appears abstruse and has invited different readings. It was generally assumed that while Satan's power was crippled by the advent of Jesus Christ, the final demise of Satan would occur at the Second Coming. Satan continued, meanwhile, his struggle against the 'Kingdom of God' and the Christian was expected to put on the whole armour of God to oppose the Devil's devices in a fight that was not 'against human foes, but against cosmic powers, against the authorities and potentates of this dark world, against the superhuman forces of evil in the heavens' (Ephesians 6 : 11–12). The sign of the cross was also supposed to banish evil powers; in early Christian thought the Devil was repeatedly denounced for fostering paganism, heresy and sorcery in his fight against the Kingdom of God and the divine plan of salvation. Through the water of Christian baptism not only was the soul believed to be redeemed of Original Sin, but also the Devil and his powers were renounced and repelled. For the Christian apologist Tertullian, the existence and opposing works of 'the Lord and his rival, the Creator and the Destroyer' could be experienced, learned and understood 'at one and the same time'.[45]

The early Christian notions of the Devil, his rebellion, fall, reign in 'this world' and final defeat were further elaborated and conceptualized by the Fathers of the Church. The fall of Satan and the angels could be attributed to their pride or to their envy of men. The parable against the king of Babylon in Isaiah 14 : 12–15 was now firmly associated with the fall of Satan and linked also to Jesus' statement in Luke 10 : 18: 'I watched how Satan fell, like lightning, out of the sky'. The king of Tyre in Ezekiel 28 : 12–19, originally all-wise and blameless, but later obsessed by lawlessness and doomed to be hurled down from the mountain of God and devoured by the fire that Yahweh had kindled within him, also came to be recognized as Satan. Michael, however, was identified as the cherub who was placed at the gates of Paradise to guard 'the way to the tree of life' (Genesis 3 : 24), and as the angel who stood like *satan* against Balaam. Venerated among the early Christians, particularly in Phrygia, as a heavenly healer and redeemer, Michael emerged as the patron of the Church and the medieval chivalric orders. Apart from leading the war against Satan in heaven, Michael was seen as being entrusted with salvaging human souls from the power of the Devil and conducting them to the place of judgement, while later Christian elaborations envisaged Satan as ruling and punishing the sinners in hell.

In the early stages of building the normative Christian satanology, where the Devil was generally believed to have been created by God but had fallen through his pride, envy and free will, the chronology and the outcome of his fall received varying treatment. According to Origen (*c.* 185–254) the final defeat of Satan would lead to the destruction of his sinful and ungodly nature, while his original angelic essence would be resurrected and he would be saved to return ultimately to God. At the same time, the early Church Fathers had vigorously to defend their orthodox tenets of evil as privation of good and Godness against the more radical, dualist solutions of the origin of evil which were advanced in the Gnostic schools of the second and third centuries.

Demiurge and Redeemer

Despite the evident dualism of spirit and flesh in early Christianity, which was inevitably associated with the Devil's status in the New

Testament as 'the ruler of this world of matter and bodies',[46] the world was viewed as a creation of the benevolent God–Creator and was not evil by nature. Though defiled by Satan and his evil spirits, it would ultimately be redeemed and purified by the Second Coming of Christ. Conversely, the multifarious Gnostic schools did share, on the whole, an anti-cosmic dualism – the material world was negated as an imperfect and evil creation of an inferior demiurgic or clearly 'Satanic' power and was opposed to the supernal spiritual world of the true but remote and unknown God. As with Orphic-Pythagorean religiosity, in Gnosticism the soul was seen as a stranger and an exile in the body, the souls of men were 'precious pearls', divine sparks from this spiritual realm and had descended into the wicked material world of the 'howling darkness' to be imprisoned in material bodies and could be released only through the redeeming mediation of *gnosis*, a revelatory knowledge of the divine secrets.[47] The divine substance was spread unevenly among men and the Gnostic schools sometimes assumed a threefold division of mankind in which the enlightened Gnostics themselves were the spiritual aristocracy, styled the Pneumatics, the Perfect or the chosen, who would be saved, as they possessed the spirit, *pneuma*. The other class, the Psychics, had soul (*psyche*) and were deficient of spirit, yet could gain some form of salvation, while the Hylics were the earthly class, the enslaved, bound to remain entrapped in matter. These three grades of being in the universe were associated with three types of 'churches': the angelic, the psychic and the earthly.

In Christian Gnosticism Christ emerged as a heavenly spiritual redeemer sent by the unknown, supreme God to mediate the *gnosis* to men (or else only to the Pneumatics) and the Demiurge vainly endeavoured to thwart his mission. Christian Gnostic traditions elaborated different versions of Christ's mission but according to most of them Christ assumed only an appearance (*dokesis*) of humanity and accordingly his Passion and Crucifixion were also apparent. This Docetic Christology distinguished the heavenly Christ from the earthly Jesus, while sometimes substitute figures like Symon of Cyrene were introduced to replace Christ at the Crucifixion.[48]

The Gnostic schools drew widely on the syncretistic heritage of antiquity and used Iranian, Jewish, Greek, Mesopotamian, Egyptian and Christian traditions to embellish their basic myths and concepts related to the creation of the world by the Demiurge, the fall of the soul, the mission of the redeemer and revealer of the *gnosis*, and finally the release and ascent of the soul to its spiritual abode. Prior to the discovery of the Coptic corpus of secret Gnostic writings at Nag Hammadi (Cheno-boskion) in Upper Egypt in 1945, the various Gnostic systems were known mainly from the hostile testimony of great Christian anti-Gnostic polemicists like Irenaeus (*c.* 130–*c.* 200), Hippolytus (*c.* 170–*c.* 236) and Epiphanius (*c.* 315–403). The Nag Hammadi texts immensely enriched the picture of the convoluted and eclectic Gnostic systems and demon-strated that Gnostic mythologies adopted and transformed some of the central themes of the Jewish apocalyptic and apocryphal corpus – like the downfall of the angels, the role of Satan in the angelic apostasy and the fall of Adam and Eve. In the Nag Hammadi tract *The Apocryphon of John*, presented in the form of a revelation granted by the resurrected Jesus to John, the descent of the angels to the daughters of men occurred after the Flood and was a mission to raise offspring of their own (29 : 10–20). The angels impregnated the daughters of men with 'the spirit of darkness which they had mixed for them and with evil' (29 : 30) to beget children out of the darkness 'according to the likeness of their spirit' (30 : 9) and enslave creation. In another important Nag Hammadi text, *On the Origins of the World* (123:4–13), as in the classical Enochic traditions, angels (demons), created by the downcast seven rulers of darkness, were charged with imparting to men the secrets of magic, idolatry, bloodshed, temple sacrifices and libations.

The fall of Adam and Eve was also subject to diverse Gnostic inter-pretations, among which the tradition of Eve's seduction by the Devil or the Demiurge gained particular prominence. While Cain seems to have been routinely recognized as Eve's son by the Devil in many Gnostic traditions, Abel could be credited with satanic or Adamic descent. The heavenly but satanic extraction of Cain also became part of Jewish lore where Samael, the angel of the Lord, was envisaged coming to Eve 'riding on the serpent' and hence Cain was conceived not by Adam's seed, nor in his image and likeness, while Eve's canonical statement after Cain's birth, 'I have gotten a man from the Lord' (Genesis, 4 : 1 *KJV*), could be transformed into 'I have acquired a man, the angel of the Lord'.[49] While Cain could be exposed as the progenitor of 'all the generations of the wicked', Seth, with his certain and legitimate Adamic parentage, could be extolled as the father of 'all the generations of the just' and the kingdom of the House of David could be described as 'planted' from him.[50] A preoccupation with Seth and his 'genealogy' is markedly evident in some Gnostic schools where the birth of Seth and the beginning of his line were praised as the institution of justice and a higher race. In *Panarion* (39:1–5,3) Epiphanius recounted the system of the Sethian Gnostics where the birth of Cain and Abel was revealed as having been caused by creative angelic powers whose war over the two brothers ultimately provoked Abel's murder. The races of Cain and Abel came to be mixed together because of their malice and Seth was sent into the world with his higher seed to bring purification of the seed of men and destruction to the angelic forces that had created the world and the first two men. The birth of Seth was attributed to the intercession of the Gnostic higher 'Mother', Sophia (Wisdom), who implanted in him the seed of the divine power which was the heavenly prototype of Seth's earthly seed. The Sethian Gnostics therefore traced their descent to the elect and incorruptible line of Seth, who was identified with Christ and was conceived as bringing cyclically to the human race his higher 'seed of power and purity'. Indeed there are some indications that Melchizedek, Jesus Christ and even Zoroaster were considered in some Gnostic circles as manifestations of the saviour and revealer Seth. It is often assumed, moreover, that on Egyptian soil some Gnostic groups applied their principle of inverse biblical exegesis, which turned the biblical God-Creator into a lower demiurge, to the Osiris–Seth duality in Egyptian religion. The poles of this duality are believed to have been reversed, converting Osiris into an oppressive demiurge figure and Seth into a redeemer, conflated with the biblical Seth and even Jesus, but the actual evidence for such Gnostic rehabilitation of the Egyptian god is not conclusive.[51] In Epiphanius' exposé of Sethian Gnosticism the Flood itself was viewed as sent by the 'Mother on high' to extinguish the evil race of Cain, while only the just progeny of Seth was meant to be saved in Noah's ark and to remain in the world. Apprehensive of the impending genocide of their 'race of wickedness', the creative angelic powers succeeded in bringing Ham into the ark; Ham preserved their race and the world was again plunged into its traditional vices and disorder. Conversely, Irenaeus in his comprehensive diatribe against Gnosticism, *Against All Heresies* (1:31.1–2), exposed certain Gnostic Cainites who extolled Cain as conceived from a superior, absolute power above. Esau, Korah and the Sodomites, who were endowed with this knowledge, were hated by the Creator but protected by Sophia and it was on behalf of his knowledge of this truth that Judas Iscariot carried through 'the mystery of betrayal'.

However divergent, the different Gnostic cosmogonies were invariably underlain by a marked anti-cosmic dualism and repeatedly identified the Gnostic Demiurge of the material universe with God the Creator of the Old Testament. In the teachings of Marcion (*d.c* AD 166), which were largely based on Paul's opposition between Law and Faith in the Epistle to the Galatians, the God of the Old Testament was a just but inferior Demiurge-god, who was neither good nor omniscient, who promulgated the law of vengeance and whose strict judgement is antithetic to the essence of Christ's gospel of love and mercy. Jesus was sent by the higher, good and 'strange' God of love and salvation to redeem man from the tyranny of the law of the lower Demiurge, who is also described as the god of this time period and who has sworn an oath – the Covenant with the Jewish people. Accordingly, whereas Christ had come to announce the existence of the superior, hidden and indescribable God, the Demiurge's own Jewish messiah is a warrior, aiming to save and establish a millennial earthly kingdom for the Jewish people of the Covenant. The Devil is recognized as a rebellious angel of the Demiurge who was expelled from the first heaven of the god and came to dwell in Matter. According to Marcion, Christ did not have a material body (it was a 'deceiving apparition') and his teachings advocated a disdain for the world of the Demiurge by preaching asceticism, Encratite abstention from meat and wine and rejection of marriage. Marcion's canon included only ten of Paul's epistles and an edited version of Luke's Gospel; his dualistic teaching of the radical opposition between the 'two Gods' and their two worlds attracted a wide following in the Roman empire while the communities of the missionary-active Marcionite Church, spread from Italy and Egypt to Armenia. Opinion is divided whether Marcion was a rationalist biblical exegete or a Gnostic or non-Gnostic heresiarch; his doctrines were further modified by his disciples. Some of the Marcionites elevated Marcion's higher, good God as a first principle, others transformed his dualistic tenets into a teaching of three principles – the good God, the intermediary Demiurge and the evil god (the Devil). Marcion's two messianic figures, respectively envoys of the higher God and the Demiurge, could be conflated into a single Christ, who, similar to the way Mithras has come to be seen in some later traditions, was described as a mediator between good and evil. One of the best known of Marcion's disciples, Appeles, acknowledged only one good and holy God above, converting the creator of the world into his angel and emanation. In the teachings of the Gnostic Basilides (second century AD) the biblical God of Abraham, Isaac and Jacob emerged as the ruler of the inferior sphere of the planets, the Hebdomad, and as he was held to rule over 365 heavens, he was also called Abrasax, a name comprising the number 365. In the convoluted system of the Gnostic teacher Valentinus (second century AD) the Father, the First Principle and his consort, Thought, begot the spiritual world of Pleroma (plenitude or fullness) which comprised fifteen pairs of aeons. A crisis in the Pleroma, the fall or else the 'abortion' of the youngest aeon Sophia, precipitated the birth of the God of Genesis in the lower spheres who in his turn created the material cosmos blind to the higher realm of Pleroma.[52]

In the Nag Hammadi treatise *On the Origin of the World* (100:3–25) the lion-like Demiurge, called Yaldabaoth (probably 'Son of Chaos') and identified with the biblical God–Creator, came into being after a descending series of emanations from the spiritual world that had already caused the emergence of matter. Yaldabaoth established the heavens and their powers and proclaimed after Deuteronomy 32:39: 'I am He and there is no god beside me', but with this 'monotheistic' proclamation he sinned against the 'immortal (imperishable) ones' (103:10–15). The initiator of his creation, Pistis Sophia, called him Samael – i.e. 'the blind god' – prophesied his downfall to his 'mother, the abyss' (100:17–33) and revealed to him 'in the water the image of her greatness'. In *The Apocryphon of John* (9:28–35; 10:1–22) the birth of Yaldabaoth was attributed to Sophia's 'desire to bring forth a likeness out of herself without the consent of the spirit' and Yaldabaoth emerged in the form of a lion-faced serpent, imperfect, created 'in ignorance', but none the less, he was the first archon who had inherited power from his mother. Among his manifold feats in *The Apocryphon of John* 24, Yaldabaoth was charged with the seduction of Eve, who begot from him two sons, Elohim and Yahweh, the first set over the fire and the wind and the second over the water and the earth, named respectively by Yaldabaoth, 'with the view to deceive' (24:25), Cain and Abel.

The episode of the 'monotheistic' claim of the Demiurge, the reproach of Sophia and the revelation of the higher divine powers occurs in several important Gnostic tracts. In her various incarnations the Gnostic Sophia was perceived sometimes as the Holy Spirit, the heavenly Eve or as a dual figure, separated into a higher Mother of the heavenly Redeemer and lower

Mother of the Demiurge of the material universe. Moreover, while the Gnostic Demiurge could be associated with the arrogant king of Babylon in the parable in Isaiah 14, his Mother could be seen in Gnostic mythology as Babylon or else as the heavenly Jerusalem.[53] It is also apparent that while the lion-headed Mithraic deity and the lion-shaped Gnostic Demiurge Yaldabaoth share essentially 'a similar function for symbolizing the same world-ruling, world-ensouling Power',[54] in Gnostic myths the cosmos of Yaldabaoth and his reign as a 'cosmocrator' were opposed to the supernal realm of the spirit and the liberation of the entrapped souls, whose salvation was mediated by a heavenly Redeemer breaking the bondage of the Demiurge.

Apart from the Gnostic tradition of one original principle and a fall in the divine realm, other Gnostic schools forged elaborate systems with three primary principles like that of the Gnostic sect of the Naassenes (from the Hebrew *nahash*, serpent), whose doctrines were expounded by Hippolytus in his *Refutation of All Heresies* (5 : 6.3–11). According to Hippolytus the Naassenes regarded the belief in one principle as the source of the world as erroneous and taught that the universe proceeded from three principles – the pre-existent, the self-originated and the outpoured chaos. All temples, rites and mysteries were viewed by the Naassenes as established for the serpent *nahash*, which was further praised as good and necessary for the existence of all things mortal and immortal. The serpent was compared with the second, self-originated principle, itself called Adamas and perceived as bisexual Man, also associated with the seed as the source of all that comes into being. In this bisexual Man was the life that was 'the light of men' (John 1 : 4), and the generation of perfect men, or else the drinking cup which the king 'uses for divination' when he drinks (Genesis 44 : 4) that was hidden and found 'in the good seed of Benjamin' (8 : 6). Moreover, the second, bisexual principle is compared with the 'Ocean', with its unceasing ebbs and fluctuations, the 'upward' flow being related to the origin of the gods and the 'downward' movement to the origin of humanity. At the same time, the Naassenes had to introduce a fourth evil power, the fiery god Esaldaios (El Shaddai), who was a Demiurge and artificer of 'this world', where he had imprisoned mankind against the will of Adamas.

Another Gnostic sect, the Peratae, exposed by Hippolytus in the *Refutation of All Heresies* (5 : 12.1–17; 13), formulated similar threefold partitions in the world: three gods, three words, three minds and three types of men. In the Peratae system the first principle is the 'unoriginate' 'perfect Goodness'; the second, the 'self-originate' good multitude of powers; and the third, the 'originate' and particular being. In another version of the Peratae triad these three principles appeared as the Father, the Son and matter. Christ was also perceived as three-natured and through his descent all that had been divided into three was to be saved and all that had been brought down from the higher realms was to ascend through him. The second, 'self-originate' principle of the Peratae was envisaged as moving constantly between the Father and matter and was identified with the serpent, which was credited with bringing the 'fully formed perfect race' up from the world. The serpent was also eulogized as the 'perfect word' of Eve or the mystery of Eden and was recognized as the sign marked on Cain to protect him from murder. The position of a fourth evil principle was effectively taken by the stars, the gods of generation and destruction, whose emanations conducted the beginnings and the end of everything in the created world, but did not have power over those who were illuminated by their *gnosis* of the perfect serpent.

Another system where the serpent occupied a prominent was elaborated by the Gnostic Ophites (from the Greek *ophis*, serpent), as recounted in Irenaeus' work *Against all Heresies* (1:30.1–15). In the Ophite system the first triad was formed by the Father of All or the First Man, the Son of Man, or the Second Man, and the feminine Holy Spirit or the First Woman, below whom were the elements of Water, Darkness, Abyss and Chaos. The female Holy Spirit united with both the First and Second Man to give birth to the Third Man, Christ, but their light overflowed on her left side. Being on the right, Christ was raised to the higher realms, while the power that had overflowed on the left fell downwards and was envisaged as a female being, variously called the Left, Sophia or Man–Woman. Sophia gave birth to Yaldabaoth who fathered his own son, and the unfolding of this generative process led to the emergence of six sons who formed, along with Yaldabaoth, the higher hebdomad. The serpent was envisaged as begetting six sons in the world below to form the lower hebdomad of the seven demons or planets of the world, who were in opposition to the human race. According to the Ophites the serpent bore two names, Michael and Samael, who appeared thus, 'fused into the positive and negative aspects of a single state of existence'.[55]

As well as the Naassenes and the Peratae, Hippolytus recounted in his *Refutation of All Heresies* (5:19.1–22) a Sethian Gnostic system which involved not only three sharply defined principles, of Light above, Darkness below, and pure Spirit between them, but also the lowest principle of darkness was already perceived as negative and maleficent, a horrible water. The division into three powers was further associated with biblical ternaries like Adam, Eve and the serpent; Cain, Abel and Seth; or Abraham, Isaac and Jacob. The multitudinous powers of the three principles were at rest when they remained in their original state but the great impact of the three principles, which had caused the creation of heaven and earth, led to their mixture and conflict. With its cunning intelligence Darkness sought to detain the elements of Light and Spirit, imprisoned in the impure and harmful 'womb of disorder', which accepted and recognized only the forms of the 'first-born' of the waters, the wind, the serpent and the beast (19 : 20). The mind of man, 'perfect god' brought down from the sublime Light, was also entrapped in wicked and dark bodies and strove in vain to free itself from the bodily prison. The perfect word of Light had to assume the form of a snake to enter the womb of Darkness and redeem the mind from its bondage and to accomplish the division and separation of everything that had been intermixed. Jesus' statement in Matthew 10:34, 'I have not come to bring peace, but a sword', was explained as an allusion to this mission of separation when the compounded elements were to return to their original abodes.

The same system of three primeval powers received dramatic mythological elaboration in the Nag Hammadi tract, *The Paraphrase of Shem*, where the gentle Spirit was again envisaged positioned between the exalted and infinite Light and the Darkness, itself a 'wind in the waters', with the mind 'wrapped in a chaotic fire' (1 : 25–35; 2:1–5). With the agitation of Darkness and the intermixture of the three roots the universe entered an era of cosmic strife which marked the creation of heaven and earth. The Gnostic saviour Derdekeas had to descend from the realm of Light and assume the form of the beast to enter the abode of Darkness and redeem the imprisoned light of the Spirit. Derdekeas' revelation of the *gnosis* to the elect brought upon him 'the wrath of the world' when the gates of fire and smoke were opened against him and he was attacked by the winds and thunder (36:12–22). Such vivid and often striking mythic imagery was used consistently to recount the unfolding of Derdekeas' redeeming mission in the world. The very time when the light was finally about to be separated from darkness was thus marked by the act of beheading the woman who was 'the coherence of the powers of the demon who will baptize the seed of darkness in severity ...' (40:24–30). In the last days, when the evil power of Darkness would be laid low and immobilized, those who had resisted 'the heritage of death', the oppressive water of darkness, would finally be separated from its body to enter the entirely redeemed light of the Spirit (48:10–30).

In the treatise *On the Origin of the World* (126–7), at the time of the final consummation the Light was prophesied to cover and wipe out the Darkness and return to its own root. Yet the essence of the opposition between the two powers of Light and Darkness could vary in the different Gnostic schools and they could be perceived as brothers deriving from one 'mystery' that retained both in itself. According to the Nag Hammadi *Gospel of Philip* (53:15–20): 'Light and darkness, life and death, right and left are brothers of one another. They are inseparable. Because of this neither are the good good nor the evil evil, nor is life life, nor death death'. In other Gnostic traditions the dualism of good and evil appeared radical and irretrievable and rather than being retained in one original trunk, the powers of Light and Darkness were perceived as two coeternal principles that were opposed from the very beginning. The absolute dualism of these traditions is in sharp contrast to Gnostic monarchian dualism that poses one first principle and the creation of the material world as a result of a crisis or discontinuity in the divine 'fullness'.

The spread of Gnosticism was more pronounced in the eastern parts of the Mediterranean world and coincided with the diffusion of Mithraism in the Roman empire, which was more concentrated in its European provinces and noticeably less evident in Greece proper. Accordingly, with their initiatory and salvationist agendas, the Mithraic societies are sometimes seen as having provided a 'western' counterpart of the Gnostic communities in the Greek world.[56] Gnosticism, moreover, shared its preoccupation with the divine knowledge, *gnosis*, the soul's search for its divine origin and its final salvation with another religio-spiritualist current whose teachings crystallized in the early Christian era, Hermeticism; but there were important differences between the two movements in the spheres of theology, cosmology and anthropology.[57] Gnostic groups also adopted and further elaborated esoteric traditions current in early Christianity and Judeo-Christianity which were believed to have been transmitted both orally in apostolic times and through apocryphal (understood as 'hidden') texts.[58] The significance of esotericism in early Christian thought was attested to by such figures as

Clement of Alexandria and Origen but the Gnostic preoccupation with and reinterpretation of esoteric traditions led to their gradual censure by the Church Fathers, a process that gained momentum by the second century and effected their disappearance or assimilation into the framework of nascent Christian mysticism.[59]

The radical Gnostic dualism of two primordial fundamental principles, the two realms of Light and Darkness, associated respectively with spirit and matter, has been defined sometimes as 'Iranian' Gnosticism. In traditional Iranian Zoroastrianism the material universe was created by Ohrmazd as a replica of the spiritual world and man himself was created as a microcosm of universe and Ohrmazd's 'material symbol' incarnation, a harmonious unity of body and soul. At the time of the final renewal of the world the resurrected body would be reunited with its soul in the reassembled and immortalized human being, as matter and spirit would finally coalesce in the life everlasting. While in Zoroastrianism both the spiritual and material world, both the soul and the body, were created as Ohrmazd's allies against the destroyer Ahriman, in Iranian Gnosticism the spirit and matter, Light and Darkness, appeared as two primordial and antagonistic principles whose coexistence and opposition determined three main epochs of a grandiose cosmic drama. Iranian Gnosticism received its elaborate and striking formulation in the system devised by the great Gnostic visionary, missionary and artist, Mani, the self-proclaimed herald of the third final age when the conflict between the powers of Light and Darkness would be consummated. The unfolding of the mission of Mani and the early fortunes of his religion coincided and were inextricably linked with the rise of the new Iranian empire of the Sassanid dynasty and the ensuing powerful renascence of Zoroastrianism.

The Throne and the Altar

In AD 226 Arsacid rule collapsed in Iran. Plagued by internal strife, it was overthrown by a Persian dynasty, the Sassanids, who had been hereditary guardians of a great temple of Anahita at Istakhar, near ancient Perse-polis. Apart from Persia the cult of Anahita enjoyed prominence in neighbouring Armenia, which had itself long been within the Iranian and Zoroastrian sphere of influence, and where a branch of the Arsacid dynasty continued to reign for another two centuries after its fall in Iran. The Parthian feudal state in Iran was replaced by the highly centralized Sassanian empire where Zoroastrianism was upheld as a well-organized and often intolerant state religion. Sassanid art and culture clearly mark the zenith of pre-Islamic Iranian civilization, but the history of the Sassanid empire was dominated by continual collisions with its western enemy, the Roman empire. The Sassanid monarchs claimed divine descent from the 'seed of the gods': from the time of Ardashir I, the founder of the dynasty, they were seen as treading in the footsteps of their Achaemenid predecessors, claiming the 'rightful inheritance' of the Achaemenid empire to recover the imperial glory of Persia. According to Ammianus Marcellinus (17:5.5–6) in about 357 the Sassanid King of Kings, Shapur II (309–79), 'partner with the Stars, brother of the Sun and Moon', was said to have written to his 'brother', the Roman emperor Constantius II (337–61), that the dominion of his forefathers had reached in the west to the River Strymon (Struma) and the borders of Macedonia and these lands belonged to and should be restored to the Persian empire. In the face of Constantius' successor, Julian the Apostate, however, Shapur II was to confront a Roman emperor who perceived himself as an incarnation of Alexander the Great, determined to meet and reconquer the Persians, who according to Julian had once subdued the whole of Asia and most of Europe, embracing the whole known world in their aspirations. Apart from the revival of paganism, the subjugation of Persia after the example of Alexander was to become Julian's ruling passion and in 363 he led his abortive campaign against Persia, where he finally met his death, mortally wounded during the retreat of his army. A Sassanid rock relief at Taq-i Bostan, western Iran, commemorating Shapur's triumph over Julian, depicts the three figures of Shapur, Ahura Mazda and Mithra trampling on the Roman emperor, who had adopted Mithras as his guardian.

Julian's war and death in Sassanid Persia were among the most dramatic episodes of the four centuries of violent intermittent warfare between the Sassanid empire and the Roman, and later the East Roman, empire for supremacy in the Near East, Armenia and the Caucasus region. The exhausting internecine struggle between the two rival empires, eulogized as 'the two eyes of the world', came to a striking climax in the early seventh century, when, under the Sassanid monarch

Chosroes II the Victorious, the westward Persian advance reached the heartlands of the East Roman (Byzantine) empire in western Asia Minor. In 614 the armies of Chosroes, who seems to have been disliked by the Zoroastrian clergy and was suspected of being a Christian convert, captured Jerusalem and took away the fragments of the 'True Cross', on which Jesus was supposed to have been crucified. As Persian conquests progressed into Syria, Anatolia and Egypt, Chosroes recovered most of the former western Achaemenid dominions and attempted a strike at the Byzantine capital, Constantinople. In 330 Constantine the Great had moved the imperial capital to Constantinople and now, in 626, Persian troops directly threatened the second Rome. The Byzantine emperor Heraclius, however, outmanoeuvred the Persian forces completely by shipping his army to the Caucasus via the Black Sea and in 628 was already campaigning deep into the Sassanid empire where he sacked Chosroes' palace. Heraclius' invasion provoked the assassination of Chosroes and Heraclius achieved a victorious truce with Chosroes' short-lived successor, Kavad-Shiruya, himself a suspected Christian, after which Byzantium regained its control over the newly lost provinces and the 'True Cross' was restored to Jerusalem. Plunged into political turmoil, the Sassanid empire lacked the breathing space to recover and withstand the new Arab menace from the south. Within fifteen years, despite vigorous Iranian resistance, it collapsed before the rising Arab tide. As the Arab conquest swept through Iran, the last Sassanid King of Kings and 'Brother of Sun and Moon', Yazdagird III – who was crowned at Istakhar, the site of the old Sassanid shrine of Anahita – was forced to flee and was assassinated in 652. A legend persisted that a daughter of Yazdagird, Shahrbanu (Lady of the Land, a cult name for Anahita), had married the third Imam of Shiah Islam, the martyr Husain, and begot the fourth Shiah Imam, bringing Sassanid royal blood into the lineage of subsequent Shiah Imams. With the fall of Sassanid Persia the Arab armies descended on the Byzantine empire: Egypt, Palestine and Syria, which long had been a bone of contention between the Roman and Sassanid monarchs, were now annexed to the Umayyad caliphate and the 'True Cross' had to be moved to Constantinople.

The protracted conflict between the Roman and Sassanid empires was also marked by a vigorous religious rivalry as the two empires sought to establish their own religious orthodoxies. The Christianization of the Roman world after Constantine's Edict of Milan of AD 313 was completed with the Theodosian laws in 380; the installation of Zoroastrianism as the official religion of the Sassanid empire began with its founder, Ardashir I, and was accomplished under Shapur II. Inevitably, while Christianity was on the rise in the Roman empire Shapur persecuted its adherents in Iran. Portrayed as 'bound by the rites of the Magi and practitioner of secrets' (Agathias 2 : 26.30), Ardashir I was credited with the saying, 'kingship and religion are twin brothers, no one of which can be maintained without the other. For religion is the foundation of kingship and kingship is the guardian of religion. Kingship cannot subsist without its foundation and religion cannot subsist without its guardian. For that which has no guardian is lost, and that which has no foundation crumbles' (*Testament of Ardashir*). The great Sassanid monarch Chosroes I, 'The Just of the Immortal Soul' (5.31–79), declared that the 'King of Kings', as ruler of the material world, was an intermediary between humanity on earth and Ohrmazd, Lord of the spiritual realm.[60]

During the reign of Shapur II, Armenia continued to be the focus of Roman–Iranian rivalry as it drifted away from the orbit of Zoroastrianism and became the first Christian state. Early in the fourth century the Arsacid king of Armenia, Tiridates IV, who began his reign as a zealous Zoroastrian, was converted to Christianity by St Gregory the Illuminator, himself from a branch of the old Arsacid royal house, and the old cultic centres of the Zoroastrian divinities, the *yazatas*, were turned into Christian sites.[61] Yet in subsequent centuries Zoroastrianism still found support among many Armenian nobles, who defended some of the Zoroastrian shrines by force, while the Sassanids launched three major campaigns to reconvert Armenia to Zoroastrianism. Within the Sassanid empire itself anti-Christian persecution was intermittent and its intensification in the fourth century was doubtless linked to the Christianization of its western rival, the Roman empire. At the same time, with the establishment of Christian orthodoxy in the Roman world, the Sassanid realm became a comparatively secure refuge for Christian movements that were condemned in the Byzantine empire. Following the condemnation at the Council of Ephesus in 431 of Nestorian Christianity, with its teaching of the two separate persons of Christ – the divine and the human – the Nestorian Church established its Patriarchal see in Sassanid Persia, where it was favoured by some Sassanid monarchs and from where it extended its mission into India, central Asia and China. Along with the Nestorian Christians, adherents of Monophysitism – the teaching of the single divine nature of

Christ, which was embraced by the Coptic and, partially, by the Armenian Church – also fled to Sassanid Persia. Apart from this Christian influx, pagan philosophers also sought refuge there following the closure of the philosophical schools in Athens by Emperor Justinian I in 529.

The establishment of Zoroastrianism as the organized state religion of the Sassanid empire occurred together with the reassembling and canonization of the Zoroastrian sacred scriptures, as well as sporadic campaigns against what was perceived as heresy, *daeva*-worship or 'Ahrimanic' sorcery. In the first century of Sassanid rule and expansion, Zoroastrian worship and fire temples were established in the newly conquered areas and regions within the Sassanid orbit of influence, such as Armenia, Georgia and Caucasian Albania. From the beginning of the Sassanid era in Iran the Zurvanite form of Zoroastrianism enjoyed intermittent prevalence, while the Zoroastrian state-church adhered to the strictly dualist form of the Good Religion. Despite the establishment of Zoroastrian orthodoxy and sporadic persecution against other faiths in the Sassanid empire, the religious climate remained diverse. Within Zoroastrianism itself a division appears to have existed between a higher, elitist and restrictive type of religion, with its esoteric and spiritualized concepts, and a common, popular type of religion, a division which was further linked with the notion of three classes of people, recognized as those who were saved, those who were not guilty and those who were guilty.[62] Although it is difficult to discern the exact targets of the constant condemnations and warnings against *yatukih* (sorcery) and *daeva*-worship during the Sassanid era, diverse magical practices undoubtedly flourished throughout the empire, remnants of *daeva*-worship being apparently still active, particularly in eastern Iranian regions like Sogdiana where Zoroastrianism anyway seems to have been of a local variety and with a pronounced Zurvanite orientation.

An important testimony of the religious situation in the Sassanid empire refers to three religious currents in Iran, the first of which advanced a system of three principles – the good, the just and the evil, an obvious reference to Zurvanism: the good principle being Ohrmazd; the just, Zurvan; and the evil, Ahriman. The other two currents were respectively the doctrine of the two principles – clearly dualist Zoroastrianism – and that of the seven principles, which still eludes identification.[63] Besides the strict Zoroastrian dualism, elevated to the status of orthodoxy in the Sassanid empire, there also existed a 'monotheistic' version of Zoroastrianism, according to which it was a supreme God that had created Ahriman and the world was thereafter subjected to their dual treatment, the good deriving from God and the evil from Ahriman. Another Zoroastrian trend during the Sassanid era sought the origin of Ahriman in a transformation in the good principle, an 'evil thought' that gave rise to its evil opposite.[64]

The Zoroastrian religious work *Denkart* ('Acts of the Religion') alluded to another type of threefold division among the religious trends in Iran: the first, the *yatukih*, recognized the creator as entirely maleficent; the second, 'the religion of false dogma', approached the creator as both maleficent and beneficent; and finally the third, 'the religion of the worshippers of Mazda or Ohrmazd', extolled the Creator as wholly beneficent.[65] The religion of the believers and worshippers of a maleficent creator, condemned by the orthodox Zoroastrians as an 'evil knowledge', was described as a hidden heresy and in its rite of the 'mystery of the sorcerers' Ahriman, the Destroyer, was praised in 'great secrecy'. The heretical sorcerers were accused of trying to spread the religion of Ahriman in the name of Ohrmazd and thus of prompting men to abandon the worship of Ohrmazd and turn to Ahriman. Their teachings were based on a drastic reversal of Zoroastrian tenets and practices; according to Zoroastrian orthodoxy Ahriman was not conciliated by their worship but was becoming more vicious and violent. Whether the heretical 'mystery of the sorcerers' differed from, coalesced with or was identical to the pre-Zoroastrian *daeva*-worship, vestiges of which survived well into the Sassanid era, can only be conjectured, but certainly both were treated as equally dangerous by Zoroastrian orthodoxy and were suppressed. The zealous Zoroastrian prelate Kartir, who was particularly influential in the late third century, conducted concerted campaigns against everything he regarded as *daeva*-worship. In his inscription at Naqsh-i Rustam, Kartir proclaimed that 'great blows and torment' befell Ahriman and the *daevas*, whose heresy 'departed and was routed from the empire', while the abodes of the *daevas* were 'made into thrones and seats of gods'.[66] Kartir's crusade against *daeva*-worship was accompanied by measures against the other religions in the Sassanid empire. The Zoroastrian priesthood was reformed; Kartir's inscription recorded that Zoroastrianism and the Magians were greatly exalted in the Sassanid empire.

Yet in the climate of a revived and militant Zoroastrianism and before the Zoroastrian reaction prevailed, the second Sassanid King of Kings,

Shapur I (240–72), followed a generally tolerant and indeed syncretistic religious policy. In the *Denkart* he was credited with collecting philosophical and scientific writings from Byzantium and India and adding them to the Zoroastrian canon. He forbade the Magian establishment to persecute the other faiths in the Sassanid empire and even patronized the founder of new universalist but essentially Gnostic religion, Mani. A tradition existed that he had proclaimed his religion of salvation on the day of Shapur's coronation; it was under Shapur's patronage that Manichaeism thrived and began its grand expansion in Asia and Europe.

Mani, who claimed that unlike the kings of the world he had to subdue cities and lands not with military might but with the word of God, identified himself with the Paraclete (Comforter), the Holy Spirit, promised to be sent in Christ's name to continue and 'call to mind' Christ's teachings (John 14 : 26). Apart from the expected Paraclete, Mani presented himself as a successor to the prophetic missions of Buddha, Zoroaster and Christ, the ultimate seal of the Prophets and 'the envoy of the true God in the Land of Babylon'.[67]

The Prophet of Babylon

Mani was born on 14 April 216 in Babylonia, with its rich, eclectic and tolerant religious climate, one decade before the fall of the old house of the Arsacids that had ruled Iran since 250 BC. Although depicted in Christian polemical tradition as the freed slave of a widow, Mani was a scion of a noble line related to the Arsacid dynasty. His father had been converted to a sect of Babylonian baptists, who were variously called *Mughtasilah* (practitioners of ablution) or *katharioi* and who have been recently identified as a branch of the Judaeo-Christian movement of the Elchasaites, named after their mysterious founder Elchasai (Hidden Power), who was active in the early second century.[68] Elchasai was said to have been in possession of a book, later called the *Book of Elchasai*, revealed by an angel of enormous size, the Son of God, accompanied by an equally large female angel, the Holy Spirit (Hippolytus, *Refutation of All Heresies* 9 : 13.1–4). Elchasai was supposed to have received this book of revelations in Parthia but the content remains largely unknown since only short and scattered quotations have been preserved. Parallels have been drawn between Elchasaite teachings and the Zurvanite school that assumed that Zurvan had generated two elements, the male principle of fire and the female principle of water, associated respectively with light and darkness, but in the Elchasaite system the poles appear reversed.[69] In his rejection of the fiery sacrifices, Elchasai preached that fire was leading to error and was to be avoided as abhorrent and strange to God, while the 'sound of the water' should be followed, as water was good and acceptable to God (Epiphanius, *Panarion* 19 : 3.7).

What seems certain is that the Elchasaites were a Judaeo-Christian baptist sect, which might have been influenced during its development by Gnosticism, but otherwise they endeavoured to live 'according to the Law', observed the Sabbath and like most Jewish Christians denounced Paul and the 'way of the Greeks'. The teachings of the *Book of Elchasai*, with its reputed secret revelations, were undoubtedly fundamental to the Elchasaite sect which apparently possessed its own version of the Gospels. The Elchasaites were said to have invoked seven elements during their baptism: 'heaven, water, the holy spirits, the angels of prayer, oil, salt and the earth' which constituted the 'astonishing, ineffable and great mysteries' of Elchasai, revealed to the worthy Elchasaite disciples (Hippolytus, *Refutation of All Heresies* 9 : 15.2). Otherwise, of the 'astonishing, ineffable and great mysteries' of Elchasai, little is known, apart from the evident Elchasaite preoccupation with astrology, some sets of magical practices and the belief in the cyclic manifestation of Christ or the 'True Prophet' in many bodies throughout the ages. In some Elchasaite circles Elchasai was considered the latest incarnation in the chain and all Elchasaites were obliged to pray not towards the east but always in the direction of Jerusalem. In *Panarion* (53 : 1.1), Epiphanius declared that the Elchasaites were not Jews, Christians or pagans, but were somewhere between them, 'keeping to the middle way'.

Within one century of Elchasai's mission, Elchasaite groups were reported in Rome, Palestine and Syria, and were said to worship as goddesses two sisters from the 'famous seed' of Elchasai, Marthous and Marthana. The Babylonian Elchasaites, joined by Mani and his father, abstained from meat and wine and observed frequent purification of food and the body by ritual ablutions with water. Indeed, Mani's conflict with the sect was provoked by his denial of the Elchasaite baptismal procedures, which he judged as preoccupied with the purification of the body, which is by its nature impure and, unlike the soul, irredeemable.

Real purity, according to Mani, could be achieved only through *gnosis*, the knowledge of the separation of Light from Darkness, life from death and the living waters from the foul waters.[70]

Although Mani tried to fortify his position with parables about Elchasai, where the prophet himself was credited with supporting the reality of Mani's innovations, his attempted dualist reformation met with outright hostility. At a special synod of the sect Mani's *gnosis* and his attack on Elchasaite ritual ablutions were vigorously denounced amid turbulent debates: even Mani's life was threatened. Some of the Babylonian baptists fell under the sway of Mani's orations and recognized him as a prophet and *didaskalos* (teacher), as a vehicle of the 'Living Word' and perhaps as an awaited incarnation of the 'True Prophet'. The Elchasaites, however, also had a prophecy predicting the advent of a young man, a new teacher, who would reverse the precepts of their religion and for most Elchasaites Mani seemed the incarnation of this false prophet. Mani himself was to declare that his new 'mysteries' had abolished and invalidated the traditional teachings and the mysteries of the Babylonian baptists.

Mani's mysteries were proclaimed to stem from revelations from his *Syzygus* (divine twin), deemed to come from the Father and from the 'good Right (Hand)'.[71] The mysteries revealed by the *Syzygus* to Mani were seen as secret knowledge that had been kept hidden from the world, forbidden for man to see or hear. In the Manichaean text *Kephalaia*, they appear as the mystery of 'the Deep and the High', of Light and Darkness, the mystery of the Destruction, 'the mystery of the Great War that was stirred up by Darkness',[72] the merging of Light and Darkness and the creation of the world. These 'mysteries' were to become the basis of Mani's new Gnostic system of the two contrary and coeternal principles of Light and Darkness and the Three Times of their original separation, fusion and cosmic struggle and, finally, their future ultimate separation.

One of the precepts of the *Syzygus*' revelations was that it was through Mani that the blessed Father would fight the kings and rulers of the world. Despite his apprehension that all religions and sects were adversaries of good and that he would encounter kings and religious leaders,[73] Mani perceived his mission as universalist – it had to reach all regions of the world, all people and all schools of religion. His self-proclaimed spiritualist vision provoked the isolationist Elchasaites to accuse him of 'going to the Gentiles' and, following the disputes during the Elchasaite synod, he was expelled from the Babylonian sect, which continued to live 'according to the Law'.

Mani began his mission as an 'Apostle of Light' with three former Elchasaites, including his father, and his initial missionary routes were directed into north-east Iran and remained within the Sassanid and Zoroastrian orbit. Soon, however, he embarked on a greater missionary journey which took him to the Indo-Iranian borderlands, north-west India and the Kushan realm, itself then apparently under Sassanid suzerainty. In its mature form Mani's Gnostic synthesis included elements not only of Gnosticism, Judaeo-Christianity and Zoroastrianism, but also of Mahayana Buddhism. The Buddhist influences on Manichaeism could date to Mani's missionary venture in India where he became acquainted with Hindu and Buddhist teachings and practices. Both as a missionary and theologian Mani was influenced by Paul; he perceived his mission as a spiritual war to recover the light imprisoned in the darkness of the world. In Manichaean apocalyptic thought Mani's missionary campaigns emerged as a continuation of the wars against 'Error' which had been waged by the previous great saviours, Zoroaster and Jesus.[74] Zoroaster had once banished the Error from Babylon and when it re-emerged among the Jews it was Jesus who was sent to cast the Error out from Jewish religion and who overturned the law, destroyed the Temple and was finally crucified. Following the destruction of the Jerusalem Temple the Error retreated to Mesopotamia, where it mastered the fire of the Magi, and now Mani was entrusted with the task of launching the new, ultimate war against its renascence and its kings and nobles, a war which was set to continue until the end of time.

During his Indian journey Mani had some missionary success with local dynasts and on his return to Iran he was soon granted audience with Shapur I. Mani was presented as a 'physician from Babylon' and his encounter with the King of Kings was to prove crucial for the early missionary expansion of Manichaeism – Mani joined Shapur's entourage and was given permission to promulgate his new religion of salvation freely in the Sassanid empire. Besides securing the favour of the *Shah-an-Shah*, Mani converted two brothers of Shapur to his 'Religion of Light' and dedicated his work *Shabuhragan*, where he expounded his teachings of the Seal of the Prophecy, the Two Principles and the Three Times, to his royal patron.

Shapur's patronage of Manichaeism has been seen as proof that at the time of his great confrontation with the Roman empire he sought the means to achieve religious cohesion in his heterogeneous realm – where Zoroastrianism coexisted with Christianity, Buddhism, Judaism and other faiths – through Mani's daring religious synthesis. Whatever the designs of Shapur, Mani certainly joined his campaigns against the Romans and in 260 might have witnessed the capture of the Roman emperor Valerian, an event commemorated on a monumental rock relief at the dynastic site of Naqsh-i Rustam near Persepolis. Valerian soon died in Persian captivity and while Zoroastrianism continued to expand its sphere of influence, Mani's 'Religion of Light' also considerably widened its missionary propaganda to 'sow the corn of life from East to West'. Apart from extending into eastern Iran, Bactria, Armenia and Georgia, the Manichaean missions also spread westwards into Egypt and Syria, penetrating the Roman empire itself, where their presence was to be lasting and feared. At the same time, the threat of Zoroastrian reaction to Mani's prominence was steadily growing but during the long rule of Shapur and the following short reign of Hormizd (Ohrmazd) I – Shapur's son from his marriage with his daughter – the 'Doctor of Babylon' and his increasing flock remained safe from persecution. The Zoroastrain reaction to Sassanid toleration of Manichaeism was imminent and the accession of Bahram I in 273 marked a drastic reversal in the fortunes of Mani and his Religion of Light, which seems to have been largely provoked by the high Zoroastrian prelate Kartir, the 'Soul-saviour of Bahram'. Apparently incited by the Zoroastrian clergy and Kartir, Bahram summoned Mani and although the Doctor of Babylon claimed that he had brought only good to the royal house by exorcizing demons and healing illness, Bahram could not be persuaded that divine revelation might be granted to Mani rather than to the King of Kings, 'The Ruler of the World'. Mani, the self-proclaimed 'Apostle of Light', was heavily fettered with seven chains and cast into prison, where he continued to instruct his disciples during his twenty-six days' Passion. On Mani's death a blazing torch was thrust through his body on Bahram's orders to ensure that the 'Seal of the Prophets' was dead and his severed head was impaled over the city gate, which came to be known as 'Mani's Gate'.

In the wake of Mani's martyrdom, with which Bahram was said to have appeased 'the Magians, the teachers of Persia, the servants of fire',[75] the Manichaeans were subjected to violent persecution and many were forced to flee eastwards to Sogdiana.[76] After ten years, amid another eruption of anti-Manichaean campaigns, apparently instigated by Kartir, Mani's successor, Sisinus, was crucified. At the height of his influence

Kartir proclaimed in his inscription at Naqsh-i Rustam that throughout the whole empire the rites of Ohrmazd had become superior, while Jews, Buddhists, Hindus, Christians and Manichaeans had been smitten in the Sassanid realm.

The Father of Greatness and the Prince of Darkness

The violent reaction of official Zoroastrianism to Mani's Religion of Light was provoked partly by his use of Zoroastrian concepts in his new and essentially Gnostic religion, where Iranian, Jewish, Christian, Buddhist and Egyptian traditions were synthesized in what is usually described as the supreme syncretistic system of late antiquity. Mani was clearly indebted to Marcion's teaching of the two Gods – the good Father of Jesus Christ and the Demiurge of the visible world, but at the same time appears to have been influenced also by Marcion's theological adversary, the heretical Christian evangelist Bardaisan of Edessa (AD 154–222).[77] In Bardaisan's system the world is composed of five primal elements – Light in the East, Wind in the West, Fire in the South, Water in the North, and their enemy Darkness in the Depths below, while their Lord is in the heavens. Following strife among the first four elements, Darkness emerged from the abyss seeking to merge with them but the pure elements were delivered by the Most High, who sent the Messiah, Christ, to hurl Darkness down to its abode below. The elements were set up in accordance with the 'mystery of the Cross', while the world was created from the amalgam of the elements with Darkness. Mani's Religion of Light, moreover, bears traces of distinct Gnostic traditions, but it remains unclear whether they were assimilated through the medium of the Elchasaite sect or during Mani's exposure to the eclectic religious currents in Mesopotamia.

The canon of the Manichaean Church comprised seven works written by Mani himself: *The Living Gospel*, *The Treasure of Life*, *Treatise*, *The Book of Secrets*, *The Book of the Giants*, *The Epistles* and *Psalms and Prayers*, while works like the *Shabuhragan* also enjoyed great prominence. Mani's writings were lost and until the discovery of authentic Manichaean manuscripts early in the twentieth century, Manichaean teachings were known mainly through the accounts of Church Fathers like Augustine, the Syrian Theodore bar Konai or Islamic authorities like al-Nadim and al-Biruni.[78] With the discovery of Manichaean texts first in Turfan, in Chinese Turkestan, and then in Egypt, the non-Manichaean observers of the Religion of Light could be compared with the genuine Manichaean records.

In Mani's synthesis the Gnostic anti-cosmic dualism of spirit and matter coalesces with the later Zoroastrian type of dualism of the two primordial, irreconcilable principles of good and evil and the Three Times or Epochs of the tripartite cosmic drama. In Mani's *gnosis* the imprisonment and the suffering of the soul are caused by the fusion of the two contrary principles of Light (spirit) and Darkness (matter) and the soul could be released from the 'great calamity' of the prison-body only through knowledge of their duality and the destinies of their struggle and final separation. According to Mani's *historia arcana* of the cosmos in the Former Time, the sublime Realm of Light was totally separated from the infernal Realm of Darkness and was ruled by the 'Father of Greatness'. One of the important elements of Manichaean missionary strategy was to adjust Manichaean teaching to the local religious terminology: in Iran the Father of Greatness was identified with Zurvan and his fourfold dignity comprised Divinity, Light, Power and Wisdom – hence he is also styled the Four-faced God. Like Zurvan, the Father of Greatness was regarded as androgynous and could be styled 'elder brother' or 'elder sister'. Mani's identification of the Father of Greatness with Zurvan shows clearly that he formulated his system when Zurvanism was strong in Iran, but otherwise the Manichaeans rejected the teaching that Ohrmazd and Ahriman were respectively the younger and first-born sons of one supreme deity.

In Manichaean cosmology the Realm of Light consisted of five elements – Air, Wind, Light, Water and Fire – and was also the abode of the splendid Tree of Life. In the Realm of Darkness five evil archons presided over its own five worlds – Smoke, Fire, Wind, Water and Darkness – from which arose five trees of evil that formed the Tree of Death. The whole Realm of Darkness was ruled by the Prince of Darkness (in Iranian Manichaeism usually Ahriman), who was sometimes depicted as a five-shaped being – with the head of a lion, the body of a serpent, the wings of a bird, the tail of a fish and the four feet of creeping animals.[79]

The fivefold domain of the Prince of Darkness was in a state of constant and disorderly agitation, plagued by destructive, internecine struggles between its hierarchies, during which some of the demonic powers broke out of the confines of their world and encroached upon the tranquil Realm of Light. The invasion of the forces of Darkness marked the beginning of the Present Time, the era when the two principles of Light and Darkness are intermingled and warring. To oppose the demonic onslaught the Father of Greatness evoked the Mother of Life, who herself evoked the Primal Man (Ohrmazd in Iranian Manichaeism), who was armed with the five elements of the Light Sphere, and sent against the Prince of Darkness with his infernal elements. In the ensuing battle the Prince of Darkness was victorious and his forces devoured a part of the five 'luminous elements', the panoply of the Primal Man who collapsed senseless in the bondage of Darkness.

Yet the defeat of the Primal Man was a sacrifice through which the Father of Greatness entrapped and stifled the aggression of the forces of Darkness who now seemed to be 'bitten by a snake', poisoned but addicted to the Light elements they had swallowed. In the Realm of Light a second generation of gods was evoked, the Friend of the Lights, the Great *Ban* (Architect or Builder) and the Living Spirit (Mithra in Iranian Manichaeism) to save the Primal Man, the 'bright one in darkness'. The Living Spirit (Mithra) released the Primal Man (Ohrmazd) by grasping his right hand to raise him from the dark bondage and the ritual greeting with the right hand, symbolizing the mystery of salvation from the Darkness, was to become a Manichaean custom. The Living Spirit then began the work of saving the Light elements, the so-called 'Living Soul', imprisoned in the 'burning house' of matter, and with his five sons defeated the archons of Darkness to create eight earths from their bodies and ten skies from their skins. The Living Spirit was the Demiurge of the visible world, which was created according to the design of the Great *Ban*, with its different regions representing various levels of blending Light and Darkness and mechanisms for the redemption of the Light elements that were to return to the new earth or paradise fashioned by the Great Architect.

While the sun and moon were created from the most pure of the recovered Light particles, the plight of the remaining entrapped Light was seen as crucifixion, the Light itself being recognized as the suffering Jesus (Jesus *patibilis*), 'hanging on every tree'. None the less, the cosmos had been designed by the Great Architect to advance the salvation of the Light elements and the Prince of Darkness had to devise new stratagems to bind them to the dark matter. In the counter-attack of the powers of Darkness the male and female archons Saclas and Namrael created Adam and Eve to fortify the imprisonment of the Light elements through the lust and reproduction of the human species. In Manichaean accounts of early human procreation, Cain was born from Eve's union with the male archon and his own incestuous intercourse with Eve generated Abel and two daughters, the 'Wise of the Ages' and the 'Daughter of Corruption'. While Abel was murdered and Cain married the 'Wise of the Ages', Adam finally begat from Eve Sethel (Seth), who was recognized as a 'stranger' to the race of the archons and was inevitably threatened with death.[80]

Prior to this entangled saga Adam had been oblivious of the Light within himself, but was awakened from his sleep by a saviour from the Realm of Light, Jesus the Splendour (sometimes identified with Ohrmazd) who released him from possession by the 'deceiving demon' and the 'great archontess'. Jesus the Splendour revealed to Adam the secret history of the cosmos, the suffering of the Light taken captive in the Darkness, and made him eat of the Tree of Life. When Adam reached full awakening he deplored the archontic creator of his body and ever after the human race remained the principal battleground between the forces of Light and Darkness. Following the mission of Jesus the Splendour a succession of redeemers, bearers of *gnosis*-power, were sent to humanity to further the work of salvation in a continuous revelation – Seth(el), Enoch, Noah, Abraham, Shem, Zoroaster, Buddha and the historical Jesus Christ. As in other Gnostic schools, in Manichaeism Jesus Christ remained a divine being, who did not assume a material body and whose incarnation, Passion, death and Resurrection were only in appearance. There existed, however, Manichaean traditions concerning the actual Jewish Messiah, but they are preserved only in scattered and obscure fragments, and Mani's lost book, *Book of the Secrets*, contained a chapter about the 'Son of the Widow', the crucified Messiah.[81] Other Manichaean texts asserted that it was the son of Mary who suffered death on the cross, not the true Son of God. At least in some Manichaean circles the son of Mary was regarded as being of the evil principle and while the Enemy or Satan had planned to crucify the Redeemer, he had actually crucified himself.

Apart from the obvious Gnostic parallels, the Manichaean teachings of Jesus' crucifixion have also been compared to the Koranic version – ' "We have killed the Messiah, Jesus son of Mary, the apostle of God" – But they did not kill him, neither did they crucify him, but a similitude was made for them' (Sura 4:156–7). Certain similarities to Manichaeism have been detected also in the Koranic vision of the eschatological 'terror' (Sura 56) and the Koranic notion of the revelation being transmitted by preceding prophets until its culmination in Mohammed, 'the Apostle of God and the Seal of the Prophets' (Sura 33:40).[82] In Manichaeism, following the mission of the heavenly Jesus, it was the 'Light-bringer' Mani, the Apostle of Jesus Christ and the announced Paraclete, who was sent to proclaim the complete and final revelation in his Religion of Light. Mani was extolled as the Seal of the Prophets who revealed the future final stages of the separation of Light and Darkness, when the number of souls trapped below would 'diminish day by day' and the world of Darkness, increasingly depleted of Light, would be plunged into a Great War. The Third Time would be marked by the second coming of Jesus as the 'Great King', his 'Last Judgement' followed by the destruction of the universe in a Great Fire lasting 1,468 years. The last Light elements released would be gathered in a 'statue' to be lifted and restored to the Realm of Light, while the Prince of Darkness and his powers would be imprisoned forever in a grave prepared by the Great Architect.

The Manichaean account of the threefold cosmic drama of the strife between Light and Darkness, good and evil, matter and spirit, is illustrated by rich, expressive and occasionally disturbing mythological imagery which undoubtedly made its appeal more forceful. At the same time, the dramatic and violent narratives provided their adversaries with material for accusations of secret, unnatural and monstrous practices. Such accusations have often been made against secretive or persecuted religious groups like the early Christians, and the Manichaeans were no exception, being charged with demon-worship, human sacrifice and the use of human skulls for divination, sexual orgies, and the like.

Mani himself was a target for anti-Manichaean polemics, and his name was often translated in derogatory terms in Syriac, Greek and Chinese, from the simple 'maniac' to 'the demonic nun'. Mani had predicted that his mission would provoke the adversity of the secular and religious powers but zealously strove to extend its sphere, as he believed that the messages of his predecessors, Buddha and Zoroaster in the east and Christ in the west, remained confined to their 'Churches' and were, moreover, distorted by their followers. As a self-proclaimed prophet from the land of Babylon, Mani clearly distinguished himself from his eastern and western apostolic predecessors and perceived himself as 'placed in the centre as uniting messenger'.[83] His highly syncretistic system was intended to reach Buddhists, Zoroastrians and Christians alike and during its spread was further enriched through contact with other religions such as Taoism in China. In his designs for a world religion Mani had hoped that his 'Church of Light' would expand both in the west and the east and would thus prove superior to all previous religions, which had remained bound either to east or west or, worse, to particular cities and countries.[84] Mani predicted that his gospel would be preached everywhere and in all languages; in the millennium that followed the Passion of the prophet of Babylon, his 'Religion of Light' was to spread from the Atlantic Ocean to the Pacific.

The Diffusion of the 'Religion of Light'

Mani's 'Church of Light' was divided into two principal and distinct classes, the elect and the listeners or auditors, and this division is variously attributed to Buddhist or Marcionite influences. The elect, the so-called 'members of Mani', were the minority elite and were associated with Seth(el), the apostle of electship.[85] The elect were entrusted with furthering Mani's vision of redeeming the Light elements from the bondage of matter and, as the 'Saviours of God', they had to observe extreme asceticism. They were bound by the rules of the 'Three Seals', the seals of mouth, hands and breast, which imposed strict abstinence from meat, wine, blasphemy, sexual intercourse and work that could damage the Light elements. The more numerous listeners followed less rigorous standards of conduct and were allowed to marry but had to avoid 'demonic' procreation. Unlike the apostolic elect, listeners could own property and had to ensure the living of the elect, who were engaged in missionary and scribal work. Upon the death of an elect his soul was supposed immediately to reach the Realm of Light, while the soul of the listener was believed to enter a series of transmigrations until reaching the ultimate goal – an incarnation as a Manichaean elect. Mani himself was said to have preached that there were three paths which divided human souls: the way of the elect led to the Gardens of Paradise; the way of the listeners, guardians of the religion and sustainers of the elect, led to the world and its horrors; the third way of the sinners led to hell.[86] The division between the elect and the listeners would persist even during the time of the Last Judgement when the elect would be transformed into angels and the listeners would be elevated to Jesus' right side.

The elect formed the Manichaean ecclesiastical hierarchy, crowned by Mani's successor, with his seat in Babylon, who was the leader of the Church of Light or the *archegos*, a title ascribed earlier to Elchasai himself. Below the *archegos* were the twelve apostles, or teachers, and this hierarchy allowed Christian polemicists to depict Mani as a type of Antichrist accompanied by 'twelve evil disciples'. The twelve Manichaean apostles were followed by seventy-two bishops or deacons and then by 360 elders or presbyters. While women could achieve the status of an elect they could not occupy a position in the hierarchy of the Church of Light.

For the Manichaean Church, and for himself, Mani was not merely the prophet who revealed the mysteries of the separation and mixture of Light and Darkness, but was seen as the Seal of Prophecy heralding the advent of the final cycle of separation and salvation. In the Manichaean eschatological chronology Mani's missionary wars against the Error and the Magi, who were recognized as reigning 'in this world', were to be followed by a vigorous revival of the Error's power, when the 'Church of Light' would be subjected to renewed suppression.[87] The renascence of the Error was expected to bring about a disastrous Great War which was, however, to be succeeded by a time of peace under the rule of the Great King, when the Manichaean Church would be fully restored and would then replace the Magi. With the liberation of Light from matter nearly accomplished, the advent of pseudo-prophets and the Antichrist would lead to the last wars against the powers of Darkness and finally the Last Judgement.

These final stages of the threefold drama of the wars between good and evil were regarded by the early Manichaeans as impending events, since they saw themselves as the last generation to have received directly the message of salvation. The great anti-Manichaean persecution launched by the Zoroastrian prelate Kartir after Mani's martyrdom was inevitably associated with the time of the renewal of Error in the Manichaean eschatological chronology. If the fourth century failed to fulfil Manichaean expectations of the restoration of the Church of Light and its triumph over the Magi, it saw the great Manichaean expansion, as Mani had predicted, into both the east and the west.

With the first serious outbreaks of persecution in the Sassanid empire many Manichaeans left Mesopotamia; none the less Babylonia remained a centre of Manichaeism and the *archegos* retained his seat there. The Religion of Light entered the Roman empire during Mani's lifetime and in the fourth century continued its advance in the Mediterranean world and particularly in North Africa. In 302, five years before hailing Mithras as the 'patron of the Empire', Diocletian issued a harsh edict against the Manichaeans in the empire, where they were accused of seeking to infect and poison like a 'malignant serpent' the Roman people with the customs and laws of the Persians. Diocletian apparently perceived Manichaeism as a Persian 'fifth column' in the empire and decreed that the sectarian leaders should be burnt with their books and their followers duly punished. The persecution of the Manichaeans, whether successful or not, was relaxed with Constantine's Edict of 312 which granted universal religious tolerance. Manichaeism then began to spread more vigorously throughout the empire and from the eastern Mediterranean provinces it entered the Balkans and Italy, spread into North Africa, and reached as far as Spain and Gaul, while the first Christian anti-Manichaean works began to appear. As witnessed by St Augustine, who for nine years (373–82) had been a Manichaean listener and had ministered to the needs of the elect, Manichaeism was well established and well organized in Rome and the network of Manichaean conventicles was widespread throughout the empire. With the increasing missionary work of the Manichaean envoys among the Christian populace of the empire, western Manichaeism came to accept even more Christian notions into its theological vocabulary.

After an imperial decree of 372 had forbidden Manichaean gatherings, the edicts of Theodosius the Great (379–95), which suppressed Arianism and paganism, contained anti-Manichaean legislation and marked the beginning of an era of intensifying persecution of the Manichaeans in both the West and East Roman empires. Throughout the fifth and the early sixth centuries the Roman papacy launched a concerted campaign against the Manichaeans in Rome and many of them were exiled and their books burnt. In the East Roman (Byzantine) empire, where becoming a

'Manichaean' was like becoming 'a citizen of a theological Persia perpetually at war with the Romans',[88] the persecution was bound to be severe and Emperor Anastasius (491–518) decreed capital punishment for the Manichaeans. The beginning of Justinian the Great's reign (527–65) saw another edict prescribing the death penalty for Manichaeans which was followed by wide-ranging searches for and execution of Manichaeans occupying imperial posts. In the *Secret History* of his contemporary, Procopius of Caesarea, Justinian was condemned as a demon-incarnate, if not the Lord of the Evil Spirits himself, whose deeds were destined to inflict great calamities upon the world. Justinian might have rebuilt the magnificent church Hagia Sophia (St Sophia), boasting that he had outdone Solomon, but Procopius' insights into his 'demonic' nature must have been shared by the Byzantine Manichaeans, as the anti-Manichaean campaigns intensified and relapsed Manichaeans were threatened with capital punishment. Under Justinian, the 'many-eyed Emperor', the Church and state joined forces more effectively than ever before; two centuries after Diocletian had launched the war against the 'malignant serpent' from Persia, the Religion of Light was extinguished in the empire and thereafter seemed to have disappeared from Europe.

While the westward course of the Manichaean mission collapsed amid the barbaric invasions and the mounting persecution in the Roman empire, it was subjected to further vicissitudes in its homeland, Babylonia. The *archegos* continued to reside in Babylonia in the Sassanid era and following the establishment of the Umayyad caliphate in 661 the Manichaeans generally received relaxed treatment and some Manichaeans returned to Mesopotamia. The succeeding Abbasids, however, took more vigorous measures against the Manichaeans and unrepentant Manichaeans were executed with their heads being left on gibbets. None the less, the Manichaean movement and its *archegos* remained active in Babylonia into the tenth century, but thereafter its fortunes in the Near East are extremely obscure. By the end of the tenth century the centre of gravity of the Religion of Light seems to have been moved finally entirely to the east, to Sogdiana and central Asia; it was this eastward course that prolonged the life of Manichaeism in Asia until the end of the Middle Ages.[89]

Manichaeism had established an early foothold in eastern Iran and the former Kushan areas in Bactria and Sogdiana, and in central Asia Manichaeism was to compete for converts with both Buddhism and Nestorian Christianity. With the persecution following Mani's death in

274 many Manichaeans were forced to flee to the east and crossed the River Oxus (Amu Darya) into Sogdiana. Amid the strong and locally coloured Zoroastrian traditions of the region and the increasing Buddhist influence, Manichaeism succeeded none the less in gaining ground in Sogdiana, which itself from the end of the third century onwards came to be invaded and dominated successively by the nomadic Chionites (Kidarites), the Hephtalites and the expanding Turkic tribes. Between the fourth and the sixth centuries Manichaeism appears to have been most prominent in the formerly Kushan-ruled areas to the south of Samarkand and in the last decades of the seventh century Sogdiana became a stepping stone for the introduction of the Religion of Light into T'ang China. Sogdian merchants played a crucial role in the spread of Manichaeism across the trade routes of Central Asia and Manichaean priests gained a reputation as skilled astrologers at local courts in the area. The rising prominence of the 'eastern' Manichaeans in Sogdiana and the eastward advance of Manichaeism was, however, accompanied by a schism between the eastern wing and the old Babylonian see in the late sixth century. The schismatic 'eastern' Manichaeans began to call themselves 'The Pure Ones', established their own *archegos* in the Samarkand area and carried their missionary work further east.

In 762 Manichaean priests succeeded in converting the Khagan of the Uighurs, then the dominant Turkic military power in Central Asia, and despite some opposition by Uighur nobles he soon imposed the Manichaean creed on the subjects of his empire. An inscription commemorating the Khagan's conversion extols this act as transforming the Uighurs from people who indulged in blood sacrifices and wanton killing into a nation that came to cultivate vegetarianism and uphold righteousness. Now Manichaeism could use Uighur political power to expand its mission in Central Asia and China, and due to the Uighur influence in Chinese internal political affairs, the T'ang government soon felt compelled to found Manichaean temples in the two capital cities, in four provinces in the Yangtze basin as well as in one of its northern strategic towns. By that time Buddhism had greatly increased its influence in China and gained T'ang royal patronage, coexisting as a foreign religion with Zoroastriansim, brought by Sassanian exiles from Arab-conquered Iran, and some Nestorian Christians. Now it was Manichaeism that earned the status of a privileged foreign religion in China but this ended when the Uighur empire collapsed in 840 under the pressure of the Kirghiz Turkic tribes. As

Manichaeism lost its powerful Uighur patronage, the Chinese Manichaean temples were closed in stages and in 843 the Manichaeans in China were subjected to massive persecution; similar drastic measures were taken two years later against Buddhism, whereas Nestorian and Zoroastrian priests were either defrocked or exiled.

In the second Uighur empire, founded in the Tarim Basin (modern north-west China), Manichaeism continued to enjoy the patronage of the Uighur court and along with the Manichaean temples the established Manichaean monasteries evolved into important centres of learning and artistic and missionary work.[90] Yet Buddhism and Nestorian Christianity were to become prevalent in the Uighur realm until the Mongol conquest in the thirteenth century and the forthcoming invasion of Islam.

The great anti-Manichaean persecution launched by the T'ang authorities around 843 did not halt completely the spread of the Religion of Light in China. Reports indicate that a Manichaean priest escaped the persecution by fleeing to a coastal town in the south Chinese province of Fukien. His apparently was not an isolated case, as Manichaeism succeeded in establishing itself in Fukien and even began to penetrate the neighbouring areas. If originally Manichaeism in China was a religion predominantly professed by foreign Sogdian merchants or envoys and Uighur mercenaries, in Fukien it was bound to become Cinicized, as the links between Fukien and Central Asian Manichaeans were virtually extinguished. Whereas relations between Manichaeism and Buddhism have often been marked by strong rivalries and Buddhist polemicists attacked the Manichaean tenets, Taoists could adopt a much less controversialist and more eclectic approach to Manichaeism, while Confucian attitudes to the Religion of Light were periodically determined by its presumed association with secret religious sects in China. In its expansion in Central Asia and the Far East Manichaeism inevitably not only came to use Buddhist and Taoist terminology as an important element of its missionary strategy but also was influenced by Buddhist and Taoist teachings, while Manichaean influences are sometimes detected in Tibetan religious traditions.[91] In the framework of the Manichaean missionary approach to other religion's notions, in Central Asia Mani could be identified with Maitreya, the would-be Buddha, and could be given the title 'Mani the Buddha of Light', as eastern Manichaeans compiled a life of Mani based on that of Buddha; at the same time in Taoist circles Mani came to be regarded as one of the avatars

of Lao-Tzu, the founder of Taoism.[92] Such identifications could allow the
Manichaeans in South China to pass off as Buddhists or Taoists and in the
eleventh century Fukien Manichaeans succeeded in persuading Chinese
commissioners to include a Chinese Manichaean work, *The Sutra of the Two
Principles and the Three Moments* (probably a version of the *Shabuhragan*
which Mani had dedicated to his royal patron, Shapur I), in the Taoist
canon,[93] which again was intended to secure the Manichaeans protection
from persecution and destruction of their literature. With its complicated
network of Manichaean cells, intended to ensure the missionary work of the
Manichaean priests and the maintenance of the Religion of Light,
Manichaeism effectively functioned as a secret religion and Manichaean
missionaries gained further renown for their presumed expertise in magic
and divination. Such associations inevitably could provoke accusations of
'black arts' practices and political subversion against the Manichaeans,
particularly in times of social unrest. The abusive term, 'Vegetarians and
Demon Worshippers', by which Manichaeans were derided by their adversaries, was also used against some Buddhist and Taoist secret sects but
almost certainly was originally forged to denote Manichaeism. Due to the
various ascetic and magical practices cultivated in such esoteric Taoist and
Buddhist sects, Manichaeism could be attacked along similar lines which
makes its history from the Sung to the early Ming periods (eleventh to
fourteenth centuries), amid the political rebellions and activities of various
secret societies, rather obscure – Manichaeans could be implicated, for
example, in forbidden sorcery and political subversion along with the
Buddhist White Lotus and White Cloud sects or other extremist esoteric
groups.[94] In 1292 Marco Polo encountered Manichaeans during his visit to
Fukien province[95] but less than a century later the founder of the Ming
dynasty (*ming-chao* – 'dynasty of light'), Chu Yüan Chang, who himself was
a leader of a society stemming from the Maitreya sect, suppressed
Manichaeism in 1370, accusing its followers, among other charges, that their
Religion of Light (*ming-chiao*) had usurped his dynastic title. While
arguments that Chu Yüan Chang chose the symbol of light as his dynastic
title under Manichaean influence are virtually impossible to prove, it
remains certain that his suppression of the Religion of Light did much to
diminish the Manichaean presence in southern China, although vestiges of
Manichaeism were still active in Fukien in the early seventeenth century.[96]
In south China the Religion of Light reached the easternmost limit of its
expansion and the extant Manichaean temple on the slopes of Hua-piao hill

in Fukien, with its surviving stone relief of Mani as the Buddha of Light, bears striking witness to the vitality of Chinese Manichaeism which not only outlasted by centuries the other Manichaean offshoots and the original see in Babylon, but may have joined with other secret religions in Fukien and persisted in syncretistic forms into modern times.[97]

The measures taken against Chinese Manichaeism were largely insti-gated because of its perception, particularly by Confucian officials, as a secret religious society, which, on a par with other sects, had 'under-ground' network of cells, with all its potential for subversion of law and order. The ascetic and other practices cultivated by the Manichaean Elect also could be seen as antagonistic to the social rules and condemned under the general term of 'Vegetarianism and Demon Worship'. But apart from this perceived association between sectarianism and social disturbance or rebellion, Confucian concerns did not include a preoccu-pation with the Manichaean religious and intellectual challenge to estab-lished religion as in the case of the Christian polemicists and adversaries of Manichaeism among the Church Fathers.[98] Yet the legacy of the popular perception of Chinese Manichaeans as adepts in divination and magic persisted in Chinese historical novels in which they can further appear as experts in martial arts, a far cry from the original Manichaean code of non-violence.[99] Similar accusations of magic and forbidden secret practices, sometimes with a similar motivation, were levelled at the Manichaeans and some Gnostic groups in the early Christian world but there these charges developed a religious and social dynamism of their own, leaving a lasting and disturbing imprint on Christian religiosity.

Heresiarch and Magus

The fusion and interpenetration of the notions of magic and heresy in early Christian thought and the resultant association between the figures of the sorcerer and the heretic, the magus and the heresiarch, had important implications for medieval and early modern European religious and intellectual history, particularly for the evolution of Christian heresiology and demonology. The early Christian formula-tions of the links between magic and heresy have occasionally been included in more general discussions of the wider problem of the relationship between magic and religion.[100] The exact nature of this relationship continues to be debated from an increasing variety of perspectives, some of which have indicated very promising directions for future research in fields ranging from comparative religion to sociology and anthropology.[101]

Among the various elements that were assembled to form the composite notion of the crime of diabolical witchcraft in the late Middle Ages particularly important was the amalgamation of the notion of harmful or maleficent magic (*maleficium*) and that of a secret, heretical anti-society, practising forbidden magical and orgiastic rites. In its final, crystallized form this amalgamation was the culmination of a lengthy process of syncretism of learned and popular traditions concerning sorcery and heresy which developed in the later Middle Ages but its earlier stages can be detected in late antiquity.

Late Roman legislation against magic and heresy, as reflected in the relevant legislation of Constantine the Great, Constantius II, the imperial constitution of Valentinian III and Marcian as well as the cumulative evidence of the Theodosian and Justinian codes, was particularly severe.[102] Indeed, earlier Roman laws against maleficent magic or *maleficium* (which besides harmful sorcery initially could refer to other kinds of 'evildoing'), from the Twelve Tablets to the edicts of Tiberius and Diocletian, could also be very harsh.[103] Apart from the inherited Roman legal attitudes to *maleficium*, the upsurge in sorcery accusations and persecution of magicians, diviners and the like under Constantius II, Valentinius and Valens have been seen as sociologically indicative of the changes and tensions affecting the imperial governing classes and the development of new social stratification.[104]

Notwithstanding the strong anti-magical stance of late Roman secular legislation, the early medieval Church had at its disposal a considerable body of patristic literature, including the influential works of Tertullian (*c.* 160–*c.* 225), Jerome (*c.* 342–420) and Augustine (354–430), dealing with the problems of magic and heresy, In its struggle against paganism, sorcery and heterodoxy the early medieval churchmen could use the relevant decrees of ecclesiastical synods and councils like the Council of Laodicaea (364) and the Council of Chalcedon (451). Collections of such decrees and papal decretals were to form the basis for ecclesiastical canon law which contained a number of sanctions concerning magicians and heretics. Collections of canon law also included excerpts from patristic writings, some of which treated the problems of magic and heresy and had developed the stereotype of a secret sect practising blasphemous and promiscuous rites.

Augustine, for example, who remained an influential source for medieval Catholic theologians, attributed to his former Manichaean co-religionists sexual malpractices and even secret infanticide,[105] but such claims appeared as early as Irenaeus (c. 130–c. 200) who declared that similar Roman accusations against the Christians were provoked by the depraved practices of heretical Gnostic groups like the Carpocratians.[106] Irenaeus stated, moreover, that the Carpocratians practised magic, possessed love potions and conjured spirits and dream senders,[107] whereas Clement of Alexandria (c. 150–c. 215) accused them of libertinism and indiscriminate orgiastic love-feasts.[108] In the next century Epiphanius (c. 315–403) charged the Gnostic Phibionites with conducting blasphemous orgiastic rites and ritual infanticide,[109] and along with Philaster (d. c. 397)[110] raised the latter charge against the non-Gnostic, ascetic and apocalyptic movement of the Montanists in Phrygia.[111] Despite being questioned by Jerome[112] and in *Praedestinatus* (c. 432–40),[113] these accusations against the Montanists were reiterated by Cyril of Jerusalem (c. 315–86)[114] and Augustine.[115]

Concerning the association between magic and heresy, early and suggestive examples may be found in early Christian elaborations of the story of Simon, who according to Acts 8:9–24 was a magus 'bewitching the people of Samaria with his sorceries'. Simon was baptized but was rebuked by Peter when he tried to purchase from the apostles the power of the Holy Ghost. The story of Simon Magus was expanded in a number of Christian legendary narratives; heresiologists like Irenaeus regarded him as the first heretic, a source of all heresies, whereas the apocryphal *Acts of Peter*[116] and the *Passion of Peter and Paul*[117] embellish the story of Simon's magical powers and trials of strength with Peter. Still more details about the magical feats and heretical teachings ascribed to him may be found in the Clementine literature[118] and in the works of authors like Justin Martyr (c. 100–65),[119] Hippolytus (c. 170–c. 236)[120] and Epiphanius;[121] sometimes his magical exploits, including miracles during his baptism, could be seen as having been accomplished with demonic help.[122] Menander of Samaria, reportedly Simon's successor, gained a similar reputation for his use of magic and his salvation-oriented magic-like baptismal rite as did the Gnostic group of the Simonians, deemed to be followers of Simon's teachings.[123]

Other Gnostic heresiarchs who according to the early Christian authors were associated with magic include Basilides and Marcus. According to Eusebius, Basilides transmitted the magic of Simon Magus in secrecy,[124] whereas Irenaeus claimed that his followers practised magic, necromancy, invocation of spirits and invented angelic names belonging to the different heavens of the Basilidean 365-heavens cosmology.[125] Hippolytus styles Marcus a 'master of magic',[126] while Irenaeus denounces the Gnostic heresiarch as proficient in magical deceit (including the making of love potions), a precursor of Antichrist', an unholy miracle-worker, whose prophetic utterances were provoked by a demon residing within him.[127] Like Simon Magus and Menander, Marcus gained renown for his redemptive baptismal rite during which he reportedly performed miracles.[128] His system comprised mystical rites of 'spiritual marriage', and another rite to be performed on those of his followers who were about to die which included invocations for the safe ascent of their 'inner nature' through the heavenly realms and for immunity against assaults by celestial powers. Similarly, the famous cosmogonic diagram of the Ophite Gnostics, representing the seven circles of the universe, also could be seen as a magic tool,[129] synthesizing the Ophite system which included magic names, formulae and 'symbols' or seals to be used by the ascending soul when passing through the gates to the realm of each circle.[130]

While these early Christian heresiological denunciations of Gnostic heresiarchs' involvement with the magic arts reflected the dual concern of the early Church with heresy and magic, accusations of sorcery against heretical or heterodox leaders could also result from the political and related agendas of the accusers. In 302 Diocletian (284–305) outlawed the followers of Manichaeism in the Roman empire with an edict that condemns the Manichaean sect as a subversive, malignant import from the Roman hereditary enemy, Persia, and links their 'abhorrent practices' with *maleficium*.[131] That Mani's association with Persia could provoke charges of proficiency in magic is also evident in the testimony of Epiphanius, who asserts that Mani was well acquainted with the practices of the Magi and his followers used astrology, amulets, phylacteries and incantations.[132] Some of these and similar accusations against the Manichaeans might have been partially provoked by Mani's reputation for magical healing and exorcism in Manichaean traditions and by Manichaean apotropaic and exorcist practices.[133] Legal and theological condemnations of Manichaeism after the Christianization of the Roman empire maintain resonances of Diocletian's sorcery accusations against the Manichaeans within the framework of the developing anti-heretical theological rhetoric and imperial legislation. Consequently, Manichaean books and prayers could be denounced as replete with sorcery and as honouring the Devil, while Mani himself could be represented as a successor to a lineage of infamous sorcerers.[134] The association between sorcery, illicit practices and Manichaeism apparently persevered both on a popular and learned level, as the severe anti-Manichaean legislation of Anastasius (491–518) and Justinian 1 (527–65) began to inflict on the Manichaeans death penalties similar to those prescribed for the practitioners of *maleficium*. The legal and theological potential of the combined accusations of Manichaeism and *maleficium* or sorcery was demonstrated by the charges raised in the 380s against Priscillian, Bishop of Avila, which included both, and led to his execution in 386 after a trial at a secular court at Trier.[135]

The harsh Justinian anti-Manichaean legislation was retained in later Byzantine law codes and the term 'Manichaean' continued to be employed as an equivalent of dualist or heretic sectarians or to condemn religious or political opponents. As with accusations of 'Manichaeism', sorcery charges, particularly at the Byzantine court, could also be used as political weapons. Such use of heresy and sorcery accusations makes the reconstruction of the history of heretical and sectarian movements, readily recognized by the Church as 'Manichaean' even more problematic. The association between magic and heresy, often resurfacing in these accusations, acquired, moreover, a lasting and menacing vitality of its own, capable of being resurrected with ease and targeted at the new sectarian or heretical groups which began to proliferate shortly after the completion of the first Christian millennium, often seen by anxious churchmen as a renascence of Manichaeism, an ancient and dangerously revived 'Great Heresy'.

CHAPTER THREE

The Thread of the Great Heresy

Following the explosion of religious and spiritual creativity during late antiquity, traces and actual transmitters of Gnostic and dualist teachings in the early Middle Ages become increasingly difficult to discern and identify. In the Near East such teachings enjoyed an uninterrupted historical prevalence within the still existing small religious group of the Mandaeans in southern Iraq and Khuzistan in Iran, rightly considered the last survivors of the great Gnostic movements of late antiquity. Mandaean doctrines certainly display links with Jewish baptismal sects, with Christianity, Manichaeism and Iranian religious traditions which almost certainly reflect stages in their history – facing persecution, by the late second century AD the Mandaeans apparently migrated from their original abodes in the eastern Jordan region to northern and thereafter to southern Mesopotamia, their present habitat. While the patterns of their encounter and interaction with Jewish, Christian and Gnostic traditions are still being established, it is obvious that Mandaeism exhibits a pronounced Gnostic dualism which opposes soul and body, the realms of light ('Lightworld') and darkness (originally a 'black watered' sea of chaos), the oppression of humanity by demonic super-natural powers, etc. The creation of the world and man is seen as the work of a demiurge, Ptahil, who was originally a light-being but came to cooperate with the demonic spirits of the 'Master of Darkness' and consequently was banished from the Lightworld. As the body of Adam was motionless, his soul was brought from the Lightworld to animate it. Unsurprisingly, the salvation and liberation of the light particles, brought into the earthly body, in the afterlife, when the soul ascends through the dangerous demon-inhabited spheres before it can re-enter the Lightworld, is a main preoccupation of Mandaean religious life. Adam was given the salvationist knowledge by a divine envoy and saviour from the Lightworld and the work of redemption was carried on by a succession of similar emissaries. Mandaeism features further a dualistic opposition between John the Baptist and Jesus – apparently, for historical reasons, John the Baptist, seen as a messenger of the king of light, was elevated as the Mandaean 'Prophet of Truth', whereas Jesus was treated as a kind of apostate Mandaean, facing the trial of purgatory.[1]

The Dualist Succession

In the early Middle Ages traces and elements of Gnostic and dualist teachings in varying degrees of intensity were also preserved in diverse apocryphal works from late antiquity which despite being banned, were preserved and maintained their circulation, mainly in the east Christian world, in heterodox, sectarian or simply learned circles. In the right circumstances these Gnostic or dualist residues in apocryphal works could stimulate a revival of related attitudes through simple borrowing of their themes or through creative interpretation spreading from these works to the canonical scriptures, with all the possibilities for the formulation of new heterodoxies and heresies.

A number of such apocryphal texts was preserved in Byzantium where the process of the creation of new apocrypha, such as apocalyptic revelations about the course of world history, also continued throughout the early Middle Ages. Moreover, Justinian's crusade against the Religion of Light might have extinguished it from the empire, but as the term Manichaean was to be repeatedly used not only to label heretics but also to stigmatize political and religious adversaries, Manichaeism continued to be feared as an unceasing threat, always capable of re-inventing itself and subverting orthodoxy. These arbitrary charges against 'Manichaeans' make the detection of any possible authentic survivals of Manichaeism after Justinian's reign extremely difficult. Yet among the array of heretical and heterodox movements in early medieval Byzantium there were two sects which have often been identified as the possible heirs of Manichaean Gnostic dualism and as crucial links in the chain supposedly connecting Manichaeism and medieval 'neo-Manichaeism' – the Massalians and the Paulicians.

The Paulicians emerged in the complicated religious world of sixth-century Armenia, which in 389 had been partitioned between Byzantium and Sassanid Persia. Despite Armenia's early adoption of Christianity, Zoroastrians continued to be active and the last Sassanid campaign to reclaim the Armenian lands for the religion of Ahura Mazda in 571 to 572 was supported by Armenian feudal nobles. By the time of this attempted Zoroastrian restoration, the Armenian Christian Church had already made itself autonomous and had adopted a version of Monophysite Christianity, defying the authority of Constantinople. The continuous Byzantine endeavours to assert the ecclesiastical supremacy of Constantinople in Armenia failed and in the mid seventh century, when the Arabs had conquered most of the Sassanid empire, Armenia had to acknowledge nominal Arab suzerainty.

With the foundation of the Umayyad caliphate, which engulfed the former Sassanid dominions, Zoroastrianism was disestablished in Iran and the advance of Islam in the Iranian world was accompanied by sporadic anti-Zoroastrian persecution and the turning of fire temples into mosques. Rather than through forceful conversions, the gradual Islamization of Iran was facilitated by the political and religious conditions in the Umayyad and later the Abbasid caliphates. The emergence of a distinct, sophisticated Persianized Islam spawned important and influential mystical and esoteric trends within Islam. None the less, in the first three centuries of the caliphate, Zoroastrianism retained its prominence in various Iranian provinces, particularly in Fars, the old Achaemenid heartland, where until the tenth century it was still stronger than Islam. After a notable religious revival in the ninth and the early tenth centuries Zoroastrianism gradually diminished to a small religious minority in Iran, while migration to India established new Zoroastrian centres in Gujarat.

Although the Good Religion of Ahura Mazda declined in Iran, Zoroastrian traditions survived in Armenia into the Middle Ages and indeed might have persisted into the modern era, even until the early twentieth century.[2] Moreover, with the establishment of Christian orthodoxy in the Roman empire, Armenia became a refuge for heretics and heterodox sectarians. Marcionite and other Gnostic groups, perhaps including Manichaeans, certainly lingered in Armenia well into the fifth century, while the Paulicians, who appeared in the following century, still present numerous problems in the study of eastern Christianity and medieval dualism. In Armenia they were accused of consorting with 'sun-worshippers' (Persians, Zoroastrians), also called Arewordik (Sons of the Sun), or of observing some Zoroastrian customs, like the exposure of the dead on rooftops or the veneration of the sun; and indeed, some Paulician groups might have adopted such practices.[3]

Later Byzantine polemical works consistently described the Paulicians as outright Manichaeans and attributed to them the radical dualist doctrine of two gods or principles, the evil creator of the present material world and the good God of the future world. The Paulicians are also described as professing Docetic Christology – Christ's incarnation was proclaimed illusory and the Virgin Mary was praised not as the mother of Christ but as the 'heavenly Jerusalem'. However, the differing readings of the references to the Paulicians in the Armenian and Byzantine sources have led to conflicting conclusions as to whether they were originally dualist or embraced dualism later in their history.[4] The influential view that Paulicianism originated as a dualist heresy has been strongly challenged by a recent wide-ranging reassessment of Paulician history and teachings which argues that both the dualist and Docetic doctrines represent late developments in the Paulician movement.[5] According to this reassessment, original Paulicianism adhered to Adoptionist teachings current in early Armenian Christianity which held that Christ had been adopted as the son of God during his baptism.[6] However, this reconstruction of Paulician religious evolution has not succeeded in explaining convincingly the timing and cause of the later Paulician doctrinal reorientation, its hypothesized scenario, that this dualist reformation was carried through by the Paulician heresiarch, Sergius, in ninth-century Byzantium[7] as well as its suggested bridging of the sources for the heresy have both met strong criticism.[8] The Byzantine reports of Paulician teachings reiterate their dualism between the recognized creator-god and ruler of this world and the concealed god of the world to come (who could be seen as lord of the heavens), but its origins have been variously traced to Manichaean, Gnostic or Marcionite influences.[9] It is, of course, wholly plausible that Paulicianism developed its dualist version of Christianity through a spiritualist and allegorical reading of the New Testament, its dualist element being influenced directly or indirectly by the various dualist residues still active on the religious scene of late antique and early medieval Armenia, ranging from Zoroastrian to Gnostic survivals.

What complicates the argument for a direct Manichaean influence on Paulicianism is the apparent lack of the crucial Manichaean division between the elect and the listener among the Paulicians, although there are some indications of esoteric teachings or mysteries, preserved for the few 'perfect in impiety' Paulicians.[10] The early Paulician organization also remains obscure; they did not observe the ascetic practices of the Manichaean elect, the strict abstinence from meat, wine and marriage. With their presence in areas adjacent to the changing Armeno-Byzantine frontiers, the Paulicians were forced into conflicts with Byzantium early in their history and like the Manichaean Uighur mercenaries in central Asia came to be renowned as aggressive and dangerous warriors who inflicted some heavy defeats on the Byzantine armies.

The Byzantine chronicler of Paulicianism, Peter of Sicily, traces the beginnings of original 'Manichaean' Paulicianism to the missionary activities of a Manichaean woman, Callinice, who taught the heresy to her two sons, as a 'viper mother' rearing 'two snakes', and preached it around Samosata in eastern Anatolia.[11] While this report about the female Manichaean heresiarch seems largely fictitious, the tradition that the formulation of actual Paulicianism as a Christian dualism should be ascribed to Constantine of Mananalis (on the upper Euphrates), active in the reign of Constans II (641–8), appears more reliable. It is almost certain that Paulicianism owed to Constantine its specific Christian dualism and Docetism, the first version of its canon (comprising the four Gospels and the epistles of Paul), the enduring veneration of Paul and the foundation of its first Church of Cibossa. Constantine was eventually accused of Manichaeism and executed; he was the first of the Paulician religious teachers and leaders, the *didaskaloi*, who continued the Paulician missionary work and sometimes came to share the fate of the first *didaskalos*. Since the beginning of its diffusion in Byzantium around the mid seventh century and for more than three centuries thereafter, Paulicianism posed a series of serious problems for the Byzantine authorities. At the height of their influence the Paulicians established seven 'churches' in Armenia and Asia Minor, among which the church of Corinth, reputedly founded by St Paul, was regarded as their mother-church. From the eighth century onwards the Paulicians also emerged as a factor in the Byzantine–Arab confrontation in eastern Anatolia and in 759 Paulician colonists entered the Balkans for the first time, having been resettled by the emperor Constantine V, along with other eastern heretics, in plague-stricken Thrace.

The heretics condemned in 719 by a council of the Armenian Church as 'sons of Satan' and 'fuel for the fire eternal' may or may not have been actual Paulicians but earlier, in the mid fifth century, it was still the Massalians who were perceived as the greatest heretical threat in Armenia. In 447 a special council announced sweeping measures against the Massalian heresy. The Massalians (the praying people), also called Enthusiasts were an anti-clerical, pietist sect about whose actual teachings not enough is known.[12] Their main belief was underlain by a peculiar type of anthropological dualism, according to which from birth in every man dwells a demon, who cannot be banished by baptism alone, but through continuous, zealous prayer and spiritual 'baptism by fire'. After a long period of strict asceticism and unceasing prayer the Massalian mystic was supposed to reach a completely passionless state, when the demon could be expelled and he could become a receptacle for the Holy Ghost. Having achieved mystical union with the Holy Ghost, the Massalian adept was believed to be able to behold the Trinity. With the demon driven away and the Holy Ghost dwelling in his soul, the Massalian adept could sin no more and could return to life in 'this world' without ascetic restrictions. The Massalians were frequently accused by their orthodox enemies of immorality and of committing various excesses – which did not prevent them from spreading their teachings and practices in the monasteries. Monasteries remained the favourite target of Massalian proselytism, although monasteries suspected of having been infected by Massalianism could be penalized and even burned.

The Massalians appear to have emerged in north-east Mesopotamia and by the end of the fourth century they had penetrated Syria and Asia Minor. Despite persecution at the hands of the ecclesiastical authorities, in the fifth century the Massalians spread further in Asia Minor and Armenia, and remained active in Syria until the seventh century. Although there are several Orthodox testimonies to their continuing activities, from that time their history is unknown and when their name was revived in the eleventh century, they were clearly associated with the Bogomils. Historical links between the early Massalians and the Manichaeans in Mesopotamia and Byzantium are not implausible but they have not been established and the repeated allusions to the Massalians after the eleventh century indicate that their name was used as a label for the new heretics, namely the Bogomils, rather than to refer to a genuine revival of the ancient sect.

It is possible that some Massalians were resettled along with the Pauli- cians during the eighth century in the Byzantine campaigns whereby

THE OTHER GOD

Syrian and Armenian heretics were sent to the Balkans. The influx of heretics into the Balkans added to the eclectic religious climate of the peninsula in the Dark Ages and complicated what was already a peculiar religious situation. Although the first Christian missions to the Balkans dated from the apostolic times and Balkan Christianity produced many martyrs during Diocletian's persecution, the process of Christianization was severely disrupted by the barbarian invasions of the fourth and the fifth centuries. The Visigoths, the Huns, the Ostrogoths and the Avars traversed and plundered the peninsula and in their wake came the great Slav colonization in the sixth and seventh centuries. While Justinian the Great, the adversary of Manichaeism, was campaigning to restore the western dominions of the old Roman empire, reconquering Italy, north Africa and parts of southern Spain, the Balkans were exposed to Slav invasions from the north.

Procopius might have fancifully attributed the natural disasters that befell Byzantium during Justinian's reign to the 'demonism' of the emperor, but he also acknowledged the increasing Slav influx into the Balkans that soon brought cataclysmic changes to the peninsula. The intermittent, heavy warfare with Sassanid Persia in the east did not allow Byzantium to take efficient measures to halt the Slav invasions and eventually the pagan Slav tribes were to penetrate deep even into Greece and its southernmost region, Peloponnesus. The complete transformation of the Balkan political and ethnic make-up was furthered also by the arrival of the Serbs and Croats, tribes which were apparently of Iranian extraction, but were Slavicized by the ninth century and played a crucial role in medieval Balkan history.[13]

The Slav colonization plunged the already weakened ecclesiastical order into further disarray. The reassertion of Byzantine authority in its Balkan domains was inevitably linked to their re-evangelization and the conversion of the pagan Slav settlers to Byzantine Orthodoxy. The Balkans were open terrain in the struggle between Rome and Constantinople, as the battle for ecclesiastical jurisdiction over the province of Illyricum in the western Balkans intensified. The process of the re-Christianization of the Balkans was extremely conducive to the emergence of heterodox movements over the centuries. In the late seventh century the Byzantine plans for political and religious reconquest of the Balkans were halted by the sudden rise of the first Bulgarian empire.

In Balkan antiquity, besides Orphism, some trends in Thracian

130

religion had cultivated a distinct religiosity, based on a dualism of soul and body, of life in this world and life after death, and had fostered ascetic practices. This spirituality 'of Balkan extraction' has been defined as 'somewhat evasive, in controversy and in opposition to the life in this world'[14] and thus was at variance with traditional biblical and Zoroastrian spirituality. It has also been noted that the Gnostic type of dualism fostered by medieval neo-Manichaeism gained prominence in those East European regions where religious dualist currents had already been influential.[15] Among these currents were enduring popular cosmogonies in which the creation of the world was ascribed to two primordial beings whose initial partnership was often depicted as evolving into rivalry and outright enmity, one of them becoming progressively recognized under Christian influence as the Devil.

The Earth Diver and the Devil

The investigation and recording of popular cosmogonic traditions in eastern Europe, Central and northern Asia and northern America in the nineteenth century demonstrated that a number of these cosmogonies share some significant motifs which are not present or are less accentuated in other areas. Like a number of other ancient creation belief systems, these cosmogonic traditions usually feature a water cosmogony according to which the earth is created from a primordial sea; sometimes the original demiurgic feat includes the crucial act of diving to the bottom of the sea and bringing earth to the surface as well as spilling this earth over the primal waters to cause the appearance of dry land. On certain occasions there exists a focus on the assumption of a bisection of a primary cosmic unity in a markedly binary cosmos, a bisection sometimes associated with the activities of two or more demiurgic figures who could be further involved in ambiguous or conflicting interrelations. In their early forms some of these cosmogonies include the theme of the earth-diving bird, itself a widespread cosmogonic motif in eastern Europe, northern and Central Asia, as well as North America. Generally, the mythic scenario underlying the earth-diver cosmogonies includes the themes of the primordial waters; God or two or more primal figures moving about on the surface of the waters; the cosmogonic dive to the bottom of the sea by God or some of the primal figures; the creation of the world by the primordial Beings (who have brought the 'seed of the earth' from the sea), who may be seen either as cooperating or as functioning in various degrees of antagonism. In some of these popular cosmogonies the earth-diver tradition is associated with the cult of the heavenly twins or two original creators, one of whom brings earth by diving into the primordial sea, but variants do abound: usually, these cosmogonies develop the theme of two or three primordial figures, such as two brothers and an earth-diving bird; sometimes one of the brothers is identified with the bird; on other occasions both brothers or two primal figures could be depicted as birds, etc.

Significantly, the activities of the second demiurge do not always lead him into outright rivalry with the first one or to producing his own counter-creations in all of these cosmogonies, but such dualist themes could appear in these systems variously developed and combined. Some of the mature East European versions of the cosmogonic scenario have retained the ornithomorphism of the earth-diver figure; however, under the influence of orthodox and/or heterodox Christian diabology in the majority of them, the two primordial beings are identified as God and Satan, and it is God who dispatches Satan to dive into the primal sea (whether in ornithomorphic form or not), upon which act there follows the antagonism between the two figures. This scenario is represented in Bulgarian, Romanian, Transylvanian Gypsy, Bukovinian, Russian, Ukrainian, Polish and Baltic variants.[16] These East European dualist cosmogonic legends vary in detail but all emphasize the role of Satan as an original companion of God and a crucial vehicle for the creation of the material world. The legends disagree most about the origin of Satan; he may be depicted as emerging from a bubble of foam from the primal sea;[17] as being born from the spittle of God,[18] as arising from the place where God threw his wand into the primordial waters[19] or indeed from God's shadow or reflection in the waters.[20]

Very similar to these variants are some of the Finno-Ugrian cosmogonic legends, but several of these have also preserved the theme of the ornithomorphism of the diving figure (a duck in the Cheremis legend,[21] iron or water bird in Vogul legends;[22] in a Samoyed myth, God sends water birds to dive but his rival is not among them and appears after the cosmogonic dive, etc.[23]). Significantly, in the Cheremis legend the duck is identified with Keremet, who is depicted as the younger brother of the highest god, Yuma, and evolves into an adversary of the first demiurge after Yuma bids him dive for earth in the sea. Following his dive Keremet not only becomes involved in the cosmogonic proceedings by creating the mountains and the rocks but also fashions his demonic forces and interferes in the anthropogonic process. The dualist cosmogonic tendencies are also pronounced in the Vogul myth in which Satan emerges from a bubble formed by God's spittle on the waters, brings up earth from the sea and becomes the creator of the mountains.[24]

In these Finno-Ugrian legends, to which one may add the Samoyed creation story in which Ngaa (Death) cooperates with the highest god, Num,[25] the theme of the earth-diving is intertwined with that of the creation of the world seen as an act of collaboration between two demiurges replaced by rivalry and hostility, as the second demiurge is often perceived as trying to spoil the creation of the first demiurge. On the other hand, the Finno-Ugrian legends that have preserved the motif of the ornithomorphic earth-diver, stand close to the Slavonic variants of the scenario where the earth-diving Satan is ornithomorphic – a loon or duck in *The Sea of Tiberias* and in some related Russian legends.[26] These Finno-Ugrian and Slavonic versions of the earth-diving cosmogonic myth have preserved its most archaic element – that of a water bird diving into and taking earth from the bottom of the sea – and this brings them closer to other archaic variants of the myth prevalent in northern and Central Asia.

Similarly archaic is the treatment of the myth in some Ukrainian Christmas carols in which three doves or peacocks bring up sand from the bottom of the sea and create the earth;[27] in another, Christianized Ukrainian variant, God, St Peter and St Paul dive to the bottom of the sea to bring up the sand of creation but it is only God who is successful[28] – in these Ukrainian variants the earth-diving birds or figures have not been subjected to diabolization. But the majority of the Slavonic and Romanian variants of the myth do identify the diving bird with Satan or dispense with the bird altogether – it is the Devil who dives and takes to God the earth of creation and subsequently challenges him as a kind of second demiurge.

These East European (Slavonic, Romanian, Finnish and Baltic) Christianized cosmogonic legends are not unique in this near-dualist reinterpretation[29] of the old cosmogonic scenario. In a cosmogonic myth recorded among the Abakan Tartars,[30] both God and his companion, whom he created and bade to dive and bring back sand, are envisaged in the shape of ducks; subsequently, the second duck begins to act as God's rival and the myth enhances further its dualist tendencies by introducing the wicked Erlik Khan, the Lord of the Underworld and corrupter of man. It is worth noting that before evolving into a lord of the lower world and the realm of darkness as well as judge of the dead, apparently in at least some Altaic traditions Erlik was originally a celestial deity. Particularly important for the history of religious dualism are those Altaic traditions in which Erlik appears as second only to the highest god, Ulgen, and as his assistant in creation and is assigned important demiurgic functions, as he not only takes part in the anthropogonic process but also begins to act in some kind of opposition against the first demiurge. In Iakut traditions Erlik is associated with the so-called 'Blue Boundlessness' and possibly with the water element, whereas in Buriat mythology he is seen as the leader of the wicked black or eastern spirits. Erlik plays a major role in Siberian Turkic and Mongol shamanistic traditions and their ideas of the afterlife (both he and his spirits could be seen as abducting souls for their realm): shamans are often depicted as invoking, offering sacrifices to and propitiating Erlik, undergoing a descent into his lower world and encountering the king of the underworld.[31]

Another myth found among the Lebed Tartars does not introduce dualist elements in the cosmogonic scenario itself – God orders a white swan to dive and it fetches up silt in its beak – but dualism is nevertheless evident in its account of creation, in which appears the figure of the Devil who makes the marshes.[32] The ornithomorphism of the diver figure has disappeared in a myth recorded among the Kuznetsk Tartars, but the dualism of the two creators seems greatly enhanced. When he descends to the primordial waters God (Ulgen) encounters a man who proclaims that he wants to create land; Ulgen bids him dive to the bottom of the sea; after he brings up a piece of earth, he duly begins to act as a rival demiurge.[33]

In an Altaian Turkic legend[34] before the creation of heaven and earth, when the whole world was covered with water, the highest of gods, Tengere Kaira Khan, created a being in his image and called him man. Tengere Kaira Khan and his companion, the man, are depicted as flying over the primordial waters in the shape of black geese; the man shows his arrogance by trying to fly higher than God and falls into the water; God sends him to bring up silt but the man attempts to keep some of the silt in his mouth – he is exposed by God and called Erlik. Subsequently, Erlik tries to seduce mankind and creates his own heaven but is banished into the underworld. In another version of this myth, which further betrays some Iranian influences,[35] the man, flying alongside God, (again, both in the form of black geese), appears as God's primordial companion who is sent to bring up earth from the bottom of the sea. God spills this earth over the sea to create land but, as in the first version of the myth, the man tries to hide some of the earth in his mouth and is exposed – God calls himself Kurbistan and names the man Erlik, telling him that because of his evil deed his future subjects are destined to be evil. In a Mongol version of the cosmogonic myth,[36] after the dive the figure of the diabolical adversary appears to oppose a pair of creator deities trying to obtain a share of the created earth. Characteristically, one of the deities of the primordial pair, the one who acts as an earth-diver, also begins to display the initial features of an arrogant, rival demiurge, priding himself on his crucial role in the cosmogonic process.

The various Siberian versions of the cosmogonic myth can display both very archaic features of the scenario, with a non-diabolic water bird as the protagonist of the diving (as in Buriat and Enisei legends)[37] and its later Christianized forms (as in some of the Iakut myths where Satan is identified as the diver figure, whether shaped as a bird or not).[38] In Siberian mythology, then, one can discern the various stages of the development of the archaic cosmogonic scenario, its earliest phase being associated with the rich bird mythology in northern and Central Asia, where birds could play a demiurgic role (sometimes related to the widespread myth of the cosmogonic egg in the primeval sea) or in ancestral and shamanistic symbolism (as demonstrated by the ornithomorphic symbols in Siberian shaman costume).[39] Similarly archaic is the Aryan Indian earth-diving cosmogonic myth, as related in *Taittiriya Samhita* (7.1.5.1f.), where Prajapati is portrayed as moving over the primordial waters and plunging into them in the form of a boar to fetch up earth.[40] The myth is obviously devoid of any dualism, and pre-Aryan Indian, Indonesian and Micronesian cosmogonies that contain the motif of the cosmogonic dive, usually performed by an amphibious animal[41] (with the exception of the two primordial spirits diving in the shape of birds in the Dyak legend from Borneo),[42] are likewise largely free of dualist tendencies.

Symptomatically, while found in a great number of North American cosmogonies in its early form which involves earth-diving birds,[43] the cosmogonic myth generally does not feature antagonism between diving birds or animals and demiurge supreme beings, even when these cosmogonies display dualist elements in other areas of their creationist mythology. However, a version of the earth-diving myth does become integrated into the dualistic scenarios of some versions of Iroquois cosmogony, with their dramatic accounts of the struggle between a good and a bad twin, their creations and counter-creations, and the evil twin becoming ultimately a king of the dead.[44]

As is made evident by the various levels of development of dualist elements in European, Asian and North American cosmogonies which include the earth-diver myth, the problem of the dating of the introduction of these elements is a notoriously difficult one. As far as the Slavonic dualist legends are concerned, at first they were regarded as stemming from dualist teachings of the heretical Bogomils[45] who came to diffuse such teachings in the form of apocryphal stories. In another view, the Slavonic legends were spread by the medieval dualist heretics, but the cosmogonic myth in the legends derived from Uralo-Altaic traditions, which themselves borrowed it from Iranian lore.[46] The dualism of the Slavonic cosmogonic legends could also be seen as reflecting a dualist phase in the development of Slavonic religious thought which could be paralleled in the evolution of other religious systems[47] or viewed as residues of a posited proto-Slavonic dualism.[48]

Consequently, a new classification of the dualist cosmogonic legends and the transformation of their two main motifs posited that the dualist myth of the Devil diving into the sea to bring out earth, and his cooperation with God in the creation of the earth followed by enmity between the two creators, was developed under the combined influence of Iranian dualism and Chaldean and Indian cosmogonic concepts.[49] In this line of reconstruction the dualist myth was further modified in Gnostic and Manichaean circles and with the expansion of Manichaeism it spread into parts of Central and northern Asia and was brought to eastern Europe by Paulician heretics from Transcaucasia.[50] According to an analogous line of enquiry the Slavonic and the related apocryphal cosmogonies present two dualist layers – an archaic Iranian one and a medieval heretical one.[51]

The view that the myth of the bird diving into the sea and challenging the creator has ultimately to represent an Iranian dualist tradition reflects a lasting tendency to regard Iran as the obligatory source for the diffusion of dualist myths and cosmogonies. However, such Iranian-centred historico-genetical approaches tend to ignore the existence of parallel developments of binary theologies and cosmogonies related, for example, to the widespread cult of the heavenly twins, and their natural evolution into dualist or near-dualist systems, not necessarily under the pressure of external factors such as missionary work or religio-political conquest. What is significant in this context is that the theme of the earth-diving bird (whether recognized as a satanic agency or not) is not prominent in Iranian lore but it is a widespread cosmogonic motif in eastern Europe, northern and Central Asia, as well as in North America. The publication of the cosmogonic accounts from these areas invalidated the earlier attempts to locate the origin of the dualist version of the cosmogonic myth in ancient Iran or Mesopotamia[52] and showed the extent of the popularity of the earth-diver theme beyond the Middle East, where it does not enjoy a particular currency. Even in the case of the Assyrian myth of the Anzu bird,[53] which develops the Near Eastern theme of the divine combat, with all its dualist potential (as apparent, for example, in some strands of early Jewish apocalyptic satanology), Anzu steals the Tablet of Destiny thus threatening the order in the universe, but the myth is not related to cosmogony.

There is an increasing amount of evidence that very early forms of the earth-diver myth certainly played an important role in the cosmogonic systems developed in prehistoric times in Central and northern Asia upon which the North American cosmogonies are evidently dependent.[54] It would be futile, however, to postulate a single line of development for the evolution or integration of the myth into dualist and near-dualist systems. It has been proposed, for example, on the basis of the Aryan-Indian myth of Prajapati diving in the shape of a boar, that in the oldest version of the myth a theriomorphic creator deity was envisaged as diving alone and unaided into the primeval waters; in later versions he was seen as summoning a companion or helpers to perform the earth-diving feat and in still later versions his companion was identified as his adversary.[55] Such reconstruction ignores the obvious interpenetration of the themes of the divine pair of heavenly twins and the earth-diver in some of the cosmogonies based on the concept of the earth-diver creation. Whereas in some cosmogonies and mythic sacred histories the divine twin pair is perceived as acting in a complementary relationship, in others there is a definite transition to dualism, as the twins came to be seen as rivals and opponents (often manifest in their creations), one of them being identified as a bad twin or a type of demiurge trickster. As the myth of divine twinship is frequently associated with dualities in the cosmological sphere, asserting the notion of the demiurgic activities of two creators behind creation, when combined with the earth-diver myth, the twinship topos can develop the dualism of the earth-diver element in those narratives in which the twins are not seen to act in complementary fashion but rather to be in conflict and opposition.

Since the various East European, Siberian and Central Asian earth-diver cosmogonies display dualist elements in different stages of development and combination, it would be safe to assume that both internal factors (such as inherited binary cosmogonies, divine twins mythology) and external influences (in the Eurasian cases: Christian diabology, with its inherent dualist tendencies; possible Zoroastrian and Manichaean influences in the Central Asian cosmogonies, etc.) conditioned the overall general movement towards dualism, as the mythic scenario came to be reinterpreted and modified, particularly in Eurasia. Thus even before the spread of medieval dualist heresies in various east European areas, some of the pre-Christian popular cosmogonic traditions there, whether indigenous or spread by migrations such as the Slavonic one, featured a legacy inherited from what is sometimes seen as a common 'Eurasian dualism',[56] particularly in the sphere of cosmogony. Furthermore, the posited existence of pre-Christian proto-Slavonic dualism, with arguments, for example, that 'the Slavs participated in the Iranian evolution into a clear-cut dualism',[57] may also have similar direct implications for the history of dualist traditions in Europe. However, the authenticity of the evidence attesting such proto-Slavonic dualism remains a highly controversial and contested area[58] and it would be premature to draw any definite conclusions about its possible implications for the spread of dualist heresies in the Orthodox Slavonic world.

What is certain is that the survival of the 'Eurasian' dualist cosmogonic inheritance in South and East Slavonic traditions could make the appeal of Christian dualist heresies stronger and allow for its interaction and interchange with survivals of pagan lore in popular belief. In the Balkans, from the late seventh century onwards the conditions for such interaction and interchange were particularly favourable, as the newly founded Bulgarian domain not only allowed the continuation of non-Christian religious trends but also the spread of Christian heretical movements and eventually, in the wake of the region's Christianization, was to became the scene of the next, crucial stage of the medieval evolution of the 'Great Heresy'.

In the late seventh century the Byzantine empire had to face the sudden rise of the first rival domain in its 'God-protected' Balkan territory. In 680 the imperial fleet and armies of Constantine IV Pogonatus ('The Bearded') had advanced to the Danube delta against the forces of the Bulgar dynast Asparukh but suffered there one of the most crucial and humiliating defeats in all Byzantine history. In the following year Constantine IV surrendered to Asparukh the imperial land to the north of the Balkan (Haemus) Mountains, already penetrated by Slav tribes, and the ensuring treaty marked imperial recognition of one of the first states in medieval Eastern Europe: the first Bulgarian empire (681–1118).

From the Steppes to the Balkans

The foundation of the Bulgarian empire in the Balkans was one of the turning points in the religious and political history of eastern Europe in the early Middle Ages, when successive migratory waves of nomadic people from the Eurasian steppes poured one after another into Europe. Stretching from the Carpathians to the Altai Mountains in Central Asia, the Eurasian steppes are traditionally regarded as a cradle of nations that served as the homeland of the Finno-Ugrian, Turco-Mongolian and arguably the Indo-European peoples. Although the ancient history of the Eurasian steppes still poses numerous unsolved problems, it is becoming increasingly apparent that this vast area had a specific cultural unity[59] in which the northern Iranians were a potent and often dominant political and cultural force until the tumultuous irruption of the Huns into Europe during the fourth century AD. In the previous century the Iranian millennial hegemony in the east European steppes had already been broken by a strong Gothic influx into the area and by the establishment of a strong Ostrogothic kingdom in modern Ukraine. The early Middle Ages was a period of continuous and bewildering movements and migrations of nomadic and semi-nomadic people in the east European extension of the Eurasian steppes. During this era the old northern

Iranian and Finno-Ugrian tribes in the steppes were frequently replaced by or entered into tribal union and federations with the nomadic Turkic-speaking newcomers and a number of them underwent linguistic as well as partial or large-scale ethnic Turkicization. This was also a process of new linguistic and cultural homogenization which had its precedent, for example, in the linguistic Iranization of peoples in western Iran and the eastern Transcaucasus around the beginning of the first millennium BC.[60] This was further a process of cultural and religious syncretism, particularly between Iranian and Turkic traditions, in which principal deities could now have both Iranian and Turkic names, while in the new nomadic federations the nomadic aristocracy comprised Iranian, Turkic and Ugrian elements existing and fighting side by side. Contemporary chronicles reflect this linguistic and ethnic confusion on the Eurasian steppe scene and could describe the same people as both 'Hunnic' and 'Scythian', which makes any generalization about a fixed ethnic identity of such people based on these texts premature and potentially highly erroneous. However, archaeological work in the nineteenth and twentieth centuries at sites ranging from Central Asia to the Caucasus, the Pontic steppes and the middle Volga area, has contributed much new evidence to our knowledge of the nomadic migrations in the early Middle Ages and allowed for the reconstruction of some of their extended and frequently erratic trajectories. The Hunnic invasion spelt the end of Iranian Sarmation power in the steppes, pushed the Ostrogoths to the west and forced the Visigoths into the lands of the Roman empire where they defeated and slew Emperor Valens (378), burned the sanctuary of Eleusis and, finally, in 410 sacked Rome itself.

In the following two centuries, along with new peoples from the steppes, the Bulgars expanded into eastern Europe and their incursions in the Balkans multiplied with a mounting intensity. As for other masters of the Eurasian steppes – the Sarmatians, the Alans, the Avars, the Khazars – much of the ancient history of the Bulgars remains obscure. The semi-legendary era of their early conquests and domains in inner and Central Asia abounds in immense gaps and riddles and is still being reconstructed from exceedingly diverse and uneven evidence. It is widely assumed that in the early Christian era most of the Bulgars inhabited areas in southern Central Asia, particularly in the Pamir region and the Sogdiana lands locked between the upper reaches of Oxus and Jaxartes, described as being between Iran and Turkestan.[61] In the political transformations of the period the former Achaemenid satrapy had retained its strong Zoroastrian traditions amid the increasing presence of Buddhism, Nestorian Christianity and Manichaeism.[62] In the turmoil of the great migrations in the fourth and fifth centuries, when the Huns achieved complete supremacy over the nomadic world for a century, the Bulgars were pushed along the westward Hunnic expansion and drawn towards the Caucasus–Caspian region and further into Europe. In early Bulgar sites nomadism and agriculture could coexist and among some Bulgar tribes there are also indications of organized urban life, but external pressure like the Hunnic westward advance could drive such semi-nomadic or urban groups into enforced nomadization. The history and the role of the Bulgars in the period of the Hunnic military tribal union and the Western Turkic Khaganate can only be conjectured but ultimately the invasion of the Huns and the Hunnic-led tribes in Europe led to the emergence of new centres of Bulgar diaspora in Pannonia and the northern Black Sea–Azov areas, while more Bulgar groups were apparently still moving from Central Asia towards the Pontic steppes. While it is not entirely certain as yet how conclusive are some recent arguments that the core of the Bulgar tribes in Central Asia were of eastern Iranian extraction and that it was later, during their westward migrations and tribal unions with other peoples that they assimilated Turkic and Ugrian elements, it is, however certain that the Bulgar settlers in the Pontic areas merged culturally and ethnically with the northern Iranian Alans, hence in scholarship, particularly in Russia, they are often referred to as Bulgar-Alan tribes.[63]

By the end of the fifth century Bulgar contingents were campaigning on the turbulent Balkan scene and their incursions eventually reached Thessaly and the Thermopylae.[64] In the early seventh century most of the Bulgars were united along with some of their allies in their realm of *Magna Bulgaria*, founded on the ruins of the old Sarmato-Alan and Hellenistic civilizations in the northern Pontic–Azov area. *Magna Bulgaria* incorporated large areas of what is today Ukraine and south-eastern Russia and has been defined as a 'new edition of the Bosphorus kingdom'[65] which now extended its sway into the north Caucasus steppes. In the previous two centuries the northern Caucasus region had been an arena of intense Sassanid–Byzantine rivalry and had been subjected to the dual penetration of Byzantine Christianity and Zoroastrianism, and was marked by the appearance of Christian sites and the distinctive square-shaped fire temples of the Zoroastrian cult.[66] While the Bulgars themselves had been exposed to the strong influence of Sassanid political and cultural traditions, the ruler of *Magna Bulgaria*, Kubrat, visited Constantinople to conclude an alliance with Emperor Heraclius, was baptized and granted the noble title of 'Patrician'. On Kubrat's death (c. 663–8), however, *Magna Bulgaria* collapsed under the vigorous pressure of the Khazars and was incorporated into the rising Khazar khaganate, a powerful steppe empire which at its height extended its authority from the Pontic–Caspian area to the Ural Mountains.

The Bulgar groups, who remained in the Pontic–Azov lands under Khazar suzerainty, continued to be a strong political force and formed a large, if not the predominant element of the population in the eastern Crimea, the Azov and the lower Don areas as well as in cities like Sarkel and Phanagoria.[67] Whereas in the case of other steppe state formations, the Khazars themselves constituted Iranian, Turkic and Ugrian elements, the ethnic and cultural synthesis between the Bulgars and the Alans continued in the Don and Azov areas, as demonstrated by the so-called Saltovo-Mayatskoe culture which developed in two main variants in the Bulgar and Alan areas of the khaganate.[68] The role of the Bulgar–Alan element in the political history of the Khazar empire is still being recon- structed but there are indications that in the turbulent period of the first half of the eighth century the Bulgar clans sought to exploit the Khazar dual kingship in an attempt to seize political power in the khaganate.[69] Despite Arab attempts to introduce Islam in the Khazar empire in the course of the eighth century the Khazar court and nobility unexpectedly embraced Judaism but in the Khazar empire, renowned thereafter as the 'Judaic domain', the Judaized elements coexisted with pagans, Christians and Muslims.[70] With its vital strategic position, the Khazar empire served effectively as a buffer shielding eastern Europe from the progress of the Muslim Holy War and, after prolonged and violent Arab–Khazar warfare, the Arab advance was finally blocked at the Caucasus.

While the Bulgars in the Khazar empire contributed significantly to the formation of its civilization, the Bulgars who escaped from Khazar overlordship separated into several branches which began to spread over Europe, from the 'Volga to the shadows of Vesuvius.'[71] A Bulgar offshoot had already sought refuge in the Merovingian dominions of *le bon roi* Dagobert I and some Bulgars were to settle permanently in northern Italy. During the latter stages of the Arab–Khazar warfare, when Arab troops advanced deep into the Khazar heartlands and the Khazar capital had to be moved to the lower Volga region, Alan, Bulgar and Turkic tribes were forced to migrate northwards from the northern Caucasus and eventually the migratory wave carried some of them to the middle Volga-Kama area, inhabited largely by Finno-Ugrians. There may have been earlier Bulgar influxes to the area and certainly further Bulgar migrations reinforced the Bulgar groups there, who, known as the 'Silver Bulgars', emerged as a powerful political force that succeeded in unifying the diverse elements in the middle Volga-Kama region in the realm of Volga Bulgaria. Volga Bulgaria developed as a strong trading domain which, in contrast to the Khazar khaganate, and struggling against its influence, was won over to Islam in the tenth century. Little is known of the religious life in Volga Bulgaria before the Islamization, although in a controversial statement in *Fihristi* the Islamic encyclopedist Ibn al-Nadim asserted that the Bulgars (the Volga Bulgars) had used the 'script of the Chinese and the Manichaeans'.[72] The art of Volga Bulgaria elaborated mainly Central Asian and Iranian traditions, which sometimes appear to echo Zoroastrian themes, along, with an array of fantastic dragon-like and sphinx-like creatures.[73] Volga or 'Silver' Bulgaria evolved as the northernmost Muslim civilization, which flourished until it was overrun by the Mongols in the thirteenth century and its vestiges were ultimately wiped out in 1552 by Ivan the Terrible, the first Grand Duke of Moscow to assume the imperial title of Tsar.

The Balkan wing of the Bulgar diaspora took full advantage of its victory over Constantine IV to consolidate its domain in the former Roman provinces in the Balkans, traditionally seen as the most contested territory in Europe. With their well-developed and complex politico-military system, which betrayed distinct Iranian influences, the Balkan Bulgars easily secured the allegiance of the Slav tribes in their expanding realm. The state-building and centralizing role of the Bulgars in the Balkans is usually compared to that of the Normans in England after 1066 or the Salian Franks in fifth-century Gaul. The Bulgar monarchy seems to have been of the dual kingship type and the sublime ruler, who bore the title Kan, apparently was regarded as an incarnation of the divine power, and combined religious and political functions. Established in close proximity to the imperial capital of the heir apparent of the old Roman empire, the Bulgar Sublime Kans were to carve out their Balkan domain with the 'ultimate ambition to create a metropolis rivalling Constantinople itself'.[74] The monumental architecture of the pre-Christian Bulgarian empire embodies architectural traditions that find their closest parallels in palace and temple cities in the Irano-Mesopotamian and Irano-Central Asian worlds, and the royal residences of the Sublime Kans are usually associated with the Sassanid palaces in Persia or with the Umayyad citadels in Syria. Bulgar art and architecture is diverse and eclectic, but with a predominant Sassanid influence, which largely supports the thesis that the Sublime Kans, who often bore Iranian-derived names like Persian or Khormesios (a Central Asian form of Hormizd or Hormuz) perpetuated in the Balkans ceremonial and architectural traditions akin to those of the Sassanid monarchs of Persia.[75]

The imposing temples and cult centres erected by the Bulgars point to a developed religion but, strangely, little is known about its exact nature and pantheon. The Bulgars brought to the Balkans a well-developed astronomo-astrological system, based on the central Asian 'animal cycle' calendar, along with an array of shamanistic beliefs and practices. Yet with a few exceptions, the study of pre-Christian Bulgar artistic and religious syncretism has not enjoyed the steady progress it deserves. This is mainly due to an unfortunate tendency to interpret this syncretism in the light of grand preconceived schemes borrowed from Central and inner Asian belief systems from different periods (elements of which it undoubtedly contained).[76] Rather, such syncretism should be assessed in its own terms and also with in the framework of the predominant influence of Iranian and Sassanian tradition in Bulgar art and architecture and should bring into the picture the Bulgar ethno-cultural symbiosis with the Pontic Sarmato-Alan tribes whose beliefs certainly displayed some Zoroastrian features, traces of which were maintained even after the Bulgar-Alan migrations to the middle Volga area. The complex evidence recovered from Bulgar religious monuments is still being examined but certainly it attests to the toleration and syncretism in religion and art that prevailed in the pagan Bulgarian empire. This is hardly surprising, as the Bulgars had traversed and settled in areas which were meeting places of competing religious traditions – Zoroastrianism, Buddhism, Nestorian Christianity, Manichaeism. The evidence of some Arabic authors, who styled the Bulgars 'Magians', seems controversial, yet the closest parallels to the specific square- and rectangular-shaped temples (furnished with a surrounding corridor) appear to be the Iranian fire temples of the Parthian and the Sassanid epochs which spread from Central Asia and the Kushan realm to northern Mesopotamia and, under the Sassanids, also appeared in north Caucasus.[77] Significantly, the square-shaped temple in one of the Bulgar centres in the Kuban area in northern Caucasus has been largely recognized as a Zoroastrian fire temple.[78] Furthermore, the Bulgar shrines have also been compared to a contemporary type of Buddhist temple in Central Asia which itself was representative of a syncretistic form of Buddhism.[79] Other elements in Bulgar pre-Christian art have given rise to arguments for Buddhist influences among the Bulgars[80] but these have met strong objections, while the appearance of a Jina image (c. tenth- to thirteenth-century) in the heartlands of the Bulgars' Balkan domain, which may even suggest a Jainist religious import, still remains to be explained.[81]

The problem of the Danube Bulgars' religion, the nature of its syncretism and to what extent the politico-cultural Iranian impact on the Bulgars was coupled with a religious one, remains one of the main unresolved and controversial questions related to the foundation of Danube Bulgaria. It emerged as a version of the so-called 'successor states' of the Dark Ages, similar in some respects to Frankish Gaul under the early Merovingians, to Anglo-Saxon England or to the Visigothic kingdom in Spain. The notable cultural achievements of the first Bulgarian empire have been defined as 'counterpart of the Carolingian culture in Western Europe' with works 'at least of the same quality'.[82] From its foundation in 681 until the end of the first Christian millennium the growth and expansion of the Bulgarian empire affected much of the political developments in south-east Europe. In central Europe its boundaries eventually met those of the Frankish empire under Charlemagne, while in the Balkans the Bulgar war-machine recurrently moved on the offensive against the Byzantine empire to beleaguer its new Rome, the 'Holy City' of Constantinople.

Kans and Emperors

The emergence of a Bulgar power block in south-eastern Europe ended Byzantine hegemony of the Balkans for more than three centuries and marked one of the great crises which affected Byzantium in the Dark

Ages. In the seventh and eighth centuries the rising tide of militant Islam engulfed the Byzantine provinces in the Near East, North Africa and south-eastern Spain, while Constantinople itself suffered two major Arab assaults. Losing Syria, Palestine and Egypt to the caliphate, Byzantium succeeded in holding on to Asia Minor but was beset by chronic political infighting and endemic palace revolutions. The religious life of the empire was strongly affected by the rise of the Iconoclastic movement in the early eighth century, which condemned the veneration of images as idolatry and won the support of many Byzantine emperors before being defeated in the council of the 'Triumph of Orthodoxy' in 843.

In the Balkans the centuries-long saga of the Bulgaro-Byzantine rivalry in the eastern part of the peninsula passed through decades of violent intermittent warfare and shaky peace, short-lived military alliances and relentless political feuding behind the scenes, Byzantine reconquests of lost Balkan provinces, sieges of Constantinople, and dynastic intermarriages. The Bulgar Kans periodically sought to exploit the volatile and convoluted internal politics in Byzantium, interfering even in the palace revolutions and in the struggles for the imperial throne. In 704 the exiled and slit-nosed ex-emperor Justinian II was restored to the throne with the crucial military support of the Bulgar Kan Tervel who was granted in return the title of Caesar, second only to the imperial title. In 717 the troops of Tervel helped beleaguered Byzantium in breaking the second great Arab siege of Constantinople, considered sometimes the most critical Arab assault on Europe, threatening her 'soft underbelly' in the south-east, fifteen years before Charles Martel halted the Saracen advance in western Europe at the battle of Tours.

In the latter part of the eighth century the great Iconoclastic emperor, Constantine V Copronymus, who was accused by his Iconophile opponents of being Paulician and Manichaean, or even Mammon himself, launched nine consecutive wars to reconquer the north-east Balkans. The recovery of the Bulgarian empire under Charlemagne's contemporary, Krum (c. 803–14), led to a series of political crises in Byzantium, as the Kan succeeded in overpowering three emperors on the battlefield, laid siege to Constantinople and even seized stocks of Byzantium's ultimate secret weapon – the 'Greek Fire'. While for the German Protestant dramatist Andreas Gryphius (1616–64) Krum was the epitome of heroic warrior, for the Byzantine chroniclers he was the 'new Sennacherib', an incarnation of the sinister Assyrian king (705–681

BC) who had destroyed Babylon and besieged Jerusalem. In 811 the Byzantine emperor Nicephorus I lost his life and army in an ill-fated campaign against Krum, in which his son and co-emperor was also wounded, to die several months later: the deaths of the two emperors dispelled the mystique of the traditional Byzantine myth of the invincible emperor. For nearly half a millennium, since Valens' death in 378, no Roman emperor had ever been killed in battle and now the skull of the 'invincible' Nicephorus was fashioned into a silver goblet for the palace feasts of the 'new Sennacherib'.

Meanwhile, the sudden papal coronation of Charlemagne as *Imperator Romanorum* on Christmas Day 800, coupled with his advance into traditional Byzantine spheres of influence, had brought him into a collision course with Constantinople, which refused to recognize his imperial title. In the wake of Nicephorus' death the new Byzantine emperor Michael I Rangabe, faced with the mounting Bulgarian menace, promptly recognized Charlemagne as his 'co-emperor of the West' to seek his alliance against the resurgent Bulgarian empire. Michael I was soon defeated disastrously by Krum and dethroned in Constantinople, which itself was now besieged by the 'new Sennacherib' and agonizingly awaited for months an assault as serious as the previous two Arab sieges of Constantinople. As a true priest-king, Krum conducted ostentatious pagan ceremonies and sacrifices before the very walls of the bastion of eastern Christendom, but at the height of his preparations died amid somewhat odd circumstances, in the words of a Byzantine chronicler, 'as if slain by an invisible hand'.[83]

The pagan ceremonies of the 'new Sennacherib' before the walls of Constantinople highlight the peculiar religious dimension of the Bulgaro-Byzantine collisions throughout the Dark Ages. Following the Islamic conquests in the Mediterranean world, the influence of early and important centres of Christianity in the Near East and North Africa, including the oriental patriarchates of Antioch, Alexandria and Jerusalem, inevitably declined. While losing its eastern and African provinces to Islam, Byzantium also suffered the loss of large parts of its 'historic' Roman territory in the Balkans to the pagan domain of the Bulgar Kans, who could now directly threaten the imperial capital of Constantinople.

Having survived the collapse of its western counterpart as the only legitimate heir of the old Roman empire, Byzantium saw itself as the only eternal and indissoluble empire, established by God, to be ruled by His earthly representative, the emperor. The rise of the Bulgarian empire in such menacing proximity to the New Rome was perceived as a chastening for Byzantine sins, while imperial propaganda correlated the reconquests of the Balkans with their reconversion to Christianity as part of the providential Christianizing mission of Byzantium. From the fifth century such a sense of divine election was to be shared by the newly Christianized Merovingian kingdom,[84] but in the pagan Bulgarian domain religion and royalty were also closely intertwined and in the person and the functions of the Sublime Kan the throne was wed to the altar. From its foundation the Bulgarian empire posed a determined challenge to Byzantium's inbred sense of imperial destiny and divine election. While Byzantine imperial propaganda strove to sanctify its campaigns against Bulgaria as more or less 'holy wars' against the 'most pagan and Christ-hating domain', Bulgar royal propaganda also sought to invoke divine sanction and providence for its confrontation with the New Rome.[85] Apart from becoming the Balkan arch-rivals of the emperors in Constantinople, the Sublime Kans adopted the imperial formula, 'divine ruler chosen by God', as well as, on occasions, the use of the cross in their inscription and regalia. Christianity had already won converts among the Bulgar nobility and court but the Kans remained largely intensely apprehensive of the universalist evangelical pretensions of the New Rome and also ever anxious to praise the virtues of their religion and its militant superiority to Byzantine Christianity. Yet the original religious policy of the Bulgar Kans was certainly tolerant, allowing for coexistence between paganism and Christianity, whether orthodox or heretical. While in Byzantium the Iconoclastic and Iconophile movements were vying to achieve the status of orthodoxy, in the pagan Bulgarian empire the meeting and syncretism of diverse religious traditions were still alive, maintaining a religious climate of complexity and eclecticism.

Paganism, Heresy and Christianity

The foundation of the pagan Bulgarian empire marked an abrupt turn in the religious history of the Balkans and opened one of its most complex and obscure periods. Any relic of the Christian ecclesiastical order which might have survived the dawning of the Balkan Dark Ages, with its devastating series of barbaric invasions, could hardly thrive in the pagan realm of the Bulgar Kans. Conversely, the early Bulgarian empire provided perfect conditions for the revival and continuation of pagan cults and traditions which had been suppressed earlier throughout the Byzantine-controlled parts of the peninsula. The very foundation of the Bulgarian domain coincided with the convocation of the Third Ecumenical Council of Constantinople (680–1) which condemned and took measures against the remains of Dionysian and other mysteries, apparently still active in the Balkans. The Bulgars themselves introduced religious influences from Central Asia and the steppes and in the following centuries the peninsula was to remain open to such influences brought by the advent of new, mainly pagan settlers and invaders from the steppes. Their mythological and magical beliefs mingled freely with various pagan survivals from antiquity to engender a rich and lasting syncretistic heritage, remnants of which can be traced even today. In the northern and eastern Balkans the Bulgars and the Slavs encountered relics of ancient Balkan paganism, like the Thracian religious cults, and perhaps vestiges of mystery religions. Various beliefs and practices associated with the old mystery cults proved unusually persistent in the Balkans, having endured through the centuries in folklore and quasi-Christian customs. Apart from the publicizing of folkloric relics of Orphic and Dionysian mysteries in certain regions in Thrace, a set of rituals preserved in the western Balkans has been shown to bear recognizable traces of the ancient cult of the Dioscuri and the classical mysteries of Samothrace.[86]

The expansion of the pagan Bulgarian empire in the eastern Balkans was bound to precipitate a revitalization of pagan residues in its newly conquered lands but also led to an increasing Christian presence in its sphere of control. But whatever the strength of Christianity in the eastern Balkans, without proper institutions and ecclesiastical control, it was certainly exposed to pagan and heretical influences. In Byzantium itself paganism might have been defeated but besides colouring Christian beliefs and practices pagan residues endured in certain areas of the empire and as late as the early tenth century Emperor Leo VI had to lead a crusade against the still strong paganism in the Peloponnesus region of Mani. Heterodox and heretical traditions also existed and were in force in the Byzantine world, particularly in Anatolian regions like Phrygia, where the enigmatic Judaizing sect of the Athingani synthesized the observance of the sabbath with astrological and magical beliefs and practices.[87] In sources hostile to iconoclasm the Emperors Nicephorus I and Michael II (820–9), who favoured the Iconoclastic movement, are alleged to have recognized and used their fortune-telling and magical ability, and Theophanes Continuatus even claims that Michael was born and brought up among the Athingani. The pagan Bulgarian domain to the north of Byzantium provided safe refuge not only for persecuted heretics but also for Jews who were reported to have fled there during the anti-Jewish persecution of Emperor Leo III in the early eighth century. The Byzantine policy of transplanting colonists from the empire's eastern provinces to Thrace further entangled the volatile religious climate of the Balkans. These colonies of Syrian and Armenian heretics were expected to form Byzantine garrisons during the intermittent Bulgaro–Byzantine wars in the disputed Thracian borderlands; while clearly failing to oppose the Bulgarian advance, some – particularly the Paulicians – established strong and lasting hotbeds of heretical agitation.

The Paulician colony, which was transplanted to Thrace in 757 by Constantine V, was probably positioned also as a counterpoise to his Iconophile opponents. Following the execution of the first religious leader of the Paulician movement, Constantine, one of his original persecutors, the imperial official, Symeon, was converted to Paulicianism. Symeon eventually succeeded Constantine as a *didaskalos* but was denounced to Justinian II and condemned to death, probably burnt at the stake at some point between 685 and 695. More anti-Paulician persecution followed but the period of the Iconoclastic crisis brought about a change in the fortunes of the movement. The reign of Leo III (717–41) witnessed the sharpening of the Iconoclastic controversy, as in 730 he decreed the destruction of religious images in the empire – Iconoclastic circles now had an imperial patron. At some stage of Leo's reign, apparently after his edict of 730, the contemporary Paulician *didaskalos*, Timothy, was summoned and examined by the patriarch and, due to the strong Iconoclastic strand in Paulicianism, apparently enjoyed a more sympathetic hearing than usual and was declared orthodox. Still, during an Iconophile revolt in 742–3 Timothy and his followers fled to Arab-held Armenian lands. During Constantine V's campaigns in eastern Anatolia he not only brought in but re-settled Christians from the Armenian lands in more western imperial territories, including the Paulician colonists transferred to Thrace, hence he was blamed for reintroducing the Paulician heretics into the empire. The Paulicians were forced into either Byzantine or Arab territory during the following Arab–Byzantine struggle for control of Armenia and exposed to its vicissitudes but were not subjected to imperial persecution even when the cult of the icons was restored under Empress Irene (797–802) and Nicephorus I (802–11) and the latter came to be suspected of professing Paulician beliefs. However, incited by Patriarch Nicephorus, Michael I (811–13) embarked upon a campaign of severe persecution with execution of the 'Manichaeans now called Paulicians' and this time the restoration of the Iconoclastic decrees under his successor, Leo v (813–20), did not bring a respite from the anti-Paulician measures and legislation. The Paulicians in Anatolia were now forced to seek refuge beyond the eastern borders of the empire and the protection of Islamic powers like the emirs of Melitene and Tarsus. The Paulician heresiarch and missionary Sergius found refuge in the lands of the emir of Meltiene in eastern Cappadocia where he founded the last Paulician churches. Indeed, the posited tenth-century transformation of Paulicianism from an Iconoclastic anti-ecclesiastical sect into a militant dualist movement has been attributed to the reforms of Sergius,[88] whose flight to the emir of Melitene, moreover, paved the way for the emergence of an aggressive Paulician principality on the upper Euphrates. Following the restoration of Iconophile orthodoxy in Constantinople in 843 the Paulicians suffered new violent persecution which in the chroniclers' inflated estimations claimed 100,000 Paulician lives. Inevitably, more Paulicians sought refuge in eastern Cappadocia and their leader, Carbeas, assumed power in a separate Arab-backed state along the upper Euphrates just to the east of the Byzantine frontier. A former imperial officer, whose Paulician father had been crucified in the persecution, Carbeas established his seat at Theprice in mountainous north-eastern Cappadocia, from where he launched a series of invasions across the eastern borders of the empire. Paradoxically, the foundation of the dualist Paulician principality in eastern Cappadocia coincided with the collapse of the Uighur empire, where Manichaeism had been the official religion for nearly a century, and the ensuing massive suppression of Manichaeism in T'ang China, which culminated in a massacre of an unknown number of Manichaean priests.

The final results of the great anti-Paulician campaigns in Byzantium thus turned out rather dubious – Paulicianism may have been extinguished from Byzantine soil but now it was established in a hostile Arab-backed theocratic state that directly threatened the eastern borders of the empire. The religious conflict between Byzantine Iconophile Orthodoxy and Paulician dualism evolved into a full-scale political and military confrontation in central-eastern Anatolia where the imperial armies suffered some heavy defeats and two emperors narrowly escaped capture by the Paulician forces.

Simultaneously, in south-east Europe, Byzantium had to confront the mounting prospect of a Franco–Bulgarian alliance with all its consequences for Byzantine interests in the Balkans. In the first half of the ninth century the Bulgar Kans successfully negotiated with Charlemagne's son, Louis the Pious, and grandson, Louis the German, for the exact delineation of the Franco–Bulgarian border in central Europe. By the middle of the century the Sublime Kans already controlled much of the territory between the Carolingian dominions, which then embraced most of western Christendom, and Byzantium, the stronghold of eastern Christendom. With its strategic position between the two great rival Christian powers, the Bulgarian domain was inevitably drawn into their imperial and ecclesiastical rivalries at the time when it had already witnessed itself the first bitter pagan–Christian conflicts that marked the opening stages of a protracted and exhaustive religious struggle.

Rome, Constantinople and Theprice

In 862 the Franco–Bulgarian alliance was finally concluded and it became apparent that the Bulgar Kan Boris (852–89) planned to receive Christianity from the west and had requested missions from Louis the German. Although the threefold partitioning of the Carolingian empire in 843 had largely diminished the Frankish threat to Byzantium, Constantinople was acutely aware of the manifold dangers of allowing Carolingian and Roman influences to filter into the Balkans via Bulgaria. The Byzantine armies had just defeated the Arabs and neutralized, for a time, the Paulicians in eastern Anatolia, although in 858 the emperor Michael III had nearly been taken captive by the forces of the Paulician leader Carbeas. The Byzantine main field army was moved to the Balkans and its massive attack against Bulgaria, presaged by a locust plague and earthquakes, compelled Kan Boris to renounce his pact with the Franks and to agree to accept Christianity from Constantinople. Early in 864 Kan Boris was baptized by Byzantine prelates and was converted into Prince Michael, taking the name of his imperial godfather, Michael III.

Yet unlike the solemn baptism of the Merovingian ruler Clovis, Boris's baptism was a 'nocturnal' ceremonial, reportedly conducted 'in secret and in the dead of the night'. Boris' fears of an inevitable pagan backlash proved prophetic: he was accused of apostasy and the threat of a Byzantine religious invasion aroused an immediate and fierce reaction among some Bulgar nobles. In his forceful collision with the pagan Bulgar nobles, Boris, depicted as a Christian thaumaturge, emerged victorious and fifty-two Bulgar houses faced outright annihilation. In addition to the strong pagan reaction the Christianization of the Bulgarian empire was further complicated by a long and exhausting struggle between Constantinople and Rome for ecclesiastical supremacy in the realm.

Successive and opposing missions from the Constantinople patriarchate and the Roman papacy turned the Bulgarian realm into a religious battleground between the Latin and Byzantine clergy. Apart from the dispute whether the Holy Spirit proceeds only from the Father or – as accepted by the western Church – from the Father 'and from the Son' (filioque), the battle for the Bulgarian Church was one of the main factors for the mounting confrontation between the Constantinople patriarchs and the Roman popes. The Greek–Latin confrontation was aggravated further by Boris' intricate moves for an autonomous Church. By 881 the patriarchate had altogether outmanoeuvred the papacy in the bid for the Bulgarian Church and Constantinople finally seemed to have succeeded in drawing the Bulgarian empire into the Byzantine religious and cultural orbit.

While competing for ascendancy in Bulgaria, Constantinople and Rome were challenged by other religious rivals. Besides the Islamic and Jewish missions, which don't seem to have achieved any tangible success, the Greek and Latin emissaries in Bulgaria must have vied with heretical preachers from the Thracian sectarian colonies. The newly Christianized Bulgarian empire was a suitable breeding ground for heretical agitation – apart from the heretical colonies in the annexed Thracian areas it had apparently served as a refuge for Byzantine heretics and discontents.

As late as the mid ninth century a prominent Byzantine 'Manichaean and sorcerer', Santabarenus, was offered sanctuary in then pagan Bulgaria, where he promptly denounced Christianity and freely began to promulgate his teachings. What is more, the Paulicians of the Cappadocian principality were apparently in contact with their co-sectarians in the Balkans and according to the Byzantine ambassador to Theprice, Peter of Sicily, they were organizing new missions to reinforce the Paulician colonies in Bulgaria in about 870.[89] Unlike the Roman and Constantinople missions, the course of the Theprice mission remains unknown, but late and distorted echoes of the dualist mission appear to have survived in a curious tradition about the two 'disciples of the Devil' from Cappadocia who infected Bulgaria with the Paulician heresy, Subotin (probably Child of the Sabbath) and Shutil (Jester).[90]

Yet following its heyday under Carbeas, the dualist Paulician state on the upper Euphrates soon succumbed to Byzantine military pressure. Carbeas himself was murdered in the Byzantine campaigns in eastern Anatolia in 863–4 but his nephew and successor, Chrysocheir (Golden Hand), also a former imperial officer, prolonged the war with Byzantium for another decade. In 869 Chrysocheir launched a raid across the whole of Anatolia to the Sea of Marmara and sacked Ephesus. Following his irruption into the Byzantine heartlands in western Anatolia Chrysocheir arrogantly proclaimed that the new emperor Basil I should abdicate as ruler east of the Bosphorus and retire to reign in the west. A former groom who murdered Boris' godfather, Michael, to ascend the imperial throne, Basil I immediately launched a retaliatory campaign against Theprice. Basil's offensive, however, ended in a total rout and he himself had a narrow escape from Chrysocheir's forces. Chrysocheir began a new series of devastating raids into central Anatolia but in 872 his Paulician army was annihilated in a carefully orchestrated Byzantine campaign and he himself was murdered and beheaded while attempting to flee to Theprice. Chrysocheir's head was sent to Constantinople where Basil celebrated his victory by having it pierced with three arrows while the imperial armies overran the Paulician dominions and annexed Theprice to Byzantium.

Chrysocheir's beheading and the capture of the dualist stronghold of Theprice delivered the death blow to the Paulician principality in Cappadocia and indeed to Paulicianism as a political and religious factor in the eastern provinces of Byzantium. Scattered and persecuted, many Paulicians fled back to Armenia or to the Near East, where later, during the First Crusade, Paulician forces fought under the banner of Islam. Despite the demise of Paulician power in Asia Minor there remained the Paulician colonies in the Balkans which were to play their significant role in the reassertion of the dualist tradition in the newly Christianized Balkan world.

It was also becoming increasingly apparent that the Byzantine religious sovereignty over the Bulgarian empire was far more fragile than it had seemed after the Constantinople Patriarchate had finally neutralized papal intervention in the eastern Balkans. In 889 Boris's eldest son and successor, Vladimir-Rasate (889–93), described as having chosen to tread in the footsteps of Julian the Apostate rather than St Peter, staged an emphatic pagan revival and sought to renew the old Bulgaro–Frankish alliance with the Carolingian king of the Eastern Franks, Arnulf. The new pagan renascence was terminated with the dethronement and blinding of Rasate in what was to be the last vicis-situde in the long and hard-fought battle between Christianity and paganism in the ninth-century Bulgarian empire. The old Bulgar pagan temples were demolished or replaced by Christian churches and the Christian records praised the abolition of the 'pagan altars, sacrifices and idols'. Yet the bitter pagan resistance to Christianization, the religious rivalry between Rome and Constantinople and the heretical proselytism had already created the religious ferment that was to provide the matrix for the resurgence of the dualist tradition in the Balkans.

The Anniversary of Zoroaster

With the turn of the last century before the first Christian millennium there began a series of religious and political upheavals that transformed the balance of forces in both the Christian and Muslim worlds and proved decisive in the shaping of later medieval geopolitics. The triumph of Christianity in the Balkans coincided with the beginning of the Christian reconquest of Muslim Spain which had been overtaken in the sweeping westward expansion of Islam in the eighth century. To oppose the Christian *reconquista* the Spanish Umayyad emir Abd ar-Rahman III unified the Moorish possessions in the Iberian Peninsula and in 929 founded the caliphate of Cordoba. Further east the rival Fatimid caliphate in North Africa, founded in 909 by a supposed descendant of Mohammed's daughter Fatima, eventually conquered Egypt in 969 and spread as far as Palestine and Syria, halting the revived Byzantine advance in the Near East. While the caliphate of Cordoba was a stronghold of Sunni Islam, the official creed of the Fatimid dynasty was Ismailism, a major Shia branch which enriched Shia traditions with Neo-Platonic and Gnostic doctrines but was condemned by its Sunni opponents as a revival of Zoroastrianism, and even Manichaeism, in Islamic garb. Ismailism achieved one of the most striking medieval religious syntheses, in which the universal religious history was seen as comprising seven great prophetic cycles of revelation, six of which had already been initiated by Adam, Noah, Abraham, Moses, Jesus and Mohammed and the last one was to be inaugurated by the advent of the final Mahdi (or Qaim), the expected seventh Imam of the Ismaili movement.

For the radical and schismatic Ismaili branch in Bahrain the coming of the final religious era appeared imminent and portended by a conjunction of Saturn and Jupiter in 928. The advent of the ultimate prophetic cycle was associated with the end of the era of Islam and also with the 1,500th anniversary of the supposed death of Zoroaster (or the 1242nd year of Alexander's era), for which old Persian prophecies had predicted the religious and political restoration of Zoroastrianism. The Qarmatian commemoration of Zoroaster's anniversary precipitated one of the major crises in medieval Islam – in 930, the very year of the anniversary, the Qarmatians sacked Mecca and took away the Black Stone of the Kaaba to herald the end of the era of Islam.

Following the capture of the Black Stone, Qarmatian rule in Bahrain passed into the hands of a young Persian, who claimed descent from the Persian Shahs and was declared to be the expected Mahdi. The chosen Mahdi ordered the worship of fire and abolished Islamic laws but was killed after eighty days, which marked the end of this ephemeral but vigorous Zoroastrian revival in the Qarmatian domain. The religious turbulence around Zoroaster's anniversary inevitably also affected the Zoroastrians in Babylonia and Iran, then under the control of the Abbasid caliphate, where the Zoroastrian chief priest himself was accused of collaboration with the Qarmatians and executed.

Zoroaster's reputed anniversary did not leave unstirred the Manichaeans in Babylonia, who apparently viewed it as the onset of an era for renewed missionary expansion. The revived Manichaean activities in the turmoil of the early tenth century obviously provoked Abbasid persecution, for at the end of the caliphate of al-Muqtadir (908–32) most of the Babylonian Manichaeans had to flee to Khurasan and further to Samarkand in Sogdiana, whereas those who remained in Babylonia kept their identity secret. In the new troubled times the Manichaean community in Mesopotamia entered a period of migration and secrecy, when the Manichaean *archegos* himself disappeared from his traditional seat in Mesopotamia and the 'Religion of Light' also seemed to vanish from the tumultuous arena of the Middle East.[91]

While in the early tenth century the Islamic world had seen the emergence of rival caliphates, in Christian Europe the Carolingian imperial traditions were in decline after Arnulf, the last Carolingian emperor, was stricken with paralysis in the wake of his coronation, and died in 899. Yet at the time when England was finally unified by the grandson of Alfred the Great, Athelstan, the founder of the German Saxon dynasty, Henry the Fowler (919–63), had already enforced the monarchical authority in the East Frankish kingdom. Following the conquests of his successor, Otto the Great, the East Frankish kingdom was transformed into the Holy Roman Empire, but the German empire-building had to confront another fresh pagan influx from the steppes – the coming of the Magyars. As the pagan Magyars pressed deep into central Europe they were subjected to gradual Christianization and the turn of the millennium saw the foundation of St Stephen's Christian kingdom of Hungary.

The Magyars were driven into central Europe by the diplomacy and campaigns of the Bulgarian ruler Symeon (893–927) whose Magyar venture was followed by thirty years of intermittent Balkan wars, during which he annexed Serbia, confronted Croatia and repeatedly invaded Byzantium, seeking at one stage an alliance with the Fatimids against Constantinople. What is more, Symeon endeavoured to manoeuvre himself into a new *Basileus*, a new type of Constantinople emperor, presiding over a united Byzantine–Bulgarian empire. While in his bid for the imperial throne Symeon was outplayed by the commander of the Byzantine fleet, Romanus Lecapenus, he finally proclaimed himself 'Emperor and Autocrat of the Romans and the Bulgars' and in 926 his imperial title was ratified by Pope John x.

The failed prospect of the unification of the Bulgarian and Byzantine empires has been seen as 'one of the great missed opportunities in history'[92] which would have allowed the Orthodox east to resist the incessant pressures from both east and west. The Bulgarian monarch was an able Greek scholar, praised as the 'new Ptolemy' and vigorously sought to promote the rich cultural heritage of Byzantine Orthodoxy in his realm. The Bulgarian empire had already adopted the legacy of St Cyril and St

Methodius, the Apostles of the Slavs – the Slavonic version of the Scriptures, liturgy and alphabet – and the literary schools patronized by Symeon made a crucial and seminal contribution to the spread of the new Slavo-Byzantine culture in eastern Europe, namely in Serbia and Russia.[93]

However, besides the translation of Byzantine sacred and secular literature, another body of translations was also beginning to find its way into the newly Christianized Bulgarian empire – secret apocryphal texts, most of which dated from the early Christian era and have been preserved and transmitted in the Christian east. Some of these apocryphal works were to prove fundamental for the shaping and elaboration of the mythology of Bogomil and Cathar dualism. Moreover, one of the outstanding Orthodox writers of Symeon's royal school, Ioan Exarkh, was already warning against the preachings of pagans and 'Manichaeans' (at that time a stock term for dualists) who taught that the Devil was the eldest son of God.[94] This notion of pagan–'Manichaean' affiliation has been seen as the 'earliest direct indication of the alliance between paganism and heresy'[95] in Bulgaria, significantly after a century of severe pagan-Christian collisions in the realm. What is more, this 'alliance' was a crystallization around a specific teaching of the Devil's genesis, which subsequently became the crux of Bogomil monarchian dualism, with its distinctive trinity – God the Father and his two sons, Satanael and Jesus Christ.

The Descent of the 'Manichaean Darkness'

Bogomilism made its first steps in the Balkans under the reign of Symeon's son, Peter (927–69), renowned as the 'monastic reign'. In 927 Symeon died suddenly and his death came to be ascribed to a bizarre act of magical regicide orchestrated by the emperor Romanus Lecapenus in Constantinople.[96] In the wake of Symeon's death the traditional segregation of the Byzantine imperial family was broken in a peace treaty with Peter which sanctioned a dynastic intermarriage of the Bulgarian and Byzantine royal houses and recognized Peter's title of emperor (Tsar). The treaty was soon followed by another shift in the Balkan balance of power – Serbia, long a focus of rivalry between the Bulgarian and Byzantine empires, in 931 moved out of the Bulgarian sphere of control and accepted Byzantine overlordship. Moreover, new nomads from the steppes, the Pechenegs, who are sometimes seen as recipients and bearers of Manichaean influences from Central Asia,[97] soon began their incursions into the Balkans from their settlements in southern Ukraine.

With the inevitable increase of Byzantine influences in Bulgaria, as in Byzantium, it witnessed a striking rise of monasticism that was patronized by the Tsar, who was himself praised as a 'teacher of Orthodoxy' and a 'Rock of Christianity'. Peter adopted the role of a 'defender of the faith' in a religious climate apparently fraught with tensions – the Byzantinization of ecclesiastical life, the repercussions of the unusual spread of monasticism and the first signs of heretical agitation. Pagan residues were still strong and Peter's younger brother, Prince Benjamin (Boyan), who was to become one of the famous medieval 'occult' personages, was an enigmatic figure, reminiscent of the traditional 'princely magus by blood' that in the early Middle Ages was still seen as a potential menace to the Church. The sketchy evidence about Prince Benjamin centres essentially on his magical expertise and his figure has inevitably attracted much romance and speculation which links him variously with Bulgar paganism, Byzantine magic and demonology or even with the rise of Bogomilism.[98]

While the first steps of Bogomilism largely remain uncharted, it is beyond dispute that by the mid tenth century it had already assumed the shape of an organized and rapidly spreading heretical movement. In the face of the rising heresy, Peter had to write twice to the princely patriarch of Constantinople, Theophylact Lecapenus, who was, however, said to spend more time in ministering to his many horses than in the cathedral. The patriarch, none the less, was able to recognize this 'ancient and newly appeared heresy' as 'Manichaeism mixed with Paulicianism' and urged Peter to burn the 'bitter and evil roots' of their teachings in the 'holy fire of truth', arming the Tsar with a list of twelve anathemas.[99] Soon after providing spiritual guidance for the Tsar, however, Theophylact suffered a grave riding accident and in the remaining few years of his life could not conduct the battle against the new Balkan heresy, or in his own words, 'that serpent-like and many-headed hydra of impiety', which signalled the revival of dualism in eastern Christendom.

Theophylact Lecapenus was not destined to become the heresiographer of the new dualist movement, but such a heresiographer did appear in the person of a Bulgarian presbyter, Cosmas, whose vehement *Sermon Against the Heretics* (*c.* 967–72)[100] disclosed the identity of its founder, the priest Bogomil, invariably charged in later Orthodox traditions with the spread of the Manichaean 'darkness' or heresy in Bulgaria. The *Sermon Against the Heretics* materialized a striking picture of the religious and social tensions, which, coupled with strong pagan remnants, allowed for the quick spread of the new heresy. The heretical preachers seemed won from 'hypocritical fasting' but concealed a 'voracious wolf' within and could venture to deceive the Orthodox either by open heretical preachings or by an ingenious simulation of Orthodoxy. The heretical homilies, which seemed puzzling and ambiguous to the presbyter, apparently comprised parables, allegories and unorthodox gospel interpretations. While the meaning of the gospel events could be completely transformed in accordance with their missionary purposes, the miracles of Jesus Christ were interpreted allegorically and the Eucharistic bread and wine were taken to represent the gospels and Acts of the Apostles. Their heretical dualism, which recognized the Devil as a fallen angel and the creator of heaven, earth and man, was also expounded through allegorical interpretations of the gospel parables. The Devil could be styled as the 'unjust steward', as he was identified with the unrighteous steward from the famous parable in Luke 16:1–9, whereas in the heretical reading of the Parable of the Prodigal Son (Luke 15 : 11–32) Christ was taken to represent the elder and the Devil the younger brother. The concept of the Devil as a creator and master of the visible world, as 'Lord of the sky, the sun, the air and the stars', was inevitably reinforced with the allusions to the 'prince of this world' in the fourth gospel.

The heretics were also described as rejecting Mosaic Law and the Old Testament prophets, denouncing the veneration of the icons and the relics of the saints, and condemning the Church hierarchy and ceremonial. The cross itself was reviled as 'God's enemy' and for Cosmas this repudiation of the cross made the heretics worse than demons, for demons feared the cross, while the sectarians were alleged to have 'cut down the Crosses to fashion tools out of them'. Not only were the crosses allegedly mutilated, but also the heretics were accused of maligning even the Virgin Mary with 'offensive words' and treating John the Baptist not as a predecessor of Jesus Christ but as a forerunner of the Antichrist.

In the tract the heretical preachers are portrayed as extreme ascetics, abstaining from marriage, meat and wine, which were condemned as coming from the Devil (Mammon). Some heretical missionaries were also arraigned for teaching their followers to defy the authority of the Tsar and the aristocracy, but there is no tangible evidence to imply that Bogomilism ever approached anything like a social or mostly peasant movement,[101] while all the available data point to a dualist sect with a strong appeal to monastic circles and the lower clergy. The tract leaves a vague and discrepant picture of Bogomil teachings and its paucity is predictably justified by falling on the authority of St Paul – 'For it is a shame even to speak of those things which are done of them in secret' (Ephesians 5 : 12, *KJV*). Yet, however confused and meagre, the exposé of the Bogomil doctrine yields some important clues to its underlying dualism, which is clearly of a monarchian type – the evil creator is not an eternal, independent principle, but a fallen angel, secondary and inferior to God. The monarchian character of early Bogomil dualism clearly contrasts with the late Paulician radical dualist dogma of the two principles, the evil creator of this world and the good Lord of the world to come. Confusingly, in the *Sermon Against the Heretics* Bogomil dualism treats Christ as God's eldest son and the Devil as his younger brother, whereas in the earlier warning of pagan–'Manichaean' teachings of the Devil he was represented as God's eldest son. Later versions of Bogomil and Cathar dualism traditionally regarded the Devil as God's eldest son, who, however, came to lose his seniority upon his rebellion and fall, after which Christ was elevated to the status of God's first-born. It is thus quite probable that the Devil's position in the dualist scheme in the *Sermon Against the Heretics* reflects the status quo in the wake of his fall when his seniority was already transferred to Christ.[102]

Apart from highlighting these intricacies of the Devil's reversible seniority in medieval monarchian dualism, the *Sermon Against the Heretics* leaves a striking testimony of the early Bogomil movement in which dualist, anticlerical and iconoclastic militancy were coupled with a strong ascetic and missionary fervour. Yet the formation and early history of Bogomilism remain complicated and obscure, the very origins of Bogomilism perhaps being the most controversial problem related to the rise and spread of medieval dualism.

The Riddle of Bogomil Beginnings

The precise time and place of the origins of Bogomilism remain unknown, although Macedonia and Thrace are traditionally regarded as the cradle of the new dualist movement. A later anathema against the

Bogomils locates the initial centre of their activities in 'Bulgarian Macedonia' and the area around Philippopolis (Plovdiv) in Thrace.[103] The crystallization and spread of Bogomil teachings apparently owed much to the personal missionary zeal and syncretistic skills of the heresiarch of the movement, the priest Bogomil. It is widely assumed that the 'turbulent priest' had synthesized elements of earlier heretical traditions, usually identified as Paulician and Massalian, but sometimes direct Manichaean, Marcionite or separate Gnostic influences are also assumed to have their impact on the formation of Bogomil dualism.[104] Besides the customary formula of 'Manichaean heresy', medieval Orthodox authorities on Bogomilism tended to denounce its heresy as an admixture of Manichaeism and Paulicianism, Paulicianism and Massalianism or else Manichaeism and Massalianism. Yet although the influence of antecedent anti-ecclesiastical and heretical movements on Bogomilism is undisputed, such clear-cut definitions of the Bogomil heresy are extremely misleading. There are considerable differences between Bogomil and Paulician dualism, both in the underlying dualist formula and its mythological elaborations. As regards the alleged Massalian influence on Bogomilism, the very existence of authentic Massalians in the medieval Balkan–Byzantine world is disputed and the epithet 'Massalian' seems to have been applied loosely to heretics, heterodox theologians and dissenters. For all its complexities and controversies, the evidence of early Bogomilism indicates that rather than being a natural evolution from Paulicianism or from the elusive Massalianism, Bogomilism emerged in the tenth century as a distinct and indigenous dualist movement, with its independent teachings and purposes.

Recent trends in research into Bogomil origins and the accelerated formation of Slavo-Byzantine Orthodox theology, culture and learning have presented strong arguments that the creation and elaboration of Bogomil theological dualism owe much to this diverse process, when the Scriptures were translated into a language more or less close to the vernacular, animating the tensions implicit in the complex interrelationships between orthodoxy, literacy and heresy in medieval Christianity.[105] In the Slavonic indexes of forbidden apocryphal books local priests were often condemned for possessing and circulating these texts, a situation that certainly reflects also the early stages of the development of Slavo-Byzantine culture and explains the wide-ranging translation and diffusion of apocryphal texts in that initial phases. Heterodox and heretical teachers could easily spread their teachings by borrowing notions from these texts and verses from the New Testament and preaching them in the vernacular. In the religious climate of the tenth-century Bulgarian state, marked both by the prominence of the monastic vocation which was coupled with the quest for the New Testament-inspired ascetic life and ideals, and by already existing dualist influences, whether Christian heretical or others, one can discern the factors conducive to the formulation of a new version of Christian dualism, stimulated by the influx of teachings, themes and notions rediscovered in the newly translated apocryphal works from late antiquity.

There have been attempts to link the rise of Bogomilism in the Balkans with the commencement of a new Manichaean diaspora from Babylonia in the wake of the religious and political agitation surrounding Zoroaster's anniversary in the early tenth century.[106] The old connections between the Bulgars and the peoples of Central Asia and the steppes have also been invoked to link early Bogomilism to the presumed Manichaean missions from the Manichaean Uighur empire following its collapse in 843.[107] The Bulgars themselves might well have encountered Manichaean missions during their period in Central Asia and Sogdiana, which then served as a stepping stone for the introduction of Manichaeism in China. There is, however, no existing evidence for direct Manichaean influences on the Bulgars in the Balkans, although the Volga Bulgars were recorded as having used the Manichaean script prior to their acceptance of Islam. The subsequent new nomadic waves from Central Asia and the steppes could also have brought Manichaean influences to the Balkans, but at present such links between Central Asian Manichaeism and medieval Balkan dualism remain conjectural.

The Bogomil trinity of God the Father and his elder and younger son, Satanael and Jesus Christ, closely approaches the analogous Zurvanite trinity of Zurvan, Ahriman and Ohrmazd to the extent that, despite the lack of strong historical evidence, no less authorities on religious history than R. Zaehner and M. Eliade have argued that it was derived from Iranian traditions.[108] More controversially, it has been suggested that early Bogomilism might have been affected by Balkan residues of Mithraism,[109] although late references to 'Mithraism' seem to allude generally to paganism; as late as the eleventh century the philosopher Michael Psellus accused monks of Chios of initiating rituals and mysteries akin to those of Mithras.

The characteristic pre-Christian temples of the Bulgars and the pronounced Iranian impact on their art certainly raises the possibility of Zoroastrian or Zurvanite influences in their religion. A local variety of Zurvanism was a noticeable presence in the religious life of Sogdiana, an early habitat of the Bulgars, and it is not impossible to reconstruct a religious development within Bulgar religiosity leading from the Zurvanite triad to the Christianized Bogomil dualist triad. However, with the present state of evidence, such religious development remains speculative and when seeking the origins of Bogomilism one needs to emphasize, in particular, the impact of earlier Byzantine heresies, of religious agitation during the Christianization of Bulgaria, of the accelerated influx of both canonical and apocryphal literature in this period, and of the spread of monasticism and the ideal of the apostolic life, while leaving open avenues for research on other possible contributory factors.

As far as the suggested legacy of the pre-Christian Slavonic religion in Bogomilism is concerned, again, the existence of a proto-Slavonic dualism between an evil and a good god remains hotly contested, and its posited role in the spread of Bogomilism in the Slavonic Orthodox world remains purely hypothetical. More significant is the persistence of the earth-diver dualist cosmogony in south and east Slavonic popular belief and the identification of the earth-diver with the Devil as a second demiurge, a topos which may have been affected both by orthodox diabology but also in some cases by direct or indirect Bogomil dualist influences. There is incontestable evidence that the popular Slavonic cosmogonies and Bogomil dualist theology interacted throughout the medieval period, thus increasing both the popular appeal of Bogomilism and its impact on Slavonic and Balkan folklore.

What compounds the ambiguity surrounding the origins of Bogomilism is the paucity of evidence about its founder, the priest Bogomil. He may be regarded as the 'greatest heresiarch of the Middle Ages' but it is not even certain that his name is, as has been commonly assumed, a Slavonic translation of the Greek 'Theophilus' (Beloved of God), while most Slavonic words containing the root *bog* (God) had largely been formed under Iranian influences.[110] Moreover, besides 'Beloved of God' the name Bogomil has also been translated as 'worthy of God's Mercy', 'one who entreats God' or 'one who implores God's Grace'. Apart from being recognized as the heresiarch of Balkan dualism, in later Orthodox testimonies the priest Bogomil was anathematized for preaching the Docetic teaching that Christ's Passion and Resurrection were illusory and for rejecting the veneration of the cross. Orthodox traditions may have depicted the priest Bogomil and his disciples as incarnations of Jannes and Jambres, the legendary Egyptian sorcerers who opposed Moses during the Exodus, but otherwise they did not shed any light on the mundane life of the heresiarch. Vague legends recount that on Bogomil's death his followers erected a chapel at the site of his grave where they gathered for prayers. Ultimately, unlike his great spiritual ancestor, Mani, Bogomil's background and rise as a heresiarch remain shrouded in opaque darkness.

The priest Bogomil has sometimes been identified with another notorious and elusive priest, who lived and wrote heterodox apocryphal works in tenth-century Bulgaria. The priest Jeremiah was to become the most popular and denounced apocryphal writer in the Slavonic Orthodox world and his famous apocryphal compilation, *The Legend of the Cross*, had been widely circulated and read from Bosnia to Russia. The possibility of Jeremiah being Bogomil's *alter ego* has been long and bitterly debated, as in Orthodox traditions Jeremiah was also denounced as a 'son' and disciple of Bogomil, who himself was condemned as an author of apocryphal works. What remains undisputed is the link between the crystallization of Bogomil doctrine and the influx of a rich and diverse apocryphal literature in tenth-century Bulgaria, some of which came to be adopted for the purposes of Bogomil propaganda.[111]

Apart from the priests Bogomil and Jeremiah, Orthodox records allude to two even more elusive figures accused of having introduced heretical books into Bulgaria – Sydor Fryazin (Sydor the Frank) and Jacob Tsentsal, who is also described as 'fryazin' (Frank).[112] The names of these two heretics suggest that they came from the west but the time of their supposed activity and the character of their heretical books remain unknown. There remains, however, the intriguing possibility of an early intercourse between eastern and western heretics prior to the first serious outbreaks of heresy in western Christendom.

Another significant problem concerning early Bogomilism is the organization and hierarchy of the Bogomil movement. In their mature form both Bogomilism and Catharism were divided into two main classes, the elite grade of the *perfecti* and the lesser grade of the believers, beneath which there apparently existed another introductory and looser class – the listeners. It has often been argued that these grades developed within later

Bogomilism, but it seems likely that they were a feature of the early Bogomil movement. The presence of an elite of Bogomil *perfecti* is implied in the *Sermon Against the Heretics* and soon there appeared a clear Orthodox testimony of distinct divisions and initiations within the Bogomil sect along with a distorted account of the rite that converted the dualist believer into a *perfectus* – the spiritual baptism, known in the west as the *consolamentum*. Similarly, given the paucity of the evidence, it cannot be established with certainty when Bogomilism developed its hierarchy. Later sources refer to Bogomil religious leaders, called 'teachers' or 'first teachers', who were assisted by a group of 'apostles' but it is not clear whether they allude to the Bogomil movement as a whole or to a separate Bogomil community or 'Church'. According to one of the proposed reconstructions, from its beginnings the movement had a religious leader assisted by an inner circles of apostles.[113] However, such a scenario cannot as yet be verified although it matches the later data about the twelfth-century Bogomil heresiarch Basil and his twelve apostles, which data, apart from the obvious Christian parallel, bear a close resemblance to the upper Manichaean hierarchy – the leader (*archegos*) and the following rank of twelve apostles.

The puzzles surrounding the organization of the early Bogomil movement also extend to the dates of the formation of the first Bogomil communities or 'churches' that were later regarded by the inquisitorial authorities as the source of all dualist churches in Europe. What remains certain is that only several decades after Patriarch Theophylact Lecapenus had sent his panoply of anti-heretical anathemas to Tsar Peter, Bogomilism had radiated into Byzantium and its spread in the empire was to be accelerated with the Byzantine reconquest of the Balkans.

The 'Time of Troubles'

In 969 the 'monastic' reign of Tsar Peter collapsed in the chaos and devastation of a sudden Russian invasion and the Tsar finally assumed 'monastic' garb. In one of the unexpected twists of Byzantine *realpolitik*, the heathen Duke of Kiev, Svyatoslav, who had already undermined Khazar power in the steppes, was bribed to invade the Bulgarian empire and his armies burst into the Balkans. Byzantium eventually felt threatened by the magnitude of Svyatoslav's Balkan conquests and for three years the Bulgarian lands became a battleground between the troops of Svyatoslav and Emperor John Tzimisces. When finally repelled from the Balkans, Svyatoslav was to meet a gruesome death back in the Ukrainian steppes at the hands of the old enemies of Kievan Russia, the Pechenegs, who turned his skull into a cup.

John Tzimisces forced Tsar Peter's successor, Boris II, to abdicate in Constantinople and the onset of the Byzantine reconquest of the Balkans was coupled with a steady eastward advance. In northern Armenia and Syria, however, John Tzimisces encountered strong Paulician communities, apparently remnants of the former Paulician principality in Cappadocia, and was advised by Patriarch Thomas of Antioch to remove them from the eastern imperial frontiers. John Tzimisces again chose resettlement in the Balkans and in about 975 or 976 numerous Paulicians, some sources mention 200,000, were moved to Thrace, particularly the area around ancient Philippopolis. The timely dualist blood transfusion into Thrace reinforced Balkan dualism in the crucial period of the early diffusion of Bogomilism and amid the cataclysms of another war in the Balkan interior.

Despite the initial success of the Byzantine conquest of the eastern Balkans, the Byzantine advance was blocked in Macedonia by the enigmatic tetrarchy of the sons of a Bulgarian *comes* (count) known as the Cometopuli – David, Moses, Aaron and Samuel. The rise of the house of the Cometopuli, linked by the Byzantine poet John Geometrus to an appearance of a comet in 968, is surrounded by much controversy which is by no means resolved by their appearance in a later chronicle, itself betraying Bogomil influences, as the royal 'sons of a widow-prophetess'.[114]

The youngest of the sons, Samuel, eventually succeeded in spreading his conquests into Albania and Greece, where he overran the ancient region of Thessaly and captured its main stronghold Larissa. In 997 Samuel was crowned Tsar of a renascent and aggressive Bulgarian empire, now centred on Macedonia, which had to face, however, the increasing military pressure of the ruthless warrior-monk Emperor Basil II (976–1025). The two great powers of Orthodox Christendom met the second millennium locked in an exceedingly fierce conflict but in 1001 Basil concluded a ten-year peace treaty with the Fatimid caliph and protagonist of the Druze faith, al-Hakim, during which his wide-ranging

Balkan campaigns gradually put Samuel on the defensive. In 1014, after achieving a decisive victory in Macedonia, Basil blinded and sent back to Samuel thousands of Bulgarian prisoners of war and at the sight of the blinded army Samuel collapsed and died within days.

Samuel's successors, Gabriel-Radomir (1014–15) and Ivan Vladislav (1015–18), resisted Basil's offensive for another four years but in 1018 the Bulgarian empire, which had long seemed 'all-powerful and invincible' to the Byzantines, was finally conquered by the Byzantine emperor. After three centuries Byzantium had recovered most of its lost Balkan provinces, while the various rulers in the Serbian, Bosnian and Croatian lands now became vassals of Basil, who in 1019 made his triumphant march through the reconquered Balkan territories and inaugurated victory celebrations in Athens and Constantinople. In a contemporary Arab chronicle Basil is credited with seeking to destroy the old Bulgaro-Byzantine enmity through intermarriage and the surviving descendants of the Cometopuli, like other Bulgarian noble families, intermarried with the Byzantine aristocracy to give rise to the noble line of the Aaronids, who were to play an important role in Byzantine history.[115]

Less than a century after Basil sanctioned these Bulgaro-Byzantine marriages Bogomilism was said to have affected the 'great houses' in Constantinople and it is possible that the Bulgarian influx into the Byzantine aristocracy might have facilitated the spread of the heresy among the Byzantine social elite.[116] Various scholars have assumed, moreover, that the Cometopuli and Samuel himself were of Bogomil inclination, although Samuel had re-established the Bulgarian patriarchate during his reign and was himself a vigorous church-builder. Yet Samuel seemed to be tolerant of the Bogomils and did not check the spread of the heresy in his war-torn dominions. What is more, in a later controversial Greek tradition some of the descendants of the Cometopuli, namely Samuel's daughter and Tsar Gabriel-Radomir (or else Tsar Ivan Vladislav), were themselves accused of being 'enemies of the cross' and followers of the Bogomil and Massalian heresies.[117] Yet claims that the Bogomils took an active part in the rising of the Cometopuli, who are sometimes seen as champions of a kind of political messianism, or that the realm of Samuel flourished due to the massive support of the Bogomils, who are accordingly regarded as one of the 'pillars' of his 'seemingly orthodox but heretical empire',[118] are greatly exaggerated.

Whatever the religious affinities of the Cometopuli 'sons of the widow', the last years of the reign of their dynasty marked the violent twilight of the first Bulgarian empire. The protracted and severe Bulgaro-Byzantine war of 977–1018 has been described by Arnold Toynbee as the Orthodox 'Time of Troubles', an 'internecine struggle', which marked the breakdown of the old and traditional Orthodox Christian civilization.[119] Although Orthodox Christianity had been established in Kievan Russia, which was thus drawn into the Byzantine religious and cultural orbit, the Byzantine reconquests in the Balkans were at the expense of severe social and economic setbacks in Asia Minor, most of which came to be lost to the Seljuk Turks by the end of the century. The recovery of the Balkans during the Orthodox 'Time of Troubles' was bound, moreover, to leave Byzantium open to the increasing missionary activities of the new Balkan dualist movement, Bogomilism, which in the early eleventh century had already struck roots in the western Anatolian regions and particularly in the old heretical seedbed of Phrygia.

The Heresy in Anatolia

The first testimony to the magnitude of Bogomil proselytism and expansion in western Anatolia is a long letter written in about 1050 by the monk Euthymius of the Peribleptos monastery in Constantinople.[120] The monastery itself had been infiltrated by four Bogomil missionaries who had led Euthymius' own disciple astray, and earlier a travelling presbyter, who turned out to be a Bogomil preacher, had attempted to convert Euthymius himself. In order to expose the Bogomil proselytizers Euthymius decided to risk another attempt at conversion at the hands of their first teacher and endured an exhausting heretical sermon with quotations from the gospels, St Paul's epistles, the Psalms, St John Chrysostom and the Church Fathers – as the monk said, 'from all scriptures'. The heretics were then imprisoned in separate cells and Euthymius questioned them individually about their teachings. What Euthymius comprehended was that the heretics' thorough knowledge of the Scriptures derived from a 'satanic force' that entered them on their heretical baptism, the so-called 'second baptism'. Euthymius also declared that during this baptism the gospel was placed on the novices' head and they were mesmerized with well-known gospel verses, while the initiating 'teachers of evil' recited a secret 'satanic incantation' presented as a 'revelation of St Peter'. This was alleged to banish the blessing of the Holy Ghost from the soul of the proselytes and replace it with the 'seal of the devil', transforming the initiates into devil-incarnates whose sole purpose was to lure Christ's flock into the 'repulsive and godless' heresy.

This short but expressive demonological exposé is in all probability Euthymius' own garbled and diabolized version of the rite that raised the dualist neophyte, the 'listener', to the rank of the dualist 'believer', which is referred to in other Orthodox accounts of Bogomilism as the *baptisma*. Euthymius confirmed that the first heretical baptism was only a prelude to a gradual initiation into the teachings that prepare the believer for the grade of the perfect or, in Euthymius' version, for the 'unholy service to the Devil and his mysteries'. For one or two years the neophyte was lured into a series of revelations of 'evil knowledge' until finally he was initiated into the 'whole heresy and madness'. Euthymius gave another exposé of the rite that was supposed to erase all traces of Christian baptism, probably the *consolamentum*, which admitted the dualist believer to the elite ascetic grade of the perfect. Later Orthodox versions of the *consolamentum* or *teleiosis* confirmed that the rite was preceeded by a period of prolonged asceticism and instruction, and that the consecration comprised laying the gospel on the head of the proselyte followed by the hands of the perfect, amid hymns of thanksgiving. Two western versions of the Cathar *consolamentum*, which was certainly formulated under Bogomil influence, have also been preserved and they present some obvious parallels to early Christian baptism.[121]

Yet for Euthymius of Peribleptos the ultimate dualist rite transformed the erstwhile heretical disciples into apostles and teachers, 'ordained by the Devil'. While denouncing them as 'apostles of darkness', 'God's enemies' and the 'Devil's henchmen', he reaffirmed that the Bogomils renounced all Church services, the veneration of the cross, the cult of relics and the efficacy of the Eucharist and baptism. Despite his claims of direct knowledge of the secret 'writings of the heresy', his exposure of the heretical teachings is scant and confused. In Euthymius' version of Bogomil cosmology, God created the seven heavens, whereas the expelled 'prince of this world', the Devil, created the eighth, visible heaven, the earth, sea, Paradise and man. In the visible universe ruled by the fallen 'prince of the world' only the sun and the soul of man are from God but were stolen by the Devil. As God's creation, however, the soul was constantly escaping from the 'satanic' body of man; finally the Devil had to resort to an ingenious technique to entrap it. He ate of the flesh of all unclean animals and emitted this impurity on the soul in order to defile it and compel it to remain in the body of Adam. These teachings evidently reflect the old Gnostic myth of the fallen demiurge coupled with the Orphic/Gnostic concept of the incarnation as an exile in a bodily prison. The heretics, moreover, apparently did not revere the traditional Christian trinity and Euthymius suspected them of worshipping some mysterious Satanic trinity in which the Holy Ghost was the 'spirit of evil', the Son was the 'son of perdition' and the Father was Satan himself. At the same time, Euthymius alluded to the claims of the Bogomil apostles of esoteric knowledge of 'God's secrets' in the gospels, hidden for the others in parables (Mark 4:11), but confusingly stated that they called themselves true Christians after 'their father, the Antichrist'. He also maintained that during the Bogomil initiation, anything taught prior to the 'second baptism' was refuted after the rite and the newly imparted Bogomil 'mysteries' were altered further following the final heretical baptism.

Besides the heretical 'mysteries' of Bogomilism, Euthymius was alarmed that the 'many-named heresy of the Bogomils' already permeated 'every region, town and diocese' in the empire. Unlike the Paulicians, whose heresy was overt and less dangerous, the Bogomils were prepared to feign Orthodoxy, build churches, worship icons and take part in services in order to further their secretive missionary work. While preaching, the Bogomil apostles were defying torture and death; the sphere of their missionary campaigns extended beyond Byzantium to the whole of Christendom, to 'all Christians under the sun'. Euthymius' report of the Bogomil missions' reach was understandably exaggerated but within a century Bogomil missionaries had already reached and spread their teachings in central and western Europe. Bogomil preaching in Anatolia was particularly successful in the Phrygian imperial district of Thracesion where it had already won over 'whole cities' to the heresy and where the Bogomil heresiarchs John Tzurillas and Raheas were active in the region around Smyrna (Izmir), the reputed site of one of the Seven Churches of Asia (Revelation 2:8). In north-west Anatolia, in the district of Opsikion, the heretics were known by the obscure name Phundagiagites, while in Cibyrrhaeot by the gulf of Antalya, in the 'west' (i.e. the Balkans) and 'in other places' the heretics were known as Bogomils.[122] There are also indications that around that time Bogomil missions had penetrated the mountainous province of Lycia in south-west Asia Minor.

It is significant that Euthymius affirms that the Bogomil message was gaining ground in monastic and even clerical circles in Asia Minor and was forming a dualist hidden world of 'pseudo-monks, teachers and godless priests' who used their knowledge of the Scriptures to beguile more souls into their heresy. Around the time of the great schism between Rome and Constantinople in 1054, the dualist underworld in Anatolia extended, on the evidence of Euthymius, from the Bosphorus to the Gulf of Antalya.

The Three Principles of the Thracian Euchites

In the epistle of Euthymius of Periblepthos the Bogomils were also associated with the Massalians, who were known by their Greek name Euchites, and continued to be seen as a heretical threat in early medieval Byzantium. Accusations of Massalianism, which actually focus on Bogomil beliefs, were to remain current in the next three centuries. Such charges occur in the tract *Dialogus de daemonum operatione*, traditionally attributed to the politician and philosopher, Michael Psellus, who around the mid eleventh century held the chair of *hypatos ton philosophon* (Consul of the Philosophers), but his authorship of the text has lately been challenged.[123] The tract condemned the deplorable beliefs and practices of certain 'god-fighting' and 'accursed' Euchites, who were apparently active in southern Thrace. It revealed that they believed in a trinity of the Father and His two Sons, who ruled respectively over the heavenly and material world – which in Orthodoxy was a belief invariably attributed to Bogomilism.

The heretical teaching of the three principles, as reported by the tract derived from Mani's teaching of the two principles – the two gods opposed to each other, the creator of good, who was also the heavenly ruler and the creator of evil, who was the prince of all evil on earth. To these the Euchites added a third and the new trinity comprised the Father, associated with the supramundane realm, the younger Son, who ruled over the heavenly sphere, and the elder Son, who presided over this world. As a formula, it paralleled the Zurvanite trinity: the Zurvanites had been defined as followers of the teaching of the three principles and were distinguished from the adherents of the two principles. For Zaehner the reference to Mani's two principles and 'the most exact correspondences' between the Euchitic and Zurvanite three principles demonstrated that the doctrine of the Thracian Euchites was 'directly dependent upon Zurvanism'.[124] Yet while the tract clearly defined the Thracian heretics as followers of the three principles it also stated that it had led to the emergence of three distinct trends among the sectarians.

The first trend admitted dual worship and revered both Sons – for although they were now disparate, they had originated from one Father and would eventually be reunited. The second worshipped the younger Son, 'as a ruler of the better and superior part', but at the same time honoured the power of the elder Son, aware of his ability to cause evil. The most extreme was the third trend adherents of which sought to separate themselves completely from the prince of the heavens and 'embrace the earthly Satanael alone'. Although Satanael, the elder Son, was a destroyer, he was invoked with many adulatory names such as 'the first-born of the Father' or 'the Creator of trees, animals and other composite beings'. The third Euchite trend did not permit worship of the younger Son but accused him of being jealous of the prince of this world and his ordering of the earth. They believed that, plagued by envy, the heavenly prince 'sends down earthquakes, hailstorms and pestilence' and for this reason he should be cursed and anathematized. Finally, the tract accused Euchites of celebrating their arcane mysteries with monstrous ceremonies, including licentious and incestuous sexual orgies, and black sacrifices.

This account of the Thracian heretics' dogma of the three principles and respective threefold division has inevitably sparked controversy, since it is difficult to disentangle the reliable evidence from the demonological clichés. The threefold partitioning of the Thracian Euchites in accordance with their mode of worship is not mentioned in any account of the Massalian or Bogomil movements. Moreover, while the Massalian sectarians had been accused of orgiastic excesses, the Bogomils were always renowned, among enemies and sympathizers alike, for their austere morality and asceticism. Yet the teachings of the first two Euchite groups have been found 'quite compatible with Bogomil doctrine',[125] as some Orthodox traditions state that the Bogomils felt forced to propitiate the 'prince of this world' as a defensive tactic to avert evil and destruction.

What remains undisputed is that the Euchite doctrine of the three principles in the tract is of Bogomil origin and the document confirms the growing influence of Bogomilism in Thrace. By 1062 Bogomilism had also appeared in the provincial Byzantine capital Athens, where the bishopric was driven to take measures to halt its spread. Thessaly and its capital Larissa, earlier occupied by Samuel, had also been penetrated by Bogomilism[126] and Patriarch Cosmas of Jerusalem had to admonish the Metropolitan of Larissa and the prelates of the neighbouring bishoprics with a letter warning against its spread. By the end of the twelfth century Bogomilism had gained a strong foothold in Constantinople, where its great heresiarch Basil the Physician strove to convert the pious emperor Alexius Comnenus.

The Crusades of Alexius Comnenus

The spread of Bogomilism in twelfth-century Byzantium coincided with the rise of new currents in Byzantine religious thought, a marked deepening of the interest in classical antiquity and the Hellenic past, heated theological debates and, last but not least, heresy trials. Byzantine mysticism had been revitalized by the writings of the influential mystic and monastic reformer, Symeon the Theologian (949–1022), elements of whose teachings, such as the cult of his spiritual father, Symeon Eulabes, aroused the opposition of the church authorities and led to his exile from Constantinople. Some of Symeon's assertions, such as his belief that a true spirituality rather than ordination is a prerequisite for acting as confessor and granting absolution, with their implicit omission of the church concept of hierarchy, or his view that not all who are baptized receive Christ through this baptism and hence sinners need a second baptism in or by the Spirit, find obvious parallels in Bogomil and, generally, dualist teachings. Other aspects of his teachings, like his veneration for the Eucharist are, of course, totally incompatible with Bogomilism, and these parallels and contrasts illustrate the points of convergence and divergence between Byzantine mysticism and

Bogomilism, in particular, and Christian mysticism and dualist heresy in general. While both Byzantine mysticism and Bogomilism shared practices such as asceticism, contemplation and divine vision and notions such as that of man's ability to ascend directly to God, there were also considerable differences between the two trends of religiosity, some of which could on occasion be blurred in the pursuit of 'pneumatic' Christianity.[127] Another trend in Byzantine Christianity, especially in its popular forms, that could on occasions approach dangerously close to dualist heresy, was Byzantine alternative demonology which often ascribed to the demons powers greater than normative Christianity could allow and of which Bogomilism was a 'particularly well structured and clearly thought out version'.[128] Bogomil preoccupation with the need to defend and purify oneself from the domination and aggression of the demonic powers in the world and the claims of the Bogomil adepts to have gained salvation from the diabolical dimension of reality through their spiritual baptism, could be popularly seen as an expertise in controlling and banishing demons and to further increase the appeal of Bogomil missionaries.[129] Moreover, as a Consul of the Philosophers, Michael Psellus and his pupils revived interest in Plato and the Neo-Platonists like Proclus and Plotinus, and it is commonly assumed that Psellus rediscovered and probably compiled in its present form the most important and seminal Hermetic texts, *Corpus Hermeticum*.[130]

However, Psellus had to defend himself against accusations of heterodoxy and in the late eleventh century some forms of Neo-Platonism were considered nearly as dangerous as Bogomil dualism itself by the conservative ecclesiastics in Constantinople. In 1082 Psellus' pupil and successor, John Italus, faced, along with his pupils, trial for their Platonic transgressions and were even threatened by a hostile mob. The trial appears to have been largely politically motivated, but in the *Synodicon of Orthodoxy* of 1082, John Italus was anathematized for paganism and heresy together with the heresiarch Bogomil and certain contemporary Bogomil preachers who were already active in Panormus (Palermo) in Sicily.[131] One of Italus' pupils, Eustratius, who was not implicated in the trial, evolved into a leading theologian and commentator on Aristotle as well as becoming Metropolitan of Nicaea, but was none the less arraigned for unorthodoxy and deposed in 1117.

Byzantium also saw the increasing activity of heterodox preachers like Nilus the Calabrian and the priest Blachernites, who had succeeded in winning converts from even the 'great houses' in Constantinople. Both preachers were eventually condemned by the Church to a 'perpetual anathema', but while Nilus was preaching some form of Monophysitism and had a strong Armenian following, Blachernites was accused of consorting with the Enthusiasts (the Massalians) and of undermining 'great houses in the capital'.[132]

The preaching and the anathematization of Nilus and Blachernites were symptomatic of the Byzantine religious climate, with its agitation and heresy trials, during the reign of the second Comnenian emperor, Alexius I Comnenus (1081–1118). In 1095 Pope Urban II had called for the recovery of the Holy Sepulchre, and the reign of Alexius was to witness the First Crusade (1095–9), the conquest of the Holy Land, the formation of the Latin Kingdom of Jerusalem and the foundation of the Knights Templar. Besides his volatile and delicate relations with the crusaders, Alexius Comnenus turned his attention to more spiritual concerns and took vigorous measures against the spread of heresies throughout Byzantium. Alexius' own mother was suspected of heresy and, with his marked predilection for theological debates, the emperor became a forceful, if not obsessive, defender of Orthodoxy to be eulogized by his daughter, the historian Anna Comnena, as second only to Constantine the Great. During the eleventh century Paulician detachments had been deployed in Byzantine military campaigns, their presence being reported as far a field as Sicily, and these Sicilian Paulician regiments took part in the battles with the Normans in southern Italy around 1041. Yet the Paulicians in Thrace continued to cause trouble for the empire in the second half of the century and some of them ventured to enter into anti-Byzantine alliances with the Pechenegs who had settled in the north-east Balkans around the middle of the century. Alexius' confrontation with the Paulician sectarians was, according to Anna Comnena, not only military but apostolic, for he tried to win them back to Orthodoxy through protracted theological discussions. Alexius focused his efforts on the area around Philippopolis in northern Thrace, where, according to Anna Comnena, nearly all the inhabitants were heretics, Armenians or 'Manichaeans' (Paulicians), so that it had become a truly 'Manichaean' city, 'a meeting place of all evils'.[133] Consequently Alexius launched an anti-heretical crusade in Thrace, where 'whole towns and districts infected by various heresies' were 'brought back by diverse means' to the Orthodox faith.[134]

Besides the heresies prevalent in Thrace the emperor also had to deal with the rising influence of Bogomilism in his imperial capital, where the 'pernicious race' of the Bogomils had arisen like 'a very great cloud' which had gone 'deep even into the great houses' and the higher clergy of Byzantium and had assaulted many souls 'like fire'.[135] In her usual imaginative style Anna Comnena likened Alexius' crusade against the Bogomils to a conjuration of 'a snake hiding in a hole' which was lurking in secrecy until the emperor 'lured it and brought it out to the light by chanting mysterious incantations'. Early in the persecution against the Bogomils it became clear that the heresy had a teacher and 'chief repre-sentative', the monk Basil, who was assisted by twelve apostles. Basil was one of the most outstanding figures in the history of the Bogomil movement who was said to have mastered the Bogomil teachings after fifteen years' training, followed by forty years of preaching, in which he had 'disseminated his wickedness everywhere'. For Anna Comnena, Basil was the 'arch-satrap' of Satanael, but for Alexius he held out an alluring promise of erudite theological debate and he finally managed to entertain him in the palace. In an encounter reminiscent of and yet very different from that between Mani and Shapur, the emperor and his brother, Sebas-tocrator Isaac, tried to convince Basil of their intention of becoming Bogomil neophytes and demanded a detailed explanation of the heretical teaching. The heresiarch began to elucidate the essentials of the Bogomil doctrine, apparently as taught to listeners, and when his long oration appeared to have come to an end, Alexius drew aside the curtains, behind which a secretary had written down Basil's account. The whole senate, the military elite and the elders of the Church were convened and the heresiarch was threatened with trial, torture and death at the stake but he welcomed the threats and remained, in the words of Anna Comnena, 'the same Basil, an inflexible and very brave Bogomil' who preferred to embrace 'his' Satanael.

Oddly, or perhaps predictably, Alexius Comnenus chose to keep Basil close to the royal palace in a specially prepared house, where the emperor indulged in theological arguments with him but the house was affected by a poltergeist-like phenomenon – a hailstorm of stones accompanied by an earthquake. Anna Comnena attributed the miracle to the wrath of Satanael's devils, enraged at the revelation of their secrets to the emperor and the fierce persecution of the Bogomils. The emperor had ordered a systematic pursuit of 'Basil's disciples and fellow-mystics from all over the world', and particularly his twelve apostles, with the goal of the heresy's total extermination in Byzantium. Many Orthodox Christians were also apprehended in the campaigns and to avoid misjudgement the emperor devised a dramatic rite of passage – two pyres were erected in the imperial *manège* on the coast of the Bosphorus, one of which had an enormous cross attached to it. The suspects were urged to choose on which pyre to martyr themselves – either on the one with the cross if they were true Christians, or on the crossless pyre if they were heretics. When the suspects had divided into two groups and were ready to be thrown on to the fire, the pyres were suddenly extinguished on Alexius' orders. Those who had chosen the pyre with the cross were released, while the intransigent heretics were sent to prison, where the emperor persisted in debating their 'hideous religion' with them.

The emperor and the patriarchate finally decided to confront Basil with a similar choice – death in the flames or recanting at the cross. With intense expectation of a miracle, a crowd saw Basil the Physician approach the pyre with the psalmic words 'But it shall not come nigh thee; only with thy eyes shalt thou behold' and finally 'the flames, as if deeply enraged against him, ate the impious man up, without any odour arising or even a fresh appearance of smoke, only one thin smoky line could be seen in the middle of the flames'.[136] For Anna Comnena the *auto-da-fé* of the Bogomil heresiarch was the culmination of Alexius' apostolic mission, 'the crowning act of the emperor's long labours and successes' which was an 'innovation of startling boldness'.

Alexius' crusade and Basil's execution *c.* 1109–111 clearly show that at the time of the First Crusade Bogomilism was regarded as the greatest heretical menace in Byzantium. About half a century after Euthymius of Acmonia warned of the dangers of Bogomil proselytism in western Anatolia, it was, according to Anna Comnena, penetrating the higher strata of Byzantine secular and ecclesiastical circles.

However, except for the speculation that the teachings of the Manichaeans (i.e. Paulicians) and the Massalians coalesced in Bogomilism, and some brief cursory comments, Anna Comnena preferred not 'to defile her tongue' with its teachings, as she was 'a woman, the most honourable of the Porphyrogeniti and Alexius' eldest scion' and alluded to the work of the 'best authority on ecclesiastical dogma', Euthymius Zigabenus.[137] Euthymius Zigabenus had been commissioned by Alexius to expound and refute the ancient and new heresies and his tract *Panoplia Dogmatica*[138] inevitably contained a refutation of Bogomilism. The anti-Bogomil section is apparently based on Basil's account of the Bogomil teachings before his imperial 'listeners', and is consequently by far the most exhaustive and systematic account of Bogomil doctrine. While largely confirming previous evidence of the monarchian nature of Bogomil dualism and its initiatory and ascetic practices, Euthymius made use of his privileged information to expound in greater depth on Bogomil cosmology and the concept of the Logos and the Trinity, the allegorical system of interpreting the Scriptures, the mystical practices of initiates and the distinctive demonology of the sect. Euthymius' evidence is complex and uneven but it shows that aspects of Bogomil teachings had developed a distinctly Gnostic-dualist character and that some of them were, moreover, seen as esoteric. His account provides some interesting clues as to how these apparently new attitudes to esotericism, a more systematic allegorical interpretation of the Scriptures and gradual disclosure of dualist theology and anthropogony could have appealed to Byzantine theological, intellectual and mystical circles at the end of the twelfth century.

Trials in Constantinople

Euthymius Zigabenus praised Alexius Comnenus' anti-heretical crusades as wars against the 'apostate Dragon', the 'great Assyrian mind', and saw in Basil's *auto-da-fé* the crushing of the head of the heretical serpent of Bogomilism. Yet, in spite of the campaigns of Alexius Comnenus, Bogomilism remained a heretical force in Byzantium and extended its influence not only into the western Balkans but also western Europe. Euthymius of Peribleptos and Anna Comnena had warned that Bogomilism was using the structures of the Orthodox Church itself in its proselytism and towards the mid twelfth century several synods were convened to expose the Bogomil presence within the Church. The series of ecclesiastical scandals culminated in 1147 when the patriarch was deposed, charged with Bogomil sympathies.

In 1140 a synod at Constantinople posthumously anathematized the monk Constantine Chrysomalus for his heretical writings, the *Golden Sermons*, which were preserved and circulated in the Constantinople monastery of St Nicholas. Some of Chrysomalus' teachings, such as the

existence of two souls – one sinful, one sinless – in man or the denial of
the spiritual efficacy of the Christian baptism by water, were denounced
as Massalian and Bogomil. Potentially more dangerous for the Orthodox
Church were the beliefs attributed to Constantine that all authority
should be denounced and that those who revere any ruler actually pay
homage to Satan, which finds obvious Bogomil parallels. On the whole,
however, his teachings seem to derive largely from the tradition of
Byzantine mysticism, as elaborated by Symeon the Theologian, and
probably were partially coloured by heretical tendencies, showing again
how extreme mysticism can develop into heterodoxy and approach
dualist heresy.[139] Whether Constantine Chrysomalus attempted a
synthesis between Byzantine mysticism and Bogomil dualism is impossible to say, but prior to his anathematization his teachings had apparently gained wide currency in Constantinople monastic circles.

Three years later another synod in Constantinople deposed and
anathematized two Orthodox bishops of Cappadocia as Bogomil
adherents. The two bishops, of the diocese of Tyana, Clement of
Sosandra and Leontius of Balbissa, preached that the miracles attributed
to the power of the cross were effected by demons and that the cross
should not be revered unless it bore the inscription, 'Jesus Christ, Son of
God'. They urged their flock towards monasticism, strongly condemned
icon-worship and had even ordained certain deaconesses and allowed
them to take part in the liturgies. Several weeks later another synod was
convened to condemn another heretical preacher from Cappadocia – the
monk Niphon who was charged with propagating Bogomilism. Initially
consigned to the monastery of Peribleptos, Niphon was finally excommunicated by another synod in 1144 and condemned to prison.

Although imprisoned, Niphon was to provoke a crisis in the patriarchate when in 1146 the patriarchal throne passed to Cosmas II Atticus,
who himself had earlier been suspected of heresy. There are indications
that during the preceding patriarchate of Michael II several Bogomils had
been sentenced to the stake in Constantinople but the new patriarch
Cosmas decided to release Niphon. What is more, he apparently
considered the heretical monk a close companion, as Niphon was
frequently entertained in the patriarchal palace and could preach freely
again. It has been argued that Niphon was actually Basil's successor in
Constantinople;[140] if this could be verified, the year of 1146 would mark
a unique affiliation between the heresiarch of Bogomilism and the

patriarch of Orthodoxy. Regardless of Niphon's position in the Bogomil movement, his presence in the patriarchal palace could not be tolerated for long in Constantinople. In 1147 the patriarch's adversaries succeeded in staging his dethronement and the reimprisonment of his Bogomil associate. At a synod attended by the new emperor, Manuel I Comnenus, Cosmas II Atticus tried to counter his enemies with excommunication but was finally deposed and disgraced as a Bogomil supporter.

Opinions vary whether the patriarch had been made the scapegoat of a political intrigue or whether he was indeed a Bogomil sympathizer. What is certain is that in the twelfth century Byzantine Orthodoxy perceived Bogomilism as its main heretical enemy and that Bogomilism could penetrate even the patriarchate in Constantinople or could convert and use Orthodox bishops in Cappadocia for its own propaganda. Cappadocia seemed to mark the easternmost reach of Bogomilism in Anatolia. The Balkan fortunes and the western course of Bogomilism in the second half of the twelfth century are better recorded, revealing important transformations in the Bogomil movement as it entered its third century of underground existence with the dethronement of a Constantinople patriarch, who had been condemned as a Bogomil adherent.

Manuel Comnenus and Stefan Nemanja

Emperor Manuel I Comnenus (1143–80) may have witnessed and even sanctioned the dethronement of Patriarch Cosmas Atticus but his prowestern affinities and overtures to the papacy often brought him into open conflict with the Orthodox Church. Despite the problems caused by the armies during the Second Crusade (1147–9) Manuel Comnenus remained one of the most Latinophile Byzantine emperors. With his grand design to restore the old *imperium romanum* and with his armies engaged at various stages in places as disparate as Cappadocia, southern Italy and Egypt, Manuel Comnenus succeeded in restoring Byzantine control over the western Balkans against the persistent encroachment of the Hungarian kingdom. By the end of his reign most of Croatia, Dalmatia and Bosnia were under his authority; the Serbian state, recently united under the Grand Zhupan Stefan Nemanja, was also defeated and accepted Byzantine suzerainty.

As well as his military campaigns, one of Manuel's ruling passions was astrology and while the poet John Camaterus dedicated a poetical tract on the twelve signs of the zodiac to him, the chronicler Michael Glykas, who criticized his astrological pursuits, was partially blinded and exiled. Later Orthodox tradition asserts that Manuel was exposed to heretical influences and it is curious that two such contemporaries – the deposed patriarch Cosmas and the reigning emperor Manuel – were to become targets of Orthodox suspicions. According to the later *Life of St Hilarion*[141] it was St Hilarion, then bishop in Macedonia, who fortified the Orthodox faith of the emperor, but the bishop also encountered numerous Manichaeans (probably Paulicians), Armenians (Monophysites) and Bogomils in his diocese. To confront the increasing influence of the heretics, who were described as 'beasts of prey' attacking and corrupting the Orthodox Church, the bishop ardently preached 'pious dogmas' to his flock and challenged the heretical preachers in heated and often violent debates. He overcame the influence of the Paulicians and the Armenian Monophysites, but he needed an imperial edict from Manuel Comnenus to purge the Bogomil heresy from his flock. Some of the Bogomils were converted (or feigned conversion) to Orthodoxy, while the unrepentant Bogomils were condemned to banishment and exile. That anti-Bogomil persecution raged during the reign of Manuel Comnenus is further confirmed by the canonist Theodore Balsamon, patriarch of Antioch (1185–90), who reported that towards the end of Manuel's reign 'whole regions and fortresses' in the Byzantine empire remained infected by the Bogomil heresy.[142] The Italian theologian Hugh Etherianus, who was Manuel's advisor on Latin theological matters, deemed it necessary to compose a polemic against the Bogomils in Byzantium and styled them 'Pathereni', which by the end of the century was the standard term for the Cathars in Italy.[143]

One of the main purposes of Hugh Etherianus' tract was to provide his imperial patron with an authoritative theological justification for the more severe prosecution and death penalties for the Bogomils which had been requested in Manuel's court. However, in the last years of his reign Manuel did not take new measures against the Bogomils; the only surviving abjuration formula for Bogomil converts into Orthodoxy probably dates from the beginning of his reign and specifies the rules for the reconciliation of Bogomils, while condemning their 'nocturnal initiatory rites'.[144] The spread of Bogomilism in Serbia, however, provoked a vigorous response from Stefan Nemanja, the founder of the Serbian Nemanjid dynasty (1168–1371), who restored Serbian independence soon after the death of Manuel Comnenus in 1180. He summoned a great assembly against the 'heretics' in Serbia, who were undoubtedly Bogomils, which condemned their teachings and strictly proscribed their activities and books. Bogomilism, however, had apparently won considerable support among the Serbian nobility and Stefan Nemanja had to conduct a military campaign to eradicate the heresy. The Bogomils suffered severe persecution – some met their death by fire, others were banished and their books were burnt.[145] While Stefan Nemanja's crusade had undoubtedly dealt a severe blow to Bogomilism in Serbia, his youngest son, St Sava, the founder of the autocephalous Serbian Church, had to continue the struggle against the Bogomils, who were still active in Serbia. The combined effort of the secular and ecclesiastical Serbian authorities seems to have been effective – the Bogomils did not regain any prominence in Serbia until the mid fourteenth century.

Persecution by Manuel Comnenus and Stefan Nemanja apparently drove Bogomil groups into the western Balkans, where Dalmatia and Bosnia emerged as centres of the heresy, and there are also indications of contemporary Bogomil migrations into Transylvanian lands.[146] The reigns of the two monarchs witnessed dramatic changes in the fortunes of medieval dualism in western Europe. At some stage during the first two centuries of their history, most probably around the beginning of the twelfth century, the Bogomils in the Balkans and Asia Minor began to establish communities or 'churches' with a developed hierarchy and ritual. Two of these churches played a decisive role in the crystallization of the Cathar movement in Italy and France and entered the inquisition archives as the source of all dualist churches in the west – *Ecclesia Drugunthiae* and *Ecclesia Bulgariae*.

CHAPTER FOUR

The Dualist Communion

Along with Gothic art and architecture, the renewed ideals of monasticism, asceticism and apostolic life, the advent of the dualist heresy in the west was symptomatic of the religious enthusiasm and permutations of the twelfth century. The diffusion of the dualist tradition in western Europe reached its climax in the growth of an organized and widespread Cathar movement in northern Italy and southern France. Contemporary Catholic accounts often refer to the crucial impact of Balkan dualism on its formation. Modern theories may differ in their estimation of the chronology and the scale of Bogomil influence on original Catharism but invariably confirm its vital role in providing a new, dualist framework for western heretical and heterodox currents. Signs of religious dissent in western Christendom do appear in the early Middle Ages and undoubtedly there were more unrecorded heterodoxies that troubled the Church in this era. However, the process of formulating and recognizing heresy *vis-à-vis* orthodoxy was to some extent delayed by the absence of genuine order and a coherent, authoritative approach to heterodoxy until about 1000. Such an approach was found in the framework of the increasing search for and exercise of religious and secular order in western societies after the beginning of the second Christian millennium,[1] when new heresies also made a more forceful entry on the west European scene.

Heresy in the West

In 991, on his consecration as Archbishop of Rheims, Gerbert of Aurillac made a solemn profession of faith in the sanctity of both the New and Old Testaments, in the legitimacy of marriage and of eating meat and the existence of an evil spirit *per arbitrarum*, not by nature but by choice.[2] Since these 'articles of faith' are in immediate opposition to the current

Bogomil and the later Cathar tenets, it has been argued that either Gerbert was declaring his opposition to some proto-Cathar movement in his province or was himself suspected of dualist transgressions and had to defend his orthodoxy. Gerbert was said to have studied in his youth in the Moorish schools in Spain; later his reputed learning in theology, mathematics and the natural sciences was popularly believed to have been achieved through magic and he was credited with having an 'oracular head'. As the first French pope, Sylvester II (999–1003), Gerbert presided over western Christendom at the turn of the millennium, but eighty years later Cardinal Benno was to attribute Gerbert's meteoric rise to his skills in sorcery. Among the feats assigned to Sylvester II was the founding of a 'papal' school of magic in eleventh-century Rome.

In the first year of Sylvester's papacy, near Châlons-sur-Marne, north-east France, a heretic named Leutard appeared who, after a dream of a 'great swarm of bees' entering his body through his genitals, entered the local church to break the cross and the image of the Saviour. Leutard declared that the cross-breaking was inspired by a revelation from God and his preachings won over adherents among the common people but, being exposed by the bishop of the diocese, he threw himself into a well.

Earlier, in the late tenth century, Vilgard, a scholar from Ravenna, indulged in pagan and classical learning to the extent that he provoked the manifestation of demons in the appearance of the poets Virgil, Horace and Juvenal, who encouraged his excessive pagan studies. Vilgard's preaching led to his condemnation as a heretic but his teachings spread in Italy and are alleged to have reached and provoked persecution in Sardinia and Spain.[3] Around 1018 'Manichaeans' appeared in Aquitaine, who rejected the baptism and the Cross and apparently observed strict asceticism.[4] Four years later ten of the canons of the Church of the Holy Cross at Orléans were accused of being 'Manichaeans' and of worshipping the Devil, first as an 'Ethiopian' and also as an 'angel of light'.[5] The canons were part of a larger anti-sacramental group of heretics comprised of eminent clerics and nobles, including the confessor of Queen Constance. Besides rejecting the sacraments of the Church, the heretics of Orléans denied the human birth of Christ by the Virgin and the reality of his Passion and Resurrection. They offered their disciples deliverance from 'the Charybdis of false belief' and illumination through the rite of imposition of hands which was deemed to grant salvation and the 'gift of the Holy Spirit'. Despite their manifest loathing of matter and human body, the Orléans heretics were accused of indulging in indiscriminate nocturnal orgies, cremating the children conceived in the debauchery and collecting and preserving the ashes with great veneration. The heretics were brought to trial before the French king Robert the Pious and an assemblage of bishops, and were consigned to the flames, not before Queen Constance struck out the eye of her former confessor.

In 1022 the bishop of Arras-Cambrai in northern France sought to convert another group of heretics in his diocese who denounced the sacraments, the veneration of the Cross and practised asceticism by restraining from 'carnal longings'. The heresy taught in Arras was of an Italian extraction and around 1025 a 'strange heresy' was disclosed at a castle above Monforte in north-west Italy.[6] The heretics, including the countess of the stronghold, were mostly nobles and were considered to have come into Italy 'from some unknown part of the world'. The heretical society at Monforte believed in a Trinity in which, besides God the eternal Father, the Son was 'the soul of man beloved of God' and the Holy Ghost – 'the comprehension of divine truths by which all things are separately governed'. In their belief Jesus Christ is the soul of man 'in the flesh born of the Virgin Mary' who is identified as the Sacred Scripture, whereas the Holy Ghost is the 'devout comprehension of the Sacred Scriptures'. The Monforte heretics observed severe asceticism and while abstaining form the 'corruption' of sexual intercourse they argued that if the human race would adhere to such abstention it 'would be begotten like bees without coition'. The castle at Monforte was taken by a strong force of knights sent by the Archbishop of Milan, Aribert; the heretics were brought to Milan, where they had to choose between a burning pyre and a 'Cross of the Lord' fixed close to the stake.

Towards the middle of the eleventh century Châlons-sur-Marne saw another outbreak of heresy, this time diffused by 'Manichaeans', who formed secret conventicles and used the rite of the imposition of hands to confer the Holy Spirit. Yet despite the label 'Manichaeans' and the charge of extreme asceticism, as with the previous outbreaks of western heresy in the century, there are no indications that the heretics adhered to any form of religious dualism. Most of these western heretical groups shared rejection of the sacraments and the clergy, invariably coupled with asceticism and often denunciation of worship of the Cross. They could be viewed as extreme manifestations of the evangelistic *Zeitgeist* of the eleventh century, with its monastic renascence and reformist zeal. Yet certain doctrines professed by the heretics – the rejection of Christ's Incarnation, Passion and Resurrection (Orléans), the denunciation of procreation as resulting from 'corruption' (Monforte), and the repeated hostility to the Cross – depart radically from Christian dogma and have often been attributed not to overstated and distorted apostolic impulses but to early penetration of Bogomil ideas in the west. It is the Byzantine colonies in southern Italy and Sicily, which were to be conquered in the late eleventh century by the Normans, that are usually considered as the stepping-stone for the early introduction of Bogomilism to the west and Bogomil preachers are known to have been active in Palermo in Sicily in about 1082.

Yet the early spread of Bogomilism to the west and the sudden outbreaks of western heresy in the eleventh century are surrounded by obscurity and unsolved problems. Earlier trends of research into the origins of these first outbreaks of early western heresies have tended to recognize behind them Bogomil influences at various degrees of intensity, but lately they are seen as developments that should be understood predominantly in the terms of the religious and social changes occurring in the eleventh to twelfth centuries in the west. While a Bogomil impact on some of these heretical groups should not be dismissed *a priori*, the development of western dissent and the notion of dangerous, hidden heresy threatening the Church were variously affected by the changing attitudes and reactions to socio-religious crises among what has been described as clerical elites, dominating both the spiritual and temporal spheres, and guarding their monopoly on literacy and power[7] (while the upsurges in popular antipathy and reaction to alleged heresies also contributed significantly to the climate of intolerance). The first anti-heretical accusations and supressions displayed, too, the first signs of powerful stereotyping and demonization of the heretics, suspected or real, and this approach was to become increasingly characteristic of the Church's response to the challenge of heresy in the twelfth and thirteenth centuries.

It was in the twelfth century that Catharism emerged as the most developed and influential form of western dualism and from its beginnings it bore the unmistakable traces of the formative influence of Balkan dualism.

The Rise of Catharism

While recounting the transgressions of Vilgard of Ravenna, the chronicler Ralph the Bald linked the emergence and the spread of his heresy to the prophecy in Revelation 20:7 of Satan's release from his prison after a thousand years. After the repeated incidents of heretical agitation in the first fifty years of the new Christian millennium, the second half of the eleventh century failed to fulfil such expectations. In the early twelfth century the popular success of the wandering preachers, with their yearning for piety, voluntary poverty and an evangelical life, was coupled with the rise and spread of new and more vigorous reformist and heretical movements often led by charismatic figures like the notorious Tanchelm of Antwerp, who was active in the Low Countries, or Henry the Monk in France. Inspired by apostolic ideals, heretical preachers and reformists attacked the Church hierarchy, sacraments and corruption. Particularly zealous among them was the apostate monk Henry, who, having plunged the northern French city of Le Mans into anti-clerical strife in 1116, moved to stir more anti-ecclesiastical agitation in the country of Toulouse which embraced most of Languedoc. There he encountered around 1133-4 another spirited and even more extreme preacher, Peter of Bruis, who rejected also the church buildings, the Old Testament and the cult of the Cross, which was denounced as the instrument of Christ's torture and death. Peter urged his followers to revenge the torments and death of Christ by breaking and burning crosses, but was hurled into one of his bonfires of crosses at St Gilles.

Towards the middle of the twelfth century a new heresy was taking shape, which would soon confront the spiritual authority of Rome in the Rhineland in the north and from Lombardy to the Pyrenees in the south: the movement of the Cathars or Cathari (the pure ones). The earliest certain indication of the rise of the Cathar heresy is the disclosure in 1143-4 of a heretical community at Cologne which was led by its own bishop.[8] The Cologne heretics regarded themselves as the true apostolic Church, as Christ's poor, who were 'not of this world'. They were divided into three grades – listeners, believers and the elect. Through the rite of the placing of hands, the listener could enter the ranks of the believers and after a probationary period could join the elect and be 'baptized in fire and the Spirit'. Women were also initiated into the grades of the believer and the elect, but marriage, except that between virgins, was condemned as fornication. Besides sexual intercourse, the Cologne heretics abstained from milk and any food born of coition and blessed their food and drink with the *Pater Noster*. They rejected the fire of purgatory after death but taught that upon death the soul was sent either to 'eternal rest or punishment' and fell back on Ecclesiastes 11:3 – 'And if the tree fall toward the south, or toward the north, in the place where the tree falleth, there it shall be' (*KJV*). The Cologne sectarians claimed that they had numerous adherents 'throughout the world', particularly among the clergy and the monks, and that their religion had persisted in secrecy 'from the time of the martyrs' in Greece (Byzantium) and elsewhere. The unrepentant Cologne heretics were burnt along with their bishop and his assistant but their emergence and suppression was just the beginning of a determined and prolonged challenge to the western Church.

The activities of the Cologne heretics were exposed in an appeal by the prior Eberwin of Steinfeld to the churchman and theologian St Bernard of Clairvaux. In 1145 St Bernard, who had already helped the elevation of the Knights Templar and his own Cistercian Order, embarked on a preaching mission to Toulouse to redeem the region from the heretical influence of the apostate monk Henry. St Bernard did not encounter the turbulent monk but wrote to the Count of Toulouse, Alphonse Jordan, who apparently patronized Henry, about the critical religious situation in the area around Toulouse – 'The churches are without congregations, congregations are without priests, priests are without proper reverence, and, finally, Christians are without Christ'.[9] St Bernard warned the count that after being expelled from all parts of France the heretical preacher had found refuge in the lands of the County of Toulouse and there 'he revels in all his fury among the flock of Christ . . .'. St Bernard's mission encountered anticlerical attitudes among some of the Languedoc nobility and detected heretical currents in Toulouse. Around the same time, the Liège clergy wrote to the pope that a new heresy seemed 'to have overflowed various regions' of France, 'a heresy so varied and manifold that it seems impossible to characterize it under one single name'. The heretical community in Liège itself, with its militant anti-ecclesiastical character, comprised the grades of the listeners and believers and had its hierarchy of 'priests' and 'prelates'.[10]

Besides anticlerical agitation in the Low Countries and Languedoc, reformist and heretical movements also appeared in Italy amid the protracted disputes between the popes and the Holy Roman emperors. Meanwhile, the Crusades had brought about cultural and commercial intercourse between east and west which, in the words of M. Lambert, 'facilitated formal and informal contacts with the underground Bogomil churches in Constantinople, Asia Minor and the Balkans',[11] while another possible route of dualist penetration of the west was via the Greek monks visiting and settling in western monasteries in the eleventh century and onwards, when Bogomilism had gained a number of converts in Byzantine monastic circles. Byzantium established stronger trading contacts with Italian cities like Venice and Genoa and with southern France, while the crusading movements, the foundation of the crusader domains, with the opening of trade routes, provided the possibilities for new religious exchanges in an era when the western spiritual climate was particularly receptive to new religious ideas. The Cologne heretics had acknowledged their Byzantine pedigree in 1143; besides Bogomil missionaries the orbit of Bogomil proselytism in the west was extended through crusaders and merchants returning from the east. While asserting that the earliest Bogomil dualist bishoprics were set up in Drugunthia (in Thrace), Bulgaria and Philadelphia (in western Anatolia), *Tractatus de hereticis* (*c.* 1266–7), ascribed to the inquisitor Anselm of Alessandria, emphasized the vital role of the Bogomil Church in Constantinople in the diffusion of dualism in the west, which led to the establishment of the first Cathar church in northern France that was probably connected to the Cathar communities in the Rhineland.[12] In Anselm's tract the dualist church in the new Rome was founded by Greeks from Constantinople, who went as merchants to Bulgaria and, being converted to Bogomilism, established a community and a 'Bishop of the Greeks' in the imperial capital. The tract also related that the Bogomil Church in Constantinople converted Bosnian merchants who preached the heresy in Bosnia and, 'having increased in number', established a bishop who was called the 'Bishop of Sclavonia or Bosnia'. French crusaders, who 'went to Constantinople to conquer the land', variously read as an allusion to the First or Second Crusade, were also converted and founded a dualist community led by their own heretical bishop in Constantinople, styled the 'Bishop of the Latins'.

Particularly important is Anselm's testimony to the spread of the dualist heresy in France, which he attributed to the French dualist crusaders returning from Constantinople who preached, 'increased in numbers' and established a 'Bishop of France'. Their teachings penetrated Provence to win over numerous adherents and four new heretical bishops were established, the bishops of Carcassonne, Albi, Toulouse and Agen. The tract explicitly stated that because the French crusaders were originally 'led astray by Bulgars . . . throughout France these persons are called Bulgarian heretics'. A dualist mission from France reached the Milan area and, in Concorezzo, converted the would-be first heretical bishop in Italy, Mark the Gravedigger, along with his associates John Judeus and Joseph. The newly converted heretics embarked on preaching missions in Lombardy as well as in Treviso to the east and Tuscany to the south. Mark the Gravedigger's mission apparently won a substantial following and as attested by the treatise *De heresi catharorum in Lombardia* (*c.* 1200–14) he was eventually elevated as bishop of all Lombard, Tuscan and Trevisan heretics.[13]

While Catharism was gaining ground in Italy, western Christendom witnessed a new series of outbreaks of heresy, some of which, besides their anticlerical tenor, also seem related to the spread of Catharism. It has been argued that German crusaders returning from the ill-fated Second Crusade, preached by St Bernard of Clairvaux in 1144, revitalized the dualist heresy in the Rhineland[14] and in 1163 another dualist group was brought to trial in Cologne and 'fiercely burned' near the Jewish cemetery outside the town. The monk, Eckbert of Schönau,[15] wrote a tract against the new Cologne heretics, which freely draws upon Augustine's anti-Manichaean writings, while the friend of his sister, St Elizabeth of Schönau, St Hildegard of Bingen recorded a vision in which she saw the emergence of the Cathars as an outcome of the release of the Devil, 'the old serpent with amulets on his vestment', from the bottomless pit, and the unleashing of the four winds at the corners of the earth, as prophesized in the Revelation. In his first sermon Eckbert claimed that the heretics, 'the hidden men', had increased in many countries and were called 'Piphli' in Flanders, 'Texerant' in France and Cathars in Germany. Names like 'Publicans' or 'Popelicans', deriving from the term Paulicians, were also becoming common in western Europe and around 1162, when Thomas à Becket was consecrated Archbishop of Canterbury, a group of Publicans reached England and embarked on propagating their heresy. William of Newburgh[16] asserted that the Publicans had spread their heresy in France, Spain, Italy and Germany but in England the Publicans were denounced at a synod in Oxford, publicly flogged, branded, driven out of the city and left to perish in the winter cold. This 'pious severity', said William of Newburgh, not only purged England of the heretical pestilence but prevented it from ever again reaching the island.

At about the same time the Archbishop of Rheims was prosecuting another group of Publicans in Flanders, while in 1167 Publicans were questioned about the secret tenets of their heresy in a trial at Vézelay and some of them were condemned to death. Towards the end of the twelfth century in Italy the term 'Patarene' was already interchangeable with Cathar; often the names given to the dualist communities were based on the regions or the towns associated with them. The Cathars from the area around Albi, where the earliest Cathar bishopric in southern France was founded, came to be known as Albigensians and this name acquired wide currency. However, in a number of cases dualist communities in the west adopted names like Bulgars and Sclavini to acknowledge the Balkan origin of their heresy.[17]

Catharism in Languedoc

By the end of the twelfth century Catharism was already well established in Languedoc, where it secured the favour not only of much of the rural aristocracy but also of great Midi nobles like Roger Trencavel II, Viscount of Béziers and Carcassonne, Raymond-Roger, Count of Foix, and Raymond VI (1194–1222), the Count of Toulouse. In contrast to the prevalent climate in western Europe, Languedoc society was markedly more tolerant and cosmopolitan and had also attained a high degree of prosperity. With its distinctive and diverse culture Languedoc was a prominent centre of the twelfth-century 'renaissance' and the cradle of the troubadour lyric poetry, which flourished under the patronage of the noble courts, including the affluent court of Raymond VI, himself a composer of lyrics. Apart from the flowering of its secular culture the region was plagued by political pressures in the wake of the departure of Raymond IV (1093–1105), Count of Toulouse and Marquis of Provence, for the Holy Land during the First Crusade. The rule of the Counts of Toulouse in Languedoc itself was affected by the specific feudal system in the region and threatened by the conflicting ambitions for sovereignty over Languedoc of the Capetian French kings, the kings of England and the kings of Aragon (the Counts of Barcelona).

While the Languedoc religious climate was unusually tolerant, the movement for reform within the Church had not left a strong imprint on the Languedoc clergy. The Jews enjoyed good treatment and later the Counts of Toulouse were often accused of appointing Jews to public offices. In the twelfth century the Provençal Jewry underwent a cultural and religious ferment and it was the Provençal Kabbalist school that produced in 1176 the first classic book of medieval Kabbalah, the enigmatic *Sepher Bahir*.[18] Indeed, religious interchange between the Cathars and some Jewish Kabbalist circles in Languedoc has been repeatedly postulated but not yet demonstrated conclusively. The sectarian and heretical preachers were rarely apprehended in Languedoc and following the anticlerical agitation in the first half of the century, a new gospel-inspired movement was spreading in the area: the Waldensians or the Poor of Lyons. The Waldensians were excommunicated as heretics by Pope Lucius III in 1184 but the reputed apostolic life of their preachers was in marked contrast to the conduct of the Languedoc clergy, which abounded in wealthy, worldly and corrupt prelates. The Languedoc Church did not enjoy a high reputation throughout the region and the lessening of her authority was to pave the way for the missionary advance of the Waldensians and the Cathars.[19]

The Languedoc clergy was exposed to the encroachment of the local aristocracy on Church land and tithes. The conflicts between the Church and the nobility further facilitated the spread of the anticlerical teachings of the Cathars, which won the support of many Languedoc nobles, who did not bar the Cathars from preaching in their fiefs and even allowed them access to their courts where the Cathar missionaries won over new sympathizers. Whereas Catharism permeated all social classes, it was the noble patronage of the Cathars that was crucial for the firm establishment of the heresy in Languedoc. The ascetic dualist faith of the Cathars flourished in the noble courts alongside the troubadour courtly love. While courtly love embellished the chivalric cult of the chosen lady, Catharism won numerous adherents among the noble ladies of Languedoc[20] who included, for example, both the wife and the sister of the nominally Catholic Count of Foix, respectively Philippa and Esclarmonda. While some noble ladies who converted to Catharism, like Esclarmonda, sought and received the rite of *consolamentum* to become important figures in the Cathar movement, the male noble patrons of the Cathars did not necessarily join the heretical ranks and when accepted as believers they usually deferred the *consolamentum* until their deathbed. Even the Count of Toulouse, Raymond VI, was later rumoured by his enemies to have maintained two Cathar *perfecti* ready to grant him the *consolamentum* when in mortal danger.

St Bernard's mission in 1145 was followed by sporadic Catholic attempts to halt the heretical agitation in Languedoc but they proved entirely unsuccessful. Raymond V of Toulouse, unlike his son Raymond VI, did not tolerate the Cathars and in 1178 appealed to Louis VII of France for forceful intervention against the growing heresy. A preaching mission was sent to Toulouse where a rich heretic was exposed and punished by flogging and three years' exile in the Holy Land. The mission, however, was openly sneered at in the streets of Toulouse and a public debate with two prominent Cathar preachers ended in their excommunication but without further punishment. Viscount Roger Trencavel, who had taken the Catholic bishop of Albi captive, and in whose fief Catharism was reported to have spread widely, was also excommunicated. In 1179, after the Third Lateran Council which condemned the teachings of the 'Cathars, Patarenes and Publicans' a new mission was dispatched to Languedoc. This time its leader, Henry, Abbot of Clairvaux, conducted a mini-crusade against Roger Trencavel who was forced to denounce the heresy and to promise persecution of the heretics in his domains.

In 1184 the Holy Roman Emperor Frederick I Barbarossa, after spending the first half of his reign in a bitter struggle with the papacy, met Pope Lucius III in Verona to establish procedures to check the growing spread of heresy which were elaborated in a joint decree, *Ad abolendam*. The Cathars and the Patarenes were anathematized and proscribed along with other sectarian movements and legal proceedings were established against both clerical and lay heretics. Convicted heretics were to be penalized with 'appropriate punishment' and bishops were entrusted to search out and charge the heretics in their dioceses, but the death penalty was not yet prescribed. While some sporadic measures were taken against the heretics in Italy, no major prosecutions were to follow in Languedoc. Roger Trencavel's pledge to suppress the heresy in his territory proved formal, while the year of 1194 saw the death of the old Count of Toulouse, Raymond V, who, apart from his appeals for action against the heresy in Languedoc, did little himself to diminish its spread. Indeed, it was during his rule that Catharism acquired its distinctive church order which was settled in a Cathar Council hosted by the Cathar congregation in the Toulouse area.

As in Bogomilism, the division between the believer and the perfect in Catharism was fundamental for the organization of the sect. Following the spiritual baptism with the placing of hands, the *consolamentum*, the new 'consoled' Cathar perfect assumed a black robe to enter a life of strict asceticism, prayer and preaching. The Catholics sometimes called the perfects 'the robed heretics', while among the Cathars they were known as 'Good Christians' or 'Good Men'. Not themselves bound by the austere standards of the Good Men, the believers, who formed the great majority in the sect, secured the livelihood and protection of the Cathar elite. Besides attending some of the ceremonies of the *perfecti*, the believers ritually saluted the Good Men with a bow and a request for a blessing and a prayer that they become 'good Christians' and be brought to a 'good end', the *consolamentum*.

The *perfecti* responded with the blessing and prayer for a final baptism and death in the Cathar sect. Crucially, the *consolamentum* was intended to secure the reunification of the soul with its heavenly spirit, restoring its heavenly status before the Fall, notions transmitted somehow to the medieval dualists from early eastern, probably Syrian Christianity; the ritual exchange between the *perfecti* and the believer hence was known as *melioramentum* (improvement), although Catholic commentators like Bernard Gui preferred to style it 'adoration'.[21] The approximate number of the Cathar *perfecti* at the beginning of the thirteenth century has been estimated at between 1,000 and 1,500; in its spread throughout Languedoc Catharism rose to virtual prevalence in the areas between Toulouse, Carcassonne and Albi.

Early Catharism in Languedoc and Lombardy inherited the monarchian dualism of the Bogomil system, where the evil creator of the material world was a power ultimately subordinate and inferior to the good Father. Following the great Cathar Council at St-Félix-de-Caraman, Catharism saw the renascence of the doctrines of absolute dualism, which posed the inexorable opposition between two coeternal and coequal powers, the good God and the evil God.

The Council at St-Félix and the Dualist Churches

As the expansion of Catharism was gaining momentum, at some point between 1166 and 1176 a crucial Cathar Council was convened at St-Félix-de-Caraman near Toulouse, which brought together a 'great multitude' of Cathar men and women. This council finally settled the administrative structure of the sect in France by instituting new heretical bishoprics, electing Cathar bishops and demarcating the boundaries between some of the Cathar dioceses. The council was presided over by the bishop of the dualist church of Constantinople, Nicetas, referred to in the *Acts* of the Council[22] as *Papa* Nicetas, who apparently had exceptional authority as he was empowered to consecrate the new bishops and even to reconsecrate the bishops of the communities which were already organized as bishoprics. *Papa* Nicetas reconsecrated the bishops of the Cathar dioceses or churches of northern France, Albi and Lombardy and consecrated the elected bishops for the new churches of Toulouse, Carcassonne and *Ecclesia Aransensis* (which is usually taken to denote not Val d'Aran but Agen).

Furthermore the Cathar *perfecti* at the council were reconsoled by receiving the *consolamentum* from Nicetas. In a separate sermon to the church of Toulouse, he elaborated on the nature, the functioning and the territorial organization of the eastern dualist 'primal churches'. Besides naming five dualist churches in the Balkan–Byzantine world, Nicetas cryptically referred to the primal 'Seven Churches of Asia' which have been viewed as an allusion to either the 'seven churches of Asia' in Revelation (1:4, 11, 20) or the seven Paulician churches in Asia Minor but they still remain a conundrum. The other five churches in his sermon – '*Ecclesiae Romanae et Dragometiae et Melenguiae et Bulgariae et Dalmatiae*' – can be traced and located with more certainty: some of them appear in inquisitorial sources with modified names.

Ecclesia Bulgariae was located in eastern Bulgaria or Macedonia, while *Ecclesia Dalmatiae* was clearly in Dalmatia in the western Balkans. *Ecclesia Dragometiae* (known also as Dugunthia or Drugunthia) is usually located in Thrace or Macedonia, and *Ecclesia Romanae* is generally believed to be the Constantinople church of *Papa* Nicetas. The Bogomil church of *Melenguiae* still eludes identification as it does not figure in the unique and elaborate list of the dualist churches in Europe presented by the Dominican friar and inquisitor Rainerius Sacchoni in 1250. Before becoming an Inquisitor, Rainerius Sacchoni had been a Cathar *perfectus* for seventeen years and in his *Summa on the Cathars and the Poor of Lyons*[23] furnished invaluable information on the beliefs, activities and locations of the dualist churches.

Rainerius listed ten western Cathar churches in France and Italy: the churches of Desenzano, Concorezzo, Bagnolo, Vicenza, the Spoletan Valley, Florence, northern France, Toulouse, Carcassonne and Albi. He also mentioned six eastern dualist churches: '*Ecclesia Sclavoniae, E. Latinorum de Constantinopoli, E. Graecorum ibidem, E. Philadelphiae in Romania, E. Burgariae* (Bulgariae), *E. Dugunthiae* (Drugunthiae)'. The church of Sclavonia is generally considered to correspond to the church of Dalmatia in Nicetas' sermon and to represent the Dalmatian and Bosnian Bogomils. Sacchoni clearly differentiated the Constantinople

Greek church, whose bishop had earlier been Nicetas, from the *Ecclesia Latinorum* in Constantinople which is usually viewed as a dualist order set up to minister to the Cathars in the Latin empire of Constantinople in the wake of the Fourth Crusade (1202–4).

Ecclesia Philadelphiae in Romania was also mentioned by Anselm of Alessandria among the first three dualist churches. It is suggestive of one of the seven churches of Asia in Revelation (I:II), the Philadelphian church, which is deemed to have been taught the mystery of the 'key of David' and was located at the ancient city of Philadelphia in Lydia, western Asia Minor. As with *Papa* Nicetas, Rainerius Sacchoni registered the Bogomil churches of Bulgaria and Drugunthia at the end of his list, with the comment: 'All (Cathar churches) stem from the last-named', confirming that *Ecclesia Bulgariae* and *Ecclesia Dugunthiae* (Drugun-thiae) were seen as the mother-churches of all European dualist churches.

Rainerius Sacchoni did not mention *Ecclesia Melenguiae* whose most plausible location is in Peloponnesus, probably in the Melangeia area in ancient Arcadia.[24] It has been argued that a mission from the Arcadian *Ecclesia Melenguiae* was behind the sudden emergence of *Paterini* (Cathars) in the former Byzantine province of Calabria in southern Italy, where the Greek presence was still strong in the twelfth century.[25] In the period of the general expansion of dualism the Calabrian *Paterini* gained adherents, but at the same time their links to the Cathar communities in central and northern Italy remain obscure. In the late twelfth century the Calabrian mystic Joachim of Fiore warned against their proselytism and referred to the division between the perfect and the believers among the Calabrian Patarenes. In his prophetic reading of Revelation Joachim predicted an unholy alliance between the Saracens and the Patarenes, respectively seen as the beasts from the sea and from the land, who would arise to plague the Church in the wake of the fall of the New Babylon, the Roman *imperium*.[26]

The Calabrian Cathars and the Arcadian *Ecclesia Melenguiae* remain the most enigmatic of the Bogomil and Cathar communities in southern Europe. Consequently it is impossible to determine the stance of the Calabrian and Arcadian heretics in the great schism that split the European dualist movement in the wake of *Papa* Nicetas' mission to the council of St-Félix-de-Caraman.

The Schism

With *Papa* Nicetas presiding at the council at St-Félix, there were bound to be repercussions that irreversibly transformed western dualism. Far from being the habitual heretical ceremonies, his rites of reconsecration and reconsolation were in essence rites of conversion in which the Cathar *perfecti* abandoned monarchian dualism, with its belief in the lesser status of the evil principle, to embrace the doctrine of the two coeternal principles, the doctrine of absolute dualism, whose apostle was *Papa* Nicetas.

At some time in the twelfth century the foremost Bogomil churches of Drugunthia and Constantinople had adopted the classical absolute dualism of the two coeval and opposed principles. The Bogomil church of Philadelphia apparently also came to accept the radical dualist creed and the bishop of the Constantinople church, Nicetas, consoled under the order of the Drugunthian church, was entrusted to produce a similar renaissance of absolute dualism in Catharism. *Ecclesia Bulgariae* and *Ecclesia Sclavoniae* in the western Balkans persevered with their adherence to the original Bogomil monarchian dualism and were now faced with an imminent schism.

What increased the danger of a split was the sudden apostolic fervour of the Drugunthian and Constantinople churches, which apparently considered the consecration and consolation under the order of the moderate dualist churches invalid. Claiming that the validity of these cardinal rites could be secured only by an absolute dualist consecrator, the mission of *Papa* Nicetas sought to reconsecrate the dualist bishops and reconsole the Cathar *perfecti* under the order of the Drugunthian church. As well as the mass conversion of the French Cathars to absolute dualism at St-Félix, *Papa* Nicetas also won over the Italian Cathars. In Lombardy he succeeded in converting Mark, the bishop of the Cathars in Lombardy, Tuscany and Treviso. Mark, who had been ordained in the *Ecclesia Bulgariae*, was persuaded to abandon the Bulgarian order and was reconsecrated in the Drugunthian order,[27] which was believed to stem from the head of *Ecclesia Drugunthiae*, the enigmatic bishop, Symeon. The bishop of the Drugunthian church undoubtedly played a major role in the schism, but his activities are shrouded in obscurity, unless Runciman is right to identify him with the Bogomil associate of the disgraced patriarch, Cosmas Atticus, the monk Niphon.[28]

The large-scale missionary campaign of *Papa* Nicetas had drawn the Cathar churches into communion with a renascent absolute dualism, which retained its hold on the Cathars in Languedoc until their final extirpation. The ascendancy of radical dualism in the west, however, was soon challenged by counter-missions sent by the moderate dualist churches of Bulgaria and 'Sclavonia'. Led by Petracius, 'with companions from across the sea', the first mission reached Lombardy and caused the initial division among the Italian Cathars.[29] Earlier the Lombard bishop Mark had been plunged into doubt over his Drugunthian consecration by rumours that *Papa* Nicetas had come to an evil end. Mark set out for the Balkans to obtain ordination from the bishop of *Ecclesia Bulgariae*, but only got as far as Calabria, where a Cathar deacon told him that a voyage across the sea was impossible. Unable to embark on his journey, Mark was thrown into prison, where he fell seriously ill. His failing health forced him to appeal for the election of a new heretical bishop; soon the newly elected John Judeus reached Mark and was confirmed as bishop. Mark himself was soon released and started out for Lombardy but died before meeting his successor again, the validity of whose office was to be questioned in a new debate whether 'Lord Mark' came to a good or an evil end.[30]

Petracius' moderate dualist mission intensified the growing divisions among the Italian Cathars and they split at first into two then into more groups that evolved into separate Cathar churches.[31] The churches of Bagnolo, Concorezzo, Desenzano and Mosio were active in Lombardy, the church of Vicenza in Veneto and the churches of Florence and Spoleto in Tuscany. According to their orientation, the Italian Cathar churches sought to send their bishops for the *consolamentum* and consecration at the major seats of the absolute or moderate dualist churches in the Balkans. The church of Desenzano, which was later also known as the church of the Albanenses and emerged as the stronghold of radical dualism in Italy, sent its bishop to the Drugunthian church, while Vicenza and Bagnolo sent their bishops for consecration to the church of Sclavonia. Concorezzo was led initially by John Judeus, who was persuaded to go to *Ecclesia Bulgariae* to legitimate his ordination. Another bishop of Concorezzo, Nazarius, went to Bulgaria for ordination in about 1190 and brought back with him the important Bogomil tract *Liber Secretum*,[32] which was to exercise a strong influence on the Italian moderate dualists and on some Albigensian circles in Languedoc.

Following the breach in Balkan dualism those churches that professed absolute dualism came to consider *Ecclesia Drugunthiae* as their mother-church, while the moderate communities claimed descent from the *Ecclesia Bulgariae.* The Cathars in Languedoc overall remained true to absolute dualism and in the communion of the Drugunthian church, whereas the Cathars of northern France identified with the monarchian dualist churches in Lombardy and reverted to moderate dualism. In 1208, when Pope Innocent III launched the infamous Albigensian Crusade against the Languedoc Cathars and the northern crusaders of Simon de Montfort burst into southern France, absolute dualism was the dominant creed in Languedoc.

Towards the end of the crusade, however, between 1223 and 1227, one of the foremost Cathar dioceses, that of Agen, came to be administered by an apparent advocate of monarchian dualism, Bishop Bartholomew of Carcassonne. In 1223 Cardinal Conrad of Porto, papal legate to Languedoc, alleged that Bartholomew was a vicar of a heretical antipope who had arisen 'in the regions of Bosnia, Croatia and Dalmatia, next to the nation of Hungary' to whom the Albigensians flocked 'so that he could answer their inquiries'.[33] Cardinal Conrad was referring in all probability to the bishop of the moderate dualist *Ecclesia Sclavoniae* in the western Balkans; he warned that the new Cathar bishop of Agen was consecrating bishops and organizing heretical churches. It has been shown that the activities of Bartholomew of Carcassonne were a concerted campaign to win back the Languedoc Cathars to monarchian dualism by the formation of alternative moderate dualist churches and the consecration of rival Cathar bishops.[34] The former Waldensian, Durand of Huesca, who became a vigorous anti-Cathar polemicist, wrote in about 1222–5 a tract against the Albigensians in Languedoc, where he referred to a threefold division in Catharism among the followers of the Greek, Bulgarian and Dragovitsan (Drugunthian) churches. Unlike *Papa* Nicetas, however, the prestige and influence of Bartholomew of Carcassonne did not survive his death in 1227. The old absolute dualist order in the church of Agen was restored in 1229 and in 1232 the see had to move to the Cathar stronghold of Montségur. In the following turbulent decades of mounting persecution and *autos-da-fé* the Cathar churches in Languedoc maintained their radical dualist doctrinal unity. The Catholic records of the Cathars refer regularly to the formula of two principles, or gods, or lords, one of good and the other of evil, existing from eternity and without end.

It is difficult to determine what was the catalyst for the sudden revival of radical dualism in the Bogomil Drugunthian order, especially when it is remembered that the heresiarch of absolute dualism, *Papa* Nicetas, firmly declared before the Cathar *perfecti* at St-Félix-de-Caraman that all Bogomil churches were operating in perfect concordance. The most plausible explanation is that the *Ecclesia Drugunthiae* comprised Paulicians from Thrace who precipitated a doctrinal reorientation. Another theory of the rise of Bogomil radical dualism seeks its origin in Byzantine intellectual, possibly monastic circles, which revived and brought into it some Origenist elements, but whatever the source of the schism the mission of *Papa* Nicetas and the ensuing supremacy of the two gods' formula in Languedoc are sometimes seen as having ultimately alienated western Christians from the concept of magnified dualism in Catharism.[35] For inquisitors like Rainerius Sacchoni the heretical transgressions of the absolute dualists, with their two-gods' belief, were inevitably graver than the 'errors' of the moderate dualists for whom the evil demiurge of the material world was secondary to the sublime Father. Medieval monarchian dualism was undoubtedly closer to the tenets of orthodox Christianity than absolute dualism, which has often been defined as a separate dualist religion altogether.

The schism remained entirely doctrinal and did not affect the concord between the moderate and absolute dualist churches, both of which maintained the crucial hierarchical differentiation of the two principal heretical grades, the *credentes*, believers, and the *perfecti* who had received the baptism in Spirit, the *consolamentum*. Both communities shared a common church order and the heretical dioceses were, in Languedoc for example, demarcated along the boundaries of the traditional Catholic sees. The Cathar diocese of Carcassonne thus embraced the Catholic sees of Carcassonne and Narbonne along with the Catholic dioceses in Catalonia. They were administered by heretical bishops, who were assisted by two coadjutors, called the elder son (*filius major*) and the younger son (*filius minor*) as well as a number of deacons. Upon the death of the dualist bishop the elder son succeeded to the bishopric, while the younger son was elevated to the position of the elder son and the *perfecti* elected a new younger son. The absolute churches maintained these three offices although they seem to reflect the triad of monarchian dualism – God the Father, His elder son, Satanael, and His younger son, Jesus Christ.[36]

CHAPTER FIVE

The Crusade Against Dualism

The last two decades of the twelfth century brought about a drastic reversal of fortune in the crusader domains and the Byzantine empire. In 1187 Saladin, the great adversary of the crusaders, crushed their forces near Hattin and recaptured Jerusalem, while one year earlier the militant and influential Bulgarian house of the Assenids had overthrown Byzantine rule in a campaign characterized by its religious and messianic overtones. The Assenids established the second Bulgarian empire (1186–1394) and Byzantine hegemony in the eastern Balkans was finally destroyed. The Fourth Crusade, launched in 1202 by Pope Innocent III (1198–1216), inflicted still greater disaster on Byzantium – diverted from their course, the crusaders stormed and sacked Constantinople in 1204. The leaders of the crusade and their Venetian creditors set up the Latin Empire of Constantinople (1204–61) while the remnants of Byzantium were divided into the 'empires' of Nicaea and Trebizond and the Despotate of Epirus.

Only one year after its foundation the empire suffered a severe blow: in April 1205 the armies of the Bulgarian Tsar Kaloyan totally routed the Latin troops of the first Latin Emperor of Constantinople, Baldwin I, near Adriannopolis. In the carnage Baldwin himself was captured and died in captivity in what became known as the Baldwin Tower in Kaloyan's capital. In the same year the Latin crusaders of Constantinople sought to instigate a crusade against the Bulgarian monarch, trying to persuade Innocent III that Kaloyan had joined forces with the Turks (the nomad Cumans) and 'other enemies of the Cross',[1] perhaps implicating heretics like the Paulicians and the Bogomils. In the previous year the Bulgarian Church had recognized the formal supremacy of the Roman See and Kaloyan himself had received his crown from Innocent III. The pope was not prepared to declare a crusade against his recent ally and over the next two years Kaloyan inflicted new defeats on the Latin armies, killing the crusaders' leader, Boniface of Montferrat, in 1207. However, while Innocent III did not launch a crusade against the alleged alliance of Kaloyan with the heretical 'enemies of the Cross', his papacy marked the beginning of Rome's counter-offensive against the resurgence of dualism in medieval Christendom, which culminated in the Albigensian Crusade in Languedoc.

Councils and Crusades

Besides authorizing the Fourth Crusade, which caused the dismemberment of the old Byzantine empire, Innocent vigorously enforced his vision of a universal papal theocracy and ascendancy over earthly monarchs. Innocent's theocratic aspirations led to his frequent interference in the affairs of Europe's secular rulers and with the unfolding of his long conflict with the English King John he did not hesitate to place England under an interdict and to excommunicate the king in 1208.

In the first year of his papacy Innocent proclaimed heresy *lèse-majesté* against God and received alarming reports of its spread in Bosnia, which was then nominally under the jurisdiction of Rome and the suzerainty of the Hungarian kingdom. According to the inquisitor Anselm of Alessandria, the heretical Church of Bosnia or Sclavonia had been established at some stage after the Second Crusade in 1147. In 1199 Innocent III was warned that the ruler (Ban) of Bosnia, Kulin (1168–1204), who sought independence from Hungary, had succumbed along with his family and 10,000 Christians to the 'significant' heresy that was seen to 'sprout' in the land.[2] In 1200 the pope was already asking the king of Hungary to take measures against heresy in Bosnia and Ban Kulin was accused of having granted asylum to Patarenes expelled from Dalmatia.[3] Two years later Innocent III wrote to the archbishop of Split that in Bosnia there was a multitude of people suspected of being adherents of the 'condemned Cathar heresy'[4] but Ban Kulin insisted that he believed they were actually Catholics. Ban Kulin sent some of the suspected Cathars to Rome for a profession of faith and accepted a papal legate commissioned to inspect the religious affairs of Bosnia. Innocent entrusted this to his chaplain, Johannes de Casamaris, who in 1203 witnessed the public abjuration of errors by Ban Kulin and the priors of

Bosnian monasteries. Besides renouncing the schism with Rome the Bosnian priors pledged to bring altars and crosses into the churches, to read from the Old Testament as well as the New Testament, to observe fasts and church services in accordance with the Catholic Church and not to admit Manichaeans and other heretics into their orders.[5]

Apart from his endeavours to strengthen Roman authority over Bosnia, in 1199 Innocent sent a Cistercian mission to deter the spread of Catharism in Languedoc and to reform the Languedoc Church. The mission won the support of King Pedro II of Aragon, but although Raymond VI pledged to drive the Cathars out of his domain, no firm action was taken against them. In 1204 and 1205 Innocent III repeatedly appealed to the supreme suzerain, the French King Philip Augustus, for military intervention in heresy-ridden Languedoc. Preoccupied with the conquest of the English dominions in France, Philip Augustus was openly reluctant to launch a campaign in the south. The preaching missions to Languedoc in 1206–8 were reinforced by the Spanish bishop Diego of Osma and Dominic of Guzmán, the would-be founder of the 'Order of the Preaching Friars', the Dominicans. The 'apostolic' preaching by 'example and word' of the two Spaniards brought some missionary successes but did not diminish the strength and vitality of Catharism in Languedoc. In 1207 the papal legate in Languedoc, Peter of Castelnau, finally felt compelled to excommunicate the Count of Toulouse.

One year before the excommunication of Raymond VI, Innocent III had sent a cardinal-legate[6] to Kaloyan's successor, Tsar Boril, apparently to urge him to take immediate action against the Bogomils. Innocent may have been the primary instigator of the ensuing anti-Bogomil council in 1211 but it was conducted along standard Orthodox lines and was presided over by the 'most pious' Tsar Boril. The records of the council, the *Synodicon of Tsar Boril*,[7] extol Boril as a defender of the faith who was inspired with divine zeal and gathered the heretics from the whole of his realm before the tribunal. Boril apparently shared the apostolic inclinations of Alexius Comnenus and summoned the Bogomils to present their teachings, which they did by resorting to numerous quotations from the Holy Scriptures, intending to 'entice' the Tsar and his entourage. The Tsar was said to have exposed their 'obloquy' and, after being 'entrapped' into theological disputes with the Tsar, the unrepentant Bogomils were imprisoned or 'otherwise punished'. The *Synodicon* anathematized the Bogomil doctrines and practices, most of which had already been anathematized in earlier synodicons, and cursed, along with the heresiarch Bogomil, some prominent Bogomil apostles. It explicitly condemned the 'nocturnal meetings and mysteries' of the Bogomils and their custom of 'practising sorcery' on 24 June, the birth of John the Baptist, and their performance of 'unholy mysteries like the hellenic pagan rites'.

While Tsar Boril was indulging in theological debates with the Bogomils, the Albigensian Crusade in Languedoc had been raging for a year and a half and the northern crusaders had already taken Béziers and Carcassonne, murdering many Catholics and Cathars at Béziers, and, as declared by Arnold Aimery, 'showing mercy neither to order nor to age nor sex'.[8] In January 1208 an attempted reconciliation between Raymond VI and Peter of Castelnau ended in acrimony and the papal legate was threatened that he would come under the surveillance of the Count of Toulouse. Peter of Castelnau was killed on 15 January 1208 and Innocent accused Raymond VI of heresy and complicity in his murder. The pope appealed for an immediate crusade against the heresy in Languedoc and proposed offering the indulgences granted to earlier crusaders as well as any land they might seize from the heretics. The Albigensian Crusade was vigorously promoted in northern France and in the early summer of 1209 northern feudal lords and prelates mustered a formidable army at Lyons. Yet the military orders of the Templars and the Hospitallers did not play an active military role in the crusade, which, in the case of the Templars, was bound to attack some of their patrons, who were renowned Cathar supporters, while Raymond VI was himself patron of the Order of the Hospitallers. Since the French king had refused to take part in the crusade, the crusaders descended on the south led by the zealous papal legate, Arnold Aimery.

The crusade soon turned into a war of conquest in which the northern barons strove to seize the fiefs of the southern nobility, who remained deplorably disunited in the face of the invasion. The projected alliance between Raymond VI and Viscount Raymond-Roger Trencavel of Béziers was not achieved and Raymond renewed his overtures to Innocent III. Around the time of the inception of the crusade Raymond VI had to make a public penance at St Gilles where he was forced to admit the various charges brought against him and was flogged by the papal legate at the altar of the cathedral.

To avert attack on his domain Raymond joined the crusaders until the fall of Carcassonne in August 1209, when Viscount Raymond-Roger was captured and died in captivity. The crusaders elected as leader a northern noble, Simon de Montfort, who also claimed the English earldom of Leicester. Simon was now proclaimed Viscount of Béziers and Carcassonne and he ruthlessly overran the Trencavel dominions, burning 140 *perfecti* at Minerve and many more heretics at Lavaur. In one of the most notorious murders of the crusade the widow Geralda of Lavaur castle was condemned as the worst of the heretics, was thrown into a well and then Simon de Montfort had her buried under stones. Meanwhile, Raymond VI was excommunicated yet again for his failure to comply with the legates' orders for turning over suspect heretics for investigation. Repeatedly accused of neglecting his obligations to purge the heretics from his lands, Raymond VI could not clear himself of the renewed charges of heresy and in the spring of 1211, after a furious encounter with the bishop of Toulouse, he expelled the prelate from the city. A direct attack on Raymond's dominions now seemed inevitable and in the summer of 1211 Simon de Montfort, supported by German crusaders, briefly and unsuccessfully laid siege to Toulouse. Following his withdrawal, Toulouse was excommunicated and Simon's army was soon reinforced with fresh French and German crusaders. After a year of assiduous campaigning Simon subdued most of the county and Raymond VI was encircled in Toulouse, retaining only the castle of Montauban.

The conquests of Simon de Montfort now directly threatened the Languedoc vassalages of King Pedro II of Aragon and he put Toulouse under his protection. For a time he succeeded in prevailing over Innocent III that the heresy of Raymond VI and southern nobles like the Count of Foix and the Viscount of Béziers had not yet been proven. The pope then tried to halt the warfare in Languedoc and to restore the crusading ideal back to its original focus – a Holy War against the infidel. Innocent's intentions were frustrated by the stern resistance of his extremist legates and he had to retreat, endeavouring to persuade Pedro that the patrons of the heresy were more dangerous than the heretics themselves. The king of Aragon was fresh from the Christian victory over the Muslim Almohades at Las Navas de Tolosa and now chose to ally himself with Raymond VI, the Counts of Foix and Comminges and the Viscount of Béarn, all newly condemned as protectors of the Cathars. In September 1213, however, Simon de Montfort, although greatly outnumbered, routed the forces of the Aragon–Toulousian alliance near Toulouse and in the carnage King Pedro was slain on the battlefield, while Raymond VI and his son found protection at the court of King John of England.

In the ecumenical council held in Rome in November 1215, Raymond VI was again accused of having protected heretics and his title and domains were ceded to Simon de Montfort, while Raymond's son inherited the Marquisate of Provence. It seemed that Innocent's plans for purging Catharism from Languedoc were soon to be achieved under Simon de Montfort, who went to Paris to be invested by Philip Augustus with the titles and lands of the disgraced Raymond VI. Within a year, however, Languedoc was plunged into renewed hostilities – Innocent III died in the summer of 1216 and amid a resurgence of Occitanian patriotism Raymond VI and his son began the reconquest of the county with help from Aragon and his noble allies from Foix and Comminges. He returned to Toulouse in September 1217, where he was acclaimed by his citizens, and repelled the first onslaughts of Simon de Montfort. In the ensuing long siege of Toulouse, Simon de Montfort, already excommunicated by the other erstwhile leader of the crusade, Arnold Aimery, launched a series of vigorous attacks on the city and was said to have pledged to reduce it to ashes. In one of the Toulousian counter-offensives, however, he was struck by a stone from a catapult and, in the words of *La Chanson de la Croisade Albigeoise*, he fell dead, 'bloodied and pallid'.[9] Simon's son, Amaury, continued the siege for four more weeks but finally retreated to Carcassonne and within one decade lost all the dominions won by his father during the first stage of the Albigensian Crusade.

The new pope, Honorius III, called relentlessly for a new Albigensian Crusade and repeatedly appealed to Philip Augustus for intervention, but besides a brief siege of Toulouse by the French royal army in 1219, it was the old House of Toulouse that was now on the offensive in Languedoc. Having recovered much of his county, Raymond VI died in 1222 but he was not allowed to be buried in consecrated ground. In 1224 his son, Raymond VII, finally drove Amaury de Montfort out of Carcassonne and Languedoc. Fifteen years after Béziers and Carcassonne had fallen to the crusaders and Viscount Raymond-Roger had died in captivity, his son Raymond Trencavel was re-established as 'Viscount of Béziers, Carcassonne, Razès and Albi'. Two years later, however, Raymond Trencavel was himself forced out of his newly restored dominions by the French king Louis VIII and had to flee to Aragon, while the Trencavel lands passed to the French crown.

Raymond VII's attempts to seek reconciliation with the Church at the Council of Bourges in 1225 were doomed by the Catholic preoccupation with the persistence of Catharism in Languedoc. In 1226 he was proclaimed a heretic, his lands were forfeited and he was excommunicated along with the Count of Foix and Raymond Trencavel. Amaury de Montfort had resigned his rights to the County of Toulouse and Honorius III and Louis VIII finally completed the Albigensian Crusade. In the summer of 1226 Louis VIII led a strong army into the Midi, seized Avignon and occupied much of Languedoc, but without attacking Toulouse itself, he returned to the north and died at the end of the year. Under the increasing pressure of the king's cousin, Humbert de Beaujeu, regent of the occupied lands, Raymond VII had to conclude with King Louis IX the 'Peace of Paris' in 1229 and was finally released from excommunication. The Peace of Paris marked the formal end of the Albigensian Crusade; Raymond VII retained the northern and western parts of the County of Toulouse, while ceding the larger territories either to the French king or to the Church. A marriage was arranged between Raymond's daughter and one of the king's brothers under regulations which ultimately secured the annexation of the whole of Languedoc by the French crown in 1271.

The final phase of the Albigensian Crusade was dominated by the expansionist policy of the French crown and thus, paradoxically, the rise and suppression of Catharism set the stage for the unification of the French north and the Midi under Capetian rule. By the Peace of Paris, moreover, Raymond VII was obliged to assist in the pursuit and prosecution of the heresy in his dominions. His coexistence with the French king, the Church and its new weapon against Catharism, the Inquisition, continued to be erratic and uneasy.

Suppression and Resistance

The Albigensian Crusade might have broken or depleted the power of many greater and lesser southern nobles, some of whom were forced to became *faidits* (rebels), but its primary aim – the eradication of Catharism – was far from accomplished. The mass burnings engulfed many *perfecti* but the reversals of the crusade did not allow extensive and lasting persecution of the Cathars. The Cathars were driven underground in the territories occupied by Simon de Montfort and many fled to Lombardy and Aragon. The beginning of the reconquest of the County of Toulouse by the two Raymonds after 1215 was bound to renew the vigour of Languedoc Catharism and led to the return of Cathar refugees who had escaped from the crusade in Catalonia and Lombardy. The Cathar ecclesiastical organization had survived the first, more devastating, phase of the crusade and in 1225, following the ephemeral restoration of Raymond Trencavel to his ancestral domains, a Cathar council established a new bishopric at Razès. The revival of Catharism prompted the papal legate Conrad of Porto to convene an ecclesiastical council at Sens and he wrote to leading French prelates about the activities of the Cathar bishop of Agen, Bartholomew, the apostle of moderate dualism in Languedoc.

Following the Peace of Paris, religious conditions in Languedoc changed radically; the Council of Toulouse in the same year prohibited the possession of the Bible in the vernacular among the laity and introduced a biannual oath of orthodoxy for the people of Languedoc. The imposition of the anti-heretical decrees of the council resulted in some prosecutions and executions but on the whole these remained irregular, if not half-hearted, and the Cathars continued to be protected by much of the rural nobility in Languedoc. In a significant legal innovation in the repression of heresy, however, between 1227 and 1235 the already existing episcopal 'inquisition' for heresy was augmented by a papal inquisition, entrusted to the two new mendicant orders, the Dominicans and the Franciscans, which eventually took centre stage in the prosecution of heretics.[10] By that time, the last Holy Roman emperor of the Hohenstaufen dynasty, Frederick II (1220–50), who called himself 'Lord of the World', had already passed laws prescribing the death penalty for intransigent heretics. In Brescia, central Lombardy, the hostility between the noble patrons of the Cathars and their enemies had flared up in 1224; indeed, military clashes and outbreaks of violence often arose from the persecution of the Cathars in Lombardy. Pope Honorius III appealed to the Lombard cities to enforce Frederick's anti-heretical legislation but it encountered strong opposition in cities like Florence and Verona. The initial onslaught of the Inquisition on Italian Catharism proceeded more slowly and was further enervated by the renewal of the papal–imperial disagreements over Lombardy in 1236 and the ensuing turmoil in Italy.[11]

In 1231 Gregory IX appointed the confessor of St Elizabeth of Hungary, Conrad of Marburg, as the first papal Inquisitor in Germany, but Conrad's flagrant excesses in the prosecution of the heretics were to cost him his life in 1233. Another notorious figure among the early Inquisitors was the Dominican friar Robert, called *le bougre* (the Bulgar) because of his Cathar past, but also called 'the hammer of the heretics' because he had consigned many of his former co-religionists to the flames. Robert the Bulgar was active between 1233 and 1239 in northern France and Flanders; Matthew of Paris recorded that in 1238, he had caused many thousands to be burned in Flanders.[12] His mission reached its climax in 1239 when he sent 183 *bulgri* to the stake at Mont-Aime for 'a fiery offering and propitiation of God'. Their bishop conferred the *consolamentum* on the believers before being burned with them.

The persecution forced the northern French Cathar Church into exile in Lombardy, while in Languedoc the Dominicans, entrusted by Gregory IX with the inquisition of heresy, faced sustained resistance. The Dominicans' founder, St Dominic, had already distinguished himself in the struggle against the spread of Catharism and his Order of the Preaching Friars, which received papal approval in 1217, provided the first inquisitors in the anti-Cathar campaign. In their inquests for heresy in suspect areas the Dominican inquisitors initially proclaimed a month of grace when those who confessed to heresy were absolved but had to disclose the identity of other heretics or their protectors. The period of grace was followed by the arraigning of the suspects, secret trials where those who confessed were subjected to various penances, while the seemingly insincere or unrepentant heretics could be cast into prison or delivered to the secular authorities for death by fire. Even dead heretics were not safe from the Inquisition – if their heresy was disclosed posthumously, their bodies were exhumed, dragged through the streets and burned.

Inevitably, from its inception the work of the Dominican Inquisition was frustrated by the overall hostile public reaction in Languedoc: in 1234 Raymond VII was already complaining to Gregory IX about their abuses. The beginning of inquisitorial pursuits in the towns of Languedoc led to protracted strife in Narbonne and the temporary expulsion of the Dominicans from Toulouse in late 1235, when Raymond VII was excommunicated again. Gregory soon negotiated with Raymond for the return of the Inquisition to Toulouse and the Dominicans came back to the turbulent city in 1236 to search out and convict heretics. The operation of the Inquisition, however, was affected by the escalating conflict between Frederick II and the pope, following the emperor's attempts to assert imperial authority over Lombardy in direct challenge to the papal interests in northern Italy. In 1237 Gregory IX, who excommunicated Frederick two years later, was in desperate need of allies and Raymond negotiated with him for the lifting of his own excommunication and the temporary suspension of the Inquisition in Toulouse, which was to continue for another three years. The Count of Toulouse could not negotiate, however, the elimination of the Dominican friars from the Inquisition in Languedoc, nor the burial of his father's body in consecrated ground.

The collision between the ageing pope and the emperor came to its climax in 1240–1 when Frederick, who had temporarily restored Jerusalem to Christendom in 1228, now directly threatened Rome. At the same time, Raymond Trencavel, who had been dispossessed on account of the long-standing association of his house with the heresy, attempted to recapture his dominions in the old Cathar heartlands in Razès and Carcassonne. He initially led a small force of knights from Aragon but after being acclaimed with enthusiasm in Razès he was joined by many rebellious lesser nobles and laid siege to Carcassonne, which was broken by the arrival of French royal troops. Raymond Trencavel was now himself besieged in Montréal in Razès but Raymond of Toulouse was able to act as an intermediary to secure his safe withdrawal to Aragon.

In the following year Raymond VII found himself engaged in the build-up of an anti-French league with the king of England, Henry III, and the count of La Marche, Hugh of Lusignan. Seeking to redraft the Paris treaty of 1229, Raymond VII was joined in his preparations for war by most of the southern nobles, including traditional allies like Raymond Trencavel and the counts of Comminges and Foix. As the war with the French armies unfolded early in the summer of 1242 the coalition suffered immediate setbacks: King Henry was defeated by King Louis at Taillebourg on 20 July and withdrew to English-held Aquitaine, while Count Hugo capitulated one month after the English defeat. Raymond of Toulouse, who was excommunicated during his campaign, had traversed Languedoc to Narbonne and had united the populace behind his cause, but with the collapse of the coalition and desertion in the ranks, he had to surrender in the autumn. Peace was concluded in early

1243 and yet again Raymond undertook the obligation to eradicate heresy in his domains.

Raymond of Trencavel's expedition in 1240 was followed by prosecution of his noble supporters and the unsuccessful war of Raymond VII decimated the power of the traditional patrons of the Cathars, the local southern nobles. Some of them, including Raymond Trencavel, joined King Louis in his crusade to Egypt in 1248; Raymond was rewarded afterwards with some land in his ancestral fiefs. Raymond VII himself attempted to serve as an intermediary between Frederick II and the new pope Innocent IV, who rescinded his last excommunication. Otherwise, his mediation was doomed, as Frederick's camp was to proclaim Innocent IV a type of papal Antichrist, uncovering the numerical value of *Innocencius papa* as 666, while the pope identified his imperial adversary with the beasts from Revelation and in 1245 declared him dethroned and a suspected heretic, calling for a crusade against Frederick in Germany.

In Languedoc, meanwhile, the Inquisition had recommenced its work in 1241 with renewed vigour in spite of the continuing antagonism between Raymond of Toulouse and the Dominican friars. Yet from the beginning of its institution in Languedoc the Inquisition was exposed to reprisals; while the Count of Toulouse was preparing for war against France, in May 1242 the *faidits* of the Cathar citadel of Montségur massacred the 'squad' of the inquisitors William Arnold and Stephen of St Thibery. Like the murder of the papal legate, Peter of Castelnau, in 1208 the reprisal against the *faidits* in 1242 was to have grave repercussions for the Cathar movement in Languedoc.

The Fall of Montségur

The impressive castle of Montségur was located in the northern Pyrenean foothills in the county of Foix and was held by Raymond of Pereille who had himself been accused of heresy in 1237. With its impregnable position it had long been a safe refuge for persecuted Cathars, particularly since the suppression of Catharism in Languedoc in the wake of the Peace of Paris in 1229. In 1232 the Cathar bishop of Toulouse, Guilhabert de Castres, and the heretical bishop of Agen, Tento I, moved their sees to Montségur, which became the centre of the Cathar movement where the *perfecti* practised Cathar ceremonies and granted the *consolamentum* to tested or dying believers. Protection from a strong garrison gathered from the *faidits* was reinforced by new rebels after the collapse of Raymond Trencavel's campaign in 1240. The commander of the castle was the son-in-law of Raymond of Pereille, the *faidit* Peter Roger of Mirapoix, who apparently maintained relations with other militant malcontents opposed to the French presence in Languedoc, like the seneschal of Raymond VII at Avignonet, Raymond of Alfaro.

Amid the flurry of expectations of Raymond VII's offensive against France, Raymond of Alfaro informed the commander of Montségur of the arrival at his castle of a group led by the two well-known and feared inquisitors, the Dominican William Arnold and the Franciscan Stephen of St Thibery. Peter Roger sent an armed force to Avignonet that was admitted into the castle and killed the two inquisitors and their nine companions but failed to bring to Peter Roger the skull of William of Arnold, which he had intended to convert into a drinking cup.

As with the fatal murder of Peter of Castelnau in 1207, rumours implicated the count of Toulouse in the killings at Avignonet but it is hardly credible that Raymond would risk his search for allies on the eve of war with France with such a flagrant act. Otherwise, in Languedoc the death of the inquisitors was met with rejoicing coupled with intense anticipation of the impending hostilities with France, while the Dominicans requested permission from Innocent IV to leave the Midi. The subsequent defeat of the anti-French coalition sealed the fate of Montségur: several months after the peace between King Louis and Raymond of Toulouse, Montségur was besieged by the royal seneschal of Carcassonne. With its impregnable position on a high plateau the castle of Montségur defied immediate conquest and the seneschal prepared for a long and exhausting siege. The besiegers could not prevent further supplies being brought into the castle or messages from other Cathar communities. At one stage, a Cathar bishop from Cremona offered refuge in Lombardy to Guilhabert de Castres' successor to the see of Toulouse, Bertrand Marty, but Bertrand preferred to stay in Montségur.

Rumours that the count of Toulouse, then mediating between Frederick II and Innocent IV, would come to the rescue were unfounded and hopes of help from mercenaries failed to materialize. After nine months the situation of the besieged Cathars and the defending *faidits* was becoming untenable and Raymond of Pereille and Peter Roger began to sue for terms. The reputed Cathar treasure, probably along with Cathar writings, had already been clandestinely carried away from Montségur,[13] according to the agreed terms of surrender the defenders from the garrison were granted amnesty and safe passage from the castle, but were to give confessions before the Inquisition. The *perfecti* were offered the choice of recanting or facing death by burning. During the negotiations about twenty people received the *consolamentum* and chose 'baptism by fire'. With the enforcement of the agreement of the surrender of Montségur three or four *perfecti* made a daring secret escape, possibly connected with the Cathar 'treasure'. More than two hundred *perfecti* remained who, besides the bishop of Toulouse, included the bishop of Razès, Raymond Aguilher. They were burned, most probably in the town of Bram, but according to tradition the mass burning took place at the foot of the mountain in the so-called 'Field of the Cremated'.

If not yet the Catholic *coup de grâce*, the fall of Montségur and the cremation of such a large section of the Cathar elite dealt a severe blow to Catharism in Languedoc. The capture of the Cathar citadel was followed by large-scale inquisitorial campaigns in Languedoc during 1245–6 which were directed from the two new centres of the Inquisition in Toulouse and Carcassonne. The officials of Raymond VII now assisted the inquisitors more readily and, after a reign which had at least delayed and obstructed the wholesale persecution of Catharism in his county, in 1249, the year of his death, he himself ordered the burning of eighty heretics at Agen. Despite his late ardour, however, Raymond VII failed to secure the Christian burial of his father and his coffin remained in the precincts of the Knights of St John outside Toulouse.

In 1237 the Inquisition had already penetrated one of the centres of refuge for the persecuted Cathars, to the south of the Pyrenees in the Catalonian dominions of Viscount Arnold of Castelbo. The viscount had been a vigorous champion of the Cathars and when his daughter Ermessinda, herself a Cathar believer, married Roger-Bernard II of Foix, the Cathars continued their activities largely unabated. However, in 1237 the Dominican friars finally initiated their inquests in the viscounty of Castelbo which led to the imprisonment of forty-five heretics and the customary exhumation and burning of their dead co-sectarians.[14]

With the Inquisition operating in Catalonia and Aragon, many Cathars were forced to flee to Lombardy, where the continuing strife between the papacy and Hohenstaufens did not permit a concerted inquisitorial campaign. In about 1250, according to the *Summa* of the inquisitor Rainerius Sacchoni, the number of Cathar *perfecti* in the old churches of Albi, Toulouse and Carcassonne – along with that of Agen, which was 'almost totally destroyed' – exceeded two hundred, matching the number burned after the fall of Montségur. In contrast, the Cathar *perfecti* in Italy, including those of the exiled Church of northern France, still numbered around 2,550.

The fall of Montségur marked the beginning of the real decline of Catharism in Languedoc. Despite intermittent resistance to the inquisitorial procedures and the tension between Innocent IV and the inquisitors in Languedoc, which led to a brief suspension of the Dominican Inquisition in the area between 1249 and 1255, Catharism was soon largely driven underground. The wandering missions of the *perfecti* were becoming exceedingly dangerous, although they had already exchanged their distinctive black robes for a black girdle worn next to the body. The centre of western dualism was now in Lombardy, while the crusading projects of the papacy against Balkan dualism had proved abortive.

Rome and the Balkan Heresy

Besides the 2,550 western dualist *perfecti* Rainerius Sacchoni reckoned that there were 500 in the eastern dualist churches of the Greeks, of Sclavonia, Philadelphia, Bulgaria and Drugunthia, while the Latin Church of Constantinople comprised less than fifty. During the anti-Bogomil council of 1211 the Bogomils were accused of performing 'unholy mysteries like the hellenic pagan rites' and the continuing Bogomil activity in Anatolia and Constantinople prompted Patriarch Germanus (1220–40) to warn the citizens of Constantinople against the 'dark mysteries' of the 'satanic Bogomil heresy'. From his residence in Nicaea he sent an encyclical to Constantinople, to be read in the churches on Sundays and feast days, where he condemned the Bogomil heresy as a 'stinging snake, pestering and corroding the body of the Orthodox Church'.[15]

The measures of the council of 1211 apparently failed to suppress *Ecclesia Bulgariae*. Pope Gregory IX eventually came to accuse the

Bulgarian Tsar Ivan Asen II (1218–41) of harbouring the heretics in his realm. To the anger of Gregory, Ivan Asen had released the Bulgarian Church from its allegiance to the Roman See and in about 1235, when he was the most powerful Balkan monarch, he directly threatened the Latin Kingdom of Constantinople. Having recently instigated the Inquisition in Languedoc, Gregory IX prevailed on the Hungarian King Bela IV to launch a crusade against the Bulgarian empire where, according to the pope, the whole land was 'infected' by heretics.[16] Bela IV accepted the role of the defender of the faith and Gregory IX praised his resolve to lead a crusade against 'the blasphemous nation, the heretics and the schismatics ruled over by Ivan Asen II'.[17] Bela IV began to muster an army in Hungary but the crusade, conceived by Gregory IX as a new 'Holy War' against heresy, was foiled by the diplomatic moves of the Bulgarian Tsar.

The projected crusade against the Bulgarian empire may have failed to materialize, but the papacy had already succeeded in summoning Hungarian arms in a crusade against the heresy in Bosnia. The reconciliation of the Bosnian ruler Kulin with Rome in 1203 had prevented the projected military intervention of the Hungarian King Henry, and in the words of F. Rački, the Catholic Church 'did not find in Kulin a Bosnian Raymond and in King Henry a Simon de Montfort'.[18] In 1211 the bishop of Bosnia was already reported to have encountered a strong presence of the Patarene heresy in the land and in about 1225 Pope Honorius III urged the Hungarian archbishop of Kalocsa, Ugrin, to take immediate measures against the spread of the heresy in Bosnia. According to Conrad of Porto's letter of 1223 a dualist antipope in the western Balkans, in all probability the bishop of *Ecclesia Sclavoniae*, was involved in the affairs of Languedoc Catharism. A crusade against Bosnia, to be led in 1227 by the Byzantine prince John Angelus, failed to be established although Archbishop Ugrin had already paid 200 marks to the prince.[19]

The crusade against Bosnia became a reality in 1235, although two years earlier the Bosnian Ban Ninoslav had followed in the footsteps of Ban Kulin and had abjured his heretical ways, embraced Catholicism and promised to persecute the heretics in Bosnia. Apparently this act had been formal, as in 1235 Gregory IX offered indulgences to the crusaders that were to fight the heretics in 'Slavonia' and a crusading army led by the son of the Hungarian King Andrew, the Duke of Croatia, Coloman, invaded Bosnia. The crusade promptly unified the Bosnian nobility in opposition to both Rome and Hungary, as in 1236 the pope referred to a

Bosnian prince and his mother as the only good Catholics in Bosnia, who, amid the heresy-infected Bosnian nobility, were like 'lilies among thorns'. The course of the crusade is rather obscure, but in 1238 Gregory IX claimed victory and was planning to erect a cathedral chapter in conquered central Bosnia at Vrhbosna (modern Sarajevo). Like the Albigensian Crusade, the crusade against Bosnia quickly became a war of conquest, but while losing territories to the Hungarians, Ban Ninoslav retained his hold on parts of the banate. Towards the end of 1238 the pope proclaimed that Ninoslav had relapsed into heresy and appealed to Duke Coloman to persecute the heretics in Bosnia. A year later Dominican friars were sent to Bosnia to fight the heresy. The persecution was confined to the Hungarian-occupied area of Bosnia and did not last more than three years, since in 1241 Hungary suffered a disastrous Tatar invasion, in which both the crusading champions of Rome, Coloman and Archbishop Ugrin, were killed on the battlefield.

The Hungarian crusaders had to withdraw from the occupied Bosnian areas; the crusade seemed to have achieved nothing but increased anti-Roman feelings in Bosnia. In 1246 Innocent IV began moves to subject the Bosnian diocese to the archbishopric of Kalocsa and appealed both to the new archbishop and King Bela IV to resume the crusade against the heretics in Bosnia. One year later, Innocent IV praised the archbishop of Kalocsa for his endeavours to eradicate – with great bloodshed and at great expense – the heresy into which the Bosnian Church had totally lapsed. The pope stated that large parts of Bosnia were captured and many heretics were banished but the Catholic fortifications still could not resist the attacks of the heretics. Little is known of the course of the Hungarian Crusade in Bosnia,[20] but what is clear is that while Languedoc had been finally subdued by the Inquisition, the crusade in Bosnia failed to reach its objective and in March 1248 it was suddenly halted by Innocent, as Ninoslav had again reconfirmed his Catholicism and claimed that he had favoured the heretics only as allies against foreign invasions.

Ninoslav's manoeuvres seemed to successfully check, for a time, the Hungarian and Catholic pressure on Bosnia, where the religious conditions remained extremely complicated. Religious tolerance was an overall characteristic of medieval Bosnian society where pagan beliefs and customs persisted side by side and mixed with Christian and heretical traditions. When the Catholic observers referred to 'heresy' in Bosnia it is not always clear whether they were alluding to outright heretical traditions like Bogomilism, to blends of Christian and pagan beliefs or to heterodox practices of the Bosnian Christians. What is certain, however, is that the Hungarian crusades were launched against the dualist movement in Bosnia and Dalmatia where, according to the testimony of the Dominican prior Suibert,[21] *Ecclesia Sclavoniae* was active and where many souls were destroyed by 'heretical errors'.

The Decline of Catharism

Upon the death of Raymond VII in 1249 the county was inherited by his daughter Jeanne and her Capetian husband Alphonse of Poitiers; when they died childless in 1270 it became part of the French kingdom. In the latter half of the thirteenth century the Inquisition perfected its machinery of suppression and enriched its procedures with the introduction in 1252 of the authorized but regulated use of torture, to be applied first in Italy and then in France. With the relentless expansion of the inquisitorial pursuits in Languedoc more Cathar *perfecti* and believers fled from Languedoc for the more secure Italy, but soon the conditions for survival in Lombardy worsened radically.

The Italian Cathars had long profited from the strife – which raged from 1236 to 1268 – between the papacy and the House of Hohenstaufen, and which was reflected in the political division between the Guelphs and the Ghibellines. Despite his harsh heresy laws and denouncement of the heretics in their seedbed of Milan, Frederick II was far from the 'hammer of the heretics', although he did use the heretical problem in his propaganda war against the papacy. The Lombardian cities, which played a major role in the papal–imperial conflict, saw only sporadic enactment of his heresy laws, while amid the battle for allies in Lombardy the papacy did not risk demands for full-scale prosecutions of the heresy.

The Cathars often associated with the imperial Ghibelline party and, as in Languedoc, their most common protectors were to be found among the rural nobility. In the aftermath of the dramatic conclusion of the battle between the papacy and the Hohenstaufen dynasty, however, the fortunes of Italian Catharism suffered severe setbacks, damaged by the more efficent anti-Cathar inquisitorial campaigns, the changing socio-political situation in the urban and rural areas it had penetrated, and the role of the lay confraternities and the Mendicant orders.[22] Frederick II died in 1250 and his successor as king of Germany, Conrad IV, continued the struggle against the great adversary of the 'Hohenstaufen eaglet', Innocent IV, but died after four years, although not before being excommunicated by the pope. Both his son Conradin and Frederick's illegitimate son Manfred met their deaths in their fight against the champion of the Guelph or papal faction, Charles of Anjou. With the fall of the House of Hohenstaufen the papal party inevitably gained ascendancy and by the end of the century the Inquisition was operating in most cities. Although the Italian Cathars retained some of their patrons and were occasionally able to fight the persecution, the series of anti-heretical trials, although not so sweeping as in Languedoc, steadily depleted the strength of the sect. As in Languedoc the severest blow to the Cathars was a strike at their major sectarian centre in the castle of Sirmione at the lake of Garda which was followed by a mass burning of 178 captured *perfecti*. Among those burned was the last acknowledged Cathar bishop of Toulouse.

Around the time of the successive anti-heretical trials in Bologna towards the end of the thirteenth century, a Cathar *perfectus*, Pierre Autier, returned to Languedoc and instigated a brief Cathar renascence centred mainly in the county of Foix.[23] Braving the vigilant and experienced organs of the Inquisition, which had just encountered renewed opposition in Albi and Carcassonne, Peter Autier endeavoured to revive Catharism in secret missionary journeys throughout Languedoc but his mission was mostly confined to the classes of the peasants and artisans. It took the Inquisition nearly fifteen years of relentless pursuit to capture the last major Cathar apostle and his companions. Peter Autier was burned in 1311, while Guillaume Bélibaste, usually considered the last Cathar *perfectus*, escaped to Catalonia, but was later enticed to return to Languedoc, betrayed to the Inquisition and burned in Toulouse in 1321. One of the last great enemies of Catharism and heresy in Languedoc, the inquisitor Bernard Gui, is recorded between 1308 and 1323 as having pronounced 930 sentences against heretics, among which forty-two were death penalties. In Italy the last known western heretical bishop was captured in 1321 and thereafter heretical communities survived in remote Pyrenean and Alpine areas, although some Cathars found refuge in Sicily during the reign of Frederico III of Aragon (1296–1337).

While the assiduous, if not always well coordinated, campaigns of the Inquisition were a major factor in the eclipse of Catharism in Languedoc, its demise was conditioned also by other developments. The rise of new spiritual currents in Catholicism and the work of the Mendicant orders seem to have counterbalanced the traditional dualist attractions of Catharism and the ascetic appeal of its *perfecti*.[24] At the same time, ever since the heretics of Orléans had been charged with unnatural practices and Devil-worship in 1022, the tendency to associate heresy with witch-craft had been growing, to lead to an amalgamation between them in fourteenth-century inquisitorial procedures. With the gradual demon-ization of the medieval dualists and the orthodox assimilation of heresy to witchcraft, Cathar dualism was to play an important role in the very shaping of the medieval concept of witchcraft, as charges brought against the heretics were to be transferred to the alleged Devil-worshipping witches. In the Catholic records descriptions appeared of 'Luciferian' sects in whose beliefs the traditional Bogomil–Cathar dualism of the evil demiurge of the material world and the transcendent good God appeared in a reversed form, and where Lucifer was revered and expected to be restored to heaven, while Michael and the archangels would duly be deposed to hell. The direct or indirect impact of the Bogomil–Cathar vision of Satan as a creator and master of the material world on the formation of the witchcraft paradigms, elaborated during the ensuing great witch-craze, seems apparent, although they represent a complete reversal of the dualist tenets of the Great Heresy.[25] Moreover, in political trials, such as the suppression of the Knights Templar in 1307–14, the accusations comprised a curious combination of allegations of witchcraft and heresy, some of which evidently reflected earlier charges against the Cathars.[26]

While in western Christendom the dualist teachings of defeated Catharism were to be assimilated in the new demonological and witch-craft models, in the Balkan cradle of medieval dualism Bogomilism endured for at least another 150 years and persistent Catholic traditions continued to allude to a supreme dualist pontiff residing in the Balkans.

The Antipope

During the suppression of Catharism by the Inquisition the activities of the Bogomil churches in the Balkan–Byzantine world understandably remained a matter of continuous inquisitorial concern. Not only did the inquisitorial authorities consider these communities as mother-churches of all dualist churches in western Europe, but they also believed, as has been attested in a number of Catholic records, that the persecuted western dualists could find the *consolamentum* and safe refuge in the eastern dualist churches. What is more, some Catholic observers believed in the existence of a secret antipope, a supreme Albigensian or Bogomil pope, whose residence was in the Balkans. While the title ascribed to the heresiarch of absolute dualism, Nicetas, 'Papa Haereticorum', is apparently a mistranslation of the Greek *papas* (priest), some scholars have maintained that the medieval dualist churches had a supreme head and it has even been argued that all southern Europe was 'parcelled out into Manichaean dioceses whose bishops paid allegiance to a Manichaean pope seated in Bulgaria'.[27]

In one of the early outbreaks of heresy in the west – the activities of the heretics from the Monforte castle in 1028 – their representative, Gerard, had proclaimed, 'There is no pontiff beside our Pontiff though he is without tonsure of the head or any sacred mystery',[28] but it is usually assumed that he was referring to the Holy Ghost. In 1143, during the first certain discernment of Catharism in Cologne, Eberwin of Steinfeld stated in his appeal to St Bernard of Clairvaux that the heretics who were called apostles had their own pope; the Calabrian mystic Joachim of Fiore also shared the belief in one supreme heretical pontiff.

The warning of Cardinal Conrad of Porto in 1223 about the rise of an Albigensian antipope in the western Balkans most probably referred to the heretical bishop of *Ecclesia Sclavoniae*.

In 1387 the Cathar Jacob Bech, from one of the last dualist communities in northern Italy (which was in constant contact with *Ecclesia Sclavoniae*), confirmed before his *auto-da-fé* that the dualists denied the authority of the Roman pope and had their own *Papa Major*.[29] As late as 1461 three heretical Bosnian noblemen were sent to Rome and among the fifty heretical articles that they rejected before Cardinal Torquemada was the belief that the heretics were the successors to the Apostles and that their heresiarch, 'the Bishop of the Church', was the true successor of Peter.[30]

The possibility that the medieval neo-Manichaen movement had a supreme leader, similar to the *archegos* of Manichaeism, has been much debated but generally the evidence is found insufficient and illustrates the lack of data about the internal history of the Bogomil movement. Yet

THE OTHER GOD

the image of the dualist antipope residing in the Balkans remained central to the Catholic perception of the movement and was reiterated by Bossuet even in the seventeenth century, while *Papa* Nicetas, the apostle of absolute dualism in the west, came to personify the image of the '*Antipape des Hérétiques Albigeois*'.

The association of the supposed heretical antipope with Bosnia, moreover, seems hardly surprising – following the final victory of Catholicism over Catharism in Languedoc and Lombardy in the early thirteenth century, Bosnia became for Rome the irredeemable land of heresy, or in the words of Pope Urban v (1362–70), 'the cesspool of heresy of all parts of the world'.[31]

The Bosnian Church and *Ecclesia Sclavoniae*

The accusations of heresy in the Bosnian lands in the 1220s and 1230s coincided with the intensification of Catholic suppression of Catharism in Languedoc and Lombardy, and indeed the alarmist warning of Conrad of Porto about the dangerous existence of a Balkan dualist antipope clearly reflects the belief that 'dualism was an international conspiracy designed to subvert Catholic religion'.[32] Papal accusations against heresy in Bosnia could take the form of exaggerated, emotional invectives: before Pope Urban v proclaimed Bosnia to be 'the cesspool' of heretics of various parts of the world, in 1221 Pope Honorius iii had appealed for a crusade against heretics in Bosnia, which land, in his analogy, was like a witch feeding them with her breasts[33] – he obviously became obsessed with this notion for he reiterated it in two other letters. These repeated themes and images of Bosnia as the European 'Manichaean' or heretical witch, as a refuge and lair of heresies were bound to influence also general perceptions of the land. Between 1235 and 1248 Bosnia was subjected to political and religious invasions but through force of circumstances and political moves, Ban Ninoslav succeeded in reversing the course of the two crusades that Rome had launched against Bosnia. Following his death in about 1250, however, Bosnia fell under direct Hungarian suzerainty and was divided into separate administrative areas or banates. With the accession of the adolescent King Ladislas (1272–90) Hungary itself entered a period of insecurity and internal strife that could hardly have been conducive to supervising Bosnian religious affairs. None the less, the papacy continued to urge the Hungarian court to take measures against the heresy in Bosnia and in 1280 the king's mother, Elisabeth, assured Pope Nicholas III of her intention to persecute heretics in her dominions, which included Bosnia. King Ladislas himself ordered persecution of various religious sects in the kingdom, particularly in the diocese of Bosnia, but if any action was taken its results remain unknown.

In 1282 the Orthodox king of Serbia, Stefan Dragutin, was forced to abdicate, but the Hungarian king entrusted him with important banates in Bosnia and he was credited with converting heretics there. He requested, moreover, aid from Rome against the heretics and their patrons and was sent a Franciscan mission charged with searching out and fighting the heresy in the western Balkans. Dragutin's son-in-law, Stjepan Kotroman, was related to the old lineage of Ninoslav and in the early fourteenth century blocked the attempts of Croatian nobles to occupy all Bosnian territory. His son, Stjepan Kotromanić, who was Orthodox by faith, was supported by the first Hungarian Anjou king, Charles I, and gradually manoeuvred himself into being Ban of Bosnia. He extended his sway into Dalmatia and, profiting from internal struggle in Serbia, in 1321 took over Serbian-ruled Hum (modern Herzegovina), then predominantly Orthodox.

By the time Bosnia had become a strong Balkan state under Kotromanić, another religious factor had entered the Bosnian scene – the Bosnian Church. The origins and nature of the Bosnian Church and its links with the continually reported outbreaks of heresy in Bosnia are still debated. It seems most likely that heresy was not indigenous to Bosnia but was imported from the Dalmatian coast, the most probable location of the Bogomil *Ecclesia Sclavoniae*. In the *Acts* of the Council of St Félix one of the primal dualist churches in the Balkan–Byzantine world is named as *Ecclesia Dalmatiae*; although at that time the name 'Dalmatia' could be used to describe regions extending beyond what is currently Dalmatia proper, the location of this dualist church can be seen as referring with a high degree of certainty to an area in the western Balkans. The *Ecclesia Dalmatiae* from the list in the *Acts* is commonly identified with the *Ecclesia Sclavoniae* in the list of dualist churches in the *Summa* of Rainerius Sacchoni,[34] written a little less than a century after the convocation of the Cathar Council. Furthermore, in the doctrinal schism that split medieval dualism into radical and moderate dualist wings, *Ecclesia Sclavoniae* represented the latter, and according to the anonymous inquisitorial tract, *De heresi Catharorum in Lombardia*, dating from the early thirteenth century, two moderate dualist bishops in Lombardy had received their ordination from 'Sclavonia' (differentiated in the text from the dualist Churches of Bulgaria and Druguntia).[35] While the name 'Sclavonia' could be used to describe different regions, the association of the dualist Church of Sclavonia with the western Balkans is confirmed in the tract of the Inquisitor Anselm of Alessandria, which describes the introduction of the dualist heresy in Bosnia via 'Sclavonian' merchants returning from Constantinople, as well as the election of a dualist bishop of 'Sclavonia, that is of Bosnia',[36] and is further confirmed by the 'Commentary' of the Dominican prior, Suibert, claiming that the heretical Church of Sclavonia is found in Bosnia and Dalmatia.[37]

As Ecclesia Sclavoniae came to operate in a territory which was to come under the nominal jurisdiction of Rome, it assumed more 'Catharist' characteristics. According to an early established and still widely held view, the Bosnian Church was a result of the evolution of the dualist movement in Bosnia – *Ecclesia Sclavoniae* of the inquisitors – into a national Bosnian Church which in about 1250 'displaced Catholicism as the established religion'.[38] This view has been subjected to sustained criticism which rejects the dualist nature of the Church of Bosnia but admits the presence of a dualist movement in the religious life of medieval Bosnia and its potential influences on the Bosnian Church.[39] In this view it emerged as a reaction against the Hungarian crusades but was based on the earlier Catholic monastic movement in Bosnia and developed in isolation from east and west. Another view posits a merger between the earlier Catholic monastic organization in Bosnia (which may actually have been a form of East Orthodox monastic order) and the dualist movement during the Hungarian crusade which resulted in the formation of the Bosnian Church, and its retention of some dualist features in its theology.[40] What is certain is that the Bosnian Church, established in an area where the spheres of influence of the western and eastern churches met, was schismatic from both Catholicism and Orthodoxy and had its own hierarchy, its head, *dyed*, presiding over the lesser ranks of *gost*, *starac* and *strojnik*. The members of the Bosnian Church were often referred to as Patarenes, the customary name for the Italian Cathars, and were sometimes associated with heterodox and heretical beliefs and practices. As with much of the religious life of medieval Bosnia, the beliefs and the practices of the Bosnian Church remain elusive but they were condemned as heretical by Rome and occasionally also by the Serbian Orthodox Church. For medieval Catholic observers the Bosnian Church was a dualist organization and in Pope Pius' opus *Europa* the Bosnian heretics were described as living in monasteries and as being 'Manichees', believers in two principles, 'the one good and the other evil'.[41] Indeed, it acquired a Slavonic ritual[42] that bears a close resemblance to the Cathar Ritual of Lyons and was certainly brought to Bosnia by Bogomil sectarians. Some of the practices attributed to members of the Bosnian Church at various stages – rejection of the veneration of icons and the cross, proscription of swearing vows – certainly betray dualist influences, but on the whole the organization, conduct and recorded beliefs of the Bosnian Church differ from those of the traditional dualist churches. Yet the dualist movement in Bosnia certainly enjoyed a high reputation among the western Cathar churches and in 1325 John XXII declared that many Cathars were flocking to Bosnia which has been seen sometimes as a dualist 'Promised Land'.[43] The last Cathar communities in Piedmont maintained contacts with Bosnia and their heresy was defined as 'the faith of the heretics of Bosnia'. The Bosnian dualist movement outlasted not only western Catharism but also the Bogomil communities to the east – but still the problem of its association with the actual Bosnian Church remains a puzzle. The evidence allows different solutions and even when regarded as an independent body from the dualist sect in Bosnia, the Bosnian Church could still have maintained relations with the dualists and may have acquired practices or beliefs from them,[44] an interchange that may have led to the emergence of the dualist currents within the Bosnian Church itself.

The problem of the origins and the nature of the Bosnian Church remains unresolved and while it is certain that it cannot be considered a typical dualist church, it is equally certain that it was not merely an offshoot of a Catholic order which had broken with Rome. The evidence indicates that members of the Bosnian Church could adhere to orthodox Christian beliefs and practices, but could, at times, also follow heretical, dualist or pagan traditions, surviving pagan elements remaining particularly active in the diverse religious world of medieval Bosnia. The view that the dualist movement and the monastic order in Bosnia fused to form the Bosnian Church in the turmoil of the Hungarian Crusade answers most of the puzzles associated with the Bosnian Church, if it is accepted, of course, that the newly formed Church gradually abandoned some of its dualist beliefs and practices on its way to becoming an established ecclesiastical body. Such an evolution would explain the coexistence of heretical and non-heretical teachings and practices ascribed to the Bosnian Church, in which dualism eventually could become 'a half understood heritage from the past',[45] Such a development is attested among the Paulician groups in Thrace that abandoned at least some of their dualist teachings towards the end of the seventeenth century and of which teachings only fragments survive in the later records of their beliefs.[46] Furthermore, dualist and orthodox Christian beliefs and practices could coexist harmoniously among the Cathars in Ferrara[47] and if this was the case in Italy, how much more would it have been possible in Bosnia, where religions heterodoxy was never extinguished. In this case the crusading designs and ventures in Bosnia not only failed but backfired by leading to a fusion of its own former monastic order with the dualist sect, which was to have been eradicated, to a creation of a rival Church in Bosnia preventing Rome from establishing firm control. At the same time, a dualist sect, with limited influence, might have remained independent from the Bosnian Church, but still capable of exerting influence on its members and perhaps of reviving dualist concepts in its theology.

Whatever the truth about its beginnings, the first certain signs of the existence of an organized Bosnian Church appeared around 1322, while three years later Pope John XXII wrote to the Bosnian Ban and the Hungarian king that numerous heretics from many different regions were flocking to the Bosnian state.[48] While it is difficult to be sure to what degree this papal letter reflects an actual heretical influx into Bosnia, it nevertheless bears testimony to papal distress over the religious situation there. Bosnia was regarded as a safe haven for heretics persecuted in western Christendom and the centre of a heretical diaspora. This evidence has led some scholars to conclude that in the period when the Inquisition was extinguishing the last traces of Catharism in the west, Bosnia may indeed have become a refuge for persecuted Cathars, and have come to be seen as a kind of a dualist 'Promised Land'; in consequence, the dualist heresy there may have acquired a 'Latin or Italian core'.[49] Several years later the Dominicans and the Franciscans began to vie for the right to send missions to Bosnia. Ultimately the inquisitorial contest was won by the Franciscans. Whatever the success of the

Franciscan mission, in 1337 Pope Boniface XII was already appealing to several strong Croatian nobles to aid the Franciscans in Bosnia with military force, as the Ban and part of the nobility were protecting the heretics. The swift military action of the Bosnian Ban prevented any Croatian interference but the Ban soon deemed it necessary to sanction the foundation of a Franciscan vicariate in Bosnia and accepted Catholicism himself.

The Bosnian state established by Kotromanić was rather decentralized and soon after his death Bosnia and Hungary found themselves vying for the fealty of vassals in northern Bosnia, and eventually his Catholic successor, Tvrtko, had to recognize the suzerainty of the Hungarian King Louis the Great in 1357. Yet warfare between Bosnia and Hungary flared up in 1363 and upon his invasion, Louis, the most notable of the Hungarian Anjou kings, pledged to annihilate what was seen as the great number of heretics and Patarenes in Bosnia. The Hungarian onslaught was repelled and during a period of political vicissitudes Tvrtko was accused by his own brother of accepting and defending heretics who flocked to his domain. Despite the continuing papal complaints of the heresy in Bosnia and appeals for Hungarian intervention, Tvrtko began to expand his sway into Serbia, annexing more Orthodox territory. After a period of ascendancy in the Balkans, Serbian power was in decline and after the death of the great Serbian ruler Stefan IV Dushan in 1355 the end of the royal Nemanjid dynasty came in 1371. On account of his relation to the dynasty, Tvrtko, already married to a Bulgarian Orthodox princess, laid claim to the Serbian kingship and in 1377 was crowned by an Orthodox metropolitan, king of Serbia, Bosnia and the 'coastal lands'.

There are many indications that while the Franciscan mission had made some headway in central Bosnia, Catholicism remained underdeveloped in the country. In 1373 the Franciscan vicar revealed to the pope that in Bosnia Catholic converts had to profess Catholicism in secret and to publicly perform heretical rites like 'adoring heretics', an obvious allusion to the Cathar rite of the *melioramentum*, described by the inquisitors as 'adoration'. However, Tvrtko tolerated different faiths in his realm and Pope Gregory IX was notified that while attending Catholic services, the Ban was sometimes accompanied by heretics and Patarenes.

That activity of the dualist movement during Tvrtko's rule is verified by the testimony of the procedures of the Inquisition against an Italian

Cathar community in Chieri, Piedmont, in 1387. The trial against the Piedmont Cathars coincided with the appearance of two Catholic polemical tracts against the Bosnian Patarenes and their dualist beliefs. One of the Piedmont Cathars, Jacob Bech, revealed before the Inquisition in Turin that he had been converted by two Italian heretics and one from 'Sclavonia' and that some of his co-sectarians had already gone to Bosnia to be initiated into the heretical teachings. Bech was sentenced for following the teachings of the Cathars and 'the heretics of Sclavonia' and later the Inquisition actually found and burned the remains of one of the Chieri Cathars who had gone to Sclavonia to accept the 'faith of the heretics of Bosnia'.[50]

Whereas the Bosnian dualists apparently maintained some contacts with the remaining Cathars in northern Italy, their relations with their Balkan co-sectarians to the east remain obscure. In a turbulent century, which was to be sealed with the momentous victories of Islam in the Balkans, the encounters between the Orthodox Church and the dualist tradition entered their final stages.

The Hesychast Mystics and the Bogomils

In 1261 the Nicaean Emperor Michael VIII restored the Byzantine empire under the Palaeologus dynasty (1261–1453), but increasingly weakened by internal civic and religious dissension it never reached its past imperial glory. In the second half of the thirteenth century the Bulgarian empire entered another 'Time of Trouble' but when it recovered towards the beginning of the fourteenth century it was overshadowed by the rise of Serbia as the dominant Balkan power.

In the first half of the fourteenth century the Orthodox Church was plagued by new theological controversies provoked by the emphatic revival of the Byzantine mystical tradition in the teachings of the Hesychast mystics. The Hesychasts elaborated the monastic contemplative tradition of the inner mystical prayer (*hesychia*) associated with the perpetual recitation of the Jesus Prayer, 'Lord Jesus Christ, Son of God, have mercy on me, a sinner'. While Hesychast doctrine and practice are emphatically contemplative, some Hesychast methods of inner prayer prescribe bodily postures and breathing control for achieving the necessary concentration during the prayer. The ultimate aim of the Hesychast contemplation was the communion with the divine and Hesychasm found its influential theological systematization in Palamism, the mystical teachings of the theologian St Gregory Palamas (1294–1357), the spiritual descendant of Symeon the Theologian. In Palamism God's essence remains inaccessible but the inner prayer could lead the mystic to a vision of God's uncreated light, transfiguration and salvation. Hesychasm was widespread in Byzantine monastic circles but its stronghold was the great monastic centre of Mount Athos in northeast Greece, the 'Holy Mountain' of Orthodoxy.

The increasing prominence of Hesychast mysticism was bitterly confronted by the anti-Palamite faction in the Orthodox Church, headed by Barlaam of Calabria, Gregory Akyndinus and the historian Nicephorus Gregoras. Among other arguments, the anti-Palamite party tried to associate the Hesychast focus on inner prayer and the deification of the mystic with Massalianism, then routinely identified with Bogomilism. Gregory Palamas himself condemned Massalianism as teaching that man could behold the unknowable essence of God and is reported to have defeated 'Massalians' in theological debates in one of the monasteries of Thrace. Indeed, the reaction to Hesychasm within the Orthodox Church also reflected the concern of some Byzantine ecclesiastical circles with the extreme monastic mysticism that was viewed as fertile ground for the emergence of heresy.

Massalian and Bogomil propaganda in the monasteries had a long history and in the first half of the fourteenth century the sectarian preachers encroached even on the spiritual bastion of Orthodox monasticism and Hesychasm, the Holy Mountain of Athos. Converted to the 'Massalian heresy' in Thessalonica, a number of Athonite monks propagated the heresy in the monasteries of Mount Athos for three years. The spread of the heresy was eventually checked by a special council which anathematized the heretics and banished them from the Holy Mountain. Following their expulsion the disgraced Athonite monks scattered from Constantinople to Thessalonica and Bulgaria. The prominent anti-Hesychast Nicephorus Gregoras alleged that even the champion of Hesychasm, Gregory Palamas, being a covert heretic himself, had to leave Mount Athos and hide in Thessalonica.

The Hesychast controversies attained political dimensions during the civil strife in Byzantium between 1341 and 1347, when Gregory Palamas was excommunicated, cast into prison and his Hesychast teachings condemned. The Council of 1347, however, released Palamas from his excommunication and supported Hesychasm, while excommunicating the prominent anti-Hesychast Akyndinos. Yet the two parties in the Church clashed again during the Council of 1351 when under Patriarch Callistus, Palamism was sanctioned anew and the 'rationalist' teachings of Barlaam of Calabria were condemned. Yet the anti-Palamite faction continued to be active and even sought to discredit Patriarch Callistus with accusations of heresy. In an episode similar to the twelfth-century deposition of Cosmas Atticus, one of Callistus' closest allies in Constantinople, the monk Niphon Scorpio, who had already been accused of Bogomilism, came to be accused of Massalianism by the Athonite monks. Niphon Scorpio had formerly spent some years at Mount Athos and the exhaustive enquiries of the Athonite monks had found evidence that he had indeed been one of the heretical monks. The patriarch faced the allegations of the anti-Hesychast faction but unlike Cosmas Atticus three centuries earlier he secured the final condemnation of his adversaries.[51] By the time Gregory Palamas, who had been raised as the archbishop of Thessalonica, was canonized in 1368, his great adversary Nicephorus Gregoras had died, anathematized and under house arrest, and his corpse had been dragged through the streets of Constantinople.

One of the key figures of the Hesychast movement, St Theodosius of Trnovo, also led the battle against Bogomilism and heresy in the fourteenth century.[52] An old ally of Patriarch Callistus, St Theodosius endeavoured to establish Hesychasm and confronted an array of heretical preachers. A monk called Theodoret attacked Hesychasm, and his own teachings, with their pagan and magical character, gained ground in the higher classes. He was banished by St Theodosius but another monk, Theodosius, after a period of asceticism, embarked on large-scale evangelization, denounced marriage and taught his adherents to follow him naked. Inevitably, he was accused of encouraging indiscriminate promiscuity, but it seems that he was preaching return to the 'paradisal state'. Even more dangerous were the preachings of two monks, Lazarus and Cyril the Barefooted, who had been ejected earlier along with the other heretical monks from Mount Athos. The two ex-Athonite monks, who were joined by a priest called Stefan, claimed to follow the ideal of apostolic poverty and incessant prayer, teaching that dreams were divine visions. They were also charged with various excessive teachings, varying from the indispensability of castration to the necessary submission to the 'natural passions'. In the Council convened in 1350 by St Theodosius, approved by the Bulgarian Tsar Ivan Alexander (1331–71), the heretical trio was accused of professing the radical dualist belief in two principles, but confusingly the recorded doctrine refers to the good God presiding over the earth and his adversary reigning in heaven. The dualism and anti-sacramentalism of the heretics were, however, drastically dissociated from the customary Bogomil asceticism and rigorous morality. Following the Council and the encounter with St Theodosius, Lazarus recanted, while the priest Stefan and monk Cyril were branded on the face and expelled from the realm.

During the decade following the Council St Theodosius had to acknowledge the rise of a powerful Judaizing movement related to a critical dynastic collision in the royal family – Tsar Ivan Alexander had cloistered his Tsaritsa in a monastery and had married a Jewess. Having succeeded in fostering the growth of Hesychasm in Bulgaria, St Theodosius eventually prevailed on the Tsar to convoke another Council in 1360 which anathematized the anti-Hesychasts along with the Bogomils and the Judaizers. The anti-Hesychasts and the Bogomils were proclaimed banished from Bulgaria, whereas the three leaders of the Judaizing movement were originally sentenced to death but were later reprieved by the Tsar; one of them repented and was converted to Orthodoxy, another was murdered by a mob and the third suffered mutilation. Some of the charges levelled against the Judaizers – the rejection of the churches, the clergy, the sacraments, the icons – reiterated traditional accusations against Bogomilism, and the Council of 1360 is accordingly seen sometimes as having been summoned against an association of the Judaizing and Bogomil movements.[53]

The banishing of the Bogomils from Bulgaria doubtless resulted in persecution but the scale and course of it remain unknown. Anti-Bogomil measures were also taken in neighbouring Serbia – a Serbian code of law, dating from the mid-fourteenth century, provided different punishments, from branding to exile, for the followers of Bogomilism, condemned in the document as the 'Babun faith'.[54] There are some indications that Bogomil refugees moved to the newly established Walachian principality to the north of the Danube and thereafter their fortunes in Bulgaria largely disappear from the records. When in 1365 the king of Hungary, Louis the Great, occupied parts of north-west Bulgaria he introduced Franciscan missions aimed at the conversion of numerous Patarenes and 'Manichaeans' to Catholicism. After his prolonged battle against the sectarian enemies of Orthodoxy St Theodosius died in 1363 but even from his deathbed he was warning against the ever-dangerous Bogomil–Massalian heresy.

During the patriarchate of one of his eminent disciples, Patriarch Euthymius (1375–93), the Bulgarian empire enjoyed a remarkably flourishing culture but heretical preachers continued to enjoy prominence. Particularly influential were the teachings of two vigorous heretical preachers, Phudul and Piropul, who shared the anti-clerical tenets of the Bogomils but were also renowned for their magic practices. Their teachings and rites of 'demonic sorcery' had won a considerable following, even among the nobility and the court, but the zealous public preachings of the patriarch were said to have extinguished 'the evil seeds of their venom'.[55]

In the last phase of the confrontation between heresy and Orthodoxy in Bulgaria the Orthodox authorities were challenged mainly by syncretistic teachings which combined the old anti-clerical and anti-sacramental attitudes of the Bogomils with pagan and magical practices. By that time the association between heresy and magic in western Christendom, forged in Catholic polemical anti-heretical writings, had produced the early versions of the theological and legal stereotypes of European diabolical witchcraft which would continue into the Renaissance and the early modern period, justifying the manifold excesses and the repeated upsurges of the witch-craze.

Heresy and Magic – East and West

When faced with the perceived threats of magic and heresy, secular and ecclesiastical authorities in the early medieval period could draw respectively on the strong anti-magical decrees of late Roman secular legislation (particularly severe against maleficient magic or *maleficium*) and the patristic literature dealing with the problems of magic and heresy. In the struggle against paganism, sorcery and heterodoxy the early medieval Church could put to use the decrees of ecclesiastical synods and councils such as the Council of Chalcedon (451). These decrees and papal decretals were assembled, together with selected patristic writings, to from the basis for ecclesiastical canon law which included sanctions against magic and heresy.

At the same time, with the progressive Christianization of Europe, a number of churchmen were certainly instrumental in assimilating pagan practices and customs, which in theory should have been condemned, in a variety of local religious and cultural syncretisms. Still, patristic views of magic as essentially demonic in nature in all its forms inevitably played a crucial role in the shaping of early medieval ecclesiastical attitudes to magic in general and *maleficium* in particular or to persistent and unassimilated vestiges of paganism. The demonization of generally pagan and specifically magical rites or customs is apparent in the decisions of the Synod of Toledo (681), the Synods of Rome (743 and 826), the Synod of Tours (813), the Synod of Paris (829) and the famous Canon Episcopi (*c.* 900).[56] On the other hand, among the factors that contributed to the increased influence of the already established link between magic and heresy was the idea of the satanic pact, popularized by the story of Theophilus, the sixth-century priest, translated from Greek into Latin by the end of the ninth century, who with the help of a Jewish magus had made a pact with the Devil to renounce Christ and the Virgin Mary in order to regain his position in the Church. Encyclo-pedist authors such as Isidore of Seville (*c.* 560–636) – in his influential *Etymologies*[57] – and later, Rabanus Maurus (774/86–856), reiterated the earlier patristic condemnation of all forms of magic, and in his exegesis of Exodus 22 : 18 the latter explicitly associated *maleficium* with heresy. Still, significantly enough, the secular Germanic law codes endorsed some of the late Roman anti-magical strictures, but apart form the anti-heretical legislation of the Visigothic kings of Spain provided few legal provisions against heresy.[58] Against the background of the prosecution and punishment of heresy, and what was to be condemned as demonic magic and witchcraft in the later Middle Ages and early modern period, on the whole the early medieval Church certainly seems less repressive in its treatment of heterodoxy, magic and heresy.

Following the appearance of reformist, heterodox and heretical groups in western Christendom during the eleventh and twelfth centuries, some of them came to be accused of secret criminal and orgiastic practices and conscious diabolism. Such accusations were brought against the heretical groups at Orleans in 1022, heretics at Châlons-sur-Marne in 1043–8[59] and 'Manichaean' heretics near Soissons around 1114.[60] These accusations of clandestine blasphemous and promiscuous rites were mostly literary stereotypes which had a long pre-medieval history, as indicated by Roman charges against the Jews and the early Christians.[61] At the same time, contemporary literary narratives concerning magicians and the source of their art, like the third book of Anselm of Besate's *Rhetori-machia* (*c.* 1050)[62] and William of Malmesbury's (*c.* 1096–1143) version of the legends about Pope Sylvester II (999–1003),[63] reinforced the notion of the magician's pact with the Devil or with demons. The chivalric romances also elaborated a number of important magical themes, many of which appear more or less Christianized, while some are further related to developing the evolution of ideas about demonic magic. The assimilation of Greek and Arabic scientific and magical learning in the west in the twelfth century increased the interest in certain forms of natural magic. However, attempts to legitimize them met strong opposition from figures like Hugh of St Victor (d. 1142), whose reiter-ation of the patristic view that not only the *maleficium* but all forms of magic were demonic, exercised a strong influence on the shaping of theological and legal opinions in the twelfth and thirteenth centuries.[64]

As heretical and heterodox movements increased their influence from the mid twelfth century, charges similar to those against heretics in the eleventh and early twelfth centuries came to be levelled against dualist Cathar and reformist Waldensian groups which helped the crystal-lization of new anti-heretical stereotypes. Accusations of secret, sacrile-gious rites and diabolism were raised against Cathar or Cathar-influenced heretics at Rheims in 1176–8[65] and, similarly, Alan de Lille asserted that the Cathars indulged in the worship of Lucifer.[66] He claimed, moreover, that the Waldensians abandoned themselves to excesses and libertinism in their assemblies,[67] whereas in a tract ascribed to David of Augsburg they are condemned for performing unholy rites in secrecy.[68] In the early 1230s the accusations of the first papal inquisitor in the German lands, Conrad of Marburg, against heretics in the Rhineland led to the issue of the bull *Vox in Rama* by Gregory IX (1227–41) in 1233, in which the heretics are depicted as worshipping Lucifer in blasphemous rites and obscene orgies and prophesying his final victory over God and the restoration of his rightful preeminence as the true creator.[69] In the fourteenth century some charges against Waldensian groups derive directly from *Vox in Rama*,[70] and similar teachings and practices were ascribed to 'Luciferan' heretics in Austria and Bohemia.[71] On the whole, in the period between the eleventh and fourteenth centuries, despite the appearance of heresiological tracts that offered more or less genuine reports of heretical doctrines and practices, they did not prevent the formation of influential anti-heretical defamatory clichés in other sources. Such accounts wove together in a variety of ways elements of actual heretical teachings, stereotypical accusations of orgiastic feasts and of unholy rites at the heretical secret assemblies with notions from contemporary learned or popular beliefs about magic, the demonic pact and Devil-worship.[72]

Meanwhile, as heretical and reformist movements spread during the high Middle Ages, both secular and ecclesiastical authorities began to impose sterner penalties on heretics. A crucial factor that contributed to this increased harshness was the revival of Roman law in the late eleventh and twelfth centuries, which revitalized the notion of heresy as treason against God to be punished by death, as formulated in the Theodosian and Justinian codes. The Decretum of Gratian (c. 1140),[73] the influential systematic synthesis of canon law, which was to become the basis for later collections of canon law, revived and re-emphasized the patristic condemnation of heresy and magic. Its selection of texts by figures like Jerome and Augustine would render it a standard source for authoritative views on heresy and magic for later theologians and canonists. Gratian's dependence upon and quotes from Augustine's strong attacks on all varieties of magic, which contributed to the notion of a pact with the Devil, played an important role in shaping subsequent theological and legal attitudes which were also influenced by the dominance of scholastic philosophy and theology from the twelfth century. Although the immediate contribution of scholasticism to the formulation of later learned notions of diabolical witchcraft should not be exaggerated,[74] with its systematic treatment of demonology and the manifold attacks of William of Auvergne (c. 1180–1249)[75] and Thomas Aquinas (c. 1225–74)[76] on magic, it created the theoretically justified intellectual and theological framework within which both magic and heresy could be directly associated with service to the Devil. Among the factors that contributed to the building of this framework were the scholastic Aristotelian opposition to natural magic; the idea of the explicit pact as an actual covenant with the Devil and of the implicit pact as tacit consent to serve the demons through magic or heresy; and the elaboration of notions concerning sexual intercourse between humans and demons. These scholastic reformulations and refinements of the idea of the pact and various elements of Christian demonology allowed for the future branding of all practitioners of the magic arts – from ritual magician dabbling in demonic or natural magic, to the peasant practitioner of low magic – as involved in actual or virtual diabolism, as apostates and heretics, who could be prosecuted via the appropriate anti-heretical legislation.

The main stages in the development of new anti-heretical legislation could be clearly charted from the late twelfth through the thirteenth centuries. Before the enforcement of new anti-heretical legal measures in the late twelfth century the ecclesiastical authorities could impose excommunication on the discovered heretics who, however, could face harsher penalties and even death at the hands of lynch mobs and the secular courts, as demonstrated by the executions of heretical groups at Orléans in 1022, Montforte in 1028 and Cologne in 1143. In 1184 Pope Lucius III (1181–85) issued the bull *Ab Abolendum*, with the concurrence of Emperor Frederick Barbarossa (1155–90), which signalled the beginning of cooperation between church and state powers in suppressing heresy. The bull decreed that bishops should conduct inquests of reported outbreaks of heresy, impose canonical penalties on proven heretics and then deliver them to the secular authorities for punishment.[77] In 1199 Innocent III (1198–1216) further specified the legal repression of heresy in the bull *Vergentis in senium* which also revived the notion of the association between heresy and treason as formulated earlier in Roman law.[78] The Fourth Lateran Council of 1215 reaffirmed and extended the legal repression of heresy[79] and these new anti-heretical provisions of the canon law were adopted in 1220 in the secular legislation of Frederick II (1220–50) which also prescribed the death penalty for convicted heretics. The repression of heresy entered a new stage when, between 1227 and 1235, the episcopal 'inquisition' for heresy was augmented by a papal inquisition, which was to be conducted by the two new Mendicant orders, the Dominicans and Franciscans.[80]

With the institutionalization of the prerogatives and procedures of the papal inquisition, sanctioned by documents like the *Ad extirpanda* (1252) of Innocent IV (1243–54),[81] inquisitors also began to show interest in prosecuting sorcery cases against the background of the general tendency to associate some of its forms with idolatry and heresy. In 1258, despite

THE CRUSADE AGAINST DUALISM

the inquisitors' requests to be granted jurisdiction over sorcery, Pope Alexander IV (1254–61) declared that the inquisition should deal only with cases of sorcery which savour of 'manifest heresy'.[82] *Maleficium* had already been explicitly associated with heresy in a twelfth-century *glossa ordinaria* of the Bible[83] and this association was reaffirmed by commentators on Gratian's *Decretum*[84] and Frederick II's constitutions of 1233.[85] Following the decline of Catharism in the early thirteenth century, the famous inquisitorial manuals of Bernard Gui[86] and Nicholas Eymeric[87] showed a marked concern with magical practices in the context of apostasy and heresy. The manuals drew together various kinds of magic and divination as illicit and punishable and Eymeric, moreover, focused upon what he considered heretical magic, including some forms of ritual magic.[88] In the 1320s Pope John XXII (1316–34) proceeded to authorize inquisitors to prosecute sorcerers and ritual magicians[89] and his bull *Super illis specula* (1326 or 1327)[90] threatened the practitioners of magical arts who, in his words, made 'pacts with hell', with the penalties of heresy (except confiscation). His authorization allowing the inquisitors to act against magicians was, however, virtually withdrawn in 1330. In the first half of the fourteenth century a number of trials of high-ranking clerics and at the French court for political sorcery,[91] as well as some of the charges brought during the trial of the Knights Templar,[92] helped to draw the crime of illicit magic into the orbit of accusations of blasphemy, idolatry, heresy, treason and anti-Christian conspiracy in the public mind.

In a theological climate which displayed an increased concern with the role and power of the Devil, certain procedures of learned ritual magic involving invocations of maleficent beings could invite accusations of *maleficium* and demon-worship and the figure of the learned magus could be diabolized. To what extent this new preoccupation with the power of the Devil resulted from the challenge of Cathar dualism is open to question,[93] but it now seems evident that the stereotype of an anti-society of Devil-worshipping witches did not result during or as a direct consequence of the Inquisition's suppression of Catharism in Languedoc and northern Italy.[94] Some of the fourteenth-century cases of political sorcery combined charges of ritual magic and *maleficium* and introduced other notions that were to coalesce in the later concept of diabolical witchcraft.[95] The assimilation of various forms of magic arts to heresy was further enhanced when, in 1398, the theology faculty of the University of

Paris proclaimed that acts of magic or superstitious practices seeking results beyond what might be expected from God and nature were accomplished through an implicit or explicit pact with the Devil, amounting thus to apostasy and heresy.[96] In the first half of the fifteenth century in a series of bulls, Popes Alexander v (1409–10), Martin v (1417–31)[97] and Eugenius iv (1431–47)[98] urged the Inquisition to proceed against magicians and diviners and it was against a back-drop of anti-heretical campaigns and witchcraft and sorcery trials that the complex notion of diabolical witchcraft began to crystallize. The outcome of a process of a long synthesis between literary and theological traditions as well as legal developments involving theologians, canon lawyers, secular magistrates and inquisitors, it contained elements deriving from high medieval anti-heretical stereotypes (secret assemblies, orgiastic feasts, collective diabolism), charges against ritual magicians and practitioners of low magic and *maleficium*, literary and popular traditions concerning womens' magical activities and cultic survivals from paganism, some of which seem to be vestiges of shamanistic practices.[99] The concept of diabolical witchcraft remained durable during the peak of European witchcraft persecutions in the sixteenth and seventeenth centuries, such persecutions varying in scope and intensity as witch scares broke out and prosecutions were brought in both Catholic and Protestant areas.[100] Witchcraft cases were tried in episcopal, secular and inquisitorial courts and recent research has indicated a number of factors that contributed to the outbreaks of witchcraft scares and the levelling of such accusations as well as their social functions. In its definitive form the figure of the diabolical witch of the early modern period owed its most important features both to the image of the medieval antinomian and devil-worshipping heretic and to that of the condemned practitioners of magic art – the learned magus and the practitioner of low magic.

This is the general background in the Christian west against which one should view the amalgamation of the notions of magic and heresy, of magus and heresiarch, in medieval eastern Christendom. As did Catholic polemicists, so Orthodox heresiologists could find precedents in patristic sources for such a fusion as well as for the stereotype of a clandestine sect indulging in blasphemous and promiscuous rites. The harsh Justinian anti-Manichaean legislation was retained in later Byzantine law codes and the term 'Manichaean' continued to be employed as an equivalent of dualist or heretic sectarian or to condemn religious or political opponents. Likewise with accusations of 'Manichaeism', sorcery charges, particularly at the Byzantine court, could also be used as a political weapon. Political factors, for example, seem to have played an important role in the sorcery accusations at the Byzantine court in the twelfth and thirteenth centuries,[101] whereas earlier, around the mid ninth century, Santabarenus was accused of being a 'Manichaean' as well as a sorcerer and had to flee to then pagan Bulgaria;[102] politically motivated charges of magic were eventually also raised against his son, the well-known supporter of Patriarch Photius (d.c. 895), Theodore Santabarenus.[103]

In their normative form early medieval Byzantine theological and legal attitudes to magic and heresy developed under the influence of the inherited Justinian legislation, the authoritative pronouncements of Church Fathers like Basil the Great and John Chrysostom and the enactments of church councils like the Sixth Ecumenical Council of Constantinople (680–1) and the Council of Trullo (691–2). However, in a process of accommodation of certain features of pagan culture, similar to that which occurred in various areas in the Latin West, the Byzantine Church Christianized some pagan ritual observances and magic-like practices. Still, the continuation of heretical and magical traditions in the Greek (and later Graeco-Slavonic) East and the ecclesiastical responses to them had their own distinctive patterns of development, which differed from those in the Latin West. Byzantine secular legislation seems to have contributed little to the inherited legal provisions against magic and divination, which increasingly became the province of Byzantine canon law with its generally less harsh penalties but with its strong condemnation of magical practices which, as in the influential Canons 65 and 72 of St Basil, could prescribe for their perpetrators penance as long as that for murderer.[104] This tendency to treat acts of magic and divination largely within the jurisdiction of Byzantine canon law has been described as a 'domestication' of the problem of magic.[105] Later commentaries on compilations of Byzantine canon law could provide more detailed accounts of magical practitioners and techniques and even make punishment dependent on the repentance of the culprit.[106] The prevalence of Byzantine canon law in the prosecution of magic is evident in the campaign against magicians and sorcerers, initiated by Patriarch John Kalekas in 1338 – the apprehended 'perpetrators of demonic sorceries, magic and incantations' faced the patriarchal court and were charged and punished in accordance with the penitential canons rather than within the secular judicial framework of high treason and grave heresy.[107]

Earlier, in the wake of the Iconoclastic crisis in Byzantium, the magic-like use of Christian signs and images was transformed,[108] whereas Icono-clastic emperors like Constantine V (741–75) and Nicephorus I (802–11) could be portrayed by their adversaries as protectors of heretical movements.[109] Although the field of the history of Byzantine magic still needs systematic study, the extant evidence and its studies so far suggest not only a survival but a certain continuity in the transmission of learned magical traditions in the Byzantine world through the Middle Ages (as demonstrated, for example, by the parallels between the collections of texts on magic from the late and post-Byzantine period and fourth- and fifth-century Greek magical papyri).[110]

Elements or accounts of learned or popular magical practices and beliefs are preserved in Byzantine theological and secular literature which portrays the different facets of the magus in Byzantine traditions – from the learned magus (who, as in the Latin West, could be a high-ranking ecclesiastic) to the unholy miracle-worker (trying to rival the miracles of the saint) and the common sorcerer or sorcerers, with their love philtres and divinatory techniques. For example, in some of the writings of his Iconophile adversaries the Iconoclastic Patriarch John the Grammarian (838–43) is cast in the role of the learned magus, mastering pagan learning and forbidden magical arts.[111] Accordingly, in one of the Byzantine marginal psalters John is depicted as being overwhelmed by the Iconophile Patriarch Nicephorus I (806–15), mirroring the nearby representation of the defeat of the figure of Simon Magus by St Peter.[112] Furthermore, the struggle and the trials of strength between the unholy magus and the saint form one of the important themes of Byzantine hagiography,[113] where the magus may appear as an impious miracle-worker, spell-binder, healer or false ascetic, contesting the saint's spiritual hegemony and expertise in dealing with the supernatural. Apart from often being involved in love magic some of the sorcerers and sorceresses in Byzantine hagiographic and literary traditions are themselves cursed with irregular and excessive sexuality. The practitioner of magic arts was commonly seen as having acquired his magical and divinatory techniques through learning rather than as an intrinsically evil figure deriving his powers from the Devil,[114] but the notion of the diabolic pact was also developed in the story of Theophilus[115] and, too, in the account of the pursuits of the magician Heliodorus in the *Vita* of Leo of Catania.[116] Female, diabolic witch-like figures appear, moreover, in the *Vita* of St Basil the Younger and some of the writings of Neophytus the Recluse (1134–after 1234).[117]

The adoption of Byzantine religious and cultural traditions in the Orthodox Slavonic world from the late ninth century onwards was accompanied by the assimilation of Byzantine magical and divinatory lore. Charms and magical prayers as well as divinatory texts like the *Brontologion* and the *Selenodronomion* were translated and preserved in florilegia and also in liturgical and biblical manuscripts[118] but there are no extant Old Slavonic translations of works of learned ritual magic comparable to *The Testament of Solomon* and *The Magical Treatise of Solomon*. Apart from the assimilated elements of Byzantine magical and divinatory traditions, the southern and eastern Slavonic magical folklore present a rich and diverse spectrum of beliefs and practices some of which preserve very archaic features.[119] Standard normative attitudes to magic in the Slavia Orthodoxa were shaped by the adopted Byzantine canon law and penitential canons but in reality the boundaries between the doctrinally defined views on and alternative or popular notions of magic and demonology could be fluid and frequently blurred at various levels of society, including in ecclesiastical circles.

The fluidity and mutability of attitudes to magic in the Byzantine and, later, Orthodox Slavonic medieval worlds are also apparent in the Orthodox developments of the inherited traditions of the association between magic and heresy, and between the figures of the magus and the heretic or heresiarch. Perhaps the clearest reports of an early medieval sect seen as blending magic and heresy concern the so-called Athingani heretics in Byzantine Phrygia between the late eighth and tenth centuries.[120] The evidence about their teachings is meagre and controversial, representing them as Judaizers who kept the Jewish Sabbath but also indulged in magic and divination.[121] In sources hostile to Iconoclasm the emperors Nicephorus I and Michael II (820–9), who favoured the Iconoclastic movement, are alleged to have recognized and used their fortune-telling and magical ability[122] and Theophanes Continuatus even claims that Michael was born and brought up among the Athingani.[123] In a formula of abjuration concerning the Athingani they are condemned for resorting to charms, divination and magic and for invoking certain demons (ruled by three demon chiefs) to draw the moon to themselves and ask various questions.[124] They are also anathematized for giving the stars men's names and seeking to instigate them one against the other, an allegation which also appears in a similar form in a heresiological tract touching on the Athingani,[125] where they are also denounced for invoking the three demon chiefs with incantations to implore them to cause certain stars to bring calamity upon designated people. Yet although they are compared to the 'old Thessalian witches' and despite their combination of astral and demonic magic as well as *maleficium*, these Orthodox reports do not apply to them anti-heretical stereotypes centring on secret orgiastic practices and ritual crimes or actual diabolism. On the other hand, the association between the name of the sectarians and various practices of magic and divination persisted – in the twelfth century the canonist Theodore Balsamon associates the 'Athingani' with charmers, fortune-tellers, ventriloquists and false prophets.[126] By that time the term 'Athingani' was correlated with 'Atzingani', the common Byzantine name for gypsies, but it is debatable whether the latter derives directly from the designation of the heretical sect.[127] It seems certain that this association arose because both the gypsies and the heretical sect came to be renowned for their fortune-telling and magical skills; indeed, an early account of the arrival of the Gypsies in Byzantium, the eleventh-century *Vita* of St George the Athonite, describes them as 'descendants of Simon Magus, famous diviners and sorcerers.[128]

Regardless of their reputation for magic and demon-control the Athingani were spared, at least in the extant evidence, accusations of clandestine, blasphemous practices but such charges were levelled at another early medieval heretical sect, the Paulicians. During a synod in 719 at Dvin the head of the Armenian Church, John IV of Ojun, condemned the doctrines of heretics that may have been identical with the Paulicians, denounced them as 'sons of Satan' and further accused them of idolatry, invocation of demons, incestuous orgies, ritual infanticide and worship of the Devil.[129] An Armenian *Catalogue of Heresies* denounced an alleged early female leader and heresiarch of the sect as a villainous witch who sanctioned homicide and ritual blood-drinking on certain 'Satanic' days and apart from indulging in infanticide induced by a vision of Satan, claimed that the souls of the murdered children appeared in witches' visions.[130] Another Armenian source described a later heresiarch of the sect as a 'soothsayer',[131] whereas a late Bulgarian legend about the origin of the Paulicians, which is replete with anachronisms, ascribed the foundation of the sect to the Devil himself and depicted its first two heresiarchs, Subotin ('Child of the Sabbath') and Shutil ('Jester') as his immediate disciples.[132]

The rise of a new Balkan dualist heresy, Bogomilism, in the newly Christianized Bulgarian kingdom in the tenth century and its subsequent spread into Byzantium led to the appearance of Bogomil-centred heresiological literature which occasionally blended first-hand information on the sect with anti-heretical stereotypes. The first detailed important source for Bogomilism, Cosmas' *Sermon Against the Heretics*,[133] outlined the dualist, ascetic, anti-clerical and iconoclastic features of early Bogomilism and, apart from certain polemical parallels between the demons and the heretics, it did not resort to extreme anti-heretical stereotypes and demonological clichés. Significantly, Cosmas did not assimilate magic and diabolism to the new Bogomil heresy and his sober polemical approach acquired further significance by the consequent circulation and influence of his work in other Slavonic Orthodox milieus, particularly Russia, where it was used by the Orthodox opponents of new heresies and also for general didactic purposes.[134]

A more pronounced concern with magic and demonology may be found in the epistle of Euthymius of Peribleptos,[135] who offers a distorted, demonizing reading of the rite of the admission of a dualist listener into the grade of believers, with its focus on the process through which the initiating 'teachers of evil' recited a secret 'satanic incantation' intended to banish the blessing of the Holy Ghost from the soul of the proselyte and substitute it with the 'seal of the Devil'. In the next stage of the initiation, after a probationary period of further gradual induction into heretical teachings, the neophyte could become one of the teachers of the heresy, completely prepared, in his words, for 'the unholy service of the Devil and his mysteries'. According to Euthymius, since the heretics claim that the Devil has created and resides in the visible eighth heaven (the upper seven heavens being created by God) when they recite the Lord's Prayer they are consequently praying to the Devil. Clearly preoccupied by the heretical 'satanic incantation' and the manner in which he converts the neophytes into those 'ordained by the Devil', 'apostles of darkness' and 'teachers of evil', he introduces a separate story about the origin of the incantation. The story includes an interlude about Simon Magus, who is alleged to have been revered by the Phundagiagitai/Bogomils as their first great apostle, and conflates several heresiological and literary traditions. The narrative recounts that a certain diabolical magus passed on the 'satanic incantation' to an earlier heresiarch, Peter, along with instructions about its secret use for accomplishing demonic possession during the heretical baptism, designed to banish the Holy Ghost from the proselytes. The story also includes animal metamorphosis: after his death by stoning the heresiarch Peter is transformed into a wolf, but regardless of his fate the 'satanic incantation' finds its way into the heretical initiation ceremonies.[136]

It is obvious that Euthymius assimilated heresy to magic and demonic possession in his treatment of the heretical baptism but this theme exhausts most of his concerns with demonic magic and the 'satanic incantation'. His allusions to the heretical 'service of the Devil' and the satanic purpose of the heretical use of the Lord's Prayer reflect his inflated polemics rather than any concrete charges of collective apostasy and diabolism, including blasphemous or monstrous rites, as in the extreme forms of the anti-heretical stereotypes of accusations. He charged, however, individual heretics with antinomian or amoral behaviour and his account of the magus, whom he sees as in obvious league with the Devil, as a source for the heretical baptismal 'incantation' explicitly associates the diabolic magus with the heresiarch. Euthymius' epistle might thus have become the first step in the demonization of the Phundagiagitai/Bogomils that directly linked demonic magic with heresy, but, as it was, the ensuing theological attacks on the Bogomils chose other venues

A different theological approach to Bogomil baptismal procedures and demonology is evident in the Bogomil section of Euthymius Zigabenus' *Panoplia Dogmatica*,[137] reportedly based on a confession of faith and cross examination of the Bogomil heresiarch Basil the Physician before Emperor Alexius Comnenus (1081–1118). Zigabenus' account is the most systematic extant of the cosmology, anthropogony, Christology and demonology of contemporary Byzantine Bogomilism along with a valuable exposition of examples of Bogomil allegorical exegesis of the New Testament. While presenting Bogomil dualist satanology and demonology Zigabenus does not demonize the heretics but refutes their beliefs with a more or less controlled theological rhetoric. His account of the two separate Bogomil baptismal rites – the first admission of the listener into the ranks of the believers (*baptisma*) and the initiation of the believer into the dualist elite grade of the *perfectus (teleoisis)* – while denouncing these heretical ceremonies, is free from demonological clichés and fanciful claims about satanic incantations and forces unleashed during the initiations.[138] Unlike Euthymius of Peribleptos, who demonizes the Phundagiagitai/ Bogomils as 'devils incarnate' doomed to remain forever 'henchmen of the Devil', Euthymius Zigabenus sees the Bogomils as impious, deluded and deranged heretics, whose confused and contradictory teachings are worthy only of ridicule but which can by their devilish tricks entrap weak souls in a 'sea of godlessness'. Zigabenus' claims that the Bogomils propitiated (for the purposes of dissimulation) what they saw as demons inhabiting the Orthodox churches and icons revered by the Orthodox,[139] clearly should not be seen as assimilation of demon-worship to heresy. Polemical utterances declaring, for example, that since the heretics cannot recognize the true God, they are left with the worship of demons, are very few and do not amount to an explicit association between demonic magic or demonworship and heresy. On the other hand, Zigabenus' intriguing statement that the Bogomils referred to themselves as 'magi' (adding that here they are right because they are sorcerers, corrupters and destroyers)[140] probably derives from his understanding of their allegorical reading of the second chapter of the Gospel of Matthew (Bogomil exegetical focus on this gospel is attested throughout the tract), but such Bogomil self-descriptions could, of course, be interpreted literally by their opponents or used for polemical purposes as by Zigabenus.

Zigabenus completes his section on Bogomilism by praising the decision of the ecclesiastical and secular powers to have Basil publicly burned, a rare event in Byzantine history. It is, however, Anna Comnena's account of the Bogomil heresiarch's auto-da-fé that communicates the atmosphere of superstitious awe and expectation of unholy miracles that accompanied the event.[141] It is not impossible that Anna Comnena's description of Basil's burning may reflect legendary traditions that grew up in the wake of the execution,[142] but it seems evident that in the public consciousness he was, or came to be seen after his death by burning, as a heretical miracle-worker.[143] Bogomil demonology, framed in accordance with its dualist theology, and the Bogomil popular reputation for controlling and banishing demons could, however, be turned against the sect in polemical attacks vilifying Bogomil beliefs and practices.

An important and suggestive example of how Bogomil dualism could be subverted so that the Bogomils could be demonized and associated with demonic magic is provided by the tract *Dialogus de daemonum operatione*.[144] The heretics, condemned in the tract, are described as adhering to a belief in a trinity of a Father and two Sons, reigning respectively over the material and heavenly worlds, a teaching commonly associated with Bogomil monarchian dualism. The tract specifies that this doctrine derived from a development of Mani's teaching of the two principles, to which the heretics added a third one and thus their system came to comprise a Father, residing in a supramundane world, a younger Son, reigning over the heavenly realm, and an elder Son, who ruled over the visible world.[145]

The heresiological innovation of the tract lies in its claims that belief in these three principles was linked to three distinct trends of worship in the sect. The first strand professed a dual worship of both Sons, claiming that despite being currently separate, they would ultimately be reunited. The second trend revered the younger Son as a ruler over the superior heavenly world, but at the same time did not reject the elder Son because of his power to inflict evil. The third trend, however, derided the younger Son and worshipped the elder one, the 'earthly Satanael', praising his as the 'first-born of the Father' and the creator of the visible world. The tract accuses, moreover, the Euchites/Bogomils of celebrating their hidden mysteries with incestuous orgies, ritual infanticide and demonic sacrifice.[146] The tract then uses and subverts the theological basis of monarchian dualism to associate its three principles with three alleged patterns of worship among the Euchites/Bogomils. It employs the sharply negative connotations of the theme of the fictitious worshippers of the third principle, Satanael, in its application to the herectics of the old stereotype of a secret sect practising clandestine magical, erotic and murderous rites. Since the later dating of the work is the more probable one, it offers important parallels to some contemporary charges against western dualist and reformist sectarians.[147] Whether the accusations in the tract actually derive from the newly developed anti-heretical clichés in western Christendom, however, must be open to question – both the tract and these clichés may have used and reinterpreted earlier, common literary and theological tradition. Be that as it may, *Dialogus de daemonum operatione* provides the most extreme case of demonization of heretics and assimilation of demonic magic to heresy in medieval Orthodox heresiology.

It is worth observing that a certain kind of transvalued dualism is attributed to the two pagan wizards or magi (*volkhvy*) who, according to the Russian Primary Chronicle, led a rebellion in 1071.[148] They are reported to have believed that heavenly God created the soul of man, but the Devil made his body and that the latter, the Antichrist, resided in the abyss – a form of dualism that reversed the spiritualist focus of traditional Gnostic and Bogomil dualism. While it is difficult to assess the historical reality behind the episode, it is clear that the chronicle associates a heretical, anti-spiritualist type of dualism with paganism and demonic magic.

As far as the dualist Bogomils are concerned, further attempts to associate them with magical and pagan practices may be discerned in the *Synodicon of Tsar Boril*, the records of the anti-Bogomil council summoned by the Bulgarian Tsar Boril in 1211.[149] In its opening section the *Synodicon* draws on the Jannes–Jambres tradition of the two magicians who opposed Moses with their sorcery at the pharaonic court, comparing them to the founder of Bogomilism, the priest Bogomil, and his pupils.[150] Among the following anathemas condemning Bogomil dualist teachings and heresiarchs, most of which derive from an earlier letter of Patriarch Cosmas of Jerusalem (1075–81)[151] concerning the Bogomils, there appears a new anathema denouncing those who practise magic and 'gather fruits' on 24 June, the Nativity of St John the Baptist, and in the same night also perform 'detestable mysteries' similar to 'pagan rites'.[152] The new anathema clearly tries to discredit the Bogomils by linking them to magical practices and cultic survivals from paganism. Still another anathema in the *Synodicon* which may relate to attempts to censure and criminalize the Bogomils, curses those who try to harm the Tsar with sorcery and poison, a charge combining the crimes of *maleficium* and high treason.[153] Still, the council did not treat the Bogomils excessively harshly: those who repented were accepted back into the Church, whereas the unrepentant were exiled or suffered unspecified punishments.[154]

During the other anti-Bogomil council around 1350 the charges against three heresiarchs and teachers of the Massalian (i.e. Euchite – by then commonly used to denote Bogomilism) heresy included accusations of antinomian and libertine preachings and practices combined with a dualist doctrine which confusingly professes that the good God rules over the earth, whereas his adversary reigns in heaven. Evidence of the council's proceedings is preserved in the *Vita* of St Theodosius of

Trnovo,[155] the eminent champion of hesychasm in Bulgaria. It further relates the struggle of St Theodosius against other heresiarchs whose teachings could combine anti-clerical and anti-sacramental attitudes with practices which are duly condemned as 'demonic sorceries'. While is difficult to assess the veracity of such accusations of a syncretism of heretical and magical traditions, it is possible that St Theodosius encountered eccentric heresiarchs and teachings which variously combined dualist or heterodox traditions with superstitious and magical practices, probably incorporating vestiges of paganism.[156] On the whole, however, the *Vita* does not consistently assimilate magical to heretical practices, but allows for syncretistic fusions, including very odd combinations of sexual immorality and asceticism, but without forming exclusive stereotypes about the association between magic and heresy.

In 1360 still another anti-heretical council banished unrepentant Bogomils from the Bulgarian kingdom;[157] in one of the articles in the contemporary Code of the Serbian Tsar Stefan Dushan (1331–55), which was drawn up between 1349 and 1354 and contained anti-heretical legislation, certain magical practices are associated with heretics.[158] In the following hundred years, as the Ottoman conquest of the Balkan Christian monarchies progressed and the last vestiges of Byzantium were subdued, extant reports of Bogomil and other heretics become increasingly sparse, although a systematic study of all the available evidence may well shed new light on the evolution of Christian heresies in the early Ottoman period. The new developments in the legal treatment of magic and witchcraft cases in Orthodox Russia during the early modern period understandably remain outside the scope of this book.[159] However, one should note the formation of an explicit association between the term 'heretic' and the terms 'magician', 'demon' and 'vampire', particularly in northern Russia, which could figure both in sorcery accusations and in popular belief.[160] While it remains unclear when and why this direct association first developed, it may have been partially affected by a tendency in late medieval Orthodox Slavonic Indexes of Forbidden Books to link heresy with divinatory texts and magical prayers.[161]

Within the general context of medieval Orthodox heresiology even Patriarch Germanus of Nicaea's (1222–40) strong denunciations of the demon-inspired Bogomils and their 'dark mysteries'[162] or Metropolitan Symeon of Thessalonica's (1410–29)[163] accusations that they served the Devil and indulged in ecstatic, secret prayer and incantations, appear merely as samples of vigorous rhetorical invective which did not lead to the formation of fixed stereotypical attitudes associating magic with heresy or the figure of the heresiarch with the (diabolic) magus. The polemical tradition of the demonic association of magic and heresy continued, of course, throughout the Middle Ages, periodically resurfacing in accusations against heretics and sorcerers. However, despite the inherited ecclesiastical and secular condemnation and criminalization of magic and heresy, medieval Orthodox heresiology neither occasioned nor contributed to a reconception or hardening of the theological and legal stance on magic and heresy and their association similar to that prevalent in late medieval Western Christendom.[164] Among the contributory factors to this contrasting attitude between Catholic and Orthodox heresiologies *vis-à-vis* the legal system and theology some differences may be highlighted: the flexible and changeable nature of Byzantine demonology,[165] which contained traditions about the diabolic pact,[166] but they never became a core element in its theory of demonic magic and rarely shaped intrinsically evil figures of sorcerers comparable to the classical stereotype of the diabolical witch; the absence of systematic legal and scholastic-type debate concerning the association between magic and heresy in Byzantium, and common in western Christendom; the generally less legalistic approach of Eastern Orthodoxy, including matters of canon law and its codification and application by various Eastern Orthodox churches.

The association, then, between the heresiarch and the magus in western and eastern Christendom followed slightly different trajectories, reflecting occasionally different dogmatic and polemical agendas. Within the framework of broader definitions of the terms 'religion' and 'magic' there emerges a question to which presently it is difficult to find an answer. To what extent did the medieval heresiarchs, particularly the dualists, revive or continue what Frances A. Yates saw as the essentially Gnostic based tradition of 'the dignity of Man as Magus', possessor of the divine creative power and capable of restoring his status of a divine being, before the tradition's reaffirmation in the figure of the Renaissance magus?[167] What is certain is that both the figure of this posited Renaissance 'Gnostic' magus and the continuing association between magic and heresy came to appear more at odds with parallel corresponding developments in the Balkan-Byzantine world once the latter was caught up in the political and religious turmoil of the Ottoman invasion and affected by the new, striking forms of religious syncretism of the early Ottoman period.

Heresy and Politics in Bosnia

The Ottoman avalanche in the Balkans found the Christian Balkan domains disunited and weakened by the usual internecine strife and the fate of the Byzantine emperor, who after 1371 was virtually an Ottoman vassal, was shared by the other Balkan monarchs. The great battle at Kosovo Polje in 1389, where allied Balkan (mostly Bosnian and Serbian) armies encountered the Ottomans, brought the deaths of Sultan Murad and the Serbian prince Lazar and opened the way for further Ottoman advance in the Balkans. In 1393 the Bulgarian patriarch Euthymius had to organize the defence of the capital, Trnovo, which fell to the Ottomans after a three-month siege and was sacked and partly burnt. The patriarch was exiled and by the end of the century most of the fragmented Bulgarian domains were engulfed by the Ottoman empire.

The first western crusade against the Ottomans, led by the Hungarian King Sigismund, ended in disaster in 1396 and the subsequent endeavours in 1444 and 1448 failed to check the Ottoman irruption into Europe. In 1453 Constantinople, after serving for more than 1,200 years as a capital of the successive Roman, East Roman and Byzantine empires, fell to the Ottomans and the cathedral of St Sophia was converted into a mosque. The residues of Serbia were annexed in 1459, while in 1517 Sultan Selim the Grim captured Cairo to assume the caliphate, and twelve years later the Ottomans besieged Vienna for the first time.

Balkan Orthodoxy had to adapt itself to Ottoman rule and Bogomilism gradually vanished from its records altogether. The last Orthodox polemist to denounce the Bogomil heresy was Symeon, Metropolitan of Thessalonica (1417–30), who launched a fierce attack on the Bogomils, whom he styled also as 'Kudugers', in his *Dialogus contra haereses*.[168] Symeon condemned the Bogomils as the most dangerous heretics in his metropoly and, echoing Psellus' allegations against the Thracian sectarians, accused them of worshipping, in 'secret and godless ceremonies', the Antichrist, the 'Archon of sin and darkness'. Around 1454 to 1456 the Constantinople patriarch Gennadius Scholarius, who was the first patriarch to be appointed by an Ottoman sultan, mentioned in one of his letters that the Bosnian Kudugers were still active and influential among the nobility and the court in Herzegovina.[169] At that time Bosnia and Herzegovina had not yet been conquered by the Ottoman armies and Rome was still continuing its struggle against what the papacy saw as 'Manichaean' heresy and 'errors' in Bosnia.

Alongside the Serbian troops, the Bosnian forces played a role in the battle with the Ottomans at Kosovo Polje, 'the Waterloo of Balkan freedom',[170] and upon the death of Sultan Murad on the battlefield the Bosnian king Tvrtko proclaimed a Christian victory and was praised in Florence as a Saviour of Christendom. Following his death in 1391, the decentralizing tendencies in the Bosnian domains prevailed again and several strong Bosnian houses came to dominate the political scene, while the succeeding Bosnian rulers found it extremely difficult to assert their authority and in the climate of political dualism were sometimes challenged by anti-kings raised by opposing noble factions. What complicated the political situation in the western Balkans further was the struggle for the Hungarian throne – between Ladislas of Naples and the would-be Holy Roman emperor, Sigismund of Luxemburg – which evolved into a war of succession that affected and divided the Bosnian nobility.

It seems certain that most of the Bosnian nobles were associated initially with the Bosnian Church, but with the gradual penetration of Catholicism into Bosnia some of them accepted the Catholic faith. In the early fourteenth century, when both Hungary and Bosnia witnessed the struggles of rival claimants for their thrones, several of the major Bosnian noble houses were closely linked with the Bosnian Church and used Patarenes for diplomatic services. Among the Bosnian nobles who took active part in the Hungarian dynastic collisions, particularly important was Duke Hrvoje Vukčić, who was himself known as a Patarene, and is traditionally described as the Bosnian king-maker.

In 1393 Sigismund of Luxemburg had forced the Bosnian king Dabisha to recognize him as successor to the Bosnian throne, but his unsuccessful bid for the Bosnian crown in 1395 had compelled many Bosnians into alliance with his rival, Ladislas. Duke Hrvoje sided initially with Ladislas and eventually became his deputy for Croatia and Slavonia, and while the Ladislas camp acknowledged that Hrvoje was a Patarene, it was declared that he would be brought back to the true faith. Whatever

Hrvoje's religious affinities and designs, in 1409, after an emphatic victory of Sigismund over the Bosnians, the Patarene duke shifted his allegiance to him and was accepted along with the Orthodox Serbian and Walachian rulers into his newly founded Dragon Order intended to fight pagans and heretics. Only three years later Sigismund suddenly charged Duke Hrvoje with plotting rebellion and stripped him of his powers in the kingdom; Hrvoje pleaded that as a member of the Dragon Order he must be judged before the Order and if found guilty would allow them to have his head. He implored to be allowed to embrace the Catholic faith, as he did not wish to end his days in a 'pagan rite',[171] a cryptic confession, made, moreover, by a member of the Dragon Order. Hrvoje's plea to be delivered from the 'pagan rite', which has not yet been decoded, was rejected and the turbulent duke now joined forces with one of the claimants to the Bosnian throne, Tvrtko II. In 1415, in a crucial battle in northern Bosnia, where Turkish mercenaries were used for the first time on Bosnian soil, he crushed Sigismund's forces and effectively terminated the sway of the future Holy Roman emperor in Bosnia.

The feats of Duke Hrvoje highlight the convoluted interrelations between 'heresy', politics and religion in Bosnia, where a Patarene noble could be an important ally of Catholic rulers like Ladislas and Sigismund, join the Dragon Order and use religion for his own ends. The early fourteenth century saw the increasing importance of the Bosnian Church in the volatile political situation in Bosnia and for a time the *dyed* acted as a councillor at the Bosnian court. Without evolving completely into a state religion proper, the Bosnian Church enjoyed the support of powerful Bosnian noble houses and was inter-mittently active in the Bosnian court. In Herzegovina, where the nobility remained largely Orthodox, the Bosnian Church had a strong patron in the house of Stefan Vukčić, who assumed the title 'Duke (Herzog) of St Sava', from which the name of the land was ultimately derived.

In 1443 the Bosnian throne passed to Stefan Tomaš, a member of the Bosnian Church, who was described by Pope Nicholas V as entrapped in the Manichaean errors before his final conversion to Catholicism. According to later Catholic tradition, upon Stefan Tomaš' accession Pope Eugene VI offered him a crown but requested persecution of the Manichaeans in Bosnia and Bosnian participation in a league against the Turks. By 1445, the year when Pope Eugene V recognized him as king,

Stefan Tomaš had promised to embrace Catholicism and had been engaged in a war with Stefan Vukčić, who had firmly opposed his election as king. The conversion of Stefan Tomaš was not followed by any immediate persecution against the Bosnian Church or heretics and the king maintained his relations with his former co-religionists. Some Bosnian nobles were also converted to Catholicism and the Franciscans were to increase their influence in Bosnia and at court. With the new advance of Catholicism in Bosnia references to dualists ('Manichaeans') multiplied and the Bosnian heresy was now firmly recognized as 'Manichaean'. Indeed, the evidence does suggest dualist agitation in Bosnia around the mid fifteenth century and the 'Manichaeans' were clearly perceived as an obstruction to the progress of Catholicism in the realm. At that time the Bosnian Church acquired the Slavonic ritual which was clearly a version of the Cathar Ritual of Lyons and the Constantinople patriarch Gennadius referred to Kudugers among the Bosnians and the nobility in Herzegovina. In 1461 three Bosnian nobles, seen as powerful ringleaders of the heresy at the royal court, were sent to Rome, renounced their 'Manichaean errors' before Cardinal Torquemada and returned to Bosnia, where one of them returned to his heresy 'like a dog to his vomit' and fled to Herzog Stefan. In contrast to the old *Ecclesia Sclavoniae*, however, the Bosnian nobles had to refute in Rome the articles of the radical dualism of the two principles, the two Gods, the supremely good one and the supremely evil one.

There have been various explanations for the apparent activation of the Bosnian dualist movement, continually mentioned in Inquisition documents during the reign of Stefan Tomaš. The view that the Bosnian Church and the dualist movement coexisted independently in Bosnia ascribes the latter renewed activity to a posited split within the Bosnian Church which led to the emergence of a dualist wing,[172] whereas the position that regards the Bosnian Church as a fusion of the earlier monastic order and the dualist sect sees in the reports a revival of dualist features in the Church inherited from this earlier merger. For Rome, the whole Bosnian Church appeared dualist, 'Manichaean', and with the conversion of King Tomaš the Catholic demands for strong action against the Bosnian heretics were mounting. In 1459 King Tomaš finally succumbed to the pressure and reversed the policy of religious tolerance, as had been generally pursued by his predecessors. The king is recorded as having offered the 'Manichaeans' in his realm the choice of conversion or exile; 2,000 chose baptism, while the others sought refuge in the neighbouring dominions of Herzog Stefan.

Herzog Stefan had already concluded peace with the Catholic king of Bosnia and besides some overtures to Rome continued to be a follower of the Bosnian Church and to use Patarene diplomats. During the Herzog's war with Dubrovnik (1451–4) he was accused by his adversaries of being a Patarene 'enemy of the Cross' and of destroying churches and crucifixes, but the peace was negotiated by Patarene diplomats. Indeed, by the time of Stefan Tomaš' persecution of the Bosnian Church, its hierarchy had apparently moved into Herzegovina.

The measures of Stefan Tomaš considerably weakened the hold of the Bosnian Church in his realm and did not meet the resistance of the pro-Patarene nobles in a period when Catholicism was finally gaining ascendancy in Bosnia. Besides traditionally Orthodox Herzegovina, the Orthodox presence in eastern Bosnia had also increased and there appeared the first visible signs of the religious contest between eastern and western Christianity in Bosnia.

Soon after the death of Stefan Tomaš in 1461 a new powerful religious factor entered the Bosnian scene – Sunni Islam. His successor, Stefan Tomašević, promptly appealed to Rome for a crown in a request that implied that the 'Manichaeans' had already been largely expelled from Bosnia. He was crowned by a papal legate in his capital but the evolution of Bosnia into a Catholic kingdom was severely curtailed only two years later when it swiftly fell to Mohammed II the Conqueror after a surprising Ottoman attack. The emphatic Catholicism of the Bosnian king and his requests for help against the Turks had failed to secure Christian aid and in the following centuries Catholicism in Bosnia lost ground to both Islam and Orthodoxy. The king himself was caught by the Turks and beheaded. Herzegovina was also initially overrun in the Ottoman attack but Herzog Stefan soon restored its autonomy and the hierarchy of the Bosnian Church retained its favoured position under his protection; he himself died in 1466, still a Patarene adherent.

The swift collapse of Bosnia and the ensuing success of Islam in the land that Rome called the 'lair of all heresies' has understandably attracted much attention and speculation. A traditional and, until recently, predominant approach to the religious history of Bosnia viewed the Bosnian Church as a thoroughly Bogomil organization and attributed both the fall and Islamization in Bosnia to religious and political strife in the aftermath of the persecution against the Patarenes under Stefan Tomaš. The hostility between Catholicism and the Bosnian Church, which intensified in 1459, is supposed to have provoked the collaboration of the Patarenes with the Ottoman conquerors. With their hostility to Catholicism, the forcibly converted Patarenes and their unconverted co-sectarians were suspected of a mass conversion to Islam which paved the way for the establishment of an important Islamic outpost in close vicinity to central Europe. As the Bosnian Church has been treated more than frequently as a wing of the Bogomil movement, the enduring collision between Catholicism and the 'Great Heresy' has been viewed as having finally secured the progress of a new religious rival in Bosnia, Islam. The supposed mass conversion of dualists in Bosnia and Herzegovina was said to have been facilitated by the alleged 'similarities' in dualist and Islamic ethics. Seen in the light of the dualist–Catholic strife and the repeated Catholic campaigns against Bosnian heresy, Bosnia has been presented as the 'best and the saddest example'[173] of the consequences of religious persecution.

Yet the Islamization of Bosnia clearly did not follow the simplistic pattern of a dualist reaction against Roman suppression of heresy and heterodoxy, through mass conversion to an advancing Islam. While there are some controversial and legendary reports of Patarene or 'Manichaean' association with Ottoman military success in Bosnia, an actual collaboration between the Ottomans and the Bosnian Church (or the dualists) cannot be substantiated. Indeed, the only figure to actively and successfully resist the Ottoman occupation of Bosnia and Herzegovina was Herzog Stefan, a notable and well-known patron and adherent of the Bosnian Church. The persecution under King Tomaš had undoubtedly greatly weakened the influence of the Bosnian Church, but resentment against continual Hungarian and Catholic interference in Bosnian affairs, particularly among the newly and forcibly converted Bosnians, certainly played its role in the advance of Islam. The characteristic lack of religious uniformity in medieval Bosnia – where Catholicism met with Orthodoxy, the Bosnian Church and the dualist heretics – allowed for a quicker spread of Islam, which was to win Catholic, Orthodox and Patarene converts. Yet the views of the early stages of Islamization in Bosnia and the fate of the Bosnian 'Krstjani', whether dualist or schismatic, continue to differ sharply and paint extremely conflicting pictures of the religious history of early Ottoman Bosnia.[174]

What seems certain is that the religious life of Bosnia prior to the mid fifteenth century, with its general toleration of religious beliefs and practices, undoubtedly favoured the longer survival of dualist traditions. After the death of the old patron of the Bosnian Church, Herzog Stefan, Herzegovina was finally annexed by the Ottomans in 1481. While Herzog Stefan's immediate successor had remained in the flock of the Patarene Church, his third son, like many Bosnian nobles, came to accept Islam and rose to be a grand vizir under the Ottoman ruler, Selim I. With the commencement of Ottoman rule in Bosnia, amid the novel religious diversity and rivalries, the traces of dualist traditions and the Bosnian Church itself become extremely elusive.

The Fate of Balkan Dualism

In both Constantinople and Rome, the last testimonies to the Balkan dualist heresy refer to Bosnia, and the Bosnian lands are sometimes credited with preserving another witness to Bogomil dualism in the curious symbolism of the monolithic medieval Bosnian tombstones, the *stećci*, often referred to as the 'Bogomil gravestones'. Estimated to be more than 50,000 in number and concentrated mainly in Bosnia, Herze-govina and the adjacent regions, the majority of *stećci* were erected in the fourteenth and fifteenth centuries in the shapes of standing slabs, sarcophagi and boxes. The *stećci* bear a rich variety of carvings: solar symbols, crescents, rosettes, swastikas, pentacles and crosses, along with figurative representations of hunting, dancing and jousting scenes. While the association of the carvings with traditional funeral symbolism has been acknowledged, many of their features have tantalized archaeol-ogists and antiquaries for more than a century. Since 1876, when Arthur Evans related the *stećci* carvings to the teachings of the Bosnian Patarene movement, a number of scholars have supplemented his theory with more material and suggestions, but it has also encountered strong opposition which has highlighted the numerous difficulties in the attempts at symbolic interpretations of the engravings, apart from the fact that *stećci* had been erected by Catholics, Orthodox and Patarenes alike.[175] The suggested links to dualist beliefs, such as the proposed parallels to Central Asian Manichaean iconography or the connection between the *stećci* depictions of the sun and moon and their significance in Manichaeism, necessarily rely on a series of conjectures, but attempts to discover such influences continue with the admissions that they are 'the least present and most difficult to prove'.[176] Yet it has been shown that some of the *stećci* carvings have retained the symbolism of ancient cults in the medieval guises of the jousting and hunting scenes or in the curious combinations of the symbols of the fleur-de-lis with crosses of the type of *crux ansata*.[177] There are indications of the survival of a medieval mystery cult in Bosnia and Herzegovina as pagan practices, which were condemned as heretical, persisted in various forms, and religious syncretism has been specified as plausibly being responsible for the continual accusations of heresy against the medieval Bosnians.[178]

In the early thirteenth century the Bogomils were accused of performing mysteries like 'hellenic rites' and the latter stages of the heresy were characterized by the emergence of teachings representing a *mélange* of dualist beliefs, magic and demonology. The patterns of symbiosis between dualist and traditional pagan beliefs in various areas of the Balkans have been indicated repeatedly by scholars.[179] Such a dualist-pagan synthesis in the *stećci* carvings cannot be excluded, particularly in the cases when the recoverable pagan symbolism allows for a dualist interpretation, as in the well-represented *stećci* motif of two horsemen opposing each other, identified as a survival of the classical theme of the Dioscuri.[180]

Following the disappearance of the Balkan Bogomils the Balkan folklore remained the repository of the old dualist beliefs and legends that had spread with the dissemination of Bogomil dualist teachings. Indeed, as late as the eighteenth century, reports occurred of schismatic Patarenes and 'Manichaeans' in Bosnia, sharing an opposition to Catholicism, the latter claiming that Jesus Christ did not die on the cross and extolling the archangel Michael.[181] Conversely, in Bulgaria itself Paulician sectarians, including those from their ancient dualist strongholds in Thrace, were converted to Catholicism in the seventeenth century, although they still practised their 'baptism by fire'. Nineteenth-century journalists' reports of the existence of Bogomil colonies in Bosnia are symptomatic of the western rediscovery of Bogomilism and the Balkans, rather than any actual survival of dualist sectarians in the Balkans.[182] The Islamization of Bosnia marked one of the very last chapters of the five-centuries-long history of medieval Balkan dualism and, indeed, the vestiges of medieval European dualism in general.

The reasons for the swift disappearance of the Bogomils in the early Ottoman period in the Balkans still remain largely unexplained and sometimes the 'Bosnian' argument is projected on to the whole Balkans – the Bogomils are supposed to have chosen to accept Islam and vanished without trace among the Islamized section of the Balkan population. The remains of the 'hidden tradition', which at the rise of its influence in Europe openly claimed descent from the apostles, are supposed to have finally fled to Islam. However, evidence for such a Bogomil influx into Islam is lacking and the obscurity surrounding their disappearance seems to result from the insufficient knowledge of the early religious history of the Ottoman empire, with its array of sectarian and syncretistic movements, still a controversial and largely unexplored field.

It is assumed sometimes that in the early Ottoman period Bogomil groups merged with the Paulicians still living in areas of Thrace and northern Bulgaria, the *pavlikiani*, who were largely converted to Catholicism after a succession of Catholic missions from the late sixteenth century.[183] The Catholic missions successfully exploited the tensions between the Orthodox populations in these areas and the Paulicians embraced Catholicism while retaining a number of their old beliefs and practices in a syncretistic version of Christianity. The problem with the thesis that among some of these Paulician groups, which survived into modern times, there may have been descendants of Bogomils is that the records of their beliefs and practices do not seem to show evidence of asceticism or Encratism, while betraying various elements inherited from their earlier dualist teachings. This apparent lack of asceticism and Encratism is in line with traditional Paulicianism and reduces the possibility of there having been any substantial Bogomil influx into these Paulician groups; however, the interesting records of their beliefs[184] may yet yield further clues concerning the possibility of such influx. Around the mid eleventh century Euthymius of Peribleptos had declared that the Paulician heresy was less dangerous, as it was evident and transmitted mostly inside the Paulican communities, while accusing the Bogomils of dissimulation and bearing many names, duplicity which made their heresy much more secret and harder to detect. In the early Ottoman era the Paulicians again retained their visible presence which has survived into the modern era, whereas, surpassing their own reputation for elusiveness, any visible traces of the Bogomils seem to vanish, although the study of the hitherto little-investigated syncretistic, sectarian and mystical movements of the early Ottoman period may well provide some of the missing clues.

What remained 'of the sway once held over the minds of men by the most powerful sectarian movement in the Balkans', wrote D. Obolensky, was a 'vague dualist tradition which has left its imprint on south Slavonic folklore'.[185] What remains also are the heretical book, brought from Bulgaria to Italy by the heretical bishop of Concorezzo, *Liber Secretum*, the fragments of the inner teachings of the Bogomils in Zigabenus' *Panoplia Dogmatica* and the dispersed fragments of dualist legends and myths of the Bogomils and Cathars in the sermons, annals, polemics and Inquisition records of their adversaries.

CHAPTER SIX

Legends, Parables and 'Secret Myths'

Medieval and modern authorities on medieval dualism agree that initiation into Bogomil and Cathar teachings proceeded gradually and that prior to the *consolamentum* the ordinary believers were not introduced to what were considered the inner doctrines, preserved for the *perfecti*, who claimed knowledge of the 'mystery of the Kingdom of God'. To their followers and sympathizers the Bogomil and Cathar *perfecti* did indeed seem like 'living icons'[1] of genuine, apostolic Christianity, guardians and repositories of the authentic teaching of Christ secretly revealed to his true apostles and transmitted in secrecy thereafter, untainted by the corrupting interference and doctoring of the official Church. As a mark of their initiation and status the *perfecti* bore the title of the Blessed Virgin Mary, *Theotokos* (God-Bearer), as they were seen as a receptacle of the Holy Spirit and as giving birth to the Word. The parable in Matthew 7 : 6, 'Do not give dogs what is holy, do not throw your pearls to the pigs', was interpreted as alluding to the need for esotericism, the pearls being 'the mysterious and precious tenets' of Bogomilism, the preserve of the *perfecti*.

However acrimonious, the Orthodox records of the Bogomil course of initiation suggest that the believers were initially introduced to teachings and ethics close to evangelical Christianity, coupled with a gradual introduction to progressively heretical precepts, until the general nature of the dualist doctrine was outlined to the neophyte. Yet according to Euthymius Zigabenus, dualist dogmas were revealed only at the end of further initiation to those believers who chose to enter upon the probationary period required before the final elevation to the highest dualist grade of the *perfecti* and receiving the *consolamentum*. The probationary period was described variously as lasting one to two or three years and after the *consolamentum* the new *perfecti* had access, in the words of Orthodox commentators, to the 'mysteries for the more advanced in impiety' and 'to the whole heresy and madness'. The elite class of the *perfecti* was fully introduced to the dualist *historia arcana*, which the Orthodox polemicists saw as the ultimate 'satanic mysteries', and, as 'accomplished theologians',[2] mastered a system of allegorical interpretation of the Scriptures which was widely used during missionary tours and the theological debates pursued by the 'teachers of the heresy'. In mature Italian Catharism, moreover, there was further a theological elite among the *perfecti* themselves, who had pursued higher learning, in some cases in universities, and thus were well prepared to combat Catholic scholasticism and may well have secreted certain aspects of what were seen as arcane doctrines for their select use.[3] Recent research has highlighted the importance of high learning in Northern French,[4] Italian[5] and Languedoc Catharism,[6] demonstrating that the Cathars participated in the broad theological and educational trends of the late twelfth and early thirteenth centuries, including the reception of Aristotle's *On Generation*,[7] and may have pioneered the use of polemical 'literature for battle' against Catholic opponents, (collections of authoritative, often New Testament passages), a practice which was to be emulated by the Catholic anti-Cathar preachers themselves.[8] Unsurprisingly, after applying to the first heretics the polemical cliché of the 'illiterate heretic', later Catholic controversialists eventually came to apply to the Cathars the other stereotype of the 'skilled' and 'cunning' heretical preacher.[9]

The Bogomil missionaries and scribes elaborated a vivid polemical dualist mythology, fragments of which have been preserved in the Orthodox accounts of the heresy and denounced as 'satanic fables', 'unholy babble', etc. Apart from the canonical scriptures, the dualist mythology made wide use of themes and imagery from the apocryphal literature circulating in the Orthodox east, which included early Christian texts and important Jewish apocalyptic texts like the *Book of the Secrets of Enoch* (2 Enoch) and the *Apocalypse of Abraham*. Among these texts, particularly important for the Bogomils was the *Vision of Isaiah*, an apocalypse from the early Christian era, which subsequently was taken over by the Cathars. To all these apocryphal texts, mostly written in late antiquity, Bogomilism owed some of its most important notions, which were to become influential in western Catharism. Among these are its multi-heaven cosmology, crucial features of its diabology (including, probably, the notion of the Devil as God's firstborn), elements of its cosmogony (such as the creation of the satanic stellar hosts from fire, itself made from stone), the theme of the Devil's planting of the 'sinful tree' in Paradise, and a number of eschatological traditions. Significantly, some of these inherited apocryphal texts have retained elements of esotericism and visionary mysticism – esotericism being characteristic of some Jewish and early Christian apocalyptic texts in which the revelations, granted during an ascent to heaven to the protagonist, are seen as secreted by necessity only to an inner group. These traditions were inherent, for example, in *The Vision of Isaiah*, and were adopted and elaborated by the Bogomils and some Cathar groups. Therefore, in a manner similar to the way in which the ancient Gnostics inherited and reinterpreted esoteric attitudes, revelations and interpretations from the Jewish apocalyptic and apocryphal literature,[10] the Bogomils absorbed, if admittedly only partially by comparison, similar attitudes and notions from the texts they adopted, a process which would explain the resurgence of a specific, if not always apparent, strand of Bogomil esotericism and visionary mysticism. The only extant Bogomil tract, *Liber Secretum* or *Interrogatio Iohannis*, was brought to Italy by the bishop of the Cathar church of Concorezzo, Nazarius, and became the basic text for Cathar moderate dualism in Lombardy, exerting further influence in Languedoc. Some of its concepts were in harmony with the teachings of absolute dualism and gained currency in radical dualist Cathar circles, while others were naturally at variance and were bitterly disputed. Indeed, debates over certain notions in *Liber Secretum* eventually caused a split in the church of Concorezzo. The Bogomil and Cathar preoccupation with apocryphal stories and myths provoked a reaction in the Cathar church of Desenzano, the bastion of absolute dualism in Italy, where some Cathar circles attempted to advance a more literal reading of scriptural passages and to furnish a philosophical foundation for radical dualism, the tract *The Book of the Two Principles*. Yet, along with the apostolic life and the ascetic conduct of the *perfecti*, the flexibility and the picturesqueness of dualist apocryphal mythology was one of the great strengths of Bogomil and Cathar propaganda and it is not surprising that distinct dualist traditions left a firm imprint and endured in Balkan folklore. The marked Bogomil and Cathar predilection for the elaboration of vivid mythic stories in support of dualist, doctrines some of which were indeed seen as belonging to the *secreta* of the *perfecti*,[11] presents another parallel to ancient Gnosticism, in which the creation of Gnostic secret myths was a crucial part of the process of 'a self-conscious re-mythologization'[12] by Gnostic teachers. Significantly, in both cases this re-mythologization and creation of a dualist mythology were accomplished through a determined inverse exegesis of the normative scriptures to produce alternative and striking accounts of cosmogony, fall and salvation of the soul.

Besides the principal dividing line between the medieval adherents of absolute and monarchian dualism, other divergencies of doctrine and scriptural interpretations inevitably emerged among the various dualist communities. Otherwise, the pattern of Cathar initiation into the inner sanctum of the *perfecti* seems essentially to parallel the Bogomil one, although there are some indications of teachings which were not shared by all *perfecti*, which might well have been a later innovation. The orthodox adversaries of medieval dualism zealously rejected the validity of the pretensions of the *perfecti* to esoteric knowledge of the 'divine mysteries' and many heretical books, both Cathar and Bogomil, were reported to have been burned. What has been actually preserved from Cathar written materials, both in fragments, quotations or references in Catholic literature, is admittedly only 'the tip of the iceberg',[13] the various reported Cathar books like the reputed *Stella* (work of the Desenzano Cathars) or the reports of many Cathar writings about the wars between God and Lucifer in Languedoc have not been preserved, perhaps unsurprisingly, since a traditional feature of St Dominic's iconography depicts him committing Cathar books to the ordeal of fire. Most of the information about the teachings of the medieval dualists is preserved in Orthodox and Catholic records, invariably hostile and vilifying. *The Book of the Two Principles* is a notable exception and so is the so-called 'Manichaean Tract'[14] preserved in the polemical *Liber contra Manichaeos*, but both expound the tenets of absolute dualism. For monarchian dualism the most important texts still remain the Bogomil *Liber Secretum* as well as the various, sometimes controversial, fragments in the Orthodox and Catholic polemical literature. While the works of inquisitors like Rainerius Sacchoni, Anselm of Alessandria or the friar Moneta of Cremona give the outlines of Cathar dualism, the anti-Bogomil exposé of the Orthodox theologian Euthymius Zigabenus sheds light on some of the inner teachings in the original Bogomil dualism. Euthymius' account provides some important clues to the *modus operandi* of Bogomil missionary preaching and its allusions to further esoteric revelations awaiting the neophyte, as his refutation of Bogomil teaching was based on the sermon of the Bogomil heresiarch, Basil the Physician, before Alexius Comnenus. The serman was recorded by Alexius' secretary and admittedly was tailored to the emperor's potential 'listener' level. Regrettably Euthymius Zigabenus did not make full use of the teaching divulged during the heresiarch's oration and admitted that he did not proceed to disprove all Basil's arguments, in his own words, to preserve his sanity in this 'enormous sea of godlessness'.

Euthymius' disquiet with this 'godlessness' appears understandable: his exposé of the Bogomil heresy revealed teachings focused on the problems that had once divided the Gnostic teachers from the Church Fathers: the nature of the creation, the identity of the Demiurge of the material world, the origins of evil and the plight of the human soul.

Christ–Michael and Samael–Satan

Medieval dualist lore resurrected many Gnostic and Manichaean-like themes and imagery and much of it was intended to reveal the hidden 'dualist reality' behind biblical accounts, like the creation, the fall of man or the flood. Yet in some dualist legends, particularly among the absolute dualists, direct dependence on the biblical text was lacking. Apart from the borrowings from apocryphal writings, preserved in eastern Christendom and medieval elaborations of the dualist scribes, the medieval dualist lore comprised traditions whose exact pedigree or background could appear elusive and untraceable.

Similar to some older Gnostic traditions, like the Valentinian school, medieval dualism claimed succession to the true Christian faith and, as with older Gnostic creation myths, the Bogomil–Cathar myths of the creation of the world revealed the mystery of the Demiurge of the visible world. The unfolding of this revelation is preserved in two main Bogomil versions – the tract *Liber Secretum* and the Bogomil section in *Panoplia Dogmatica*. The two accounts epitomize the monarchian strand in Bogomil–Cathar dualism,[15] where the Demiurge, the Lord of the Old Testament, is exposed as evil, but subordinate to the higher one God, while the establishment and activation of the material universe is inextricably linked to the story of his fall. Traditionally, Satan or Samael was

God's first-born and was originally the more powerful elder brother of Christ, the Logos. In *Liber Secretum*, at the beginning Satan presided over the virtues in heaven and was 'regulator of all things', sitting with the God-Father. Satan's power was described as descending from heaven to hell and even to the throne of the Father. Similarly, in the Bogomil satanology expounded in *Panoplia Dogmatica*, Samael was the heavenly vice-regent of the good God–Father and sat on a throne at his right side as second only to him, the creator of the angelic hosts, and possessed a similar image and 'garment'. The traditional cause of Satan's fall was his pride and inevitably the parable in Isaiah about the king of Babylon (14 : 13–14) – 'I will set my throne high above the stars of God . . . I will rise high above the cloud-banks and make myself like the Most High' – was thought to reveal the 'evil plots' of his real aspirations. To further his designs for exaltation and eternal rule Satan proceeded to subvert the angels of the 'Father invisible' and ascended as far as the fifth heaven. Exposed by a voice from the throne of the Father, Satan was cast out of heaven along with the ensnared angels who were stripped of their garments, thrones and crowns. According to *Liber Secretum*, with his fall Satan was deprived of the light of his glory and his face became human, albeit like 'an iron glowing from the fire', while his seven tails drew away a third of God's angels. In the alternative version of the Bogomil myth Satan still possessed his divine image and 'garment' after his downfall and having retained his creative potency he decided to 'make a second heaven like a second God'.

Echoing some of the themes of the archaic earth-diver cosmogonies, according to *Liber Secretum*, Satan was first inflamed by a sudden demiurgic élan during one of his descents when he was diving through the portals of the gates of the realm of the waters and reached the earth, itself covered with water and carried by two fish yoked together. Indeed, the ensuing rebellion and seduction of angels by Satan begin with the subversion of the pair of angels presiding respectively over the air and water, to whom he promises that with their help he will raise some of the waters above the firmament and gather the rest into seas, so that the earth will be free of waters and he can reign with them over it for eternity. After his expulsion and fall to the firmament, he takes his seat there and proceeds with his planned division of the waters with the help of the angelic pair. Satan bids the angel of the waters to stand upon the two earth-carrying fish and to lift with his head the earth upwards, bringing about in this way the appearance of dry land. Then Satan takes the crown of the angel of the air and from half of it forges a throne for himself, creating from the other half the light of the sun. Satan also divides the crown of the angel of the water, fashioning from half of it the light of the moon and from the other half the light of the day.

After a series of more demiurgic feats such as ordering the earth to bring forth all living beings and creating the heavenly hosts, his ministering angels, from fire, Satan initiates the creation of man, again involving both the angel of air and the angel of water, who originally were not sexually differentiated. *Liber Secretum* develops the Bogomil version of the old Orphic and Gnostic notions of the exile of the divine soul in the prison-body which completely parts with the canonical anthropogonic story in Genesis 4. Satan fashions man in his likeness from clay and compels the angel of the second heaven to enter the clay. With a part of man's body Satan creates the body of a woman and bids the angel of the first heaven to enter it. The introduction of sexual differentiation thus means also exile in flesh, as the angels of the first and second heavens are condemned to suffer bodily imprisonment in mortal, respectively male and female form. In the alternative version of the Bogomil myth Satan's task proved more onerous and his creature Adam, made out of earth and water, was far from perfect – a flow of water out of his right foot and forefinger twisted on the earth and took on the shape of a serpent. In Satan's attempt to breathe spirit into Adam, the spirit followed the same course, animating the serpent that inevitably became the most subtle creature, enlivened as it was by the spirit of Satan himself. Now Satan, the second Creator, was forced to appeal to the good Father to send His Spirit to his creature, pledging that both would become masters of man and that some of his progeny would eventually fill the heavenly abodes made void by the fall of the rebellious angels. The good God consented and breathed the 'spirit of life' into man. Eve was created and animated in the same manner. The Bogomil accounts of man's creation clearly reiterated the old Gnostic soul–body dualism, where the divine soul was seen as imprisoned in the body created by the Demiurge. Another tradition, which had been current in both Gnostic and Jewish traditions, also found its elaboration in medieval dualism: Eve's seduction and corruption by Satan.

Following the creation of the first human couple Satan proceeded to defile Eve by assuming the shape of the serpent and enticing her into intercourse. The stories of the seduction of Eve also varied. In *Liber Secretum* after planting a bed of reeds in Paradise, Satan forbade Adam and Eve to eat the fruit of good and evil but lured Eve into sin. With Eve's desire 'glowing like an oven' the Devil emerged from the reeds in the serpent's shape and satisfied his lust. Adam was also tricked into debauchery with Eve, who begot together the 'children of the Devil and of the serpent' and Satan's reign, dependent on procreation, would last until the end of the world. In the alternative Bogomil version of the seduction of Eve by the Demiurge she begot twins, Cain and his sister Calomena, from Samael–Satan while Abel was born after her human union with Adam. Cain, the 'seed of Samael', slew Abel, 'the seed of Adam', and brought murder and death into the world. However, after his shape-changing and intercourse with Eve, Samael–Satan lost his creative potency, even his divine form, to become dark and abhorrent.

Yet Samael–Satan continued to be master of his creation and his cruel reign allowed only a few to join the good Father and ascend into the ranks of the archangels. In *Liber Secretum* Satan was permitted by the Father to reign for seven ages, during which he sent his ministering fiery angels to men, while the sacrificial rites were initiated to hide the kingdom of heaven from men. As in the older Gnostic works Satan made the futile 'monotheistic' proclamation: 'I am He and there is no god beside me' (Deuteronomy 32:39). Satan revealed his divinity to Moses, granted him the Law and sent him to deliver the children of Israel from Egypt, leading them through the Red Sea on dry ground.

The Bogomil mythology further embellished the story of the angels' downfall and in its version, aware of Samael–Satan's promise to fill their former heavenly abode with the sons of men, the fallen angels took wives from among the daughters of men. The giants born of the union began to struggle against Samael–Satan, who, enraged by their rebellion, brought the flood over the earth to destroy every living being, sparing only the life of his minister, Noah. From Adam to Christ, only Jesus' antecedents enumerated in the genealogies in Matthew and Luke were saved, along with the sixteen prophets and the martyrs who died rather than succumb to idolatry.

In Bogomil Christology the mission of Christ was to announce the name of the Father and it is in precognition of this mission that Satan gave Moses three pieces of wood for Christ's crucifixion. In one of the strands of Bogomil Christology, after 5,500 years God the Father felt compassion for the suffering of his creation, the human soul, under the satanic reign and sent the 'Son–Logos'. He was also recognized as the archangel Michael, described as an archangel because he was the most divine of all angels, Jesus because he healed every illness or affliction and Christ because his body was 'anointed'. He descended from heaven and entered the Virgin through the right ear to assume the semblance of a human body. While his Passion, death and Resurrection were unreal, he was victorious in his battle against the rebellious Samael–Satanael. In this version of Bogomil Christology it was after the victory of Christ–Michael over Satanael that the God's first-born lost his last 'divine syllable' -el (Lord) and was cast fettered into the pit, while Christ–Michael ascended to Satanael's former throne to the right of the Father. It has been assumed sometimes that with his fall Satanael's seniority had automatically passed to the Son–Logos and following his triumph and the imprisonment of the God's first-born, Christ–Michael returned to his ultimate source, the good Father.

In *Liber Secretum*, before the advent of Christ, God sent His angel, called Mary, so that Christ could be received by her through the Holy Spirit but Satan also sent his angel, the prophet Elijah, now in the incarnation of John the Baptist, who baptized with water. Upon his descent Christ entered and emerged from Mary's ear to be recognized by John the Baptist as the one who baptized with the Holy Spirit and with fire, the one able to save and destroy. As in Manichaeism, baptism by water was vigorously rejected in Bogomilism and Catharism, but according to *Liber Secretum* the world had accepted John's baptism rather than Jesus' baptism by fire and thus the actions of many people remained evil, as they avoided coming to the light.

A recurrent idea that emerged both in Bogomil and Cathar thought held that the only Old Testament figures who were saved, recognized as the sixteen prophets and Jesus' ancestors listed in the genealogies in Matthew and Luke, rose again on the death of Christ and received the *consolamentum* from Christ himself. In their trinitarian system the Son was traditionally regarded as lesser in Godhood than the Father, and the Holy Ghost lesser than the Son. Another distinct Bogomil teaching, expounded in *Panoplia Dogmatica*, concerned the way the Son and the Holy Ghost proceeded from the Father – the Son was viewed as a light emanating from the right side of the head of the Father, while the Holy Ghost emanated from the left side. The emanation was initiated 5,500 years after the creation of the world when the Father assumed these three faces. With the return of the Son and the Holy Ghost to the Father he resumed his 'one-faced' form. The process in which the Father begot the Son and the Son begot the Holy Spirit was continued by the Holy Spirit who begot Judas and the apostles. The beginning of Jesus' genealogy in Matthew 1:2, 'Abraham begat Isaac; and Isaac begat Jacob; and Jacob begat Judas and his brethren' (*KJV*) was taken as referring to the emanatory processes within the Holy Trinity

Bogomil monarchian dualism had an eschatological character – Satan was expected to be ultimately conquered in the last days and *Liber Secretum* furnished a vivid account of the Last Judgement, with imagery dependent on the canonical Revelation and other extra-canonical apocalypses. After a period when Satan would be 'loosed out of his prison' (Revelation 20:7, *KJV*) the Son of Man would conduct the Last Judgement and separate His just from the sinners and Satan and his hosts would be cast into a lake of fire. The Son of God would then occupy for ever the place of the first-born, on the right hand of the Father and reign with his Holy Father in all eternity.

The cosmogonic and anthropogonic sections of *Liber Secretum* inevitably show indebtedness to earlier dualist doctrinal and apocryphal traditions, the latter represented by several early Jewish and Christian apocryphal apocalypses still in circulation in the medieval Byzantine-Slavonic world, which were refashioned to become the constituent elements of Bogomil monarchian dualism. However, not all cosmogonic notions in the tract find immediate parallels in this inherited and rich Judaeo-Christian heritage. The themes of Satan diving to the bottom of the sea prior to his rebellion and the execution of his demiurgic plans, as well as that of a satanic angelic agency bringing earth from the sea which then becomes the basis for the creation of the earth, are adopted from the popular earth-diver cosmogonies. The cosmogony of *Liber Secretum*, therefore, represents the fusion of two distinct cosmogonic traditions: the first derives from a dualist interpretation of canonical and apocryphal works, whereas the second stems from creation myths associated with the archaic themes of the earth-diver and the divine twins; in the tract the themes of diving into the primal sea and bringing up earth from the sea are respectively attributed to Satan and to his subordinate companion, the angel of the water.[16]

Another distinctive feature of the cosmogonic synthesis of the tract is the interrelationship between the earth diving, the primordial angelic pair and the introduction of sexual polarity into the human world. As such polarity is not envisaged in the divine world and is introduced through the imprisonment of the angelic pair in respective male and female forms, its role in the overall dualist theology and anthropology of the tract seems somewhat subdued, particularly in the context of earlier Gnostic elaborations of the theme. In *Liber Secretum* God the Father has a definite masculine image and there do not seem to be attempts to look for a sexual polarity or feminine element in the divine world. This would differentiate the Bogomil 'Secret Book' from Gnostic teachings such as Valentinian Gnosticism, for example, with its emphasis on the notion of the divine dyad, the 'Primal Father' and the 'Mother of All',[17] the latter also being praised as 'eternal, mystical silence'.[18] This dyad begets the spiritual world of the Pleroma consisting of fifteen pairs of aeons, the youngest of which, the feminine power of Sophia (Wisdom), precipitates a crisis in the divine world by trying to conceive by herself and becomes 'the great creative power by whom all things originate', bringing forth the would-be creator-God of the physical world. Other Gnostic systems that elaborate the theme of the ultimate divine source as an archetypal androgyne include, for example, that of Marcus[19] and Nag Hammadi Gnostic tracts such as *The Trimorphic Protennoia.*[20]

Nor does the Bogomil apocryphon dwell on another favoured Gnostic theme, the interpretation of the coupling of Adam and Eve as an inter-action between the soul and the spirit; Eve sometimes being identified with the soul that needs to be reunited with the higher spiritual self, Adam,[21] and on other occasions being recognized as the higher spiritual intelligence reawakening the soul, Adam, to its spiritual dimension,[22] achieved through a mystical marriage. In *Liber Secretum* the introduction of sexual differentiation leads to the imprisonment of the angels of the first and second heaven, respectively in a male and female body, but they are not seen as residing in some kind of primordial unity or marriage in the divine world before their fall. Yet this very duality of angelic agencies who are forced to enter bodies of clay, as well as the duality of the angelic powers who acted as demiurgic companions to Satan, already contained the possibility for a dualist reinterpretation of the cosmogonic story by employing these angelic dualities for the introduction of a sexual divide in the divine world itself.

Such a reinterpretation eventually was ventured by the bishop of the dualist church of Concorezzo, Nazarius, whose staunch reliance on the *Liber Secretum* was challenged by the second man in the hierarchy of the church, Desiderius.[23] Desiderius attempted to formulate a more somatic version of Bogomil–Cathar Christology by asserting that Jesus assumed a body of 'the stuff of Adam',[24] a teaching which parted with traditional Bogomil–Cathar Docetic doctrine that Christ never took an actual physical body, but did so only in appearance. Desiderius, moreover, manifested a very non-dualist concern with the whereabouts of the physical body of Jesus Christ, which, he claimed, was put in a terrestrial paradise, where also resided the Virgin Mary and John the Evangelist along with the souls of the righteous dead. According to Desiderius this righteous company will stay in the terrestrial paradise until the Day of Judgement when Christ will put it again to rise and judge all good and evil.[25] Perhaps in reaction to the emergence of these teachings, within the ranks of his own dualist bishopric, with their markedly non-dualist preoccupation with the earthly paradise and Jesus' physical body there, Nazarius intensified the already strong mythic element in the cosmogony of *Liber Secretum*. In his interpretation of this cosmogony Nazarius identified the angels of the first and second heavens, whose souls animated respectively the bodies of Adam and Eve, with the angelic pair who assisted Satan in his creation exploits; thus the sexual differentiation between Adam and Eve in the human world was projected into the divine world itself where they came to appear in the position of a primordial couple.[26] According to Nazarius' cosmogonic innovations, Satan made the sun from the crown of Adam and fashioned the moon from one half of the crown of Eve and from the other half made his throne.[27] In Nazarius' system, therefore, the angel of the water, who according to *Liber Secretum* lifted earth from the sea so that Satan could reign over the newly appeared dry land, was identified with Eve, whose role in the plan of material creation was thus greatly enhanced, functionally approaching the role of the earth-diver in the popular eastern Christian cosmogonies that influenced the Bogomil compilers of *Liber Secretum*.

Accentuating the sexual connotations of his projection of male/female polarity into the divine world, Nazarius further taught that the sun and moon, created respectively from the crowns of Adam and Eve, were animate beings who copulated every month.[28] Nazarius also asserted that dew and honey came from this lewdness of the sun and the moon, hence he rejected the eating of honey. Through his reinterpretation of the notions of a second demiurge and the duality of the sexually undifferentiated angelic pairs in *Liber Secretum*, Nazarius not only introduced a sexual divide into heaven but related it to the old mythic theme of the sexual union of the sun and moon.

Apart from these angelological and mythic innovations, Nazarius is not known (at least according to the scant evidence concerning his teachings) to have reinterpreted Bogomil angelology and traditions concerning the Virgin Mary. Against the claims of the somatically minded Desiderius, who maintained that the Virgin Mary had a real, physical body, Nazarius taught that she was an angel, obviously sent to the world so that Christ can assume an angelic or celestial body – a Mariological teaching he was said to have received from the bishop and elder son (second in the hierarchy of the medieval dualist order) of the dualist Church of Bulgaria.[29] Nazarius' dualist and exegetical career demonstrates how Bogomil–Cathar teachings could be disseminated both through apocryphal written works such as *Liber Secretum* and oral preachings, with all the potential for transformations and imaginative elaborations of the received apocryphal and doctrinal traditions, which could achieve the form of new 'secret myths' and fuel further theological controversies in the dualist communities.

The Cathar versions of moderate dualism generally followed the Bogomil prototypes, although understandably different interpretations appeared. Cathar monarchian dualism emphatically postulated that while the one higher Father created primordial matter, it was the Prince of this World, Satan, himself created by God, who divided it into four elements. Sometimes the higher God was regarded as the creator of the primal elements but invariably it was the Devil who divided the elements. The creation of man could be elaborated with various new details – in one variant God the Father sent a heavenly angel to observe how Lucifer had divided the elements and it was this angel that Lucifer captured and subjected to human flesh in the body-prison.[30] As in Bogomilism, the parable of the unjust steward in Luke 16:1–9 remained one of the principal parables in Catharism of the actions and fortunes of Satan, the present Prince of the world and the former Prince of the Angels.

According to some Cathar esoteric embellishments of the myth of Lucifer's fall, in the beginning there existed a certain evil four-faced spirit, the four faces being respectively those of a man, bird, fish and beast and when he was still good Lucifer encountered this evil spirit. The evil spirit was devoid of creative power but Lucifer was struck with wonder and ventured to converse with him, was led astray and prompted to seduce the angels.[31]

While charting the feats of Satan as the Lord of the Old Testament the Cathar accounts are as explicit as those of the Bogomils, recounting that Satan sent prophets to men and through their prophecies precipitated animal sacrifices, the blood offerings through which he was honoured as god. In the Bogomil account of the flood, moreover, Noah is not a thoroughly negative figure, as he ministered to Satan and was saved by the fallen Demiurge without knowing about his apostasy, whereas in one Cathar version it was the 'Holy God' who saved Noah and 'all living creatures' from Satan's flood.[32]

The fact that in the Bogomil *Liber Secretum* the power of Satan seems more limited than in the external sources has sometimes been taken to indicate that original Bogomil dualism, or a version of it, was even more mitigated (or 'mono-principal' to use Rottenwöhrer's expression) than in the Orthodox polemical records. Accordingly, it has been argued that Orthodox polemicists misunderstood the 'subtlety' of Bogomil theology, whose original version treated Satan, the firstborn angel of God, only as an 'architect' and not at creator of the world, who divided the elements created by God and began to organize the material universe, after being granted a kind of 'peace' by God, as narrated in *Liber Secretum*.[33] In this view Bogomilism cannot be treated as a dualism proper, it is an original 'pseudo-dualism' which is not that far removed from Orthodox Christian diabology.[34] With the present state of evidence it is impossible to substantiate this view that Orthodox polemicists misrepresented Bogomil theology and cosmogony, but it is possible that there existed slightly divergent trends in Bogomilism some of which may have professed an even more mitigated version of Bogomil moderate dualism.

Furthermore, Bogomil cosmogony and sacred history comprise notions that find interesting precedents in the history of religious dualism. According to *Liber Secretum*, God allows Satan to rule in the world for seven ages, during which Satan tries to lead men astray and persuade them that he is the only god. This divine permission for a finite period of satanic reign finds immediate parallels in God's appointment (by his 'inscrutable design') of a time of domination for the Angel of Darkness in the Qumran Community Rule and in the Zurvanite notion of a finite period of Ahriman's rule in the world, fixed in a treaty with

Zurvan. The theme of a treaty or a contract between the First Principle and the secondary 'satanic' power is further developed in the other version of Bogomil anthropogony in *Panoplia Dogmatica* in which after Satan's plea God breathes the 'spirit of life' into Satan-created man, so that the sons of men can fill the heavenly abodes left vacant by the fall of the angels. In this account God and Satan are seen virtually to cooperate in the creation of man, but Satan breaks the 'contract' by impregnating Eve to establish his race and to try to dominate the seed of Adam and prevent its growth. The Bogomil notions of Satan's divinely permitted finite rule and a contract with God concerning the creation of man again highlight the monarchian character of Bogomil dualism, showing that in the history of religious dualism it stands close to dualist systems which accentuate the inferior and derivative nature of the second principle or to essentially monistic teachings with strong dualist tendencies in its cosmology and sacred history.

Two of the themes present in moderate Bogomil and Cathar dualism, moreover, the monotheistic boasting of the satanic demiurge and his seduction of Eve as well as the notion of the heavenly, angelic descent of Mary, have been seen as sufficient (along with the idea that the soul is imprisoned in the body made by the evil creator) to define these aspects of Bogomilism/ Catharism as representing a medieval form of Gnosticism.[35] To these parallels between Gnostic and Bogomil notions one can add a few more, but one should also be aware that the important difference between the Bogomil-Cathar movement and the ancient Gnostic systems was that the crucial significance of the *consolamentum* for the salvation of the Bogomil or Cathar follower made their religion a sacramental one, comparable to the normative Church but at variance with most Gnostic traditions.[36] On the other hand, some Gnostic-like elements in certain trends of moderate Bogomil and Cathar dualism may have been magnified due to the individual interpretative efforts of the *perfecti* resulting from their use of apocryphal traditions or doctrinal innovations.

Yet, despite the variances, Satan in Bogomil and Cathar monarchian dualism was created by the higher God and because of his rebellion was cast out of heaven and created the material cosmos. Conversely, in medieval radical dualism Lucifer proceeded immediately from the eternal principle of evil, from an evil god, who was coeternal and coexistent with the good God.

The Good God, the God of Evil and the Divine Feminine

The western accounts of medieval absolute dualism are considerably more elaborate than the eastern records[37] and it was in Italy that the radical dualist doctrines received their theological and sometimes novel formulation in *The Book of the Two Principles*. The traditional accounts of Cathar radical dualism postulated the belief in two principles, existing for all eternity, without beginning or end. The principle of good was recognized as the Father of Christ, the God of Light, while the principle of evil was the God of Darkness, who blinded the minds of the unbelievers.

In some Cathar accounts the God of Darkness was regarded as the Lord of Genesis, the creator of the four elements, the visible heaven, the sun, the moon, the stars and everything on earth; He was the God of Moses. The God of Light was the creator of everlasting, eternal things and created four alternative elements of his own and another heaven, sun, moon and stars.[38]

The God of Light also created his heavenly people, comprising the body, soul and spirit, the spirit being outside the body and serving as the custodian of the soul. Satan was believed to have been envious of the God of Light and having ascended into his sublime heavens he led astray the souls created by the good God and lured them to earth and the 'murky clime'. When Satan ascended into the heavens with his legions, war ensued in heaven and he was defeated by the archangel Michael and his hosts, as recounted in Revelation. Upon his expulsion from heaven Satan entrapped the deceived souls in the prison of the body; Jesus' mission was to deliver these souls from Satan's enslavement.

Only through the *consolamentum* could the imprisoned soul receive back its heavenly custodian spirit and when, in the last days, all the ensnared souls would achieve their penance they would ascend back to their heavenly abodes and regain their heavenly bodies. This was deemed to be the resurrection of the dead in the Scriptures, not the resurrection of physical bodies but of spiritual bodies. In one form of Italian absolute dualism the Devil imprisoned the deceived souls daily in human and animal bodies and conducted their transmigration from one body to another until they – also called 'the people of God' and the 'sheep of

Israel' – were to be recovered back to heaven.[39] The Desenzano Cathars, who had their consecration in the Drugunthian order, advanced a more elaborate version of the invasion of the heavenly realm of the good Lord by the powers of darkness.[40] In their belief Lucifer, the son of the evil Lord, ascended to the heavenly abodes and transformed himself into an angel of light and gained the admiration of the angels who prevailed on the good Lord to install him as a steward over the angels. There followed Lucifer's corruption and seduction of the angels, the battle in heaven and his fall along with the third part of the angels who were believed to have body, soul and spirit. The slain bodies of the angels, recognized as Ezekiel's 'dry bones', remained in heaven, while the souls were taken captive by Lucifer and imprisoned in bodies.

Some versions of this radical dualist cosmogony and satanology intriguingly introduce the figure of a divine consort or wife of the God of Light, and the resultant notion of a divine pair in the world of good diverges dramatically from both moderate dualism and normative Christianity. Significantly, such teachings have been recorded as professed both by Italian and French Cathar groups. The quest for the sources of these teachings, which in effect establish a divine primordial and sexually differentiated pair in the realm of light, is not made easier by the fact that they are sometimes described in Catholic accounts as being perceived as 'secret', possibly being mastered only by the Cathar *perfecti* of the relevant Cathar communities.

The teaching and the history of the divine wife of the God of Light is indeed described as 'the great secret', obviously one of the secret myths of the Italian radical dualist church of Descenzano or the Albanenses.[41] As in other versions of this dualist history of the celestial wife of the good God, the Desenzano narrative focuses on the theme of sexual interrelations between supernatural figures from the realm of light and the kingdom of darkness, but also has Christological associations. According to the Desenzano story Lucifer, who was the son of the evil god, ascended into heaven and discovered the celestial wife of the good God without her divine husband. Despite her initial resistance, she finally yielded to him when he promised that she would beget from him a son whom Lucifer would make a god in his kingdom and have him 'worshipped like a god'. Falling on the authority of Revelation 11:15: 'The Kingdom of this world is become our Lord's', the Desenzano teaching asserts that it was from this sexual union that Jesus was born and in this way he was able to assume and bring his flesh down from heaven. This peculiar Christology, which is described as a 'great secret', remains Docetic and angelic: Christ continues to be regarded as an angel incarnate and his Passion is seen as having occurred only in appearance, as he did not assume or ascend in actual human flesh but ascended in the flesh that he had brought from heaven, which itself was a product of Lucifer's intercourse with the wife of the celestial God of good.

The dualist bishops of the Desenzano church received their ordination, *consolamentum* and, presumably, the core of their absolute dualist doctrines from the very prominent radical dualist Balkan Bogomil Church of Drugunthia, which also seems to have had affiliations with radical dualist Paulician communities that had settled earlier in Thrace. However, no evidence has as yet been found for teachings containing anything similar to the Desenzano story of Lucifer's seduction of the divine wife of the good God. In one of the versions of the Bogomil teaching of Eve's seduction by Satanael (Samael), which invites parallels with earlier Gnostic and Jewish traditions, she begets from him twins, Cain and Calomela.[42] It is not improbable, although impossible to prove, that the Desenzano Cathars adopted similar traditions about Satanael and Eve and projected the story of Eve's seduction into the divine world, possibly associating Eve with the celestial wife of the good God; a further association with the Virgin Mary (with her angelic or celestial associations in some versions of Bogomil–Cathar Mariology) may have generated the above particular brand of Desenzano Christology.

The Albigensian absolute dualist circles in Languedoc shared the belief in the transmigration of souls and apparently had teachings that were held to be esoteric. While it is extremely difficult to establish with any certainty the doctrinal and exegetical affiliations of the Desenzano story of Lucifer's assault on the divine feminine in the realm of light, the genealogy of an otherwise similar French Cathar narrative[43] seems even more elusive, as the pattern of sexual invasion and assault is entirely reversed – it envisages that it was the good God who broke into the realm of darkness and seduced the wife of the malign god. It was, moreover, this sexual manoeuvre of the good God that provoked the onslaught of the evil god on the world of light. Another exposition of French Cathar teachings[44] contains a cosmogonic account which similarly attributes the initial act of invasion to the God of good and, again, focuses on his dealings with female beings from the kingdom of evil. It stated that the Albigensian 'elders' taught in 'secret meetings' that it was the evil god who made his creatures first, two male and two female, a lion, a bee-eater, an eagle and a spirit. Subsequently, the good Lord took from the evil god the spirit and eagle for his act of creation and from them he fashioned his own things. Plagued by this despoilment the evil god decided to avenge himself and sent his son, Lucifer, with a host of brilliant men and women to the court of the good god, where Lucifer beguiled him and was appointed a 'prince, priest and steward' over his people. The good god also gave Lucifer a testament for the people of Israel, but in his absence the son of the evil god led them astray and scattered them throughout his dominions, while the most noble were sent to this world, styled 'the last lake', 'the farthest earth' and 'the deepest hell'. The souls were sent to this world, the bodies, abandoned by the spirit, were left in the desert and these were 'the lost sheep of the house of Israel' (Matthew 15 : 24) who are the focus of Christ's saving mission. Christ himself was born in the sublime 'land of the living' of Joseph and Mary, who are identified with Adam and Eve, and it was there that his Passion, Resurrection and Ascension to the good Father took place. Christ was deemed to have passed, with His testament, disciples, father and mother, through seven realms to free His people. The good god was believed to have two wives, Collam (Oholah) and Colibam (Oholiba) – the two courtesans in Ezekiel 23 : 4, symbolizing respectively Samaria and Jerusalem – and to have engendered sons and daughters from them.

According to the same tract another teaching that these Albigensian circles regarded as esoteric and again was taught in their 'secret meetings' claimed that Mary Magdalene was in reality the wife of Christ and she was also recognized as the Samaritan woman to whom he said, 'Call thy husband.' She was the woman whom Christ freed when the Jews were trying to stone her and she was his wife as she was alone with him in three places, the temple, at the well and in the garden. This Albigensian belief in Mary Magdalene as Christ's wife is confirmed by two additional Catholic tracts on the Cathar heresy, although in their versions the Cathar attitudes to the 'terrestrial' Christ and Mary Magdalene were modified by dualism applied to the gospel story itself.

In these two exposés the precepts of absolute dualism were transposed on the nature of Christ and there appeared two Christ figures – the celestial and the terrestrial, the latter being an evil or pseudo-Christ. In the first version[45] the terrestrial Christ, who was born in the earthly Bethlehem and was crucified in Jerusalem, was virtually an evil Christ and Mary Magdalene was his concubine. The other version[46] confirms the teaching of the two wives of the good god, adding that it was his relationship with the wife of the evil god that prompted the latter to send his son to the court of the good god. The son of the evil Lord deceived the good god and seized human and animal souls that were dispersed among his seven realms, to which Christ was sent with his redeeming mission and suffered seven times. There was a division between the true Christ, who was born in the celestial Jerusalem and suffered there, 'betrayed by His brothers', while the Christ who appeared in 'this world' was a pseudo-Christ and had pseudo-apostles. The declared belief that Mary Magdalene was Christ's wife seems to refer to the celestial Christ, although in this dualist line of argument one might have expected two distinct figures of Mary Magdalene, celestial and terrestrial.

The origins of the teachings of the two wives of the good god and particularly of Mary Magdalene's marital status appear rather obscure. The teaching of Mary Magdalene as the 'wife' or 'concubine' of Christ appears, moreover, an original Cathar tradition which does not have any counterpart in the Bogomil doctrines. These fragments of Cathar teachings envisaging Jesus Christ and Mary Magdalene as a terrestrial pair, in which the physical Jesus could be viewed as a negative figure, seem somewhat confused and as obscured fragments of a more coherent tradition of a dualist exegesis of the New Testament. What is more, they do not have any counterpart in the extant evidence of Bogomil Christology and New Testament exegesis. On the other hand, Mary Magdalene played a very prominent role in earlier Gnostic traditions presented in Gnostic works such as *The Gospel of Mary, Pistis Sophia, The Dialogue of the Saviour* and *The Gospel of Philip*, where she is extolled as a chief disciple of Christ, a visionary and mediator of Gnostic revelations. In these Gnostic revelatory works she is praised as 'the woman who knew the All' (*The Dialogue of the Saviour*),[47] 'the inheritor of light' (*Pistis Sophia*), associated with the symbol of divine Wisdom (*Pistis Sophia* and the Manichaean Coptic psalm attributed to Herakleides).[48] *The Gospel According to Philip* recognizes her as the *koinonos* (companion or consort)[49] of Christ whom he loved more than all the other disciples, and the spiritual union between Christ and Mary Magdalene is described in slightly erotic terms. Within the general framework of Gnostic cosmology and sacred history, as a terrestrial companion of the Saviour in *The Gospel of Philip*, she could indeed have been seen as a 'counterpart of the celestial Sophia'.[50]

The extant fragments of Cathar traditions about Mary Magdalene, significantly, described in the polemical sources as being secret or taught in secrecy, invite obvious parallels with the Gnostic traditions that identified her as a companion of Christ and sometimes used erotic imagery to depict her spiritual union with Christ. But in view of the lack of any evidence of textual transmission of actual Gnostic works from late antiquity to the medieval dualists these parallels must remain typological. Given the attested Bogomil–Cathar preoccupation with angelic Christology and Mariology, it is not impossible to reconstruct a line of dualist exegesis envisaging two parallel Jesus Christ–Mary Magdalene pairs, a celestial one (where Mary Magdalene could indeed have been seen as a figure comparable to the Gnostic Sophia) and a terrestrial one (involved in the actual Gospel events). Such exegetical parallelism may explain some of the contradictions in the evidence but given its scanty nature such reconstruction remains conjectural. The Cathar views on Mary Magdalene's role in the Gospel need further comparative investigation in the light of Gnostic as well as early and medieval Christian (heterodox and mainstream) approaches to Mary Magdalene to establish with more certainty the genealogy or the exegetical provenance of these Cathar traditions.

It is curious that the evidence of Cathar beliefs concerning Mary Magdalene appears in accounts which also focus on the radical dualist Cathar teachings of divine female companions of the coeternal gods of good and evil, as well as on their abduction or seduction of primordial female beings from their opposite realm. These accounts advance a new version of Cathar radical dualism which postulates some kind of sexual contact between the divine pairs in the kingdoms of light and darkness as the beginning, the starting point, of the war in heaven which provokes the cosmic drama of the perpetual battle between the powers of good and evil.

It is not certain whether this new development of Cathar theology and cosmology, which established primordial and sexually differentiated divine pairs in the realms of light and darkness, presents features of inherited dualist cosmogonies or was predominantly the result of entirely novel exegesis. There are no exact parallels to these teachings of divine wives of the two masculine causal principles in the scanty evidence of radical dualist doctrines in the Balkan-Byzantine East. Typologically, these Cathar teachings would invite parallels with the Gnostic traditions, which envisaged sexually differentiated dyads in the heavenly world. On the other hand, the association of the beginning of the creation process with sexual activity focused on a divine feminine figure may invoke analogies, again typological, with the ambiguous sexual connotations of Sophia's 'fall' in Valentinian Gnosticism (although, of course, she is not subjected to the onslaught of a masculine causal principle).

In Iranian Manichaeism itself the king of light, the so-called Father of Greatness, was identified with Zurvan, the four-fold supreme first principle of Zurvanism, and in Iranian milieus may have inherited some of the ambiguities surrounding the primal feminine element, the 'mother' of Ohrmazd and Ahriman.[51] In some versions of the myth she could be seen as a separate entity alongside Zurvan and in others as an entity within the primeval, androgynous Zurvan.[52] Accordingly, it has been argued that in eastern Manichaeism the Manichaean Father of Greatness could sometimes have been seen as a similarly androgynous figure, referred to as both the 'elder brother' and 'the elder sister'.[53] Furthermore, in Manichaean theology, after he suffered an attack initiated by the causal principle of evil, the Prince of Darkness, he evoked from himself a feminine figure, the Mother of All, thus beginning a series of defensive emanations against the violent onslaught of the evil forces. Consequently, arguments have been presented that the Manichaean Mother of Life, inferior only to the Father of Greatness (Zurvan) in the Manichaean pantheon, was associated with the 'mother' of Ohrmazd and Ahriman who had evolved into a separate entity in Zurvanite mythology.[54]

These Gnostic and Manichaean antecedents of Cathar teachings of primordial male/female pairs in the divine world do not shed an immediate light on the actual provenance of these Cathar beliefs, as there is no evidence of an unbroken tradition or transmission of texts between the Gnostics or Manichaeans of late antiquity and the medieval dualists. The comparative study of these primary dyads and divine feminine figures in Gnosticism and Catharism can, however, at least illuminate the dynamics behind the resurgence of Gnostic/dualist attempts to 'redis- cover' the bisexual nature of the divine world. It is, for example, conceivable that the radical–dualist conceptualization of the causal divine spheres of the worlds of light and darkness as masculine–feminine dyads emerged during the early doctrinal disputes with the moderate dualists as a reaction against the formula of God the Father and his two divine sons, Satanael and Jesus Christ. Some radical dualists might have attempted to counterbalance this triadic formula by generating further dyadic parallelisms in their radical dualist cosmology and Christology, although this would not necessarily explain the introduction of sublime feminine divinities alongside the two male primordial principles.

In this context it may be worth considering an analogous development in the Castilian school of early Kabbalah in the thirteenth century, namely in Rabbi Isaak ben Jacob-ha-Kohen's tract, *On the Left Emanation*[55] (seen sometimes as introducing a 'full blown Gnostic dualism into Kabbalistic symbolism[56]), with its consistent endeavours to formulate parallelisms between sexual pairs in the world of evil, on one hand, and the good and evil powers in general, on the other. His system forges a parallelism between the pairs of Samael–Grand Matron Lilith (who are seen as being born as a hermaphrodite, like Adam and Eve) and Asmodeus–Younger Lilith. According to the tract, the relationship between the pairs is affected by Samael's jealousy of Asmodeus because of the Younger Lilith. Moreover, the notion of two systems of divine emanations, respectively good and evil, as specified in the tract, confirms that in certain contexts its worldview can indeed be described as stating that 'all existence is governed by the antagonism between pairs of similar structure and conflicting content'.[57] Such a worldview would invite immediate parallels to the above discussed Cathar radical dualist cosmologies, with their symmetrical, primordial pairs in the parallel universes of light and darkness. Indeed, on the basis of other doctrinal analogies, a religious interchange between Cathar groups and Jewish Kabbalists in southern France, with the original influence coming from the dualists, has been postulated, but the arguments presented so far are not conclusive. Still, the similarities between Rabbi Isaac's tract and medieval dualist cosmologies do require a thorough reassessment of the evidence. This would certainly help to clarify whether they were the result of actual contact between dualist and kabbalistic circles, or the outcome of independent, parallel developments in Kabbalah and Catharism, or derived from earlier dualist tendencies in Judaism in southern France, attested, for example, in the ninth-century writings of Agobard of Lyons[58] (which would add another intriguing avenue for the exploration of the pre-history of western Christian medieval dualism).

Moderate and radical dualism, therefore, offer some interesting differences in their treatment of the male/female duality in the divine and human worlds. Whereas the monarchian dualism of *Liber Secretum* introduces sexual differentiation as late as the anthropogonic process, in Nazarius' reinterpretation of its cosmogony, the male/female duality is projected into the heavenly world, differentiating the sexually neutral angelic pair, assisting Satan in his demiurgic exploits, and becomes associated with archaic mythic and erotic themes, based on the male/female polarity. It is far more difficult to identify the provenance or the exegetical dynamics behind the radical dualist Cathar cosmologies that establish divine male/female pairs in the opposed realms of light and darkness, asserting thus the bisexual nature of the divine world as well as their possible relation to the emergence of Cathar traditions treating Jesus Christ and Mary Magdalene as a kind of paradigmatic gospel couple. Further comparative study of these Cathar teachings is certainly necessary to try to uncover their roots, whether in antecedent (and possibly diverse) traditions or in novel dualist exegesis that crystallized during the polemical disputes with Catholics and monarchian dualists.

Indeed, the sources for some of the doctrines taught in Cathar absolute dualist circles still prove elusive. Apart from the principal difference in the dualist formula, there are some further differences between moderate and absolute dualist teachings in the various spheres of dualist belief. Moderate dualism appears to have subscribed to the theory of Traducianism, according to which the human soul is transmitted to the children by the parents, whereas radical dualism largely followed the belief in the pre-existence and transmigration of souls.[59] The latter feature is one of the few that radical dualist Catharism shares with ancient Origenism, which has led to repeated arguments for Origenist influences on absolute dualist Catharism[60] that are still impossible to prove, despite recent suggestions that these may have been mediated by Byzantine monastic dualist circles.[61] It is thus equally plausible that some of these theological features were largely original creations of medieval radical dualism. Some of the theological and mythological elaborations of radical dualism in Italian Catharism were also original and sometimes reformist, as attested by the influential views of John de Lugio, who, for example, came to accept the whole Bible as 'written in another world.[62] John de Lugio restored the attribution of some of the events in the Old Testament, like the sending of the flood, to the true God, but argued that the acts of punishment sent upon Israel in Judaea and the Promised Land were provoked by his adversary. According to John de Lugio the evil god has attacked the true God and his Son for all eternity and he falls upon Yahweh's words to Satan in the Book of Job: 'Thou movest me against him, to destroy him without cause' (2:3). *The Book of the Two Principles*, sometimes attributed to John de Lugio himself, advanced a wide-ranging polemic against both Catholicism and monarchian dualism, attacking the doctrine of free will to present the paradigm of the absolute and eternal opposition between good and evil. The doctrine of the two creators was elaborated at some length and the good creator was defined as omnipotent over good things, while the evil creator was charged with engendering evil and wickedness which were manifested in the Old Testament. The old argument of how a good god could permit the existence of evil in his creation was invoked against monarchian dualists, with their teaching of a one higher God who had created the inferior Demiurge. Finally, the tract elaborated on the inevitability of persecution for all who 'live godly in Christ Jesus'. The tract relied heavily on its dualist readings of the Scriptures, a peculiarity which, indeed, characterized the older Bogomil system of an allegorical interpretation of the gospels and parts of the Old Testament.

Bethlehem and Capernaum

The Bogomil predilection for using parables in their sermons was attested early on, but it is Zigabenus' *Panoplia Dogmatica* that sheds light on the fuller range of Bogomil allegorical readings of the Scriptures. Besides the parable of the unjust steward, all-important for Bogomil–Cathar satanology, gospel themes and images could be used to support Bogomil teachings and propaganda. The Bogomil preachers proclaimed their Church to be true Bethlehem, as it was viewed as the cradle of the 'word' and the true faith, while the Orthodox Church was styled Herodes, as it tried to exterminate the true 'word'. The Pharisees and the Saducees coming for John's baptism in Matthew 3:7 were identified with the Orthodox, while the two violent men possessed by devils who 'came out of the tombs' to confront Jesus in Gadarenes (Matthew 8:28) were recognized as epitomes of the clergy and monks.

Besides the polemic against the Church, allegoric readings of the gospels were used to furnish scriptural support for Bogomil teachings. In Matthew's description of John the Baptist (3 : 4), the rough coat of camel's hair and the locusts were seen as the commandments of the Law of Moses, while his leather belt and the wild honey were seen as symbolizing the gospel. 'Eye for eye, tooth for tooth' certainly invited a dualist interpretation and accordingly the two eyes were the Law of Moses and the Law of the Gospel respectively whereas the two teeth represented the broad way of Moses' Law and the narrow way of the gospel. In Jesus' precept, 'You are not to swear at all – not by heaven, for it is God's throne, not by earth, for it is his footstool, nor by Jerusalem, for it is the city of the great King' (Matthew 5 : 35), the great King was inevitably recognized as the Devil, the Prince of this World; the woman who 'suffered from haemorrhages' for twelve years (Matthew 9 : 20) was the Jerusalem church bleeding from the blood offerings among the twelve tribes of Israel and healed by Jesus and by his destruction of Jerusalem. Jerusalem was indeed seen as the old seat of Satan but following its destruction he had to move to the cathedral of St Sophia in Constantinople, the 'Queen of Cities'.

Particularly interesting is the Bogomil translation of Rachel's 'weeping for her children' (Matthew 2 : 18) after Herod's killing of the innocents. Rachel, otherwise the biblical mother of Joseph and Benjamin, was seen as a widow and mother of two daughters whom she unwisely dressed in men's clothes and sent to meet their death at the hands of Herod, mistaking the purpose of his search for the male infants. The widow Rachel, who had caused the death of her children in this short Bogomil story, is identified with the heavenly Father, the daughters/sons of the widow with the souls of Adam and Christ, and Herod, naturally, with the Prince of the World.

The Cathars retained this use of parables and allegories for the illustration of their dualist teachings. The parable in Luke 10 : 30, 'A certain man went down from Jerusalem to Jericho', was seen as an allusion to Adam's descent from the heavenly Jerusalem to the world, while, 'And fell among thieves which stripped him of his raiment' (*KJV*), was read as Adam's fall among evil spirits who stripped him of his light.[63]

Yet the extant Bogomil and Cathar parables and allegories represent only fragments of what was certainly a more developed system of scriptural interpretation. The Bogomil preachers claimed that Christ's departure from Nazareth to Capernaum (Matthew 4:13) meant the departure from the established orthodox Church to their underground and persecuted church where he had chosen to dwell. Whatever the validity of these claims for apostolic succession, until there is some substantial discovery of genuine Bogomil texts like, for example, the momentous findings of Manichaean works in the sands of Turfan early in the twentieth century, most of the legends, parables and 'secret myths' of this 'Capernaum' church will remain unknown and unfathomable.

The War of Labels

In concluding this book, one needs to reiterate that despite using a chronological framework, this book was not intended to reconstruct the development of religious dualist currents in antiquity and the Middle Ages as a historically uninterrupted chain, running from Zoroastrianism or Orphism through Gnostic teachings in late antiquity to the medieval dualist heresies. On the contrary, it has frequently tried to demonstrate the impossibility of such continuity and the paucity of evidence of actual historical contacts between such currents. On the other hand, the book has been guided by the assumption that the phenomenon of the emergence of a religious dualism or dualist tendencies in a given religious tradition, can be better understood when treated against the background of similar processes in other religions, rather than in the isolated framework of early and medieval Christianity, for example.

Through one's use of terminology, moreover, one perpetuates received attitudes and perceptions. To repeat a point made some time ago, in the case of medieval dualist heresies, one should speak of dualist sects (or in some respects, of an alternative, protest and Gospel-inspired Church) rather than of a dualist religion, as the latter may reflect the legacy of medieval Catholic polemics and obscure the reality that they were Christian, if not emphatically Christian, and New Testament-inspired in essence. Still, the arguments that some forms of radical dualist Catharism represented a separate or parallel religion to medieval Christianity are bound to continue, regardless of this perceived legacy of Catholic controversialism. Also bound to continue are the counter-arguments that Bogomilism and Catharism epitomized a noble and pneumatic version of Christianity, focused on the future salvation of man, which tend to ignore some of the more intense implications of their dualist theodicy. These two positions exemplify one of the frontlines of the enduring war of the labels over ancient and medieval dualism.

One is caught up in this war of the labels, of course, by the very use of the terms 'heresy' and 'heretics', reflecting the views of normative religion on dissent and, occasionally, reform. One could choose instead to use some of the self-designations of the medieval Bogomils and Cathars such as 'true Christians', 'lilies of the field', 'magi' or 'bonshommes' but this does not make scholarly enquiry any clearer. Even terms like 'cathars' ('pure ones') and 'bogomils' ('worthy of God's grace') carry the inevitable, but not so obvious, weight of self-labelling and its related attitudes but are, of course, preferable.

Certainly, medieval Bogomil and Cathar adepts did not see themselves as 'dualists' (to reiterate, the term was first introduced by Hyde in 1700), although it is conceivable that the followers of the Cathar theologian John of Lugio, apart from seeing themselves as essentially Christian, may have been able to define themselves as believers in the existence of 'two principles'. The use of the term 'dualism' is, then, a theological and scholarly convention for discussing certain religious ideas, ideally without a confessional or ideological bias.

Such a lack of confessional or ideological bias has not been the rule in the study of ancient and medieval dualist religions. Nineteenth-century studies of versions of Iranian religions that could generally be described as 'dualist' along the lines of Hyde's definition have been on occasions accompanied by an actual or subconscious missionary tendency to find in all forms of religious thought a movement towards what Mary Boyce had described as 'desirable monism'. Consequently, the war of labels over the nature of Zoroastrianism has raged unabated and has generated yet more labels, ranging from 'the first monotheism' to 'the first dualism' and from 'dualist monotheism' to 'monotheistic dualism'. Parallel to this war of definitions, there evolved the process of a cultural appropriation of Zoroaster by figures such as Voltaire, Goethe, Kleist and Shelley, while Nietzsche, who originally adopted Zoroaster as his mouthpiece and stepping stone for his 'transvaluation of all values', ultimately praised him as the most truthful of all thinkers. This cultural and philosophical focus on Zoroaster and his religion was to lead to the curious notion that Zoroastrianism can emancipate modern man from Christianity and the even more curious sympathy of positivism for the ancient creed.

The war of the labels over medieval dualist heresy has a longer history and has its roots in Catholic–Protestant debates over the nature and teachings of medieval heretical, dissenting and reformist groups which began as early as the sixteenth century. Protestant scholars who viewed the Cathars as reviving the spirit of early Christian communities against the corruption of the medieval Church, as the ancestors of the Waldensians and hence precursors of the Reformation, also viewed the descriptions of their dualist and Docetic doctrines as polemical misrepresentations by their Catholic opponents.[1] Medieval Catholic polemicists saw the medieval eastern dualists as inheritors of Manichaean teachings and as their transmitters to the western dualists, the Cathars;[2] Protestant scholarship tended to downplay the existence of dualist (routinely defined as 'Manichaean') teaching among the eastern dualists, as through their impact on the Cathars they were seen as the ultimate forebears of the Waldensians and the later reformed churches. Catholic authors like Benoist or Bossuet also could recognize such genealogy leading from the eastern dualists to the Cathars and then to the Hugenots but with the intention of undermining their Protestant adversaries theologically and politically through the posited Albigensian connection;[3] at the same time Catholic authors could also indicate the differences between the Albigensians and Waldensians.[4]

Such reconstructions of doctrinal and sectarian genealogies were shown to be spurious in Charles Schmidt's critical history of the Cathars and Albigensians published in 1848–9.[5] Schmidt interpreted the references to heretics in late medieval Bosnia as allusions to the Bogomils.[6] Around the time of the publication of his book the discussion of the medieval Bosnian state and its religious affinities were also beginning to absorb the new Slavophile or Slavophile-influenced approaches, but it achieved wider prominence only in the wake of the dramatic changes in the Balkans in the 1870s and the opening of a new phase in the so-called 'Eastern Question'. One may consider in this connection the cases of two influential books that appeared in this period and whose contrasting treatment of Bogomilism and medieval Bosnian history largely through the prism of Catholic–Protestant controversies over medieval heresy, shaped public opinion and have continued to influence trends of research – Johann von Asboth's *Official Tour through Bosnia and Herzegovina*[7] and Arthur Evans's *Through Bosnia and Herzegovina on Foot during the Insurrection.*[8]

Arthur Evans makes his sympathies and approach very clear in the beginning of his historical introduction: the western followers of the Bulgarian and Bosnian dualist heretics were the first Protestants in western Europe, bearers of 'Gnostic Puritanism'. This persecuted 'Protestant

Christendom' looked to the Ban of Bosnia for its protection since, in the days of Ban Kulin, Bosnia indeed directed the great Protestant movement in western Europe; even the 'cultured sons of Provence' turned for spiritual guidance to the early Protestants of Bosnia. All this demonstrates the crucial role of Bosnia in European history; it presents the 'unique phenomenon' of a Protestant state within the limits of the Holy Roman Empire, a kind of religious Switzerland in medieval Europe and one cannot exaggerate 'the single service that it has rendered to the freedom of the intellect' by its stand against Rome and the arms of Hungary. On the question of Islamization, Evans declared that the Protestant population of Bosnia preferred the dominion of the more tolerant Turks to the 'ferocious tyranny of Catholic kings, magnates and monks', adding that there was never a clearer case of Nemesis which follows on the heels of religious persecution. Evans urges even the most devout Protestants to acknowledge the religious obligation to their spiritual, if Manichaean, forefathers in Bulgaria and Bosnia from whom Western Europe had gained much through the purging and elevating influence of these early Balkan Puritans.[9]

Evans' book enjoyed an enthusiastic reception in England and Asboth, himself an Austro-Hungarian official, accused him of trying to awaken an interest for Bosnia in Protestant England. But Asboth's sympathies are not precisely hidden between the lines. To Evans' vision of medieval Bosnia as a kind of proto-Switzerland heroically fighting against Rome's spiritual tyranny and Hungarian crusades, Asboth's comments on the emergence of Bosnia as a political entity in the late twelfth century are as follows: 'Bosnia sought and found in the Hungarian crown a protection against the aggressions of Byzantium, Serbia and Ragusa; it followed the Hungarian Kings in times of war ... it gained in these relations the protection of its national independence and freedom in the exercise of religion'. While accusing Evans of exaggeration, Asboth himself declares that the attempts of the Bosnian ruler, Tvrtko, to establish a large kingdom were doomed, as 'the violent South Slavonic tribes would not tolerate the supremacy of one state over the other', claiming at the same time, that around 1387 Tvrtko's troops consisted exclusively of Bogomils. In Asboth's account this comes as no surprise, as Tvrtko emerges very much as an anti-hero, severing the ancient, sacred link between Bosnia and Hungary. Since Asboth is keen to see in Duke Hrvoje Vukčić a devout Bogomil, the duke's manoeuvres *vis-à-vis* Sigismund of Hungary and the Ottomans are interpreted as the earliest indications of the looming, general alliance between the Bogomils and the Turks, which indeed becomes a central theme in Asboth's narrative. According to Asboth, in the early fourteenth century not only were the Bogomil Bosnians threatening to coalesce with the Turks but the first Turkish invasion of Hungary should be attributed to Bosnia. While admitting that the persecutions of heretics under Stefan Tomaš had 'evil effects', Asboth still argues that the accomplishment of unity of Christendom was a priority at the time when the Bogomil Bosnians were anyway coalescing with the Turks.[10] Asboth advances his account of Bosnian history along the lines of the simple pattern that he had described early in his book: 'The Bogomils founded the Bosnian state and through the Bogomils it was destroyed'.[11]

Both Evans and Asboth use the sweeping generalizations of medieval Catholic polemical literature to advance further sweeping generalizations and this is a pattern followed in other subsequent works on Bogomilism and Bosnian religious history. Both books were influential in shaping certain approaches to Bogomilism and medieval Bosnia and both are quoted, for example, in Munroe's survey of Bosnian antiquities which also ventured to introduce the novel notion that apart from Catholics and Orthodox Christians, Moslems also persecuted the Bogomils.[12] He also insisted that the phenomenon of the Bosnian gravestones, the *stećci*, needed to be urgently investigated in view of the presumed Bogomil Bosnian–European Protestant association.[13]

Meanwhile, during the nineteenth century, the study of Bogomilism itself was influenced by the newly emerging paradigms of the Slavophile movement. Bogomilism seemed an indispensable source for a historical verification of these paradigms, whether interpreted as a sinister and destructive force eroding the essence of Slavonic Orthodoxy or as a bearer of 'primordial' Slavonic values, presumably akin to those of apostolic Christianity. Inevitably, both Bogomilism and medieval Bosnian history became a major theme in the new Slavophile discourse on heresy and Balkan religious history and its later developments which came to incorporate socio-economic or Marxist approaches. On many occasions, Bogomilism and religious life. in medieval Bosnia were viewed first through the prism of medieval Catholic polemical literature, second, through their emergence in Catholic–Protestant debate in the early modern period, and third, through their reassertion in new religio-historical contexts in the nineteenth century.

These reassertions had to meet, of course, the challenge of the growing critical investigation of the sources for Bogomilism and medieval dualist heresy in general. However, the various paradigms concerning the nature of medieval dualism, introduced or reasserted in the early modern and modern Catholic–Protestant controversies, retained their vitality and their protean capacity to be resurrected and used during periods of intensification of Balkanist discourse.[14] As has been lately demonstrated, such discourse can anachronistically associate Bogomilism, Orthodoxy, Catholicism and the religious life of medieval and modern Bosnia in parochial and religiously exclusivist, if visionary, reconstructions.

Indeed, currently the politico-intellectual debates over the posited medieval 'Bogomil' identity of Bosnia *vis-à-vis* envisaged Catholicism and Orthodoxy have reached a level of intensity only attainable in the very much post-Cathar Occitania in the unlikely event of a realization of the old Occitan dream of a Trans-Pyrenean Occitan state, destroyed by the Albigensian Crusade, through some kind of symbolic counter-crusade in the area. On the other hand, the saga of the collision between Catharism and Catholicism has long been one of the most favoured subjects for research, myth-making, romance and controversy. The fall of the Cathar citadel of Montségur and the ensuing mass burning of the Cathar *perfecti*, reputedly at the 'Field of the Cremated', is often deemed to represent what Lawrence Durrell called 'the Thermopylae of the Gnostic soul', and the Cathars, whether maligned or romanticized, still retain their peculiar mystique and long-lasting hold on the European imagination.

Since the beginning of the nineteenth century at least the perceptions of Catharism have been strongly affected by what Michel Roquebert has styled 'a wave of esoteric revisionism', implicated in the time-honoured and ever fashionable 'historical mysteries', in particular those concerning the alleged heretical guilt and fortunes of the Knights Templar, the Holy Grail cycle, etc. This superficial revisionism has obscured the very real need to study the actual historical links between Catharism and the Holy Grail romances in which the Grail myth could be used against the Cathars,[16] the origins and evolution of the Bogomil/Cathar tradition of allegorical scriptural exegesis (understood in the words of Lambert as 'an authentic, underground tradition of correct interpretation,[17] of the New Testament), or the provenance of some of the Bogomil/Cathar 'secret myths' – all this highlighting the urgent necessity articulated by Antoine

Faivre to incorporate Catharism in the scholarly study of comparative Western esotericism.[18]

The uses and abuses of the terms 'dualist', 'Manichaean', 'Cathar', etc., then, have a venerable and continuing history in the war of the labels in religious and political controversies. An attempted summary of the development of religious dualism, without indulging in labelling its currents, may take the following form: in antiquity certain religious traditions identified an already existing, often trickster-like, or indeed new deity (or supernatural agency) as an all-evil bringing power, especially active in the sphere of moral evil. This new figure could further be associated exclusively with the 'negative' set from the pairs of opposites inherited from the earlier systems of dual symbolic classifications which thus were separated and seen as acting in oppositional terms, a development which contrasted these traditions both with religious monism and systems like Taoism in which the pairs of opposites are complementary. The all-evil deity or superhuman power could be seen as operating exclusively in the supernatural world and enjoying a kind of parasitic existence in the material universe, or else as mostly associated with matter. In late antiquity alternative traditions functioning in parallel to what was emerging as normative Christianity and Judaism, came to claim that beyond the public Judaeo-Christian god, there existed another, hidden and spiritual god, bringing salvation to the soul imprisoned in matter by the demiurge – in the orthodox perception of these two different notions of the two 'other' gods, they could interweave and coalesce in bewildering formations. In the Middle Ages some of these alternative traditions, whether transmitted through sectarian circles or revived through new scriptural interpretations, were often perceived as 'esoteric', both in view of the manner in which they could be revealed through a gradual initiation or *vis-à-vis* the persecution of the normative religion. During this persecution some of the notions inherent in these traditions were misinterpreted and distorted in theological and legal frameworks and in this twisted form were integrated in a number of the enduring, haunting and aggressive stereotypes of the witch-craze era.

All these religious currents, ancient or medieval, have brought about many upsurges of religious, spiritual and cultural creativity, and contemporary religion, culture and philosophy owe to them a number of the so-called eternal themes. Insofar as these religious currents frequently produce logical and structured explanations for the origin of evil, which, for a variety of socio-religious reasons, periodically have seemed more influential and justified than their monistic counterparts, it is likely that monism will have periodically to encounter and resume its battle against the theologically dying and rising 'other god'.

Abbreviations

Quotes from the Bible are taken from the New English Bible except in some instances where the King James Version has been used. These are followed by the abbreviation *KJV*. Other abbreviations used in the notes and bibliography are:

AASH	*Acta Antiqua Academiae Scientiarum Hungaricae*
ACSS	*Ancient Civilizations from Scythia to Siberia*
Acta Ir.	*Acta Iranica*
ADAW	*Abhandlungen der Deutschen Akademie der Wissenschaften*
AFP	*Archivum fratrum praedicatorum*
AIPHOS	*Annuaire de l'Institut de Philologie et d'Histoire des Orientales et Slaves*
AMH	*American Historical Review*
ANRW	*Aufstieg und Niedergang der Römischen Welt*
AO	*Archiv orientalni*
AOC	*Archives de l'Orient chrétien*
AOf	*Archiv für Orientsforschung*
AoF	*Altorientalische Forschungen*
AOH	*Acta Orientalia Hungarica*
AP	*Archiv für Papyrusforschung*
APAW	*Abhandlungen der königlichen Preussischen Akademie der Wissenschaften*
ARB-BL	*Académie Royale de Belgique, Bulletin Classe de Lettres*
AS	*Année Sociologique*
Aul.O	*Aula Orientalis*
AUSKO-CRSBID	*Annuaire de l'Université de Sofia 'Kliment Ohridski', Centre de recherches Slavo-Byzantines 'Ivan Duičev'*
B	*Byzantion*

BÄBA	*Beiträge zur ägyptischen Bauforschung und Altertumskunde*
BAI	*Bulletin of the Asia Institute*
BBA	*Berliner byzantinische Arbeiten*
BBg	*Byzantinobulgarica*
BF	*Byzantinische Forschungen*
BIFAO	*Bulletin de l'Institut français d'archéologie orientale*
BISIAM	*Bolletino dell'instituto storico italiano per il Medio Evo e archivio Muratoriano*
BMGS	*Byzantine and Modern Greek Studies*
BPH	*Bulletin philologique et historique du comité des travaux historiques et scientifiques*
BSl	*Byzantinoslavica*
BSOAS	*Bulletin of the School of Oriental and African Studies*
BSt	*Balkan Studies*
ByzSt	*Byzantine Studies*
BZ	*Byzantinische Zeitschrift*
CAJ	*Central Asiatic Journal*
CBQ	*Catholic Biblical Quarterly*
CC(L)	*Corpus Christianorum, Series Latina*
CCSA	*Corpus Christianorum, Series Apocrypha*
CdÉ	*Chronique d'Égypte*
CF	*Cahiers de Fanjeaux*
CHC	*Cahiers d'études cathares*
CHR	*Catholic Historical Review*
CMC	*Cologne Mani Codex*
CSCO	*Corpus Scriptorum Christianorum Orientalium*
CSEL	*Corpus Scriptorum Ecclesiasticorum Latinorum*
CSHB	*Corpus Scriptorum Historiae Byzantinae*
DOP	*Dumbarton Oak Papers*
DWAW.PHC	*Denkschriften der Akademie der Wissenschaften in Wien. Philologisch-Historische Classe*
EB	*Etudes balkaniques*
ECR	*Eastern Churches Review*
HCDH	*Christian Dualist Heresies in the Byzantine World c.650–c.1450*, eds J. Hamilton and B. Hamilton (Manchester, 1998)
HR	*History of Religions*

HTR	Harvard Theological Review
IA	Iranica Antiqua
IIJ	Indo-Iranian Journal
IOS	Israel Oriental Studies
JA	Journal Asiatique
JARCE	Journal of the American Research Center in Egypt
JBL	Journal of Biblical Literature
JEA	Journal of Egyptian Archaeology
JEH	Journal of Ecclesiastical History
JHS	Journal of Hellenic Studies
JIABS	Journal of the International Association of Buddhist Studies
JJS	Journal of Jewish Studies
JMH	Journal of Medieval History
JMS	Journal of Mithraic Studies
JNES	Journal of Near Eastern Studies
JRAI	Journal of the Royal Anthropological Institute
JRAS	Journal of the Royal Asiatic Society
JRS	Journal of Roman Studies
JSAI	Jerusalem Studies in Arabic and Islam
JSJ	Journal for the Study of Judaism
JTS	Journal of Theological Studies
JWCI	Journal of the Warburg and Courtauld Institutes
MGH Leg.	Monumenta Germaniae Historica, Leges
MGH Quellen	Monumenta Germaniae Historica, Quellen zur Geistesgeschichte des Mittelalters
MGH SS	Monumenta Germaniae Historica, Scriptores
MIO	Mitteilungen des Instituts für Orientforschung
MS	Medieval Studies
MVAG	Mitteilungen der Vorderasiatisch-Ägyptischen Gessellschaft
NT	Novum Testamentum
OC	Oriens christianus
OCP	Orientalia Christiana Periodica
OLZ	Orientalistische Literaturzeitung
PG	Migne, Patrologiae cursus completus, series Graeca
PL	Migne, Patrologiae cursus completus, series Latina
PP	Pliska-Preslav

RB	*Revue Biblique*
REB	*Revue des études Byzantines*
RHR	*Revue d'Histoire des Religions*
RMS	*Reading Medieval Studies*
RS	*Ricerche Slavistiche*
RSCI	*Rivista di storia della Chiesa in Italia*
RSI	*Rivista Storica Italiana*
RSLR	*Rivista di storia e letteratura religiosa*
RSO	*Rivista di studi orientali*
SA	*Sovetskaia arkheologiia*
SAS	*South Asian Studies*
SBAW	*Sitzungsberichte der Bayerischen Akademie der Wissenschaften*
SBE	*Sacred Books of the East*
SBNU	*Sbornik za narodni umotvoreniia, nauka i knizhnina*
SCH	*Studies in Church History*
SE	*Sovetskaiia etnografiia*
SEER	*Slavonic and East European Review*
SH	*Social History*
SJA	*Southwestern Journal of Anthropology*
SMAE	*Sbornik Muzeiia Antropologii i Etnografii pri Imperatorskoi Akademii Nauk*
SORIAS	*Sbornik Otdeleniia russkogo iazyka i slovesnosti Imperatorskoi Akademii Nauk*
SR	*Slavic Review*
St.Ir.	*Studia Iranica*
StP	*Studia Patristica*
T&M	*Travaux et mémoires*
UGÄ	*Untersuchungen zur Geschichte und Altertumskunde Ägyptens*
VC	*Vigilae Christianae*
VT	*Vetus Testamentum*
VV	*Vizantiiskii vremennik*
ZÄS	*Zeitschrift für Ägyptische Sprache und Altertumskunde*
ZAW	*Zeitschrift für die Alttestamentliche Wissenschaft*
ZDMG	*Zeitschrift der deutschen morgenländischen Gesellschaft*
ZKG	*Zeitschrift für Kirchengeschichte*
ZPE	*Zeitschrift für Papyrologie und Epigraphik*

ABBREVIATIONS

ZRGG	*Zeitschrift für Religions- und Geistesgeschichte*
ZSP	*Zeitschrift für Slavische Philologie*
ZThK	*Zeitschrift für Theologie und Kirche*
ZVSORAO	*Zapiski Vostochno-Sibirskogo Otdela Russkogo Arkheologicheskogo Obshtestva*

Notes

1 The Bridge of the Separator

1 Thomas Hyde, *Historia religionis veterum Persarum* (Oxford, 1700), cap. 9, p. 164.

2 Christian Wolff, *Psychologia rationalis* (Frankfurt, 1734), § 37.

3 For definitions of religious dualism in a strict religio-historic context, see U. Bianchi, 'Le dualisme en histoire des religions', *Revue de l'histoire des religions*, 159, I, 1961, pp. 6 ff.; *idem*, 'Il dualismo come categoria storico-religiosa': *Rivista di storia e letteratura religiosa*, IX, 1 (1973), pp. 4 ff.; *idem, Il dualismo religioso: saggio storico et ethnologico*, 2nd edn (Rome, 1983), pp. 7 ff.; for a wider definition and application of the term 'dualism', cf., for example, S. Pétrement, *Le Dualisme dans l'histoire de la philosophie et des religions* (Paris, 1946); *idem, Le Dualisme chez Platon, les Gnostiques et les Manichéens* (Paris, 1947); P. F. M. Fontaine, *The Light and the Dark: A Cultural History of Dualism* (Amsterdam, 1986), vol. 1, pp. xii, 263: in the subsequent 14 volumes of his study (1986–98) focusing predominantly on the Greek, Roman and Jewish worlds, Fontaine applies his broader definition of the term 'dualism' to a variety of religious, cultural, political and social phenomena in antiquity, such as dualism in Greek social and political history in the fourth to fifth centuries BC, Roman imperialism, interior politics and social life, etc. As this book is concerned primarily with developments in religious thought the term 'dualism' is used in its stricter religio-historic sense, as employed in the above works of Bianchi.

4 On the phenomenon of dual symbolic classification *vis-à-vis* physical reality, see, for example, C. Lévi-Strauss, *Anthropologie structurale* (Paris, 1958); C. E. R. Lloyd, *Polarity and Analogy: Two Types of Argumentation in Early Greek Thought* (Cambridge, 1966); C. P. Hallpike, *The Foundation of Primitive Thought* (Oxford, 1979), pp. 224–35; R. Needham (ed.), *Right and Left: Essays on Dual Symbolic Classification* (London, 1973); *idem, Symbolic Classification* (Santa Monica, Calif., 1979), pp. 31–2, 51–3; *idem, Counterpoints*

(London, 1987), pp. 200–21; *The Attraction of Opposites: Thought and Society in the Dualistic Mode*, ed. D. Maybury-Lewis and U. Almagor (Ann Arbor, 1989); S. Curletto, *La Norma e il suo rovescio: coppie di opposti nel mondo religioso antico* (Genoa, 1990). For the contribution of Russian scholarship to the study of dual symbolic classification, see for example, V. V. Ivanov and V. N. Toporov, *Issledovaniia v oblasti slavianskikh drevnostei* (Moscow, 1974), pp. 259–305; V. V. Ivanov, 'Dvoichnaia simvolicheskaia klassifikatsiia v afrikaknskikh i aziatskikh traditisiiakh', *Narody Azii i Afriki*, vyp. 5, 1969; A. Ia. Syrkin and V. N. Toporov, 'O triade i tetrade', *Semiotika. Tezisy i doklady na tret'ei letnei shkole po vtorichnym modeliruiushtim sistemam* (Tartu, 1968). For attempts to relate dual symbolic classification to the bicamerality of human mind and the asymmetrical and unbalanced differentiation of its functions, see, for example, V. V. Ivanov, *Chet i nechet. Asimetriia mozga i znakovykh sistem* (Moscow, 1968); I. P. Coulianu, *Le Gnoses dualistes de Occident, Histoire et mythes* (Paris, 1990), pp. 43–6; idem, *The Tree of Gnosis, Gnostic Mythology from Early Christianity to Modern Nihilism* (San Francisco, 1992), p. 46.

5 For the figure of the demiurge-trickster in non-literate cosmologies with dualist tendencies, cf., for example, Bianchi, *Il dualismo religioso*, pp. 57–147; idem, 'Edschou, le *trickster* divin yoruba', *Paideuma*, 24 (1978), pp. 121–9; H. Rousseau, *Le Dieu du mal* (Paris, 1963), pp. 7–13; P. Radin, *The Trikster. A Study in American Mythology* (London, 1956); A. C. Blanc, 'Considerazioni sulla "preistoria" del dualismo religioso', *Rivista Storica Italiana*, 22(1960), pp. 1–22; M. Eliade, *The Quest. History and Meaning in Religion* (Chicago, 1969), pp. 156 ff.; M. Griaule and G. Dieterlen, *Le renard pâle*, vol. 1, *Le mythe cosmogonique* (Paris, 1965).

6 Generally, on the tradition of divine twinship, see, for example, J. R. Harris, *The Cult of the Heavenly Twins* (Cambridge, 1906); U. Bianchi, *Il dualismo religioso, passim* pp. 57–194; R. Kuntzmann, *Le symbolisme des jumeaux au Proche-Orient ancien* (Paris, 1983). For a discussion of the relevant Eurasian material in this connection, see A. Zolotarev, *Perezhitki totemizma v narodov Sibiri* (Moscow, 1934); idem, *Rodovoi stroi i pervobytnaiia mifologiia* (with a discussion of North American Indian traditions); specifically, on North American divine twin mythologies, see P. Radin, 'The Basic Myths of the North American Indians', *Eranos-Jahrbuch*, Zurich, 1949, 17, pp. 359–419; Eliade, *The Quest*, pp. 141–58; for Dogon and Egyptian traditions, see, for example, U. Bianchi, 'Pour l'histoire du dualisme: un Coyote africain, le Renard Pale' in *Liber Amicorum. Studies in Honour of Professor Dr. C. J. Bleeker* (Leiden, 1969), pp. 27–43; 'Seth, Osiris et l'ethnographie', *RHR*, 179, 2, 1971, pp. 113–35, and below; for Iranian traditions, see, for example, U. Bianchi, *Zaman i Ohrmazd: Lo zoroastrizmo nelle sue origini e nella sua essenza* (Turin, 1958); J. Duchesne-Guillemin, *Ohrmazd et Ahriman, L'Aventure dualiste dans l'Antiquité* (Paris, 1953), and below.

7 For the connection between divine twinship and diarchic mythologies,

binary and dualist notions on one hand, and dual social organization, on the other, in a variety of traditions, cf. G. Dumézil, *Mitra Varuna: Essay sur deux représentations Indo-Européennes de la souveraineté* (Paris, 1948); C. Lévi-Strauss, *Les structures élémentaires de la parenté* (Paris, 1949); *idem*, 'Les organisations dualistes, existent-elles?', *Bijdragen tot de Taal-Land-en Volkenkunde*, 112(1956), pp. 99–128; the various contributions in *The Attraction of Opposites*, ed. Maybury-Lewis and Almagor.

8 For this typology of religious dualism, see Bianchi, 'Le dualisme'; *idem*, *Il dualismo religioso*; for other attempts to formulate a typology of dualism, see S. Pétrement, *Le Dieu séparé* (Paris, 1984), pp. 245–59 (on the basis of Gnostic, Manichaean and Zoroastrian dualism); cf. H. Jonas, *The Gnostic Religion* (Boston, 1958), pp. 236–7; J. Duchesne-Guillemin, 'Gnosticisme et dualisme', in J.Ries (ed.), *Gnosticisme et monde hellénistique* (Louvain, 1982), pp. 89–102; J. Frey, 'Different Patterns of Dualistic Thought in the Qumran Library: Reflections on their Background and History', in M. Berstein *et al.* (eds), *Legal Texts and Legal Issues: Proceedings of the Second Meeting of the International Organization for Qumran Studies, Cambridge, 1995, Published in Honour of J. M. Baumgarten* (Leiden, 1997), pp. 280–5 (distinguishing between 'metaphysical dualism', understood as signifying the opposition between two coeternal and causal powers of equal standing, and 'cosmic dualism', defined as the 'division of the world and humanity into two opposing forces of good and evil' but without considering them as coeternal or 'strictly causal'; the latter cosmic dichotomy can be related to other aspects of dualistic thought like spatial, ethical, anthropological and psychological dualism, pp. 282–3). See also Couliano, *The Tree of Gnosis*, p. 45, for arguments that Bianchi's scheme needs to accommodate another dichotomy, antihylic (against matter) versus prohylic dualism; according to Couliano, religious systems in which the second principle somehow derives from the first cannot be defined as dualist (p. 24) – Couliano's typology, therefore, effectively does not recognize mitigated dualist teachings as belonging to the tradition of religious dualism.

9 See the Coffin Text reference to the eight deities in P. Lacau, *Sarcophages antérieurs au nouvel empire* (Cairo, 1902), I, p. 270, 58. Cf. the cosmogonic system and the allusions to *kek* (darkness) in Coffin Text Spell 76 in R. O. Faulkner, *The Ancient Egyptian Coffin Texts* (Warminster, 1973), vol. 1, pp. 77–80.

10 Text in K. Sethe, *Amun und die acht Urgötter von Hermopolis, Eine Untersuchung über Ursprung und Wesen des ägyptischen Götterkönigs*, APAW, 4, Berlin, 1929, p. 76.

11 H. Rineggren, 'Light and Darkness in Ancient Egyptian Religion', in *Liber Amicorum*, p. 142.

12 See Pyramid Texts, §605, in *The Ancient Pyramid Texts*, tr. R. O. Faulkner, (Oxford, 1969), p. 118.

13 See the discussion of this Coffin Texts' treatment of the themes of light and darkness in the context of the deceased's progress in the netherworld in Rineggren, 'Light and Darkness in Ancient Egyptian Religion', pp. 143–5.

14 See the funerary text in A. Piankoff (tr. and intr.), *Mythological Papyri*, vol. 1, *Texts* (New York, 1957), p. 199.

15 See, for example, the texts quoted in Rineggren, 'Light and Darkness in Ancient Egyptian Religion', pp. 147–8.

16 For the Egyptian origins of these cosmogonic notions in the first Hermetic treatise, *Poimandres* (and the image of the 'outer darkness' as a serpent in the Gnostic *Pistis Sophia*), cf. E. Iversen, 'Horapollon and the Egyptian Conception of Eternity', *RSO*, 38(1963), pp. 177–86; *Egyptian and Hermetic Doctrines* (Copenhagen, 1984), pp. 29–30; P. Kingsley, 'Poimandres: the Etymology of the Name and the Origins of Hermetica', *JWCI*, 56(1993), pp. 16–17 (with parallels to the depiction of the emergence of the sun in Hermetic fragment 33).

17 For a discussion of these Egyptian influences on Hermetic cosmogonic notions, see Iversen, *Egyptian and Hermetic Doctrines*, pp. 9–13, 30–1, 39–41, 51–3.

18 R. Anthes, 'Egyptian Theology in the Third Millennium B. C.', *JNES*, 18 : 3, July 1959, p. 170.

19 H. Frankfort, *Kingship and the Gods: A Study of Ancient Near Eastern Religion and the Integration of Society and Nature* (Chicago, 1948), p. 19; Cf. H. Kees, *Ancient Egypt, A Cultural Topography*, tr. I. F. D. Modrow (London, 1961), p. 150; I. M. E. Shaw and P. T. Nicholson, *British Museum Dictionary of Ancient Egypt*, 'Duality' (London, 1995), p. 88; B. J. Kemp, *Ancient Egypt: Anatomy of a Civilization* (London, 1989), pp. 27–8, 50–1; M. Rice, *Egypt's Legacy: The Archetypes of Western Civilization* 3000–30BC (London, 1997), pp. 35–6, 95.

20 For the dynamics of the relationships between Osiris, Seth and Horus, in which Seth ultimately emerges as a brother of both Osiris and Horus, see, for example, Anthes, 'Egyptian Theology in the Third Millennium B. C.', pp. 199–200.

21 For surveys of the theories regarding the identity of the Seth-animal and the difficulty of its identification, cf., for example, P. H. Boussac, 'L'animal sacré de Set-Typhon et ses divers modes d'interprétation', *RHR*, 82, 1920, pp. 189–208; P. E. Newberry, 'The Pig and the Cult-Animal of Seth', *JEA*, 14, 1928, pp. 211–25; H. Te Velde, *Seth, God of Confusion* (Leiden, 1967), pp. 13–27.

22 See the text of the 'The Memphite Theology', in *Ancient Egyptian Literature, A Book of Readings*, vol. 1, *The Old and Middle Kingdoms*, tr. M. Lichtheim (Los Angeles, 1973), pp. 51–8.

23 See K. Sethe, *Urgeschichte und älteste Religion der Ägypter* (Leipzig, 1930), pp. 70–133; cf. the arguments for Seth being the principal god of the indigenous

Upper Egyptian people from the Ombos (near modern Nagada) area before their posited subjection by a Horus-worshipping dynastic race in W. B. Emery, *Archaic Egypt* (Harmondsworth, 1961), pp. 120 ff.; cf. also, S. A. B. Mercer, *The Religion of Ancient Egypt* (London, 1949), pp. 50, 57–8.

24 See S. Schott, *Mythe und Mythenbildung im alten Ägypten*, Untersuchungen zur Geschichte und Altertumskunde Ägyptens, 5, Leipzig, 1945, pp. 64–71; *Bemerkungen zum ägyptischen Pyramidenkult*, *BÄBA*, 5, Cairo, 1950, pp. 165 ff.

25 See the analysis of the evidence and the conclusions in J. G. Griffiths, *The Conflict of Horus and Seth* (Liverpool, 1960), pp. 131–6; on the stability of this alliance or federation, cf. H. Kees, *Der Götterglaube im alten Aegypten* (Leipzig, 1941), pp. 187–214.

26 See J. H. Breasted, 'The Predynastic Union of Egypt', *BIFAO*, 30, 1930, pp. 709–24.

27 See Griffiths, *The Conflict of Horus and Seth*, pp. 137–8.

28 See, for example, P. E. Newberry, 'The Set Rebellion of the IInd Dynasty', *Ancient Egypt*, 1922, pp. 40–6; cf. also the views of R. Weill, 'Notes sur l'histoire primitive des grandes religions égyptiennes', *BIFAO*, 47, 1948, pp. 59ff, 87, who argues that the formulation of the mythical story of the opposition and reconciliation of Horus and Seth, with its basis in the recent political and dynastic struggles, was carried out during the time of the late Second or early Third Dynasty. On the elevation of Seth under Peribsen, see now T. A. H. Wilkinson, *Early Dynastic Egypt* (London and New York, 1999), pp. 89–90, 294–5. It is worth noting that Newberry, 'The Set Rebellion', interpreted the Horus legends of Edfu (texts in H. W. Fairman, *The Triumph of Horus: An Ancient Egyptian Sacred Drama* (Berkeley, 1974) as a reflection of the Second Dynasty Sethian 'time of troubles'; cf. the analysis of other theories and the conclusions of J. G. Griffiths, 'The Interpretation of the Horus-Myth of Edfu', *JEA*, 44, 1958, pp. 75–86; on the celebration of the Horus festivals at Edfu, see now B. Watterson, *The House of Horus at Edfu: Ritual in an Ancient Egyptian Temple* (Stroud, 1998), pp. 113–23.

29 See the suggested chronology of the sequence of these conflicts and reconciliations in Griffiths, *The Conflict of Horus and Seth*, pp. 141–2; for recent discussions of the evidence for Egyptian pre-dynastic rulers, the process of state-formation and the unification of Upper and Lower Egypt at the end of the Predynastic period, see, for example, M. A. Hoffman, *Egypt before the Pharaohs, The Prehistoric Foundations of Egyptian Civilization* (New York, 1979; 2nd edn London, 1984), pp. 264–348; B. G. Trigger, 'The Rise of Egyptian Civilization', in *Ancient Egypt: a Social History*, ed. B. G. Trigger *et al.* (Cambridge, 1983), pp. 13–52; F. Hassan, 'The Predynastic of Egypt', *Journal of World Prehistory*, 2, 1988, pp. 135–85; M. Rice, *Egypt's Making* (London and New York, 1990), pp. 82–169; A. J. Spencer, *Early Egypt, The Rise of Civilization in the Nile Valley* (London, 1993), pp. 48–98; K. A. Bard,

'The Egyptian Predynastic: a Review of the Evidence', *Journal of Field Archaeology*, 21, 1994, pp. 265–88; C. K. Maisell, *Early Civilizations of the Old World, The Formative Histories of Egypt, the Levant, Mesopotamia, India and China* (London and New York, 1999), pp. 58–65; Wilkinson, *Early Dynastic Egypt*, pp. 28–70; B. Midant-Reynes, *The Prehistory of Egypt*, tr. I. Shaw (Oxford, 2000), pp. 231–55.

30 Frankfort, *Kingship and the Gods*, p. 21.

31 Te Velde, *Seth, God of Confusion*, p. 63; cf. W. Helck, 'Herkunft und Deutung einiger Züge des frühägyptischen Königsbildes', *Anthropos*, 49, 1954, pp. 961–91.

32 Frankfort, *Kingship and the Gods*, p. 20. See also H. Kees, *Ancient Egypt*, p. 150. Kemp, *Ancient Egypt*, pp. 27–8, 41–3. Cf. the views of A. Zolotarev, *Rodovoi stroi i pervobytnaia mifologiia* (Moscow, 1964), who also rejects an actual historico-political foundation of the myth of the Horus–Seth conflict and argues that Egypt was divided into Upper Egyptian and Lower Egyptian fraternities whose tradition of ritual fights or hostilities was accompanied by dualities in the spheres of state and royal ideology; Zolotarev sees in the myth of the Horus–Seth conflict traces of the divine twinship mythology, see V. Ivanov's discussion of the unpublished Egyptological part of Zolotarev's book, 'Dual'naia organizatsiia pervobytnykh narodov i proizkhozhdenie dualisticheskikh kosmogonii', *SA*, 4, 1965, pp. 276–87, esp. 281–2.

33 Frankfort, *Kingship and the Gods*, p. 22; *idem, Ancient Egyptian Religion* (New York, 1948), p. 129.

34 Cf., for example, Griffiths, *The Conflict of Horus and Seth*, pp. 122, 128; te Velde, *Seth, God of Confusion*, p. 70; J. B. Russell, *The Devil: Perceptions of Evil from Antiquity to Early Christianity* (New York, 1977), p. 82; for views tending to generalize Seth as an evil power, see A. Piankoff, *The Tomb of Rameses* (New York, 1954), p. 40; Mercer, *The Religion of Ancient Egypt*, p. 51; for Egyptian theodicy, see, for example, S. Morenz, *Egyptian Religion*, tr. A. E. Keep (London, 1973), pp. 58–60; Iversen, *Egyptian and Hermetic Doctrines*, p. 43; Russell, *The Devil*, pp. 76–7.

35 Anthes, 'Egyptian Theology in the Third Millennium B. C.', pp. 198–209.

36 Cf., for example, J. H. Breasted, *Development of Religion and Thought in Ancient Egypt* (New York, 1912), pp. 21–5; E. A. W. Budge, *From Fetish to God in Ancient Egypt* (Oxford, 1934), p. 140; cf. A. Scharff, *Die Ausbreitung des Osiriskultes in der Frühzeit und während des Alten Reiches, SBAW*, Munich, 4 (1947), pp. 7–11, 25–7; Anthes, 'Egyptian Theology in the Third Millennium B.C', p. 199; L. H. Lesko, 'Ancient Egyptian Cosmogonies and Cosmology', in B. E. Shafer (ed.), *Religion in Ancient Egypt: Gods, Myths, and Personal Practice* (London, 1991), p. 93. For a survey of the evidence and theories related to Osiris' association with water and vegetation, see J. G. Griffiths, *The Origins of Osiris and his Cult* (Leiden, 1980), pp. 151–73.

37 G. A. Wainwright, *The Sky-Religion in Egypt, its Antiquity and Effects* (Cambridge, 1938), p. 100; Mercer, *The Religion of Ancient Egypt*, p. 51.

38 For arguments for the solar affiliations of Osiris and Horus and the role of the lunar god, Thoth, in the myth, see, for example, W. Max Müller, *Egyptian Mythology, Mythology of All Races*, vol. 12 (Boston, 1918), pp. 28–30, 62 ff., 85–91; see also H. Junker, *Die Onurislegende, DWAW.PHC*, 59, 1–2, Vienna, 1917, pp. 134 ff. For Junker's later position, see n. 42 below.

39 See, for example, H. Brugsch, 'Eine Mondfinsterniss', *ZÄS*, 6, 1870, pp. 29–35; P. Boylan, *Thoth the Hermes of Egypt* (Oxford, 1922), p. 30; cf. the views of Breasted, *Development of Religion and Thought in Ancient Egypt*, p. 40 (defining the Horus–Seth fight as a 'solar accident', Seth being equated with darkness); cf. also Mercer, *The Religion of Ancient Egypt*, p. 60; for a recent detailed exposition of the theory, see J. B. Sellers, *The Death of Gods in Ancient Egypt* (London, 1992), pp. 51–60, 64, 67, 77–8, 132, 241–2, 250–4, 275–92, 314, 317, 319, 337–41; for Sellers' postulated reconstruction of the stellar correlation of Seth, see p. 116.

40 See the calculations concerning the circumpolar movement of the Great Bear in G. A. Wainwright, 'A Pair of Constellations', *Studies Presented to F. Ll. Griffith* (London, 1932), p. 379, and the stellar map, Pl. 58, p. 384; cf. the stellar map in R. A. Biegel, *Zur Astrognosie der alten Ägypter*, inaugural dissertation, University of Zurich, Faculty of Philosophy, Zurich, 1921, Pl. 8.

41 See, for example, H. Kees, 'Zu den ägyptischen Mondsagen', *ZÄS*, 60, 1925, 1–15; Griffiths, *The Conflict of Horus and Seth*, p. 125.

42 See, for example, L. Speelers, *Comment faut-il lire les textes des Pyramides égyptiennes?* (Brussels, 1934), pp. 3 ff.; H. Junker, *Die politische Lehre von Memphis, APAW*, Berlin, 1941, pp. 16 ff.; Griffiths, *The Conflict of Horus and Seth*, p. 127.

43 See the quotations from the Pyramid Texts assembled in Griffiths, *The Conflict of Horus and Seth*, p. 23; see also Frankfort, *Kingship and the Gods*, pp. 115, 121.

44 See the quotations from the Pyramid Texts in Griffiths, *The Conflict of Horus and Seth*, p. 25.

45 On this ceremony, see, for example, A. H. Gardiner, 'Horus the Behdetite', *JEA*, 30, 1944, pp. 23–60; 'The Baptism of the Pharaoh', *JEA*, 36, 1950, pp. 3–12; Griffiths, *The Conflict of Horus and Seth*, pp. 122–3.

46 Frankfort, *Kingship and the Gods*, p. 21. Cf. E. Hornung, 'Seth. Geschichte und Bedeutung eines ägyptischen Gottes', *Symbolon*, n.f., 2, 1974, pp. 58–9.

47 Frankfort, *Kingship and the Gods*, p. 22. On Horus and Seth in early dynastic Egyptian iconography and titulary see now Wilkinson, *Early Dynastic Egypt*, pp. 183–229, *passim*.

48 Griffiths, *The Conflict of Horus and Seth*, p. 122.

49 See, for example, H. Kees, *Horus and Seth als Götterpaar I, MVAG*, 28, Berlin,

p. 45; *Horus und Seth als Götterpaar II, MVAG,* 29, Berlin, 1924, pp. 14, 17ff. A. de Buck, 'De tegenstelling Noord-Zuid in Oud-Egypte', *Akademie-dagen, Koninklijke Nederlandsche Akademie van Wetenschappen,* 5, 1952, pp. 35 ff.; te Velde, *Seth, God of Confusion,* pp. 68–71. On the Egyptian phenomenon of the association of gods in pairs and trinities, see, for example, Morenz, *Egyptian Religion,* pp. 142–7; see also, Kees, '*Horus und Seth als Götterpaar I*', pp. 27–38.

50 For the allusions to the Great Bear in the Pyramid Texts, see Pyramid Texts §13–14, §458; *The Ancient Pyramid Texts,* pp. 3–4, 91. For the role of the Great Bear in Egyptian astronomy and related beliefs, see *Egyptian Astronomical Texts,* vol. 3, *Decans, Planets, Constellations and Zodiacs,* Part 1, *Text,* pp. 3, 24, 51, 52 (Fig. 13), 183, 189, 190; J. N. Lockyer, *The Dawn of Astronomy, A Study of the Temple Worship and Mythology of the Ancient Egyptians* (New York and London, 1894), pp. 309, 341, 354, 360; Biegel, *Zur Astrognosie der alten Ägypter,* pp. 17 ff.; Wainwright, 'A Pair of Constellations', pp. 373–84; Wainwright, *The Sky-Religion in Egypt,* p. 13; A. Pogo, 'The Astronomical Ceiling-decoration in the Tomb of Senenmut (XVIIIth Dynasty)', *Isis,* 14, 1930, pp. 301–25, *passim,* Pll.16–19; H. Chatley, 'Egyptian Astronomy', *JEA,* 26, 1940, pp. 120–26, *passim;* Z. Zaba, *L'orientation astronomique dans l'ancienne Égypte et la précession de l'axe du monde* (Prague, 1953), pp. 14–44 (a survey of earlier research) *passim,* pp. 45–73 *passim;* K. Làszló, *Egyptomi és antik csillaghit* (Budapest, 1978), pp. 51–5; C. Leitz, *Studien zur ägyptischen Astronomie,* 2nd edn (Wiesbaden, 1991), pp. 14ff, 35 ff. (discussion of Senenmut's astronomical ceiling decoration), 48, 64 ff.; *Altägyptische Sternuhren* (Leuven, 1995), pp. 53, 250, 252.

51 For the presentation of the slaughtered ox's foreleg to the statue/mummy of the deceased and the opening of the mouth with the ceremonial adze, see respectively Figs 3 and 4 in A. M. Blackman, 'The Rite of the Opening the Mouth in Ancient Egypt and Babylonia', *JEA,* 10, 1924, pp. 54, 55. For discussions of the association between the notions of the Great Bear as a sign of Seth, the bull's foreleg as a weapon in Osiris' murder and the ritual of the Opening of the Mouth, cf. G. A. Wainwright, 'A Pair of Constellations', pp. 374–5; te Velde, *Seth, God of Confusion,* pp. 86–90; 'Fingers, Stars, and the "Opening of the Mouth": The Nature and Function of the *ntrtj*-Blades', *JEA,* 79, 1993, pp. 70–1. On the ceremonies involved in the rite of the Opening of the Mouth, cf. A. M. Blackman, 'The Rite of the Opening the Mouth in Ancient Egypt and Babylonia', pp. 47–60; A. J. Spencer, *Death in Ancient Egypt* (Harmondsworth, 1982), pp. 52–5; A. M. Roth, 'The *psš-kf* and the 'Opening of the Mouth Ceremony', *JEA,* 78, 1992, pp. 113–49 (with suggestions that the specific shape of the forked *psš-kf* knives used in the rite may be connected, among other models, with the distinctive erect and often forked tail of the Seth-animal); 'Fingers, Stars, and the "Opening of the

Mouth": The Nature and Function of the *ntrwj*-Blades', pp. 57–81.

52 See Pyramid Texts § 13–14, *The Ancient Pyramid Texts*, pp. 3–4.

53 See, for example, S. Schott, 'Altägyptische Vorstellungen vom Weltende', *Studia biblica et orientalia*, vol. 3, *Oriens Antiquus* (Rome, 1959), pp. 319–30; see te Velde, *Seth, God of Confusion*, pp. 86 ff.

54 Plutarch, *De Iside et Osiride*, ed. and tr. J. W. Griffiths, *Plutarch's De Iside et Osiride* (Cardiff, 1970), 21.359c, p. 151; 62.376b, p. 217.

55 *The 'Mithras Liturgy'*, ed. and tr. M. W. Meyer (Missoula, 1976), p. 18; see the comments of A. Dietrich, *Eine Mithrasliturgie* (Leipzig, 1903), pp. 76 ff.; A. D. Nock, 'Greek Magical Papyri', *JEA*, 15 (1929), p. 231.

56 Pyramid Texts § 587e, see translation in K. Sethe, *Übersetzung und Komentar zu den altägyptischen Pyramidentexten* (Glükstadt and Hamburg, 1935), vol. 3, p. 91, commentary, p. 97; cf. *Ancient Pyramid Texts*, p. 115.

57 te Velde, *Seth, God of Confusion*, p. 96, see also pp. 94, 97–8.

58 For the prominence of Seth-worship during the Hyksos period, cf. te Velde, *Seth, God of Confusion*, pp. 118–29; J. Van Seters, *The Hyksos: a New Investigation* (New York and London, 1966), pp. 97–103; 171–80; Hornung, 'Seth', p. 51; on the Seth–Baal association, see, for example, Morenz, *Egyptian Religion*, p. 238.

59 For Seth's role and changing functions and attributes in Egyptian magic, see F. Lexa, *La magie dans l'Égypte antique, de l'ancien empire jusqu'à l'Époque copte*, vol. 1, *Exposé* (Paris, 1925), pp. 49, 57, 89, 125, 161ff., 166; vol. 2, *Les textes magiques*, pp. 29, 30, 38, 41, 42, 49, 56, 63, 71, 77, 79, 101, 105, 108, 146; vol. 3, *Atlas*, Pl. LXIX, fig. 159; B. de Rachewiltz, *Egitto magico-religioso* (Turin, 1961), pp. 121–2, 129; G. Roeder, *Die ägyptische Religion in Text und Bild*, vol. 4, *Der Ausklang der ägyptischen Religion mit Reformation, Zauberei und Jenseitsglauben* (Zurich, 1961), pp. 177, 179; G. Onasch, 'Der ägyptische und der biblische Seth', *AP*, 27 (1980), pp. 102–5, 115–17; C. Jacq, *Egyptian Magic*, tr. J. M. Davis (Warminster, 1985), pp. 79–82, 115, 124; L. Kákosy, *La magia in Egitto al tempi dei Faraoni* (Modena, 1985), pp. 51, 63 ff., 128; *idem.*, *Zauberei im alten Ägypten* (Budapest, 1989), pp. 51, 69 f., 88–9; R. B. Ritner, *The Mechanics of Ancient Egyptian Magical Practice* (Chicago, 1993), pp. 65–6, 84–7, 103–5, 134–5, 147–51, 157, 165–8, 172–3, 185–7, 208–12; G. Pinch, *Magic in Ancient Egypt* (Austin, 1994), pp. 30–1, 42, 73, 86, 96, 141; K. Nordh, *Aspects of Ancient Egyptian Curses and Blessings, Conceptual Background and Transmission* (Uppsala, 1996), pp. 45, 63, 90, 119, 190 (with observations of the gradual identification of Seth on a par with Apophis with the mythical prototype of the 'enemy of the order' or the 'criminal' that has to be magically punished by the curse).

60 For the trickster characteristics of Seth, see H. te Velde, 'The Egyptian God Seth as a Trickster', *JARCE*, 7, 1968, pp. 37–40; U. Bianchi, 'Seth, Osiris et l'ethnographie', *RHR*, 179, 2, 1971, pp. 113–35.

61 Cf. E. Meyer, *Set–Typhon, Eine religionsgeschichtliche Studien* (Leipzig, 1875), pp. 62 ff.; B. Gunn and A. H. Gardiner, 'New Rendering of Egyptian Texts 2. The Expulsion of the Hyksos', *JEA*, 5, 1918, pp. 45 ff.; H. Kees, *Der Götterglaube im alten Aegypten*, pp. 412 ff; te Velde, *Seth, God of Confusion*, pp. 143–7; cf. the views of Max Müller, *Egyptian Mythology*, p. 302 (arguments for Babylonian influences behind the process of the demonization of Seth).

62 See the discussion of the ceremony in the Brooklyn Papyrus in J. G. Griffiths, 'Royal Renewal Rites in Ancient Egypt', *Atlantis and Egypt: with other selected essays* (Cardiff, 1991), pp. 177–8.

63 See J. Capart, 'Contribution à l'iconographie du dieu Seth', *CdÉ*, 21, No. 41, 1946, pp. 29–31, fig. 3.

64 See PGM IV. 175ff in H. D. Betz (ed.), *The Greek Magical Papyri in Translation*, 2nd edn (Chicago and London, 1992), p. 41.

65 'The Memphite Theology', *Ancient Egyptian Literature*, tr. Lichtheim, p. 53.

66 Jacq, *Egyptian Magic*, p. 80.

67 R. C. Zaehner, *The Dawn and Twilight of Zoroastrianism* (London, 1961), p. 170.

68 M. Boyce has argued consistently for early dates of Zoroaster, ranging from 1700–1500 BC to 1400–1060 BC: *Zoroastrians: Their Religious Beliefs and Practices* (London, 1979), p. 18; *idem, A History of Zoroastrianism*, (2nd ed., Leiden, 1985) vol. 1, pp. 190–1) and vol. 2 (Leiden, 1982), p. 3. An eighth-century date (784–707 BC) has been suggested by O. Klima, 'The Date of Zoroaster', *AO*, 27 (1959), p. 564. The Iranian chronology of Zoroaster's prophetship in relation to the 12,000 years' 'life of the world' remains highly controversial, and has been accepted as historical by, among others, E. Herzfeld, 'The Traditional Date of Zoroaster' in J. D. C. Pavry (ed.), *Oriental Studies in Honour of C. E. Pavry* (Oxford, 1933), pp. 132–6; Zaehner, *The Dawn and Twilight*, p. 33; cf. W. Malandra, *An Introduction to Ancient Iranian Religion* (Minneapolis, 1983), p. 17 (cf. J. Duchesne-Guillemin, *Religion of Ancient Iran* (Bombay, 1973), pp. 99–100) but forcefully rejected by, for example, G. Gnoli, *Zoroaster's Time and Homeland: A Study on the Origins of Mazdaism* (Naples, 1980), pp. 163–75; M. Molé, *Culte, mythe et cosmologie dans l'Iran ancien* (Paris, 1963), pp. 530 ff. For the construction of this late date of Zoroaster see A. S. Shahbazi, 'The "Traditional Date" of Zoroaster Explained', *BSOAS*, 40, 1(1977), pp. 25–35; P. Kingsley, 'The Greek Origin of the Sixth-Century Dating of Zoroaster', *BSOAS*, 53, 2(1990), pp. 245–65.

69 Gnoli, *Zoroaster's Time*, pp. 167–75; M. N. Dhalla, *History of Zoroastrianism* (New York, 1938), pp. 11ff. See also the counter-arguments in Boyce, *A History of Zoroastrianism*, vol. 2, pp. 1–4.

70 The classical references placing Zoroaster in Bactria or western Iran have been assembled in A. V. W. Jackson, *Zoroaster the Prophet of Ancient Iran* (New York, 1899), respectively pp. 186–8 and 189–91, while he also compiled a valuable list of the classical passages alluding to Zoroaster, pp. 226–73. In

modern Zoroastrian tradition Bactria may similarly be seen as Zoroaster's homeland (P. D. Mehta, *Zarathushtra* (Shaftesbury, 1985), pp. 7–8).

71 The Iranian traditions about the death of Zoroaster are listed in Jackson, *Zoroaster the Prophet*, pp. 127–32.

72 W. Jaeger, *Aristotle: Fundamentals of the History of His Development*, tr. R. Robinson, 2nd edn (Oxford, 1948), pp. 133–4.

73 The traditions of Zoroaster as king of Bactria and his mythical wars with Assyria and Semiramis have been collected in Jackson, *Zoroaster the Prophet*, pp. 154–7, 186–7, 274–8, while an elaborate version of the Ninus–Semiramis legend is recounted in Diodorus 2 : 4.1–20.

74 Characteristic Christian traditions concerning Zoroaster are contained, for example, in the Clementine Recognitions 4 : 27–9 (*PG*, vol. 1, cols 1326ff.); the Clementine Homilies 9 : 4ff. (*PG*, vol. 2, cols 244ff.), as well as in later works like Georgius Cedrenus, *Historiarum Compendium.*

75 Peter Comestor, *Historia scholastica*, *PL*, vol. 198, col. 1090.

76 Marsilio Ficino, *Platonica Theologia*, ed. and tr. R. Marcel (3 vols Paris, 1964–70), vol. 3, p. 148.

77 F. Nietzsche, *Gesamtausgabe in Großoktav*, ed. C. G. Naumann, and later A. Kröner (19 vols, Leipzig, from 1894), vol. 14, p. 303.

78 The texts of the *Avesta* have been translated into English by J. Darmesteter and L. H. Mills in *Zend-Avesta*, *SBE* (Oxford 1880–7, repr. Delhi, 1965), vols. 4, 23 and 31. Apart from Mills' translation of the *Gathas* in *Zend-Avesta: Yasna*, *SBE*, vol. 31, there exist several direct and indirect English translations of the *Gathas*, such as H. Humbach and P. Ichaporia, *The Heritage of Zarathusttra: A New Translation of his Gathas* (Heidelberg, 1994). For attempts to deny Zoroaster's authorship of the *Gathas*, see, for example, M. Molé, 'Réponse à J. Duchesne-Guillemin', *Numen*, 8, 1961, pp. 51–64; J. Kellens and E. Pirart, *Les Textes vieil-avestique*, vol. 1 (Wiesbaden, 1988); for a persuasive defence of the prevalent views of Zoroaster's authorship and the integrity of the *Gathas*, see, for example, M. Schwartz, 'Coded Sound Patterns, Acrostics, and Anagrams in Zoroaster's Oral Poetry', in R. Schmitt and P. O. Skiærvø, *Studia Grammatica Iranica: Festschrift für Helmut Humbach* (Munich, 1986), pp. 327–93; The following quotations from the *Gathas* are from the recent translation by S. Insler, *The Gathas of Zarathustra* (Leiden, 1975).

79 Insler, *Gathas*, p. I. It has been argued that certain teachings of the *Gathas* represent esoteric and initiatory traditions associated with Zoroastrian elites and differ from the 'public' or state Zoroastrian cult in successive Persian empires. See, for example, G. Gnoli, 'Politica religiosa e concezione della regalità sotto i Sassanidi' in *La Persia nel Medioevo* (Rome, 1971), pp. 225–55. Arguments for esotericism in the *Gathas* have been advanced in Mole, *Culte*, pp. 61–70 and G. Messina, *Die Ursprung der Magier und die zarathustrische Religion* (Rome, 1930), pp. 80ff.

80 Apart from provoking varying theological readings within Zoroastrianism, the Gathic dualism of the two primal spirits has been a subject of continuing scholarly controversy, as the *Gathas* offer both monotheistic and dualist statements. According to Boyce, in the *Gathas* Ahura Mazda is directly opposed to Angra Mainyu who is likewise uncreated and could in no way be seen as proceeding from him: Boyce, *A History of Zoroastrianism*, vol. 1, pp. 192 ff.; *idem, Zoroastrians*, pp. 19–20, 213; 'Zoroastrianism', in J. R. Hinnells, (ed.) *A Handbook of Living Religions* (London, 1984, repr. 1991), p. 177; *idem, Zoroastrianism: Its Antiquity and Constant Vigour* (Costa Mesa, Calif., 1992), pp. 72–4; similarly, U. Bianchi, 'Aspects of Modern Parsi Theology', in *Selected Essays on Gnosticism, Dualism and Mysteriosophy* (Leiden, 1978), pp. 409–10. According to an alternative position Ahura Mazda, the supreme god, appears in the *Gathas* as a 'father' of the twin Spirits: R. C. Zaehner, 'Zoroastrianism' in *The Concise Encyclopaedia of the Living Faiths*, 4th edn (London, 1988), pp. 204–5; Gnoli, *Zoroaster's Time*, pp. 210–13, and a similar theological position can be found in modern Parsi theology: see Dhalla, *History of Zoroastrianism*, pp. 36–8; P. J. Shroff, 'The Sublime teachings of the Gāthās', in D. N. D. Minochehr-Homji and M. F. Kanga (eds), *Golden Jubilee Volume of the Bombay K. R. Cama Oriental Institute* (Bombay, 1960), pp. 154 ff. These controversies often focus on the search for a correct rendering of *Yasna* 30 : 3 stating the opposition between the twin fundamental spirits, 'the good and the bad'; for a comparative survey of the different translations of the Gathic statement, see D. K. Choksy, 'Doctrinal Variations within Zoroastrianism', *K. R. Cama Oriental Institute, Second International Congress Proceedings* (5th to 8th January 1995), (Bombay, 1996), p. 107 (Choksy adopts the view that Zoroaster's *Gathas* profess an ethical but not a cosmic dualism, p. 100). Cf. also S. Shaked, 'Cosmogony and Dualism', *Dualism in Transformation: Varieties of Religion in Sasanian Iran* (London, 1994), pp. 24–6.

81 The view that the twin Spirits had free will and became respectively Holy and Destructive by free choice is supported in Zaehner, 'Zoroastrianism', p. 204; *The Dawn and Twilight*, pp. 50–2; Gnoli, *Zoroaster's Time*, p. 213; I. Gershevitch, 'Zoroaster's Own Contribution', *JNES*, 23 (1964), p. 13. The alternative position, according to which the twin Spirits manifested in their primordial choice their innate nature and activated their inherent opposition, is advanced in Boyce, *Zoroastrians*, pp. 20–1; Bianchi, *Selected Essays*, pp. 361–89, 415–16, where the choice of the twin Spirits is seen not as the cause but as the effect of them being respectively good and evil. According to Boyce, in the 'ancient and well-defined' dualism of genuine Zoroastrianism the twin, opposed Spirits were Ahura Mazda and his great adversary, Angra Mainyu (*A History of Zoroastrianism*, vol. 2, p. 232) and their identification as Spenta Mainyu and Angra Mainyu, the Holy Spirit and Evil Spirit, emanating from Ahura Mazda, represents the attempts of modern European

scholars, 'seeking to interpret Zoroastrianism according to their own ideas of desirable monism' (Boyce, *A History of Zoroastrianism*, vol. 2, p. 232).

82 The demotion of the *daevas* has been discussed in G. Widengren, *Les Religions de l'Iran* (Paris, 1968), pp. 36ff., 97ff.; E. Benveniste, *The Persian Religion According to the Chief Greek Texts* (Paris, 1929), pp. 39ff.; Boyce, *Zoroastrians*, pp. 21–2, who argues that the *daevas* were wicked both by nature and by choice. Cf. J. Duchesne-Guillemin, *Religion*, pp. 133ff.

83 In his *Naissance d'archanges* (Paris, 1945), Chaps 2–4, G. Dumézil argues that the Amesha Spentas appear as substitutes for some of the principal gods of the archaic Indo-Iranian pantheon (see also his *Idéologie tripartie des Indo-Européens* (Brussels, 1958), pp. 40ff.), a view shared by J. Duchesne-Guillemin, *The Western Response to Zoroaster* (Oxford, 1958), Chap. 3, but rejected entirely by some Iranists, like Zaehner, *The Dawn and Twilight*, pp. 49–50. Cf. Boyce, *A History of Zoroastrianism*, vol. 1, pp. 192–229; P. Clark, *Zoroastrianism: An Introduction to an Ancient Faith* (Brighton, 1998), pp. 30–55. The *yazatas* included the *yazata* Tishtrya, who represented the star Sirius and was elevated as a 'lord and overseer over all stars' (*Yasht* 8 : 44). On the development of the Tishtrya–Sirius *yazata*, see now A. Panaino, *Tištrya*, Part 1, *The Avestan Hymn to Sirius* (Rome, 1990); Part 2, *The Iranian Myth of the Star Sirius* (Rome, 1995). The Amesha Spentas themselves came to be seen as forming the celestial cortège of Ahura Mazda and each of them was perceived as a protector of one of the seven creations that comprise the Good Creation.

84 Gnoli, *Zoroaster's Time*, pp. 193–7; M. Eliade, 'Spirit, Light and Seed' in *Occultism, Witchcraft and Cultural Fashions* (Chicago, 1976), pp. 103–5; on the development of the ecstatic and illumination-bringing aspects of the Zoroastrian cult and the ritual acquisition of the state of *maga*, see Gnoli, 'Lo stato di "maga" ', *Annali dell'Instituto Orientale di Napoli*, n.s., 15, 1965, pp. 105–17; 'La gnosi iranica: Per una impostazione nuova del problema', in U. Bianchi (ed.), *Le Origine dello Gnosticismo* (Leiden, 1967), pp. 281–90; 'Licht-symbolik in Alt-Iran: Haoma Ritus und Erlöser-Mythos', *Antaios*, 8, 1967, pp. 528–49. Cf. H.-P. Scmidt, 'Gathic Maga and Vedic Magha', *K. R. Cama Oriental Institute, International Congress Proceedings* (Bombay, 1991), pp. 220–40; Pre-Zoroastrian Iranian religion and cults have received extensive treatment in Boyce, *A History of Zoroastrianism*, vol. 1, pp. 22–181; vol. 2, pp. 14–40; see also R. Petazzoni, *La religione di Zarathustra: nella storia religiosa dell'Iran*, Bologna, pp. 38–70; Widengren, *Les Religions de l'Iran*, pp. 23–78.

85 The summary of Parsi beliefs quoted in J. Duchesne-Guillemin, *Symbols and Values in Zoroastrianism* (New York, 1966), pp. 3–5, illuminates sufficiently this theological position. Parsi translations of the Gathic teachings of the twin Spirits in terms of (modern) theosophic and Hegelian dialectics are discussed in U. Bianchi, 'Aspects of Modern Parsi Theology' in *Selected Essays*, pp. 410–16. Fragments from Parsi theosophical fragments have been included by Boyce in

the chapter on modern Zoroastrianism in her *Textual Sources for the Study of Zoroastrianism* (Manchester, 1984), pp. 135–9. A brief account of the rise of the theosophic currents among the Parsis may be found in K. Mistree, 'The Breakdown of the Zoroastrian Tradition as Viewed from a Contemporary Perspective' in S. Shaked (ed.), *Irano-Judaica* (Jerusalem, 1990), pp. 234–40.

86 Distinguishing between Zoroaster's original teachings and what seem to be later religious developments in Zoroastrianism poses notoriously difficult problems that remain far from resolved. The following account of Zoroastrian sacred history and eschatology makes use of later Zoroastrian (Pahlavi) texts, like the *Greater Bundahisbn* and the *Selections of Zadspram*, without entering into the controversial questions of the time and background of the formulation of what may appear to be novel Zoroastrian concepts or beliefs. Principal Pahlavi books have been translated by West in the *Sacred Books of the East* (vols 5, 18, 24, 37 and 47) and new, more reliable, translations of some Pahlavi texts are also available. For the quotations of Pahlavi texts here the following translations are used: *Select Counsels of the Ancient Sages*: R. C. Zaehner, *Teachings of the Magi* (London, 1956); the *Selections of Zadspram*: R. C. Zaehner, *Zurvan: A Zoroastrian Dilemma* (Oxford, 1955); *The Testament of Ardashir* (an Arabic version of a Sassanid work): Shaked, 'Esoteric Trends in Zoroastrianism'.

87 Zaehner, *The Dawn and Twilight*, pp. 59–60; Boyce, *Zoroastrians*, pp. 27–9.

88 The principal collection of relevant Orphic fragments remains O. Kern, *Orphicorum fragmenta* (Berlin, 1922), and some important Orphic fragments have been translated in W. K. C. Guthrie, *Orpheus and Greek Religion*, 2nd edn (London, 1952), pp. 59–62, 137–42. The Orphic hymns have been edited by G. Quandt, *Orphei Hymni* (Berlin, 1941), and recently re-edited and translated by A. N. Athanassakis, *The Orphic Hymns* (Missoula, Montana, 1977).

89 The tradition of Orpheus' Dionysian dynasty and initiations and the ensuing association between the Dionysian and Orphic mysteries is illustrated by the fragment in Kern, *Orphicorum fragmenta*, pp. 8ff. E. Rohde's discussion of the 'The Thracian Worship of Dionysus' in his *Psyche: The Cult of Souls and Belief in Immortality among the Greeks*, tr. (from the 8th edn) W. B. Hillis (London, 1925), Chap. 8, still remains a classic account of the cult of Dionysus in Thrace. Thracian religion has not yet been reconstructed sufficiently but R. Pettazzoni, 'The Religion of Ancient Thrace' in *Essays on the History of Religions* (Leiden, 1954), pp. 81–94, U. Bianchi, 'Dualistic Aspects of Thracian Religion', *History of Religions*, 10:3 (1971), pp. 228–33, and A. Fol and I. Marazov, *Thrace and the Thracians* (London, 1977), pp. 17–37, illuminate most of the recoverable characteristic features of Thracian religion. In his recent book, *Trakiiskiiat Dionis*, vol. 1 (Sofia, 1991), Fol distinguishes sharply between the archaic Thracian Dionysus, as a focus of Palaeo-Balkan religious tradition, and the later Hellenic Dionysus, protagonist of Greek literary tradition.

90 According to Herodotus (4:94) the Getae claim to immortality was based on the belief that they did not die but only left this life to go to Zalmoxis. On 'immortalization' among the Getae and the figure and cult of Zalmoxis see M. Eliade, *Zalmoxis, the Vanishing God* (Chicago, 1972), pp. 21–75, and for a discussion of the ascetic and spiritualist trends among the Thracians and the Getae, pp. 61ff.; also Rohde, *Psyche*, pp. 263ff., 360; D. Popov, *Zalmoxis* (Sofia, 1989), pp. 90–110, 177–93. The shamanistic features of the figure of Orpheus and their connections with shamanistic beliefs and practices in the Thracian and Scythian world have been considered in E. R. Dodds, *The Greeks and the Irrational* (Berkeley and London, 1951), pp. 147ff.; W. Burkert, *Lore and Science in Ancient Pythagoreanism*, tr. E. Mihar, Jr (Cambridge, 1972), pp. 163–5; M. L. West, *The Orphic Poems* (Oxford, 1983), pp. 4–6, 146–50; B. Bogdanov, *Orfei i drevnata mitologiyia na balkanite* (Sofia, 1991), pp. 80–91.

91 Bianchi, 'Dualistic Aspects', p. 231. The thesis that the belief in the immortality and divinity of the soul emerged in Thracian worship of Dionysus and entered Greece from Thrace has been advanced in Rohde, *Psyche*, pp. 254ff., 263ff., and W. K. C. Guthrie, *The Greeks and Their Gods* (London, 1950), pp. 174–7, 179ff., 317ff.

92 The tradition of Orpheus' solar affiliation and Dionysus' reaction was the subject of Aeschylus' lost play, the *Bassarides*; see Kern, *Orphicorum fragmenta*, p. 33 (fragment 113). The traditions about the death of Orpheus are assembled in pp. 33–41 (testimonies 113–35). In Guthrie's reconstruction of Orpheus' association with Apollo (*Orpheus and Greek Religion*, pp. 44–9), Orpheus is seen as a Hellenic missionary in Thrace, a champion of Apollo-worship, opposed to the excesses of the Thracian cult of Dionysus; also in his *The Greeks and Their Gods*, pp. 315ff.

93 M. Detienne, 'Orpheus', in M. Eliade (ed.), *Encyclopedia of Religion* (New York, 1987), vol. II, p. 114.

94 Olympiodorus' comment is included in Kern, *Orphicorum fragmenta*, p. 232 (fragment 211). The view that Orpheus or the Orphics acted as reformers of Dionysian mysteries is supported, for example, in Guthrie, *Orpheus and Greek Religion*, pp. 39–46; M. Nilson, 'Early Orphism and Kindred Religious Movements', *HTR*, 28 (1935), pp. 203ff.

95 For Bacchic concern with the afterlife see, for example, W. Burkert, *Greek Religion*, tr. J. Raffan (Oxford, 1985), pp. 293–6; *Ancient Mystery Cults* (Cambridge, Mass., 1987), pp. 22–3; see also P. Kingsley, *Ancient Philosophy, Mystery and Magic: Empedocles and Pythagorean Tradition* (Oxford, 1995), pp. 261–5.

96 The antiquity of the myth has been debated, as it is preserved by later authors like Olympiodorus and Proclus, although it seems apparent that early authors like Plato alluded to the story, as argued in Dodds, *The Greeks and the Irrational*, p. 156; Bianchi, 'Péché originel and péché antécédent', *RHR*, 170

(1966), pp. 118ff. Moreover, according to Bianchi, the myth of Dionysus–Zagreus and the crime of the Titans as well as Plato's utterance about the rebellious and deceitful 'Titanic nature' (*Laws* 3 : 701c–d) allude to an antecedent sin of divine beings preceding the existence of humanity. Arguments for the antiquity of the myth of the dismemberment of Dionysus and that it was deliberately kept secret as 'a doctrine of mysteries' are presented in Burkert, *Greek Religion*, p. 298. The Orphic cosmogonies and theogonies are discussed in Guthrie, *Orpheus and Greek Religion*, Chap. 4 (with a translation of fragments, pp. 137–42); L. J. Alderink, *Creation and Salvation in Ancient Orphism* (Chico, California, 1981), Chap. 2; M. L. West, *The Orphic Poems*, Chaps 3–7, pp. 143–51, presents further suggestions for a shamanistic background of the myth of the death and rebirth of Dionysus, a pattern of ritual initiation that is thought to have been brought into the Greek world from Thrace and Scythia. Assertions that Orphism might owe its cosmogonical and salvation beliefs to Zoroastrian influences can be found, for example, in Boyce, *A History of Zoroastrianism*, vol. 2, pp. 162, 232.

97 Rohde, *Psyche*, pp. 341ff.; Guthrie, *Orpheus and Greek Religion*, pp. 156ff.; Nilsson, 'Early Orphism', pp. 207, 229ff.; A. D. Nock, *Essays on Religion and the Ancient World* (Oxford and Cambridge, Mass., 1972), vol. I, p. 297; Bianchi, 'Psyche and Destiny', in E. Sharpe and J. Hinnells (eds), *Man and His Salvation: Studies in Memory of S. G. F. Brandon* (Manchester, 1973), pp. 53–65.

98 Alderink, *Creation and Salvation*, pp. 65–72, 76–7, 83–5, 92–3. For reconstructions of Orphic teachings on the afterlife, judgement and fate of the soul see Guthrie, *Orpheus and Greek Religion*, pp. 156–71, and *The Greeks and Their Gods*, pp. 322–5; Rohde, *Psyche*, pp. 344ff.; Nilsson, 'Early Orphism', pp. 216ff.; but for Alderink's alternative position, see *Creation and Salvation*, pp. 74–80, 87ff.

99 In *Laws*, 6 : 782c, Plato refers to the vegetarianism required by the 'Orphic life', while Aristophanes alludes to the Orphic ban on killing, a prohibition introduced by the initiations of Orpheus (*Frogs* 1032). Modern views of the Orphic way of life are to be found in Guthrie, *Orpheus and Greek Religion*, pp. 196–201; Burkert, *Greek Religion*, pp. 301–4; Alderink, *Creation and Salvation*, pp. 80–5. Alderink questions the widely accepted position that Orphism comprised the doctrine of the transmigration of the soul, *Creation and Salvation*, pp. 57ff., 83ff. Another controversy surrounds the supposed existence of an Orphic 'church' or sect. While authorities like Guthrie, *Orpheus and Greek Religion*, pp. 204ff., or M. P. Nilsson, *A History of Greek Religion*, tr. F. J. Fielden, 2nd edn (London and New York, 1945), p. 218, accept that the Orphics effectively formed a sect, others strongly deny the existence of a sectarian type of organization. According to Eliade the 'secret groups' of Orphic initiates could be compared to the similarly secret associations of the Tantric adepts (*History of Religious Ideas*, tr. W. R. Trask (Chicago, 1982), vol. 2, p. 488).

100 Bianchi, 'Dualistic Aspects', p. 231; On Plato's indebtedness to Orphic traditions, see now Kingsley, *Ancient Philosophy*, pp. 112–33.

101 On Dionysus as a saviour-god see Alderink, *Creation and Salvation*, pp. 69–70; Guthrie, *Orpheus and Greek Religion*, p. 83. The thesis that Orphism introduced the dualism of soul and body into Greek religious thought is advanced, for example, by Nilsson, *A History of Greek Religion*, p. 229, where Orphism is credited with formulating the new idea of the body as the tomb of the soul with the inevitable re-evaluation of 'this life as compared with the other life'. Similarly, Dodds, *The Greeks and the Irrational*, p. 139, assigns to Orphism the initiation of a new, fateful religious pattern which credited man with 'an occult self of divine origin' and set soul and body in opposition. While arguing that Orphic anthropological dualism did not imply opposition between soul and body, Alderink, *Creation and Salvation*, p. 88, indicates that the Orphics 'were among the first – if not the first – to make a distinction between body and soul and to speculate about their relations'.

102 The teaching of the four spiritual constituents of man is expounded in the Pahlavi work *Denkart* (Acts of the Religion) 3 : 218, while the doctrine of man's three parts with their three subdivisions is advanced in another important Pahlavi text, the *Selections of Zadspram*. Both teachings have been analysed in detail in Sir Harold Bailey, *Zoroastrian Problems in the Ninth-century Books* (Oxford, 1943), which presents further material on the Zoroastrian doctrine of man and his spiritual constitution, pp. 78–119. The relationship between soul and body in Zoroastrianism has been examined, with translations of relevant fragments, in Zaehner, *The Dawn and Twilight*, pp. 268–79; Shaked, *Dualism*, pp. 52–71.

103 This is illustrated by the *Denkart* fragment translated in Zaehner, *The Dawn and Twilight*, p. 274. See also the text of the Pahlavi fragment and discussion in Shaked, *Dualism*, p. 55.

104 S. Shaked, 'Some Notes on Ahreman, the Evil Spirit, and his Creation', in *Studies in Mysticism and Religion Presented to G. G. Scholem* (Jerusalem, 1969), p. 230. Shaked sees the essence of Ahriman's creation as a corruption of Ohrmazd's creation (p. 233), while the 'coming into being of the material world out of the conceptual, *menog*, is only made possible through the negative participation of the evil principle' (p. 234). For an overview of the Zoroastrian treatment of notions of *menog* and *getig* as presented in Pahlavi Texts and their role in Zoroastrian eschatology, see Shaked, 'The Notions *mēnōg* and *gētīg* in the Pahlavi Texts and their Relation to Eschatology', reprinted in *From Zoroastrian Iran to Islam* (Aldershot, 1995), II, pp. 59–108 (with translations of relevant fragments from the Pahlavi sources); on the notions of the 'non-existence' of Ahriman, his lack of material existence and endeavours to attach his evil spirituality to the material, cf. H. P. Schmidt, 'The Non-Existence of Ahreman and the Mixture (*gumezisn*) of Good and

Evil', in *K. R. Cama Oriental Institute, Second International Congress Proceedings* (5th to 8th January 1995), pp. 79–96 (with parallels and suggestions for a connection between the idea of the 'non-existence' of Ahriman and the Neo-Platonic notion of the non-being of evil, p. 85); cf. also the suggestion that in this context evil appears as a kind of 'anti-body' on account of its lack of corporeality and destructive and parasitic presence in A. V. Williams, 'The Body and the Boundaries of Zoroastrian Spirituality', *Religion*, 19 (1989), pp. 227–39.

105 Benveniste, *The Persian Religion*, pp. 20–1. According to Pliny, *Natural History*, 30:3, both Eudoxus and Aristotle held that Zoroaster lived 6,000 years before Plato; Benveniste thought this chronological relation served to link Zoroastrian and Platonic dualism in a cyclical scheme which reflected the Iranian cycle of 12,000 years and its division into two eras of six millennia – the first period is marked by the advent of Zoroaster, while the end of the second has to bring back 'a representative of the same idea', Benveniste, *The Persian Religion*, p. 20. According to Herzfeld, *Zoroaster and his World*, vol. I, p. 3, Eudoxus' figure of 6,000 years between Zoroaster and Plato implies 'the Zoroastrian doctrine of messianic return' and combines the notions that Zoroaster would reappear after 6,000 years and that Plato is Zoroaster's incarnation.

106 Jaeger, *Aristotle*, p. 136. Jaeger wrote: the 'originality of Eudoxus lay solely in putting Zarathustra 6,000 years ago', while it was Aristotle who, 'led by his doctrine of the periodical return of all human knowledge, first specifically connected this figure with the return of dualism, and thereby put Plato in a setting that corresponded to his profound reverence for him'. The cycle of 6,000 years between Zoroaster and Plato thus served to indicate that 'Zarathustra and Plato are obviously two important stages in the world's journey towards its goal, the triumph of the good', Jaeger, *Aristotle*, pp. 134–5.

107 Hippolytus, *Refutation of All Heresies*, 6:23.2.

108 The possibility of Zoroastrian influences on Orphism and Pythagoreanism is discussed, for example, by Duchesne-Guillemin in his *Ormazd et Ahriman*, p. 87. Zoroastrian impact on Orphic cosmogony and teachings of salvation is suggested by Boyce (see above, n. 96). The parallels between Zoroastrian traditions and the concepts of Heraclitus, along with a survey of the earlier studies and approaches to the problem, have been examined at great length in M. L. West, *Early Greek Philosophy and the Orient* (Oxford, 1971), pp. 165–202. In Chap. 7, 'The Gift of the Magi', pp. 203–42, West offers a strong argument for active Iranian influence on the development of Greek thought in the period 550–480 BC. For earlier endorsements of similar views, see, for example, R. Eisler, *Weltenmantel und Himmelszelt* (Munich, 1910), and for criticism, see J. Kerschensteiner, *Platon und der Orient*

(Stuttgart, 1945). Iranian influences on early Ionian philosophical and religious movements are discussed, also in Boyce, *A History of Zoroastrianism*, vol. 2, pp. 153–63. The parallels between the concepts of Empedocles and Zoroastrian thought are examined, for example, in Bidez and Cumont, *Les Mages hellénisés*, vol. 1, pp. 238ff, with the suggestion that they reflected Empedocles' Pythagorean affinities. Cf. Duchesne-Guillemin, *Religion of Ancient Iran*, p. 152; Kingsley, *Ancient Philosophy*, pp. 226–7; 'Meetings with Magi: Iranian Themes among the Greeks, from Xanthus of Lydia to Plato's Academy', *JRAS*, Series 3, 5, 2, 1995, pp. 173–210. For Plato's contacts with the Iranian world, see now A. D. H. Bivar, 'Plato and Iran', in *The Personalities of Mithra in Archaeology and Literature* (New York, 1998), pp. 67–89; on Plato's dualism cf., for example, Pétrement, *Le dualisme chez Platon*, Chaps 1–3; Fontaine, *The Light and the Dark*, vol. 3, 1988, pp. 167–82.

109 The Achaemenid empire, the fifth 'Great Oriental Monarchy' in Rawlinson's *Seven Great Oriental Monarchies of the Ancient World* (3 vols, New York, 1885), has been given a further full-length treatment in A. T. Olmstead, *History of the Persian Empire* (Chicago, 1948), and more recently in J. Cook, *The Persian Empire* (London, 1983), while R. N. Frye, *The Heritage of Persia* (London, 1967), pp. 16–78, offers a survey of pre-Achaemenid Iranian traditions. A. Kuhrt, H. Sancisi-Weerdenburg, *et al.* (eds), *Achaemenid History* (5 vols, Leiden, 1984–9) contains important recent contributions to the historiography of the Achaemenid empire. Somewhat differing accounts of the history of Zoroastrianism and its relationship with the Achaemenids may be found in Boyce, *A History of Zoroastrianism*, vol. 2; Zaehner, *The Dawn and Twilight*, Part I, Chap. 7, 'Achaemenids and Magi'; Gershevitch, 'Zoroaster's Own Contribution'; Duchesne-Gulleimin, *The Western Response to Zoroaster*, pp. 52ff.; *Religion of Ancient Iran*, pp. 110–22; Molé, *Culte*, pp. 26ff; G. Gnoli, 'La religion des Achéménides', in *De Zoroastre à Mani, Quatre leçons au College de France* (Paris, 1985), pp. 53–73; for an overview of the problem see now Shaked, 'Aspects of Iranian religion in the Achaemenid Period', *K. R. Cama Oriental Institute, International Congress Proceedings*, pp. 90–101.

110 E. J. Bickerman, 'Persia' in *Encyclopaedia Judaica*, vol. 13 (Jerusalem, 1971), p. 304. Apart from the accounts in Greek historiography, the Graeco-Persian wars have received detailed treatment in works like A. R. Burn *Persia and the Greeks: the Defence of the West, c. 567–478*, 2nd edn (London, 1984); H. Bengston (ed.), *The Greeks and Persians from the Sixth to the Fourth Centuries* (London, 1968).

111 J. Wellard, *By the Waters of Babylon* (London, 1973), p. 188. The tradition of Xerxes' destruction of Esagila and removal of Marduk's statue has been subjected to strong criticism and rejected in A. Kuhrt and S. Sherwin-White, 'Xerxes' Destruction of Babylonian Temples' in Kuhrt and Sancisi-

Weerdenburg, *Achaemenid History*, vol. 2, pp. 69–78. cf. M. Dandamaev, 'Xerxes and the Esagila Temple', in C. A. Bromberg (ed.), *Bulletin of the Asia Institute*, 7, 1993, *Iranian studies in Honor of A. D. H. Bivar*, pp. 41–6.

112 The inscriptions of Darius and other Achaemenid monarchs have been edited and translated in R. G. Kent, *Old Persian: Grammar, Texts, Lexicon*, 2nd edn (New Haven, 1953). According to Boyce, Cyrus' religion was indeed Zoroastrianism, *A History of Zoroastrianism*, vol. 2, pp. 43ff., 51–3; M. Boyce, 'The Religion of Cyrus' in Kuhrt and Sancisi-Weerdenburg, *Achaemenid History*, vol. 3, pp. 5–31. The role of the Achaemenid ceremonial capital of Persepolis is discussed in Frye, *The Heritage of Persia*, p. 100; Olmstead, *History of the Persian Empire*, pp. 172–85; A. U. Pope, 'Persepolis, a Ritual City', *Archaeology*, 10 (1957), pp. 123–30.

113 Kent, *Old Persian*, p. 138; Boyce, *Textual Sources*, p. 105. Darius' Mazda-worship, as reflected in his inscriptions, is discussed in Zaehner, *The Dawn and Twilight*, pp. 155–8; Gershevitch, 'Zoroaster's Own Contribution', pp. 16–19; Boyce, *A History of Zoroastrianism*, vol. 2, pp. 118–24.

114 Kent, *Old Persian*, pp. 150–1; Boyce, *Textual Sources*, p. 105. The historical significance of Xerxes' inscription has provoked debate and varying interpretations in, for example, Zaehner, *The Dawn and Twilight*, pp. 159ff.; Gershevitch, 'Zoroaster's Own Contribution', p. 18; Boyce, *A History of Zoroastrianism*, vol. 2, pp. 173–7; M. Papatheophanes, 'Heraclitus of Ephesus, the Magi and the Achaemenids', *Iranica Antiqua*, 20 (1985), pp. 107–11; H. S. Nyberg, *Die Religionen des alten Iran*, tr. H. Schaeder (Leipzig, 1938), pp. 337ff.

115 There is a considerable literature and divergence of opinion on the Magi – from the surmise in G. Messina, *Die Ursprung der Magier und die zarathus-trische Religion* (Bologna, 1930), and Molé, *Culte*, that the Magi were Zoroaster's disciples and heirs, to the opinion of R. Pettazzoni, *La religione di Zarathustra* (Rome, 1920), p. 84, that the Magi were the priests of the *daevas*. The problem of the Magi and Zoroastrianism has been approached and illuminated from different angles in Bidez and Cumont, *Les Mages hellénisés*; E. Benveniste, *Les Mages dans l'ancien Iran* (Paris, 1938); Widengren, *Les Religions de l'Iran*, pp. 134ff., 147ff.; Zaehner, *The Dawn and Twilight*, pp. 161ff.; Papatheophanes, 'Heraclitus of Ephesus'; Boyce, *A History of Zoroastrianism*, vol. 2, pp. 19ff., 21, 43, 46–8, 154–5; Gershevitch, 'Zoroaster's Own Contribution', pp. 24ff., 29–31; Gnoli, *Zoroaster's Time and Homeland*, pp. 206ff.

116 The question of the religious eclecticism of the Magi and their role in the religious syncretism of the Achaemenid era has been examined in Gnoli, *Zoroaster's Time and Homeland*, pp. 209ff.; Papatheophanes, 'Heraclitus of Ephesus', pp. 111 ff.; Gershevitch, 'Zoroaster's Own Contribution', pp. 24ff.; Frye, *The Heritage of Persia*, pp. 75–7. Zaehner, *The Dawn and Twilight*, pp.

97–144, offers a detailed, if controversial, account of the fortunes of Mitra-worship in pre-Zoroastrian and pre-Achaemenid Iran and its reintegration into the Good Religion. The promotion of the cult of Anahita under Artaxerxes is discussed in Boyce, *A History of Zoroastrianism*, vol. 2, pp. 201–4. According to Frye, Mithra and Anahita were always revered by the Achaemenid house (*The Heritage of Persia*, p. 269, n. 91). Perhaps significantly, Mithras is not acknowledged by name in the *Gathas* (on this silence, see for example, M. Boyce, 'On Mithra's Role in Zoroastrianism', *BSOAS*, 32, 1969, pp. 14f.); for arguments that the pair Ahura(Mazda)–Mithra had the same significance, balance and double orientation as the Vedic pair Varuna–Mithra (which would link Ahura Mazda with Varuna), see Dumézil, *Mitra–Varuna*, pp. 60–4; on Mithra in Indo-Iranian belief and his relationship and pairing with Varuna, see also, for example, J. Gonda, *The Vedic God Mithra* (Leiden, 1972); P. Thieme, 'The concept of Mitra in Aryan belief', in J. R. Hinnels (ed.), *Mithraic Studies*, vol. 1 (Manchester, 1975), pp. 21–40; H.-P. Schmidt, 'Indo-Iranian Mitra Studies: The State of the Central Problem', in J. Duchesne-Guillemin (ed.), *Études mithriaques* (Leiden, 1978), pp. 345–95.

117 The Magi have been identified as authors of the Ohrmazd-versus-Ahriman formula in Gershevitch, 'Zoroaster's Own Contribution', pp. 29ff., where it is defined as 'an original and elegant heresy'; and in Gnoli, *Zoroaster's Time and Homeland*, pp. 210ff., with arguments for Mesopotamian influences in the creation of the new dualist opposition. On the association between Spenta Mainyu and Ahura Mazda, cf., for example, Boyce, *History of Zoroastrianism*, vol. 1, pp. 193 ff.; P. Kreyenbroek, 'On Spenta Mainyu's Role in Zoroastrian Cosmogony', in Bromberg (ed.), *Bulletin of the Asia Institute*, 7, pp. 97–103.

118 The figure of the 'Accursed Whore', her wickedness and her 'defection' to Ahriman are discussed in Zaehner, *The Dawn and Twilight*, pp. 231–4; *Zurvan*, pp. 74–5, 183ff.

119 Zaehner, *The Dawn and Twilight*, p. 267.

120 See, for example, Boyce, *A History of Zoroastrianism*, vol. 1, p. 149, 'Zoroaster the Priest', *BSOAS*, 33, 1970, pp. 22–38, esp. pp. 26 ff, 31 ff.; cf. P. Kreyenbroek, 'Mithra and Ahreman, Binyāmin and Malak Tawūs: Traces of an Ancient Myth in the Cosmogonies of two Modern Sects', *Recurrent Patterns in Iranian Religions: From Mazdaism to Sufism*, ed. P. Cignoux (Paris, 1992), pp. 57–79, esp. p. 61.

121 For an exposition of this reconstruction of the pre-Zoroastrian cosmogonic scenario, see Kreyenbroek, 'Mithra and Ahreman, Binyāmin and Malak Tawūs'; 'Mithra and Ahriman in Iranian cosmogonies', in J. R. Hinnels (ed.), *Studies in Mithraism* (Rome, 1994), pp. 173–82; *idem, Yezidism – its Background, Observances and Textual Tradition* (Lewiston, 1995), pp. 57–61.

122 See Kreyenbroek, 'Mithra and Ahreman, Binyāmin and Malak Tawūs', pp. 62–5, 72–7; 'Mithra and Ahriman in Iranian cosmogonies', pp. 180–1; *Yezidism*, pp. 57–62. For the demiurge-trickster characteristics of Indra *vis-à-vis* Mithra, see, for example, U. Bianchi, 'Mithra and the Question of Iranian Monotheism', in Duchesne-Guillemin, *Études mithriaques*, pp. 24–38.

123 A. D. H. Bivar, 'Religious Subjects on Achaemenid Seals' in J. R. Hinnells (ed.), *Mithraic Studies*, vol. 1 (Manchester, 1975), pp. 95ff. Bivar contends that the Zoroastrian dualist antithesis between Ahura Mazda and Ahriman could 'to some extent reflect tensions which had arisen in neo-Babylonian religion and was not merely an abstract psychological antithesis but a concrete fact of religious history' (p. 96). In Accadian sources Nergal is identified with Moloch (Molech) and two relatively recent books have demonstrated that rather than being a technical name for human sacrifice by fire, 'Molech' was indeed the name of a Canaanite chthonic deity. See: G. Heider, *The Cult of Molek* (Sheffield, 1985); J. Day, *Molech: A God of Human Sacrifice in the Old Testament* (Cambridge, 1989).

124 Bivar suggests that a cult similar to those of the Semitic underworld deities Nergal and Moloch made headway in Iran during the era of Median supremacy prior to the rise of Cyrus the Great ('Religious Subjects on Achaemenid Seals', pp. 103ff.; 'Mithra and Mesopotamia' in Hinnells, *Mithraic Studies*, vol. 2, pp. 275–89). In 'Mithra and Mesopotamia' Bivar presents arguments for a blending of features of the cult of Nergal with pre-Zoroastrian Iranian religious traditions, such as Mithra-worship, in a syncretistic religion which in the early Achaemenid era was suppressed and forced westwards, eventually providing the basis of later Roman Mithraism (pp. 285–9). While much of Bivar's hypothesis remains conjectural, evidence exists of a local identification of Nergal and Mithra in Cilicia (Boyce, *A History of Zoroastrianism*, vol. 2, p. 273). See also Bivar, *The Personalities of Mithra*, pp. 31–67.

125 The theory that Zurvanism was a pre-Zoroastrian religion which evolved in western Iran and was re-interpreted in Zoroastrianism is advanced by Benveniste in Chap. 4, 'Theopompus and Plutarch', of *The Persian Religion*, pp. 69–117, and, similarly, Nyberg regarded Zurvan as an ancient western Iranian deity, indeed the god of the Median Magi, *Die Religionen des alten Iran*, pp. 105, 380ff. (cf. I. V. Rak, *Mify drevnego i rannesrednevekovogo Irana* (St Petersburg and Moscow, 1998), pp. 115 ff.). According to Widengren, during the Parthian era (250 BC to AD 226) in Iran Zurvanism was independent of Zoroastrianism (*Les Religions de Iran*, pp. 240f., 310f.), but the weight of evidence indicates that Zurvanism did emerge as a religious trend in Zoroastrianism and was affected by Babylonian astronomical and astrological speculations – see, for example, U. Bianchi, *Zaman i Ohrmazd:*

lo zoroastrismo nelle sue origini e nella sua essenza (Turin, 1958), pp. 130–89 and Boyce, *A History of Zoroastrianism*, vol. 2, pp. 232–43 (both putting its beginnings in the Achaemenid period); cf. the approach of R. Frye, 'Zurvanism Again', *Harvard Theological Review*, 1959, pp. 65 ff., who dates it to the Sassanian period. For the eclectic position of Zaehner, see *Zurvan*, pp. 5, 19–20, 80 ff., 239–42. Gnoli also argues that the dualist formula of Ohrmazd-versus-Ahriman was itself a feature of the Zurvanite system (*Zoroaster's Time and Homeland*, p. 212). Boyce offers arguments that Zurvanism was promoted by Persian Magi in Babylon, who in the latter half of the fifth century combined new interpretations of the Gathic teaching of the twin Spirits with elements of Babylonian astronomical–astrological lore and the new movement gained the support of Darius II (*A History of Zoroastrianism*, vol. 2, pp. 240ff.). The influence of Zurvanism seems to have been particularly strong and lasting in western Iran and Asia Minor (F. Cumont, *Textes et monuments figurés relatifs aux mystères de Mithra* (Brussels, 1896–9), pp. 9–10).

126 The principal Zurvanite myth is preserved in non-Zoroastrian works like the work of the Armenian Christian apologist Eznik of Kolb, *Wieder die Sekten*, tr. J. M. Schmidt (Vienna, 1900); and in *Zurvan* Zaehner reproduces the four parallel versions of the myth (pp. 419–29). The second part of Zaehner's book (pp. 257–453) reproduces fragments from the *Avesta*, from extra-Avestan Zoroastrian texts and from polemical (Christian, Manichaean and Islamic) works relevant to Zurvanism and Zurvanite myths.

127 This account of the alternative 'garments', 'implements' or 'weapons' of Ohrmazd and Ahriman follows Zaehner's reconstruction of the Zurvanite myth of their investiture, *Zurvan*, pp. 113–25, which is based on fragments from the *Greater Bundahishn*, *The Selections of Zadspram* and the *Denkart*. Zaehner's argument seems to demonstrate that the forms of Ohrmazd's creation from the substance of light, 'a form of fire – bright, white, round, and manifest afar', and the 'black and ashen' form of Ahriman's creation from the substance of darkness in the *Greater Bundahishn* (1 : 44–9) were seen in Zurvanism as 'gifts' of Zurvan to his two sons who invested them with their respective 'selfhood' or 'essence' (Zaehner, *Zurvan*, pp. 116ff., 124ff.). The Denkart fragment reproduced by Zaehner, *Zurvan*, pp. 374–8, elaborates the myth of the alternative weapons of Ohrmazd, the robe of priesthood, his brilliance and 'shining white garment' versus Ahriman's weapon, the robe of false priesthood, 'the ordering of evil in its pure estate', the ash-coloured garment associated with Saturn. The fragments from *The Selections of Zadspram* that allude to the 'implement' or 'form' delivered by Zurvan to Ahriman are reproduced in Zaehner, *Zurvan*, pp. 342ff. and 351, and while the first passage describes the implement as fashioned from the 'very substance of darkness mingled with the power of Zurvan', in the second

fragment the form brought by Zurvan to Ahriman is 'the black and ashen garment', the implement 'like unto fire, blazing, harassing all creatures, that hath the very substance of Az (greed or lust)'. The second fragment alludes also to the treaty by which Ahriman's creation is doomed to be devoured by Az if Ahriman fails to fulfil his threat to make all material creation hate Ohrmazd and love him, which is seen as 'the belief in the one principle' that identifies the increaser and destroyer.

128 The myth of the creation of the luminaries through heavenly incest after Ahriman's instruction is preserved in Eznik's *Wieder die Sekten* and a translation of the relevant fragment may be found in Zaehner, *Zurvan*, pp. 438ff. Eliade suggests that the myth was introduced to justify the renowned incestuous practices of the Magi, see *A History of Religious Ideas*, vol. 2, p. 525.

129 Zaehner, *Zurvan*, p. 78. This Zurvanite system, in which the creation of fire and water precedes the creation of Ohrmazd and Ahriman, is preserved in the tract, *Ulema i Islam* (Zaehner, *Zurvan*, pp. 409–16). The fatalist and materialist Zurvanite circles are discussed in Zaehner, *The Dawn and Twilight*, pp. 197ff., 205ff.

130 M. Eliade, *The Two and the One* (London, 1965), p. 83. Zurvanism is defined as a 'major heresy' by Zaehner, *Zurvan*, p. 5; Boyce sees it as a 'deep and grievous heresy', *Zoroastrians*, p. 69, heretical monistic development from the original Zoroastrian dualism under the late Achaemenids, *A History of Zoroastrianism*, vol. 2, p. 232; heterodox monism radically opposed to orthodox dualism, *A History of Zoroastrianism*, vol. 3, pp. 333, 367, 412; *Zoroastrianism*, p. 142 (in relation to Iranian divine trinities such as Ahura Mazada, Mithra, Anahita Boyce acknowledges a predilection for triads in Iranian religious history in 'Great Vayu and Greater Varuna', Bromberg (ed.), *Bulletin of the Asia Institute*, 7, p. 39). Zurvanism is similarly defined as a monistic heterodoxy in N. Cohn, *Cosmos, Chaos and the World to Come* (New Haven and London, 1993), p. 221. According to Shaked, Zurvanism was not considered heretical but was a 'fairly inoffensive variant of the Zoroastrian myth of creation', seen by its opponents as 'mildly deviant', S. Shaked, 'The Myth of Zurvan: Cosmogony and Eschatology', in I. Gruenwald, S. Shaked, G. A. G. Stroumsa (eds), *Messiah and Christos* (Tübingen, 1992), pp. 232–3; Shaked defines Zurvanism also as a 'triangular kind of dualism' ('Mihr the Judge', repr. in *From Zoroastrian Iran to Islam*, IV (Aldershot, 1995), p. 17) which was not a monotheistically inclined Zoroastrianism but a dualist Zoroastrianism with a different version of the creation story, *Dualism*, p. 18, in which the introduction of a third figure mitigated the starkness of the dualist system, p. 23.

131 The Bon triad, its Zurvanite colouring and the question of Iranian religious influences in Tibet are discussed, for example, in G. Tucci, *The Religions of Tibet*, tr. G. Samuel (London/Berkeley, 1980), pp. 214ff.; M. Eliade, *A*

History of Religious Ideas, tr. A. Hitelbeitel and D. Aspostolos-Cappadona (Chicago, 1985), vol. 3, pp. 267, 270 (see also the account of Bon cosmology in H. Hoffmann, 'The Ancient Tibetan Cosmology', *Tibetan Journal*, 2:3–4, 1977, pp. 13–17; on the figure of the divine saviour in Bon, see the text in H. Hoffmann, 'An Account of the Bon Religion in Gilgit', *CAJ*, 13, 1969, pp. 137–46). On the traditions linking Bon with Iran cf. T. Wylie, ''O-lde-spu-rgyal and the Introduction of Bon to Tibet', *CAJ*, 8, 1963, pp. 93–104, esp. pp. 101–2; D. Snellgrove and H. Richardson, *A Cultural History of Tibet* (London, 1968), p. 99, R. A. Stein, *Tibetan Civilization*, tr. J. E. S. Driver (London, 1972), pp. 49, 231–2, 236, 240–1; N. Norbu, 'Bon and Bonpos', *Tibetan Review*, 15:12, 1980, pp. 8–11, esp. p. 9; B. L. Bansal, *Bon, Its Encounter with Buddhism in Tibet* (Delhi, 1994), pp. 27, 34, 50–1; for further arguments for Iranian (most often seen as Zurvanite) influences on Tibetan Bon and popular religious traditions, see H. Hermanns, *Das National-Epos der Tibeter. Gling König Ge sar* (Regensburg, 1965), pp. 130–2; H. Hoffmann, *Tibet. A Handbook* (Bloomington, 1975), pp. 102–3, 106–7; A.-M. Blondeau, 'Les religions du Tibet', in H.-C. Puech, *Historie des religions III* (Paris, 1976), pp. 233–329, esp. pp. 313–14; S. G. Karmay, 'A General Introduction to the History and Doctrines of Bon', *Memories of the Research Department of the Toyo Bunko*, No. 33, 1975, pp. 171–218, esp. pp. 194–5; P. du Breuil, 'A Study of Some Zoroastrian and Buddhist Eschatological Features', *K. R. Cama Oriental Institute, International Congress Proceedings*, pp. 57 ff.; arguments that Tibetan Bon religion was influenced by Iranian Mithra-worship have been advanced, particularly by L. Gumilev and B. I. Kuznetsov – see, for example, L. Gumilev, 'Velichie i padenie drevnego Tibeta', *Strany i narody Vostoka*, 8, Moscow, 1969, p. 157; *Searches for an Imaginary Kingdom: The Legend of the Kingdom of Prester John* (Cambridge, 1987), pp. 274–6; B. Kuznetsov, 'Who Was the Founder of Bon Religion', *Tibetan Journal*, 1:1, 1975, pp. 113–15; 'The Highest Deities of the Tibetan Bon Religion', *Tibetan Journal*, 6:2, 1981, pp. 47–53 (with arguments that the highest deities of the Bon religion were associated with the Iranian triad of Ahura Mazda, Mithra and Anahita). For counter-arguments against the latter theory, see N. L. Zhukovskaia, *Lamaism i rannie formy religii* (Moscow, 1977), pp. 90 ff. See also P. Kvaerne, 'Dualism in Tibetan Cosmogonic Myths and the Question of Iranian Influence', in C. I. Beckwith, *Silver on Lapis, Tibetan Literary Culture and History* (Bloomington, 1987), pp. 163–75, who argues that a possible dualist substratum in Tibetan religion may have been reinforced by a contact with Iranian religions or that dualism in Tibetan cosmogony may have been a result of an internal development (while acknowledging the fact that 'Tibetan Bonpos, perhaps for a thousand years, have been unanimous in claiming, on the authority of their sacred texts, that Stagzig – i.e. Iran in one sense or another – is the holy land from which their religion spread', p. 173).

132 Such presentation by the priesthood of the king as a heretic has been defined
as 'a novelty in Mesopotamian religious politics', A. I. Oppenheim, 'The
Babylonian evidence of Achaemenian rule in Babylonia', in I. Gershevitch
(ed.), *Cambridge History of Iran* (Cambridge, 1985), vol. 2, p. 541. Apart from
the *Cyrus Cylinder* (published by H. C. Rawlinson in *The Cuneiform Inscriptions of Western Asia*, 101.5, plate 35, tr. in J. B. Pritchard, *Ancient Near Eastern
Texts Relating to the Old Testament*, 3rd edn with suppl. (Princeton, 1969), pp.
315–16) and the *Verse Account of Nabonidus* (published by S. Smith,
Babylonian Historical Texts Relating to the Capture and Downfall of Babylon
(London, 1924), pp. 27–97, tr. in Pritchard, *Ancient Near Eastern Texts*, pp.
312–15). Another cuneiform document that recounts the story of
Nabonidus' reign and Cyrus' conquest of Babylon in a less prejudiced
manner is the *Nabonidus Chronicle* (published in Smith, *Babylonian
Historical Texts*, pp. 110–18, tr. in Pritchard, *Ancient Near Eastern Texts*, pp.
305–7; A. K. Grayson, *Assyrian and Babylonian Chronicles* (Locust Valley,
New York, 1975), pp. 104–11). Cyrus' assumption of Babylonian kingship in
the context of Babylonian royal ideology and his ceremonial acts on
assuming the duties of the Babylonian kings are discussed in A. Kuhrt,
'Usurpation, Conquest and Ceremonial: From Babylon to Persia', in D.
Cannadine and S. Price (eds), *Rituals of Royalty* (Cambridge, 1987), pp.
48–67.

133 The problem of Nabonidus' religious reforms has been examined in detail in
P.-A. Beaulieu, *The Reign of Nabonidus, King of Babylon 556–539 BC* (New
Haven and London, 1989), where the exaltation of Sin in Nabonidus'
inscriptions is described on pp. 43–65 and the proclamation of Esagila and
Ezida as temples of Sin on pp. 61ff. In the last years of his reign, 'Nabonidus
was no longer hesitant to publicize his fanatical devotion to Sin and his
intention to relegate Marduk to nearly total oblivion' (Beaulieu, *The Reign
of Nabonidus*, p. 62). However, the promotion of serious religious reforms
under Nabonidus and his conflict with the Babylonian priesthood have
been questioned by A. Kuhrt, 'Nabonidus and the Babylonian Priesthood',
in A. Beard and J. North (eds), *Pagan Priests* (Ithaca, NY, 1990), pp. 117–55.

134 Although questioned by some scholars, the authenticity of Cyrus' edict has
been well established in E. J. Bickerman, 'The Edict of Cyrus in Ezra' in
Studies in Jewish and Christian History (3 vols, Leiden, 1976–86), vol. 1, pp.
72–108, where he demonstrates that Cyrus' proclamation was intended to
legitimize his succession to the Davidic throne (pp. 94ff.). In 'The Biblical
Portrayal of Achaemenid Rulers' (Kuhrt and Drijvers, *Achaemenid History*,
vol. 5, pp. 1–17), Ackroyd recognizes in Ezra's narrative of Cyrus' actions
both Persian and Jewish perspectives: from the first 'it can be seen to
constitute a claim for Cyrus to be the legitimate successor to the Davidic

line' and from the latter 'the claim that Cyrus is moved in this by the command of Yahweh, God of heaven' (p. 3). A. Netzer argues that Yahweh's recognition of Cyrus as 'his anointed' (Isaiah 45 : 1) gives Cyrus a 'true place in the line of David' and makes him a 'legitimate king of Israel', A. Netzer, 'Some Notes on the Characterization of Cyrus the Great in Jewish and Judeo-Persian Writings', *Commémoration Cyrus, Hommage Universel* II (Teheran and Liège, 1974), p. 41. Later Jewish traditions concerning Cyrus and the Throne of Solomon are assembled in L. Ginzburg, *The Legends of the Jews*, vol. 6 (Philadelphia, 1946), pp. 433ff, 453ff.

135 The contrasting historical fortunes of the Jews under Babylonian and Persian rule and the developments in exilic and post-exilic Judaism are charted in P. R. Ackroyd, *Israel under Babylon and Persia* (Oxford, 1970), while his *Exile and Restoration* (London, 1968) traces the principal themes in the prophecy of the exile and restoration. The phenomenon and the evolution of the prophetic tradition in Israel have been the subject of numerous studies. See, for example, J. Lindblom, *Prophecy in Ancient Israel* (Oxford, 1962), or the more recent R. Coggins, A. Phillips and M. Knibb (eds), *Israel's Prophetic Tradition: Essays in Honour of Peter R. Ackroyd* (Cambridge, 1982). The figures and reforms of Nehemiah and Ezra have been examined, sometimes with different conclusions, in W. Rudolph, *Esra und Nehemiah* (Tübingen, 1949); Ackroyd, *Israel under Babylon and Persia*, pp. 173–96; M. Smith, 'Palestinian Judaism in the Persian Period' in Bengston, *The Greeks and the Persians*, pp. 386–401. Among the studies of Jewish messianism see, for example, S. Mowinckel, *He That Cometh* (Oxford, 1959), pp. 155–87, for the belief in the Davidic messiah. Various theories have been put forward to explain the sudden disappearance of the Davidic scion Zerubbabel from the biblical narrative: according to Smith, 'Palestinian Judaism', p. 391, the messianic claims of Zerubbabel led to his assassination in a conspiracy organized by other members of the House of David.

136 Boyce provides an interesting historical parallel between the situation of the Jews in the Achaemenid empire and the Parsis in British India, which allowed their continuous exposure to and unconscious assimilation of Zoroastrian and Christian influences respectively, *A History of Zoroastrianism*, vol. 2, p. 195.

137 The continuous influence of Iranian law on Judaism in the Achaemenid era and later is discussed, for example, in R. N. Frye, 'Iran and Israel' in G. Wiessner (ed.), *Festschrift für Wilhelm Eilers* (Wiesbaden, 1967), pp. 74–85. Given the problems of identifying with precision the time and background of a number of Zoroastrian theological and apocalyptic notions, the problem of Iranian religious influences on post-exilic Judaism has provoked much controversy and literature, most of which is referred to in D. Winston, 'The Iranian Component in the Bible, Apocrypha and Qumran: A Review of the

Evidence', *HR*, 5 (1966), pp. 183–216; Duchesne-Guillemin, *Religion*, pp. 178–82; Cohn, *Cosmos, Chaos and the World to Come*, pp. 222–27, 263–5 (nn. 1–10). A more detailed treatment of postulated Zoroastrian influences on Jewish eschatological, angelological and demonological notions in Jewish writings, from the canonical Daniel to the Qumran scrolls, may be found in Boyce *A History of Zoroastrianism*, vol. 3, pp. 389–436. The chronological problem affecting the studies of the religious contacts between Iran and Israel has been dealt with, for example, by S. Shaked in 'Qumran and Iran: further considerations', *IOS*, 2 (1972), pp. 433–46.

138 J. B. Russell, *The Devil*, pp. 176ff. Russell does not exclude Iranian influence on the emergence of the concept of the Devil in Hebrew thought (p. 218) and defines finally the Hebrew theodicy as standing 'between the monism of the Hindus and the dualism of the Zoroastrians' (p. 220). Similarly, according to P. S. Alexander, 'Satan appears to be an objectification of the dark side of God' – 'Demonology in the Dead Sea Scrolls', in P. W. Flint and J. VanderKam (eds), *The Dead Sea Scrolls after Fifty Years: A Comprehensive Assessment* (Leiden, 1999), p. 342. According to A. Coudert, the development of an elaborate angelology and satanology in post-exilic Judaism was conditioned by the Babylonian exile and the impact of Zoroastrianism, after which the angelic entourage of the Old Testament God began to resemble that of Ahura Mazda, being envisaged as warrior angels fighting against the demonic hosts of evil, led by Satan, who 'gradually assumes the characteristics of the archfiend, Angra Mainyu', 'Angels', in Eliade, *Encyclopedia of Religion*, vol. 1, p. 283. The evolution of the concept of Satan in the Old Testament is the subject of R. S. Kluger's *Satan in the Old Testament*, tr. H. Nagel (Evanston, 1967), where the principal thesis is that the influence of Ahriman on the figure of Satan was exercised not on the Old Testament level but at the further, Judeo-Christian, stage of development (p. 157). Kluger also suggests that there might have been Persian influences in the later version of the Satan figure in Chronicles and that 'Ahriman in his polar opposition to Ahura Mazda may have been a prototype for the Old Testament Satan detaching himself from the personality of God' (p. 158). However, Persian influence on the figure of Satan is accepted as certain only after 'the detachment of Satan from God, who is then "cleansed" of his darkness' (p. 159), a differentiation process in which 'the decisive factor is the immanent development as a prerequisite for such influence' (p. 158). N. Forsyth, in his *The Old Enemy: Satan and the Combat Myth* (Princeton, 1987), advances the thesis that the newly independent figure of Satan in Chronicles, who 'substitutes for God as the *agent provocateur* in human affairs' (p. 121), came to be fused in Jewish apocalyptic literature with the figure of the adversary of the combat mythology of the ancient Near East, pp. 124ff. (On Satan in Chronicles, cf P. L. Day, *An Adversary in Heaven:*

sātān in the Hebrew Bible (Atlanta, 1988), Chap. 7, pp. 149–50.) More recently, Cohn in his *Cosmos, Chaos and the World to Come* offers further arguments that the Judeo-Christian Satan/Beliar/Devil owes much to Zoroastrian notions, most probably through the Zurvanite medium which 'could be more easily harmonized with Jewish belief', p. 221).

139 The Enochic apocalyptic cycle and its role in early Jewish apocalyptic thought have been widely debated and studied but many important problems concerning the origins of the Enochic traditions have not yet been resolved. Some new studies of the Enochic traditions have reinforced the traditional theory about the Mesopotamian background of the figure of Enoch. See. P. Grelot, 'La légende d'Hénoch dans les apocryphes et dans la Bible: son origine et signification', *Recherches de science religieuse*, 46 (1958), pp. 5–26, 181–210; J. C. VanderKam, *Enoch and the Growth of an Apocalyptic Tradition* (Washington, 1984) and H. Kvanvig, *Roots of Apocalyptic: the Mesopotamian Background of the Enoch Figure and the Son of Man* (Neukirchen-Vluyn, 1988). J. Charlesworth (ed.), *The Old Testament Pseudepigrapha* (vol. 1, New York and London, 1983), includes new translations of the oldest Enochic apocalyptic cycle of 1 (Ethiopic Apocalypse of) Enoch, 2 (Slavonic Apocalypse of) Enoch and 3 (Hebrew Apocalypse of) Enoch. 2 Enoch, a much debated and often enigmatic Enochic apocalypse, has been preserved only in the Slavonic Orthodox world and influenced important Bogomil teachings. The Books of Enoch and the development of Enochic traditions have been treated comprehensively, sometimes controversially, in J. T. Milik and M. Black, *The Books of Enoch* (Oxford, 1976). See also M. Knibb, *The Ethiopic Book of Enoch* (2 vols, Oxford, 1978); M. Black, *The Book of Enoch or 1 Enoch: A New English Edition with Commentary and Textual Notes* (Leiden, 1985); M. Stone, 'The Books of Enoch and Judaism in the Third Century B.C.E.', *CBQ* 40 (October 1978), pp. 479–92; Sacchi, 'Il "Libro di Vigilanti" e l'apocalittica', *Henoch* 1, 1979, pp. 42–92; J. VanderKam, *Enoch, a Man for All Generations* (Columbia, S.C., 1995). On the types of dualism in 1 Enoch, see, for example, G. W. E. Nickelsburg, 'The Apocalyptic Construction of Reality in 1 Enoch', in J. J. Collins and J. H. Charlesworth (eds), *Mysteries and Revelations. Apocalyptic Studies since the Uppsala Colloquium* (Sheffield, 1991), pp. 51–65. 1 Enoch and the Sibylline Oracles, The Martyrdom and Ascension of Isaiah and The Testaments of the Twelve Patriarchs are quoted from the translations in Charlesworth, *The Old Testament Pseudepigrapha*, vols 1 and 2. The account of the teachings of the 'two ways' and Belial in the Testaments of the Twelve Patriarchs on pp. 60–1 is based on the Testament of Asher 1:3–5; Testament of Judah 20:1–2; 25:3; Testament of Dan 5:6–11; 6:2; Testament of Gad 4:7; 5:1; Testament of Benjamin 7:1–2.

140 The theme of Satan poisoning the tree is developed in the Life of Adam and

NOTES

Eve 19, while the tree was planted by Satan in 3 Baruch, or the Greek Apocalypse of Batuch, which dates from the early Christian era and has been
preserved in Greek and Slavonic versions. The apocalyptic narrative of 3
Baruch, with its rich and complex imagery, came to influence some Bogomil
beliefs in the Middle Ages. See the new English translation and commentary
of the apocalypse, H. E. Gaylord Jr, '3 (Greek Apocalypse of) Baruch', in
Charlesworth, *The Old Testament Pseudepigrapha*, vol. 1, pp. 653–81; see also
the new study of D. C. Harlow, *The Greek Apocalypse of Baruch (3 Baruch) in
Hellenistic Judaism and Early Christianity* (Leiden, 1996). For discussions of
the dualism in the Book of Jubilees, see, for example, P. von der Osten-
Sacken, *Gott und Belial: Traditionsgeschichtliche Untersuchungen zum
Dualismus in den Texten aus Qumran* (Göttingen, 1969), pp. 197–200; M.
Testuz, *Les Idées religieuses du livre des Jubilés* (Paris, 1960), pp. 75–99 (cf.,
however, B. Z. Wacholder, *The Dawn of Qumran, The Sectarian Torah and
the Teacher of Righteousness* (Cincinnati, 1983), p. 82).

141 The Martyrdom and Ascension of Isaiah is a work with a complicated
structure and its last section (Chaps 6–11) came to be circulated as an
independent apocalyptic text, which, known as The Vision of Isaiah and
preserved in Latin and Slavonic translations, was to enjoy considerable
popularity among the Bogomils and the Cathars. See its new edition and
commentary in E. Norelli *et al.* (eds), *Ascensio Isaiae: Textus* (Turnhout,
1995); idem, *Ascensio Isaiae: Commentarius* (Turnhout, 1995).

142 See, for example, the later *Sibylline Oracles*, Book 3, verses 63–74 in J. J.
Collins. 'Sibylline Oracles', in Charlesworth, *The Old Testament Pseude-
pigrapha*, vol. 1, p 363. For a discussion on the traditions concerning the
'Persian Sibylline Oracles' and the Zoroastrian influences in the Jewish-
Christian Sibylline Oracles, see Boyce, *A History of Zoroastrianism*, vol. 3, pp.
371–87 and 389–401 respectively.

143 A discussion of and references to the publications of and concerning the
Dead Sea Scrolls and the unfolding debates focused on their manifold
relevance to the study of apocalyptic Judaism and early Christianity are
obviously beyond the scope of this book, so the following references are
confined to the different and sometimes conflicting approaches to the dualist
notions in the Scrolls, mostly the Community Rule and the War Rule,
discussed in the main text below: A. Dupont-Sommer, *Aperçus préliminaires
sur les manuscrits de la Mer Morte* (Paris, 1950), pp. 107, 113, 119; *Idem,
Nouveaux aperçus sur le manuscrits de la Mer Morte* (Paris, 1953), pp. 157–72;
K. G. Kuhn, 'Die Sektenschrift und die iranische Religion', *ZThK*, 49, 1952,
pp. 296–316; H. Wildenberger, 'Der Dualismus in den Qumranschriften',
Asiatische Studien, 8, 1954, pp. 163–77; M. Burrows, *The Dead Sea Scrolls*,
London, 1956, pp. 257–61; idem, *More Light on the Dead Sea Scrolls: New
Scrolls and New Interpretations with Translations of Important Recent*

Discoveries (New York, 1958), pp. 281, 290ff.; J. Duchesne-Guillemin, 'Le Zervanisme et les manuscrits de la Mer Morte', *IIJ*, 1, 1957; *Western Response*, pp. 91–4; H. W. Huppenbauer, *Der Menschen zwischen zwei Welten. Der Dualismus der Texte von Qumran (Höhle I) und der Damaskusfragmente. Ein Beitrag zur Vorgeschichte des Evangeliums* (Zurich, 1959); Zaehner, *The Dawn and Twilight*, p. 52; L. Mowry, *The Dead Sea Scrolls and the Early Church* (Chicago, 1962), pp. 28–30, 80, 146–8, 150–1, 171–2, 179; G. R. Driver, *The Judean Scrolls: The Problem and a Solution* (New York, 1965), pp. 550–62; P. von der Osten-Sacken, *Gott und Belial*; Shaked, 'Qumran and Iran: further considerations', pp. 433–46; P. R. Davies, 'Dualism and Eschatology in the Qumran War Scroll', *VT*, 28, 1978, pp. 28–36; 'Eschatology at Qumran', *JBL*, 104, 1985, pp. 39–55; J. J. Collins, 'The Mythology of Holy War in Daniel and the Qumran War Scroll: A Point of Transition in Jewish Apocalyptic', *VT*, 25, 1975, pp. 596–612; 'Was the Dead Sea Sect an Apocalyptic Movement?', in L. H. Schiffmann (ed.), *Archaeology and History in the Dead Sea Scrolls, The New York University Conference in Memory of Yigael Yadin* (Sheffield, 1990), pp. 16, 35ff, 42–6; 'The Origin of Evil in Apocalyptic Literature and the Dead Sea Scrolls', repr. in *Seers, Sybils and Sages in Hellenistic-Roman Judaism* (Leiden, 1997), pp. 287–301; *Apocalypticism in the Dead Sea Scrolls* (London and New York, 1997), pp. 41–52; *The Apocalyptic Imagination: An Introduction to Jewish Apocalyptic Literature*, 2nd edn (Cambridge, 1998), pp. 153–6; J. L. Duhaime, 'La Rédaction de 1QM XIII et l'évolution du dualisme à Qumrân', *RB*, 84, 1977, pp. 237–8; P. J. Kobelski, *Melchizedek and Melchireša* (Washington, 1981), pp. 84–98; B. Z. Wacholder, *The Dawn of Qumran*, pp. 81–3, 88–9, 97; Fontaine, *The Light and the Dark*, vol. 3, 1992, pp. 217–21, 222–3; J. C. VanderKam, *The Dead Dea Scrolls Today* (Michigan, 1994), pp. 110–11, 182–3; L. Schiffmann, *Reclaiming the Dead Sea Scrolls: The History of Judaism, the Background of Christianity, and the Lost Library of Qumran*, (Philadelphia, 1995), pp. 149ff; G. Widengren, A Hultgård and M. Philonenko, *Apocalyptique iranienne et Dualisme Qoumrânien* (Paris, 1995); J. Frey, 'Different Patterns of Dualistic Thought in the Qumran Library: Reflections on their Background and History', pp. 275–335. H. Shanks, *The Mystery and Meaning of the Dead Sea Scrolls* (London, 1998), pp. 75–6, 94–5. F. G. Martinez, 'Apocalypticism in the Dead Sea Scrolls', in J. J. Collins (ed.), *Encyclopedia of Apocalypticism*, vol. 1: *The Origins of Apocalypticism in Judaism and Christianity* (New York, 1999), pp. 166–72; the quotes in the text are taken from: G. Vermes, *The Dead Sea Scrolls in English*, rev. and ext. 4th edn (London, 1995), pp. 69–90, 123–46; T. Gaster, *The Scriptures of the Dead Sea Sect* (London, 1957), pp. 49–71; 261–85.

144 Shaked, 'Qumran and Iran', pp. 436–8; cf. also the comments in R. N. Frye, 'Qumran and Iran: The State of Studies' in J. Neusner (ed.), *Judaism, Christianiy and Other Graeco-Roman Cults: Studies Dedicated to Morton Smith*

(Leiden, 1975), vol. 3, pp. 167–73 and particularly pp. 172–3. According to Zaehner in *The Dawn and Twilight*, p. 52, God's attitude to the spirits of truth and falsehood in the Community Rule offers 'an exact parallel' to Ahura Mazda's attitude to the Holy and Destructive Spirits. Cf. the views of A. Dupont-Sommer, *Aperçus préliminaires sur les manuscrits de la Mer Morte*, pp. 107, 113, 119; *idem*, *Nouveaux aperçus sur le manuscrits de la Mer Morte*, pp. 157–72; K. G. Kuhn, 'Die Sektenschrift und die iranische Religion', pp. 296–316; F. M. Cross, *The Ancient Library of Qumran* (Sheffield, 1995), 3rd edn, pp. 151–6 (suggestions that the Qumran dualism and angelology developed 'partly under Iranian influence', pp. 154–5); Collins, 'The Origin of Evil in Apocalyptic Literature and the Dead Sea Scrolls', pp. 291–6 (arguments that the underlying myth of the Qumran teachings of the Two Spirits is the myth of Persian dualism, pp. 293 ff.); *idem*, *The Apocalyptic Imagination*, pp. 153 ff. (arguments that the 'distinctive teaching on two Spirits of Light and Darkness . . . is clearly derived from Zoroastrian dualism . . . inevitably modified in its Jewish context', p. 153); M. Philonenko, 'Mythe et histoire qoumrânienne des deux Esprits: ses origenes iraniennes et ses prolongements dans le judaisme essénien et le christianisme antique', in Widengren *et al.*, *Apocalyptique Iranienne et Dualisme Qoumrânien*, pp. 163–211; Martinez, 'Apocalypticism in the Dead Sea Scrolls', pp. 170ff. (with conclusions that the author of the Qumran Community Rule is 'deeply indebted to some form of Zoroastrian thought' p. 170).

145 Parallels between Zurvanite and Qumranite myths, including the focus on predestination, are discussed in Duchesne-Guillemin, *The Western Response to Zoroaster*, pp. 92–4; *idem*, 'Le Zervanisme et les manuscrits de la Mer Morte'. Arguments for Zurvanite influence on Qumran are presented in H. Michaud, 'Un mythe zervanite dans un des manuscrits de Qumran', *VT*, 5 (1955), pp. 137–47; D. Dimant, 'Qumran Sectarian Literature', in M. E. Stone (ed.), *Jewish Writings of the Second Temple Period* (Philadelphia, 1984), pp. 538, 546; Boyce, *A History of Zoroastrianism*, vol. 3, pp. 422–5 (arguments that the Qumran teaching of the Two Spirits is at least partially of Zurvanite inspiration).

2   The Time of Mixture

1 J. M. Balcer, 'Alexander's Burning of Persepolis', *Iranica Antiqua*, 13 (1978), p. 133. According to Balcer, 'Fundamental to Alexander's sovereignty of Asia, the key regal centres of Memphis, Thebes and Babylon bound him within the agelong mythological ceremonies of ancient Near Eastern cosmic kingship, to rule as the Achaemenid "Great King, King of Kings, King of Many

Countries" ' but the 'Achaemenid resistance to Alexander's invasion and usurpation of the kingship of Asia denied this assumption to rule' (p. 126). In this line of argument the burning of Persepolis led not only to the 'conclusive disruption of the Achaemenid cycle of cosmic kingship' (p. 131) but also prevented Alexander from 'obtaining the sovereignty of Asia' and opened the millennium of Persian 'resistance to Hellenism and the West' (p. 133). Literature and views on the figure and the conquests of Alexander are abundant, from W. W. Tarn's *Alexander the Great* (2 vols, Cambridge, 1948), where Alexander is credited with the ideal of the 'union of mankind', to more recent works like R. Lane Fox, *Alexander the Great* (London, 1973) and A. B. Bosworth, *Conquest and Empire* (Cambridge, 1988).

2 The Persian tradition of Alexander and his association with Ahriman appears in later Pahlavi texts like *Arda Viraf Namak* 1:3–11 or the *Bahman Yasht* 2:19, and is discussed from a Parsi perspective by Dhalla, in *History of Zoroastrianism*, p. 293; there are further comments in S. K. Eddy, *The King is Dead* (Lincoln, 1961), pp. 11–19; Boyce, *A History of Zoroastrianism*, vol. 3, pp. 384ff. Eddy's book reconstructs, sometimes controversially, the patterns of Near Eastern reaction to the penetration of Hellenism and touches upon the origins of the alternative Persian tradition, recorded in the *Shah Nameh* 18:3–4, which converts Alexander into a son of Darius III and a Macedonian princess (pp. 73ff.).

3 The Iranian apocalyptic tradition of Macedonian rule as the fourth and final age is discussed in Boyce, *A History of Zoroastrianism*, vol. 3, pp. 384–7; D. Flusser, 'The four empires in the Fourth Sibyl and in the Book of Daniel', *IOS*, 11 (1972), pp. 148–75. Pahlavi fragments alluding to Alexander's burning of the Avesta are assembled in Bailey, *Zoroastrian Problems*, pp. 151–7, while the story of Alexander's visit to and restoration of Cyrus' tomb is narrated in Arrian (6:28.4–8) and Strabo (730). Further controversies surround the antiquity of various strands of Iranian apocalypticism and their interrelations with Jewish and Christian apocalypticism; cf. the views and approaches in Boyce, *A History of Zoroastrianism*, vol. 3, pp. 361–491 *passim*; 'On the Antiquity of Zoroastrian apocalyptic', *BSOAS*, 47:1, 1984, pp. 57–75; D. Flusser, 'Hystaspes and John of Patmos', in S. Shaked (ed.), *Irano-Judaica* (Jerusalem, 1982), pp. 12–75; S. Shaked, 'The notions *mēnōg* and *gētīg*'; *idem*, 'Eschatology and Vision' in *Dualism*, pp. 27–52; A. Hultgård, 'Forms and Origins of Iranian Apocalypticism', in D. Hellholm (ed.), *Apocalypticism in the Mediterranean World and the Near East. International Colloquium on Apocalypticism. (Uppsala 1979. Proceedings)* (Tübingen, 1983), pp. 387–411; 'Bahman Yast: A Persian Apocalypse', in Collins and Charlesworth, *Mysteries and Revelations*, pp. 114–34; 'Persian Apocalypticism', in Collins (ed.), *Encyclopedia of Apocalypticism*, vol. 1, *The Origins of Apocalypticism in Judaism and Christianity*, pp. 39–84; P. Gignoux, 'L'apocalyptique iranienne est-elle

vraiment la source d'autres apocalypses?', *AASH*, 31, 1985/88, pp. 67–78; *idem*, 'Nouveaux regards sur l'apocalypse iranienne', *Comptes-rendus des Séances de l'Académie des Inscriptions et Belles-lettres*, Paris, 1986, pp. 334–46; for a balanced survey of the debates surrounding the antiquity of the earliest layers of the important Iranian apocalypse, *Zand Ī Wahman Yasn*, see C. Cereti, *The Zand Ī Wahman Yasn: A Zoroastrian Apocalypse* (Rome, 1995), pp. 11–27.

4 The Hellenistic age and civilization have been surveyed in works like W. W. Tarn, *Hellenistic Civilization*, 3rd edn (London, 1952); M. Hadas, *Hellenistic Culture: Fusion and Diffusion* (New York and London, 1959); C. Schneider, *Kulturgeschichte des Hellenismus* (2 vols, Munich, 1967–9); while F. E. Peters' *Harvest of Hellenism* (New York, 1967) charts the history of the Near East from the time of Alexander's conquests to the victory of Christianity over paganism in the fourth Christian century. The history of the Hellenistic kingdoms has received extensive treatment, including works on individual Hellenistic states, such as E. J. Bickerman, *Institutions des Seleucids* (Paris, 1938), but new studies continue to shed fresh light on various aspects of the Hellenistic civilization; see, for example, the contributions in A. Kuhrt and S. Sherwin-White (eds), *Hellenism in the East* (Berkeley, 1987), on subjects like the Seleucid rule in Babylonia or the interaction of Greek and non-Greek elements in the art and architecture of the Hellenistic east. An overview of the approaches and stereotypes in the study of the Greek mysteries and the 'mystery religions' and the attempts at dating the latter can be found in W. Burkert, *Ancient Mystery Cults* (Harvard, 1987), pp. 1–4, which offers a 'comparative phenomenology' of the mysteries of Eleusis, Dionysus, Meter, Isis and Mithras. Burkert's book (pp. 2ff.) and the earlier, classic work of R. Reitzenstein, *Hellenistic Mystery Religions*, tr. J. Steely (Pittsburgh, 1978), Chap. 2, 'Oriental and Hellenistic Cults', pp. 169–237, offer two different approaches to the Oriental influences in Hellenistic religions (cf. also J. Godwin, *Mystery Religions in the Ancient World* (London, 1981)). From the publication of F. Cumont's work, *The Oriental Religions in Roman Paganism* (Chicago and London, 1911) to the more recent studies of J. Ferguson, *Religions of the Roman Empire* (London, 1970); R. Macmullen, *Paganism in the Roman Empire* (New Haven/London, 1981); Turcan, *The Cults of the Roman Empire*, most of the cults have received extensive separate treatment in other works: see M. P. Nilsson, *The Dionysiac Mysteries of the Hellenistic and Roman Age* (Lund, 1957); M. J. Vermaseren, *Cybelea and Attis: The Myth and the Cult*, tr. A. M. H. Lemmers (London, 1977); R. Merkelbach, *Isisfeste in Griechisch-römischer Zeit* (Meisenheim-am-Glan, 1963); R. E. Witt, *Isis in the Greco-Roman World* (London, 1971); R. A. Wild, *Water in the Cultic Worship of Isis and Sarapis* (Leiden, 1981); J. Teixidor, *The Pagan God: Popular Religion in the Greco-Roman Near East* (Princeton, N.J., 1977), M. Speidel, *The*

THE OTHER GOD

Religion of Jupiter Dolichenus in the Roman Army (Leiden, 1978). See also the studies of various aspects of the cults in the Graeco-Roman world in A. D. Nock, *Essays on Religion and the Ancient World*, 2 vols (Oxford, 1972); A. Momigliano, *On Pagans, Jews and Christians* (Middletown, Conn., 1987). On the regional spread of oriental cults see, for example, the thorough survey of their diffusion in the Thracian lands in M. Tacheva-Hitova, *Oriental Cults in Moesia Inferior and Thracia* (Leiden, 1983).

5 These missions to the Hellenistic world were proclaimed in the Thirteenth Major Rock Edict of Ashoka; the five kings alluded to in the edict are identified as the Seleucid Antiochus II, Ptolemy II of Egypt, Antigonus Gonatas of Macedonia, Magas of Cyrene and Alexander of Epirus (G. P. Carratelli, *Gli editti di Aśoka* (Florence, 1960), pp. 40–2). The legends about Ashoka are discussed in E. J. Thomas, *The History of Buddhist Thought* (London, 1932), Chap. 3, and further in Chap. 12, with an assessment of Ashoka's Buddhism, pp. 153ff.

6 Early standard works on the Greeks, Scythians and the Sarmatians in the north Pontic area, such as E. H. Minns, *Scythians and Greeks* (Cambridge, 1913) and M. I. Rostovtzeff, *Iranians and Greeks in South Russia* (Oxford, 1922), have been followed by numerous new publications, particularly in Russian, on the history of the Graeco-Iranian coexistence and interchange in the area. The remarkable Scythian art is well represented in M. Artamonov, *The Treasures in the Scythian Tombs* (London, 1969), while many recent Russian works have illuminated further aspects of the history of the Scythians, Sarmatians and the Hellenistic Bosphorus kingdom: for a brief recent survey of Scythian and Sarmatian history, see A. I. Melyukova, 'The Scythians and the Sarmatians', in D. Sinor (ed.), *The Cambridge History of Early Inner Asia* (Cambridge, 1990), pp. 97–118 (with updated bibliography, including recent important Russian and East European publications, on pp. 435–41); see also the various contributions treating aspects of Scythian and Sarmatian history and culture in B. Genito (ed.), *The Archaeology of the Steppes: Methods and Strategies* (Naples, 1994), and J. Davis-Kimball *et al.* (eds), *Nomads of the Eurasian Steppes in the Early Iron Age* (Berkeley, 1995). Much obscurity surrounds Scythian and Sarmatian religious beliefs; Scythian religious traditions are discussed, for example, in V. I. Abayev, 'Kul't semi bogov u skifov', *Drevnii mir*, ed. N. V. Pugulevskaia *et al.* (Moscow, 1962), pp. 445–50; B. N. Grakov, *Skify* (Moscow, 1971), Chap. 6, pp. 80–8; D. S. Raevskii, *Model' mira skifskoi kul'tury: problemy mirovozzreniia iranoiazy-chnykh narodov evraziiskikh stepei I tysiacheletiia do n.e.* (Moscow, 1985); for the Scythian world-view *vis-à-vis* the Zoroastrian reform of Iranian religious traditions, see V. I. Abayev, 'Skifskii byt i reforma Zoroastra', *AO*, 24, 1956, pp. 23–56; for surveys of Sarmatian religious beliefs see, for example, K. F. Smirnov, *Savromaty* (Moscow, 1964) pp. 247–57 and T. Sulimirski, *The*

Sarmatians (London, 1970), pp. 34–8 (with suggestions for Zoroastrian influences on p. 255 and p. 35 respectively). For an up-to-date survey of the
religious syncretism (mostly Graeco-Iranian) in the Bosphorus kingdom, see
now Y. Ustinova, *The Supreme Gods of the Bosporan Kingdom: Celestial
Aphrodite and the Most High God* (Leiden, 1999).

7 A fresh overview on Hellenism in the Seleucid kingdom is offered in Kuhrt
and Sherwin-White, *Hellenism in the East*, while the conflict between the
Jewish Hellenizers and the Hassidim and Antiochus IV's measures against
Judaism have been treated extensively in early works such as V. Tcherikover,
Hellenistic Civilization and the Jews (Philadelphia, 1959), and E. J. Bickerman,
Der Gott der Makkabäer (Berlin, 1937). The history of the Graeco-Bactrian
kingdom is surveyed, sometimes with differing conclusions, in W. W. Tarn,
The Greeks in Bactria and India, 2nd edn (Cambridge, 1951), and A. K.
Narain, *The Indo-Greeks* (Oxford, 1957). Boyce's discussion of the religious
aspects of the Graeco-Iranian encounter in Central Asia at the time of the
Graeco-Bactrian kingdom (*A History of Zoroastrianism*, vol. 3, pp. 157–93)
summarizes the evidence of the crucial recent archaeological discoveries in
Bactria.

8 On the history of Parthia, the sixth 'Oriental Monarchy' in Rawlinson's *Seven
Great Oriental Monarchies of the Ancient World*, N. C. Debevoise's *A Political
History of Parthia* (Chicago, 1938) remains the standard work, while more
recent and updated surveys are offered in A. Bivar, 'The Political History of
Iran under the Arsacids' in E. Yarshater (ed.), *The Cambridge History of Iran*,
vol. 3 (1) (Cambridge, 1983), pp. 21–100 and R. N. Frye, *The History of Ancient
Iran* (Munich, 1984), pp. 205–49. Many problems and controversies plague the
study of the religious situation in the Parthian empire and the evolution of
Zoroastrianism in the Arsacid era: compare Boyce, *Zoroastrians*, pp. 80–100
and J. Duchesne-Guillemin, *La Religion de l'Iran ancien* (Paris, 1962), pp.
224ff. Among the studies of Graeco-Iranian syncretism in Commagene a
recapitulation can be found in J. Duchesne-Guillemin, 'Iran and Greece in
Commagene' in *Études mithriaques* (Leiden, 1978), pp. 187–201.

9 The connection between the Yueh-Chih movement into Bactria and the
Sarmatian migration to the Pontic area is made in J. Harmatta, *Studies in the
History and Language of the Sarmatians* (Szeged, 1970), pp. 31–4, 40; see also
A. M. Mandelshtam, *Pamiatniki kochevnikov kushanskogo vremeni v severnoi
Baktrii* (Leningrad, 1975), p. 148; A. S. Skripkin, 'The Sarmatian
Phenomenon', in Genito, *The Archaeology of the Steppe*, pp. 279–87. There
are many uncertainties about the identity and early history of the Yueh-Chih
and opinion has been divided over their original ethnic identity but now their
Indo-European extraction seems more or less established; see, for example, A.
K. Narain, 'Indo-Europeans in Inner Asia', in Sinor (ed.), *The Cambridge
History of Early Inner Asia*, pp. 151–77; A. N. Zelinsky and Y. G. Rychkov,

'On the Question of the Ethnic Anthropology of the Kushans', in B. Gafurov *et al.*, *Kushan Studies in the U.S.S.R.* (Calcutta, 1970), pp. 178–80. A reconstruction of the nomadic influx and conquest in Bactria may be found, for example, in Tarn, *Greeks in Bactria*, pp. 270–311; cf. A. M. Mandelshtam, 'Archaeological data on the origins and early history of the Kishans', in Gafurov, *Kushan Studies*, pp. 165–7; B. N. Mukherjee, 'Ta-Hsia and the Problems concerning the Advent of Nomadic Peoples in Greek Bactria', in A. Guha (ed.), *Central Asia: Movement of Peoples and Ideas from Times Prehistoric to Modern* (New York, 1970), pp. 121–30; B. Staviskii, *La Bactriane sous les Kushans*, tr. P. Bernard, M. Burda, F. Grenet, P. Leriche (Paris, 1986), pp. 21–8, 101–47; The translation of the name Yueh-Chih as 'Lunar Race' is suggested by J. M. Rosenfield, *The Dynastic Art of the Kushans* (Berkeley, 1967), pp. 7–8, with arguments for its connection with the mythology and the lunar emblems in the costumes of the Yueh-Chih, whose pre-Bactrian history is reviewed briefly on pp. 9ff. The reconstruction of the early history of the Yueh-Chih in Narain, 'Indo-Europeans in Inner Asia', associates the Yueh-Chih problem with that of the supposed Inner Asian homeland of the Indo-Europeans (pp. 152–4).

10 Frye, *History of Ancient Iran*, p. 257. With reference to the Kushan king Kanishka, see p. 58. On Kushan history an overview is provided in Staviskii, *La Bactriane sous les Kushans*, pp. 127–57.

11 An extensive survey of the complex Kushan pantheon, as recovered from Kushan coinage, can be found in Rosenfield, *The Dynastic Art of the Kushans*, pp. 60–104, which is a good guide to the uniquely syncretistic character of Kushan civilization, in both the fields of culture and religion. For a complex picture of the religious and cultic traditions in Kushan Bactria general orientation is provided in Staviskii, *La Bactriane sous les Kushans*, pp. 195–231. On the role of Mithra in the Kushan pantheon, see D. W. MacDowel, 'The Role of Mithra among the Deities of the Kushan Coinage', in J. Hinnells, *Mithraic Studies*, vol. 1, (Manchester, 1975), pp. 142–51; 'Mithra's Planetary Setting in the Coinage of the Great Kushans', in *Études mithriaques*, pp. 305–17; H. Humbach, 'Mithra in the Kusāna period', in Hinnells, *Mithraic Studies*, vol. 1, pp. 135–42. On the enduring tradition of Mithra as a divine protector of Kushan sovereigns, see V. G. Lukonin, *Drevnii i rannesrednovekovii Iran. Ocherki istorii kul'tury* (Moscow, 1987), p. 138. On the problem of whether the Iranian deities in the Kusha pantheon represent Zoroastrian, pre-Zoroastrian or local Iranian gods, see Rosenfield, *The Dynastic Art of the Kushans*, pp. 70ff; MacDowel, 'The Role of Mithra among the Deities of the Kushan Coinage', pp. 142 ff; Humbach, 'Mithra in the Kusāna period', pp. 136ff.; Staviskii, *La Bactriane sous les Kushans*, pp. 195ff; for Rosenfield's arguments that deities of the Kushan pantheon served as divine companions and supporters of the Kushan monarchy, see *The Dynastic Art of the Kushans*, pp. 69–70.

12 There are various valuable surveys of Mahayana Buddhism, for example, E.
Conze, *Buddhist Thought in India* (London, 1962), pp. 195–237; B. L. Suzuki,
Mahayana Buddhism, 4th edn (London, 1981). On the role of the Kushan
kingdom in the spread of Buddhism in Central Asia and China, see, for
example, B. Litvinskii, 'Outline History of Buddhism in Central Asia', in
Gafurov, *Kushan Studies*, pp. 53–135 *passim*; L. S. Vasil'ev, 'The Kushans and
the Penetration of Buddhism into China', in Gafurov, *Kushan Studies*, pp.
192–3; A. N. Zelinsky, 'The Kushans and Mahāyāna', in Gafurov, *Kushan
Studies*, pp. 156–8; T. V. Grek, and N. V. D'yakonova, 'The conception of
dharmakāya in the fine arts (contribution to the problem of the development
of the Mahayana dogmatics in the Kushan empire)', in Gafurov, *Kushan
Studies*, pp. 146–8; in Staviskii, *La Bactriane sous les Kushans*, pp. 201–15; and
M. Tardieu, 'La diffusion du boudhisme dans l'empir kouchan, l'Iran et la
Chine, d'après un *Kephalaion* manichéen inédit', *St. Ir.*, 17, 1988, pp. 153–82.
The teaching of the Bodhisattva has also received extensive treatment in
works like H. Dayal, *The Bodhisativa Doctrine in Buddhist Sanskrit Literature*
(London, 1932), with arguments for Zoroastrian influence on the Bodhisatma
doctrine and the cult of sun-worship in India, p. 39. Iranian influence on the
Bodhisattva teaching is also proposed, for example, in M. T. de Mallmann,
Introduction à étude d'Avalokiteçvara (Paris, 1948); du Breuil, 'A Study of Some
Zoroastrian and Buddhist Eschatological Features', p. 54. For the Iranian
influences on Buddhist iconography and notions, see, for example, J. Hackin,
Les Antiquités boudhiques de Bamiyan (Paris and Brussels, 1928); Duchesne-
Guillemin, *Religion*, pp. 168–9 (on the instances of artistic syncretism of
Buddha and Mazda, see, for example, B. Staviskii, 'Buddha-Mazda from
Kara-tepe', *JIABS*, 3/2, 1980, pp. 89–94.; M. M. Rhie, *Early Buddhist Art of
China and Central Asia*, vol. 1 (Leiden, 1999), p. 189). The influence of the
Zoroastrian teaching of the Saoshyant on the emergence of the Maitreya
belief in northern Buddhism is put forward, for example, in Boyce, *Zoroas-
trians*, p. 84; Gnoli, 'Saoshyant' in Eliade, *Encylopedia of Religion*, vol. 13, p.
68; Mithraic influence on the figure of the Maitreya is proposed, for example,
in A. M. Dani, 'Mithraism and Maitreya' in *Études mithriaques*, pp. 91–9; cf.
E. Lamotte, *Histoire du boudhisme indien des origines à 1ère Saka* (Louvain,
1958), pp. 782 ff.; J. Nattier, 'The Meaning of the Maitreya Myth, A
Typological Analysis', in A. Sponberg and H. Hardacre (eds), *Maitreya, the
Future Buddha* (Cambridge, 1988), pp. 23–51, esp. 34–6; Duchesne-
Guillemin, *Religion*, p. 169; Frye, *History of Ancient Iran*, p. 269. For
arguments for Iranian religious influences on the Tibetan Buddhist *Bardo
Thodol* (the Tibetan Book of the Dead), see du Breuil, 'A Study of Some
Zoroastrian and Buddhist Eschatological Features', pp. 58–61. There is
extensive literature on the syncretism of the Gandhara art school and
differing conclusions as to the source of the western influences in Gandhara

which are variously recognized as Roman or Graeco-Bactrian. For catalogues of the Gandhara art, see, for example, K. V. Trever, *Pamiatniki greko-baktriiskogo iskusstva* (Leningrad, 1940); I. Lyons, *Gandharan Art in Pakistan*, intr. and desciptive catalogue by H. Ingholt (New York, 1957); W. Zwalf, *A Catalogue of the Gandhara Sculpture in the British Museum*, 2 vols (London, 1996). For the unfolding of the debates concerning the evolution of the Gandhara school and its pioneering elaboration of the Buddha image, cf., for example, J. Marshall, *The Buddhist Art of Gandhara* (Cambridge, 1960); B. Staviskii, *Iskusstvo srednei Azii* (Moscow, 1974), pp. 72–112; G. A. Pugachenkova, *Iskusstvo Baktrii epokhi kushan* (Moscow, 1979); M. Bussagli, *L'arte del Gandhāra* (Turin, 1984); F. Tissot, *Gandhâra* (Paris, 1985); and the recent contributions in R. Allchin *et al.* (eds), *Gandhâran Art in Context: East-West Exchanges at the Crossroads of Asia* (New Delhi, 1997).

13 The offerings to Ahriman, as described by Plutarch, are seen by Boyce as a 'conscious inversion' of the 'sacred rituals of the *yasna*', *A History of Zoroastrianism*, vol. 3, p. 457. She also suggested that this 'dark rite' might have 'owed something to what appears to have been a recognized observance of the Old Iranian religion, namely the making of offerings to chthonic beings in shady places' (pp. 457–8). Plutarch's version has been read as an authentic form of Zurvanism by Benveniste, *The Persian Religion*, p. 113, where the position of Mithras as a mediator between the forces of good and evil is regarded as a Zurvanite idea (pp. 89ff.). F. Cumont, whose views on Mithraism have lately been subjected to strong criticism, argues that the 'ancient Magi' revered Mithra as a god of light, inhabiting the middle zone between heaven and hell, and serving as a mediator between the unapproachable God above and the human race below, a position that made him comparable to the Alexandrian logos and to Christ's status of an intermediary between the celestial father and men, Cumont, *The Mysteries of Mithra*, tr. T. McCormack (New York, 1956), pp. 127–9, 191–2. According to G. Widengren, in Mithra's myth and ritual system, some aspects of which were independent of Zoroastrianism, Mithra was 'something of a mediator between good and evil . . . in the midst of the good and evil, between these two opposite forces', which was reflected in Plutarch's testimony, G. Widengren, 'The Mithraic Mysteries in the Graeco-Roman world with special regard to their Iranian background', *La Persia e il mondo Greco-Romano* (Rome, 1966), pp. 433–4. Shaked shows that an Iranian term denoting judiciary functions was applied to Mithra and to his role as a judge in the cosmic struggle between Ohrmazd and Ahriman (and may indeed lie behind Plutarch's reference to Mithra), but this does not imply that in any versions of Zoroastrianism he was seen to be impartial or literally as occupying a middle ground between the two adversaries – he was a mediator in the 'technical sense of judge', 'Mihr the Judge', pp. 18–19; see also pp. 14–15 (cf. Boyce, *A History of Zoroastrianism*, vol. 3, pp. 478–9). On the other hand,

Zaehner sees in Plutarch's 'description a "half-way house" between catholic Zoroastrianism and Roman Mithraism', *The Dawn and Twilight*, pp. 123–5.

14 Cumont, *The Mysteries of Mithra*, p. vi.

15 E. Renan, *Marc-Aurèle et la fin du monde antique* (Paris, 1923), p. 579. It is worth noting that Julian's adherence to Mithraism has been questioned by R. Turcan in his *Mithras Platonicus* (Leiden, 1975), but his objections have been met by P. Athanassiadi, 'A Contribution to Mithraic Theology: The Emperor Julian's *Hymn to King Helios*', *JTS*, 28 (1977), pp. 360–71. On the problem of some parallels and posited interrelations between Mithraic and Christian doctrines and ritual practices, cf., for example, G. Widengren, *Iranisch-Semitische Kulturbegegnung in partischer Zeit* (Cologne-Opladen, 1960), Chap. 8; J. Duchesne-Guillemin, 'Die Magier in Bethlehem und Mithras als Erlöser?', *ZDMG*, 3, 1961, pp. 472–5; *idem*, *Religion*, pp. 180–1; M. Deman, 'Mithras and Christ: some iconographical similarities', in Hinnells (ed.), *Mithraic Studies*, pp. 507–18; M. Gerveres, 'The Iconography of the Cave in Christian and Mithraic Traditions', in U. Bianchi (ed.), *Mysteria Mithrae* (Leiden, 1979), pp. 579–601; G. Lease, 'Mithraism and Christianity', pp. 1307–31; L. Martin, 'Roman Mithraism and Christianity', *Numen*, 36, 1989, pp. 2–15.

16 It would be impossible to refer here to all theories that try to trace the beginnings of the Mithraic Mysteries (for a recent survey of Mithraic cult sites, see M. Clauss, *Cultores Mithrae: die Anhängerschaft des Mithras-Kultes* (Stuttgart, 1992). Yet mention should be made of some interesting recent theories such as the attempt to associate early Mithraism with the Bosphorus kingdom: see P. Beskow, 'The Routes of early Mithraism', *Études mithraiques*, pp. 7–19 (for arguments that the Most High God of the Bosphorus kingdom assimilated characteristics of Mithra, see Ustinova, *The Supreme Gods of the Bosporan Kingdom*, pp. 270–5, 287; whereas the arguments for a solar cult of Mithra in the Kushan empire and its potential affiliations with Roman Mithraism occur in MacDowall, 'Mithra's Planetary Setting in the Coinage of the Great Kushans', pp. 305–17; A. D. H. Bivar, 'Mithraic Images of Bactria: Are they related to Romian Mithraism?' in Bianchi, *Mysteria Mithrae*, pp. 741–61. For arguments that western Mithraism emerged in the Balkans, see G. Wikander, *Études sur les mystéres de Mithras* (Lund, 1950), pp. 41–6 (on the spread of Mithraism in south-eastern Europe, see, for example, V. Najdenova, 'Mithraism in Lower Moesia and Thrace', *ANRW*, W. Hasse *et al.* (eds), II, 18, 2, 1989, pp. 1397–419; L. Zotović, *Mitraizam na tlu Jugoslavije* (Belgrade, 1973); on the problem of the presence of Mithraic cultic traditions in Graeco-Roman Egypt, see, for example, Meyer, *The Mithras Liturgy*; Betz, *The Greek Magical Papyri*, pp. 48–65; W. Brashear, *A Mithraic Cathechism from Egypt* (Vienna, 1992). For arguments that the origins of the Mithraic Mysteries should be sought in pre- and non-Zoroastrian Mithraic tradition preserved in

THE OTHER GOD

western Iranian lands, see Kreyenbroek, 'Mithra and Ahreman, Binyāmin and Malak Tāwūs'; *idem*, 'Mithra and Ahriman in Iranian cosmogonies', *Yezidism*, pp. 57–61; Bivar, 'Mithra and Mesopotamia'; *idem*, 'Religious Subjects on Achaemenid Seals', *idem*, *The Personalities of Mithra*, pp. 22, 64, 68 (for arguments for a prominence of Mithra's cult in Media and attempts to link the Mithraic Mysteries with the legendary lore of Cyrus' life (defined as a 'Mithras-King'), see R. Merkelbach, *Mithras* (Königstein, 1984), pp. 31–4; similarly, R. Turcan, *The Cults of the Roman Empire*, tr. A. Nevill (Oxford, 1996), pp. 197–8. The traditional Anatolian theory is referred to below.

17 R. N. Frye, 'Mithra in Iranian history' in Hinnells, *Mithraic Studies*, vol. 1, p. 64. The claim for a 'proto-Mithraic cult' in the Persian army has been advanced on the basis of Aramaic inscriptions in Persepolis in R. A. Bowman, *Aramaic Ritual Texts from Persepolis* (Chicago, 1970). According to G. Widengren, 'The Mithraic Mysteries in the Graeco-Roman world with special regard to their Iranian background', *La Persia e il mondo Greco-Romano*, pp. 433–6, Mithra was indeed the high god of the 'warrior societies' who had their 'military forms of initiation' and these were the source of the initiatory rites in the Mithraic Mysteries of the Roman age. The theses of Bowman and Widengren have met much resistance, but in regard to a cult of Mithra among the Persepolis soldiers Frye remarks that 'there is no reason why such a kind of special organization or cult should not exist within the Mazdayasnian religion at Persepolis' (p. 64). In his *The Personalities of Mithra* Bivar goes further by suggesting that what he styles non-Zoroastrian or esoteric Mithraism (p. 12) lived on to exist as 'a secret cult' in Achaemenid military society and survived, 'tolerated . . . to a greater or lesser extent' into the Sassanid period (pp. 52–3); (for these Mithraic survivals in Sassanid times, see also his 'Towards an integrated picture of ancient Mithraism', pp. 69–73). See also the objections to the above arguments in Boyce, 'Priests, cattle and men', *BSOAS*, 50 : 2, 1987, pp. 508–26.

18 Bivar, 'Religious subjects on Achaemenid seals'; 'Mithra and Mesopotamia'. Some of Bivar's arguments have been subjected to criticism by H. J. W. Drijvers, 'Mithra at Hatra' in *Études mithriaques*, pp. 151–87.

19 This reconstruction of the symbolism of the *tauroctonia* follows the interpretation of J. Hinnells, 'Reflections on the bull-slaying scene', in *Mithraic Studies*, vol. 2, pp. 290–313; 'The Iranian Background of Mithraic Iconography', *Commemoration Cyrus, Hommage Universel*, 1 (Teheran/Liége, 1974), pp. 242–50, which rejects Cumont's thesis of the *tauroctonia* as a reflection of the Iranian theological dualism of good and evil in a specific Mithraic version in which Mithra sacrifices the primeval bull to create the world but creation and life are attacked, as in the *Greater Bundahishn*, by Ahriman and his demons (Cumont, *The Mysteries of Mithra*, pp. 136ff.; M. J. Vermaseren,

340

Mithras the Secret God, tr. T. and V. Megaw (London/Toronto, 1963), pp. 67–70). Drawing on the evidence of the autumn *Mihragān* festival, the culmination of which represents a sacrifice of a bull to Mithra, Hinnells argues that Mithra was indeed associated with the myth of bull sacrifice in Iranian thought and soteriology and this association, expressing old Iranian notions of sacrifice and salvation, lies behind the *tauroctonia* of Roman Mithraism. While admitting that Mithra's sacrifice may have been seen as the primeval sacrifice from which the creation of the world began, Hinnells rejects Cumont's presupposition that there existed a pre- or non-Zoroastrian myth in which Mithra instead of Ahriman slays the primeval bull, acting as a creator of the world, and points to the lack of conclusive evidence that Mithra was ever thought of as a demiurge. The debate concerning Mithra's role in pre-Zoroastrian beliefs and his posited demiurgic functions in relation to the bull-sacrifice has been re-opened by Kreyenbroek, 'Mithra and Ahreman, Binyāmin and Malak Tāwūs'; *idem*, 'Mithra and Ahriman in Iranian cosmogonies'. For another approach to the associations between Mithra, archaic Iranian ideas of bull sacrifice and the Mithraic *tauroctonia*, see Zaehner, *The Dawn and Twilight*, Chaps 4 and 5. See also I. Gershevitch, *The Avestan Hymn to Mithra* (Cambridge, 1959), who argues that Ahriman's murder of the bull was transferred to Mithra in a cult of 'Ahrimanian Mithraism', representing Iranian *daeva*-worshippers, who viewed Mithra as the chief god and Ahriman as a chief demon and after being supressed by Xerxes moved westwards to generate eventually the Mithraic Mysteries (pp. 61–6). According to Boyce, in its pre-Zoroastrian form, the myth of the slaying of the bull might have been referring to a sacrifice, its death being considered 'a creative and useful act' which led to the generation of 'all other good creatures and plants' and may have been the prototype of the yearly sacrifice offered to Mithra during the *Mihragān* feast of the autumn equinox (*A History of Zoroastrianism*, vol. 1, pp. 139, 172–3). For another approach to the *tauroctonia* that seeks to explain it as a ritual development of the traditions of the primal hunt, see Merkelbach, *Mithras*, p. 4; see also L. Martin's arguments that as a ritual sacrifice the *tauroctonia* serves as an 'apt formalization and focalization for Mithraic military culture', invoking the 'universal sphere of Roman political and military aspirations', 'Reflections on the Mithraic Tauroctony as Cult Scene', in Hinnells, *Studies in Mithraism*, p. 224.

20 On the complexity of the symbolism of Mithraic iconography, see, for example, the studies of R. Gordon, 'The sacred geography of a *mithraeum*; the example of Sette Sfere', *JMS* 1, no. 2, 1976, pp. 119–65; 'Ritual, evocation and boundary in the Mysteries of Mithra', *JMS* 3, nos 1–2, 1980, pp. 19–99; 'Authority, salvation and mystery in the Mysteries of Mithra', in J. Huskinson *et al.* (eds), *Image and Mystery in the Roman World. Three Papers Given in Memory of J. Toynbee* (Cambridge, 1988), pp. 45–80; 'Mystery, metaphor and

doctrine in the Mysteries of Mithra', in Hinnells, *Studies in Mithraism*, pp. 103–25; R. Beck, *Planetary Gods and Planetary Orders in the Mysteries of Mithra* (Leiden, 1988).

21 For a brief survey of earlier attemps to identify series of constellations in the bull-slaying scene, see M. P. Spiedel, *Mithras–Orion: Greek Hero and Roman Army God* (Leiden, 1980), pp. 6–7; this approach to the symbolism of the *tauroctonia* was reintroduced first in modern scholarship mostly in the studies of J. Beck, 'Cautes and Cautopates: Some Astronomical Considerations', *JMS* 2, 1977, pp. 1–17; S. Insler, 'A New Interpretation of the Bull-Slaying Motif', in M. D. de Boer and T. A. Edridge (eds), *Hommages á M. J. Vermaseren*, vol. 2 pp. 519–38, and followed by other studies.

22 Spiedel, *Mithras–Orion*, pp. 4–28.

23 Spiedel, *Mithras–Orion*, pp. 42–5.

24 D. Ulansey, *The Origins of the Mithraic Mysteries, Cosmology and Salvation in the Ancient World* (Oxford, 1989), Chap. 5.

25 Ulansey, *The Origins of the Mithraic Mysteries*, Chaps 6 and 7.

26 Ulansey, *The Origins of the Mithraic Mysteries*, Chap. 6. Ulancey seeks the origin of the Mithraic Mysteries predominantly in Hellenistic astral, philosophical and theological speculations. For arguments that the *tauroctonia* may have been based on an Iranian version of the Hellenistic star map, itself based on a Babylonian prototype, see A. D. H. Bivar, 'Towards an Integrated Picture of Ancient Mithraism', in Hinnells, *Studies in Mithraism*, pp. 61–74, esp. pp. 68 ff.

27 R. Beck, 'In the Place of the Lion: Mithras in the Tauroctony', in Hinnells, *Studies in Mithraism*, pp. 29–51.

28 Beck, 'In the Place of the Lion', pp. 46–50.

29 The reliability of Porphyry's text regarding the Mithraic Mysteries is questioned in Turcan, *Mithras Platonicus: Recherches sur l'Hellénization Philosophique du Mithra* (Leiden, 1975), but considered pivotal in the studies of R. Beck (see, for example, *Planetary Gods and Planetary Orders*) and R. Gordon (see, for example, 'The sacred geography of a *mithraeum*').

30 On the relationship between the Mithraic grades, their order and their respective planets, cf., Vermaseren, *Mithras the Secret God*, pp. 138–53; U. Bianchi, 'The religio-historical question of the mysteries of Mithra', in Bianchi, *Mysteria Mithrae*, pp. 31–47;; L. A. Campbell, *Mithraic Iconography and Ideology* (Leiden, 1968), pp. 304–15; A. Schütze, *Mithras – Mysterien und Urchristentum* (Stuttgart, 1972), pp. 103–34; Beck, *Planetary Gods and Planetary Orders*; M. Clauss, *Mithras: Kult und Mysterien* (Munich, 1990), pp. 138–48; I. P. Couliano; 'The Mithraic Ladder Revisited' in Hinnells, *Studies in Mithraism*; for arguments for certain correspondences between the emblems and attributes of the divinities represented on the Kushan coinage and grades of Roman Mithraism, see Macdowall, 'Mithra's Planetary Setting

in the Coinage of the Great Kushans', pp. 313–15; for a pioneering theory trying to identify an Iranian provenance for the Mithraic initiatory grades, see Bivar, *The Personalities of Mithra*, pp. 25–31.

31 J. P. Arendzen, 'Mithraism' in *The Catholic Encyclopedia*, vol. 10 (New York, 1911), p. 403.

32 U. Bianchi, 'The religio-historical question of the mysteries of Mithra', in Bianchi, *Mysteria Mithrae*, p. 27, though he argues that the 'dynamic and heroic Mithra of the Roman mysteries is not without connexion with the Iranian Mithra' (p. 27). In *Mithras Platonicus*, Turcan argues that by the second century Greek philosophical circles were well acquainted with Mithraic teachings and began the process of accommodating Mithras into the Platonic system (cf. Merkelbach, *Mithras*, Chap. 9, and Couliano, 'The Mithraic Ladder Revisited', in Hinnells, *Studies in Mithraism*, pp. 75–92; for the opposite view, stating that Plato was influenced by ancient, pre-Roman Mithraist teachings, see Bivar, *The Personalities of Mithra*, pp. 40–1). The traditional theory that Mithraism was essentially a Roman version of Zoroastrianism (through the medium of Anatolian Zurvanite traditions) and its dualist myth of creation, can be found in Cumont, *The Mysteries of Mithra*. Cumont's reconstructions of Mithraic doctrines as reflecting Zoroastrian dualism were followed by a number of scholars (see, for example, A. D. Nock, 'The Genius of Roman Mithraism', *JRS*, 27, 1937, pp. 108–13; F. Legge, *Forerunners and Rivals of Christianity* (New York, 1965); Campbell, *Mithraic Iconography and Ideology*, but subjected to a systematic and well-founded criticism by Wikander, *Études sur les mystéres de Mithras*, pp. 19–32 and R. L. Gordon, 'Franz Cumont and the doctrines of Mithraism', in Hinnells, *Mithraic Studies*, vol. 1, pp. 215–49. See also the criticism of Cumont's views in Hinnells, 'Reflections on the bull-slaying scene and 'The Iranian Background of Mithraic Iconography'; while accepting that in the late Achaemenid period Zurvanism became well established in Asia Minor, Boyce regards its contribution to western Mithraism as doubtful, 'Some further reflections on Zurvanism', E. Skaervø *et al.* (eds), *Papers in Honour of E. Yarshater, Acta Ir.*, 29, 1990, pp. 20–9; Boyce, *A History of Zoroastrianism*, pp. 470, 474.

33 J. F. Hansman, 'Some Possible Classical Connections in Mithraic Speculation', in Bianchi, *Mysteria Mithrae*, p. 610.

34 Bivar, 'Mithra and Mesopotamia', p. 280; U. Bianchi, 'Mithraism and Gnosticism' in Hinnells, *Mithraic Studies*, vol. 2, p. 458.

35 The identification of the lion-man with Aion–Zurvan is suggested, for example, in Cumont, *The Mysteries of Mithra*, pp. 107ff., where he is regarded as being 'at the pinnacle of the divine hierarchy and at the origin of things', and 'Lord and master of the four elements that compose the universe', who 'creates and destroys everything' (p. 109). His identification with Ahriman has

been accepted by Zaehner, *The Dawn and Twilight*, p. 129; Duchesne-Guillemin, *Ormazd et Ahriman*, pp. 126ff. (where he is held to represent both Aion and Ahriman); Duchesne-Guillemin, *The Western Response to Zoroaster*, p. 95 (where the lion-headed figure, 'this cruel, ugly deity, clearly appears with his serpent, his signs of the Zodiac, his four wings, as the master of the world'). The association with the lion-headed portrayals of Nergal is in Bivar, 'Religious subjects on Achaemenid seals'; 'Mithra and Mesopotamia'; this Mesopotamian, 'Nergalian' background of the Mithraic lion-headed statues is supported by H. von Gall, 'The Lion-Headed and the Human-Headed God in the Mithraic Mysteries', *Études mithriaques*, p. 515.

36 A J. Hansman, 'A Suggested Interpretation of the Mithraic Lion-Man Figure', *Études mithriaques*, pp. 215–27, 'Some Possible Classical Connections in Mithraic Speculations', pp. 608ff. 'Bivar, who presents arguments that the Mithraic lion-headed god predates the Roman form of Mithraism and can be traced to Achaemenid times, suggests that Plato's description indicates his knowledge of esoteric Mithraism and the incoherence of the passage may be attributed to Plato's reluctance to reveal a cult secret, *Personalities of Mithra*, pp. 11–12. Jaeger sees Plato's 'bad world-soul that opposes the good one in the Laws' as a 'tribute to Zoroaster' (*Aristotle*, p. 132).

37 Hansman, 'A Suggested Interpretation', p. 226.

38 The relevant fragments from the *Denkart*, 182. 6ff.; 211.1; 355.6, after D. Madan (ed.), *Dinkard* (Bombay, 1911) and the *Greater Bundahishn* concerning the religion of the sorcerers and the rite of the 'mystery of the sorcerers' are translated and discussed in Zaehner, *Zurvan*, pp. 14ff. Duchesne-Guillemin supports the identification of the 'Ahrimanic' sorcerers with the 'Magians' described by Plutarch ('Notes on Zervanism in the light of Zaehner's *Zurvan*, with additional references', *JNES*, 15:2 (1956), p. 110).

39 Zaehner, *The Dawn and Twilight*, pp. 128ff.; *Zurvan*, pp. 19ff. Similarly, Duchesne-Guillemin (n. 35, above) sees 'the master of this world' in the lion-headed figure.

40 Bianchi, 'The religio-historical question of the mysteries of Mithra', pp. 24ff.; and 'Mithraism and Gnosticism'; R. L. Gordon, 'Franz Cumont and the doctrines of Mithraism' in Hinnells, *Mithraic Studies*, vol. 1, p. 222. For arguments that the Mithraists professed a 'cultic' and 'social' dualism, that has to be distinguished from theological dualism proper, see S. Laeuchli, 'Mithraic Dualism', in Laeuchli (ed.), *Mithraism in Ostia: Mystery Religion and Christianity in the Ancient Port of Rome* (Evanston, Ill., 1967), pp. 47–67, esp. pp. 64–6. Yet for G. Widengren, the very presence of Ahriman among Mithraic deities is a 'sufficient indication' of its dualistic character, 'Babakiyah and the Mithraic Mysteries', in *Mysteria Mithrae*, p. 692. While arguing that the lion-headed god represents 'the divine fire from which the world emerged and to which it must one day return, like the souls whose spark, at the end of

NOTES

the sidereal cycle, would rejoin their original element', Turcan, *The Cults of the Roman Empire* (p. 232), also admits that his identification with Ahriman raises the question of dualism (p. 232).

41 Bianchi, 'The religio-historical question of the mysteries of Mithra', p. 39.

42 H. M. Jackson, 'The Meaning and Function of the Leontocephaline in Roman Mithraism, *Numen*, 32 (1985), pp. 19, 33, with a detailed overview of the evidence and theories concerning the nature of the lion-headed god in the Mithraic Mysteries. Ulansey also sees the lion-headed god as embodying a cosmic power or the cosmos itself but he links him with the Gorgon killed by Perseus – drawing a parallel between Perseus' overpowering of the Gorgon and Mithras' subjugation of the associated cosmic force, Ulansey, *The Origins of the Mithraic Mysteries*, pp. 116–24. An astrological reading is provided by R. Beck according to whom the lion-headed and snake-encircled Mithraic deity was modelled on the description of the being (with the form of a lion's mask and snake body) associated with the first decan of the sign of Leo and the related 'person' of Saturn, *Planetary Gods and Planetary Orders*, pp. 99–100.

43 The notions of *yester ha-tov* and *yester ha-ra* are discussed in E. Urbach, *The Sages: Their Concepts and Beliefs* (Jerusalem, 1975), vol. 1, pp. 471–83. The 'heretical' tradition of the 'Two Heavenly Powers', as attested in the rabbinic records, has received extensive treatment in A. Segal, *Two Powers in Heaven* (Leiden, 1977), while according to I. P. Coulianu, 'The Angels of the Nations and the Origins of Gnostic Dualism' in R. Van den Broek and M. J. Vermaseren (eds), *Studies in Gnosticism and Hellenistic Religions* (Leiden, 1981), pp. 78–92, its transformations in the first century AD could have influenced Gnostic dualism. Later Jewish lore about Satan and the powers of evil is surveyed in J. Trachtenberg, *The Devil and the Jews* (New Haven, 1943); *Jewish Magic and Superstition* (New York, 1939); L. Jung, *Fallen Angels in Jewish, Christian and Mohammedan Literature* (Philadelphia, 1926).

44 In 3 Enoch Samael appeared as Prince of the Satans (14:2) and Prince of Rome (26:12), while in the quoted rabbinics, Samael was styled the 'great prince in heaven' in Pirke de-Rabbi Eliezer 13, 'Samael the Wicked' prince of the evil angels in Deuteronomy Rabbah II, and was portrayed as standing alongside Michael before the *Shekhinah* during the Jewish Exodus in Exodus Rabbah 18:5. Samael's war against Michael, his defeat, fettering and surrender to Israel were recounted in Bereshit Rabbah, whereas he appeared as the angel of death, for example, in Abodah Zarah 20b, and in Jewish astrological literature was associated with Mars. Michael was given the title Prince of the World in Pirke de-Rabbi Eliezer 27 and his association with the 'foundation' of Rome is brought forward in Shir ha-Shirim Rabbah (1:6,4). A convergence between the figures of Satan, the 'Prince of the World' (as chief of the national angels) and Samael (as an angel of death and Rome) is posited in Coulianu, 'The Angels', pp. 84ff., which might have changed the Prince of

the World into Creator of the World and further an evil Creator of the World in a dualist system (Coulianu, 'The Angels', p. 91).

45 Quoted after J. B. Russell, *The Prince of Darkness* (London, 1989), p. 70. In an earlier book, *The Devil*, Russell provided an instructive summary of the features of the Devil in the New Testament, while in *Satan: The Early Christian Tradition* (New York, 1981), he surveyed in detail the perception of the Devil and evil in early Christian thought. Among other studies of the role of the Devil and the powers of evil in the New Testament and the early Christian tradition, are: A. Frank-Duquesne, 'Réflexions sur Satan en marge de la tradition Judéo-Chrétienne', in B. de Jésus-Marie (ed.), *Satan* (Paris, 1948), pp. 179–315 *passim*; F. X. Gokey, *The Terminology for the Devil and Evil Spirits in the Apostolic Fathers* (Washington, DC, 1961); T. Ling, *The Significance of Satan* (London, 1961); N. Forsyth, *The Old Enemy: Satan and the Combat Myth* (Princeton, 1987), pp. 248–307; J. Hick, *Evil and the God of Love* (New York, 1966); J. W. Boyd, *Satan and Māra: Christian and Buddhist Symbols of Evil* (Leiden, 1975), Pt 1; H. Haug, *Teufelsglaube* (Tübingen, 1980), 2nd edn, 'Satan und das Böse im Neuen Testament', pp. 271–389; S. R. Garrett, *The Demise of the Devil: Magic and the Demonic in Luke's Writings* (Minneapolis, 1989, Chap. 2, pp. 101–6); E. Pagels, *The Origins of Satan* (New York, 1995) (an exploration of the legacy of Jewish apocalyptic satanology and vison of the cosmic struggle, involving the split of society into two opposing forces, in the early Christian tradition, focusing mainly on the social implications of the figure of Satan); T. H. van der Hoeven, *Het imago van Satan* (Leiden, 1998); 'Het imago van Satan in de het Nieuwe Testament', pp. 165–213; see also pp. 213–27.

46 J. B. Russell, *The Devil*, p. 256. According to Russell, early Christianity developed an inner tension between monism and dualism which led to 'inconsistencies in Christian theodicy' but also to theological creativity, p. 228; similarly, according to A. Sharma, 'Satan', in Eliade, *Encyclopedia of Religion*, vol. 13, p. 82, while stopping short of professing that the Devil is utterly evil in essence, early Christianity developed a 'tension between explicit monotheism and implicit dualism', characteristic also of Judaism.

47 It is impossible to survey here the development of the study of Gnostic origins, revolutionized with the discovery of the Nag Hammadi Library of Gnostic Coptic codices in 1945, and the existing theories about the phenomenon of Gnosticism. The contributions to the Messina Colloquium on the origins of Gnosticism – U. Bianchi (ed.), *Le origini dello Gnosticismo: Colloqio di Messina 13–18 Aprile 1966* (Leiden, 1967) highlighted the multifarious approaches to the problem (for a definition of Gnosticism, see pp. xxvi–xxix; for recent attempts to redefine Gnosticism, see B. A. Pearson, 'Introduction' in B. A. Pearson, *Gnosticism, Judaism, and Egyptian Christianity* (Minneapolis, 1990), pp. 7–8; M. A. Williams, *Rethinking Gnosticism:*

An Argument for Dismantling a Dubious Category, (Princeton, 1996); A. H. B. Logan, *Gnostic Truth and Christian Heresy: A Study in the History of Gnosticism* (Edinburgh, 1996), pp. xxix–xxx). While for the early Church the Gnostic sects largely represented forms of Christian heresy that had to be combated, in modern Gnostic studies opinions about the nature of Gnosticism have varied widely – from those defining it as a Hellenization of Christianity (Harnack – who still treated it mostly within a church-historical context), to those regarding it as a pre-Christian phenomenon rooted in Iranian mysticism and redemption myths (Bousset, Reitzenstein, Widengren, etc.; for a strong criticism of the Iranian myth of a 'redeemed redeemer', proposed by Reitzenstein, and its influence on Gnosticism, see C. Colpe, *Die religionsgeschichtliche Schule: Darstellung und Kritik ihres Bildes vom gnostischen Erlösermythus* (Göttingen, 1961), but see more recently H.-M. Schenke, 'Marginal Notes on Manichaeism from an Outsider', in P. Mirecki and J. BeDuhn (eds), *Emerging from Darkness: Studies in the Recovery of Manichaean Sources* (Leiden 1997), p. 290, anticipating that further research of the Nag Hammadi texts may lead to a 'revival of the classical hypothesis concerning the redeemed redeemer'). Other theories have proposed an explanation of Gnosticism as an outcome of a crisis in Jewish apocalyptic thought following the destruction of the Second Temple in AD 70 (Grant), and the presence of Jewish and Jewish–Christian apocalyptic traditions in Gnostic systems has been acknowledged in recent studies whether by focusing on the posited Jewish provenance of important Gnostic notions or Jewish origins of trends in Gnosticism (Quispel, Schenke, Pearson, Turner, Stroumsa, etc.); Samaritan influence has also been postulated (Fossum, Beltz, etc.) and the presence of Orphic and Platonic influences in Gnosticism has also been variously emphasized. A differentiation between non-(or pre-) Christian, Christianized and purely Christian Gnostic works in the Nag Hammadi Library has been proposed (Krause, Rudolph, Robinson, etc.) but has provoked continuous debates and has been challenged by proponents of the view that Gnosticism represents essentially an inner Christian development or that the principal Gnostic myths can be understood best in terms of Christian doctrines, as argued with differing degrees of emphasis by S. Pétrement, *A Separate God, The Christian Origins of Gnosticism,* tr. L. Harrison London, 1990 and Logan, *Gnostic Truth.* Yet, while the origins of Gnosticism remain controversial, with the publication and the studies of the texts of the Nag Hammadi Library it is becoming increasingly apparent that at least mature Gnosticism, in the words of J. M. Robinson, 'seems not to have been in its essence just an alternate form of Christianity' but 'a new syncretistic religion', 'drawing upon various religious heritages', *The Nag Hammadi Library in English,* 4th rev. edn (Leiden, 1996), p. 10. The Nag Hammadi texts referred to below are quoted from the translations in *The Nag Hammadi Library.*

48 An overview of the figure of Christ in Gnostic systems and Gnostic Christologies can be found in K. Rudolph, *Gnosis*, ed. and tr. R. McL. Wilson
(Edinburgh, 1983), pp. 148–71; also in G. Filoramo, *A History of Gnosticism*,
tr. A. Alcock (Oxford, 1990), pp. 116–27; see also Pétrement, *A Separate God*,
pp. 140–57; P. Perkins, 'Gnostic Christologies and the New Testament', *CBQ*,
43, 1981, pp. 590–606; *Gnosticism and the New Testament* (Minneapolis,
1993), Pt 3; Gnostic Docetism is discussed, for example, by U. Bianchi,
'Docetism: A Peculiar Theory about the Ambivalence of the Presence of the
Divine' in his *Selected Essays on Gnosticism, Dualism and Mysteriosophy*
(Leiden, 1978), pp. 303–11; Pétrement, *A Separate God*, pp. 144–57; for
discussions of the highly controversial problems related to the links between
Gnosticism, on one side, and early Christianity and the New Testament, on
the other, see, for example, R. M. Grant, *Gnosticism and the Early Christianity*
(New York, 1966), 2nd edn.; R. McL. Wilson, *Gnosis and the New Testament*
(Oxford, 1968); K.-W. Tröger (ed.), *Gnosis und Neues Testament, Studien aus
Religionswissenschaft und Theologie* (Berlin, 1973); W. Schmithals, *Neues
Testament und Gnosis* (Darmstadt, 1984); Pétrement, *A Separate God*; Perkins,
Gnosticism and the New Testament; Logan, *Gnostic Truth*; and the contribu-
tions in A. H. B. Logan and A. J. M. Wedderburn (eds), *The New Testament
and Gnosis, Essays in Honour of R. McL. Wilson* (Edinburgh, 1983); C. W.
Hedrick and R. Hodgson (eds), *Nag Hammadi, Gnosticism and Early Chris-
tianity* (Peabody, Mass., 1986); for a recent overview and critical analysis of
the arguments for pre-Christian Gnosticism based on Nag Hammadi texts,
see E. Yamauchi, 'The Issue of Pre-Christian Gnosticism Reviewed in the
Light of Nag Hammadi texts', in J. D. Turner and A. McGuire (eds), *The Nag
Hammadi Library after Fifty Years, Proceedings of the 1995 Society of Biblical
Literature Commemoration* (Leiden, 1997), pp. 72–89.

49 The tradition of Eve's seduction by Samael, who comes to her, 'riding on the
serpent', to beget Cain is recorded in Pirke de-Rabbi Eliezer 22. The tradition
that Eve had conceived the angel from Samael and declared that with the
birth of Cain she had acquired the angel of the Lord as a man occurs in
Targum-Pseudo-Jonathan 5: 1–3, where Cain is described 'as those on high,
not like those below' (quoted after J. Bowker, *The Targums and Rabbinic
Literature* (Cambridge, 1969), p. 132). For Gnostic elaborations of the theme
of Eve's seduction or attempted seduction by the demiurge, his oppressive
archons or the chief archon in the Nag Hammadi tracts, see *The Apocryphon
of John* 24:8–28; *The Apocalypse of Adam* 66 : 25–66 : 10; *The Hypostasis of the
Archons* 89 : 17–28; *On the Origin of the World* 116:5–117 : 20. For further
evidence concerning Gnostic and Gnostic-related teachings about Eve's
seduction by the demiurge or his archons (or authorities), which maintained
their currency among the schismatic Audians in the Holy Land (on the
Audians, see now G. A. G. Stroumsa, 'Jewish and Gnostic Traditions among

the Audians', in G. G. Stroumsa and A. Kofsky, *Sharing the Sacred: Religious Contacts and Conflicts in the Holy Land, First–Fifteenth Centuries CE* (Jerusalem, 1998) pp. 97–109; see H.-C. Puech, 'Fragments retrouvés de l'Apocalypse d'Allogéne', repr. in Puech, *En quête de la Gnose*, vol. 1, pp. 271–300. For a comparative survey of the theme of Eve's seduction in Gnostic (original and reported) and Jewish traditions, see G. A. G. Stroumsa, *Another Seed: Studies in Gnostic Mythology* (Leiden, 1984), pp. 35–53.

50 The duality between Cain, as father of the generations of the wicked, and Seth, as father of the generations of the just, is emphasized in Pirke de-Rabbi Eliezer 22, while the notion of the kingdom of the House of David as planted by Seth is discussed in Stroumsa, *Another Seed*, p. 74. On Gnostic attitudes to and creative exegesis of the biblical text as well as use of Jewish apocryphal traditions, see also, for example, G. W. MacRae, *Some Elements of Jewish Apocalyptic and Mystical Tradition and their Relation to Gnostic Literature*, 2 vols (Ph.D. dissertation, Cambridge University, 1966); R. McL. Wilson, 'Old Testament Exegesis in the Gnostic Exegesis on the Soul', in M. Krause (ed.), *Essays on the Nag Hammadi Texts: In Honour of Pahor Labib* (Leiden, 1975), pp. 217–25; K.-W. Tröger (ed.), *Altes Testament-Frühjudentum-Gnosis, Neues Studien zu Gnosis und Bible* (Berlin, 1980); E. Pagels, 'Exegesis and Exposition of the Genesis Creation Accounts in Selected Texts from Nag Hammadi', in Hedrick and Hodgson, *Nag Hammadi, Gnosticism and Early Christianity*, pp. 257–87; B. E. Pearson, 'Jewish Sources in Gnostic Literature', in M. E. Stone (ed.), *Jewish Writings of the Second Temple Period* (Philadelphia, 1984), pp. 443–81; I. S. Gilhus, *The Nature of the Archons: A Study in the Soteriology of a Gnostic Treatise from Nag Hammadi CGII, (4)* (Wiesbaden, 1985), pp. 12–37; G. P. Luttikhuizen, 'The Thought Pattern of Gnostic Mythologizers and Their Use of Biblical Tradition', in Turner and McGuire, *The Nag Hammadi Library*, pp. 89–105.

51 For arguments for an association between the biblical and Egyptian Seth and a Gnostic rehabilitation of the Egyptian god, see, for example, H. Bonnet, *Reallexicon der ägyptischen Religionsgeschichte* (Berlin, 1952), p. 715; J. Doresse, *The Secret Books of the Egyptian Gnostics*, tr. P. Mairet (London, 1960), pp. 104–5 (n. 93); C. J. Bleeker, 'The Egyptian Background of Gnosticism', in Bianchi, *Le origini dello gnosticismo*, p. 236; the theory of the assimilation of the Egyptian to the biblical Seth is shown to lack conclusive evidence by B. A. Pearson, 'The Figure of Seth in Gnostic Literature', in Pearson, *Gnosticism, Judaism, and Egyptian Christianity*, pp. 80–3 (with a discussion of other possible influences of the Egyptian cult of Seth in the Nag Hammadi *Gospel of the Egyptians* and indirect Egyptian influence of the Thoth lore on Gnostic Seth traditions) and J. Fossum and B. Glazer, 'Seth in the Magical Texts', *ZPE*, 100, 1994, pp. 87ff. The notion of the Gnostic spiritual race as the 'children' or 'seed' of Seth appeared in Nag Hammadi tracts like *The*

Apocryphon of John. The Three Steles of Seth and *The Gospel of the Egyptians*, being identified along with *The Thought of Norea, Marsanes, Allogenes, The Apocalypse of Adam, Zostrianos, The Trimorphic Protennoia, The Hypostasis of the Archons* and *Melchizedek* as belonging to the so-called 'Sethian Gnosticism' (the texts have been divided into three groups: non-Christian, secondarily Christianized and Christian tracts). The nature of 'Sethian' Gnosticism has been explored in the contributions in B. Layton (ed.), *The Rediscovery of Gnosticism: Proceedings of the International Conference on Gnosticism at Yale, New Haven, Connecticut, March 28–31, 1978*), vol. 2, *Sethian Gnosticism* (Leiden, 1981), esp. H.-M. Schenke, 'The Phenomenon and Significance of Gnostic Sethianism'; J. M. Robinson, 'Sethians and Johannine Thought'; Stroumsa, *Another Seed, passim*; J. D. Turner, 'Sethian Gnosticism: A Literary History', in Hedrick and Hodgson *Nag Hammadi, Gnosticism, and Early Christianity*, pp. 55–86; H.-M. Schenke, 'Gnosis: Zum Forschungen unter besonderer Berücksichtigung der religions-geschichtlichen Problematik', *Verkündigung und Forschung*, 32, 1987, pp. 2–22; Perkins, *Gnosticism and the New Testament*; J.-M. Severin, *Le dossier baptismal séthien: Etudes sur la sacramentaire gnostique* (Québec, 1986) (exploration of the baptismal aspects of Sethian Gnosticism). For a criticism of the arguments for the existence of non- (or pre-) Sethian Gnosticism, see, for example, Pétrement, *A Separate God*, pp. 420–82, *passim*; Logan, *Gnostic Truth, passim*; Yamauchi, 'The Issue of Pre-Christian Gnosticism'. In Epiphanius' account of the Sethian Gnostic system Jesus Christ was identified with Seth, while the Nag Hammadi treatise *Melchizedek* implied that Melchizedek might have been regarded as Seth's incarnation. The equation between Seth and Zoroaster is discussed in W. Bousset, *Hauptprobleme der Gnosis* (Göttingen, 1907), pp. 379–82; also by B. A. Pearson, 'The Figure of Seth in Gnostic Literature' in Layton, *The Rediscovery of Gnosticism*, vol. 2, pp. 494, 498. For arguments for Zoroastrian influences in the Nag Hammadi *The Apocalypse of Adam*, see A. Böhlig, 'Die Adamsapocalypse aus Codex V von Nag Hammadi als Zeugnis jüdisch-iranischer Gnosis', *OC*, 48, 1964, pp. 47–8; A. Welburn, 'Iranian Prophetology and the Birth of the Messiah: the Apocalypse of Adam', *ANRW*, II.25.4, 1988, pp. 4572–94.

52 The main Christian sources for the Gnostic theology of Valentinus were the polemical writings of Irenaeus, Hippolytus and Epiphanius, Tertullian's *Against Valentinus* and others. Some of the Nag Hammadi texts like *The Gospel of Philip* betray Valentinian influences, while *The Gospel of Truth* is sometimes attributed to Valentinus himself. Valentinian Gnosticism has received extensive treatment in A. Orbe, *Estudios valentinianos*, 4 vols(Rome, 1955–61); more recently in the contributions in Layton, *The Rediscovery of Gnosticism*, vol. 1, *The School of Valentinus*; C. Markschies, 'Valentinian Gnosticism: Toward the Anatomy of a School', in Turner and McGuire, *The*

Nag Hammadi Library after Fifty Years, pp. 401–39; *Valentinus Gnosticus?: Untersuchungen zur valentinianischen Gnosis; mit einem Kommentar zu den Fragmenten Valentins* (Tübingen, 1992). The teachings of the Alexandrian theologian Basilides are known from the differing versions of Irenaeus, Hippolytus and Clement of Alexandria (for a recent survey of the evidence of Basilides teachings, see W. A. Löhr, *Basilides und seine Schule* (Tübingen, 1996)). Marcion's writings have been lost but accounts of his teachings are presented in the works of anti-heretical polemicists like Irenaeus and Tertullian. The view that Marcion was largely a rationalist and reformist biblical exegete was advanced in A. Harnack's classic treatment of Marcion's doctrines *Marcion: Das Evangelium vom fremden Gott*, 2nd edn (Leipzig, 1924) (with arguments that Marcion was in some respects a forerunner of Protestant reformist theology). Harnack's position is shared, among others, by R. J. Hoffmann, *Marcion: On the Restitution of Christianity* (Chico, Calif., 1984); the viewpoint that Marcion's dualism is of Gnostic character has been defended, for example, in E. G. Blackmann, *Marcion and his Influence* (London, 1948); U. Bianchi, 'Marcion: théologien biblique ou docteur gnostique', repr. in Bianchi, *Selected Essays*, pp. 320–8; B. Aland, 'Marcion. Versuch einer neuen Interpretation', *ZThK*, 70, 1973, pp. 420–47. For a discussion of the parallels and differences between Marcion's and Gnostic dualism, see also Coulianu, *The Tree of Gnosis*, pp. 145–56.

53 The association between the portrayal of the Demiurge as an arrogant archon and Isaiah's parable against the king of Babylon has been demonstrated in N. A. Dahl, 'The Arrogant Archon and the Lewd Sophia' in Layton, *The Rediscovery of Gnosticism*, vol. 2, pp. 689–713, with further arguments for Sophia herself being cast in the role of the 'virgin daughter of Babylon'. On the figure of the Gnostic Sophia, see, for example, G. W. MacRae, 'The Jewish Background of the Gnostic Sophia Myth', *NT*, 12, 1970, pp. 86–101; G. S. Gasparro, 'Il personaggio di Sophia nel Vangelo secondo Filipo', in Gasparro, *Gnostica et hermetica* (Rome, 1982), pp. 73–121; Gilhus, *The Nature of the Archons*, pp. 95–104; D. J. Good, *Reconstructing the Tradition of Sophia in Gnostic Literature* (Atlanta, 1987); K. Rudolph, 'Sophia und Gnosis. Bemerkungen zum Problem "Gnosis und Frühjudentum" ', in *Gnosis und spätantike religionsgeschichte* (Leiden, 1996), pp. 170–90; Coulianu, *The Tree of Gnosis*, Chap. 3; S. La Porta, 'Sophia-Mĕtĕr: Reconstructing a Gnostic Myth', in Turner and McGuire, *The Nag Hammadi Library after Fifty Years*, pp. 188–208. On the figure of the demiurge in Gnostic traditions, see, for example, G. Quispel, 'The Demiurge in the "Apocryphon of John" ' in R. McL. Wilson (ed.), *Nag Hammadi and Gnosis* (Leiden, 1978), pp. 1–34; B. Barc, 'Samaél-Saklas-Yaldabaôth. Recherche sur la genèse d'un mythe gnostique', in Barc (ed.), *Colloque international sur les textes de Nag Hammadi (Québec, 22–25 août)* (Québec, 1981), pp. 123–51; Filoramo, *A History of*

Gnosticism, Chap. 5; Coulianu, *The Tree of Gnosis*, Chap. 4; M. A. Williams, 'The Demonizing of the Demiurge. The Innovation of Gnostic Myth', in M. A. Williams *et al.* (eds), *Innovation in Religious Traditions* (Berlin, 1992), pp. 73–107.

54 Jackson, 'The Meaning and Function of the Leontocephaline in Roman. Mithraism', p. 32. G. Quispel argues for the influence of the Orphic teriomorphic Demiurge Phanes, sometimes described as a roaring lion, on both the Mithraic lion-man and on Yaldabaoth, 'The Demiurge in the "Apocryphon of John" ' in Wilson, *Nag Hammadi and Gnosis*, pp. 1–34. According to Jackson, however, it is impossible to establish any genealogy between the three figures, which are seen as the result of 'independent development of late Roman representatives of celestial eternity on solar and/or Saturnine exemplars' (p. 32).

55 A. J. Welburn, 'Reconstructing the Ophite Diagram', *NT* 23 : 3 (1981), p. 271.

56 See, for example, W. Liebeschuetz, 'The expansion of Mithraism among the religious cults of the second century', in Hinnells, *Studies in Mithraism*, p. 196.

57 For a survey of the parallels between Gnosticism and Hermeticism, see R. van den Broek, 'Gnosticism and Hermeticism: Two Roads to Salvation', in van den Broek, *Studies in Alexandrian Christianity and Gnosticism* (Leiden, 1996), pp. 3–22; see also J.-P. Mahé, 'Gnostic and Hermetic ethics', in R. van den Broek and W. Hanegraaff, *Gnosis and Hermeticism from Antiquity to Modern Times* (Albany, NY, 1997), pp. 21–37; G. G. Stroumsa, 'Gnostic Elements in Hermetic Traditions', in Stroumsa, *Another Seed*, pp. 137–45; G. S. Gasparro, 'La gnosi ermetica come iniziazione e mistero', in Gasparro, *Gnostica et hermetica*, pp. 309–31.

58 On the Gnostic adoption and development of early Christian and Jewish esoteric traditions, see now G. G. Stroumsa, *Hidden Wisdom: Esoteric Traditions and the Roots of Christian Mysticism* (Leiden, 1996), esp. Chap. 3, 'Gnostic Secret Myths'.

59 See, for example, B. McGinn, *The Foundation of Mysticism* (New York, 1991), pp. 98–9; Stroumsa, *Hidden Wisdom*, Chaps 8 and 9.

60 Quoted from the *Denkart* fragment in Zaehner, *The Dawn and Twilight*, p. 301. The link between Zoroastrianism and the Sassanid empire is discussed on pp. 284ff., while a survey of the religious situation in the Sassanid period in Iran is advanced in Zaehner, *Zurvan*, pp. 35–53; cf. Boyce's arguments that the Sassanid dynasty was of Zurvanite orientation, *Zoroastrians*, pp. 118ff. The concepts of royalty and religious policy in the Sassanid empire have been surveyed in G. Gnoli, 'Politica religiosa e concezione della regalità sotto i Sassanidi', in *La Persia nel Medioevo*, pp. 225–51.

61 J. R. Russell, *Zoroastrianism in Armenia* (Harvard Iranian Series v, Cambridge, Mass., 1987), p. 126, with an account of the Christian–Zoroastrian encounter in Armenia and a scrutiny of Zoroastrian traditions in

Armenia and their survival, pp. 113–53. 'Iranian' Armenia has been the subject of two pioneering studies by N. G. Garsoïan, reprinted in her *Armenia between Byzantium and the Sasanians*. (London, 1985): 'Prolegomena to a Study of the Iranian Elements in Arsacid Armenia' and 'Then Locus of the Death of Kings: Iranian Armenia – the Inverted Image'.

62 Quoted after Shaked's translation, *The Wisdom of the Sasanian Sages (Denkard VI)*, p. 79. The notion of threefold religious hierarchy in Sassanid Zoroastrianism is scrutinized by Shaked in his 'Esoteric Trends in Zoroastrianism' where he demonstrates its association with a 'hierarchy of religious truths' and the division between popular and higher Zoroastrianism, some aspects of the latter being considered restricted religious mysteries; see also Shaked, *Dualism in Transformation*, pp. 60–6.

63 This threefold division is reported by Eznik of Kolb in his work *Against the Sects*, in Schmidt's translation, *Wieder die Sekten*, p. 87. The interpretation of the adherents of the three principles as Zurvanites follows Zaehner's reading of Eznik's report in *Zurvan*, pp. 28–9.

64 These two forms of Zoroastrianism are attested by later Islamic writers like al-Baghdadi and al-Shahrastani and their evidence is discussed in Zaehner, *The Dawn and Twilight*, pp. 180–1.

65 Madan, *Dinkard*, p. 154, quoted after Zaehner's translation of the names of the sects in *Zurvan*, p. 13.

66 Quoted from the recent translation of Kartir's inscription by D. N. Mackenzie in *Iranische Denkmäler, Reihe* 2, *Lief* 13 (Berlin, 1989), p. 58.

67 al-Biruni, *Chronology of the Ancient Nations*, tr. E. Sachau (London, 1879), p. 190; on Mani's life and career, see, for example, H.-Ch. Puech, *Le Manichèisme. Son fondateur, sa doctrine* (Paris, 1949), Chap. 1; G. Widengren, *Mani and Manichaeism*, tr. C. Kessler (London, 1965), Chaps 1 and 2; O. Klima, *Manis Zeit und Leben* (Prague, 1962); L. J. R. Ort, *Mani: A Religio-Historical Description of a Personality* (Leiden, 1967); F. Decret, *Mani et la tradition manichéenne* (Paris, 1974), pp. 44–74; M. Tardieu, *Le Manichéisme* (Paris, 1981); Gnoli, *De Zoroastre à Mani*, Chap. 4; S. N. C. Lieu, *Manchaeism in the Later Roman Empire and Medieval China*, 2nd rev. edn (Tübingen, 1992), Chap. 2.

68 The Babylonian sectarians, joined by Mani's father, are called *Mughtasilah* by al-Nadim, in *The Fihristi of al-Nadim*, tr. B. Dodge (2 vols, New York, 1970), p. 774; and *katharioi* in the Manichaean work *Kephalaia*, ed. and tr. H. J. Polotsky and A. Böhlig (vol. 1, Stuttgart, 1940), 1.27, p. 44 (see new edition by I. Gardner, *The Kephalaia of the Teacher, The Edited Coptic Manichaean Texts in Translation with Commentaries* (Leiden, 1995). They have been identified with the Elchasaites on the basis of the recently deciphered *Cologne Mani Codex* (see n. 70 below). On some parallels between the organization of Mani's Elchasaite community and that of the Qumran sect, see J. C. Reeves,

'The "Elchasaite" Sanhedrin of the Cologne Mani Codex in Light of Second Temple Jewish Sectarian Sources', *JJS*, XLII/1, 1991, pp. 68–91. Hippolytus' *Refutation of All Heresies* along with Epiphanius' *Panarion* are the principal sources for Elchasai and the Elchasaites. The relevant passages are quoted from the translations provided in A. F. Klijn and G. J. Reinink, *Patristic Evidence for Jewish-Christian Sects* (Leiden, 1973), pp. 54–67. On the Elchasaites, see, for example, L. Cirillo, *Elchasai e gli Elchasaiti, Un contributo alla storia della communitá giudeo-cristiane* (Cosenza, 1984); on the 'Revelation of Elchasai', see G. P. Luttikhuizen, *The Revelation of Elchasai, Investigation into the Evidence of a Mesopotamian Jewish Apocalypse of the Second Century and its Reception by a Judaeo-Christian Propagandist* (Tübingen, 1985); 'The Book of Elchasai: A Jewish Apocalypse', *Aul.O*, 5, 1, 1987, pp. 101–6; J. M. Baumgarten, 'The Book of Elkezai and Merkabah Mysticism', *JSJ*, 17, 2, 1986, pp. 212–23.

69 These Zurvanite-Elchasaite parallels are emphasized in Bousset, *Hauptprobleme der Gnosis*, pp. 153, 156; and critically discussed in Zaehner, *Zurvan*, pp. 72ff.

70 Mani's Elchasaite background and his conflict with the Elchasaites came to light with the recent decipherment and publication by A. Henrichs and L. Koenen of the important Greek document, the *Cologne Mani Codex (CMC)*, now available in L. Koenen and C. Römer (eds), *Der Kölner Mani-Codex* (Opladen, 1988), which is used for the references below. The document relates the account of Mani's childhood, his revelations and the crystallization of his sense of mission, the customs and the purification rituals of the Elchasaites, Mani's collision with Elchasaite traditionalists and his breaking with the sect. His arguments against the Elchasaite ablutions and purifications are contained in *CMC* 80 : 18–83, 19, pp. 55–7. The account of Mani's conflict with the Elchasaites follows the evidence of the *CMC* 80 : 22ff. On this conflict see further A. Henrichs, 'Mani and the Babylonian Baptists: A Historical Confrontation', *Harvard Studies in Classical Philology*, 77, 1973, pp. 23–59; L. Cirillo, 'Elchasaiti e Battisti di Mani: i limiti di un confronto delle fonti', in L. Cirillo and A. Roselli (eds), *Codex Manichaicus Coloniensis, Atti del Simposio Internazionale (Rende-Amantea 3–7 settembre 1984)* (Cosenza, 1986), pp. 97–141; J. Ries, 'La doctrine de l'âme du monde et des trois sceaux dans la controverse de Mani avec les Elachasaïtes', in Cirillo and Roselli, *Codex Manichaicus Coloniensis*, pp. 169–83.

71 *CMC* 18:8–19 : 1. On Mani's celestial Twin and revelations see Henrichs, 'Mani and the Babylonian Baptists', pp. 33–5; W. Sunderman, 'Mani's Revelations in the Cologne Mani Codex and in Other Sources', in Cirillo and Roselli, *Codex Manichaicus Coloniensis*, pp. 205–15; J. C. VanderKam and W. Adler (eds), *The Jewish Apocalyptic Heritage in Early Christianity* (Assen, 1996), pp. 11ff., 17–21.

72 Quoted after *CMC* 26:7–15; 43:3–7 and *Kephalaia*, vol. I, ed. and tr. Polotsky and Böhlig, 15:3ff. The esotericism in Elchasaite and Manichaean thought has been well demonstrated by G. Stroumsa in his 'Esotericism in Mani's Thought and Background' in Cirillo and Roselli, *Codex Manichaicus Coloniensis*, pp. 153–69.

73 *CMC* 102:5ff.; 108:17ff. The diverse sources for Manichaean apocalypticism and its syncretic character are surveyed by L. Koenen in his 'Manichaean Apocalypticism at the Crossroads of Iranian, Egyptian, Jewish and Christian Thought' in Cirillo and Roselli, *Codex Manichaicus Coloniensis*, pp. 285–333. See also Puech, *Le manichéisme*, pp. 84ff; Widengren, *Mani*, pp. 64–70; F. Decret, 'Le "globus horribilis" dans l'eschatologie manichéenne, d'apres les traités de saint Augustine', repr. in *Essais sur l'Église maichéenne en Afrique du Nord et à Rome au temps de saint Augustin, Recueil d'études* (Rome, 1995), pp. 7–15; G. G. Stroumsa, 'Aspects de l'eschatologie manichéenne', *RHR* 197, 1981, pp. 63–81; N. E. Pedersen, *Studies in the Sermon on the Great War* (Aarhus, 1993), Chap. 3; E. Smagina, 'Manichäische Eschatologie', *Gnosis-forschung und Religionsgeschichte, Festschrift für K. Rudolph zum 65. Geburtstag*, eds H. Preissler und H. Seiwert (Marburg, 1994), pp. 297–307; M. Heuser, 'The Manichaean Myth According to the Coptic Sources', in M. Heuser and H.-J. Klimkeit, *Studies in Manichaean Literature and Art* (Leiden, 1998), pp. 18–25, 49–82; Mani's views of individual salvation included the doctrine of reincarnation – on its sources in Manichaean teachings, see, for example, W. Sunderman, 'Mani, India, and the Manichaean Religion', *SAS*, 2, 1986, pp. 11–19; G. Cassadio, 'The Manichaean Metempsychosis: Typology and Historical Roots', in G. Wiessner and H.-J. Klimkeit (eds), *Studia Manichaica. II. Internationaler Kongress zum Manichäismus* (Wiesbaden, 1992), pp. 131–51.

74 This apocalyptic scheme is recounted in the 'Great War Sermon' in H. J. Polotsky (ed.), *Manichäische Homilien* (Stuttgart, 1934), 7:8–42:7.

75 C. R. C. Alberry (ed.), *A Manichaean Psalm Book*, Part 2 (Stuttgart, 1938), p. 16.

76 al-Nadim, *Fihristi*, p. 802.

77 Bardaisan rejected and polemicized against Marcion's teaching of two gods. On the intriguing figure of Bardaisan, his system and teachings of fate and free will, see H. J. W. Drijvers, *Bardaisan of Edessa* (Assen, 1966); see also B. Aland, 'Mani und Bardesanes – Zur Enstehung des manichäischen Systems', in A. Dietrich (ed.), *Syncretismus im syrisch-persischen Kulturgebiet* (Göttingen, 1975), pp. 123–44.

78 Among the principal non-Manichaean sources for Manichaeism are: Alexander Lycopolitanus' opus against Manichaeism; the *Acta Archelai*, Augustine's works such as *Contra Faustum PL*, vol. 42, Cols. 207–518; Theodore bar Konai's *Liber Scholiorum*; al-Nadim's account of Manichaeism

in his *Fihristi*. The Turfan fragments were written in various languages (Middle Persian, Sogdian, Parthian, Uighur, Bactrian), while the Coptic finds included the Manichaean *Psalm Book, Homilies, Kephalaia* (Discourses) – the sayings of Mani collected after his death. Along with the decipherment of the *Cologne Mani Codex*, the discovery and publication of these Manichaean documents were of crucial importance for testing the validity of the non-Manichaean accounts of the Manichaean system and for providing new insights into the teachings and history of the Manichaean Church and its founder, Mani. On Manichaean literature in general and in the relevant languages, see, for example, Widengren, *Mani*, Chap. 5; J. P. Asmussen, *Manichaean Literature, Representative Texts Chiefly from Middle Persian and Parthian Writings* (New York, 1975); M. Boyce, 'The Manichaean Literature in Middle Iranian', *Handbuch der Orientalistik*, IV, 2, 1 (Leiden, 1968), pp. 67–76; L. Clarke, 'The Turkic Manichaean Literature', in Mirecki and BeDuhn (eds), *Emerging from Darkness*, pp. 89–143. For collections and editions of and commentaries on Manichaean texts (apart from those already quoted), see, for example, P. Alfaric, *Les écritures manichéennes*, 2 vols (Paris, 1918–19); M. Boyce, *The Manichaean Hymn-Cycles in Parthian* (London, 1954), *A Reader in Manichaean Middle Persian and Parthian, Text with Notes* (Leiden, 1975); A. Adam (ed.), *Texte zum Manichäismus*, 2nd edn (Berlin, 1969); A. Böhlig and J. P. Asmussen, *Die Gnosis*, III, *Der Manichäismus* (Zurich and Munich, 1980); H. Schmidt-Glintzer, *Chinesische Manichaica, Mit textcritischen Anmerkungen und einem Glossar* (Wiesbaden, 1987); W. Sunderman, *Mittelpersische und parthische kosmogonische und Parabeltexte der Manichäer* (Berlin, 1973); *Mitteliranische manichäische Texte kirchenges-chichtlichen Inhalts* (Berlin, 1981); P. Zieme, *Manichäisch-türkische Texte* (Berlin, 1975); J. Hamilton, *Les ouïghours du ixe–xe siècle de Touen-houang*, 2 vols (Paris, 1986); S. Giversen (ed.), *The Manichaean Coptic Papyri in the Chester Beatty Library*, 4 vols (Geneva, 1986–8); M. Hutter, *Manis Kosmogo-nische Šābuhragān Texte* (Wiesbaden, 1992); *Dictionary of Manichaean Texts*, vol. 1, *Texts from the Roman Empire (texts in Syriac, Greek, Coptic and Latin)*, ed. S. Clackson *et al.* (Turnhout, 1998); H.-J. Klimkeit, *Gnosis on the Silk Road. Gnostic Texts from Central Asia* (San Francisco, 1993); G. Wurst (ed.), *Die Bema Psalmen*, Corpus fountum Manichaeorum, Series Coptica 1, Manichaean Coptic papyri in the Chester Beatty Library, Psalm Book, Part II, Fasc. 1 (Turnhout, 1996); S. G. Richter, *Die Aufstiegspsalmen des Herak-leides: Untersuchungen zum Seelenaufstieg und zur Seelenmesse bei den Manichäern* (Wiesbaden, 1997). For the recent sensational discoveries of Manichaean texts in Coptic, Greek and Syriac in the village of Kellis in the Dakhle Oasis, Egypt, see P. Mirecki *et al.*, 'Magical Spell, Manichaean Letter', in Mirecki and BeDuhn (eds), *Emerging from Darkness*, pp. 1–33; for editions of the Kellis texts, see *Greek Papyri from Kellis, I*, ed. K. A. Worp *et al.*

(Oxford, 1995); *Kellis Literary Texts, I*, ed. I. Gardner (Oxford, 1996); *Coptic Documentary Texts from Kellis*, ed. A. Alcock and I. Gardner (Oxford 1999). For more publications of Manichaean texts, see S. N. C. Lieu, 'Working Catalogue of Published Manichaean Texts', in *Manichaeism in Central Asia and China* (Leiden, 1998), pp. 196–247. On the development of Manichaean studies in relation to the successive discoveries of primary sources and changing trends of scholarly and theological approaches to Manichaeismn, see J. Ries, *Les études manichéennes. Des controverses de la réforme aux découvertes du XXe siècle* (Louvaine-la Neuve, 1988).

79 al-Nadim, *Fihristi*, p. 778; this description of the lion-headed and serpent-bodied Manichaean Prince of Darkness presents clear parallels to that of the lion-headed demiurge, Yaldabaoth and the Mithraic *Deus Arimanius* (see n. 54 above). The studies of Manichaean dualism and satanology have variously discerned (opinions about the time and the scope of these influences often vary) Gnostic, Jewish–Christian, Christian and Zoroastrian influences. For studies highlighting the Jewish–Christian, Christian and Gnostic influences on Manichaeism, see, for example, Lieu, *Manchaeism*, pp. 51–70; A. Böhlig, 'The New Testament and the Concept of Manichaean Myth', in Logan and Wedderburn, *The New Testament and Gnosis*, pp. 90–104; for studies highlighting the Zoroastrian influences, see, for example, Widengren, *Mani*, Chaps 3 and 4; *idem, The Great Vohu Manah and the Apostle of God. Studies in Iranian and Manichaean Religion* (Uppsala and Leipzig, 1945) (for Widengren's arguments for Mesopotamian influences on Manichaeism, see his *Mesopotamian Elements in Manichaeism, Studies in Manichaean, Mandean and Syrian Gnostic Religion* (Uppsala and Leipzig, 1946)); Gnoli, 'La gnosi iranica'; M. Hutter, 'Das Erlösungsgeschichte im manichäisch-iranischen Mythos. Motiv- und traditionsgeschichtliche Analysen', in K. M. Woschitz *et al., Das manichäische Urdrama des Lichtes* (Vienna, 1989), pp. 153–239; Rudolph, 'Mani und der Iran', in Rudolph, *Gnosis und spätantike religionsgeschichte*, pp. 698–714; U. Bianchi, 'Zoroastrian Elements in Manichaeism, the Question of Evil Substance', in P. Bryder (ed.), *Manichaean Studies, Proceedings of the First International Conference on Manichaeism* (Lund, 1988), pp. 13–19. On Manichaean dualism, cf., for example, Pétrement, *Le dualisme*, pp. 200–5, 208–307 *passim*; G. G. Stroumsa, 'König und Schwein. Zur Struktur des manichäischen Dualismus', in J. Taubes (ed.), *Gnosis und Politik* (Munich, 1984), pp. 141–53; L. Koenen, 'How Dualistic is Mani's Dualism?', in L. Cirillo (ed.), *Codex Manichaicus Coloniensis. Atti del Secondo Simposio Internazionale* (Cosenza, 1990), pp. 1–34; Lieu, *Manchaeism*, pp. 187–91; U. Bianchi, 'Sur le dualisme de Mani', in A. van Tongerloo and S. Giversen (eds), *Manichaica Selecta. Studies Presented to Prof. J. Ries on the Occasion of his Seventieth Birthday* (Louvain, 1991), pp. 9–19; W. Sunderman, 'How Zoroastrian is Mani's Dualism?', in L. Cirillo and A. van Tongerloo (eds),

THE OTHER GOD

Manichaean Studies III, Atti dei terzo congresso internazionale di studi 'Manicheismo e Oriente Cristiano antico' (Louvain, 1997), pp. 343–61.

80 al-Nadim, *Fihristi*, pp. 783–6; for the indebtedness of the Manichaean accounts of the aggression of the archons and their oppression of mankind to Jewish Enochic literature (the Manichaean *Book of the Giants* clearly had a Jewish Enochic prototype), see, for example, W. M. Henning, 'The Book of the Giants', *BSOAS*, XI/1, 1943, pp. 52–74; J. Milik and M. Black, *The Books of Enoch* (Oxford, 1976), pp. 298–339; J. C. Reeves, *Jewish Lore in Manichaean Cosmogony* (Cincinnati, 1992); 'Jewish Pseudepigrapha in Manichaean Literature: The Influence of the Enochic Library' in J. C. Reeves (ed.), *Tracing the Threads: Studies in the Vitality of Jewish Pseudepigrapha* (Atlanta, Ga, 1994), pp. 184–91; L. T. Stuckenbruck, *The Book of Giants from Qumran, Text, Translation, and Commentary* (Tübingen, 1997), *passim*. On Manichaean pseudepigraphy see also VanderKam and Adler (eds), *The Jewish Apocalyptic Heritage in Early Christianity*, pp. 11ff., 17–21; D. Frankfurter, 'Apocalypses Real and Alleged in the Mani Codex', *Numen*, 44, 1997, pp. 60–73. On the characteristic use of astrological notions in Manichaean cosmogonic accounts, see, for example, Widengren, *Mani*, pp. 69–74; Lieu, *Manichaeism*, pp. 177–80; I. Coulianu, 'The Counterfeit Spirit in Manichaeism', in Tongerloo and Giversen, *Manichaica Selecta*, pp. 53–9; A. Panaino, 'Visione della volta celeste e astrologia nel Manicheismo', in Cirillo and Tongerloo, *Manichaean Studies*, pp. 249–97.

81 al-Nadim, *Fihristi*, p. 798. For studies of Manichaean Christology (for the relevant texts, see, for example, Asmussen, *Manichaean Literature*, pp. 98–113) see E. Waldschmidt and W. Lentz, *Die Stellung Jesu in Mänichaismus*, Abhandlungen der königlichen Presussischen Akademie der Wissenschaften, 1926, 4; Puech, *Le manichéisme*, pp. 82ff; E. Rose, *Die Manichäische Christologie* (Wiesbaden, 1979); Böhlig, 'The New Testament and the Concept of Manichaean Myth'; Decret, *Mani*, pp. 94–101; 'La christologie manichéenne dans la controverse d'Augustin avec Fortunatus', in *Essais sur l'Église manichéenne*, pp. 269–81; N.-A. Pedersen, 'Early Manichaean Christology' in Bryder, *Manichaean Studies*, p. 157–91 (with an examination of the Jesus figures in Manichaeism and their parallels in Gnosticism, Marcionism, etc.); I. Gardner, 'The Manichaean Account of Jesus and the Passion of the Living Soul', in Tongerloo and Giversen, *Manichaica Selecta*, pp. 71–87; J. Ries, 'Jesus Christ dans la religion de Mani', *Augustiniana*, 14, 1964, pp. 437–54; 'Jésus la Splendeur, Jésus patibilis, Jésus historique dans les textes manichéens occidentaux', in Preissler and Seiwert, *Gnosisforschung*, pp. 235–47.

82 T. Olsson, 'The Manichaean Background of Eschatology in the Koran' in Bryder, *Manichaean Studies*, pp. 273–82; on the significance of the Manichaean notion of the 'Seal of the Prophets', cf. G. G. Stroumsa, ' "Seal of the Prophets". The Nature of a Manichaean Metaphor', *JSAI*, VII, 1986, pp. 61–74.

83 Pedersen, 'Early Manichaean Christology', p. 169.

84 *Kephalaia* 154, tr. I. Stevenson, *A New Eusebius* (London, 1968), p. 282. For the Mani's views of mission and its pursuit, see, for example, Widengren, *Mani*, pp. 28–37; Asmussen, *Manichaean Literature*, Chap. 2; Lieu, *Manichaeism*, pp. 86–106; 'From Mesopotamia to the Roman East – The Diffusion of Manichaeism in the Eastern Roman Empire (with a contribution by D. A. Montserrat)', in Lieu, *Manichaeism in Mesopotamia and the Roman East* (Leiden, 1994), pp. 22–6; W. Sunderman, 'Zur frühen missionarischen Wirksamkeit Manis' and 'Weiteres zur frühen missionarischen Wirksamkeit Manis', *AOH*, 24, 1971, pp. 79–125 and pp. 371–9. On Manichaean missionary strategy, see, P. Bryder, 'The Zebra as a Chameleon, Manichaean missionary technique', in Preissler and Seiwert, *Gnosisforschung*, pp. 49–55; on the problems concerning the reconstruction of Mani's original teaching caused by the Manichaean translation technique of using loan terms from other religions, see H. H. Schaeder, 'Urform und Fortbildung des manichäischen System', *Vorträge der Bibliothek Warburg*, 1924–5 (1927), pp. 65–157; P. Bryder, 'Problems Concerning the Spread of Manichaeism from One Culture to Another', in Wiessner and Klimkeit, *Studia Manichaica*, pp. 334–42. For a study of the Manichaean terminology in the Coptic sources for Manichaeism, see P. V. Lindt, *The Names of Manichaean Mythological Figures, A Comparative Study on Terminology in the Coptic Sources* (Wiesbaden, 1992); for the Manichaean cosmogonic and eschatological terminology in Middle Iranian, see S. N. C. Lieu and A. van Tongarloo (eds), *Dictionary of Manichaean Terms and Concepts, 1, Cosmogonic and Eschatological Terms in Middle Persian* (Leuven, 1993). For a study of Manichaean symbolism and metaphors, see V. Arnold-Döben, *Die Bildersprache des Manichäismus* (Cologne, 1978).

85 B. A. Pearson, 'The Figure of Seth in Manichaean Literature' in Bryder, *Manichaean Studies*, pp. 153–5. Sethel (i.e. Seth) was praised as an 'Apostle of Electship' in *A Manichaean Psalm Book*, p. 144. On the two classes and ecclesiastical organization of Manichaeism, see, for example, Widengren, *Mani*, Chap. 6; Decret, *Mani*, pp. 106–25; Lieu, *Manichaeism*, pp. 27ff.; apart from the arguments for Marcionite and Buddhist influences on the division between the two grades of elect and listeners in Manichaeism, recently suggestions have been made that Jainism may have also influenced the rules and principles associated with the Manichaean elect, see R. N. Frye, 'Manichaean Notes', in Wiessner and Klimkeit, *Studia Manichaica*, pp. 93–8, esp. pp. 95–6. On Manichaean ecclesiastical organization, see also C. Römer, 'Die manichäische Kirchenorganization nach dem Kölner Mani-Kodex', in Wiessner and Klimkeit, *Studia Manichaica*, pp. 181–9. On Manichaean monasticism, see, for example, S. N. C. Lieu, 'Precept and Practice in Manichaean Monasticism', repr. in *Manichaeism in Central Asia and China*, pp. 76–99.

86 al-Nadim, *Fihristi*, p. 796.

87 This eschatological chronology is developed in the 'Great War Sermon' in the *Manichaische Homillien*, pp. 12–14 1. 11. See the new detailed study of N. A. Pedersen, *Studies in The Sermon on the Great War* (Aarhus, 1993).

88 Lieu, *Manichaeism*: Lieu's book presents a detailed and updated survey of the history of Manichaeism in the Roman empire (pp. 115–21, Chap 4), the subject also of an earlier general work, E. de Stoop, *Essai sur la diffusion du manichéisme dans l'empire romain* (Ghent, 1909); P. R. L. Brown, 'The Diffusion of Manichaeism in the Roman Empire', in *Religion and Society in the Age of St Augustine* (London, 1972), pp. 94–118; on the diffusion of Manichaeism in the Eastern Roman empire, see Lieu, 'From Mesopotamia to the Roman East – The Diffusion of Manichaeism in the Eastern Roman Empire'; for Roman anti-Manichaean polemical literature, see Lieu, 'Some themes in Later Roman anti-Manichaean polemics', repr. in *Manichaeism in Mesopotamia and the Roman East*, pp. 156–203 (see also W. Klein, *Die Argumentation in den griechisch-christlichen Antimanichaica* (Wiesbaden, 1991)); for the Theodosian anti-Manichaean legislation, see P. Beskow, 'The Theodosian Laws against Manichaeism', in Bryder, *Manichaean Studies*, pp. 1–13; for a survey, texts and translations of Greek and Latin formulas for abjuration of Manichaeism, see Lieu, 'An early Byzantine formula for the renunciation of Manichaeism', repr. in *Manichaeism in Mesopotamia and the Roman East*, pp. 203–306. For studies of the development of Augustine's religious and intellectual stance *vis-à-vis* Manichaeism, see P. Alfaric, *L'évolution intellectuelle de saint Augustine, I, Du manichéisme au néoplatonisme* (Paris, 1918); Lieu, *Manichaeism*, Chap. 5 *passim*; J. van Ort, *Jerusalem and Babylon, a Study into Augustine's 'City of God' and the Sources of his Doctrines of the Two Cities* (Leiden, 1991), pp. 199–234; 'Augustinus und der Manichäismus', in A. van Tongerloo and J. van Ort, *The Manichaean ΝΟΥΣ, Proceedings of the International Symposium Organized in Louvain from 31 July to 3 August 1991* (Louvain, 1995), pp. 289–309; N. J. Torchia, *Creatio ex nihilo and the theology of St Augustine: the anti-Manichaean polemic and beyond* (New York, 1999).

89 On the Islamic records concerning the fortunes of Manichaeism in the Islamic world, see, for example, M. Guidi, *La lotta tra l'Islām e il Manicheismo* (Rome, 1927); H. S. Nyberg, 'Zum Kampf zwischen Islam und Manichäismus', *OLZ*, 32, 1929, cols 425–41; G. Vajda, 'Die zindīqs im Gebiet des Islam zu Beginn der Abbasidenzeit', repr. in G. Widengren (ed.), *Der Manichäismus* (Darmstadt, 1977), pp. 418–64; C. Colpe, 'Anpassung des Manichäismus an den Islam (Abū 'Isā al-Warrāq), repr. in Widengren, *Der Manichäismus*, pp. 464–79; A. Abel, 'Les sources arabes sur le manichéisme', *Annuaire de l'Institut de Philologie et d'Histoire Orientales et Slaves*, 16, 1961–2, pp. 31–73. The study of the eastward expansion of Manichaeism received a

massive impetus with the discoveries of Manichaean texts at Tun-huang and Turfan, and the study of the history of Manicheism in China was consequently enhanced by the works of Chavannes, Pelliot and Noyé; followed after the Second World War by the studies of G. Messina, *Cristianesimo, Buddismo, Manicheismo nell'Asia Antica* (Rome, 1947); H. H. Schaeder, 'Der Manichäismus und sein Weg nach Osten', *Glaube und Geschichte – Festschrift für F. Gogarten* (Giessen, 1948), pp. 236–54; J. P. Asmussen, 'People and Religions in Central Asia', in *X ᵘāstānīft Studies in Manichaeism* (Copenhagen, 1965), pp. 130–66; and the studies of Henning, Klimkeit, Sunderman, Lieu, Bryder and other scholars referred to in the notes below.

90 For the Middle Iranian and Turkic Manichaean literature from Central Asia see, for example, the studies collected in W. B. Henning, *Selected Papers*, 2 vols (Teheran and Liège, 1977); L. Clark's recent overview, 'Turkic Manichaean Literature', in Mirecki and BeDuhn, *Emerging from Darkness*, pp. 89–143; the texts in Klimkeit, *Gnosis on the Silk Road*; Lieu, 'Manichaean art and texts from the Silk Road', repr. in *Manichaeism in Central Asia and China*, pp. 1–59; for other publications, see the recent critical bibliography of earlier and new studies added to the new edition of H.-J. Polotsky, *Il Manicheismo, gnosi di salvezza tra Egitti e Cina*, ed. C. Leurini, A. Panaino and A. Piras (Rimini, 1996), pp. 86–93. On the use of Christian apocryphal texts by the Manichaeans in Central Asia, see W. Sunderman, 'Christliche Evangelientexte in der Überlieferung der iranisch-manichäischen Literatur', *MIO*, 14, 1968, pp. 386–405; H.-J. Klimkeit, 'Apocryphal Gospels in Central and East Asia', in Heuser and Klimkeit, *Studies*, pp. 189–212; on Manichaean art in Central Asia, see the classic work of A. van de Coq, *Die buddhistische Spätantike II, Die manichäische Miniaturen* (Berlin, 1923); among the studies of H.-J. Klimkeit, see, for example, his *Manichaean Art and Calligraphy* (Leiden, 1982); 'Hindu deities in Manichaean art', *Zentralasiatische Studien*, 14, 1980, pp. 179–99; 'On the Nature of Manichaean Art' and 'Manichaean art on the Silk Road: New and Old Discoveries', in Heuser and Klimkeit, *Studies*, pp. 270–91 and pp. 300–14; Z. Gulácsi, 'Identifying the Corpus of Manichaean Art among the Turfan Remains', in Mirecki and BeDuhn, *Emerging from Darkness*, pp. 177–217. On the intriguing association between Manichaeism and kingship ideology in Central Asia during the period of Uighur supremacy and its implications, see Klimkeit, 'Manichaean Kingship: Gnosis at Home in the World' and 'Temporal and Spiritual Power in Central Asian Manichaeism', in Heuser and Klimkeit, *Studies*, pp. 212–29 and pp. 229–37.

91 On the question of Manichaean influences on Tibetan religious traditions, cf., for example, J. H. Edgar, 'A suspected Manichaean stratum in Lamaism', *Journal of the West China Border Research Society*, 6, 1933–4, pp. 252–7; 'Did Manichaeism influence Lamaism?', *Journal of the North China Branch of the Royal Asiatic Society*, 60, 1935, pp. 127ff.; Hermanns, *Das National-Epos der*

Tibeter, pp. 130–1; Hoffmann, *Tibet*, pp. 106–7; *idem*, 'Kalacakra Studies I. Manichaeism, Christianity and Islam in the Kālacakra Tantra', *CAJ*, 13, 1969, pp. 52–73; 'Addenda et corrigenda', *CAJ*, 15, 1971, pp. 289–301; Blondeau, 'Les religions du Tibet', p. 313; G. Uray, 'Tibet's Connections with Nestorianism and Manichaeism', in E. Steinkellner and H. Tauscher (eds), *Contributions on Tibetan Language, History and Culture* (Vienna, 1983), pp. 399–429.

92 On the representation of Mani (as the Paraclete) as Maitreya, see Lieu, *Manichaeism*, pp. 300–1 (with arguments that this representation is not sufficient to justify the posited links between Chinese Manichaeism and the messianic Maitreya societies); Natier, 'The Meaning of the Maitreya Myth', pp. 36–7 (with references to the relevant primary sources); Klimkeit, 'Jesus' Entry into Parinirvāna: Manichaean identity in Buddhist Central Asia', in Heuser and Klimkeit, *Studies*, pp. 257–8; on Mani as the Buddha of Light, see Lieu, *Manichaeism*, pp. 255–7; for the text of Buddhist-based life of Mani, see the recent translations in Schmidt-Glintzer, *Chinesische Manichaica*, pp. 69–77; N. Tajadod, *Mani le Bouddha de Lumière. Catéchisme manichéen chinois* (Paris, 1990), on Mani's assimilation to Lao-Tzu, see Lieu, *Manichaeism*, pp. 259–61 (with arguments that the assimilation was conceptualized in Taoist circles); on the eastern Manichaean use of Buddhist and Taoist terminology, see Lieu, *Manichaeism*, Chaps 7–9 *passim*: specifically, on the use of Buddhist terms in Chinese Manichaean writings, see P. Bryder, *The Chinese Transformations of Manichaeism: A Study of Chinese Manichaean Terminology* (Lund, 1985); H. Schmidt-Glintzer, 'Das buddhistische Gewand des Manichäismus. Zur buddhistischen Terminologie in den chinesischen Manichaica', in W. Haussig and H.-J. Klimkeit (eds), *Synkretismus in den Religionen Zentralasiens, Ergebnisse eines Kolloquiums vom 25 bis 26 mai 1983 in St. Augustin bei Bonn* (Wiesbaden, 1987), pp. 76–90; see also H. J. Klimkeit, 'Manichäische und buddhistische Beichtformeln aus Turfan', *ZRGG*, 29/3, 1977, pp. 193–228; 'Adaptations to Buddhism in East Iranian and Central Asian Manichaeism', in Heuser and Klimkeit, *Studies*, pp. 237–54; S. N. C. Lieu, 'From Parthian into Chinese: Some Observations on the *Traktat (Traité) Pelliot*', repr. in *Manichaeism in Central Asia and China*, pp. 59–76.

93 On the circumstances of the inclusion of this work in the canon, see Lieu, *Manichaeism*, pp. 268–70.

94 For a survey and critical discussion of the sources for Manichaean history from Sung to early Ming China and the current state of research, see Lieu, *Manichaeism*, Chaps 8 to 9; *The Religion of Light – an Introduction to the History of Manichaeism in China* (Hong Kong, 1979), II. 'Manichaeism as a Secret Religion in China', pp. 27–35; on the association between the White Lotus sect and Manichaeism, see B. ter Haar, *The White Lotus Teachings in Chinese Religious History* (Leiden, 1992), pp. 47–56.

95 On Marco Polo's encounter with Manichaeans in Fukien see L. Olschki, 'Manichaeism, Buddhism and Christianity in Marco Polo's China', *Zeitschrift der schweizerischen Gesellschaft für Asienkunde*, 5, 1951, pp. 1–21; S. N. C. Lieu, 'Nestorians and Manichaeans on the South China coast', repr. in *Manichaeism in Central Asia and China*, pp. 177–96, *passim*.

96 For an analysis of Chu Yüan Chang's supression of Manichaeism, see Lieu, *Manichaeism*, pp. 298–302 (with a criticism of the theory that he may have come earlier under Manichaean influences, p. 300, and a discussion of the last reliable reports concerning Manichaean activities in Fukien in the early seventeenth century, pp. 303–4).

97 For the Manichaean temple on Hua-piao hill, see P. Bryder, 'Where the faint traces of Manichaeism disappear', *AoF*, 15, 1988, pp. 201–8; 'Cao'an Revisited', in Tongerloo and Giversen, *Manichaica Selecta*, pp. 35–43. For the possibility of Manichaean survivals in modern times in south China, see L. Wushu's survey of Chinese and Western studies of the diffusion of Manichaeism in Fukien, 'On the Spreading of Manichaeism in Fujian', in Wiessner and Klimkeit, *Studia Manichaica*, pp. 342–56 (with suggestions that Manichaeism did not disappear in the early seventeenth century but 'lost its position of an independent religion, and joined into other secret religions' in the area and may have survived into modern times, pp. 353–6.

98 For a discussion of Chinese polemics against and Confucian attitudes to Manichaeism, see Lieu, *Manichaesim*, Chaps 8–9 *passim*; 'Polemics against Manichaeism as a subversive cult in Sung China (*c.* 960–*c* 1200)', repr. in *Manichaeism in Central Asia and China*, pp. 126–77, esp. pp. 154–77; *Religion of Light*, II. 'Manichaeism as a Secret Religion in China', *passim*; 'A lapsed Chinese Manichaean's correspondence with a Confucian official in the late Sung dynasty (1260): a study of the *Ch'ung-shou-kung chi* by Huang Chen', repr. in *Manichaeism in Central Asia and China*, pp. 98–126.

99 Lieu, *Religion of Light*, p. 21.

100 The formerly influential sets of distinctions between magic and religion developed in the works of E. B. Tylor, James Frazer and L. Thorndike (a coercion/supplication line of differentiation had been argued as early as in Protestant anti-Catholic polemics, cf. K. Thomas, *Religion and the Decline of Magic* (New York, 1971), pp. 51–77) have been superseded by a number of new attempts to redefine and reinterpret the relationship between magic and religion which often have reached very conflicting conclusions. Some of these attempts have been influenced by earlier arguments for the similarity or lack of distinction between magic and religion (particularly in their early stages), as presented, for example, by M. Mauss and H. Hubert, 'Esquisse d'une théorie générale de la magie', *AS*, 7 (1902–3) pp. 1–146; R. Marett, *The Threshold of Religion* (London, 1914), pp. 27–8; R. H. Lowie, *Primitive Religion* (London, 1925), pp. 136–53. E. Durkheim's sociological criterion for

distinguishing magic from religion in his *Les formes élémentaires de la vie religieuse*, 2nd edn (Paris, 1925), pp. 58–66, has also been subjected to continuous criticism. The problem of the magic/religion dichotomy has been a central concern of anthropological studies following the pioneering field research of anthropologists like B. Malinowski and E. E. Evans-Pritchard. In his *Magic, Science and Religion* (Glencoe, 1948), pp. 67–72, Malinowski argues that religion is related to the fundamental human values, while magic deals with immediate and concrete aims, whereas Evans-Pritchard, *Theories of Primitive Religion* (Oxford, 1965), p. 111, dwells on the insurmountable difficulties in trying to understand magic 'as an idea in itself', insisting that it becomes intelligible only when related to belief systems and empirical realities. Another influential anthropologist, Claude Lévi-Strauss, also presents his views on the contrast between magic and religion in *La pensée sauvage* (Paris, 1962), p. 291–302. Some approaches to the problem have partially reiterated and redefined the earlier posited distinctions between magic and religion – see, for example, W. F. Goode, 'Magic and Religion: A Continuum', *Ethnos*, 14 (1949), pp. 172–82; W. A. Lessa and E. Z. Vogt (eds), *Reader in Comparative Religion*, 2nd edn (Evanston, Ill., 1965), pp. 298–300; R. Horton, 'A Definition of Religion and its Uses', *JRAI*, 90 (1960) pp. 201–20. Other approaches have followed on from the earlier posited emphasis on the similarity between magic and religion in terms of beliefs and practices, sometimes reinforced by application of the structural–functional methods in anthropology – see, for example, M. and R. Wax, 'The Notion of Magic', *Current Anthropology* 4 (1963) pp. 495–518; D. E. Aune, 'Magic in Early Christianity', *ANRW*, II.23.2 (1980), pp. 1507–57; cf. also M. Smith, 'How Magic was Changed by the Triumph of Christianity', *Graeco-Arabica* 2 (1983), pp. 51–8. These latter types of approach often accentuate the social function of magic accusations and the deviant or subversive nature of magical practices *vis-à-vis* normative religion. For a summary and discussion of both the essentialist and function-alist approaches, see H. S. Versnel, 'Some Reflections on the Relationship Magic – Religion', *Numen* 38 (1981), pp. 177–97; for the development of anthropological theories of religion and magic see, for example, Evans-Pritchard, *Theories of Primitive Religion*; S. J. Tambiah, *Magic, Science, Religion and the Scope of Rationality* (Cambridge, 1990).

101 Following the publication of E. E. Evans-Pritchard's seminal work, *Witchcraft, Oracles and Magic among the Azande* (Oxford, 1937) the study of magic has broadened its scope to include investigations of the social, cultural and psychological dimensions of ritual and magical activities and has influenced a number of classicists, New Testament scholars, medievalists, etc. The sociological approach, focusing on the socially regulating role and distribution of sorcery accusations, has proved very useful in different historical contexts – for its

application to the Graeco-Roman world, see P. Brown, 'Sorcery, Demons and the Rise of Christianity: from Late Antiquity into the Middle Ages' in M. Douglas (ed.), *Witchcraft Confessions and Accusations* (London, 1970), pp. 17–45; J. Smith, 'Good News is No News' in *idem, Map is not Territory, Studies in the History of Religions* (Leiden, 1978), pp. 190–207. Cf. A. Segal, Hellenistic Magic: Some Questions of Definitions' in R. Van den Broek and M. J. Vermaseren (eds), *Studies in Gnosticism and Hellenistic Religions: Studies presented to G. Quispel on the occasion of his 65th birthday* (Leiden, 1981), pp. 349–75. For the use of anthropological models in other socio-historical contexts, see the articles in Douglas, *Witchcraft Confessions*; A. D. J. Macfarlane, *Witchcraft in Tudor and Stuart England: a regional and comparative study* (London, 1970). For a linguistic investigation of magical language, see, for example, S. J. Tambiah, *Culture, Thought and Social Action. An Anthropological Perspective* (Cambridge, Mass, 1985), I.1 'The Magical Power of Words'. On the strategies of selection and definition of practices as 'religious' and 'magical', see J. Neusner, E. S. Frerichs and P. V. M. Flesher (eds), *Religion, Science and Magic in Concert and in Conflict* (Oxford, 1989). A detailed survey of other interpretative viewpoints is outside the scope of the present book – for its purposes, the term 'magic' will be defined in an heresiological context as ritual activities and belief systems concerning relations and dealings with the supernatural that remained outside the norms and authority of the orthodox religious system (Christianity) and accordingly could be seen as involving demonic help, delusions, pseudo-miracles, etc.

102 For the legislation of Constantine the Great presented in the Theodosain Codex, see its edition by T. Mommsen *et al.* (eds), *Theodosiani libri XVI cum Constitutionibus Sirmondianis* (Berlin, 1905), vol. 1.2; 19.6.1–3, pp. 460–1; for the laws of Constantius see *ibid.*, 9.16.4–6; for further legislation against magic see *ibid.* 9.16.7–12, pp. 462–3. For the edict of Valentinian III and Marcian against pagan sacrifices see *Codex Iustinianus* I.11.7 in *Corpus Iuris Civilis*, ed. P. Krueger, vol. 2 (Berlin, 1915), p. 63; for legislation against magic in *Codex Iustinianus* 9.18 see *ibid.*, pp. 379–80. On the legal treatment of magic in the Christianized Roman empire, see, for example, F. R. Trombey, *Hellenic Religion and Christianization c. 370–529* (Leiden, 1993), Chap. 1, IV; R. MacMullen, *Enemies of the Roman Order* (Cambridge, Mass., 1966), Chaps 3 and 4.

103 For earlier Roman legislation against magic see, for example, E. Massonneau, *La Magie dans l'antiquité romaine* (Paris, 1934), Part II: 'La Repression de la Magie'; MacMullen, *Enemies of the Roman Order*, Chaps 3 and 4.

104 See P. Brown, 'Sorcery, Demons and the Rise of Christianity'; cf. the criticism of Brown's arguments by J. O. Ward, 'Witchcraft and sorcery in the later Roman empire and the early Middle Ages: an anthropological comment', *Prudentia* 13 (1981) pp. 93–108. See also Segal, 'Hellenistic Magic', pp. 359–75.

105 See, for example, Augustine, *De Moribis Manichaeorum*, 18, 19, *PL.*, vol. 32, cols 1372–6; *De Haeresibus* 46, *PL*, vol. 42, cols 34–8; *De Natura Boni* 45, 47, *ibid.*, cols 569, 570–1. On Augustine's treatment of accusations against the Manichaeans, see, for example, Alfaric, *L'évolution intellectuelle de saint Augustine*, p. 165; A. A. Moon (ed. and tr.), *The De Natura Boni of Saint Augustine* (Washington, DC, 1955), pp. 239–44, 253–5.

106 Irenaeus, *Adversus Haereses*, 1.25.3, *PG*, vol.7, col.682.

107 Irenaeus, *Adversus Haereses*, 1.25.3, cols 681–2.

108 Clement of Alexandria, *Stromata*, III, ii, ed. O. Stählin, vol. 2, *Stromata. Buch I–VI* (Leizpig, 1906), pp. 197–206.

109 Epiphanius, *Panarion* 26.4.1–5.8, ed. K. Holl, vol. 1 (Leipzig, 1915), pp. 280–2.

110 Philastrius, *Diversarum hereseon liber*, XLIX.4, *Sancti Filastrii episcopi Brixiensis Diversarum hereseon liber*, ed. F. Marx (Vienna, 1898), p. 26.

111 Epipahnius, *Panarion* 48.14.6, ed. K. Holl and J. Dummer, vol.2 (2nd rev. edn, Berlin, 1980), p. 240.

112 Jerome, *Epistula* 41.4.1, *Epistularum, Pars I, Epistulae I–LXX*, ed. I. Hilberg (Vienna, 1996), p. 314.

113 *Praedestinatus* 26, *PL*, vol. 53, col. 596.

114 Cyril of Jerusalem, *Catechesis*, XVI, *PG*, vol. 33, cols 927–30.

115 Augustine, *De Haeresibus*, XXVI, *PL*, vol.42, col.30.

116 Texts in R. A. Lipsius, *Acta Apostolorum apocrypha*, vol. 1 (Hildesheim, 1959), pp. 45–103.

117 Text in Lipsius, *Acta Apostolorum apocrypha*, pp. 118–77.

118 See, for example, *Clementine Homilies* 2.22.2–41–1, 3.29.1–58.2, ed. B. Rehm, *Die Pseudoklementinen. I. Homilien* (Berlin, 1969), pp. 43–52, 67–78; *Clementine Recognitions* 2.7.1–13.3, 3.46f., ed. B. Rehm, *Die Pseudoklementinen. II. Recognitionen* (Berlin, 1965), pp. 55–8, 80f.

119 Justin Martyr, *Prima Apologia* 26.1–3, ed. G. Kruer (Tübingen, 1915), pp. 20–1. On the sources for the traditions about Simon Magus, see K. Beyschlag, *Simon Magus und die christliche Gnosis* (Tübingen, 1974), Chap. 2; G. Ludeman, *Untersuchungen zur simonianischen Gnosis* (Göttingen, 1975).

120 Hippolytus, *Refutatio omnium haeresium*. VI.6.1–19.8, ed. M. Markovich (Berlin, 1986), pp. 213–27.

121 Epiphanius, *Panarion* 21.1.1–21.4.5, vol. 1, pp. 240–3.

122 Pseudo-Cyprian, *De rebaptismate* 16, in *Tertulliani De baptismo et Ps.-Cypriani De rebaptismate*, ed. G. Rauschen (Bonn, 1916), pp. 69–70.

123 On Menander, see Irenaeus, *Adversus Haereses* 1.23.5, col.673; Epiphanius, *Panarion* 22.1f., vol. 1, pp. 247f.; Tertullian, *De Anima* 50.2f., ed. J. H. Waszink (Amsterdam 1947), p. 68. On Simonian Gnosis, see Beyschlag, *Simon Magus*, Chap. 5;

124 Eusebius, *Historia Ecclesiastica* 4.7.9, ed. E. Schwartz, *Eusebius Kirchengeschichte*, 2nd edn (Leipzig, 1914), p. 130.

125 Irenaeus, *Adversus Haereses* 1.24.5, col. 678.

126 Hippolytus, *Refutatio* 6.39.1, p. 256; see also *ibid.* 6.39–55, pp. 256–78.

127 Irenaeus, *Adversus Haereses* 1.13, cols 578–92; see also *ibid.* 1.14–21, cols 594–657.

128 Ireneaus, *Adversus Haereses* 1.13.6, cols 587–92; Hippolytus, *Refutatio* 6.42, pp. 259–61; Epiphanius, *Panarion* 34:1, vol. 2, pp. 6–8.

129 See Origen, *Contra Celsum*, 6.31, ed. M. Borret, *Contre Celse*, vol. 3 (Paris, 1969), pp. 254–8.

130 For a description of the Ophite diagram and system, see Origen, *Contra Celsum* 6.24–38, pp. 238–70. For an attempt to reconstruct the diagram, see Welburn, 'Reconstructing the Ophite Diagram'.

131 *Lex Dei sive Mosaicarum et Romanarum legum collatio* XV, 3, ed. J. Baviera *et al.*, *Fontes Iuris Romani Anteiustiniani*, vol. 2 (Florence, 1940), pp. 580–1.

132 Epiphanius, *Panarion* 66.13.7, vol. 3, ed. K. Holl and J. Dummer (2nd rev. edn, Berlin, 1985), pp. 35–6.

133 See, for example, J. D. BeDuhn, 'Magical Bowls and Manichaeism' in M. Meyer and P. Mirecki (eds), *Ancient Magic and Ritual Power* (Leiden, 1995), pp. 420–35; P. Mirecki, I. Gardner, A. Gardner, 'Magical Spell, Manichaean Letter', in Mirecki and BeDuhn, *Emerging from Darkness*, pp. 1–33.

134 See *Acta Archelai* 14, 40, 62, ed. C. H. Beeson (Leipzig, 1906) pp. 22–3, 58–60, 90–2; for anathematization of Manichaean books as replete with sorcery and offering worship of the Devil, see the published anti-Manichaean text (going back to a sixth-century source), *The Seven Chapters* 2,50 in M. Richard (ed.), *Iohannis Caesariensis presbyteri et grammatici opera quae supersunt* (Turnhout, 1977), p. xxxiv; see *ibid.* 7.216f. and 7.219f., p. xxxix for anathematization of their 'abominable and magical prayers' and 'unholy and magic-filled mysteries'.

135 On the religious and social context of the accusations against Priscillian, cf., for example, E.-Ch. Babut, *Priscillien et le priscillianisme* (Paris, 1909), pp. 60–96; H. Chadwick, *Priscillian of Avilla. The Occult and the Charismatic in the Early Church* (Oxford, 1976), Chaps 3 and 4; V. Burrus, *The Making of a Heretic. Gender, Authority and the Priscillianist Controversy* (Berkeley, 1995).

3 The Thread of the Great Heresy

1 The publications of Mandaean texts and the study of Mandaean doctrines in the pioneering works of E. S. Drower (see, for example, *The Book of the Zodiac (Sfar Malwašia)* (London, 1949); *The Mandaeans of Iraq and Iran*

(Oxford, 1937; repr. Leiden, 1967)) have been followed by systematic studies of Mandaean teachings and cult in, among others, K. Rudolph, *Die Mandäer* I, *Prolegomena: das Mandäerproblem*; II, *Der Kult* (Göttingen, 1960–1). On dualism in Mandaean cosmogony and anthropogony, see, for example, K. Rudolph, *Theogonie, Kosmogonie und Anthropogonie in der Mandäeischen Schriften* (Göttingen, 1965); M. V. Cerutti, *Dualismo e ambiguità, Creatori e creazione nella dottrina mandea sul cosmo* (Rome, 1981); see also the articles assembled in Rudolph, *Gnosis und spätantike religionsgeschichte*, II. 'Mandaica', pp. 301–629.

2 The evidence for the late survival of Zoroastrian traditions in Armenia is examined in Russell, *Zoroastrianism in Armenia*, pp. 514–39. On the presence of Iranian traditions in Arsacid Armenia and their subsequent enduring residues in Armenia, see also N. Garsoïan, 'Prolegomena to a Study of the Iranian Elements in Arsacid Armenia' and 'The Locus of the Death of Kings: Iranian Armenia – the Inverted Image', repr. in *Armenia between Byzantium and the Sasanians* (London, 1985), esp. pp. x and xi.

3 The Arewordik are discussed in Russell, *Zoroastrianism in Armenia*, with allusions to the allegations of Paulician association with the 'Sons of the Sun'. According to N. G. Garsoïan, *The Paulician Heresy* (The Hague and Paris, 1967), p.95, n. 46, although the Arewordik remained distinct from the Paulicians, the two sects may have been in 'close relation with each other, since the Paulicians were favoured by the Persian authorities', while it is possible that some Paulician groups adopted Persian practices.

4 For a discussion of the posited references to and discussions of Paulicianism in the Armenian sources, cf., R. M. Bartikiian, *Istochniki dlia izucheniia istorii pavlikianskogo dvizhenii* (Erevan, 1961), Chap. 1; Garsoïan, *The Paulician Heresy*, Chap. 2; on the Byzantine sources for Paulicianism, cf. H. Grégoire, 'Les sources de l'histoire des Pauliciens', *ARB-BL*, 5e serie, 22, 1936, pp. 95–114; Bartikiian, *Istochniki*, Chap. 2, pp. 55–102; Garsoïan, *The Paulician Heresy*, Chap. 1; P. Lemerle, 'L'Histoire des Pauliciens d'Asie Mineure d'après les sources grêcqucs', *T&M*, 5, 1973, pp. 1–137, esp. pp. 17–49. The Byzantine sources have been edited and collected in C. Astruc *et al.* (eds), 'Les sources grecques pour l'histoire des Pauliciens d'Asie Mineure', *T&M*, 4, 1970, pp. 1–227. A valuable selection of Byzantine sources for Paulician history and teachings has been translated, with commentaries, in *Christian Dualist Heresies in the Byzantine World c. 650-c.1450*, ed. J. Hamilton and B. Hamilton, assisted with the translation of the Old Slavonic texts by Yuri Stoyanov (Manchester, 1998), (*HCDH*), pp. 57–114, 139–42, 166–75, 259–60.

5 Garsoïan, *The Paulician Heresy*, with a proposed critical reconstruction of Paulician history, Chap. 3, pp. 112–51, and of Paulician doctrine, Chap. 4, pp. 151–86.

6 Garsoïan, *The Paulician Heresy*, Chap. 5, pp. 186–231.

7 Garsoïan, *The Paulician Heresy*, pp. 183–5.

8 See, for example, Lemerle, 'L'Histoire des Pauliciens', pp. 12ff. *passim*; L. Barnard, 'The Paulicians and Iconoclasm', in A. Bryer and J. Herrin (eds), *Iconoclasm: Papers Given at the Spring Symposium of Byzantine Studies, March, 1975* (Birmingham, 1977), pp. 75–83, esp. p. 81; Coulianu, *The Tree of Gnosis*, pp. 192–4; *HCDH*, Appendix 2, 'Armenian Sources and the Paulicians', pp. 292–8 (with up-to-date discussion of the vexed problem of the relationship between the Paulicians and the Armenian Tondrakian sectarians and the eighteenth-century text, *The Key of Truth*).

9 The allegations that Paulician dualism derives from Manichaeism are repeatedly reiterated in the Byzantine sources for the heresy; for arguments that Manichaeism was in many respects a direct precursor of Paulicianism which experienced also some Marcionite influences, see D. Obolensky, *The Bogomils. A Study in Balkan Neo-Manichaeism* (Cambridge, 1948), pp. 44–7, followed by D. Angelov, *Bogomilstvoto* (Sofia, 1993), pp. 83, 97, n. 57; for arguments that Paulician dualism may have been a development of Marcionite teachings, cf., Harnack, *Marcion*, pp. 382–3 (with reservations); Grégoire, 'Les sources'; J. Anastasiu, *Oi paulikianoi* (Athens, 1959), pp. 153 ff.; M. Loos, 'Le mouvement paulicien à Byzance', *BSl*, 25, 1964, pp. 55–6; *Dualist Heresy in the Middle Ages* (Prague, 1974), pp. 34–5; for arguments for Gnostic influences on Paulician dualism, see I. Döllinger, *Beiträge zur Sektengeschichte des Mittelalters* (Munich, 1890), vol. 1, pp. 2–3; H. Söderberger, *La Religion des Cathares: études sur le gnosticisme de la basse antiquité et du moyen âge* (Uppsala, 1949), pp. 52 ff.; cf. the views of Coulianu, *The Tree of Gnosis*, pp. 190–6, who, while treating Paulicianism as a 'popular Marcionism', argues that the Marcionite influence need not have been a direct historical one. See also Lemerle, 'L'Histoire des Pauliciens', pp. 132–5, for a discussion of the parallels and the important differences between Marcionism and Paulicianism, and an emphasis on Paulician reinstatement of evangelical Christianity and the Pauline tradition.

10 Petrus Siculus, *Historia*, 33, ed. C. Astruc *et al.*, *T&M*, 4, 1970, p. 19; a distinction between an exoteric teaching, focused on the New Testament, for the use of the ordinary members of the Paulician sects and an esoteric one comprising a Paulician dualist interpretation of the Scriptures following a 'secret and oral tradition of the initiates' is emphasized by Obolensky, *The Bogomils*, p. 33; similarly, Loos, *Dualist Heresy*, p. 35, argues that the Paulician teaching of the salvation of man was a secret teaching 'revealed only to the Paulician initiates' and that this esotericism represented a 'development away from Marcionism'.

11 Petrus Siculus, *Historia*, 85–6, pp. 37–9.

12 For discussions of the evidence concerning the teachings of the Massalians,

see, for example, H. Hausherr, *Études de spiritualité orientale* (Rome, 1969), pp. 64–96; R. Staats, *Gregor von Nysa und die Messalianer* (Berlin, 1968); L. Gribomont, 'Le dossier des origines du messalianisme', in *Epektasis, Mélanges patristiques offerts au cardinal J. Daniélou* (Beauchesne, 1972), pp. 611–27; A. Guillamont, 'Le baptême de feu chez les Messaliens', in *Mélanges d'histoire des religions offerts à H.-C. Puech* (Paris, 1974), pp. 517–25; A. Louth, 'Messalianism and Pelagianism', *StP*, 17.1, 1982, 127–35 (with comments on the role of the Massalians in eastern Christian spirituality *vis-à-vis* the Augustinian trend in western Christian spirituality). According to S. Runciman, *The Medieval Manichee: A Study of the Christian Dualist Heresy* (Cambridge, 1946), p. 24, the Massalians were 'the agents that were to keep alive the rich Gnostic tradition in Byzantium' and had 'preserved for the heretics of the future a vast bulk of Gnostic literature', but this is difficult to ascertain; on the Massalians against the background of the complicated picture of sectarian and heretical trends in the early medieval Near East and Byzantium, see Obolensky, *The Bogomils*, pp. 48–51; D. Dragojlović's treatment of the Massalians in his *Bogomisltvo na Balkanu i u Maloi Aziji, I Bogomilski rodonachalnitsi* (Belgrade, 1974) is marred by the fact that he regards references to the Massalians from the eighth century onwards as authentic, and as some of them reflect the later heresiological equation between Massalianism and Bogomilism, he attributes to the Massalians the Bogomil theological dualism and anthropogony, see, for example, pp. 99–113.

13 The background to the Serbs' and the Croats' arrival in the Balkans, their Iranian origins and Slavicization, can be found in J. V. A. Fine, Jr, *The Early Medieval Balkans: A Critical Survey from the Sixth to the Late Twelfth Century* (Ann Arbor, 1983), pp. 49–59. On the Sarmatian origins of the Serbs and Croats see also R. Browning, *Byzantium and Bulgaria* (London, 1975), p. 44; Sulimirski, *The Sarmatians*, pp. 188–94; 'Sarmatians in the Polish Past', *Polish Review*, 9 : 1, 1964, pp. 47–51; F. Dvornik, *The Slavs: Their Early History and Civilization* (Boston, 1956), pp. 26–7. For recent politicized interpretations of the Croats' Iranian origins, see, for example, S. Sakač, 'The Iranian Origins of the Croats according to C. Porphyrogenitus', in A. F. Bonifačić and C. S. Mihanovich, *The Croatian Nation in its Struggle for Freedom and Independence* (Chicago, 1955); and some of the contributions in *Etnogeneza Hrvata, Ethnogenesis of the Croats*, ed. N. Budak (Zagreb, 1996). The extensive Iranian influences on the Slavs and Slavonic religion are treated more generally in Dvornik, *The Slavs*, pp. 47ff.; M. Gimbutas, *The Slavs* (London, 1971), pp. 151–70; I. Dujčev, 'Il mondo slavo e la Persia nell'alto medioevo' in *Medioevo bizantino-slavo*, 3 vols (Rome, 1965–71), vol. 2, pp. 321–424; R. Jacobson, 'Slavic Mythology' in M. Leach and P. Freund (eds), *Funk and Wagnalls Standard Dictionary of Folklore, Mythology and Legend* (New York, 1949–50), vol. 2, p. 1025ff.

14 Bianchi, 'Dualistic Aspects of Thracian Religion', p. 231.

15 Bianchi, 'Dualism' in Eliade, *Encylopedia of Religion*, vol. 4, p. 511.

16 For the Bulgarian material, see the sixteen Bulgarian legends, displaying various dualist tendencies printed in V. V. Ivanov, *Bogomilski knigi i legendi* (Sofia, 1925), pp. 328–57 (for the literary version of the south and east Slavonic cosmogonic legend, the apocryphon, *The Sea of Tiberias*, see the texts published on pp. 287–311); for discussions of the legends, cf. Dragomanov, 'Zabelezhki vŭrkhu slaviianskite religiozno-eticheski legendi', *SBNU*, 8, 1892, pp. 257, 276, and pp. 257–63; O. Dänhardt, *Natursagen, Eine Sammlung Naturdeutender Sagen, Märchen, Fäbeln und Legende 1: Sagen zum Alten Testament* (Leipzig and Berlin, 1907), pp. 2–7; W. Schmidt, *Der Ursprung der Gottesidee* (Münster, 1955), 12, pp. 72–6; for the Romanian legends see the text in Fl. Marianu, *Insectele în limba credinţele şi obiceiuvile Românilor* (Bucharest, 1903), p. 122; for an early discussion of the cosmogonic legend see N. Cartojan, *Cărţile populare in literatura româneasca* (Bucharest, 1929), vol. 1 pp. 37–9; for a more recent analysis and a summary of the Romanian publications and studies on the subject, see M. Eliade, *De Zalmoxis à Gengis-Khan* (Paris, 1970), pp. 81–3; for the Transsylvanian Gypsy variant see the text published in H. Wislocki, *Märchen und Sagen Transsylvanische Zigeuner* (Berlin, 1892), p. 1; for the Bukovinian version, see the text published in *Zeitschrift für deutsche Mythologie*, 1, p. 178 f.; for publications and discussions of the Russian legends, cf. A. N. Veselovskii, 'Razyskaniia v oblasti russkogo dukhovnogo stikha,' 11 (Dualistich-eskiia pover'ia o mirozdanii), *SORIAS*, 46, 1890, pp. 1–117; Dänhardt, *Natur-sagen*, 1, pp. 44–8; Schmidt, *Der Ursprung*, 12, pp. 50–62; for an updated discussion, see V. S. Kuznetsova, 'Dualisticheskie legendi o sotvorenii mira', PhD dissertation, Russian Academy of Science, A. M. Gor'ki Institute of World Literature, Moscow, 1995, Chaps 2 and 7; 'Sotvorenie mira v vostochnoslavian-skikh dualisticheskikh legendakh i apokrificheskoi knizhnosti' in V. Petrukhin *et al.* (eds), *Ot Bytiia k Iskhodu. Otrazhenie bibleiskikh siuzhetov v slavianskoi i evreiskoi narodnoi kul'ture* (Moscow, 1998), pp. 64–74; for early publications and discussions of the Ukrainian legends, see M. Dragomanov, *Malorusskiia narodnyia predaniia i razskazy* (Kiev, 1876), 1, p. 89; P. Chubinskii, *Trudy etnografichesko-statisticheskoi ekspeditsii v zapadno-russkii krai . . . Iugo-zapadnyi otdel. Materialy i izsledovaniia sobrannyia P. P. Chubinskom* (St Petersburg, 1872), 1, p. 145; for new discussions of the legends, see Kuznetsova, 'Dualisticheskie legendy', Chaps 2 and 7; 'Sotvorenie mira', pp. 60–1; for the Polish legends, see the texts published by I. Piatowska, 'Obyczaje ludu ziemi sieradzkiez', *Lud*, 4 : 4, 1898, pp. 414–15, and B. Gustawicz, 'Kilka szczegòlow ludoznawczych w powiatu bobreckiego', *Lud*, 7 : 3 1902, pp. 267–8; for the Baltic versions, see, for example, the Estonian legend published in O. Loorits, *Grundzüge des estonischen Volksglauben* (Uppsala and Lund, 1949), pp. 455–6.

17 This diabology is recorded in the legend from Bukovina, published in

Zeitschrift für deutsche Mythologie, 1, p. 178 f., and in the Polish variant published by Piatowska, 'Obyczaje ludu ziemi sieradzkiez'.

18 This tradition is presented in a Vogul legend published in A. Strauss, *Die Bulgaren* (Leipzig, 1898), pp. 14 ff.; cf. the Mordvinian legend published *ibid.*, pp. 17–19.

19 This tradition is attested in the Transylvanian Gypsy legend published in Wislocki, *Märchen und Sagen Transylvanische Zigeuner*. For arguments that the legend presents parallels to Altaian and Iranian traditions, see Dänhardt, *Natursagen*, pp. 35–6.

20 This tradition is presented in a Bulgarian legend published by M. Drinov, *Periodichesko spisanie*, 8, 1884, pp. 124–6.

21 Published in Veselovskii, 'Razyskaniia', p. 7; Strauss, *Die Bulgaren*, p. 16; Dänhardt, *Natursagen*, p. 60.

22 Published respectively in L. Adam, *Revue de philologie et d'ethnographie*, 1, 1874, p. 9 and Dänhardt, *Natursagen*, 1, p. 63.

23 Published in T. Lehtisalo, 'Entwurf einer Mythologie der Jurak-Samojeden', *Mémoires de la Société finno-ougrienne*, 53, 1927, pp. 8 ff.

24 See the Vogul legend published in Strauss, *Die Bulgaren*, pp. 14 ff.

25 See the Samoyed legend published in Lehtisalo, 'Entwurf einer Mythologie der Jurak-Samojeden', pp. 9 ff. in which the opponent of God, Ngaa (Death), cooperates in the creation of the world from the beginning and attacks the newly created first man – the myth preserves echoes of the theme of the bringing up of earth from the primal waters which is duly performed by Ngaa. Another Samoyed myth in P. I. Tretiakov, *Turuchanskii krai, ego priroda i zhiteli* (St Petersburg, 1871), pp. 201–2, associates the themes of the earth-diving and the flood.

26 See, for example, the northern Russian legend published in Veselovskii, 'Razyskaniia', p. 69, and the legend in Schmidt, *Der Ursprung*, 12, p. 56. For the interrelationship between the Russian cosmogonic legends of this kind and Finno-Ugrian as well as Uralo-Ugrian cosmogonic myths, see N. Korobka, 'Obraz ptitsy, tvoriashtei mir v russkoi narodnoi poezii i pis' menosti', *Izvestiia Otdela russkoi iazyka i sloves 'nosti*, 14, No. 4, pp. 193–4; A. M. Zolotarev, *Rodovoi stroi i pervobytnaia mifologiia* (Moscow, 1964), pp. 278–81; V. V. Napol'skikh, 'Mify o voznikoveniia zemli v praural'skoi kosmogonii: rekonstruktsii, paraleli, evoliutsiia', *Sovetskaia etnografiia*, 1990, 1, pp. 65–74; 'Drevneishie finno-ugorskie mify o vozniknovenii zemli', in *Mirovozzrenie finno-ugorskikh narodov*, ed. I. N. Gemuev (Novosibirsk, 1990).

27 Published in Ia. Golovatskii, *Narodnyia pesni galitskoi i ugorskoi Russi* (Moscow, 1878), 2, p. 5.

28 Published in A. Nowosielski, *Lud ukrainski* (Vilnus, 1857), 1, pp. 103 ff. Cf. the discussions of the text in Veselovski, 'Razyskaniia', pp. 2–3; Dragomanov,

'Zabelezhki', 10, pp. 26–65; Dobrev, *Proizkhod i znachenie*, pp. 116–18, 125–6, 129; Kuznetsova, 'Dualisticheskie legendi', Chap. 3.

29 M. Eliade defines this intensification of the dualist tendencies in these East European cosmogonic legends as 'dualist hardening' of the myth, see *A History of Religious Ideas*, tr. A. Hiltelbeitel and D. Apostolos-Cappadona (Chicago, 1985), pp. 10, 29 ff.

30 Published in W. Radloff and H. T. Katanov, *Proben der Volksliteratur der türkischen Stämme* (St Petersburg, 1907), vol. 9, pp. 522–8; on the Abakan Tatars, see the up-to-date discussion and references in S. I. Vainshtein's notes to the Russian translation of W. Radloff, *Aus Sibirien: lose Blätter aus dem Tagebuche eines reisenden Linguisten* (Leipzig, 1883); V. V. Radlov, *Iz Sibiri: stranitsy dnevnika* (Moscow, 1989), tr. K. D. Tsivina and B. E. Chistova, edited with, notes and aferword by S. I. Vainshtein, pp. 586–7; see also pp. 589, 600, 609, 610, 644, 645, 658, 660, 661.

31 For reports of beliefs and material concerning Erlik and his links with shamanism and afterlife, see G. N. Potanin, *Ocherki severo-zapadnoi Mongolii*, 4 (St Petersburg, 1884), pp. 62, 64, 71, 79, 88, 91, 129, 180, 241–5, 259, 290–1, 327–8, 415, 481, 516, 616, 738, 761, 868; A. V. Anokhin, *Materialy po shamanstvu u altaitsev, Sbornik Muzeiia antropologii i etnografii*, 4, vyp. 2 (Leningrad, 1924), p. 88; B. E. Petri, *Staraia vera buriatskogo naroda* (Irkutsk, 1928), p. 20; V. Diószegi, 'Pre-Islamic Shamanism of the Baraba Turks and Some Ethnogenetic Conclusions', in *Shamanism in Siberia*, ed. V. Diószegi and M. Hoppál (Budapest, 1978), pp. 122–4; U. Marazzi (ed.), *Testi dello Sciamanesimo siberiano e centroasiatico* (Turin, 1984), pp. 114–16, 131–7, 153–4, 158, 182, 197–8, 389, 405, 434; M. B. Kenin-Lopsan, *Shamanic Songs and Myths of Tuva*, ed. M. Hoppál, with the assistance of C. Buckbee (Budapest, 1997), pp. 9, 14–15, 20, 64, 74. For the different treatment of Erlik in Buriat and Iakut shamanism, cf. T. M. Mikhailov, *Iz istorii buriatskogo shamanizma* (Novosibirsk, 1980), pp. 168–71, and G. R. Galdanova, *Dolamaistkie verovaniia buriat* (Novosibirsk, 1987), pp. 62–3. For discussions of Altaic traditions about Erlik, cf. U. Harva, *Die religiösen Vorstellungen der altaischen Völker* (Porvoo, 1938), pp. 343–63, *passim*; M. Eliade, *Le Chamanisme et les techniques archaïques de l'extase* (Paris, 1951), pp. 148, 162, 184ff., 199–200; N. A. Alekseev, *Shamanizm tiurkoiazychnykh narodov Sibiri* (Novosibirsk, 1984), pp. 52–63; J.-P. Roux, *La religion des Turcs et des Mongols* (Paris, 1984), pp. 126, 129.

32 Published in Radloff, *Aus Sibirien*, vol. 1, p. 360. On the Lebed Tatars see the up-to-date discussion and references in Vainshtein, 'Primechaniia', in Radlov, *Iz Sibiri*, p. 594; see also pp. 593, 608, 619, 620, 657.

33 Published in G. N. Potanin, *Ocherki severo-zapadnoi Mongolii*, 4 (St Petersburg, 1884), pp. 218–21; on the Kuznetsk Tatars, see Veinshtein, 'Primechaniia', in Radlov, *Iz Sibiri*, p. 582; see also pp. 589, 590, 595.

34 Published in Radloff, *Aus Sibirien*, vol. 2, pp. 3–5.
35 Radloff and Katanov, *Proben der Volksliteratur* (St Petersburg, 1866), vol. 1,
pp. 175–84. On the Iranian influences on archaic Turkic religious traditions,
see J.-P. Roux, 'Turkic Religions', in Eliade *et al.*, *Encyclopedia of Religion*, vol.
15, p. 88; Roux, *La religion des Turcs et des Mongols*, pp. 26, 28–32, B. Ögel,
Türk mitolojisi (Ankara 1971), pp. 419–31; on the strong Iranian and Zoroastrian residues in the beliefs of the Uzbeks in Khoresm, see G. P. Snesarev,
Relikty domusul'manskikh verovanii i obriadov u uzbekov Khorezma (Moscow,
1969), pp. 30–3, 56–62, 68–70, 283–4. On the Iranian origin of the name of
the Mongol sky deity Khormusta (and its Central Asian and Siberian variants
such as Kurbistan) and its association with the Iranian Ahura Mazda, see A.
Schiefner's introduction in Radloff, *Proben der Volksliteratur*, vol. 1, p. x; D.
Banzarov, *Chernaia vera, ili Shamanstvo u mongoli*, in *Sobrannye sochineniia*
(Moscow, 1955), pp. 56, 59–60; N. L. Zhukovskaia, *Lamaism i rannie formy
religii* (Moscow, 1977), p. 100; W. Heissig, 'Mongol Religion', in Eliade *et al.*,
Encyclopedia of Religion, vol. 10, 1987, p. 54 (who considers Khormusta Tengri
an Iranian Zoroastrian import in Mongol popular religion); on Khormusta in
Mongolian Buddhist traditions, see A. M. Pozdneyev, *Religion and Ritual in
Society: Lamaist Buddhism in 19th-Century Mongolia*, ed. J. R. Krueger, tr. A.
Raun and L. Raun (Bloomington, 1978), pp. 107, 113, 147, 373, 380, 481.
36 The Mongol myth is published in Potanin, *Ocherki*, pp. 220–4; on the figures
of the rival demiurge and God's adversary in this Mongol myth, see, for
example, Bianchi, *Il dualismo religioso*, p. 162.
37 See the Buriat myths published in S. Shashkov, *Shamanstvo v Sibiri* (St
Petersburg, 1884), p. 30, and in *Skazaniia buriat, zapisannyia raznymi
sobirateliami*, Zapiski Vostochno-Sibirskogo Otdela Russkogo arkheologich-
eskogo obshchestva, I, 2 (Irkutsk, 1890), pp. 65–7; see the myths of the Enisei
Evenki (with strong dualist elements) in G. V. Vasilevich, *Sbornik materialov
po evenkiiskomu tunguskomu fol'kloru* (Leningrad, 1936), pp. 29–32; 'Rannie
predstavleniia o mire u evenkov', in *Issledovaniia i materialy po voprosu
pervobytnykh i religioznykh verovanii* ((Moscow, 1959), p. 173; see also the
Enisei Ostiak myth in V. Anuchin, *Ocherk shamanstva u eniseiskikh ostiakov*,
Sbornik Muzeiia Antropologii i Etnografii pri Imperatorskoi Akademii Nauk
(St Petersburg, 1914), p. 14.
38 See the Iakut myths published in V. I. Priklonskii, 'Tri goda v Iakutskoi
oblasti', *Zhivaia starina*, 4, 1891, p. 66, and V. L. Seroshevskii (W. L.
Sieroszewski), *Iakuti* (St Petersburg, 1896), I, p. 653.
39 It would be impossible to include here references to studies of the role of birds
generally in archaic cosmogonies and systems of belief, hence the following
references will be confined to Central Asia and Siberia. On the cosmic bird in
cosmogonic traditions in Central Asia, see, for example, Iu. A. Rapoport,
'Kosmogonicheskii siuzhet na khorezmiiskikh sosudakh', *Sredniaia Aziia v*

drevnosti i srednovekovie, ed. B. G. Gafurov and B. A. Litvinskii (Moscow, 1977), pp. 58–72 (with a discussion of Indian and Iranian parallels); on the water bird in earlier Scythian art and mythology, see D. S. Raevskii, 'O semantike odnogo iz obrazov skifskogo izkusstva', *Novoe v arkheologii. Sbornik posviashtennyi 70-letiu A. B. Artsikhovskogo* (Moscow, 1972); on the role of birds in shamanistic beliefs, practices and costume in Central Asia and Siberia, see, for example, Seroshevskii, *Iakuti*, pp. 632, 646; U. Holmberg (Harva), *Finno-Ugric Siberian Mythology*, in J. A. MacCulloch (ed.), *Mythology of All Races* (Boston, 1927), vol. 4, pp. 498–500, 509, 514–16; *Die religiösen Vorstellungen*, pp. 103–4; Eliade, *Le Chamanisme et les techniques archaïques de l'extase*, pp. 149 ff.; G. M. Vasilevich, *Evenki* (Leningrad, 1969), pp. 214–15, 219, 223, 254–5; S. V. Ivanov, 'Some Aspects of the Study of Siberian Shamanism', in *Shamanism in Siberia*, ed. V. Diószegi and M. Hoppál, pp. 33, 36; E. A. Alekseenko, 'Categories of the Ket Shamans', *ibid.*, p. 256; 'Dances of Yakut Shamans', *ibid.*, p. 304; 'Notes on Selkup Shamanism', *ibid.*, p. 380; T. M. Mikhailov, *Buriatskii shamanizm* (Novosibirsk, 1987), pp. 23, 27, 108–9; 'Buriat shamanism', in *Shamanism. Soviet Studies of Traditional Religion in Siberia and Central Asia*, ed. M. M. Balzer (New York and London, 1990), pp. 58, 106.

40 On the Aryan Indian earth-diving myth, cf. the comments in Dragomanov, 'Zabelezhki', pp. 284–5; F. B. J. Kuiper, 'An Austro-Asiatic Myth in the Rig-Veda', *Mededelingen der koninklijke Nederlandse Akademie van Wetenschappen*, new series, 13, 7, 1950, pp. 163–82; Eliade, *De Zalmoxis*, pp. 116–19.

41 For Pre-Aryan cosmogonic earth-diving traditions, see, for example, the Bihor myth in R. B. S. C. Roy, *The Bihors, a Little Known Jungle Tribe of Chota Nigpur* (Ranchi, 1925), pp. 398–400, and the Munda (Savara) myth in V. Elwin, *The Religion of an Indian Tribe* (Oxford, 1955), pp. 86–7. Generally, for a discussion of the earth-diving cosmogonic traditions in India and Indochina within the framework of the other Asian traditions, see L. Walk, 'Die Verbreitung des Tauchmotifs in der Urmeerschöpfungs- (und Sinflut-) Sagen, *Mitteilungen der anthropologischen Gesellschaft in Wien*, 63, 1933, pp. 60–76; cf. Eliade, *De Zalmoxis*, pp. 119–23.

42 For the Dyak myth from Borneo, see W. Schmidt, *Grundlinien einer Vergleichung der Religion und Mythologie der austronesischen Völker* (Vienna, 1910), p. 7.

43 The earth-diver myth can be found in a variety of forms in many areas of North American except for Arizona and New Mexico; for the distribution of the myth among the North American Indians, see A. B. Rooth, 'The Creation Myths of the North American Indians', *Anthropos*, 52, 1957, pp. 497–508. For North American Indian versions of the myth, see, for example, the myths in J. MacLean, 'Blackfoot Mythology', *Journal of American Folklore*, 1883, 6, pp. 166–7; J. Mooney, *Myths of the Cherokee. 19th Annual*

Report of the Bureau of Ethnology, Pt. 1 (Washington DC, 1897–8), pp. 239–40; R. H. Lowie, 'The Assiniboine', *Anthropological Papers of the American Museum of Natural History* (New York, 1909), 4 (1), p. 1. As in the abovementioned Samoyed myth (n. 25), some North American cosmogonies bring together the motifs of the earth-diving and the flood; see, for example, the myths in H. P. Alexander, *North American Mythology, Mythology of All Races*, 10 (Boston, 1916), pp. 42 ff.

44 For Iroquois cosmogonic myths, incorporating the earth-diver theme and the motif of the divine twins, see the Onondaga, Seneca and Mohawk creation stories in J. N. B. Hewitt, *Iroquois Cosmology* (Washington DC, 1899–1900), 1, pp. 141–339; cf. W. Muller, *Die Religionen der Waldlandindianer Nordamerikas* (Berlin, 1956), pp. 119 ff.; cf. also the Huron myth in H. Hale, 'Huron Folklore', *Journal of American Folklore*, 1888, 1, pp. 175–83. For early arguments that the Iroquois myth of the good and bad twin betrays an Iranian influence, see Dänhardt, *Natursagen*, 1, pp. 10–11, 79; see, however, the observations of M. Eliade, *The Quest: History and Meaning in Religion* (Chicago, 1969), pp. 147–9; A. Hultkranz, *Les Religions des indiens primitifs de l'Amérique: Essai d'une synthèse typologique et historique* (Stockholm, 1963), pp. 41 ff.

45 A. N. Veselovskii, *Slavianskie skazaniia o Solomone i Kitovrase i zapadnye legendy o Morol'fe i Merline* (St Petersburg, 1872), p. 164.

46 Veselovskii, 'Dualisticheskie poveriia o mirozdanii', pp. 4–5.

47 Veselovskii, 'K voprosu o dualisticheskikh kosmogoniiakh', p. 123.

48 See note 58 below.

49 Dragomanov, 'Zabelezhki vŭrkhu slavianskite narodno-eticheski legendi. 2. Dualistichesko mirotvorenie', *SBNU*, 10, 1894, pp. 10–62; see also his 'Zabelezhki vŭrkhu slaviianskite religiozno-eticheski legendi', *SBNU*, 8, 1892, pp. 257, 276; see also the similar views of Dänhardt, *Natursagen*, pp.7, 14, 37; Harva, *Die religiösen Vorstellungen*, p. 108.

50 Dragomanov, 'Zabelezhki vŭrkhu slaviianskite narodno-eticheski legendi', p. 9.

51 See, for example, A. Veselovskii, Razyskaniia, v oblasti russkago dukhovnogo stikha', 11, pp. 4–5; cf. also Dänhardt, *Natursagen*, 1, pp. 7ff., 34 ff.; 34 ff.; Cartojan, *Cărţile populare*, p. 39, in which the archaic layer is defined as 'Indo-Iranian'.

52 For arguments that the origins of the earth-diver theme are to be found in Iran, see Dänhardt, *Natursagen*, 1, pp. 14ff; for an opinion that it spread from India, see Harva, *Die religiösen Vorstellungen*, p. 108; *Finno-Ugric, Siberian Mythology*, pp. 328, 331; Dragomanov argues that the myth is a combination of Chaldean–Indian cosmogonic traditions and Iranian dualist notions, 'Zabelezhki', 8, p. 278 – for this Indo-Iranian theory, see also Cartojan, *Cărţile populare*, p. 39; cf. J. Feldmann, *Paradies und Sundenfall* (Leipzig and

Berlin, 1907), pp. 337 ff., 381 ff. For early attempts to classify the earth-diving myths and arguments for a maritime (island) origin of the oldest versions, see H. de Charencey, *Une Legende cosmogonique* (Havre, 1884); for a similar thesis that the motif originated in a coastal or island area like that of eastern Asia, see Rooth, 'The Creation Myths', p. 500; for arguments that the myth was part of the belief systems of the Paleolithic and Neolithic peoples of Northern Asia from where it spread to South Asia and North America, see Schmidt, *Der Ursprung*, 6, pp. 40 ff., 233; 12, pp. 166 ff.; J. Haekel, 'Prof. Wilhelm Schmidts Bedeutung für die Religionsgeschichte des vorkolumbischen Amerika', *Saeculum*, 7, 1956, pp. 26 ff.; cf. also G. Hatt, *Asiatic Influences in American Folklore* (Copenhagen, 1949), p. 30.

53 The Mesopotamian myth of the feats of the lion-headed thunderbird, Anzu, is extant in two main versions: texts in B. Hrǔska, *Der Mythenadler Anzu in Literatur und Vorstellung* (Budapest, 1975), pp. 107–74; see also H. W. F. Saggs, 'Additions to Anzu', *Archiv für Orientsforschung*, 33, 1986, pp. 1–29. The relationship between the Anzu-bird in the Old/Standard Babylonian versions and Imdugud (the Sumerian form of the name of the thunderbird) in the Sumerian *Epic of Lugalbanda* (where it has different characteristics) remains controversial and in dispute: cf. S. N. Kramer, *History Begins at Sumer* (New York, 1959), p. 203; Hrǔska, *Der Mythenadler Anzu*, pp. 35–77; T. Jacobsen, *Toward the Image of Tammuz and Other Essays* (Cambridge, Mass., 1970), pp. 3–4, 57, 207; *Treasures of Darkness: A History of Mesopotamian Religion* (New Haven, 1976), pp. 115, 132, 135, 127–8; H. W. F. Saggs, *The Encounter with the Divine in Mesopotamia and Israel* (London, 1978), pp. 59, 101. For the place of the myth of the Anzu-bird in the ancient Near Eastern divine combat mythic narratives, see N. Forsyth, *The Old Enemy. Satan and the Combat Myths* (Princeton, NJ, 1987), pp. 50–4.

54 For the Asiatic origin of the North American earth-diver myths and the problem of the dating of the Asiatic influence, cf. Hutt, *Asiatic Influences in American Folklore*; E. W. Count, 'The Earth-Diver and the Rival Twins: A Clue to Time Correlation in North-Eurasiatic and North American Mythology', *Selected Papers of the XXIXth International Congress of Americanists*, ed. S. Tax, 3 (Chicago, 1952), pp. 55–62; Rooth, 'The Creation Myths', p. 500; Schmidt, *Der Ursprung*, 6, pp. 40 ff., 233; 12, pp. 166 ff.; Haekel, 'Prof. Wilhelm Schmidts Bedeutung'.

55 Eliade, *De Zalmoxis*, pp. 126–9.

56 For an attempt to locate the areas of 'Eurasian dualism' as a part of a larger tradition of cosmogonic dualism found also in Australia, Oceania, etc., see Bianchi, *Il dualismo religioso*, Chap. 2, pp. 26–57; cf. the objections of Couliano to the diffusionist aspect of Bianchi's reconstruction of the spread of this cosmogonic dualist tradition in his *Tree of Gnosis*, pp. 45 ff; see also Bianchi's later treatment of the theme in 'Dualistische Mythologien in

Nordasien und Amerika', in Preissler and Seiwert, *Gnosisforschung*, pp. 379–89.

57 Jacobson, 'Slavic Mythology', p. 1025.

58 The theory of proto-Slavonic dualism was based on Helmold's statement concerning the alleged existence of a dualism of a good and a bad god among the twelfth-century Polabian pagan Slavs: *Helmoldi Presbyteri Chronica Slavorum*, in C. H. Meyer, *Fontes historiae religionis slavicae* (Berlin, 1931), 1, col. 52. For early formulations of the theory of this dualism and its supposed influence on medieval dualism and the Slavonic cosmogonic legends, see A. Afanas'ev, *Poeticheskie vozzreniia slavian na prirodu* (Moscow, 1865) ii, p. 485; G. Schmidt, *Histoire et doctrine de la secte des Cathares ou Albigeois* (Paris and Geneva, 1849), 1, p. 7; 2, pp. 271 ff. For an early criticism and later refutations of the theory see, for example, V. M. Mochulskii, 'O mnimom dualizme v mifologii slavian', *Russkii filologicheskii vestnik*, 17, 1887, pp. 173–7; Ivanov, *Bogomilski knigi*, pp. 361–4; A. Brückner, *Mitologia Slava* (Bologna, 1924), pp. 203 ff.; Vynckie, 'The Religion of the Slavs', pp. 648–66, esp. pp. 658, 664–5. For recent attempts to rehabilitate Helmold's testimony of proto-Slavonic dualism, see, for example, V. Pisani, *La religioni dei Celti e dei Balto-Slavi* (Milan, 1940), pp. 40ff.; Jacobson, 'Slavic Mythology', pp. 1025ff.; I. Dobrev, *Proizkhod i znachenie na praslaviianskoto konsonantno i diftongichno sklonenie* (Sofia, 1982), pp. 124–37; see also the commentary on Slavic 'dualism' in Eliade, *De Zalmoxis*, pp. 93–7.

59 Frye, *The Heritage of Persia*, p. 159, with a discussion of the Iranian presence and cultural influence in the steppes prior to the advent of the Huns. On nomadism in the Eurasian steppes and its main types in general, see, for example, A. M. Khazanov, *Sotsialnaia istoriia skitov* (Moscow, 1969); *The Nomads and the Outside World*, 2nd edn, tr. J. Crookenden (Madison, 1994), pp. 17–25, 233–63 (discussion of nomadic statehood in the Eurasian steppes, cf. I. Boba, *Nomads, Northmen and Slavs* (Wiesbaden and The Hague, 1967), pp. 46–56); G. E. Markov, *Kochevniki Azii* (Moscow, 1976), pp. 8–49; S. Pletneva, *Kochevniki srednovekoviia* (Moscow, 1982); the relevant recent contributions in Genito, *The Archaeology of the Steppes: Methods and Strategies* and Davis-Kimball, *Nomads of the Eurasian Steppes*. For further classifications of the principal types of nomad pastoralism, see also R. Patai, 'Nomadism: Middle Eastern and Central Asian', *SJA*, 7:4, 1951, pp. 401–14; E. Bacon, 'Types of Pastoral Nomadism in Central and Southwest Asia', *SJA*, 10:1, pp. 44–68; C. Rathjens, 'Geographische Grundlagen und Verbreitung des Nomadismus', in W. Kraus (ed.), *Nomadismus als Entwicklungsproblem* (Bielefeld, 1969), pp. 19–28.

60 See, for example, D. Eremeev and M. Semashko, 'Pastoral and Nomadic People in Ethnic History', in G. Seaman (ed.), *Foundation of Empire, Archeology and Art of the Eurasian Steppes* (Los Angeles, 1989), pp. 223–33, esp. pp. 230–2; on the

process of the Turkicization of the older Iranian and Ugrian groups in the Eurasian steppes in the early Middle Ages, see, for example, P. Golden, *Khazar Studies* (Budapest, 1980), vol. I, pp. 14, 21, 28–9; A. P. Novosel'tsev, *Khazarskoe gosudarstvo i ego rol' v istorii Vostochnoi Evropy i Kavkaza* (Moscow, 1990), pp. 69–71, 80–1. On the late period of Sarmatian culture in the Eurasian steppes (mid-first to fourth centuries AD), including its latter stages, when Sarmatian power was undermined by Gothic and then Hunnic expansion in the steppes, see Sulimirski, *The Sarmatians*, Chap. 5; V. I. Kostenko, *Sarmaty Samarsko-Orelskogo mezhdurechiia III v. do n.e. – IV v. n. e.* (Dnepropetrovsk, 1986); M. Moshkova, 'Pozdnesarmatskaia kultura', in A. I. Meliukova (ed.), *Stepi evropeiskoi chasti SSSR v skifo-sarmatskoe vremiia* (Moscow, 1989), pp. 191–202 (see also O. Dashevskaia's chapter on the late Scyths, pp.125–47); 'Late Sarmatian Culture', in Davis-Kimball, *Nomads of the Eurasian Steppes*, pp. 149–65; I. B. Sergackov, 'The Sarmatians of the Volga-Don Steppes and Rome in the First Centuries AD', in Genito, *Archaeology of the Steppes*, pp. 263–79.

61 The Bulgars were placed between Iran and Turkestan in a seventh-century Armenian geographical tradition; see text in S. T. Eremiian, *Armeniia po 'Ashharashuitzu' (Armianskaia geografia VII v.)*, (Erevan, 1963), p. 101, which alludes to four Bulgar tribes residing in the Caucasus–Azov–Caspian area. There is evidence for what seems to be a late sixth-century Bulgar migration from the Pamir region to the Azov–Don area in the chronicle of Michael the Syrian, see J. Marquart, *Osteuropäische und ostasiatische Streifzüge* (Leipzig, 1903), pp. 479–80, 484–5; J.-B. Chabot, *Chronique de Michel le Syrien, patriarche Jacobite*, 4 vols (Paris, 1899–1924), vol. 2, pp. 363–4. There is also evidence of an early Bulgar presence in Armenia (see the reference in the fifth-century chronicle of Moses of Khorene, *Istoriia Armenii Moiseiia Khorenskogo*, newly tr. N. O. Emin (Moscow, 1893), pp. 55–6, 62) and in the northern Caucasus, where they were reported to have founded their own cities in Zacharias Rhetor's *Ecclesiastical History* (mid sixth-century): Zacharias Rhetor, *Die Sogenannte Kirchengeschichte des Zacharias Rhetor*, XII, 7, tr. K. Ahrens and G. Krüger (Leipzig, 1899), p. 253.

62 For the religious situation in Central Asia during late antiquity and the early Middle Ages, characterized by competition and interchange between Zoroastrianism, Buddhism, Nestorian Christianity and Manichaeism, see the up-to-date general discussion in *History of Civilisation in Central Asia*, vol. 3, *At the Crossroads of Civilisations* AD 250 to 750, ed. B. A. Litvinsky *et al.* (Paris, 1996), Chap. 18, 'Religion and Religious Movements'; on the socio-political development of Sogdiana *vis-à-vis* its diverse religious climate, see O. I. Smirnova, *Ocherki iz istorii Sogda* (Moscow, 1970) Chap. 1. On the unsolved questions concerning the encounter between Zoroastrianism and Buddhism in Central Asia, see R. N. Frye, 'Buddhism, Competitor of Zoroastrianism in Central Asia', in *K. R. Cama Oriental Institute, Second International Congress*

Proceedings, pp. 238–43; on the interrelationship between Buddhism and Manichaeism in the region, see n. 92 to ch. 2 above and on the character of this interrelationship in Turkic Buddhist and Manichaean milieu, see H.-J. Klimkeit, 'Buddhism in Turkish Central Asia', *Numen*, 37, 1990, pp. 53–70; on the presence of Zoroastrian traditions in the culture of Ferghana, see the summary of the evidence in N. G. Gorbunova, *The Culture of Ancient Ferghana VI Century BC–VI Century AD* (Oxford, 1986), p. 196; on the Zoroastrian influences on the Iranian-speaking Saka groups in the Pamir mountains area, see B. A. Litvinskii, *Drevnie kochevniki 'kryshi mira'* (Moscow, 1972), pp. 149–56.

63 On the ethnic and cultural symbiosis between the Bulgars and the Alans in the Pontic steppes and the use of the term 'Alan-Bulgar', see, for example, S. Pletneva, *Ot kochevii k gorodam* (Moscow, 1967), pp. 4–7, 184–9; *Khazary* (Moscow, 1976), pp. 55–7; 'O sviazakh alano-bolgarskikh plemen podon'a so slavianami v VIII–IX vv.', *SA*, 6, 1, 1962, pp. 83–5; G. A. Fedorov-Davydov, *Kochevniki Vostochnoi Evropy pod vlast' iu Zolotoordynskikh khanov* (Moscow, 1966), pp. 163–6 (discussing the latter period of the tenth to the fourteenth centuries); V. S. Flerov, 'Rasprostranenie loshtenoi keramiki na territorii Saltovo-Maiatskoi kul'tury', *PP*, 2 (Sofia, 1981), pp. 170–82. V. Gjuzelev, 'The Protobulgarians, A Pre-History of Asparouhian Bulgaria', in *Medieval Bulgaria, Byzantine Empire, Black Sea–Venice–Genoa*, (Villach, 1988), p. 14; Novosel'tsev, *Khazarskoe gosudarstvo*, p. 84. The controversy surrounding the origins of the Bulgars still continues and is likely to continue; for recent reinstatements of the three influential theories that the Bulgars were predominantly of Iranian, Turkic or Ugrian stock, see respectively, Ts. Tafradzhiiska, 'Orientalistikatai prabŭlgaristikata', in *Istoriia na bŭlgarite: potrebnost ot nov podhod, Preotsenki*, 1 (Sofia, 1998), pp. 91–107; I. Bozhilov and H. Dimitrov, 'Protobulgarica', *BBg*, 9, 1995, pp. 7–62; Novosel'tsev, *Khazarskoe gosudarstvo*, pp. 72–3. A recent reassessment of the problem has taken into account the complex situation in the Eurasian steppes and the Bulgars' previous participation in steppe federation, presenting strong arguments that while the Bulgar aristocracy comprised Bulgar, Ugrian and Turkic elements, the rest of the Danubian Bulgar tribes were predominantly of 'east European Iranian extraction', R. Rashev, 'Za proizkhoda na prabŭlgarite', in *Studia protobulgarica et mediaevalia europensia, V chest na Prof V. Beshevliev* (Veliko Tŭrnovo, 1993), pp. 23–35. The related problem of the original Bulgar language has proven equally controversial and cannot be considered solved, as demonstrated by its entirely conflicting classifications, among others, by A. Baksakov, *Altaiskaia sem'ia iazykov i ee izucheniia* (Moscow, 1981), p. 17; K. H. Menges, *Introduction to Turkic Studies* (Cleveland, 1963), p. 88. Such classifications are usually based on the fragmentary remains of 'Volga Bulgar' language dating from the period of the linguistic Turkicization of the state of

Volga Bulgaria and thus represent a very unsafe basis for generalizations concerning the nature of the original language (on the difficulty of establishing the nature of the original languages of nomadic Eurasian people after their partial of full linguistic Turkicization, cf. V. F. Genning and A. H. Halikov, *Rannie bolgari na Volge* (Moscow, 1964), pp. 184, 190–1; L. Gumilev, *Drevniaia Rus' i Velikaia step'* (Moscow, 1989), p. 47. On the Iranian element in the remnants of Bulgar language and titles, cf., for example, V. Beshevliev, *Pŭrvobŭlgarite, Bit i kultura*, (Sofia, 1981), pp. 41ff.; 'Iranski elementi u pŭrvobŭlgarite', in *Antichnoe obshchestvo, Trudy konferentsii po izucheniiu problem antichnosti* (Moscow, 1967), pp. 237–48; F. Altheim, *Geschichte der Hunnen*, 5 vols (Berlin, 1962–75), vol. 1, pp. 37, 50–51, 214–15, vol. 4, p. 39, n. 6; B. Von Arnim, 'Turkotatarische Beiträge 2. Prinzipielles zur Frage nach Sprache und Volkstum der Urbulgaren', *ZSP*, 10, 1933, pp. 349–51; P. Tsvetkov, *A History of the Balkans. A Regional Overview from a Bulgarian Perspective* (San Francisco, 1995), pp. 10–57, 66–7 *passim*, etc.

64 Evidence for these Bulgar incursions and campaigns may be found in: Marcellinus Comes, *Chronicon, MGH A. A.*, 9, pp. 94, 96, 103, 104, 108; Ioannes Zonaras, *Epitome historiarum*, ed. Th. Büttner-Wobst (Bonn, 1897), vol. 3, pp. 137, 140–1, 144; Theophanes Confessor, *Chronographia*, ed. C. de Boor (Leipzig, 1883), pp. 143, 147, 217–19; Procopius Caesariensis, *Opera omnia*, ed. J. Haury and G. Wirth, 4 vols (Leipzig, 1963–4), vol. 1, pp. 163–4, 602–3; vol. 2, pp. 114–15, 162–3 *passim*.

65 O. Pritsak, *The Origin of Rusi*, vol. 1, *Old Scandinavian Sources Other than the Sagas* (Cambridge, Mass., 1981), p. 61, with extensive discussion of the cultural and religious situation in the Eurasian steppes in the period (pp. 56–73). According to Pritsak, in the Eurasian steppes and particularly in the Bosphorus area, Hellenism, understood as a 'marriage of cultures', survived the decline of classical Mediterranean Hellenism after 31 BC and 'continued to flourish until the tenth and eleventh centuries' (*The Origin of Rus*, p. 72); see also his 'The Role of the Bosporus Kingdom and Late Hellenism as the Basis for the Medieval Cultures of the Territories North of the Black Sea', in *Islamic and Judaeo-Christian World*, pp. 3–22.

66 B. B. Piotrovskii (ed.), *Istoriia narodov severnogo Kavkaza is drevneishikh vremen do kontsa XVIIIv.* (Moscow, 1988), pp. 112–14, 136–7.

67 See the discussion of the archaeological evidence in, among others, Pletneva, *Ot kochevii k gorodam*, pp. 5ff., 48, 186 ff.; 'Drevnie bolgary v basseine Dona i Priazovia', in *PP*, 2, 1981, pp. 9–18; *Khazary*, p. 52; I. A. Baranov, 'Nekotorye itogi izuchennia tiurko-bolgarskikh pamiatnikov Kryma', *PP*, 2, pp. 57–71; M. Artamanov, *Istoriia Khazar* (Leningrad, 1962), pp. 288–323; P. Iuhas, 'Kŭde da tŭrsim tiurksko-bŭlgarskiia grad Bakat' (tr. D. Boliarov), *Tiurko-bŭlgari i madzhari* (Sofia, 1985), pp. 230–1.

68 See, for example, N. Merpert, *K voprosu o dreveneishikh bolgarskikh plemenakh*

(Kazan, 1957); Artamanov, *Istoriia Khazar*, pp. 309 ff.; Pletneva, *Ot kochevii k gorodam*; *Khazary*, pp. 43 ff.; S. Vaklinov, *Formirane na staro-búlgarskata kultura VI–XI vek* (Sofia, 1977), pp. 29–31.

69 Pletneva, *Ot kochevii k gorodam*, pp. 183–4; *Khazary*, pp. 56–8 (for arguments that the Bulgaro-Alan nobility sought to exploit the dual kingship system of the khaganate by establishing a permanent hold on the seat of the khagan's secular co-ruler, bek or khagan-bek, and by surrounding the khagan himself with a system of taboos). On Khazar dual kingship, see Artamanov, *Istoriia Khazar*, pp. 409 ff.; Golden, *Khazar Studies*, pp. 98 ff. On Khazar kingship, see further D. Ludwig, *Struktur und Gesellschaft des Chazaren-Reiches im Licht der schriftlichen Quellen*, Phil. Diss., Univ. zu Münster (Westf.), (Münster, 1982), pp. 112–202.

70 On the circumstances of the Khazar court and nobility's adoption of Judaism, see Artamonov, *Istoria Khazar*; pp. 262–82; Pletneva, *Khazary*, pp. 61 ff.; O. Pritsak, 'The Khazar's Kingdom's Conversion to Judaism', *Harvard Ukrainian Studies*, 2, 1978, pp. 261–81; Golden, *Khazar studies*; pp. 97–107 *passim*; M. G. Magomedov, *Obrazovanie khazarskogo kaganata* (Moscow, 1983), pp. 173 ff. (with a discussion of the spread of Christianity in the khaganate on pp. 158–73); Novosel'tsev, *Khazarskoe gosudarstvo*, pp. 141–73 *passim*; see also N. Golb and O. Pritsak, *Khazarian Hebrew Documents of the Tenth Century* (Ithaca and London, 1982). On Judaism in Khazaria, see also Ludwig, 'Struktur und Gesellschaft', pp. 328–33.

71 S. Runciman, *A History of the First Bulgarian Empire* (London, 1930), p. 21. Runciman's book still remains the standard full-length treatment of the First Bulgarian empire in English. More recent surveys in English can be found in D. M. Lang, *The Bulgarians* (London, 1976), 'From Khanate to Imperium'; R. Browning, *Byzantium and Bulgaria* (London, 1975), a comparative study of Bulgaria and Byzantium in the ninth to the tenth centuries; Fine, *The Early Medieval Balkans*, Chaps 3–6; Tsvetkov, *A History of the Balkans*, pp. 95–147.

72 al-Nadim, *Fihristi*, pp. 36–7. In a recent work, I. Zimonyi, *The Origins of the Volga Bulgars* (Szeged, 1990), examining the evidence for the Volga Bulgars in Islamic sources, the author suggests that al-Nadim had confused the Bulgars with the Manichaean Uighurs, whereas R. G. Fahrutdinov, *Ocherki po istorii volzhskoi Bulgarii* (Moscow, 1984), argues that al-Nadim was referring to the runic script used in Volga Bulgaria – both suggestions rely on conjectures.

73 The art of Volga Bulgaria and its indebtedness to Sarmato-Alan culture has been examined in considerable detail in F. H. Valeev, *Drevnee i srednevekovoe iskusstvo srednego povolzhia* (Joshkar Ola, 1975), with references to some Zoroastrian themes in Volga Bulgar art, seen as indications of the Sarmato-Alan influence, pp. 76, 78–9, 97–9, cf. S. M. Chervonnaia, *Iskustvo Tatarii* (Moscow, 1987), pp. 61–2; on early Volga Bulgar art, see also E. P. Kazakov, *Kul'tura rannei Volzhkoi*

Bolgarii (Moscow, 1992); Fahrutdinov, *Ocherki*, pp. 63–85; on urbanism in Volga Bulgaria, see G. A. Fedorov (ed.), *Gorod Bolgar, ocherki istorii i kul'tury* (Moscow, 1987); *Gorod Bolgar, ocherki remeslennoi deiatel'nosti* (Moscow, 1988); *Biliar – stolitsa domongolskoi Bulgarii*, ed. P. N. Starostin *et al.* (Kazan, 1991).

74 Lang, *The Bulgarians*, p. 121. The imperial structure of the Bulgar state is surveyed in detail in Beshevliev, *Pŭrvobŭlgarite*, pp. 39–66, with a discussion of the possible dual-kingship type of Bulgar monarchy (pp. 45–50) and some significant parallels between the Sassanid and Bulgar classes of nobility (p. 41); *Die protobulgarische Periode der bulgarischen Geschichte* (Amsterdam, 1981), pp. 333–55; see also S. Stanilov, *Bŭlgarskata monarkhiia prez srednite vekove* (Varna, 1994), pp. 9–71 *passim*; I. Bozhilov, 'Razhdaneto na Srednovekovna Bŭlgariia (nova interpretatsiia)', in *Sedem etiuda po Srednovekovna istoriia* (Sofia, 1995), pp. 49–56.

75 Lang, *The Bulgarians*, p. 121. The strong Sassanid influence on Bulgarian art and architecture has also been recognized and discussed by, among others, D. Talbot Rice, 'Persia and Byzantium', in A. J. Arberry (ed.), *The Legacy of Persia* (Oxford, 1953), p. 49; 'Persian Elements in the Arts of Neighbouring Countries'; A Protich, 'Sasanidskata khudozhestvena traditsiia u prabŭlgarite', *Izvestiia na arkheologicheskiia institut*, 4, 1926–7, p. 217; B. Fiov, *Geschichte der altbulgarischen Kunst bis zur Eroberung des bulgarischen Reiches durch die Türken* (Berlin and Leipzig, 1932), pp. 5–35; Dujčev, 'Il mondo slavo e la Persia nell'alto medioevo', pp. 413 ff.; Vaklinov, *Formirane* pp. 92–3, 148–9; O. Minaeva, *Madarskiiat konnik* (Sofia, 1990), pp. 81–96, 110–25. The thesis that Sassanid elements of design might have reached Byzantium through the Bulgarian medium has been advanced by Talbot Rice, 'Persia and Byzantium', p. 49. On the Iranian names of a number of Bulgar Kans, see for example, Beshevliev, 'Iranski elementi' (with references to the relevant literature); for the derivation of the name Khormesius from the Central Asian (Uighur) variants, Khormusda or Khormyzda of the Iranian Hormizd or Hormuz (as in the Mongol translation of Ahura Mazda (Ohrmzad) as Khormusta), see K. H. Menges, 'Altaic Elements in the Protobulgarian inscriptions', *B*, 1951, p. 117.

76 A Bulgar inscription in Greek, alludes, for example, to a sacrifice offered to 'Tengri', possibly the Central and Inner Asian sky deity popular among Turkic and Mongol peoples (see text in V. Beshevliev, *Pŭrvobŭlgarski nadpisii* (Sofia, 1979), p. 123 (No. 6), but one has to bear in mind also other possibilities, since in the second half of the first millennium AD old Turkic inscriptions refer to various deities named *tengri* and there is virtually no evidence about their functions and relationship to the sky deity (*tengri* could be used further as a divinizing or adulatory adjective as well as in Central Asian Buddhist and Manichaean traditions and terminology; see, for example, J.-P. Roux, 'Tangri, Essai sur le ciel-dieu des peuples altaïques', *RHR*, 149,

pp. 49–82; 150, pp. 27–54, 173–212). This remains an isolated reference to Tengri and there are no other 'direct and certain indications' of his cult in Bulgar art, as argued, among others, by D. Ovcharov, 'Kultura i izkustvo, kulturniiat geroi ot bŭlgarskiia epos i Tangra', *AUSKO-CRSBID*, 1, 1987, pp. 387–8; Rashev, 'Za proizkhoda', pp. 23–4, and attempts to position him in Bulgar belief have to rely and have relied on sweeping conjectures. In religious and cultural syncretism between Iranian and Turkic traditions in the Eusrasian steppes in the early Middle Ages, moreover, a revered deity could be known both by its Turkic name, 'Tengri Khan', and by its Iranian name, 'Aspandiat' (see, for example, Moses Kalankatvatsi, *Patmuiun alvanits ashharh* (Erevan, 1983), pp. 248–50). Other aspects of Bulgar pre-Christian beliefs, which have roots in Central Asia, such as shamanistic and astronomo-astrological traditions, have been charted with more certainty in works such as Beshevliev, *Die protobulgarische Periode*, pp. 355–93.

77 These parallels have been well demonstrated by B. Brentjes, 'On the Prototype of the Proto-Bulgarian Temples at Pliska, Preslav and Madara', *East and West*, Rome, new series, vol. 21, 1971, pp. 213–16; G. R. H. Wright, 'Square Temples, East and West, *Vth International Congress of Iranian Art and Architecture* (Teheran, 1972); 'Temples at Shechem', *ZAW*, 80, 1, 1968, p. 2, Fig. 2; Vaklinov, *Formirane*, pp. 112–15; for the recently discovered new Bulgar pagan temple in Danube Bulgaria, see T. Totev and B. Bonev, 'Novorazkrit prabŭlgarski khram v Preslav', *PP*, 6, pp. 222–31; for the recently explored Bulgar rectangular-shaped sanctuary in what was Volga Bulgaria, see G. A. Fedorov-Davidov, 'Bolgarskoe gorodishe-sviatilishte X–XI vv.' *SA*, 3, 1960, pp. 122–43. Arab evidence defining the Bulgars as Magians can be found in Marquart, *Osteuropäische und ostasiatische Streifzüge*, pp. 204–5. On the development and spread of the early Iranian fire temple in the Irano-Mesopotamian world, see D. Stronach, 'On the Evolution of the Early Iranian Fire Temple', in *Acta Ir.*, *Papers in Honour of Prof. M. Boyce* (Leiden, 1985), pp. 605–28; on the typology of square and rectangular-shaped forms of monumental architecture in the Irano-Mesopotamian and Central Asian world, see G. A. Pugachenkova, 'K tipologii monumental'nogo zodchestva drevnikh stran sredneaziatskogo regiona', *IA*, 17, 1982, pp. 20–40 (cf. the classification of fire temples and their plans in Central Asia in V. L. Voronina, 'Doisliamskie kul'tovye sooruzheniia Srednei Azii', *SA*, 2, pp. 42–56; see also Pugachenkova's study of the remains of Zoroastrian fire temples and their plans in Transoxiana, 'The Antiquities of Transoxiana in the Light of Investigation in Uzbekistan', *ACSS*, pp. 3–38 (with arguments that they represented local versions of Zoroastrianism); on the recently explored rectangular-shaped fire temple in southern Uzbekistan, see A. Askarov and T. Shirikov, 'Drevnebaktriiskii khram ognia v Iuzhnom Uzbekistane', in G. A. Pugachenkova, *Gradoustroitel' stvo i arkhitektura* (Tashkent 1989), pp. 7–25;

cf. the plan of the Erkurgan temple site discussed in R. H. Suleimanov, 'Obshchestvennye sooruzheniia Erkurgana osevogo kompozitsionno-planirovochnogo tipa', in Pugachenkova, *Gradoustroitel'stvo*, pp. 25–35.

78 See H. H. Bidzhiev and A. V. Gadlo, 'Issledovaniia 1974 g. na Humarinskom gorodishte v Karachaevo-Cherkesii', *Tez. dokl. V Krupnovskikh chtenii po arkheologii Severnogo Kavkaza* (Mahachkala, 1975), p. 72; H. H. Bidzhiev, 'Humarinskoe gorodishte', in *Sbornik v chest na Prof. S. Vaklinov* (Sofia, 1984), pp. 115–25; Piotrovskii, *Istoriia*, p. 136.

79 Brentjes, 'On the Prototype of the Proto-Bulgarian Temples', p. 215; Vaklinov, *Formirane*, p. 159.

80 See the evidence and arguments in A. Iavashev, *V-i Otchet na Razgr. arkheo-logichesko druzhestvo za 1927* (Razgrad, 1927), pp. 8–11; Brentjes, 'On the Prototype of the Proto-Bulgarian Temples', p. 215; E. Esin, *A History of pre-Islamic and early-Islamic Turkish Culture* (Istanbul, 1980), p. 86. For the reported finds of Buddhists statuettes in the territory of Danube Bulgaria, see R. Rashev, 'Za tibetskite usporeditsi na Madarskiia konnik', *Arkheologiia*, 20, 3, 1978, pp. 24–29, esp. p. 27 (with a criticism of the theory of Tibetan Buddhist religious influence on the Bulgars).

81 See Iavashev, *Otchet*; Brentjes, 'On the Prototype of the Proto-Bulgarian Temples', pp. 215–16; L. Kvinto, 'Otnovo za indiiskata statuetka ot Razgrad-skiia muzei', *Arkheologiia*, 33, 1, 1991, pp. 56–60.

82 M. Kiel, *Art and Society of Bulgaria in the Turkish Period* (Assen, 1985), p. 1, with a brief survey of the history of medieval Bulgaria until the Ottoman conquest in the late fourteenth century.

83 *Scriptor incertus*, in Leo Grammaticus, *Chronographia*, ed. I. Bekker (Bonn, 1842), p. 348. Browning, *Byzantium and Bulgaria*, p. 50, argues that Krum did not intend to take Constantinople but was waiting instead for a *coup d'état* in the besieged city.

84 In the Salic law, compiled during the reign of the first Christian Merovingian king, Clovis I (481–511), the Franks were extolled as an 'illustrious tribe', 'of immaculate purity', established by God the Creator, converted to Catholicism and 'free of heresy'. See H. Fichtenau, *The Carolingian Empire* (Oxford, 1963), pp. 1–3.

85 The numerous monumental inscriptions in Greek, left by the Bulgar Kans, traditionally praised their deeds and theocratic rule. Concerning the Kans' collisions with Byzantium, Bulgar royal propaganda used formulas such as 'May God grant the divine ruler that he tramples underfoot the emperor . . .', while an inscription of Kan Persian (836–52) states: 'The Bulgars rendered many favours to the Christians [i.e. the Byzantines] and the Christians forgot but God sees all', Beshevliev, *Pŭrvobulgarskite nadpisi*, pp. 132–9, 200–9.

86 Folkloric relics of the Thracian worship of Dionysus in modern Thrace are examined in K. Kakouri, *Dionysiaka: Aspects of the Popular Thracian Religion*

of To-day (Athens, 1965); vestiges of Thracian Orphism in south-eastern Thrace are treated in A. Fol, *Trakiiskiiat Orfizŭm* (Sofia, 1986); M. Wenzel, 'The Dioscuri in the Balkans', *Slavic Review*, 26 (1967), pp. 363–81, argues that a complex of rituals preserved in the western Balkans includes surviving relics from the mysteries of Samothrace.

87 This evidence pertaining to the teachings of the Athingani is preserved in a formula of abjuration of the sect, *PG*, vol. 106, cols 1333–5 and a tract on the Melchisedekites, Theodotians and Athingani, edited by G. Ficker, 'Ein Sammulung von Abschwörungsformeln', *ZKG*, 26 (1906), pp. 450–2. On the history of the Athingani, see J. Starr, 'An Eastern Christian Sect: The Athinganoi', *HTR*, 29 (1936), pp. 93–106; I. Rochow, 'Die Häresie der Athinganer im 8. und 9. Jahrhundert und die Frage ihres Fortlebens', *BBA*, 51 (1983), pp. 163–78.

88 See the theory presented in Garsoïan, *The Paulician Heresy*, pp. 183–5; 'Byzantine Heresy. A Reinterpretation', *DOP*, 25 (1971), pp. 87–114, esp. pp. 101 ff. (with arguments that the Paulician adoption of dualism was effected by a movement towards dualism in extreme Iconoclastic circles in Constantinople); see the objections to Garsoïan's theory in Lemerle, 'L'Histoire des Pauliciens', pp. 12ff. *passim*; Couliano, *The Tree of Gnosis*, pp. 192–4; see also *HCDH*, Appendix 2, 'Armenian Sources and the Paulicians', pp. 292–3; for a discussion of Paulicianism during the Iconoclastic period, see further J. Gouillard, 'L'Héresie dans l'empire byzantin jusq'au xiie siècle', *T&M*, 1, 1965, pp. 307–13 (with a discussion of other heresies and heterodoxies of the period); Barnard, 'The Paulicians and Iconoclasm', pp. 75–83, with a discussion of the important differences between Paulicianism and Iconoclasm, p. 81.

89 Petrus Siculus, *Historia*, 5, p. 9.

90 The 'Paulician' legend and its relation to the Paulician influx in Bulgaria are discussed in Ivanov, *Bogomilski knigi i legendi*, pp. 10–12.

91 al-Nadim, *Fihristi*, pp. 802–3, acknowledged the rapid decline of Manichaeism after al-Muqtadir's caliphate: in the mid tenth century he knew 300 Manichaeans in Baghdad, but around twenty-five years later there were not even five Manichaeans left, while the *archegos* himself 'sought out any place where he could be safe'.

92 Browning, *The Byzantine Empire*, (London, 1980), p. 82; cf. the position of A. Toynbee, *Constantine Porphyrogenitus and His World* (London, 1973), p. 367, with the conclusion that if Symeon's imperial designs had succeeded, his reign might 'have seen the beginnings of a fusion between the East Roman empire and Bulgaria with a minimum of resistance and bloodshed'. In 913, with his troops at the gates of Constantinople, Symeon was indeed crowned a *Basileus* by Patriarch Nicholas I Mysticus (although it remains unclear whether he was crowned *Basileus* of the Bulgars or co-emperor with the young Constantine VII) but the validity of his coronation was rejected after the ensuing Constantinople

coup. Inevitably, Symeon's coronation in Constantinople and his bid for the imperial throne have attracted much comment and differing conclusions: see, for example, Fine, *The Early Medieval Balkans*, pp. 148ff.; D. Obolensky, *The Byzantine Commonwealth: Eastern Europe* 900–1453 (London, 1971), pp. 108–15.

93 The circumstances of the adoption of the Slavonic liturgy in Bulgaria following the collapse of the mission of the Apostles of the Slavs in Moravia are expounded in F. Dvornik, *Les Slaves, Byzance et Rome au IXe siècle* (Paris, 1926), pp. 312–13; D. Obolensky, 'Sts. Cyril and Methodius, Apostles of the Slavs', *St Vladimir's Seminary Quarterly*, 7 (1963), pp. 6–7, with a discussion of the role of the literary movement under Symeon for the transmission of the Slavo-Byzantine culture to the Russians and the Serbs and making 'Byzantine sacred and secular literature accessible to all Slavs'.

94 Text in Ivanov, *Bogomilski knigi i legendi*, p. 20.

95 Obolensky, *The Bogomils*, p. 95; Cf. the different approach of M. Loos, 'Le prétendu témoignage d'un traité de Jean Exarque intitulé "Šestodnev" et relatif aux Bogomiles', *BSl*, 13 (1952–3), pp. 59–67; for arguments that the allusion to the 'Manichaeans' in Ioan Exarkh's tract refers to Paulicians or Paulician missionaries in Bulgaria, see Angelov, *Bogomilstvoto*, pp. 88–9; B. Hamilton, 'Historical Introduction', in *HCDH*, p. 26 (with a clarification that this specific view of the Devil as the eldest son of God did not derive from Paulicianism).

96 According to Theophanes Continuatus, *Chronographia*, pp. 411–12, Romanus Lecapenus was persuaded by a certain astrologer that one of the statues in the Constantinople quarter of Xerolophus was in reality Symeon's double and ordered its decapitation, which caused the immediate death of Symeon.

97 Arguments for Manichaean influences among the Pechenegs can be found in V. G. Vasilevskii, 'Vizantiia i Pechenegi 1048–1094', in *Trudi* (St Petersburg, 1908), pp. 38–57. Cf. the views of O. Pritsak, *The Pechenegs: A Case of Social and Economic Transformation* (Lisse, 1976), p. 24, and Ivanov, *Bogomilski knigi i legendi*, pp. 19–20 (with suggestions for Zoroastrian influences on the Pechenegs); E. Tryjarski, 'Les religions des Petchenégues', in *Traditions religieuses et para-religieuses des peuples altaïques* (Paris, 1972), pp. 139–49.

98 In *Antapodosis* (3 : 29), Liudprand of Cremona, Otto the Great's ambassador to Constantinople, portrayed Benjamin (Boyan) as an adept of magic, who could transform himself into a wolf or any other shape: see *Die Werke Liudprands von Cremona*, ed. J. Becker (Hanover and Leipzig, 1915), p. 88. The figure of the 'princely magus by blood' has been discussed in V. Flint, *The Rise of Magic in Early Medieval Europe* (Princeton, 1991), pp. 350–55. I. Dujčev, 'Boian Magesnik' in *Prouchvaniia vŭrhu bŭlgarskoto srednovekovie* (Sofia, 1945), pp. 9–51, associated the pursuits of the Prince with the Byzantine secret arts, while V. Pundev, *Boian Magiosnik* (Sofia, 1925), p. 18, attempted to link the Prince with the Bogomil heresy.

99 Theophylact's letter to Tsar Peter, the earliest certain evidence for the rise of Bogomilism, has been edited and discussed in I. Dujčev, *Medioeva bizantino-slavo* (Rome, 1965), vol. 1, pp. 283–315; see the translation of the text in *HCDH*, pp. 98–102. Only two of the anathemas in Theophylact's letter do not derive from Peter of Sicily's text on the Paulicians and thus apply specifically to the new heretics: one of them condemns their moderate dualist teaching that the Devil is the creator and ruler of matter and the visible world, whereas the other denounces their rejection of marriage and procreation.

100 New edition of the text in Iu. Begunov, *Kozma prezviter v slavianskikh literaturakh* (Sofia, 1973). Translation into French and comments in H.-C. Puech and A. Vaillant, *Le Traité contre les Bogomiles de Cosmas le prêtre* (Paris, 1945); partial translation of the anti-Bogomil section of the tract into English in E. Peters (ed.), *Heresy and Authority in Medieval Europe* (London, 1980), pp. 108–17; new translation of the anti-Bogomil section of the tract in *HCDH*, pp. 114–34.

101 The statement that Bogomil preachers taught their followers to defy the Tsar and nobility has been voluminously developed and over-elaborated in Marxist historiography, which largely treats the Bogomil sect as a broad social movement against 'feudal oppression', while notions of the Bogomils as vehicles of social protest occur in some general works on Bulgarian or Balkan history. The lack of evidence for such theses and for the speculation that the Bogomils might have been a strong social or peasant movement have been well demonstrated in J. Fine, 'The Bulgarian Bogomil Movement', *East European Quarterly*, 11 : 4 (1977), pp. 385–412.

102 Puech and Valliant, *Le Traité contre les Bogomiles*, pp. 190–2.

103 Text in a Serbian version of the Synodicon of Orthodoxy, published by V. A. Moshin, 'Srbskaia redaktsiia Sinodika v Nedeliu Pravoslaviia', *VV*, 17 (1960), pp. 347–8.

104 For a view that Bogomilism represents a direct continuation of old Manichaeism, see, for example, A. Sharenkoff, *A Study of Manichaeism in Bulgaria with Special Reference to the Bogomils* (New York, 1927); for the view that Bogomilism derived from Messalianism, see, for example, J. C. L. Gieseler, *Lehrbuch der Kirchengeschichte*, II (Bonn, 1848), p. 679; for the view that Bogomil dualism was predominantly influenced by Paulicianism, see Runciman, *The Medieval Manichee*, pp. 66–8; for a dual Paulician–Massalian influence on Bogomilism, see Obolensky, *The Bogomils*, p. 110; for a view that Bogomilism represented a direct continuation of previous heresies in Anatolia such as the Athingani, see Loos, *Dualist Heresy*, pp. 60 ff. (and in other Loos' publications); for arguments for a significant Gnostic strand in Bogomilism, see Söderberg, *La religion des cathares* p. 68 *passim*.

105 Lidia Denkova, 'Bogomilism and Literacy', *EB*, 1 (1993), pp. 90–7; 'Les Bogomiles: ontologic du Mal et orthodoxie orientale', *Heresis*, 13–14 (1990), pp. 65–81; P. Dimitrov, 'Bogomil' and 'Bogomilski skazaniia i legendi', in *Petŭr Chernorizets* (Shumen, 1995), resp. pp. 116–40, 140–67; D. Dimitrova, 'Tainata kniga na bogomilite v sistemata na starobŭlgarskata literatura', *Preslavska knizhovna shkola* 1 (Shumen, 1995), pp. 59–69; Angelov, *Bogomilstvoto*, pp. 76–9, 161–3 (in a change of emphasis from earlier works, Angelov states that Bogomil doctrines were originally conceptualized among 'a narrow circle of theologians – mostly priests and monks', p. 235); on the role of apocryphal literature in the formulationa and elaboration of Bogomil doctrines, cf. Ivanov, *Bogomilski knigi i legendi*; E. Turdeanu, 'Apocryphes bogomiles et apocryphes pseudo-bogomiles' in *RHR*, 138 (1950), No. 1, pp. 22–52, No. 2, pp. 176–218; N. Minissi, 'La tradizione apocrifa e la origini del bogomilismo', *RS*, 3 (1954), pp. 97–113. Thus, the notion of the Devil as God's firstborn angel could have been borrowed by the Bogomils from the apocryphal work, *The Questions of Bartholomew*, Greek text in *Questiones s. Bartholmaei apostoli*, ed. A. Vassiliev, *Anecdota graeco-byzantina* (Moscow, 1893), pp. 17–21; for the Slavonic manuscripts of the work, see A. de Santos Otero, *Die handschriftliche Überlieferung der altslavischen Apokryphen* (Berlin and New York, 1981), vol. 2, pp. 58–9.

106 E. Esin, 'The Conjectural Links of Bogomilism with Central Asian Manichaeism', in *Bogomilstvoto na balkanot vo svetlinata na najnovite istrajuvanja* (Skopje, 1982), p. 108.

107 See, for example, I. Dujčev, 'I Bogomili nei paesi slavi e la loro storia', in *L'Oriente Cristiano nella storia della civiltà* (Rome, 1963), p. 628.

108 Zaehner, *Zurvan*, pp. 70, 450, where the related doctrine of the three principles of the Thracian 'Euchites' is defined as dependent on Zurvanism; Eliade, *The Two and the One*, pp. 83–4; the parallels between Zurvanism and Bogomilism are also noted by Toynbee, *Constantine Porphyrogenitus*, p. 657, where the mythologies of the two religious systems are defined as 'identical in essence', although affiliation between them is being rejected.

109 I. Dujčev, 'Aux origines des courants dualistes à Byzance et chez les Slaves méridionaux', *Revue des Études Sud-est Européennes*, 1 (1969), pp. 57ff.

110 Sulimirski, 'Sarmatians', pp. 7–8; 'Bogomil' may have been further an assumed name, indicating the attainment of a more elevated spiritual status; cf. the views of Obolensky, *The Bogomils*, pp. 119–20; Puech, *Le Traité*, pp. 27, 282–3; E. Werner, 'Theophilos-Bogumil', *BS* 7 (1966), pp. 49–60.

111 Runciman, *The Medieval Manichee*, p. 91, considers Jeremiah a 'co-founder of the Bogomils' along with Bogomil, while D. Mandić, *Bogomilska crkva bosanskih krstjana* (Chicago, 1962), p. 127, argues that Jeremiah was the first leader of the heretical Church in Bosnia under the name of Eremis. Jeremiah is more commonly seen, however, as an author and compiler of apocryphal

legends; cf. Obolensky, *The Bogomils*, pp. 271–4.

112 The evidence of the activities of the two 'Franks' appears in an index of forbidden books and is reprinted and discussed in Ivanov, *Bogomilski knigi i legendi*, pp. 50–1.

113 D. Angelov, 'Rationalistic Ideas of a Medieval Heresy' in *Bulgaria's Share in Human Culture* (Sofia, 1968), p. 69; for a survey of the evidence concerning Bogomil hierarchy, see D. Dragojlović, *Bogomilstvo na Balkanu i u Maloi Aziji, II Bogomilstvo na pravoslavnom vostoku* (Belgrade, 1982), pp. 162–6; Angelov, *Bogomilstvoto*, pp. 238 ff.; K. Onasch, 'Zur Frage der Hierarchie in der Bogomilenkirche', in *Studien zum Menschenbild in Gnosis und Manichäismus* (Halle, 1979), pp. 211–22; on the problem of the dating of the Bogomils' adoption of episcopal government, see A Borst, *Die Katharer* (Stuttgart, 1953), pp. 202–3 (dating it to the first half of the twelfth century and relating to Bogomil expanding missionary work); for similar dating, see Hamilton, 'Historical Introduction', *HCDH*, p. 44; cf. M. Lambert, *The Cathars* (Oxford, 1998), p. 34.

114 *The Bulgarian Apocryphal Chronicle* 13, published and discussed in Ivanov, *Bogomilski knigi i legendi*, pp. 273–87, with comments on the Bogomil elements in the work (pp. 275–6).

115 Although the early Aaronids were often implicated in mutinies and plots, the lineage intermarried with the prominent Byzantine houses of the Ducas and Comneni and by the end of the twelfth century had already given two imperial wives to Comnenian emperors, Catherine and Irene Ducaina. Two of Irene's female scions soon entered the new royal house of Jerusalem by marrying the Angevin kings of Jerusalem, Baldwin III (1143–62) and Amalric I (1162–74).

116 Cf. Eliade, *A History of Religious Ideas*, vol. 3, p. 182, with arguments that following the influx of Bulgarian nobles into Constantinople Bogomilism penetrated Byzantine aristocratic and monastic circles and shaped their theology. Basil's design for defeating Bulgaro-Byzantine hostility through intermarriage is reported in Yachya of Antioch, *Historiae*, quoted after the translation in V. P. Rozen, *Imperator Vasili Bolgaroboïtsa* (St Petersburg, 1883), p. 59.

117 These controversial accusations are advanced in a Greek version of the *Life of St Vladimir*, which abounds in errors, and are usually regarded as unreliable. The evidence of the religious situation under Samuel allows various interpretations and some scholars continue to consider Samuel a Bogomil supporter. Obolensky, *The Bogomils*, p. 151, suggests that in the course of his wars with Byzantium Samuel tolerated the Bogomils for political reasons and this toleration gave rise to popular legends, associating him with Bogomilism; cf. also Fine, *The Early Medieval Balkans*, pp. 196–7.

118 D. Tashkovski, *Bogomilism in Macedonia* (Skopje, 1965), p. 88; for claims of

massive Bogomil support for Samuel's rule, see N. Derzhavin, *Istoriia Bolgarii*, (Moscow, 1946), II, p. 35; for arguments that the Bogomils took active part in the rising of the Cometopuli, see D. Dragojlović, 'Ulogata na bogomilite vo vostanichko dvizhenje na Makedonskite sloveni za vremeto na tsar Samoil', in *Iljiada godini od vostanieto na komitopulite i sozdavaneto na Samoilovata drzhava* (Skopje, 1971), pp. 95–110; Tashkovski, *Bogomilism in Macedonia*, pp. 81–2, 87–8. For a criticism of the above views, see S. Pirivatrić, *Samoilova drzhava, obim i karakter* (Belgrade, 1997), pp. 160–1, n. 78; cf. S. Antolyak, *Samuel and His State* (Skopje, 1985), pp. 106–9. For the political messianism of the Cometopuli, see P. Pavlov, 'Ot Presian 1 do Presian II', in T. Totev (ed.), *1100 godini Veliki Preslav, 1* (Shumen, 1995), pp. 240–50, esp. p. 241.

119 A. Toynbee, *A Study of History* (London, 1939), vol. 4, p. 72.

120 The letter is contained in *PG*, vol. 131, cols 47–58, but is erroneously attributed to a later theologian, Euthymius Zigabenus. Another edition is to be found in G. Ficker, *Die Phundagiagiten: Ein Beitrag zur Ketzergeschichte des byzantischen Mittelalters* (Leipzig, 1908), pp. 3–86; English translation in *HCDH*, pp. 142–64. Euthymius of Periblepots equates the Bogomils he targets in his letters with the 'Massalian' heretics, a term that by that time could be used against heretical and heterodox groups or against mystical preachers who put too much stress on spiritual illumination or perceptible manifestation of the Holy Spirit. On the development of the equation between Bogomilism and Massalianism, see A. Rigo, 'Messalianismo= Bogomilismo: un equazione dell'ereseologia medievale bizantina', *OCP*, 56 (1990), pp. 53–82; for a discussion of the 'cases' and accusations of 'Massalianism' in the framework of developments in the Byzantine mystical tradition and its equation with Bogomilism, see Gouillard. 'L'hérésie', pp. 319–23.

121 The text of the eleventh-century Bogomil liturgy, partially described and quoted by Euthymius, has not survived. The descriptions of the ritual in Byzantine sources find immediate parallels in the two extant texts, Latin and Provençal, of the Cathar *Ritual* which are commonly derived from a Bogomil original. The two texts of the Cathar *Ritual* have been published in C. Thouzellier, *Rituel cathare* (Paris, 1976). An English translation of both versions of the Cathar ritual can be found in Wakefield and Evans, *Heresies of the High Middle Ages*, pp. 468–94. Part of a later Slavonic Bosnian *Ritual* written by Radoslav the Christian parallels closely the Cathar *Ritual* of Lyons and was certainly used by fifteenth-century dualists in Bosnia; see the English translation of its text by Y. Stoyanov in *HCDH*, pp. 289–92. For suggestions that the Bogomils may have inherited their *Ritual* (with an archaic and generally Orthodox character) from the Paulicians to whom it was transmitted by the schismatic Novatians, who called themselves *katharoi*

(later used in reference to the medieval dualists in western Europe), see B. Hamilton, 'The Cathars and the Seven Churches of Asia', in J. Howard-Johnston (ed.), *Byzantium and the West c.* 850–c. 1200 (Amsterdam, 1988), pp. 269–95, esp. pp. 291–5; for the use of the name *katharoi* among the Novatians, see H. Grégoire, 'Cathares d'Asie Mineure, d'Italie et de la France', *AOC*, 1 (1948), pp. 142–51.

122 According to M. Angold, *Church and Society in Byzantium under the Comneni 1081–1261* (Cambridge, 1995), pp. 47, 2–7, the Phundagiagites were not identical with the Bogomils, the direct continuation between the original Bogomil heresy in Bulgaria and Byzantine Bogomilism is not certain and John Tzurillas may have been a follower of Eleutherius of Paphlagonia (d.950), whose mystical teachings may have evolved into a heresy. There are, however, some important differences between the reported teachings and practices of Tzurillas and those of Eleutherius of Paphlagonia; see Hamilton, 'Historical Introduction', pp. 32–3. Euthymius' letter, however, evidences that Anatolian groups of Bogomils had absorbed some Paulician traditions; see Hamilton, 'Historical Introduction', p. 35, and some of the reported teachings display absolute dualist tendencies, see Angold, *Church and Society*, pp. 475–6.

123 P. Gautier, 'Le *De Daemonibus* du Pseudo-Psellus', *REB*, 38 (1980), pp. 105–94; text and French translation: pp. 132–78; for Gautier's view of authorship and the date of the tract, see pp. 128–31 (cf. Angold, *Church and Society*, p. 496); earlier edition: Michael Psellus, *Dialogus de daemonum operatione*, *PG*, vol. 122, cols 819–76. The English translation of the relevant section of the tract is in *HCDH*, pp. 227–33. Given the uncertainty surrounding the date of the tract, the section dealing with it below follows that on Euthymius of Peribleptos' epistle, this time not for chronological reasons but for thematic ones, conditioned by the parallels between the demonological material in the two texts.

124 Zaehner, *Zurvan*, p. 450, with a reproduction of the relevant fragment.

125 Obolensky, *The Bogomils*, p. 186, with an analysis of the teachings that could be considered Bogomil and those which seem to have been imposed by the tract on the Euchites. The demonology in the tract, including the third trend, is more commonly attributed to its indebtedness to Chaldean systems through Neo-Platonic authors like Porphyry and Proclus, but some scholars accept the existence of a third 'satanic' trend among the Thracian sectarians. See, for example, M. Wellnhofer, 'Die Thrakischen Euchiten und ihr Satan-skult im Dialoge des Psellos', *BZ*, 30 (1929–30), pp. 477–84, with Near Eastern parallels.

126 J. Gouillard, 'Une source grecque du Sinodik de Boril, la lettre inédité du Patriarche Cosmas', *Travaux et mémoires*, 4 (1970), pp. 361–74. English translation of the text in *HCDH*, pp. 165–7.

NOTES

127 On the 'narrowing' or 'thinning' of the borders between Christian asceticism/mysticism and dualist heresy, see, for example, Obolensky, *The Bogomils*, p. 21; Garsoïan, 'Byzantine Heresy', pp. 109–13; Angold, *Church and Society*, pp. 472–3, 478. For the parallels and differences between the teachings of Symeon the New Theologian and Bogomilism, see H. J. M. Turner, 'St. Symeon the New Theologian and Dualist Heresies – Comparisons and Contrasts', *St. Vladimir's Theological Quarterly*, 32, 4 (1988), pp. 359–66; *St Symeon the New Theologian and Spiritual Fatherhood* (Leiden, 1990), pp. 66–8.

128 R. P. H. Greenfield, *Traditions of Belief in Late Byzantine Demonology* (Amsterdam, 1988), p. 175, with a general discussion of Bogomil demonology on pp. 166–76.

129 Greenfield, *Traditions of Belief*, p. 169; cf. Angold, *Church and Society*, p. 470; Hamilton, 'Historical Introduction', pp. 42–3.

130 In 1463 a copy of the *Corpus Hermeticum* was brought to the founder of the Platonic Academy in Florence, Cosimo de'Medici, where it was translated by the Platonist Marsilio Ficino. A survey of the recoverable history of the manuscript of the *Corpus Hermeticum* and the role of Psellus can be found in W. Scott, *Hermetica* (Oxford, 1924), vol. I, pp. 25ff.

131 Gouillard, 'Le Synodicon de l'orthodoxie', *T&M*, 2 (1967), pp. 59–61. English translation in *HCDH*, pp. 134–6 (with a discussion of the problem related to the location of Panormus, p. 135, n. 3). For another reference linking Bogomilism with Sicily, see the anathema against the priest Bogomil and certain Theodor of Sicily in a Russian synodicon from the sixteenth to seventeenth centuries in Begunov, *Kozma prezviter*, p. 122. For the Paulician contingents in Sicily in the mid eleventh century and their participation in the Byzantine anti-Norman campaigns in southern Italy, see *Annales Barenses*, *MGH SS* 9, p. 248 (English translation in *HCDH*, pp. 139–41). According to Obolensky, *The Bogomils*, p. 202, there seems to have been contact between Italus' disciples and Bogomilism and through similar encounters with philosophical ideas in Byzantium during the eleventh and twelfth centuries Bogomilism 'assumed the character of a philosophical sect'.

132 Anna Comnena, *The Alexiad*, tr. E. Dawes (London, 1928), p. 236. On Nilus, cf. Gouillard, 'Le synodicon', pp. 202–6; N. Garsoïan, 'L'abjuration du moine Nil de Calabre', *BSI*, 35 (1974), pp. 12–27 (with arguments that Nilus was a 'neo-Paulician'); on Blachernites, see J. Gouillard, 'Quatre procès de mystiques à Byzance (vers 960–1143). Inspiration et autorité', *REB*, 36 (1978), pp. 19–28; Angold, *Church and Society*, p. 478.

133 Comnena, *The Alexiad*, p. 385.

134 Comnena, *The Alexiad*, p. 386.

135 Comnena, *The Alexiad*, p. 412 (the following quotations are from Dawes's translation, pp. 412–15). See also the new English translation of the relevant

section of Anna Comnena's text in *HCDH*, pp. 175–80. On Bogomilism in
Constantinople, cf. Obolensky, *The Bogomils*, pp. 197–220; Runciman, *The
Medieval Manichee*, pp. 70ff.; D. Gress-Wright, 'Bogomilism in Constantinople', *B*, 47 (1977), pp. 163–85; Angold, *Church and Society*, pp. 479–88
136 Comnena, *The Alexiad*, p. 418.
137 Comnena, *The Alexiad*, p. 415.
138 Euthymius Zigabenus, *Panoplia Dogmatica*, *PG*, vol. 130. The Bogomil
section is edited by Ficker in *Die Phundagiagiten*, pp. 89–111. See the English
translation of the relevant section in *HCDH*, pp. 180–207. Angold considers
Zigabenus' account of the burning of Basil more plausible, arguing that
Anna Comnena's version reflects a legendary lore that grew around Basil's
execution, even a Bogomil myth about the death and the ascent of the
theotokos, *Church and Society*, pp. 486–7. On the process of Basil, see also A.
Rigo, 'Il processo del Bogomilo Basilio (1099 ca.): una riconsiderazione',
OCP, 58 (1992), pp. 185–212.
139 For the influence of the mystical teachings of Symeon the Theologian on
Contantine Chrysomalus, see J. Gouillard, 'Constantin Chrysomallos sous
le masque de Syméon le Nouveau Théologien', *T&M*, 5 (1973), pp. 313–27;
'Quatre procès', pp. 29–39; Angold, *Church and Society*, pp. 487–91; for
arguments that Constantine's stance decrying all authority as 'satanic' has a
Bogomil character, see Puech, *Le Traité*, pp. 137, 275; cf. Obolensky, *The
Bogomils*, pp. 219–20. See also the English translation of the official
posthumous trial of Contantine Chrysomalus in *HCDH*, pp. 212–15.
140 Runciman, *The Medieval Manichee*, pp. 72–3. It is worth noting that the
association between Niphon and Patriarch Atticus is presented as a much
closer relationship in Joannes Cinnamus, *Historiae*, ed. A. Meineke, *CSHB*,
Book 2 (1836), pp. 63–6, than in Nicetas Choniates, *De Manuele Commeno*,
in *Historia*, ed. I. Bekker, *CSHB*, Book 2 (1835), p. 107, where it was used by
Atticus' adversaries in their intrigues against the patriarch. English translations of both accounts can be found in *Deeds of John and Manuel Comnenus*,
C. M. Brand (tr.), (New York, 1976), pp. 56–8, and H. J. Magoulias, *O City
of Byzantium: Annals of Niketas Choniates* (Detroit, 1984), pp. 4–7. See also
the texts in *HCDH*, pp. 219–25.
141 An important source for the encounters between Orthodoxy and heretical
movements in Macedonia, *The Life of St Hilarion*, was edited by E.
Kalužniacki in *Werke des Patriarchen von Bulgarien Euthymius* (Vienna,
1901), pp. 27–58. English translation of the relevant sections is in *HCDH*,
pp. 225–7.
142 Theodore Balsamon, *Photii Patriarchae Constantinopolitani Nomocanon*, *PG*,
vol. 104, col. 1148.
143 Hugh Etherianus and his work against the heretics in Byzantium has been
surveyed by A. Dondaine in 'Hugues Ethérien et Léon Toscan' *Archives d'his-*

toire doctrinale et littéraire du moyen âge, 27 (1952) pp. 67–113, with fragments of the text itself. See the English translation in *HCDH*, pp. 234–50.

144 The abjuration formula has recently been edited by P. Eleuteri and A. Rigo, *Eretici, dissidenti, musulmani ed ebrei a Bisanzio, Una raccolta eresiologica del xii secolo* (Venice, 1993), pp. 125–53; the English translation is in *HCDH*, pp. 207–11.

145 Stefan Nemanja's campaign against the heretics is recorded in his *Life*; see the text, *Život Sv. Symeona od Krále Štěpána*, in P. J. Šafařík, *Památky Dřevního Písemníctvy Jihoslovanův* (Prague, 1873), pp. 6ff. The Bogomil identity of the heretics persecuted by Stafan Nemanja is sometimes questioned but the evidence suggests that their heresy was indeed most likely Bogomilism, see S. Ćircović, 'Dualistichka heterodoksija u ulozi zemaljske tsrkve: Bosanska tsrkva', in *Rabotnitsi, vojnitsi, duhovnitsi, drushtva srednjovekovnog Balkana* (Belgrade, 1997), p. 216.

146 For arguments for such Bogomil influx into Transylvania, see V. Tufesco, 'O mărunta populaţie balcanica', *Balcania*, 4 (1941), pp. 513 ff.; for arguments for early Bogomil influx in Romanian lands, see R. Constantinescu, 'Une formule slave pour la réception des Bogomiles', *EB*, 2 (1982), pp. 69–83; for arguments for the diffusion of Bogomil-influenced apocryphal traditions, see A. Balota, 'Bogomilismul si kulturo-maselor din Bulgaria si tarile Romine', *Romanoslavica*, 10 (1964), pp. 19–71; cf. the articles assembled in E. Turdeanu, *Apocryphes Slaves et Roumains de L'Ancien Testament* (Leiden, 1981).

4   The Dualist Communion

1 For this reconstruction of the relationship between heresy and orthodoxy in the early medieval era, see J. B. Russell, *Dissent and Order in the Middle Ages. The Search for Legitimate Authority* (New York, 1994), pp. 1–10 (with a discussion of the evidence for early medieval heresy in the period between the Council of Chalcedon in 451 and 1050, pp. 9–21). On the development and variety of medieval views on western heresy, see, for example, the contributions in W. Lourdaux and D. Verhelst, *The Concept of Heresy in the Middle Ages (11th–13th Centuries)* (Louvain, 1976); the relevant contributions in P. Biller and A. Hudson (eds), *Heresy and Literacy* (Cambridge, 1994); J. L. Nelson, 'Society, Theodicy and the Origins of Heresy: towards a Reassessment of the Medieval Evidence', *SCH*, 11, *The Materials, Sources and Methods of Ecclesiastical Society*, ed. D. Baker, (Oxford, 1975), pp. 65–77; R. I. Moore, *The Origins of European Dissent* (Oxford, 1977; 2nd edn. 1985);

idem, *The Formation of a Persecuting Society* (Oxford, 1987); T. Assad, 'Medieval Heresy: an Anthropological View', *SH*, 11, 1986, pp. 354–62; see also the insights on the functioning of medieval dissenting and heretical groups as 'textual communities' in B. Stock, *The Implications of Literacy: Language and Models of Interpretation in the Eleventh and Twelfth Centuries* (Princeton, NJ, 1983).

2 J. Havet (ed.), *Les Lettres de Gerbert* (Paris, 1889), No. 180, pp. 161–2. Among the historians suspecting heretical inclinations in Gerbert are Runciman, *The Medieval Manichee*, p. 117; I. da Milano, 'Le eresie popolari', in *Studi Gregoriani*, 2, pp. 44–6.

3 The incidents with Leutard and Vilgard are reported in Raoul Glaber (the Bald), *Historiarum libri quinque* 2: 11–12, in *Raoul Glaber: Les cinq livres de ses histoires [900–1044]*, ed. M. Prou (Paris, 1886), pp. 49–50; on the use of literary conventions in Glaber's report, see M. Lambert, *Medieval Heresy, Popular Movements from the Gregorian Reform to the Reformation*, 2nd edn (Oxford, 1992), pp. 29–30 (with a discussion of previous views concerning the provenance of Leutard's heresy); for a discussion of Glaber's report about Leutard within the framework of the eleventh-century concept of literacy and heresy, see R. I. Moore, 'Literacy and the Making of Heresy, *c.* 1000–*c.* 1500', in Biller and Hudson, *Heresy and Literacy*, p. 22.

4 The Aquitanian 'Mainichaeans' are reported in Adémar of Chabannes, *Chronique* 3 : 49, ed. J. Chavanon (Paris, 1897), p. 173. On the circumstances behind the appearance of Adémar's reports of 'Mainichaeans' in Aquitaine, see Lambert, *Medieval Heresy*, pp. 20ff.; R. I. Moore, 'Heresy, Repression, and Social Change in the Age of Gregorian Reform', in S. L. Wagh, and P. D. Diehl (eds), *Christendom and its Discontents* (Cambridge, 1996), pp. 31–3. On Adémar see now, R. Landes, *Relics, Apocalypse and the Deceits of History, Adémar of Chabannes, 989–1034* (Cambridge, Mass., 1995).

5 Among the accounts of the Orléans heretics a short version is provided in Adémar of Chabannes, *Chronique* 3 : 59, pp. 184–5; while a longer account appears in Paul of Saint Père de Chartres, *Gesta synodi Aureliansis*, in M. Bouquet (ed.), *Recueil des historiens des Gaules et de la France*, vol. 10, pp. 536–9; for a discussion of the religious and political factors underlying the discovery and the trial of the Orléans heretics, see Lambert, *Medieval Heresy*, pp. 9–17 (with a survey of the scholarly positions accepting Bogomil influences on the Orléans heretics versus those who favour a western interpretation of their heresy, pp. 15–16, n. 21); cf. R. H. Bautier, 'L'hérésie d'Orléans et le mouvement intellectuelle au début du xiᵉ siècle', *Actes de 95ᵉ Congrès National des Sociétés savantes (Rheims, 1970): Section philologique et historique* (Paris, 1975), 1, pp. 63–88; Moore, *Origins*, pp. 285–9; H. Fichtenau, *Ketzer und Professoren: Häresie und Vernunftglaube im Hochmittelalter* (Munich, 1992), pp. 33–43; G. Rottenwöhrer, *Der Katharismus*, Bd. III, *Die Herkunft*

der Katharer nach Theologie und Geschichte (Bad Honnef, 1990), pp. 151–72;
for a discussion of the suggested Neo-Platonic influences on the Orléans
heretics, see Moore, 'Heresy', pp. 26–7.

6 The Monforte episode is recorded in Ralph Glaber, *Historiarum* 4 : 2, in *Raoul
Glaber*, ed. Prou, pp. 94–6 and Landulf the Elder, *Historia Mediolanensis*,
2 : 27, *MGH SS*, vol. 8, pp. 65–6, quoted after the translation in Wakefield
and Evans, *Heresies of the High Middle Ages*, pp. 86–9. On the Monforte
heretics, see Moore, *Origins*, pp. 31–5; Lambert, *Medieval Heresy*, pp. 16–20;
E. Peretto, *Movimenti spirituali laicali del medioevo: Tra ortodossia ed eresia*
(Rome, 1985), pp. 38–53; for arguments that the Monforte heretics were influenced by the Neo-Platonism of Eriugena, see R. Gorre, *Die ersten Ketzer im
11. Jahrhundert: Religiose Eiferer–Soziale Rebellen* (Constance, 1985), pp.
185–204; cf. Fichtenau, *Ketzer*, p. 46.

7 For a forcefully argued exposition of this process, see Moore, *The Formation of
a Persecuting Society, idem,* 'Heresy', *idem,* 'Literacy'; for earlier arguments for
a decisive Bogomil influence on the the earliest appearances of heresy in
medieval western Christendom, see A. Dondaine, 'L'Origine de l'hérésie
mediévale: A propos d'un livre récent', *RSCI*, 6, 1952, pp. 47–78; for references
to the works of the main supporters of the Bogomil and western interpretation
of the origins of early western heresy, see Lambert, *Medieval Heresy*, pp. 15–16,
n. 21. In the first edition of his book (*Medieval Heresy* (London, 1977), p.33)
Lambert defined early western heresy as 'proto-dualism' and a 'half-way house
between Western dissidence and Eastern Dualism' but this position is superseded by his new analysis in the second edition, where he puts the emphasis
on the western factors that 'fostered dissidence in the eleventh century', p. 16.
Cf. H. Grundmann, *Religiöse Bewegungen* (Hildesheim, 1935, 2nd edn, 1961),
pp. 476–83; da Milano, 'Le eresie popolari', pp. 43–89; Rottenwöhrer, *Der
Katharismus*, Bd. III, *Die Herkunft*, pp. 131–227, 255–81; J. B. Russell, *Dissent
and Reform in the Early Middle Ages* (Berkeley, 1965), p. 215; *idem, Dissent and
Order*, Chap. 3, pp. 21–43; for arguments that a possible Bogomil influence on
eleventh-century western outbreaks of heresy still should be taken into consid-
eration, see B. Hamilton, 'Wisdom from the East', in Biller and Hudson,
Heresy and Literacy, pp. 39–41.

8 An account of the beliefs and practices of the Cologne heretics is given in the
letter of Eberwin of Steinfeld to St Bernard of Clairvaux, *PL*, vol. 182, cols
676–80.

9 Bernard's letter to Alphonse Jordan is reproduced in *PL*, vol. 182, cols 434–6;
the quotations are from the translation provided in Wakefield and Evans,
Heresies of the High Middle Ages, pp. 122–4.

10 The letter is reproduced in *PL*, vol. 179, cols 937–8; the quotations are from
the translation in Wakefield and Evans, *Heresies of the High Middle Ages*, pp.
140–1.

11 Lambert, *Medieval Heresy*, 1st edn, p. 43; for suggestions that Greek monks visiting and settling in western monasteries in the eleventh century and onwards may have been transmitters of heterodox and dualist beliefs, see Hamilton, 'Wisdom from the East', pp. 39–40.

12 Anselm of Alessandria, *Tractatus de hereticis*, ed. A. Dondaine, 'l'Hiérarchie cathare en Italie', Pt 2: 'Le "Tractatus de hereticis" d'Anselme d'Alexandrie', *Archivum Fratrum Praedicatorum*, 20, 1950, pp. 308–24. The quotations are from the translation in Wakefield and Evans, *Heresies of the High Middle Ages*, pp. 168–70. On the significance of the emergence of a heretical Latin church in Constantinople, where translation of texts from Greek into Latin could be pursued in scholarly and bilingual milieux, see Hamilton, 'Wisdom from the East', pp. 46–52; Lambert, *The Cathars*, p. 37. On the dating of the episode of the conversion of French crusaders to dualism in the aftermath of the First Crusade, see Hamilton, 'Wisdom from the East', pp. 44–5; P. Biller, 'William of Newburgh and the Cathar Mission to England', in D. Wood (ed.), *Life and Thought in the Northern Church c. 1100–c. 1700, Essays in Honour of C. Cross* (Woodbridge, 1999), pp. 23–5 (with a discussion of the vital role on north French Cathars in the early history of Catharism); cf. the views of Lambert, *The Cathars*, pp. 35–36; Moore, *Origins*, pp. 172–3.

13 *De heresi catharorum in Lombardia*, ed. A. Dondaine, 'L'Hiérarchie cathare en Italie', Pt I, *Archivum Fratrum Praedicatorum*, 19 (1949), pp. 305–12.

14 C. Thouzellier, 'Hérésie et croisade au xiie siècle', *Revue d'histoire ecclésiastique*, 49 (1954), pp. 855–72.

15 See the thirteen sermons of Eckbert of Schönau, *Sermones tredecim contra Catharos*, PL, vol. 195, cols 11–107; on Eckbert's anti-Cathar semons, see Borst, *Die Katharer*, pp. 6–7, 94–5; R. Manselli, 'Ecberto di Schönau e l'eresia catara in Germania alla metà del secolo XII', in *Studi sulle eresie del secolo XII* (Rome, 1975), pp. 191–211; Fichtenau, *Ketzer*, pp. 85, 102–3, 129, 158; Rottenwöhrer, *Der Katharismus*, Bd. I, vol. 1, *Quellen zum Katharismus*, pp. 90–1; vol. 2, *Anmerkungen* (1982), pp. 292–6; on the importance of the dates, which St Hildegard relates to the recorded apocalyptic events, for the dating of the earliest emergence of Catharism in the Rhineland, see Hamilton, 'Wisdom from the East', pp. 42–5, making further the necessary point that the discovery of the Cologne Cathar groups in 1143 was certainly preceded by an apparently lengthy process of Bogomil missionary influx in western Christendom, p. 44; Cf. Borst, *Die Katharer*, pp. 89–96; Lambert, *Medieval Heresy*, pp. 55 ff.; *idem, The Cathars*, pp. 32 ff.; Coulianu, *The Tree of Gnosis*, p. 214 (who estimates that Bogomil dualism had penetrated western areas by the beginning of the twelfth century).

16 William of Newburgh, *Historia rerum anglicarum* 1:13, ed. R. Howlett, *Chronicles of the Reigns of Stephen, Henry II and Richard I* (London, 1884), vol. 1, pp. 131–4. On William of Newburgh's report see now Biller, 'William of

Newburgh and the Cathar Mission', with a discussion of other reported Cathar-related incidents in England and the role of Cistercian information networks in England and France in the struggle against Catharism.

17 On the names given to Cathar groups, see Borst, *Die Katharer*, pp. 240–53; J. Duvernoy, *Le Catharisme I: La Religion des Cathares* (Toulouse, 1976), pp. 297–313; Lambert, *The Cathars*, p. 43.

18 G. Scholem, *The Origins of the Kabbalah*, tr. A. Arkush (Princeton, N. J. 1987), esp. pp. 12–18, draws attention to some interesting parallels between Cathar and early Kabbalistic themes, but studies and debates on this matter continue without any clear conclusions as yet. See, for example, S. Shahar, 'Écrits cathares et commentaire d'Abraham Abulafia sur "Le Livre de la Création", Images et Idées Communes', in *Juifs et Judaïsme de Languedoc, CF*, 12 (Toulouse, 1977), pp. 345–63, and the criticism of Shahar's views in M. Idel, *Studies in Ecstatic Kabbalah* (New York, 1988), pp. 33–45. See also C. P. Hershon, *Faith and Controversy: The Jews of Medieval Languedoc* (Birmingham, 1998), pp. 33–44.

19 On the diverse conditions favouring the spread of Catharism in Languedoc in the second half of the twelfth century, see, for example, C. Thouzellier, *Catharisme et valdéisme en Languedoc à la fin du XIIe et au début du XIIIe siècle, Politique pontificale-controverses*, 2nd rev. edn (Paris, 1969), Chaps 1 and 2, pp. 11–81; 'Hérésie et croisade au XIIe siècle', in *Hérésie et hérétiques: Vaudois, cathares, patarins, albigeois* (Rome, 1969), pp. 17–39; M. Roquebert, *L'Épopée cathare*, vol. 1, *1198–1212: L'invasion* (Toulouse, 1970), Chaps 3 to 5; ; J. Duvernoy, *Le Catharisme II: L'Histoire des Cathares* (Toulouse, 1979), pp. 195–237; P. Labal, 'L'Église de Rome face au catharisme', in *Les Cathares en Occitanie* (Paris, 1982), pp. 11–205; E. Griffe, *Les débuts de l'aventure cathare en Languedoc (1140–1190)* (Paris, 1969); M. Costen, *The Cathars and the Albegensian Crusade* (Manchester, 1997), Chap. 2; Lambert, *The Cathars*, pp. 60–81; on the presence of Catharism, in its early and mature forms in the various levels of Occitan society, see A. Brenon, *Le vrai visage du catharisme* (Poret-sur-Garonne, 1988), Pt. 2, pp. 100–95; see also Duvernoy, *Le Catharisme I: La Religion*, pp. 245–89, *passim*; A. Roach, 'Cathar Economy', *RMS*, 12, 1986, pp. 51–71, etc.; various aspects of the religious, political, social and cultural conditions in Languedoc during the period of Cathar presence in the area have been illuminated in the contributions to the conferences at Fanjeaux published in the successive *Cathiers de Fanjeaux*.

20 On the role of noble ladies and women in general in Languedoc Catharism, cf. the sometimes differing views of Brenon, *Le vrai visage*, pp. 166–95; *Les Femmes Cathares* (Paris, 1992); M. Barber, 'Women and Catharism', *RMS*, 3, 1977, pp. 45–62; R. Abels and E. Harrison, 'The Participation of Women in Languedoc Catharism', *MS*, 41, 1979, pp. 215–51; P. Biller, 'The Common Woman in the Western Church in the Thirteenth and early Fourteenth

Centuries', *SCH*, 27, 1990, pp. 127–57; J. Mundy, *Men and Women at Toulouse in the Age of the Cathars* (Toronto, 1990), *passim*; B. Hamilton, 'The State of Research. The Legacy of Charles Schmidt to the Study of Christian Dualism', *JMH*, 24:2, 1998, pp. 200–1. On the troubadour culture in Occitan society, see now L. M. Paterson, *The World of the Troubadours: Medieval Occitan Society, c.* 1100–1300 (Cambridge, 1993); on the way courtly love could be seen as religious dissent, see J. B. Russell, 'Courtly Love as Religious Dissent', *CHR*, 51, 1, 1965, pp. 31–44.

21 Bernard Gui, *Manuel de l'inquisiteur*, ed. G. Mollat, 2 vols (Paris, 1926–7), vol. 1, p. 20; for an important analysis of the notions inherent in the *consolamentum*, its parallels in early eastern Christianty and the possible role of the Massalians as the possible transmitters of the rite to the medieval dualists, see R. van den Broek, 'The Cathars: Medieval Gnostics', in *Studies in Alexandrian Christianity and Gnosticism*, pp. 157–78, esp. pp. 169–77; on the common use of the *consolamentum* and other religious practices among the Bogomils and the Cathars, see Hamilton, 'Wisdom from the East', pp. 46–9; Lambert, *The Cathars*, pp. 29–33; F. Sanjek, 'Le catharisme: l'unité des rituels. Apport des sources bosniaques', *Heresis*, 21, 1993, pp. 29–47; Rottenwöhrer, *Der Katharismus*, Bd. III, *Die Herkunft*, pp. 102–15, *passim*; Y. Hagman, 'Le rite d'initiation chrétien chez les cathares et les bogomiles', *Heresis*, 20, 1993, pp. 13–33; on the Cathar *perfecti* in Languedoc and the nature of Cathar rites such as the *melioramentum*, see the excellent discussion in Lambert, *The Cathars*, pp. 141–58; on the *consolamentum* and other Cathar ritual practices, see further Duvernoy, *Le Catharisme I: La Religion*, Chap. 3, pp. 143–70; Brenon, *Le vrai visage*, pp. 76–85; 'Les fonctions sacramentelles du consolament', *Heresis*, 20, 1993, pp. 33–55; Rottenwöhrer, *Der Katharismus*, Bd. II, *Der Kult, die Religiöse praxis, die Kritik am Kult und Sakramenten der Katholischen Kirche*, vol. 1, *Der Kult* (Bad Honnef, 1982).

22 The *Acts* were published by G. Besse in *Histoire des ducs, marquis et comtes de Narbonne* (Paris, 1660), pp. 483–6. Their authenticity has been conclusively established by A. Dondaine in 'Les Actes du concile albigeois de Saint-Félix-de-Caraman', *Miscellanea Giovanni Mercati*, vol. 5, *Studi e Testi*, Vatican City, 125 (1946), pp. 324–56. The text of the *Acts* has been reproduced by B. Hamilton in 'The Cathar Council of Saint-Félix Reconsidered', *Archivum Fratrum Praedicatorum*, Rome, 48 (1978), pp. 51–3.

23 Rainerius' tract has been printed in Dondaine, *Un traité néo-manichéen*, pp. 64–78; with the list of the Cathar and Bogomil churches on p. 70. The locations of the various Bogomil churches have provoked much debate and conflicting decisions; see, for example, Obolensky, *The Bogomils*, pp. 156–64; Dragojlović, *Bogomilstvo na Balkanu*, pp. 176–83; D. Angelov, *Bogomilstvoto v Bŭlgariia*, 3rd edn (1980), pp. 355ff.; Angold, *Church and Society*, pp. 493–4; B. Hamilton, 'The Origins of the Dualist Church of Drugunthia', *ECR*, 6, 1974, pp. 115–24;

'Historical Introduction', pp. 44–5. For arguments for a Paulician background of Nicetas' allusion to the 'seven churches of Asia', see Hamilton, 'The Cathars and the Seven Churches'; on the figure of Nicetas, see D. Obolensky, 'Papa Nicetas: a Byzantine Dualist in the Land of the Cathars', *Harvard Ukrainian Studies*, 7, 1983; pp. 489–500; Fichtenau, *Ketzer*, pp. 151–3.

24 See, for example, Dondaine, 'Les Actes', p. 345; J. Duvernoy, 'L'eglise dite bulgare du catharisme occidental et le problème de l'unité du catharisme', *BBg*, 6, 1980, p. 138, n. 91; Hamilton, 'Cathar Council', pp. 38–9; recently Angold, *Church and Society*, pp. 493–4, revived the old theory of C. Schmidt, *Histoire et doctrine de la secte des Cathares et Albigeois*, 2 vols (Paris and Geneva, 1848–9), vol. 1, p. 57, n. 5 that *Ecclesia Melenguiae* should be associated with the town of Melnik in the Struma valley in eastern Macedonia.

25 Hamilton, 'The Cathar Council', p. 39.

26 Joachim of Fiore, *Expositio in Apocalypsum* (Venice, 1527), f. 134r–v.

27 *De heresi catharorum in Lombardia*, p. 306. Lambert, *The Cathars*, pp. 46–7, suggests confusion in the sources, arguing that Mark should have received his reconsoling and episcopate from Nicetas back in Italy. For arguments that the reconsoling at St-Félix did not imply that the previous order was superseded by Nicetas in the framework of a schismatic division, see Brenon, *Le vrai visage*, pp. 108–9; see the criticism of this approach to Nicetas' rites of reconsolation at St-Félix in Lambert, *The Cathars*, pp. 46–7, n. 6; see also the views of A. Brenon that the intellectual divergences between the absolute and moderate dualists did not have implications for the validity of the *consolamentum*, 'Le faux problème du dualisme absolu', *Heresis*, 21, 1993, pp. 61–75.

28 Runciman, *The Medieval Manichee*, p. 73; on the possible role of Symeon in initiating radical dualism in the Drugunthian church, see Rottenwöhrer, *Der Katharismus*, Bd. III, *Die Herkunft*, pp. 565–7.

29 *De heresi catharorum in Lombardia*, p. 306.

30 Mark's doubts, journey, imprisonment and death are recounted in Anselm's *Tractatus de hereticis*, pp. 309–10.

31 The split of Italian Catharism into separate churches and their missions to the Balkan mother-churches is recorded in *De heresi catharorum in Lombardia*, pp. 306–8. For arguments that the Catholic sources have exaggerated the schismatic divisions among the Italian Cathar churches, see Duvernoy, *Le Catharisme I: La Religion*, pp. 58, 83, 329–47; cf. however, Rottenwöhrer, *Der Katharismus*, Bd. III, *Die Herkunft*, pp. 528–9. For arguments that the divisions among the Italian Cathars led to increasing intellectual activity in Cathar circles amid the unfolding doctrinal disputes, see L. Paolini, 'Italian Catharism and Written Culture', p. 88, cf. in this context Lambert, *The Cathars*, pp. 55–6. The most pronounced doctrinal divisions were between the absolute dualist church of Desenzano and the moderate dualist church of

Concorezzo (see below); on Desenzano and Concorezzo versions of dualism and beliefs, see Rottenwöhrer, *Der Katharismus*, Bd. IV, *Glaube und Theologie der Katharer*, vol. 1 (1993), resp. pp. 31–165 and pp. 310–427; on the schism and the diverging systems of belief of Cathar absolute and moderate dualists, see further Duvernoy, *Le Catharisme I: La Religion*, pp. 105–20.

32 Published for the first time by J. Benoist, *Histoire des Albigeois et des Vaudois ou Barbets* (Paris, 1691), vol. 1, pp. 283–96. Benoist's text was reprinted in *Fortgesetzte Sammlung von alten und neuen theologischen Sachen* (Leipzig, 1734), pp. 703–13; J. C. Thillo, *Codex apocryphus Novi Testamenti* (Leipzig, 1832), vol. 1, pp. 884–96; C. U. Hahn, *Geschichte der Ketzer im Mittelalter* (Stuttgart, 1847), vol. 2, pp. 815–20. The Carcassonne version was published alongside the Vienna version by M. Sokolov, *Slavianskaia kniga Enokha pravednago* (Moscow, 1910), pp. 165–75; also by I. Ivanov, *Bogomilski knigi i legendi*, pp. 73–87, R. Reitzenstein, *Die Vorgeschichte der christlichen Taufe* (Leipzig and Berlin, 1929), pp. 297–311, and in the most recent critical edition of the text, E. Bozoky, *Le livre secret des cathares* (Paris, 1980), pp. 41–94. For the other two manuscripts of this version see their description in Bozoky, *Le livre secret*, pp. 19–21; one of these manuscripts, that from the Dole library, is used as a representative of the Carcassonne version in Bozoky's critical edition.

33 The letter exists in two versions, reproduced in J. D. Mansi, *Sacrorum conciliorum nova et amplissima collectio* (54 vols, reprint of 1901–27 edn, Graz, 1960–1), vol. 22, cols 1201–2, 1203–6.

34 Hamilton, 'The Cathar Council', pp. 46ff.

35 See, for example, Borst, *Die Katharer*, pp. 98, 108, 142. According to Obolensky, *The Bogomils*, pp. 157–62, the Drugunthian church was actually the Paulician Balkan church, with its traditional absolute dualist orientation (see, however, his revised position on this issue in 'Papa Nicetas', pp. 496–7). For arguments that Bogomil radical dualism was conceptualized in Byzantine monastic circles 'with intense nostalgia for Origenism', see Coulianu, *The Tree of Gnosis*, p. 214 (on the posited Origenist elements in Cathar radical dualism, see M. Dando, *Les origines du catharisme* (Paris, 1967); Duvernoy, *Le Catharisme I: La Religion*, pp. 60, 296, 364, 367–77). A recent synthesis of the evidence concerning Bogomil radical dualism in B. Hamilton, 'The Origins of the Dualist Church of Drugunthia', has demonstrated the Bogomil character of the Drugunthian church and indicated that the schism in Balkan dualism followed cultural lines: 'the Byzantine areas of Drugunthia in Thrace and Constantinople accepted absolute dualism, while Slavonic areas in Bulgaria and Bosnia remained faithful to the traditional moderate dualist teaching of Pop Bogomil' (p. 121).

36 Cf. Hamilton, 'The Origins of the Dualist Church of Drugunthia', p. 119; 'Historical Introduction', p. 44.

5 The Crusade Against Dualism

1 A. Theiner, *Vetera monumenta Slavorum Meridionalium historiam illustrantia* (Rome, 1863), vol. I, p. 41. The religious and messianic overtones of the Assenid rebellion and restoration of the Bulgarian monarchy are discussed in Dujčev, *Prouchvania*, pp. 46ff. Alternatively, Nicetas Choniates, *Historia*, p. 485, stated that the rebels were incited by 'demoniacs' and 'soothsayers' who prophesied that God had assented to their freedom. On the ethnicity of the rebels, see J. V. A. Fine, Jr, *The Late Medieval Balkans* (Ann Arbor, 1987), pp. 12–14.

2 See the letter of Vukan to Pope Innocent III in T. Smičiklas, *Codex diplomaticus regni Croatiae, Dalmatiae et Sclavoniae* (Zagreb, 1904), vol. 2, pp. 333–4.

3 See Innocent's letter in Smičiklas, *Codex diplomaticus*, vol. 2, p. 350–2.

4 Letter in Smičiklas, *Codex diplomaticus*, vol. 3, pp. 14–15.

5 See the text of the abjuration, for example, in Smičiklas, *Codex diplomaticus*, vol. 3, pp. 24–5.

6 Alberic of Trois-Fontaines, *Chronica*, p. 886.

7 The *Synodicon of Tsar Boril* has been edited by M. G. Popruzhenko in *Bŭlgarski Starini* (Sofia, 1928), vol. 8. The English translation is in *HCDH*, pp. 260–3. On the source for the *Synodicon*, see J. Gouillard, 'Une Source grecque du synodik de Boril', *T&M*, 4 (1970), pp. 361–74. On the organization and proceedings of the council, see now N. Shivarov, 'Otnosno niakoi saobrazheniia i motivi za svikvaneto na Tŭrnovskiia sŭbor ot 1211 i za negoviia obrazets', *AUSKO-CRSBID*, 1 (1987), pp. 89–100, which concludes that the council was Orthodox in character, had certain political implications and was deployed in accordance with contemporary papal measures against Catharism – consequently, the Bulgarian Church maintained its links with Rome and the Bulgarian bishopric was invited to take part in the Fourth Lateran Council in 1215.

8 Arnold Aimery, *PL*, vol. 216, col. 139. On the massacre at Bézier, see now *'Tuez-les tous, Dieu Reconnaîtra les siens', Le massacre de Bézier (22 juillet 1209) et la croisade contre les Albigeois vus par Césaire de Heisterbach* (Poret-sur-Garonne, 1994).

9 E. Martin-Chabot (cd. and tr.), *La Chanson de la Croisade Albigeoise*, 3 vols (Paris, 1931–61), vol. 3, pp. 208–9. There exists a considerable literature on the crusade in French: a recent exhaustive treatment of the theme is M. Roquebert, *L'Épopée cathare. I. 1198–1212: L'invasion. II. 1213–1216 Muret ou la dépossession. III. 1216–1229. Le lys et la croix. IV. Mourir à Montségur* (Toulouse, 1971–89). Among the accounts of the Albigensian Crusade in English, see J. R. Strayer, *The Albigensian Crusade* (New York, 1971);

B. Hamilton, *The Albigensian Crusade* (London, 1974); J. Sumption, *The Albigensian Crusade* (London, 1978); M. Costen, *The Cathars and the Albegensian Crusade.*

10 On the establishment of the papal inquisition and its first stages, see, for example, H. I. Lea, *A History of the Inquisition in the Middle Ages* (New York, 1888), vol. 1, Chap. 7; H. Maisonneuve, *Études sur le origines de l'inquisition* (Paris, 1942), Chap. 8; E. Duvernoy, *Le Catharisme II: L'Histoire,* pp. 267–79; B. Hamilton, *The Medieval Inquisition* (New York, 1981), pp. 31–72; E. Peters, *Inquisition* (New York, 1988), pp. 44–71; W. Wakefield, *Heresy, Crusade and Inquisition in Southern France* (London, 1974); J. Griffe, *Les Cathares et l'Inquisition (1229–1329)* (Paris, 1980).

11 For the development of Italian Catharism in the late twelfth and during the thirteenth century and the initial inquisitorial campaigns against Italian Cathars, cf. M. D'Alatri, *Eretici e inquisitori in Italia, Studi e documenti,* 2 vols (Rome, 1986–7); R. Manselli. *L'eresia del male* (Naples, 1961); 'La fin du Catharisme en Italie', *Effacement du Catharisme? (XIIIe–XIVe siècles), CF,* 20 (1985), pp. 101–18; 'Per la storia dell'eresia catara nella Firenze del tempo di Dante', *BISIAM,* 62 (1950), pp. 123–38; C. Violante, 'Hérésies urbanies et hérésies rurales en Italie du 11e au 13e siècle', in J. Le Goff, (ed.) *Hérésies et sociétés dans l'Europe pré-industrielle,* 11e–18e siècles (Paris, 1968), pp. 171–202; L. Paolini, *L'eresia catara alla fine del duecento,* vol. 1, *L'eresia a Bologna fra XIII e XIV secolo* (Rome, 1975); G. Zanella, 'L'eresia catara fra XIII e XIV secolo: in margine al disagio di una storigrafia', repr. in *Hereticalia: Temi e discussioni* (Spoleto, 1995), pp. 127–44; *Itinerari ereticali: patari e catari tra Rimini e Verona* (Rome, 1986); G. Merlo, 'Eretici nel mondo communale italiano', repr. in *Ereticie e eresie medievale* (Bologna, 1989), pp. 233–59; Lambert, *The Cathars,* Chaps 8, 11; C. Lansing, *Power and Purity, Cathar Heresy in Medieval Italy,* (New York, 1998).

12 Matthew of Paris, *Historia Anglorum,* ed. F. Madden, 3 vols (London, 1868–91), vol. 3, p. 278; cf. vol. 2, pp. 338, 415. The mass burning at Mont-Aime is recorded in Alberic of Trois-Fontaines, *Chronica,* pp. 944–5. On Robert le Bougre, see C. H. Haskins, 'Robert le Bougre and the beginning of the Inquisition in Northern France', in *Studies in Medieval Culture* (Cambridge, Mass., 1929), pp. 193–224.

13 On the historical evidence concerning the Cathar treasure and its later mythological elaborations, see M. Roquebert, 'Napoléon Peyrat, le trésor et le "noveaux Montségur"', in *Catharisme: l'édifice imaginaire, Actes du 7ème colloque du Centre d'Études Cathares/René Nelli* (Carcassonne, 1998), pp. 345–77. On the Avignonet assassination, see Y. Dossat, 'Le massacre d'Avignonet', *CF,* 6, pp. 343–59. On the siege of Montségur, see Z. Oldenburg, *Massacre at Montségur,* tr. P. Green (London, 1961), Chap. 12; Roquebert, *L'Épopée cathare, IV, Mourir á Montségur,* pp. 130–57; 'Montségur', refuge ou

quartier general?' in *La Persécution du Catharisme XIIème–XIVème siècles*, *Collection Heresis*, VI (Arques, 1996), pp. 159–92; Duvernoy, *Le Catharisme II: L'Histoire*, pp. 286–95; Oldenburg, *Massacre at Montségur*, Chap. 12. On the Inquisition work in the area, see J. Duvernoy (ed. and tr.), *Le Dossier de Montségur: interrogatoires d'inquisition 1242–47* (Toulouse, 1998).

14 The events in Catalonia are reconstructed by J. V. Subirats, 'Le catharisme en Catalogne', *Cahiers d'études cathares*, 14 (1963), 2e serie, No. 19, pp. 3–25; cf. Loos, *Dualist Heresy in the Middle Ages*, p. 204. On Catharism in Spain, which was mostly present in Catalonia, see 'El catarismo en Cataluña', *Boletin de la real academia de buenas letras de Barcelona*, 28 (1959–60), pp. 75–168; L. Vones, 'Krone und Inquisition'; A. Cazenave, 'Les Cathares en Catalogne et Sabarthès après les registres d'Inquisition:la hiérarchie Cathare en Sabarthès après Montségur', *BPH Année 1969*, 1972, pp. 387–436; C. A. Esteve, *Cātaros y Occitanos en el reino de Mallorca* (Palma de Mallorca, 1978); A. M. A. I Tasis and P. C. i Roca, *Càtars i Catarismea a Catalunya* (Barcelona, 1996).

15 Germanus' encyclical is published in Ficker, *Die Phundagiagiten*, pp. 115–26. English translation in *HCDH*, pp. 267–75; on Germanus' encyclical, see A. Rigo, 'Il patriarca Germano II (1223–1240) e i Bogomili', *REB*, 51 (1993), pp. 91–110.

16 Gregory's letter to Bela is reproduced in A. Theiner, *Vetera monumenta historica Hungariam sacram illustrantia*, 2 vols (Rome, 1859–60) vol. I, pp. 159–60.

17 Theiner, *Vetera monumenta historica*, vol. I, pp. 166–7.

18 F. Rački, '*Bogomili i Patareni*', *Rad jugoslovenske akademije znanosti i umjetnosti*, Zagreb, 7 (1869), p. 144.

19 Theiner, *Vetera monumenta historica*, pp. 55, 72.

20 An overview of the evidence and reconstruction of the course of the crusade is provided in J. V. A. Fine, *The Bosnian Church: A New Interpretation* (New York and London, 1975), pp. 137–48. The failure of the crusade is apparent in Innocent's statement in 1247 that the Bosnian Church had relapsed 'totally into heresy' (Theiner, *Vetera monumenta historica*, pp. 204–5).

21 *Commentariorum de provinciae Hungariae originibus, Monumenta Ordinis Fratrum Praedicatorum Historica I*, ed. B. M. Reichert (Louvain, 1896), pp. 305–8.

22 On the fortunes of Italian Catharism during the thirteenth and early fourteenth centuries, amid the anti-Cathar inquisitorial campaigns, the changing socio-political situation in the urban and rural areas where Catharism had a following and the role of the lay confraternities and the Mendicant orders in the eclipse of Italian Catharism, cf. D'Alatri, *Eretici e inquisitori in Italia, Studi e documenti*, vol. 2; S. Savini, *Il catarismo italiano ed i suoi vescovi nei secoli XIII e XIV* (Florence, 1958); Manselli, 'La fin du Catharisme en Italie'; D. Corsi, 'Aspetti dell' inquisizione fiorentina nel

'200'', in D. Maselli, *Eretici e ribelli del XIIIe secolo* (Pistoia, 1974), pp. 65–71; Paolini, *L'eresia a Bologna fra XIII e XIV secolo*; L. Paolini and R. Orioli, *Acta Sancti Officii Bononie ab a. 1291 usque ad 1310* (Rome, 1982); N. J. Housley, 'Politics and Heresy in Italy: Anti-Heretical Crusades, Orders, Confraternities, 1200–1500', *JEH*, 32 (1982), pp. 193–208; Zanella, 'L'eresia catara fra XIII e XIV secolo; *Itinerari ereticali*; F. Zambon, 'L' hérésies cathare dans la société et la culture italienne du XIIIe siècle', in *Europe et Occitanie: les pays Cathares, Collection Heresis V* (Arques, 1995), pp. 27–52; Lambert, *The Cathars*, Chap. 11; Lansing, *Power and Purity*, Part III.

23 On Pierre Autier and his mission to revive Catharism, see J. Duvernoy, 'Pierre Autier', *CHC*, 21 (1970), pp. 9–49; Lambert, *The Cathars*, Chap. 10; H. C. Stoodt, *Katharismus im Untergrund, Die Reorganisation durch Petrus Auterii* (Tübingen, 1996).

24 On the inquisitorial anti-Cathar campaigns in Languedoc after the fall of Montségur in the second half of the thirteenth and early fourteenth centuries, see B. Hauréau, *Bernard Délicieux et l'Inquisition albigeoise, 1300–1320* (Paris, 1877); reissued Poret-sur-Garonne, 1992); R. W. Emery, *Heresy and Inquisition in Narbonne* (New York, 1941); Y. Dossat, *Les crises de l'Inquisition toulousaine au XIIIe siècle (1233–1273)*, (Bordeaux, 1959); J. Duvernoy (ed.), *La registre d'Inquisition de Jacques Fournier èveque de Pamiers (1318–1325)*, (Toulouse, 1965); *Le Catharisme II: L'Histoire*, pp. 297–335; *Le Dossier de Montségur*; E. Griffe, *La Languedoc cathare et l'Inquisition* (Paris, 1980). C. W. Davis, *The Inquisition at Albi*, 1299–1300 (New York, 1948; repr. 1974); J. H. Mundy, *The Repression of Catharism at Toulouse, The Royal Diploma of 1279* (Toulouse, 1985); A. P.-Gobilliard, *L'Inquisiteur Geoffroy d'Ablis et les cathares du comté de Foix* (Paris, 1984); the contributions in Part 2 of *Effacement du Catharisme, CF*, 20 (1985) and *La Pérsecution du Catharisme XII*-*XIV* *siècles, Collection Heresis*, VI (Arques, 1996); J. B. Given, *Inquisition and Medieval Society, Power, Discipline, and Resistance in Languedoc* (Ithaca, N Y, 1997); A. Friedlander, *The Hammer of the Inquisitors, Brother Bernard Délicieux and the Struggle Against the Inquisition in Fourteenth-Century France* (Leiden, 2000), Chap. 2, pp. 39–66.

25 See the sub-chapter 'Heresy and Magic – East and West' below pp. 232–50

26 Cf. Barber, *The Trial of the Templars*, pp. 181, 186–8. See also n. 91 below.

27 F. Legge, 'Western Manichaeism and the Turfan Discoveries', *JRAS* (1913), p. 73.

28 Quoted after the translation provided in Wakefield and Evans, *Heresies of the High Middle Ages*, p. 88; this reference, of course, predates the first recorded emergence of Cathar groups but it is suggestive of the way mystical or ambiguous statements made by framed or real heretics could be interpreted literally to generate a belief in the existence of a heretical pontiff. For a discussion of the evidence concerning the belief in the existence of an heretical anti-pope, see Borst, *Die Katharer*, pp. 209–11.

29 Bech's statement may be found in I. von Döllinger, *Beiträge zur Sektenge-schichte des Mittelalters* 2 vols (Munich, 1890 repr. 1968), vol. 2, p. 206.

30 The Patarene articles are refuted in Juan Torquemada, *Symbolum pro informatione manichaeorum*, ed. N. L. Martines and V. Proano (Burgos, 1958). A translation of the articles can be found in Fine, *The Bosnian Church*, pp. 355–7, with a commentary that questions their relevance for the Bosnian Church.

31 Theiner, *Vetera monumenta historica*, vol. 2, p. 91.

32 B. Hamilton, 'Catholic Perceptions of East European Dualism in the Twelfth and Thirteenth Centuries', in his *Crusaders, Cathars and the Holy Places* (Ashgate, 2000), XIV, p. 8.

33 See Honorius' letter in Smičiklas, *Codex Diplomaticus*, vol. 3, pp. 196.

34 Rainerius Sacconi, *Summa*, ed. A. Dondaine, in *Un Traité néo-manichéen*, p. 70.

35 *De heresi Catharorum in Lombardia*, p. 308.

36 Anselm of Alessandria, *Tractatus de hereticis*, p. 308.

37 *Commentariorum de provinciae Hungariae*, pp. 305–8.

38 B. Hamilton, *Religion in the Medieval West* (London and New York, 1986), p. 177; for an early development of this thesis, see F. Rački, *Bogomili i Patareni, Rad Jugoslavenske akademie Znanosti i umjetnosti*, Zagreb, 7 (1869), p. 84–179; 8 (1869), pp. 121–87; 10 (1870), pp. 160–263. Rački's reconstruction of the history and nature of the Bosnian Church has been followed and elaborated in a number of scholarly and popular works.

39 Fine, *The Bosnian Church*, esp. pp. 148 ff. Fine's views have also gained the support of a number of scholars and have been developed in scholarly and general works, see, for example, the recent treatment of the theme in N. Malcolm, *Bosnia. A Short History* (London, 1994), chap. 3. Views, similar to those of Fine, that the Bosnian Church developed independently of the dualist heresy in Bosnia, have been articulated earlier but in a less systematic manner. For a particular view that the Bosnian Church evolved separately from eastern Bogomilism and western Catharism, but as a continuation of Manichaeism from 'the East' (a thesis which is impossible to prove), see S. H. Alić, 'Bosanski krstjani i pitanje njihovog porjekla i odnosa prema manihejstvu', *Bogomilstvoto na Balkanot*, pp. 153–94.

40 Circović, 'Die Bosnische Kirche', *L'Oriente cristiano nella storia della civiltà* (Rome, 1964), pp. 552–5; *Istorija srednjovekovne bosanske drzave* (Belgrade, 1964), pp. 58–69, and more recently in his 'Dualistichka heterodoksija'. A similar thesis has recently been argued very persuasively in Lambert, *The Cathars*, pp. 297–314. For arguments that the Bosnian monks forced to conduct the public abjuration of errors under Ban Kulin belonged to an East Orthodox-derived monastic organization under the rule of St Basil (whose existence is itself a controversial problem), see M. Miletić, *I 'Krstjani' di Bosnia alla luce dei loro monumenti di pietà* (Rome, 1957); cf. discussion in Malcolm, *Bosnia*, pp.

34–6; for arguments that the Bosnian Church was influenced by the mysticism and structure of eastern monasticism, see D. Dragojlović, *Kristjani i jeretička crkva bosanska* (Belgrade, 1987). For a different set of arguments, which are impossible to substantiate, that the Bosnian Church was a non-ecclesiastical diplomatic-arbitrary body under the jurisdiction of the Serbian Orthodox Church, see M. M. Petrović, *Kudugeri-bogomili u vizantijskim i srpskami izvorima i 'crkva bosanska'* (Belgrade, 1998).

41 Pius II, *Europa Opera quae extant omina*, ed. M. Hopperus (Basel, 1551), p. 407.

42 The so-called Radoslav ritual; see n. 121 to Chapter 3 above. Cf. Fine, *The Bosnian Church*, p. 83; F. Sanjek, *Les Chrétiens bosniaques et le mouvement cathare XIIe–XVe siècles*, (Paris, 1976), pp. 185ff.; see the English translation of its text by Y. Stoyanov in *HCDH*, pp. 289–92.

43 Loos, *Dualist Heresy*, p. 298. On the letter of John XXII, see n. 47 below.

44 Fine, *The Bosnian Church*, pp. 151, 295–6.

45 Lambert, *The Cathars*, p. 301, with a summary of the evidence showing that at least some features of the Bosnian Church were heretical, p. 301, n. 15. Lambert defines the Bosnian Church as a 'syncretistic Church, with a top-hamper of doctrine and ritual inherited from dualist infiltration', p. 310.

46 This process has been explored in a valuable recent survey of Paulician settlements in Bulgaria during the fifteenth to eighteenth centuries in I. Iovkov, *Pavlikiani i pavlikianski selishta v bŭlgarskite zemi XV–XVIII v.* (Sofia, 1991), pp. 55–102.

47 See the evidence discussed in Lansing, *Power and Purity*, pp. 94 ff.

48 T. Smičiklas, *Codex Diplomaticus*, vol. 9, p. 234.

49 S. Circović, 'The Bosnian Patarenes and Western Heresies' (unpublished paper read at the *Heresy in Eastern Europe conference*, SSEES, University of London, August, 1994), p. 14. Cf. Hamilton, *Religion in the Medieval West*, p. 177. For Bosnia as a kind of a dualist promised land, cf. Loos, *The Dualist Heresy*, pp. 221, 298; Lambert, *The Cathars*, pp. 298–9, 302, 313.

50 Quoted after the documents published in M. Esposito, 'Un Auto-da-fé à Chieri en 1412', *Revue d'histoire ecclésiastique*, 42 (1947), pp. 422–32.

51 The events surrounding the accusations against Niphon Scorpio and Callistus' defence were told by Nicephorus Gregoras, *Historia Byzantinae*, vol. 3, pp. 260–1, 532–46; whereas the penetration of heresy into Mount Athos is discussed in vol. 2, pp. 714, 718–20. For the evidence concerning Gregory Palamas and the Bogomils, see the texts translated in *HCDH*, pp. 278–82. For a critical analysis of the sources for and the historico-religious background to the complex interrelationship between monasticism, Hesychasm and Bogomilism, see now A. Rigo, *Monasi esicasti e monasi bogomili*, (Florence, 1989).

52 The account of Theodosius' struggles against heresy follows the version of these

events in the *Life of St Theodosius*, ed. V. Zlatarski, *SBNU*, 20(1904), pp. 1–44. See the English translation of the relevant sections by Y. Stoyanov in *HCDH*, pp. 282–6; for arguments that the absolute dualist teachings ascribed to the two Bogomils expelled from Athos derived from the doctrines of the Drugunthian (Dragovitian) Church, see Hamilton, 'Historical Introduction', p. 54.

53 Obolensky, *The Bogomils*, p. 264.

54 *Zakonik Stefana Dushana, cara Srpskog*, ed. S. Novaković (Belgrade, 1898). New edition and English translation, D. Krstić, *Dushan's Code. The XIV Century Code of Serbian Tsar Stephan Dushan*, 2nd edn (Belgrade, 1989).

55 The episode of Euthymius' struggle with the two heretical sorcerers is examined in D. Angelov, *Bogomilstvoto v Bŭlgaria*, pp. 426–31, with observations on the growing popularity of magic and demonology in this period.

56 See the text in Regino of Prum, *Libri duo de Synodalibus causis et disciplinis Ecclesiasticis*, ed. F. G. A. Wasserschleben (Leipzig, 1840), p. 355. On its later inclusion in corpuses of canon law see E. Peters, *The Magician, the Witch and the Law* (Sussex, 1978), pp. 72–4; Russell, *Witchcraft*, pp. 75–80, 146–7, 291–3; N. Cohn, *Europe's Inner Demons* (London, 1975), pp. 211–13.

57 *Isidori Hispalensis Episcopi Etymologiarum*, ed. W. M. Lindsay, 2 vols (Oxford, 1911), VIII, ix, *De Magis*.

58 Rabanus Maurus, *Commentaria in exodum*, PL, vol. 108, col.121. On Rabanus' attitudes to magic see Peters, *The Magician*, pp. 16–7.

59 The 'Manichaean' heretics at Châlons-sur-Marne are accused of performing 'shameful religious rites' in *Herigeri et Anselmi Gesta episcoporum Leodiensium*, II.62–4, ed. R. Koepke, in *MGH SS*, vol. 8, pp. 226–8.

60 The accusations against the 'Manichaean' heretics near Soissons are reported in *Guibert de Nogent: Histoire de sa vie (1053–1124)*, III.xvii, ed. G. Bourgin (Paris, 1907), pp. 212–15.

61 For descriptions of Jewish rites as 'base and abominable' and permitting all that was abhorrent to Romans, see Tacitus, *Histories*, 5:4–5; Tacitus' account draws on earlier anti-Jewish Alexandrian writers like Lysimachus and Apion; for the anti-Jewish stories of Apion (which included accusations of ritual human sacrifice), see the account of Josephus in *Contra Apionem*, II, 65–103, ed. L. Blum, *Contre Apion* (Paris, 1930), pp. 69–76. For examples of anti-Christian accusations, see, for instance, the description of Minucius Felix, *Octavius*, cap. IX, ed. J. Beaujeu (Paris, 1960), pp. 12–14.

62 *Gunzo Epistola ad Augiensis und Anselm von Besate Rhetorimachia*, MGH Quellen, ed. K. Manitius, II, (Weimar, 1958), pp. 170–6; see also *ibid.*, pp. 124–5, 25, 129–30, 142–5. On Anselm's description of magical practices, see Peters, *The Magician*, pp. 21–7.

63 William of Malmesbury, *Gesta Rerum Anglorum*, II, 167–71, *PL*, vol. 179, cols 1137–44.

64 *Hugonis de Sancto Victore Didascalicon de studio legendi*, ed. C. H. Buttimer

(Washington, 1939), VI, xv, pp. 132–3. On Hugh of St Victor's views om magic, see, for example, L. Thorndike, *A History of Magic and Experimental Science* (New York, 1923), vol. 2, pp. 11–16; on his influence on subsequent attitudes to magic, see Peters, *The Magician*, pp. 66–7.

65 The accusations against the heretics at Rheims appear in the chronicle of Ralph of Coggeshall: see *Radulphi de Coggeshall Chronicon Anglicanum*, ed. J. Stephenson (London, 1875), pp. 121–5; see also the practices ascribed to 'Patarines' (Cathars) in Walter Map, *De nugis curialium*, I, XXX, ed. M. R. James (Oxford, 1914; rev. edn 1983), pp. 117–23.

66 Alain de Lille, *De fide catholica contra haereticos sui temporis*, I, lxiii, in Migne, *PL*, vol. 210, col. 366; for Alain of Lille's claim that the Cathars worship Lucifer in the form of a cat (from which he derives their name), cf. Walter of Map, *De nugis curialium*, p. 120.

67 Alain de Lille, *De fide catholica*, II, i, *PL*, vol. 210, col.380.

68 *Tractatus de haeresi Pauperum de Lugduno*, in E. Martene and U. Durand, *Thesaurus novus anecdotorum* (Paris, 1717), vol.5, cols 1781–2; otherwise the tract rejects the charge of Devil-worship.

69 Text in Martene and Durand, *Thesaurus*, vol. 1, cols 950–3.

70 See, for example, the accusations against Waldensians in the chronicle of John of Winterthur, *Chronica Iohannis Vitodurani, MGM SS*, new series, vol.III, ed. F. Baethngen (Berlin, 1955).

71 See, for example, the charges against 'Luciferan' heretics in *Gesta archiepiscoporum Magdeburgensium*, in *MGH SS*, vol. 14, pp. 434–5.

72 On the formation of anti-heretical stereotypes in this period, cf. H. C. Lea, *Materials Toward a History of Witchcraft*, ed. by A. Howland (Philadelphia, 1937; repr. New York, 1957), vol. 1, pp. 201–26; Russell, *Witchcraft*, pp. 86–95, 120–32, 176–92; Cohn, *Europe's Inner Demons*, pp. 22–59; Kieckhefer, *European Witch Trials*; R. I. Moore, *The Formation of a Persecuting Society* (Oxford, 1987); B. P. Levack, *The Witch-hunt in Early Modern Europe* (London, 1987), Chap. 2; Ginsburg, *Storia notturna*, pp. 63–86.

73 Edited by Ae. Friedberg, *Corpus Iuris Canonici . . . Pars Prior, Decretum Magistri Gratiani* (Leipzig, 1879).

74 Views inherited from nineteenth-century studies that posit a supposedly crucial role for scholasticism in the formation of the intellectual foundations of later witch beliefs have been strongly challenged in the dissertation of C. E. Hopkin, *The Share of Thomas Aquinas in the Growth of Witchcraft Delusion* (Philadelphia, 1940); cf. also Russell, *Witchcraft*, pp. 142–7; Peters, *The Magician*, pp. 95–8.

75 William of Auvergne's views on magic are elaborated in his *De legibis* and *De universo*: see *Guilelmi Alverni . . . Opera Omnia*, 2 vols (Paris, 1674), *De legibis*, vol. 1, fols 18–102 (particularly, fols 67–99); *De universo*, vol. 1, fols 593–1074 (particularly, fols 947–1074). On William of Auvergne's attitudes to magic, see, for example, Thorndike, *A History of Magic and Experimental*

Science, pp. 338–71; on his views concerning the distinction between natural and demonic magic, see *ibid.*, pp. 346–8; R. Kieckhefer, *Magic in the Middle Ages* (Cambridge, 1989), pp. 12, 182.

76 For Thomas Aquinas' views on magic see his *Summa Contra Gentiles*, III, ii, Chaps civ–cvi, in *Opera Omnia*, vol. 14 (Rome, 1926), pp. 325–35; *Summa Theologica*, I, cxiv, in *S. Thomae Aquinatis Doctoris Angelici Summa Theologica* vol. 1 (Turin, 1922), pp. 717–22; *ibid.* II, ii, xcii–cv, vol.3, pp. 531–3; *Quaestiones de Quodlibet, Quodlibetum 11, Quaestio IX, Art. X, in S. Thomae Aquinatis Doctoris Angelici ord. praed. Quaestiones Quodlibetales*, vol. 1 (Paris, 1926), pp. 419–21.

77 Text in J. D. Mansi, *Sacrorum conciliorum nova et amplissima collectio* (repr. of 1901–27 edn; Graz, 1960–1), vol. 22, cols 476–8.

78 Text in *PL*, vol. 214, cols 537–9.

79 For the anti-heretical legislation of the Fourth Lateran Council, see Mansi, *Sacrorum conciliorum*, vol. 22, cols 986–90.

80 See note 10 above.

81 Text in Mansi, *Sacrorum conciliorum*, vol. 23, cols 568–9.

82 Text in J. Hansen, *Quellen und Untersuchungen zur Geschichte des Hexenwahns und der Hexenverfolgung.* (Bonn, 1901), p. 1.

83 *Glossa ordinaria*, vol. 113 : 1, col. 261 (and Exodus 22 : 18); on the importance of the gloss, see Peters, *The Magician*, p. 68.

84 *Die Summa Decretorum des Magister Rufinus* ed. H. Singer (Paderborn, 1902), pp. 423–8; on the views of other commentators on the *Decretum*, see Peters, *The Magician*, pp. 75–8.

85 For the anti-heretical legislation of Frederick 11, see *Constitutiones regni Sicialiae, MGH Leges. Sectio 5. Constitutiones*, T.2, ed. W. Sturner (Hanover, 1996) pp.149–52, 458–60.

86 Bernard Gui, *Manuel de l'inquisiteur*, ed. and tr. G. Mollat, 2 vols (Paris, 1926–7).

87 Written in 1376, Nicholas Eymeric's manual subsequently became very influential and in the late sixteenth century appeared in a number of printed editions; see, for example, *Directorium inquisitorum* (Rome, 1587).

88 Nicholas Eymeric, *Directorium inquisitorum*, pp. 235–6, 338–43.

89 The texts of John xxii's letters of authorization to inquisitors may be found in Hansen, *Quellen*, pp. 2–5.

90 Text in Hansen, *Quellen*, pp. 5–6.

91 In the early fourteenth century charges of demonic magic were raised against such high-ranking ecclesiastics as Pope Boniface viii (1294–1303) and Guichard, bishop of Troyes, while sorcery accusations at the French court were brought against figures like Mahaut of Artois, mother-in-law of Philip v, and Enguerrand de Marigni. For other political trials or accusations of sorcery in this period and their religio-political context, see Peters,

The Magician, pp. 112–25; Russell, *Witchcraft*, pp. 193ff.; W. R. Jones, 'Political Use of Sorcery in Medieval Europe', *The Historian* 34 (1972), pp. 670–87.

92 For the accusations against the Templars raised during their suppression in 1307–14, see, for example, Cohn, *Europe's Inner Demons*, Chap. 5; M. Barber, *The Trial of the Templars*; Peters, *The Magician*, pp. 125–30; Russell, *Witchcraft*, pp. 194–8.

93 For arguments that Cathar dualist emphasis on the Devil's role in the material world encouraged the development of a preoccupation with diabology and witch beliefs, see Russell, *Witchcraft*, pp. 101, 111, 123–5, 272–89; *idem.*, *A History of Witchcraft* (London, 1980), pp. 60–1; G. P. Quaife, *Godly Zeal and Furious Rage* (New York, 1987), p. 54; cf. the more cautious approach of Levack, *The Witch Hunt*, pp. 37–8, and Cohn, *Europe's Inner Demons*, pp. 57–8; Chap. 4. Cf also A. G. Bernstein, 'Teaching and Preaching in Thirteenth-Century Paris', in A. Ferreiro (ed.), *The Devil, Heresy and Witchcraft in the Middle Ages, Essays in Honor of Jeffrey B. Russell* (Leiden, 1998), pp. 111–31, esp. pp. 128–30.

94 Assumptions that the stereotype emerged during and as a consequence of the inquisitorial prosecution of fourteenth-century Cathar groups are based on records of their trials and confessions which, however, have recently been shown to be forgeries; see Cohn, *Europe's Inner Demons*, Chap. 7; Kieckhefer, *European Witch Trials*, pp. 16–18.

95 The accusations against Bishop Guichard of Troyes, for example, advanced the notion of the incubus, while the trial of Dame Alice Kytler in 1324–5 combined charges of *maleficium*, collective apostasy of a secret sect, demonic sacrifices and copulation with demons.

96 On the declaration of the theology faculty of the University of Paris, see Lea, *A History of the Inquisition*, vol. 3, pp. 464–5.

97 Alexander v's bull of 1409 concerning the prosecution of sorcerers and diviners was reiterated in 1418 by Martin v; text in Hansen, *Quellen*, pp. 16–17.

98 The texts of Eugenius iv's bulls concerning the prosecution of sorcerers and invokers of demons may be found in Hansen, *Quellen*, pp. 17–19.

99 This is not the place for detailed bibliographical references to the development of witchcraft scholarship since the demolition of M. Murray's thesis that European witchcraft was an ancient fertility religion, as advanced in her *Witch-cult in Western Europe* (London, 1921). For recent arguments that certain elements of witchcraft beliefs betray traces of pagan, cultic and shamanistic traditions, see, for example, Ginsburg, *Storia notturna*; G. Klaniczay, 'Shamanistic Elements in Central European Witchcraft' in *idem.*, *The Uses of Supernatural Power* (Cambridge, 1990), pp. 129–51; G. Henningsen, ' "The Ladies from Outside": An Archaic Pattern of the Witches' Sabbath', in Ankarloo and Henningsen, *Early Modern European Witchcraft*, pp. 191–218.

100 On Protestant literature on demonology and witchcraft, see, for example, S. Clark, 'Protestant Demonology: Sin, Superstition and Society (c.1520–c.1630)', in Ankarloo and Henningsen, *Early Modern European Witchcraft*, pp. 45–83.

101 See R. Greenfield, 'Sorcery and politics at the Byzantine court in the twelfth century: interpretation of history', in R. Beaton and C. Rouche (eds), *The Making of Byzantine History: Studies dedicated to D. M. Nicol* (Aldershot, 1993), pp. 73–86; *idem.*, 'Sorcery Accusations as a Political Weapon at the Byzantine Court in the Twelfth and Thirteenth Centuries' in *Seventeenth Annual Byzantine Studies Conference, November 8–10, 1991: abstracts of papers* (Madison, 1991), p. 26.

102 Mansi, *Sacrorum conciliorum*, vol. 16, col. 432.

103 Cf. *Vita Ignatii Patriarchi, PG*, vol. 105, col. 568; *Vita Euthymii* 1.29–30, ed. P. Karlin-Hayter (Brussels, 1970), p. 5.

104 Basil, *Kanones*, G. Rhalles and M. Potles (eds), *Syntagma ton theion kai hieron kanonon* (Athens 1854), vol. 4, pp. 232–3; see also pp. 221–2, 250–2.

105 M. T. Fögen, 'Balsamon on Magic: From Roman Secular Law to Byzantine Canon Law', in Maguire, *Byzantine Magic*, p. 115.

106 Fögen, 'Balsamon on Magic', p. 108.

107 For the acts and trials of magicians before the patriarchal court during the fourteenth century, see F. Miklosic and J. Müller, *Acta et Diplomatica Graeca Medii Aevi* (repr. Aalen, 1968), vol. 1, pp. 180–2, 184–7, 188–90, 301–6, 317–18, 342–4, 541–50, 560, 594–5. On these campaigns against magicians, see C. Cupane, 'La magia a Bizanzio nel secolo XIV: Azione e reazione', *Jahrbuch der Österreichischen Byzantinistik* 29 (1980), pp. 237–62; Forgen, 'Balsamon on Magic', pp. 112–15.

108 See H. Maguire, 'Magic and the Christian Image', in Maguire, *Byzantine Magic*, pp. 51–73.

109 For claims that Constantine v was a Paulician heretic, see Georgius Monachus, *Chronicon*, ed. C. de Boor (Leipzig, 1904), p. 751; for similar claims about Nicephorus I, see Theophanes, *Chronographia*, ed. C. de Boor (Leipzig, 1883), vol. 1, p. 488.

110 On these parallels, see, for example Greenfield, *Traditions of Belief*, pp. 153–64; *idem.*, 'A Contribution to the Study of Palaeologan Magic' in Maguire, *Byzantine Magic*, pp. 129ff.; D. Pingree, 'Some Sources of the Ghaya al-hakim', *Journal of the Warburg and Courtauld Institute* 43 (1980), pp.10–12.

111 See, for example, *Vita Nicephori Patriarchi a.Ignatio* 36, *PG*, vol. 100, col. 81; *Vita Theodori Grapti* 18, *PG*, vol. 116, col. 667; *Vita Theodori Studiti* A 32, *PG*, vol. 99, cols. 277–79.

112 See the reproduction of the scene from the Khludov Psalter in K. Corrigan, *Visual Polemics in the Ninth-Century Byzantine Psalters* (Cambridge, 1992), fig. 38, p. 258; for a discussion of the representation, see *ibid.*, pp. 2, 27–8.

113 See D. de F. Abrahamse, 'Magic and Sorcery in the Hagiography of the Middle Byzantine Period', *Byzantinische Forschungen* 7 (1982), pp. 3–17; Kazhdan, 'Byzantine Hagiography and Sex in the Fifth to Twelfth Centuries', pp. 140–3.

114 On these Byzantine notions concerning the figure of the sorcerer, see, for example, Abrahamse, 'Magic and Sorcery', pp. 15–17; Greenfield, *Traditions of Belief*, pp. 249ff.; *idem.*, 'A Contribution', pp. 119ff.

115 For the Greek literary tradition and texts of the story of Theophilus, see L. Radermacher, *Grechische Quellen zur Faustsage* (Vienna, 1927), pp. 41–71, 152–220.

116 New edition, A. A. Longo, 'La vita di s.Leone vescovo di Catania e gli incantesimi del mago Eliodoro', *Rivista di studi bizantini e neoellenici* 26 (1989), pp. 3–98; text, pp. 80–99.

117 See the description of a female witch-like figure in the *Vita* of Basil the Younger in S. G. Vilinskii, *Zhitie sv. Vasillia Novago v russkoi literature* (Odessa, 1913), pp. 320ff; on the female witch-like figures in the writings of St Neophytus the Recluse, see G. S. Galatariotou, 'Holy Women and Witches: Aspects of Byzantine Conceptions of Gender', *BMGS*, 9 (1984–5), pp. 55–95, esp. pp. 62–9. See also the description of the sorceresses in the romance of *Libistros and Rhodamne*, ed. J. A. Lambert (Amsterdam, 1935), pp. 221ff., and the romance of *Kallimachus and Chrysorrhoe*, M. Pichard (ed.), *Le romance de Callimaque et de Chrysorrhoe* (Paris, 1956).

118 On the Orthodox Slavonic adoption of Byzantine magical and divinatory traditions, see Mathiesen, 'Magic in Slavia Orthodoxa'; specifically, on the Slavonic reception of Byzantine divinatory texts, see A. Angusheva-Tikhanova, *Gadatelnite knigi v starobbŭlgarskata literatura* (Sofia, 1996); W. F. Ryan, *The Bathhouse at Midnight, Magic in Russia* (Stroud, 1999), *passim*.

119 A large folklorist literature exists on folk magic in the Slavonic Orthodox world, but mostly in the relevant Slavonic languages; for an English-language introduction to the material, see the publications of J. L. Conrad, 'Magic Charms and Healing Rituals in Contemporary Yugoslavia', *Southeastern Europe/L'Europe du sudest* 10.2 (1983), pp. 99–120; 'Bulgarian Magic Charms: Ritual, Form and Content', *Slavonic and East European Journal* 31 (1987), pp. 548–672; 'Russian Ritual Incantations: Tradition, Diversity and Continuity', *ibid.*, 33 (1989), pp. 422–44. See also E. Pocs, *Fairies and Witches at the Boundary of South-Eastern and Central Europe* (Helsinki, 1989).

120 On the history of the Athingani, see Starr, 'An Eastern Christian Sect: The Athinganoi', pp. 93–106; Rochow, 'Die Häresie der Athinganer', pp. 163–78.

121 This evidence pertaining to the teachings of the Athingani is preserved in a formula of abjuration of the sect, *PG*, vol. 106, cols 1333–5, and a tract on the Melchisedekites, Theodotians and Athingani, edited by G. Ficker, 'Eine

Sammlung von Abschworungsformeln', *Zeitschrift für Kirchengeschichte* 26 (1906), pp. 450–2.

122 For claims for an association between the Athingani and Nicephorus I, see Theophanes, *Chronographia*, p. 488; for similar claims about Michael II, see Genesius, *Regum libri quattuor*, ed. A. Lesmueller-Werner and I. Thurin (Berlin and New York, 1978), pp. 22–3.

123 Theophanes Continuatus, *Chronographia*, ed. I. Bekker, *CSHB*, 1838, pp. 42, 52.

124 See *PG*, vol. 106, cols 1333–6.

125 Cf. *PG*, vol. 106, cols 1333–6 and Ficker, 'Eine Sammlung', pp. 450–1.

126 Rhalles and Potles, *Syntagma*, vol. 2, pp. 444–5, 458.

127 See G. C. Soulis, 'The Gypsies in the Byzantine Empire and the Balkans in the Late Middle Ages', *DOP*, 15 (1961), pp. 145–9.

128 Latin translation in P. Peeters, 'Histoires monastiques georgiennes', *Analecta Bollandiana* 36–7 (1917–19), pp. 102–4.

129 Original text and Latin translation in *Domini Johannis Philosophi Ozniensis Armeniorum Catholici Opera*, ed. and tr. J.-B. Aucher (Venice, 1834), pp.85ff. See also the accusations against the Paulicians in C. Astruc *et al.* (eds), 'Les sources grecques pour l'histoire des Pauliciens del'Asie Mineure', *T&M*, 4 (1970), pp. 92–3, 130–1, 188–9, 200–1, 204–5.

130 See the translation of the relevant extract in Garsoïan, *The Paulician Heresy*, p. 112.

131 See the translation of the relevant fragment from Nerses Snorhali's 'Confession of Faith' in Garsoïan, *The Paulician Heresy*, p. 147.

132 Text in I. Ivanov, 'Proizkhod na Pavlikianite spored dva bŭlgarski rakopisa', *Spisanie na Bŭalgarskata Akademiia na Naukite* 24 (1922), pp. 20–31.

133 See note 100, Chap. 3 above.

134 Texts and commentary in Begunov, *Kozma presviter*, Chaps 1, 2 and 3, pp. 393–483.

135 See note 120, Chap. 3 above.

136 Ficker, *Die Phundagiagiten*, pp. 50–7.

137 See note 138, Chap. 3 above.

138 Euthymiuz Zigabenus, *Panoplia Dogmatica. XXVII: Kata Bogomilon*, *PG*, vol. 130, col. 1311; *De haeresi Bogomilorum narratio*, ed. G. Ficker, *Die Phundagiagiten*, pp. 100–1. In another reference to the gradual initiation into Bogomil teachings and sectarian hierarchy, however, Zigabenus employs the cliché of 'introduction into the diabolical mysteries' – *Kata Bogomilon*, col. 1321; *De haeresi*, p. 101.

139 *Kata Bogomilon*, col. 1309; *De haeresi*, p. 97.

140 *Kata Bogomilon*, col. 1321; *De haeresi*, p. 103.

141 Anna Comnena, *Alexiad* XV.10.3–4, ed. B. Leib, vol. 3 (Paris, 1945), pp. 227ff.

142 Angold, *Church and Society*, pp. 486–7.

143 Cf. A. Kazhdan, 'Holy and Unholy Miracle Workers' in Maguire, *Byzantine Magic*, pp. 76–7.

144 See note 123 to Chap. 3 above.

145 Gautier, 'Le *De Daemonibus*,' pp. 135–7.

146 Gautier, 'Le *De Daemonibus*', pp. 139–41.

147 See Gautier, 'Le *De Daemonibus*', p. 131; Greenfield, *Traditions of Belief*, pp. 256–7; on the demonology of the tract, see, for example, Greenfield, *Traditions of Belief*, pp. 182–3, 203–7, 210–12, 214–17, 233–4; on its treatment of demonic magic, see *ibid.*, pp. 256–7, 262, 266, 292.

148 *Lavrent'evskaia letopis (Die Nestor-Chronik)*, ed. D. Tschizewskij (Wiesbaden, 1969), pp. 169–76. For a discussion of the episode, see, for example, S. Franklin, 'The Reception of the Byzantine Culture by the Slavs', *The 17th International Byzantine Congress Major Papers* (New Rochelle, 1986), pp. 386–8, 391; R. Zguta, 'The Pagan Priests of Early Russia: Some New Insights', *SR*, 33 (1974), pp. 259–66; Ryan, *The Bathhouse at Midnight*, pp. 38, 70–2.

149 See note 7 above.

150 Popruzhenko, *Sinodik*, p. 79.

151 See Gouillard, 'Une source grecque du synodik de Boril'.

152 Popruzhenko, *Sinodik*, pp. 44–5.

153 Popruzhenko, *Sinodik*, pp. 73–4. On the anathema, cf. *ibid.*, pp. 169–70; Obolensky, *The Bogomils*, pp. 247–8.

154 Popruzhenko, *Sinodik*, p. 80.

155 See note 51 above.

156 On the syncreticism of mysticism, heresy and vestiges from paganism in the teachings of the heresiarchs condemned by St Theodosis, cf. Obolensky, *The Bogomils*, pp. 259–67; Angelov, *Bogomilstvoto v Bŭlgariia*, pp. 426–31. For a discussion of the comparable process of regeneration of pagan rituals in Russian sectarian circles as a result of their anti-clerical stance, see Iu. M. Lotman and B. A Uspenskij, 'The Role of Dual Models in the Dynamics of Russian Culture (Up to the End of the Eighteenth Century', in Iu. M. Lotman and B. A. Uspenskij, *The Semiotics of Russian Culture*, ed. A. Shukman (Ann Arbor, 1984), pp. 12ff.

157 Zlatarski, *Zhitieto*, pp. 25–7.

158 For the association between heresy and magical practices in Stefan Dushan's Code, see Krstić, *Dushan's Code* pp. 14–15, 23, 40–1, 44–5, 60–1.

159 For the legal treatment of magic and witchcraft in early modern Russia, see the pioneering studies of R. Zguta, 'Witchcraft Trials in Seventeenth-century Russia', *AMH*, 82, 5 (1977), pp. 1187–1207; V. A. Klievson, 'Through the Prism of Witchcraft: Gender and Social Change in Seventeenth-Century Moscow', in B. Evans *et al.* (eds), *Russia's Women: Accommodation, Resistance,*

Transformation (Berkeley, 1991), pp. 74–94. See the major new reassessment of Zguta's and Klievson's arguments on the basis of a wide range of primary sources in Ryan, 'Witchcraft Hysteria in Early Modern Europe', *SEER*, 76, 1 (1998), pp. 1–36.

160 For examples of explicit associations of the terms 'heretic' and 'magician' (or 'vampire') in Russian popular belief and notions of sorcery, see, for instance, the material compiled in P. N. Rybnikov, *Pesny sobrannye P. N. Rybnikovym* (Moscow, 1910), vol. 3, pp. 189–90; A. Zvonkov, 'Ocherk verovanii krest'ian Elatomskogo uezda', *Etnograficheskoe obozrenie*, 2, 1989, pp. 77–8; K. Danilov, *Drevnie rossiskie stikhotvorennia, sobrannye Kirsheiu Danilovym* (Moscow and Leningrad, 1958), pp. 79, 81. On this association between 'heretic' and 'sorcerer', see D. Zelenin, *Russische (ostslavische) Volkskunde* (Berlin and Leipzig, 1927), p. 395; F. J. Oinas, 'Heretics as Vampires and Demons in Russia', in *Essays on Russian Folklore and Mythology* (Columbus, Oh., 1985), pp. 121–30.

161 The association between heresy and magical prayers and practices appears in some of the late versions of the Slavonic Indexes of Forbidden Books (from the fifteenth century onwards); for the relevant manuscripts, see A. Iatsimirskii, *Bibliograficheskii obzor apokrifov v iuzhoslavianskoi i russkoi pis'menosti, I; Apokrifi vethozavetnye* (Petrograd, 1921), pp. 10, 14, 19, 21, 26; for the relevant readings in the texts, see *ibid.*, pp. 70–3. Cf. also the link between magic and heresy made in another version of the index in A. Gorskii and K. Nevostruev, *Opisanie slavianskikh rukopisei Moskovskoi sinodal'noi biblioteke* (Moscow, 1867), II, 3, p. 641.

162 See note 15 above.

163 See note 165 below.

164 On sources for Byzantine demonology, see, for example, P. Gautier, 'Pseudo Psellos, *Graecorum opiniones de daemonibus*, *REB*, 46 (1988), pp. 85–117. On the evolution and interaction of 'standard' and 'alternative' demonology, see Greenfield, *Traditions of Belief*. See also C. de Mantos, 'Psellos et le monde d'Irrationel', *T&M*, 6 (1976), pp. 325–49.

165 On Byzantine notions of the diabolical pact, see Greenfield, *Traditions of Belief*, pp. 250, 255–7; on the figure of the sorcerer and the notion of super-natural evil, respectively in the middle and late Byzantine period, see Abrahamse, 'Magic and Sorcery', pp. 16–17; Greenfield, *Traditions of Belief*, pp. 249–53.

166 F. A. Yates, *Giordano Bruno and the Hermetic Tradition* (London, 1964), p. III.

167 Symeon of Thessalonica, *Dialogus contra haereses*, PG, vol. 155, cols 33–176.

168 *Oeuvres complètes de Gennade Scholarios*, ed. L. Petit, X. Sideridès, M. Jugie (Paris, 1935), vol. 4, p. 200.

169 W. Miller, *The Balkans* (New York and London, 1896), p. 287.

170 Fine suggests that the term 'pagan' could have been 'a pejorative term for members of the Bosnian Church' (*The Bosnian Church*, p. 235). An overview of Hrvoje's career is provided in *ibid.*, pp. 232–7.

171 Fine, *The Bosnian Church*, p. 295, with further suggestions that the religious situation might have been misunderstood in Rome or was a 'deliberate frame-up' of the Bosnian Church, pp. 297–9.

172 W. Miller, *Essays on the Latin Orient* (Cambridge, 1921).

173 A critical overview of the evidence alleging Patarene cooperation with the Ottomans can be found in Fine, *The Bosnian Church*, pp. 338–41, along with a brief survey of Bosnian religious history after the Turkish conquest, pp. 375–87, and criticism of the theory of Patarene mass conversion to Islam, p. 385. Cf. S. Džaja, *Die 'Bosnische Kirche' und das Islamisierungsproblem Bosniens und der Herzegowina in den Forschungen nach dem Zweiten Weltkrieg* (Munich, 1978). Still other interpretations and conclusions are presented in M. Hadžijahić, *Porijeklo bosanskih Muslimana* (Sarajevo, 1990) and S. Balić, *Das unbekannte Bosnien* (Cologne, 1992), pp. 90–127.

174 The Bosnian gravestones were associated with Bogomilism by A. J. Evans, *Through Bosnia and Herzegovina on Foot during the Insurrection* (London, 1876), pp. 174–7, and the theory was developed further by A. Solovjev in 'Le symbolisme des monuments funéraires bogomiles', *Cahier d'Études Cathares*, 18 (1954), pp. 92–114; 'Les Bogomiles vénéraient-ils la Croix?', *Bulletin de l'Académie royale de Belgique, Classe des lettres*, 35 (1949), pp. 47–62; O. Bihalji-Merin and A. Benac, *Steine der Bogomilen* (Vienna and Munich, 1964), pp. viiiff., and others. Among the opponents of the Bogomil thesis is M. Wenzel who has published and catalogued the motifs on the *stećci*, with maps showing the distribution of each motif, in *Ukrasni motivi na stećcima* (Sarajevo, 1965). Along with other scholars, M. Wenzel links some of the *stećci* with the horse-breeding Vlach clans, who were numerous and influential in medieval Bosnia and Herzegovina.

175 Ćircović, 'Dualistichka heterodoksija', p. 234; on the theory of Manichaean influences in the *stećci*, see Solovjev, 'Le symbolisme', p. 100; a discussion of the themes of *stećci* symbolism in the light of Central Asian Manichaean iconography can be found in Esin, 'The conjectural links', pp. 109–14. The thesis that the symbolism of the *stećci* reflects medieval dualist teachings has been developed also in G. Wild, *Bogomilen und Katharer in ihrer Symbolik I* (Wiesbaden, 1970), and revived recently in L. Harris, *The Secret Heresy of Hieronymus Bosch* (Edinburgh, 1995).

176 The survival of classical cultic symbolism in some figurative and ornamental *stećci* carvings has been demonstrated in a series of publications of M. Wenzel, 'O nekim simbolima na dalmatinskim stećcima', *Prilozi povijesti umjetnosti u Dalmaciji* (Split) 14 (1962), pp. 79–94; *idem*, 'The Dioscuri in the Balkans'.

177 Fine, *The Bosnian Church*, p. 10, with a discussion of the strong pagan survival in Bosnia, and a suggestion for the late survival of a classical mystery cult, p. 18. The evidence for a medieval mystery cult in Bosnia is presented in M. Wenzel, 'A Medieval Mystery Cult in Bosnia and Herzegovina', *JWCI*, 24 (1961), pp. 89–107, with suggestions of links between the cult and the underground chambers in the castle of the Patarene duke, Hrvoje Vukčić, pp. 103–5.

178 Cf., for example, Kakouri, *Dionysiaka*, with a discussion of the association between heresy and the survival of Dionysian worship in Thrace; pp. 61ff.; R. Vulcanescu, *Mitologie Romana* (Bucharest, 1985), pp. 233–4.

179 Wenzel, 'Medieval Mystery Cult'; *idem*, 'The Dioscuri in the Balkans'.

180 The eighteenth-century evidence of the Patarenes and 'Manichaeans' in Bosnia is discussed in Fine, *The Bosnian Church*, pp. 376–7.

181 Nineteenth-century references to alleged current Bogomil remains in Bosnia were discussed in J. Asboth, *An Official Tour through Bosnia and Herzegovina* (London, 1890), pp. 98–100.

182 See, for example, C. A Frazee, *Catholics and Sultans, The Church and the Ottoman Empire 1453–1923*, (Cambridge, 1983), pp. 108–11 (who assumes that the Paulician groups that converted to Catholicism were largely Bogomil); D. P. Hupchick, *The Bulgarians in the Seventeenth Century, Slavic Orthodox Society and Culture Under Ottoman Rule* (Jefferson, N.C. and London, 1993), pp. 74–84, who estimates that in the seventeenth century around 1,000 of the 7,000 *pavlikianii* were the descendants of the medieval Bogomils, p. 78. Cf. Iovkov, *Pavlikiani*, pp. 55–102. Documents relating to the Catholic missions in the Paulician areas have been published in B. Primov *et al.* (eds), *Dokumenti za katolicheskata deinost v Bŭlgariia prez XVII vek* (Sofia, 1993). For the course of Catholic missions to one of these Paulician communities, see the discussion in B. Dimitrov, *Minaloto na grad Rakovski*, Sofia, 1989.

183 See, for example, the material assembled in Miletich, 'Nashite pavlikiani', *SBNU*, 19 (1903), pp. 1–369; 21 (1905), pp. 1–155.

184 Obolensky, *The Bogomils*, p. 267.

6 Legends, Parables and 'Secret Myths'

1 Phrase used in reference to the Cathar *perfecti* in Fichtenau, *Ketzer*, pp. 86–7.
2 D. Obolensky, *The Byzantine Commonwealth: Eastern Europe 500–1453* (London, 1971), p. 123, with the observation that the Bogomil leaders were 'mostly drawn from the lapsed clergy and monks'. Obolensky also discusses

what he styles the 'occultism' of the Bogomils, in which the 'doctrines of the sect had an outward and inward esoteric aspect' and the 'latter was communicated only to a relatively small group of initiates' (p. 123). Similarly, according to Loos, *Dualist Heresy*, p. 89, the account by Euthymius Zigabenus of the Bogomil doctrines revealed 'some of the hidden depths – the things which the sect kept carefully hidden from the uninitiated'.

3 Paolini, 'Italian Catharism', p. 94.

4 See P. Biller, 'Northern Cathars and Higher Learning', in P. Biller and B. Dobson, *The Medieval Church: Universities, Heresy, and the Religious Life, Essays in Honour of G. Leff* (Woodbridge, 1999), pp. 25–52.

5 Paolini, 'Italian Catharism', pp. 87–103.

6 P. Biller, 'The Cathars of Languedoc and written materials', in Biller and Hudson, *Heresy and Literacy*, pp. 61–82, esp. pp. 80–2.

7 Biller, 'Northern Cathars and Higher Learning', pp. 27–40, 50–1.

8 See R. Morghen, 'L'eresia nel Medioevo', in *Medioevo cristiano* (Bologna, 1968), p. 229; Paolini, 'Italian Catharism', p. 92.

9 For this shift in Catholic polemic, see P. Biller, 'Heresy and Literacy: earlier history of the theme', in Biller and Hudson, *Heresy and Literacy*, pp. 1–19; Paolini, 'Italian Catharism', pp. 84–6.

10 On this process of transmission of esoteric attitudes and notions from Jewish apocalyptic literature to Gnosticism, see, for example, G. A. G. Stroumsa, 'Gnostic Secret Myths', in *Hidden Wisdom*, pp. 46–63, esp. p. 56 ff.

11 Paolini, 'Italian Catharism', pp. 92–6; cf. A. Greco, 'Per una riconsiderazione dei miti catari', in G. G. Merlo (ed.), *Storia ereticale e antiereticale del medioevo* (Torre Pellice, 1997), pp. 77–95.

12 Stroumsa, 'Gnostic Secret Myths', p. 54.

13 'The Cathars of Languedoc and written materials', p. 68, with a thorough survey of the evidence of extant and lost Cathar written materials, pp. 61–82. On the sources for Catharism in general, see Rottenwöhrer, *Der Katharismus*, Bd.I/1, *Quellen zum Katharismus* (1982); Bd.I/2, *Quellen zum Katharismus, Anmerkungen* (1982).

14 The 'Manichaean Tract' was copied into the *Liber contra Manichaeos* of the anti-Cathar polemicist Durand de Huesca for the purpose of refutation, see *Un Traité cathare inédit du début du XIIIe siècle, d'après le 'Liber contra Manicheos' de Durand de Huesca*, ed. C. Thouzellier (Louvain, 1964), pp. 87–113. See also Thouzellier's discussion of the tract in *Catharisme et valdèisme*, pp. 303–75.

15 On Bogomil and Cathar monarchian dualism, cf., for example, Söderberg, *La religion des cathares*, chap. 6, pp. 84–109; Duvernoy, *Le Catharisme I: La Religion*, Part 1, Chaps 2–6 *passim*; Coulianu, *The Tree of Gnosis*, pp. 198–210, 217–21; Rottenwöhrer, *Der Katharismus*, Bd.IV/1, *Glaube und Theologie der Katharer* (1993), pp. 310–427; Bd. IV/2 (1993), pp. 413–35; Bd. IV/3 (1993),

pp. 114ff, 239–77; Lambert, *The Cathars*, pp. 25ff., 204–7. On the position of the Bagnolo church, originally close to moderate dualism but moving towards the absolute dualist strand, see Rottenwöhrer, *Der Katharismus*, Bd.IV/1, *Glaube und Theologie der Katharer*, pp. 442–50.

16 On this process, see Y. Stoyanov, 'The Transformations of Binary Theologies and the Theme of the Divine Pair in Medieval Dualism and East Christian Cosmogonic Legends' (forthcoming).

17 Irenaeus, *Adversus haereses*, 1.11.1.

18 Irenaeus, *Adversus haereses*, 1.13.6.

19 Irenaeus, *Adversus haereses*, 1.18.2.

20 *Trimorphic Protennoia*, 35.1–24, 42.4–26, 45.2–10, ed. J. D. Turner, in *Nag Hammadi Codices XI, XII, XIII*, ed. C. W. Hedrick (Leiden, 1990), pp. 402, 416, 422.

21 See, for example, the Nag Hammadi tract *The Expository Treatise on the Soul*, 133:1–9, ed. W. C. Robinson, in *Nag Hammadi Codex II, 2–7*, ed. B. Layton (Leiden, 1989), p. 156.

22 See, for example, the Nag Hammadi tract *The Apocryphon of John*, II 23.2–33, ed. M. Waldstein and F. Wisse, *The Apocryphon of John. Synopsis of Nag Hammadi Codices II, 1; III, 1; and IV, 1 with BG 8502, 2* (Leiden, 1995), pp. 133–5; and *The Hypostasis of the Archons*, 89.1–17, ed. B. Layton, in *Nag Hammadi Codex II, 2–7*, p. 240.

23 Anselm of Alessandria, *Tractatus de hereticis*, p. 311.

24 Anselm of Alessandria, *Tractatus de hereticis*, p. 311.

25 Anselm of Alessandria, *Tractatus de hereticis*, pp. 311–12.

26 Anselm of Alessandria, *Tractatus de hereticis*, p. 312.

27 Anselm of Alessandria, *Tractatus de hereticis*, p. 312.

28 Anselm of Alessandria, *Tractatus de hereticis*, p. 312.

29 Rainerius Sacconi, *Summa*, p. 76.

30 The Cathar teaching of the angel, sent by God and imprisoned in a prison-body, was recorded by Moneta of Cremona, *Adversus Catharos et Valdenses libri quinque*, ed. T. Richini (Rome, 1743), Bk 2, Chap. I, p. 110; on Moneta's tract, see G. S. Vackenberg, *Grundlehren katharischer Sekten des 13.Jahrhunderts, Eine theologische Untersuchung mit besonderer Berücksichtigung von 'Adversus Catharos et Valdenses des Moneta von Cremona* (Munich, 1971); see also Rottenwöhrer, *Der Katharismus, Quellen zum Katharismus, Anmerkungen*, pp. 134–88.

31 This doctrine is recorded in the *De heresi catharorum* and was professed by two groups of Italian Cathars, whose bishops, Caloiannes and Garattus, drew their consecration from Sclavonia and Bulgaria respectively. See Coulianu's attempted interpretation of the mythical evil four-faced spirit as a synthesis of the well-known four symbols of the Evangelists and some distorted recollection of the five-faced Manichaean 'King of Darkness', *The Tree of Gnosis*, p. 218.

32 Moneta, *Adversus Catharos*, Bk 2, Chap. 1.2, p. 112, referred to a Cathar belief that when Satan proceeded to destroy the human race, God saved Noah, his wife, sons, etc.

33 Coulianu, *The Tree of Gnosis*, pp. 200, 208 ff.

34 Coulianu, *The Tree of Gnosis*, pp. 208ff.

35 van den Broek, 'The Cathars: Medieval Gnostics?', pp. 160–9, 176–7.

36 van den Broek, 'The Cathars: Medieval Gnostics?' pp. 169–77.

37 On Bogomil and Cathar radical dualism, see, for example, Borst, *Die Katharer*, pp. 254–318; Söderberg, *La religion des cathares*, Chap. 5, pp. 44–84; R. Nelli, *La philosophie du catharisme* (Paris, 1975), Chap. 4, pp. 125–37; Duvernoy, *Le Catharisme I: La Religion*, Part 1, Chap. 2–6, *passim*; Coulianu, *The Tree of Gnosis*, pp. 207 ff., 221–7; Rottenwöhrer, *Der Katharismus*, Bd.IV/1, *Glaube und Theologie der Katharer*, pp. 31–310; Bd. IV/2, pp. 17–413; Lambert, *The Cathars*, pp. 196–205; on the problem of later reports alleging absolute dualism among the Bosnian Patarenes, cf. Fine, *The Bosnian Church*, Chap. 2, *passim*, Duvernoy, *Le Catharisme I: La Religion*, p. 353; Coulianu, *The Tree of Gnosis*, pp. 207ff.

38 This system of Cathar absolute dualism is recorded in Moneta, *Adversus Catharos*, Bk 1, Preface, pp. 2–4.

39 Rainerius Sacchoni, *Summa*, p. 71.

40 The beliefs of the Desenzano Cathars were recorded in *De heresi catharorum*, pp. 308–10. On Desenzano absolute dualism, see Rottenwöhrer, *Der Katharismus*, Bd.IV/1, *Glaube und Theologie der Katharer*, pp. 31–65; Lambert, *The Cathars*, pp. 196–204.

41 The heresy of the Albanenses is recorded in the treatise *Brevis summula contra herrores notatos hereticorum*, ed. C. Douais, *La Somme des authorités à l'usage des prédicateurs méridionaux au XIIIe siècle* (Paris, 1896), pp. 114–43. The quotations are from the translation provided in Wakefield and Evans, *Heresies of the High Middle Ages*, pp. 353–61.

42 Euthymius Zigabenus, *Panoplia Dogmatica*, XXVII, vol. 130, col. 1297.

43 The polemical account of these Languedoc Cathar teachings is published in J. N. Garvin and J. A. Corbett (eds), *The Summa contra haereticos. Ascribed to Praepositinus* (Notre Dame, 1958), Appendix B, p. 292.

44 The exposition is printed in A. Dondaine, 'Durand de Huesca et la polemique anti-cathare', *AFP*, 29(1959), pp. 268–71.

45 Peter of Vaux-de-Cernay, *Historia albigensis*, Part 1, 2, ed. P. Guébin and E. Lyon, *Petri Vallium Sarnii monachi Historia albigensis*, 3 vols (Paris, 1926–39), vol. 1, pp. 11–12.

46 Garvin and Corbett, *The Summa contra haereticos*, p. 292.

47 *The Dialogue of the Saviour*, 139.12–13, ed. S. Emmel, *Nag Hammadi Codex III.5. The Dialogue of the Saviour* (Leiden, 1984), p. 78 (where the text is translated as 'a woman who had understood completely').

48 'Psalms of Herakleides', in *A Manichaean Psalm Book*, Part 2, vol. 2, ed. R. C. Allberry (Stuttgart, 1938), p. 187. On Herakleides, cf. P. Alfaric, *Les écritures manichéennes* (Paris, 1918), 2, p. 114.

49 *The Gospel According to Philip*, 63:30–4, ed. B. Layton, in *Nag Hammadi Codex II, 2–7*, pp. 166–8.

50 Filoramo, *A History of Gnosticism*, pp. 176, 224. For further observations on the role of Mary Magdalene in Gnostic speculations, see, for example, E. Pagels, *The Gnostic Gospels* (London, 1979), pp. 22, 49, 64–7; S. Hasking, *Mary Magdalene: Myth and Metaphor* (New York and London, 1993), pp. 33–58; S. Petersen, 'Zerstört die Werke der Weiblichkeit!', *Maria Magdalena, Salome und andere Jüngerinnen Jesu in christlich-gnostischen Shriften* (Leiden, 1999).

51 For the feminine figure beside Zurvan, 'mother' of Ohrmazd and Ahriman, see the parallel presentation of the accounts of the Zurvanite myth by Eznik of Kolb, Theodore ben Konai and Yohannan ben Penkaye in Zaehner, *Zurvan*, pp. 422–3.

52 For an interpretation of Zurvan as a hermaphrodite deity, see Eznik of Kolb, *Against the Sects*, Vienna, 1926, p. 149; for an interpretation of the feminine figure as Zurvan's divine wife, see Theodore Abu Qurra, *On the True Religion*, in Zaehner, *Zurvan*, p. 428; on the role of this figure, cf., for example, H. S. Nyberg, 'Questions de cosmogonie et de cosmologie mazdéennes', *JA*, ccxix (1931), p. 83; Zaehner, *Zurvan*, pp. 62–7.

53 A. von Coq, *Türkische Manichäica aus Chotscho* (Berlin, 1911), I, p. 22; cf. Nyberg, 'Questions', p. 83; Zaehner, *Zurvan*, pp. 64–5.

54 Nyberg, 'Questions', p. 83; Zaehner, *Zurvan*, pp. 64–6.

55 Published in G. Scholem, *Mada ey ha-Yahadut*, I, 1926, pp. 244–64.

56 J. Dan, 'Introduction', in J. Dan (ed.), *The Early Kabbalah* (New York, 1986), p. 37; on the 'Gnosticism' of the Kohen brothers, see also G. Scholem, *Kabbalah* (Jerusalem, 1974), pp. 55–6.

57 J. Dan, 'Samael, Lilith, and the Concept of Evil in Early Kabbalah', *Association for Jewish Studies Review*, 5, 196 (1980), p. 40; see also his recent treatment of the tract in 'Samael and the Problem of Jewish Gnosticism', in A. Ivry, E. Wolfson and A. Arkush (eds), *Perspectives on Jewish Thought and Mysticism* (Amsterdam, 1997), pp. 267, 274–5.

58 I owe this reference to Professor Moshe Idel; see his analysis of Agobard's writings in this context in 'The Evil Thoughts of the Deity' (Hebrew), *Tarbiz*, 3–4 (1980), pp. 356–65.

59 On the roots and interpretations of this belief in radical Cathar dualism, see R. Poupin, 'De métempsycose en réincarnation ou la transmigration des âmes des temps cathares à nos jours', in *Catharisme: l'édifice imaginaire*, pp. 145–65.

60 Dando, *Les origines du catharisme*; Duvernoy, *Le Catharisme I: La Religion*, pp. 60, 296, 364, 367–77; Coulianu, *The Tree of Gnosis*, pp. 227–30; see also

the objections to this theory in van den Broek, 'The Cathars: Medieval Gnostics?' p. 158, n. 4.

61 Coulianu, *The Tree of Gnosis*, p. 214.

62 This dualist system of John de Lugio is recorded in Rainerius Sacchoni, *Summa*, pp. 72–6; on John de Lugio, see Rottenwöhrer, *Der Katharismus*, Bd.IV/1, *Glaube und Theologie der Katharer*, pp. 165–211; Lambert, *The Cathars*, pp. 196–208, *passim*. On the opposition between the 'mythological' strand in Nazarius' type of dualist speculation and John de Lugio's focus on speculative and systematic theology, see, for example, Hamilton, 'Wisdom from the East', pp. 56 ff.

63 Moneta, *Adversus Catharos*, Bk 2, Chap. 1 : 1, p. 110.

Epilogue: The War of Labels

1 For early Protestant views on the connections between eastern/western dualist sects and the reformist movement, see, for example, J. Chassanion, *Histoire des Albigeois: touchant leur doctrine & religion & de la . . . guerre qui leur a este faite* (Geneva, 1595), pp. 29ff.; J. Perrin, *Histoire des Vaudois et des Albigeois* (Geneva, 1618), *passim*; J. Léger, *Histoire générale des églises évangéliques vaudoises des vallées de Piemon: Ou Vaudoises* (Leiden, 1669), I, pp. 18, 126–31, II, p. 328; E. Gibbon, *Decline and Fall of the Roman Empire*, ed. J. B. Bury (London, 1902), vol. 6, pp. 111–15, 124–5 (1st edn 1776–88); J. L. Oeder, *Dissertatio inauguralis prodromum historiae Bogomilorom criticae exhibers* (Göttingen, 1743). For a recent survey of Protestant attitudes to medieval heresy, see A. Friesen, 'Medieval Heretics or Forerunners of the Reformation: the Protestant Rewriting of the History of Medieval Heresy', in Ferreiro, *The Devil*, pp. 165–91.

2 For the development of post-Reformation Catholic approaches to eastern/western dualist connections with the reformist movements, see, for example, C. Du Cange, *Glossarium ad scriptorem mediae et infimae latinitatis* (Graz, 1954) (1st edn 1678), I, pp. 688, 722; VI, pp. 211, 412; C. Baronio, *Annales Ecclesiastici*, 12 vols (Antwerp, 1597–1612), vol. 9, pp. 28–30, 235, 502, 577; vol. 10, pp. 24, 740; vol. 11, pp. 57, 59, 195, 215; vol. 12, pp. 659–60, 663, 714–15, 716–18; J. B. Bossuet, *Histoire des variations des églises protestantes* (Paris, 1688), vol. 2, pp. 146–7, 154–5, 201; C. Fleury, *Histoire ecclésiastique* (Paris, 1858; 1st edn 1722), III, pp. 223, 225–7, 229, 243–4, 259, 319, 487–8, 645; L. A. Muratori, 'Dissertatio LX, Quaenam haereses saeculis rudibus Italiam divexarint', *Antiquitates Italicae Medii Aevi* (Milan, 1741), V, pp. 79–153.

3 J. Benoist, *Histoire des Albigeois et des Vaudois* (2 vols, Paris, 1691); Bossuet, *Histoire des variations des églises protestantes*, vol. 2, pp. 121, 144, 155, 162, 200, 244.

4 See, for example, Fleury, *Histoire ecclésiastique*, IV, p. 767.

5 C. Schmidt, *Histoire et doctrine de la secte des Cathares et Albigeois* (2 vols, Paris and Geneva, 1848–9).

6 Schmidt, *Histoire et doctrine*, vol. 1, pp. 104–20.

7 Johann von Asboth, *Bosnien und die Herzegowina. Reisebilder und Studien* (Vienna, 1888); English translation from the Hungarian: *An Official Tour through Bosnia and Herzegovina: with an account of the history, antiquities, agrarian conditions, religion, ethnology, folk lore and social life of the people* (London, 1890).

8 A. Evans, *Through Bosnia and Herzegovina on Foot during the Insurrection, August and September 1875* (London, 1876).

9 Evans, *Through Bosnia and Herzegovina*, quotes respectively from p. xliv; pp. xlvi–xlvii; p. xlviii; p. l; pp. lvi–lvii; p. lv; p. lviii.

10 Asboth, *Bosnien*, quotes respectively from p. 28; p. 42; quote from the English translation, *An Official Tour*, p. 42; p. 61; quote from the English translation, *An Official Tour*, p. 66; p. 58; p. 70; p. 83; p. 87.

11 Asboth, *Bosnien*, p. 28; quote from the English translation, *An Official Tour*, p. 30.

12 R. Munro, *Rambles and Studies in Bosnia-Herzegovina and Dalmatia: with an account of the proceedings of the Congress of Archaeologists and Anthropologists held in Sarajevo, August 1894* (Edinburgh, 1895), p. 381.

13 Munro, *Rambles and Studies*, p. 383.

14 For the evolution and fluctuations of the Balkanist discourse *vis-à-vis* the Orientalist discourse, see now the pioneering work of M. Todorova, *Imagining the Balkans* (New York, 1997).

15 Roquebert, 'Napoléon Peyrat', English summary, p. 473.

16 See, among others, M. Roquebert, *Les Cathares et le Graal* (Toulouse, 1994).

17 Lambert, *The Cathars*, p. 25.

18 A. Faivre, *Access to Western Esotericism* (New York, 1994), p. 299 (see also p. 53).

Select Bibliography

Abrahamse, D. de F., 'Magic and Sorcery in the Hagiography of the Middle Byzantine Period', *BF*, 7 (1982), pp. 3–17.

Ackroyd, P. R., *Exile and Restoration*, London, 1968.

— *Israel under Babylon and Persia*, Oxford, 1970.

Acta Bosnae potissimum ecclesiastica, ed. E. Fermendžin, in *Monumenta spectantia historiam Slavorum meridionalium*, vol. 23, Zagreb, 1892.

Acta Bulgariae ecclesiastica, ed. E. Fermendžin, in *Monnumenta spectantia historiam Slavorum meridionalium*, vol. 18, Zagreb, 1887.

Adam, A., *Texte zum Manichäismus*, Berlin, 1954.

Adémar of Chabannes, *Chronique*, ed. J. Chavanon, in *Collection de textes pour servir à l'étude et à l'enseignement de l'histoire*, vol. 20, Paris, 1897.

Afanas'ev, A. N., *Poeticheskie vozzreniia slaviian na prirodu*, 3 vols, Moscow, 1865–9.

Alberic of Trois-Fontaines, *Chronica Albrici monachi Trium Fontium a monachi novi monasterii Hoiensis interpolata*, ed. P. Scheffer-Boichorst, *MGH SS*, vol. 23, cols 631–950.

Alberry, C. R. C. (ed.), *A Manichaean Psalm Book*, Part 2, Stuttgart, 1938.

Alderink, L. J., *Creation and Salvation in Ancient Orphism*, Chico, California, 1981.

Alexander Lycopolitanus, *Contra Manichaei opiniones disputatio*, ed. A Brinkmann, Leipzig, 1895.

Alexander, P. J. 'Religious Persecution and Resistance in the Byzantine Empire of the Eighth and Ninth Centuries: Methods and Justifications', *Speculum*, 52 (1977), pp. 238–64.

Alfaric, P., *Les écritures manichéennes*, 2 vols, Paris, 1918–19.

Altheim, F. and R. Stiehl (eds), *Geschichte Mittelasiens in Altertum*, Berlin, 1970.

Angelov, D., *Bogomilstvoto v Bŭlgariia*, 3rd edn, Sofia, 1980.

— *Bogomilstvoto*, Sofia, 1993.

Angold, M., *The Byzantine Empire 1025–1204: a political history*, London, 1984.

— *Church and Society in Byzantium under the Comneni 1081–1261*, Cambridge, 1995.

Anklesaria, B. T. (ed. and tr.), *Zand-Akasih, Iranian or Greater Bundahishn*, Bombay, 1956.

— *Zand-I Vohuman Yasn and Two Pahlavi Fragments*, Bombay, 1957.

— *The Pahlavi Rivayat of Aturharnbag and Franbag-Sros*, 2 vols, Bombay, 1969.

Annales S. Medardi Suessionnenses, ed. G. Waitz, *MGH SS*, vol. 26, pp. 518–22.

Anthes, R., 'Egyptian Theology in the Third Millennium B. C.', *JNES*, 18:3, July 1959, pp. 169–212.

Arberry, A. J., (ed.), *The Legacy of Persia*, Oxford, 1953.

Arnold-Döben, V., *Die Bildersprache des Manichäismus*, Cologne, 1978.

Artamonov, M., *Istoriya Khazar*, Leningrad, 1962.

Asboth, J., *An Official Tour through Bosnia and Herzegovina*, London, 1890.

Assmussen, J. P., *Xᵘāstānīft, Studies in Manichaeism*, Copenhagen, 1965

— *Manichaean Literature*, New York, 1975.

Athanassakis, A. N. (ed. and tt.), *The Orphic Hymns: Text, Translation and Notes*, Missoula, Montana, 1977.

Attaliates, Michael, *Historia*, ed. I. Bekker, *CSHB*, 1853.

Babut, E.-Ch., *Priscillien et le priscillianisme*, Paris, 1909.

Bailey, Sir Harold, *Zoroastrian Problems in the Ninth-century Books*, Oxford, 1943.

Bansal, B. L., *Bon, Its Encounter with Buddhism in Tibet*, Delhi, 1994.

Barber, M., 'Women and Catharism', *RMS*, 3, 1977, pp. 45–62.

— *The Trial of the Templars*, Cambridge, 1978.

Barc, B., (ed.), *Colloque international sur les textes de Nag Hammadi (Québec, 22–25 août)*, Québec, 1981.

Baronio, C., *Annales Ecclesiastici*, Antwerp, 12 vols, 1597–1612.

Bartikiian, R. M., *Istochniki dlia izucheniia istorii pavlikianskogo dvizhenii*, Erevan, 1961.

Bautier, R. H., 'L'hérésie d'Orléans et le mouvement intellectuel au début du *xiᵉ siécle*', *Actes de 95ᵉ Congrès National des Sociétés savantes (Rheims, 1970): Section philologique et historique*, Paris, 1975, 1, pp. 63–88.

Beaulieu, P.-A., *The Reign of Nabonidus, King of Babylon 536–539 BC*, New Haven and London, 1989.

Beck, H.-G., *Kirche und theologische Literatur im byzantinischen Reich*, Munich, 1959.

Beck, R., *Planetary Gods and Planetary Orders in the Mysteries of Mithra*, Leiden, 1988.

Begunov, Iu., *Kozma prezviter v slavianskikh literaturakh*, Sofia, 1973.

Bengston, H. (ed.), *The Greeks and the Persians from the Sixth to the Fourth Centuries*, London, 1968.

Benoist, J., *Histoires des Albigeois et des Vaudois*, 2 vols, Paris, 1691.

Benveniste, E., *The Persian Religion According to the Chief Greek Texts*, Paris, 1929.

— *Les Mages dans l'ancien Iran*, Paris, 1938.

Berlioz, J., '*Tuez-les tous, Dieu reconnaîtra les siens*', *Le massacre de Bézier (22 juillet*

1209) et la croisade contre les Albigeois vus par Césaire de Heisterbach, Poret-sur-Garonne, 1994.

Berlioz, J. and J.-C. Hélas (eds), *Catharisme: l'édifice imaginaire, Actes du 7ᵉ colloque du Centre d'Études Cathares/René Nelli*, Carcassonne, 1997.

Bernard Gui, *Manuel de l'inquisiteur*, ed. and tr. G. Mollat, *Les Classiques de l'histoire de France au moyen âge*, 8, 9, 2 vols, Paris, 1926–7.

Berstein, M., *et al.* (eds), *Legal Texts and Legal Issues: Proceedings of the Second Meeting of the International Organization for Qumran Studies, Cambridge, 1995, Published in Honour of J. M. Baumgarten*, Leiden, 1997.

Beshevliev, V., *Die Protobulgarische Periode der bulgarischen Geschichte*, Amsterdam, 1981.

—*Pŭrvobŭlgarite*, Sofia, 1981.

Betz, H. D., (ed.), *The Greek Magical Papyri in Translation*, Chicago and London, 1992.

Bianchi, U., *Il dualismo religioso, Saggio storico ed etnologico*, Rome, 1958, 2nd edn., Rome, 1983

—'Le dualisme en histoire des religions', *RHR*, 159, 1 (1961), pp. 1–46.

—(ed.), *Le Origine dello Gnosticismo*, Leiden, 1967.

—'Dualistic Aspects of Thracian Religion', *HR*, 10:3 (1971), pp. 228–333.

—'Il dualismo come categoria storico-religiosa', *RSLR*, IX, 1 (1973), pp. 3–16.

—*Selected Essays on Gnosticism, Dualism and Mysteriosophy*, Leiden, 1978.

—(ed.), *Mysteria Mithrae*, Leiden and Rome, 1979.

—'Dieu unique et création double: pour une phénoménologie du dualisme', *Orientalia J. Duchesne-Guillemin emerito oblata, Acta Ir.*, 23, Leiden (1984), pp. 49–61.

Bickerman, E. J., *Studies in Jewish and Christian History*, 3 vols, Leiden, 1976–86.

Bidez, J. and F. Cumont, *Les Mages hellénisés*, 2 vols, Paris, 1938.

Biller, P. and A. Hudson (eds), *Heresy and Literacy 1000–1530*, Cambridge, 1994.

Biller, P. and B. Dobson (eds), *The Medieval Church: Universities, Heresy, and the Religious Life, Essays in Honour of G. Leff*, Woodbridge, 1999.

—'Northern Cathars and Higher Learning', in P. Biller and B. Dobson, *The Medieval Church: Universities, Heresy, and the Religious Life, Essays in Honour of G. Leff*, Woodbridge, 1999, pp. 25–52.

—'William of Newburgh and the Cathar Mission to England', in D. Wood (ed.), *Life and Thought in the Northern Church c. 1100–c.1700, Essays in Honour of C. Cross*, Woodbridge, 1999, pp. 11–31.

al-Biruni, *Chronology of the Ancient Nations*, tr. E. Sachau, London, 1879.

—*Alberuni's India*, tr. E. Sachau, 2 vols, London, 1988.

Bivar, A. D. H., 'The Absolute Chronology of the Kushano-Sasanian Governors in Central Asia', in J. Harmatta (ed.), *Prolegomena to the Sources on the History of Pre-Islamic Central Asia*, Budapest, 1979.

— *The Personalities of Mithra in Archaeology and Literature*, New York, 1998.

Black, M. (ed.), *The Scrolls and Christianity*, London, 1969.

Blackmann, E. G., *Marcion and his Influence*, London, 1948.

Blanc, C., 'Considerazioni sulla "preistoria" del dualismo religioso', *RSI*, 22, 1960, pp. 1–22.

Bogomilstvoto na Balkanot vo svetlinata na nai novite istrazivany, Skopje, 1982.

Böhlig, A., *Kephalaia*, vol. 2, Stuttgart, 1966.

Böhme, R., *Orpheus*, Bern, 1970.

Bonacursus, *Manifestatio haeresis catharorum quam fecit Bonacursus*, PL, vol. 204, pp. 775–92.

Borst, A., *Die Katharer*, Stuttgart, 1953.

Bossuet, J. B., *Histoire des variations des églises protestantes*, 2 vols, Paris, 1688.

Bottrich, C., *Weltweisheit, Menschheitethik. Urkult*, Tübingen, 1992.

Bousset, W., *Hauptprobleme der Gnosis*, Göttingen, 1907.

Bowker, J., *The Targums and Rabbinic Literature*, Cambridge, 1969.

Boyce, M., *The Manichaean Hymn-cycles in Parthian*, London, 1954.

—*A Persian Stronghold of Zoroastrianism*, Oxford, 1977.

—*Zoroastrians: Their Religious Beliefs and Practices*, London, 1979.

—*Textual Sources for the Study of Zoroastrainism*, Manchester, 1984.

—*A History of Zoroastrianism*: vol. 1, *The Early Period*, 2nd edn with corrections, Leiden, 1989; vol. 2, *Under the Achaemenians*, Leiden, 1982; (and F. Grenet), vol. 3, *Zoroastrianism under Macedonian and Roman Rule*, Leiden, 1991.

—*Zoroastrianism: Its Antiquity and Constant Vigour*, Costa Mesa, 1992.

Boyd, J. and D. A. Crosby, 'Is Zoroastrianism Dualistic or Monotheistic?', *Journal of the American Academy of Religion*, 47 : 4, 1978, pp. 557–88.

Boylan, P., *Thoth the Hermes of Egypt*, Oxford, 1922.'

Bozoky, E., *Le Livre secret des cathares*, Paris, 1980.

Brand, C. M., *Byzantium Confronts the West, 1180–1204*, Cambridge, Mass., 1968.

Brashear, W., *A Mithraic Cathechism from Egypt*, Vienna, 1992.

Breasted, J. H., *Development of Religion and Thought in Ancient Egypt*, New York, 1912.

—'The Predynastic Union of Egypt', *BIFAO*, 30 (1930), pp. 709–24.

Brenon, A., *Le vrai visage du catharisme*, Poret-sur-Garonne, 1988.

—*Les Femmes cathares*, Paris, 1992.

—*Le catharisme, vie et mort d'une Église chrétienne*, Paris, 1996.

Brevis summula contra herrores notatos hereticorum, ed. C. Douais, *La Somme des authorités à l'usage des prédicateurs méridionaux au XIIIe siècle*, Paris, 1896.

Broek, R. van den, *Studies in Alexandrian Christianity and Gnosticism*, Leiden, 1996.

Broek, R. van den and M. J. Vermaseren (eds), *Studies in Gnosticism and Hellenistic Religions Presented to G. Quispel on the Occasion of his 65th Birthday*, Leiden, 1981.

Broek, R. van den and W. Hanegraaff, *Gnosis and Hermeticism from Antiquity to*

Modern Times, Albany, 1997.

Brown, P. R. L., *Religion and Society in the Age of St Augustine*, London, 1972.

Browne, E. G., *Literary History of Persia*, Cambridge, 1928.

Browning, R., *Byzantium and Bulgaria*, London, 1975.

— *The Byzantine Empire*, London, 1980.

Brückner, A., *Mitologia Slava*, Bologna, 1924.

Bryder, P., *The Chinese Transformations of Manichaeism: A Study of Chinese Manichaean Terminology*, Lund, 1985.

—(ed.), *Manichaean Studies: Proceedings of the First International Conference on Manichaeism*, Lund, 1988.

Bryer A. and J. Herrin (eds), *Iconoclasm: Papers Given at the Spring Symposium of Byzantine Studies, March, 1975*, Birmingham, 1977.

Buber, M., *Good and Evil*, New York, 1952.

Burkert, W., *Lore and Science in Ancient Pythagoreanism*, tr. E. Mihar, Jr, Cambridge, 1972.

— *Greek Religion*, tr. J. Raffan, Oxford, 1985.

— *Ancient Mystery Cults*, Harvard, 1987.

Burkitt, F. C., *The Religion of the Manichees*, Cambridge, 1925.

Burn, A. R., *Persia and the Greeks: The Defence of the West, c. 567–478*, 2nd edn, London, 1984.

Burrus, V., *The Making of a Heretic. Gender, Authority and the Priscillianist Controversy*, Berkeley, 1995.

Burstein, S. M. (tr.), *The Babyloniaca of Berossus*, Malibu, 1978.

Bury, J. B., *A History of the Later Roman Empire from Arcadius to Irene*, 2 vols, London, 1889.

— *A History of the Eastern Roman Empire from the Fall of Irene to the Accession of Basil I (AD 802–867)*, London, 1912.

—(ed.) *The Early History of the Slavonic Settlements in Dalmatia, Croatia and Serbia*, London, 1920.

Campbell, L. A., *Mithraic Iconography and Ideology*, Leiden, 1968.

Cartojan, N., *Cărţile populare in literatura românesca*, vol. 1, Bucharest, 1929.

Les Cathares en Occitanie, Paris, 1982.

Cedrenus, Georgius, *Historiarum Compendium*, ed. I. Bekker, 2 vols, *CSHB*, 1838–9.

Cereti, C., *The Zand Ī Wahman Yasn: A Zoroastrian Apocalypse*, Rome, 1995.

Cerutti, M. V., *Dualismo e ambiguità, Creatori e creazione nella dottrina mandea sul cosmo*, Rome, 1981.

Chadwick, H., *Priscillian of Avilla. The Occult and the Charismatic in the Early Church*, Oxford, 1976.

La Chanson de la Croisade Albigeoise, (ed. and tr.), E. Martin-Chabot, 3 vols, Paris, 1931–61.

Charles, R. H. (ed.), *The Apocrypha and Pseudepigrapha of the Old Testament*, 2 vols, Oxford, 1913.

Charlesworth, J. (ed.), *The Old Testament Pseudepigrapha*, 2 vols, New York and London, 1983–5.

Chassanion, J., *Histoire des Albigeois*, Paris, 1595.

Ch'en, K., *Buddhism in China: A Historical Survey*, New Jersey, 1964.

Choksy, J., *Triumph over Evil: Purity and Pollution in Zoroastrianism*, Austin, Texas, 1989.

Christensen, A., *L'Iran sous les Sassanides*, Copenhagen, 1936.

Cignoux, P. (ed.), *Recurrent Patterns in Iranian Religions: From Mazdaism to Sufism*, Paris, 1992.

Cinnamus, Joannes, *Historiae*, ed. A. Meineke, *CSHB*, 1836.

Ćircović, S., *Istorija srednjovekovne bosanske drzave*, Belgrade, 1964.

—*Rabotnitsi, vojnitsi, duhovnitsi, drushtva srednjovekovnog Balkana*, Belgrade, 1997.

Cirillo, L., *Elchasai e gli Elchasaiti. Un contributo alla storia della communitá guideo-cristiane*, Cosenza, 1984.

Cirillo, L. and A. Roselli (eds), *Codex Manichaicus Coloniensis, Atti del Simposio Internazionale (Rende-Amantea 3–7 settembre 1984)*, Cosenza, 1986.

—*Codex Manichaicus Coloniensis. Atti del Secondo Simposio Internazionale*, Cosenza, 1990.

Cirillo, L. and A. van Tongerloo (eds), *Manichaean Studies III, Atti dei terzo congresso internazionale di studi 'Manicheismo e Oriente Cristiano antico'*, Louvain, 1997.

Clackson, S., *et al.* (eds), *Dictionary of Manichaean Texts*, vol. 1, *Texts from the Roman Empire (texts in Syriac, Greek, Coptic and Latin)*, Turnhout, 1998.

Clark, P., *Zoroastrianism: An Introduction to an Ancient Faith*, Brighton, 1998.

Clauss, M., *Mithras: Kult und Mysterien*, Munich, 1990.

—*Cultores Mithrae: die Anhängerschaft des Mithras-Kultes*, Stuttgart, 1992.

Clemen, C., *Fontes historiae religionis persicae*, Bonn, 1920.

Cohn, N., *The Pursuit of the Millennium*, London, 1957.

—*Europe's Inner Demons*, London, 1975.

Colledge, M. A. R., *The Parthians*, London, 1967.

Collins, J. J., *Seers, Sybils and Sages in Hellenistic-Roman Judaism*, Leiden, 1997.

—*Apocalypticism in the Dead Sea Scrolls*, London and New York, 1997.

—*The Apocalyptic Imagination: An Introduction to Jewish Apocalyptic Literature*, 2nd edn, Cambridge, 1998.

—(ed) *Encyclopedia of Apocalypticism*, vol. 1, *The Origins of Apocalypticism in Judaism and Christianity*, New York, 1999.

Collins, J. J. and J. Charlesworth (eds), *Mysteries and Revelations*, Sheffield, 1991.

Colpe, C., *Die religionsgeschichtliche Schule: Darstellung und Kritik ihres Bildes vom gnostischen Erlösermythus*, Göttingen, 1961.

Commentariolum de provinciae Hungariae originibus, Monumenta Ordinis Fratrum Praedicatorum Historica I, ed. B. M. Reichert, Lovanii, 1896.

Comnena, Anna, *Alexias*, ed. L. Schopen and L. Reifferscheid, 2 vols, *CSHB*, 1839–78; also in J. Migne, *PG*, vol. 131; *The Alexiad*, tr. E. Dawes, London, 1928.

Constitutiones regni Sicialiae, MGH Leges. Sectio 5. Constitutiones, T.2, ed. W. Sturner, Hanover, 1996.

Conybeare, F. C. (ed.), *The Key of Truth: A Manual of the Paulician Church in Armenia*, Oxford, 1898.

Corbine, H., *Spiritual Body and Celestial Earth: From Mazdean Iran to Shi'ite Iran*, tr. N. Pearson, London, 1990.

Ćorović, V., *Bosna i Hercegovina*, Belgrade, 1925.

Corrigan, K., *Visual Polemics in the Ninth-Century Byzantine Psalters*, Cambridge, 1992.

Costen, M. D., *The Cathars and the Albigensian Crusade*, Manchester, 1997.

Coulianu, I. P., *Les Gnoses dualistes d'Occident: histoire et mythes*, Paris, 1990.

Count, E, W., 'The earth-diver and the rival twins' in *Indian Tribes of Aboriginal America. Selected Papers of the XXIXth International Congress of Americanists*, Chicago, 1952, pp. 55–62.

Cross, F. M., *The Ancient Library of Qumran*, New York, 1961; 3rd edn 1995.

Cumont, F., *Textes et monuments figurés relatifs aux mystères de Mithra*, 2 vols, Brussels, 1896–9.

— *The Oriental Religions in Roman Paganism*, Chicago and London, 1911.

— *Lux Perpetua*, Paris, 1947.

— *The Mysteries of Mithra*, tr. T. McCormack, New York, 1956.

Cupane, C., 'La magia a Bizanzio nel secolo XIV: Azione e reazione', *Jahrbuch der Österreichischen Byzantinistik* 29 (1980), pp. 237–62.

Curletto, S., *La Norma e il suo rovescio: coppie di opposti nel mondo religioso antico*, Genoa, 1990.

D'Alatri, M., *Eretici e inquisitori in Italia, Studi e documenti*, 2 vols, Rome, 1986–7.

Dan, J. (ed.), *The Early Kabbalah*, New York, 1986.

— 'Samael and the Problem of Jewish Gnosticism', in A. Ivry, E. Wolfson and A. Arkush (eds), *Perspectives on Jewish Thought and Mysticism*, Amsterdam, 1997, pp. 267–75.

Dando, M., *Les origines du catharisme*, Paris, 1967.

Dänhardt, O. *Natursagen, Eine Sammlung Naturdeutender Sagen, Märchen, Fabeln und Legende 1: Sagen zum Alten Testament*, Leipzig and Berlin, 1907.

Daniélou, J., *Theology of Jewish Christianity*, tr. and ed. J. A. Baker, London, 1964.

Darmesteter, J. (tr.), *Le Zend-Avesta*, 3 vols, Paris, 1892–3.

— (tr.), *The Zend-Avesta*: Part I, *The Vendidad, SBE*, vol. 4, Oxford, 1895, repr. Delhi, 1965; Part 2, *The Sirozahs, Yashts and Nyayaesh, SBE*, vol. 23, Oxford, 1883, repr. Delhi, 1965.

Davis, C. W., *The Inquisition at Albi, 1299–1300*, New York, 1948, repr. 1974.

Davis-Kimball, J., *et al.* (eds), *Nomads of the Eurasian Steppes in the Early Iron Age*, Berkeley, 1995.

Day, P. L., *An Adversary in Heaven: Sātān in the Hebrew Bible*, Atlanta, 1988.

Dean-Otting, M., *Heavenly Journeys*, Frankfurt, 1984.

Debevoise, N. C., *A Political History of Parthia*, Chicago, 1938.

Decret, F., *Mani et la tradition manichéenne*, Paris, 1974.

— *L'Afrique manichéenne*, 2 vols, Paris, 1978.

— *Essais sur l'Église manichéenne en Afrique du Nord et à Rome au temps de saint Augustin, Recueil d'études*, Rome, 1995.

Dhalla, M. N., *Zoroastrian Theology*, New York, 1914.

— *History of Zoroastrianism*, New York, 1938.

Dietrich, A., *Eine Mithrasliturgie*, Leipzig, 1903.

Dimitrov, P., *Petŭr Chernorizets*, Shumen, 1995.

Dobrev, I., *Proizkhod i znachenie na praslavianskoto konsonantno i diftongichno sklonenie*, Sofia, 1982.

Dodds, E. R., *The Greeks and the Irrational*, Berkeley and London, 1951.

— *Pagans and Christians in an Age of Anxiety*, Cambridge, 1965.

Döllinger, I. von, *Beiträge zur Sektengeschichte des Mittelalters*, 2 vols, Munich, 1890, repr. 1968.

Dondaine, A., *Un traité néo-manichéen du XIIIe siècle: Le Liber de doubus principiis, suivi d'un fragment de rituel cathare*, Rome, 1939.

— 'Nouvelles sources de l'histoire doctrinale du néo-manichéisme au moyen âge', *Revue des sciences philosophiques et théologiques*, 28 (1939), pp. 465–88.

— 'Les Actes du concile albigeois de Saint-Félix-de-Caraman', in *Miscellanea Giovanni Mercati*, vol. 5, *Studi e Testi*, Vatican City, 125 (1946).

— 'Le Manuel de l'inquisiteur (1230–1330)', *AFP*, 17 (1947), pp. 85–194.

— 'L'Hiérarchie cathare en Italie': Part I, 'Le "De heresi catharorum in Lombardia" ': Part 2, 'Le "Tractatus de hereticis" d'Anselme d'Alessandrie', *AFP*, 19 (1949), pp. 280–312, 20 (1950), pp. 234–324.

— 'L'Origine de l'hérésie médiévale: À propos d'un livre récent', *RSCI*, 6 (1952), pp. 47–78.

— 'Durand de Huesca et la polémique anti-cathare', *AFP*, 29 (1959), pp. 228–76.

Doresse, J., *The Secret Books of the Egyptian Gnostics*, New York, 1960.

Dossat, Y., *Les crises de l'Inquisition toulousaine au XIIIe siècle (1233–1273)*, Bordeaux, 1959.

Dougherty, R. P., *Nabonidus and Belshazzar: A Study of the Closing Events of the Neo-Babylonian Empire*, New Haven, 1929.

Douglas, M. (ed.), *Witchcraft Confessions and Accusations*, London, 1970.

Dragojlović, D., *Bogomilstvo na Balkanu i u Maloj Aziji*: vol. I, *Bogomilski rodonacalnici*, Belgrade, 1979; vol. 2, *Bogomilstvo na pravoslavnom istoku*, Belgrade, 1982.

Dragojlović, D. and V. Antić, *Bogomilstvoto vo srednovekovnata izvorna graga*, Skopje, 1978.

Drijvers, H. J. W., *Bardaisan of Edessa*, Assen, 1966.

Drower, E. S., *The Mandaeans of Iraq and Iran*, Oxford, 1937.

Duchesne-Guillemin, J., *Ormazd et Ahriman: L'aventure dualiste dans l'antiquité*, Paris, 1953.

— *The Hymns of Zaratushra*, tr. from the French by M. Henning, London, 1953.

— *The Western Response to Zoroaster*, Oxford, 1958.

— *La Religion de l'Iran ancien*, Paris, 1962.

— *Symbols and Values in Zoroastrianism*, New York, 1966.

— (ed.) *Études mithriaques*, Leiden, 1978.

— 'Gnosticisme et dualisme', in J. Ries (ed.) *Gnosticisme et monde hellénistique*, Louvain, 1982, pp. 89–102.

Dujćev, I., 'I Bogomili nei paesi slavi e la loro storia', *L'Oriente Cristiano nella storia della civiltà*, Rome, 1963, pp. 619–41.

— *Medioevo bizantino-slavo*, 3 vols., Rome, 1965–71.

— 'Aux origines des courants dualistes à Byzance et chez les Slaves méridionaux', *Revue des Études Sud-est Européennes*, I (1969), pp. 51–62.

Dumézil, G., *Naissance d' archanges*, Paris, 1945.

— *Mitra–Varuna: Essai sur deux représentations Indo-Européennes de la souveraineté*, Paris, 1948.

Dunlop, D. M., *The History of the Jewish Khazars*, Princeton, NJ, 1954.

Duvernoy, J., (ed.), *La registre d'Inquisition de Jacques Fournier èvêque de Pamiers (1318–1325)*, Toulouse, 1965.

— *Le Catharisme I: La Religion des Cathares*, Toulouse, 1976.

— *Le Catharisme II: L'Histoire des Cathares*, Toulouse, 1979.

— *Cathares, Vaudois et Beguins du pays d'Oc*, Toulouse, 1994.

— (ed. and tr.), *Le Dossier de Montségur: interrogatoires d'inquisition 1242–47*, Toulouse, 1998.

Dvornik, F., *Les Slaves, Byzance et Rome au IXe siècle*, Paris, 1926,

— *The Slavs: Their Early History and Civilization*, Boston, 1956.

Eberwin of Steinfeld, *Epistola ad S. Bernardum*, PL, vol. 182, pp. 676–80.

Eckbert of Schönau, *Sermones tredecim contra Catharos*, PL, vol. 195, cols 11–102.

Eddy, S. K., *The King is Dead*, Lincoln, 1961.

Eisler, R., *Weltenmantel und Himmelszelt*, Munich, 1910.

Eliade, M., *The Quest: History and Meaning in Religion*, Chicago, 1969.

— *De Zalmoxis à Gengis-Khan*, Paris, 1970.

— *Occultism, Witchcraft and Cultural Fashions*, Chicago, 1976.

Emery, R. W., *Heresy and Inquisition in Narbonne*, New York, 1941.

Emery, W. B., *Archaic Egypt*, Harmondsworth, 1961.

Esteve, C. A., *Cātaros y Occitanos en el reino de Mallorca*, Palma de Mallorca, 1978.

Europe et Occitanie: les pays Cathares, Collection Heresis V, Arques, 1995.

Euthymius of Acmonia, 'Euthymii monachi coenobii Peribleptae epistula invectiva contra Phundagiagitus sive Bogomilos haereticos', ed. G. Ficker, in *Die Phundagiagiten*, Leipzig, 1908, pp. 3–86.

—*Euthymii monachi coenobii Peribleptae liber invectivus contra haeresim exsecrabilium et impiorum haereticorum qui Phundagiatae dicuntur, PG*, vol. 131, cols 47–58.

Evans, A. J., *Through Bosnia and Herzegovina on Foot during the Insurrection*, London, 1877, repr. New York, 1971.

Evans-Pritchard, E. E., *Theories of Primitive Religion*, Oxford, 1965.

Eznik of Kolb, *Wieder die Sekten*, tr. J. M. Schmidt, Vienna, 1900.

Fairman, H. W., *The Triumph of Horus: An Ancient Egyptian Sacred Drama*, Berkeley, 1974.

Faivre, A., *Access to Western Esotericism*, New York, 1994.

Fallon, F. T., *The Enthronement of Sabaoth: Jewish Elements in Gnostic Creation Myths*, Leiden, 1978.

Faulkner, R. O., (tr.), *The Ancient Pyramid Texts*, Oxford, 1969.

—*The Ancient Egyptian Coffin Texts*, Warminster, 1973.

Ferreiro, A., (ed.), *The Devil, Heresy and Witchcraft in the Middle Ages, Essays in Honor of Jeffrey B. Russell*, Leiden, 1998.

Fichtenau, H., *Ketzer und Professoren: Häresie und Vernunftglaube im Hochmittelalter*, Munich, 1992.

Ficker, G., *Die Phundagiagiten: Ein Beitrag zur Ketzergeschichte des byzantinischen Mittelalters*, Leipzig, 1908.

Filoramo, G., *A History of Gnosticism*, tr. A. Alcock, Oxford, 1990.

Fine, J. V. A., Jr, *The Bosnian Church: A New Interpretation*, New York and London, 1975.

—*The Early Medieval Balkans*, Ann Arbor, Michigan, 1983.

—*The Late Medieval Balkans*, Ann Arbor, Michigan, 1987.

Fischer, G., *Eschatologie und Jenseitserwartung im hellenistischen Diasporajudentum*, Berlin and New York, 1978.

Fleury, C., *Histoire ecclésiastique*, Paris, 1858 (1st edn 1722).

Flint, P. W., and J. VanderKam (eds), *The Dead Sea Scrolls after Fifty Years: A Comprehensive Assessment*, Leiden, 1999.

Flusser, D., *Judaism and the Origins of Christianity*, Jerusalem, 1988.

Fol, A., *Trakiiskiat Dionis*, I, Sofia, 1991.

Fol, A. and I. Marazov, *Thrace and the Thracians*, London, 1977.

Fontaine, P. F. M., *The Light and the Dark: A Cultural History of Dualism*, 15 vols, Amsterdam, 1986–98.

Forsyth, N., *The Old Enemy: Satan and the Combat Myth*, Princeton, NJ, 1987.

Frankfort, H., *Ancient Egyptian Religion*, New York, 1948.

—*Kingship and the Gods: A Study of Ancient Near Eastern Religion and the Integration of Society and Nature*, Chicago, 1948.

Frazee, C. A., *Catholics and Sultans, The Church and the Ottoman Empire 1453–1923*, Cambridge, 1983.

Friedlander, A., *The Hammer of the Inquisitors, Brother Bernard Délicieux and the Struggle Against the Inquisition in Fourteenth-Century France*, Leiden, 2000.

Frye, R. N., *The Heritage of Persia*, London, 1962.

— *The History of Ancient Iran*, Munich, 1984.

Gabain, A. von, *Das uigurische Königreich von Chotscho 850–1250*, Berlin, 1961.

Gafurov, B., *et al.*, *Kushan Studies in the U.S.S.R.*, Calcutta, 1970.

Galatariotou, S. G., 'Holy Women and Witches: Aspects of Byzantine Conceptions of Gender', *BMGS*, 9 (1984–5).

Gardner, I., *The Kephalaia of the Teacher, The Edited Coptic Manichaean Texts in Translation with Commentaries*, Leiden, 1995.

Garsoïan, N. G., *The Paulician Heresy*, The Hague and Paris, 1967.

— 'Byzantine Heresy: A Reinterpretation', *DOP*, 25 (1971), pp. 85–113.

— *Armenia between Byzantium and the Sasanians*, London, 1985.

Garvin, J. N. and J. A. Corbett (eds), *The Summa contra haereticos. Ascribed to Praepositinus*, Notre Dame, 1958.

Gasparro, G. S., *Gnostica et hermetica*, Rome, 1982.

Gaster, M., *Ilchester Lectures on Greco-Slavonic Literature and its Relation to the Folklore of Europe during the Middle Ages*, London, 1887.

Gaster, T. H. (tr.), *The Scriptures of the Dead Sea Sect*, London, 1957.

Gemuev, I. N., (ed.), *Mirovozzrenie finno-ugorskikh narodov*, Novosibirsk, 1990.

Genesius, *Regum libri quattuor*, ed. A.Lesmueller-Werner and I. Thurin, Berlin and New York, 1978.

Genito, B. (ed.), *The Archaeology of the Steppes: Methods and Strategies*, Naples, 1994.

Genning, V. F. and A. H. Halikov, *Rannie bolgari na Volge*, Moscow, 1964.

Georgius Monachus, *Chronicon*, ed. C. de Boor, Leipzig, 1904.

Germanos II, 'Germani Patriarchae Constantinopolitani epistula ad Constantinopolitanos contra Bogomilos', ed. G. Ficker, in *Die Phundagiagiten*, Leipzig, 1908, pp. 115–25.

Gershevitch, I., *The Avestan Hymn to Mithra*, Cambridge, 1959.

— 'Zoroaster's Own Contribution', *JNES*, 23 (1964), pp. 12–38.

Gibbon, E., *The History of the Decline and Fall of the Roman Empire*, ed. J. B. Bury, 7 vols, 1909–14.

Gilhus, I. S., *The Nature of the Archons: A Study in the Soteriology of a Gnostic Treatise from Nag Hammadi, CGII, 4*, Wiesbaden, 1985.

Gimbutas, M., *The Slavs*, London, 1971.

Given, J. B., *Inquisition and Medieval Society, Power, Discipline, and Resistance in Languedoc*, Ithaca, NY, and London, 1997.

Glycas, Michael, *Annales*, ed. I. Bekker, *CSHB*, 1836.

Gnoli, G., *Zoroaster's Time and Homeland: A Study on the Origins of Mazdaism and Related Problems*, Naples, 1980.

—*De Zoroastre à Mani, Quatre leçons au Collège de France*, Paris, 1985.

Gokey, F. X., *The Terminology for the Devil and Evil Spirits in the Apostolic Fathers*, Washington, D. C., 1961.

Gonda, J., *The Vedic God Mithra*, Leiden, 1972.

Good, D. J., *Reconstructing the Tradition of Sophia in Gnostic Literature*, Atlanta, 1987.

Gordon, R., 'The sacred geography of a *mithraeum*; the example of Sette Sfere', *JMS 1*, 2, (1976), pp. 119–65.

—'Ritual, evocation and boundary in the Mysteries of Mithra', *JMS 3*, 1–2 (1980), pp. 19–99.

Gorre, R., *Die ersten Ketzer im 11. Jahrhundert: Religiose Eiferer – Soziale Rebellen*, Constance, 1985.

Gouillard, J., 'L'hérésie dans l'empire byzantin des origines au XIIe siècle', in *T&M*, I (1965), pp. 299–324.

—'Le Synodicon de l'orthodoxie' in *T&M*, vol. 2 (1967), pp. 1–316.

—'Une Source grecque du synodik de Boril', *T&M*, 4 (1970), pp. 361–74.

—'Constantin Chrysomallos sous le masque de Syméon le Nouveau Théologien', *T&M*, 5 (1973), pp. 313–27.

Grant, R. M., *Gnosticism and the Early Christianity*, 2nd edn., New York, 1966.

Gratian, *Decretum*, in *Corpus Iuris Canonici . . . Pars Prior, Decretum Magistri Gratiani*, ed. Ae. Friedberg (Leipzig, 1879).

Grayson, A. K., *Assyrian and Babylonian Chronicles*, Locust Valley, New York, 1975.

Greenfield, R. P. H., *Traditions of Belief in Late Byzantine Demonology*, Amsterdam, 1988.

—'Sorcery and politics at the Byzantine court in the twelfth century: interpretation of history', in R. Beaton and C. Rouche (eds), *The Making of Byzantine History: studies dedicated to D. M. Nicol*, Aldershot, 1993, pp. 73–86.

Grégoire, H., 'Les sources de l'histoire des Pauliciens', *ARB-BL*, 5e serie, 22 (1936), pp. 95–114.

Gregoras, Nicephorus, *Byzantina Historia*, ed. L. Schopen and I. Bekker, 3 vols, *CSHB*, 1829–55.

Gress-Wright, D., 'Bogomilism in Constantinople', *B*, 47 (1977), pp. 163–85.

Griaule, M. and G. Dieterlen, *Le renard pâle*, vol. 1, *Le mythe cosmogonique*, Paris, 1965.

Griffe, J., *Les débuts de l'aventure cathare en Languedoc (1140–1190)*, Paris, 1969.

—*Les Cathares et l'Inquisition (1229–1329)*, Paris, 1980.

Griffiths, J. G., *The Conflict of Horus and Seth*, Liverpool, 1960.

—*The Origins of Osiris and his Cult*, Leiden, 1980.

Gruenwald, I., *Apocalyptic and Merkavah Mysticism*, Leiden, 1980.

Gruenwald, I., S. Shaked, and G. A. G. Stroumsa (eds), *Messiah and Christos*, Tübingen, 1992.

Grundmann, H., *Religiöse Bewegungen*, Hildesheim, 1935; 2nd edn, 1961.

Guha, A. (ed.), *Central Asia: Movement of Peoples and Ideas from Times Prehistoric to Modern*, New York, 1970.

Gumilev, L., *Searches for an Imaginary Kingdom: The Legend of the Kingdom of Prester John*, Cambridge, 1987.

Guthrie, W. K. C., *The Greeks and Their Gods*, London, 1950.

— *Orpheus and Greek Religion*, 2nd edn, London, 1952.

Gyuzelev, V., *Kniaz Boris Pŭrvi*, Sofia, 1969.

Hahn, C. U., *Geschichte der Ketzer im Mittelalter*, 2 vols, Stuttgart, 1847.

Hallpike, C. P., *The Foundation of Primitive Thought*, Oxford, 1979.

Hamilton, B., *The Medieval Inquisition*, New York, 1981.

— *Religion in the Medieval West*, London and New York, 1986.

— *Crusaders, Cathars and the Holy Places*, Ashgate, 2000.

Hamilton, J., *Les Ouïghours du ix⁰–x⁰ siècle de Touen-houang*, 2 vols, Paris, 1986.

Hansen, J., *Quellen und Untersuchungen zur Geschichte des Hexenwahns und der Hexenverfolgung*, Bonn, 1901.

Hanson, P. D., *The Dawn of Apocalyptic*, Philadelphia, 1975.

Harlow, D. C., *The Greek Apocalypse of Baruch (3 Baruch) in Hellenistic Judaism and Early Christianity*, Leiden, 1996.

Harmatta, J., *Studies in the History and Language of the Sarmatians*, Szeged, 1970.

— (ed.), *Prolegomena to the Sources on the History of Pre-Islamic Central Asia*, Budapest, 1979.

Harnack, A., *Marcion: Das Evangelium vom fremden Gott*, 2nd edn, Leipzig, 1924.

Harris, J. R., *The Cult of the Heavenly Twins*, Cambridge, 1906.

Hasking, S., *Mary Magdalene: Myth and Metaphor*, New York and London, 1993.

Haug, H., *Teufelsglaube*, Tübingen, 2nd edn, 1980.

Hauréau, B., *Bernard Délicieux et l'Inquisition albigeoise, 1300–1320*, Paris, 1877; reissued Poret-sur-Garonne, 1992.

Hausherr, I., *Études de spiritualité orientale*, Rome, 1969.

Haussig, H. W., *A History of Byzantine Civilization*, tr. J. Hussey, London, 1971.

Haussig W. and H.-J. Klimkeit (eds), *Synkretismus in den Religionen Zentralasiens, Ergebnisse eines Kolloquiums vom 25 bis 26 mai 1983 in St. Augustin bei Bonn*, Wiesbaden, 1987, pp. 76–90.

Hedrick, C. W. and R. Hodgson (eds), *Nag Hammadi, Gnosticism and Early Christianity*, Peabody, Mass., 1986.

Hegemonius, 'Acta Archelai', ed. C. H. Beeson, in *Die Griechischen Christlichen Schriftsteller der ersten drei Jahrhundert*, vol. 16, Leipzig, 1906.

Hellholm, D. (ed.), *Apocalypticism in the Mediterranean World and the Near East, International Colloquium on Apocalypticism (Uppsala 1979, Proceedings)*, Tübingen, 1983.

Hengel, M., *Judaism and Hellenism*, 2 vols, Philadelphia, 1974.

Henneke, E. and W. Schneemelcher (eds), *New Testament Apocrypha*, 2 vols, Philadelphia, 1963–5.

Henning, W. B., *Zoroaster, Politician or Witch-Doctor?*, Oxford, 1951.

— *Selected Papers*, 2 vols, Teheran and Liège, 1977.

Henrichs, A., 'Mani and the Babylonian Baptists', in *Harvard Studies in Classical Philology*, 77 (1973), pp. 23–59.

Herrmann, G., *The Iranian Revival*, Oxford, 1977.

Hershon, C. P., *Faith and Controversy: The Jews of Medieval Languedoc*, Birmingham, 1998.

Herzfeld, E., *Zoroaster and His World*, 2 vols, Princeton, N.J., 1947.

— *The Persian Empire*, Wiesbaden, 1968.

Heuser, M. and H.-J. Klimkeit, *Studies in Manichaean Literature and Art*, Leiden, 1998.

Hick, J., *Evil and the God of Love*, New York, 1966.

Himmelfarb, M., *Ascent to Heaven in Jewish and Christian Apocalypses*, New York and Oxford, 1993.

Hinnells, J. R., 'Zoroastrian Saviour Imagery and its Influence on the New Testament', *Numen*, 16 (1969), pp. 161–5.

— *Persian Mythology*, London, 1973.

— (ed.), *Mithraic Studies*, 2 vols, Manchester, 1975.

— *Zoroastrianism and the Parsis*, London, 1981; repr. Bombay, 1996.

— (ed.), *Studies in Mithraism*, Rome, 1994.

Hoeven, T. H. van der, *Het imago van Satan*, Leiden, 1998.

Hoffman, M. A., *Egypt before the Pharaohs, The Prehistoric Foundations of Egyptian Civilization*, New York, 1979; 2nd edn, London, 1984.

Hoffmann, R. J., *Marcion: On the Restitution of Christianity*, Chico, Calif., 1984.

Hopkin, C. E., *The Share of Thomas Aquinas in the Growth of Witchcraft Delusion*, Philadelphia, 1940.

Horst, P. W. van der and J. Mansfeld, *An Alexandrian Platonist Against Dualism*, Leiden, 1974.

Hosch, E., *The Balkans*, tr. T. Alexander, New York, 1972.

Humbach, H., *The Gathas of Zarathustra and the Other Old Avestan Texts* (in collaboration with J. Elfenbein and P. O. Skærvø), Parts 1 and 2, Heidelberg, 1991.

Humbach, H. and Ichaporia, P., *The Heritage of Zarathushtra: A New Translation of his Gathas*, Heidelberg, 1994.

Hupchick, D. P., *The Bulgarians in the Seventeenth Century, Slavic Orthodox Society and Culture Under Ottoman Rule*, Jefferson, N. C., and London, 1993.

Huppenbauer, H. W., *Der Mensch zwischen zwei Welten. Der Dualismus der Texte von Qumran (Höhle I) und der Damaskusfragmente. Ein Beitrag zur Vorgeschichte des Evangeliums*, Zurich, 1959.

Huskinson, J. *et al.* (eds), *Image and Mystery in the Roman World. Three Papers Given in Memory of J. Toynbee*, Cambridge, 1988.

Hussey, J. M., *Church and Learning in the Byzantine Empire 867–1185*, London, 1937.

— *The Orthodox Church in Byzantium*, Oxford, 1986.

Hyde, Thomas, *Historia religionis veterum Persarum*, Oxford, 1700.

Idel, M., 'The Evil Thoughts of the Deity', *Tarbiz*, 3–4 (1980), pp. 356–65.

Insler, S., *The Gathas of Zarathustra*, Leiden, 1975.

Iovkov, I., *Pavlikiani i pavlikianski selishta v bŭlgarskite zemi XV–XVIII v.*, Sofia, 1991.

Isidore of Seville, *Isidori Hispalensis Episcopi Etymologiarum*, ed. W. M. Lindsay, 2 vols, Oxford, 1911.

Ivanov, I., *Bogomilski knigi i legendi* [Bogomil Books and Legends], Sofia, 1925 (French tr.: *Livres et légendes bogomiles*, Paris, 1976).

Ivanov, V. V., *Chet i nechet. Asimetriia mozga i znakovykh sistem*, Moscow, 1968.

Ivanov, V. V. and V. N. Toporov, *Issledovaniia v oblasti slavianskikh drevnostei*, Moscow, 1974.

Iversen, E., 'Horapollon and the Egyptian Conception of Eternity', *RSO*, 38, 1963, pp. 177–86.

— *Egyptian and Hermetic Doctrines*, Copenhagen, 1984.

Jackson, A. V. W., *Researches in Manichaeism with Special Reference to the Turfan Fragments*, New York, 1932.

Jacobsen, T., *The Treasures of Darkness*, New Haven and London, 1976.

Jacq, C., *Egyptian Magic*, tr. J. M. Davis, Warminster, 1985.

Jaeger, W., *Aristotle: Fundamentals of the History of His Development*, tr. R. Robinson, 2nd edn, Oxford, 1948.

James, M. R. (tr.), *The Apocryphal New Testament*, Oxford, 1924.

John of Winterthur, *Chronica Iohannis Vitodurani, MGM SS*, new series, vol. 3, ed. F. Baethngen, Berlin, 1955.

Jonas, H., *The Gnostic Religion*, Boston, 1958.

Jones, W. R., 'Political Use of Sorcery in Medieval Europe', *The Historian*, 34 (1972), pp. 670–87.

Juan de Torquemada, *Symbolum pro informatione manichaeorum* (*El Bogomilismo en Bosnia*), ed. N. L. Martines and V. Proano, Burgos, 1958.

Juifs et Judaïsme de Languedoc, CF, 12, Toulouse, 1977.

Jung, L., *Fallen Angels in Jewish, Christian and Mohammedan Literature*, Philadelphia, 1926.

Junker, H., *Die politische Lehre von Memphis, APAW*, Berlin, 1941.

Kakouri, K. J., *Dionysiaka: Aspects of the Popular Thracian Religion of To-day*, Athens, 1965.

Kallimachus and Chrysorrhoe, ed. M. Pichard, *Le romance de Callimaque et de Chrysorhoe*, Paris, 1956.

Kalužniacki, E., *Werke des Patriarchen von Bulgarien Euthymius*, Vienna, 1901.

Kees, H., *Horus und Seth als Götterpaar*, I, II, *MVAG*, 28 and 29, Berlin, 1923–4.

—*Der Götterglaube im alten Aegypten*, Leipzig, 1941.

—*Ancient Egypt, A Cultural Topography*, tr. I. F. D. Modrow, London, 1961.

Kellens, J. and E. Pirart, *Les textes vieil-avestique*, 3 vols, Wiesbaden, 1988–91.

Kelly, H. A., *The Devil, Demonology, and Witchcraft*, New York, 1974.

Kemp, J., *Ancient Egypt: Anatomy of a Civilization*, London, 1989.

Kent, R. G., *Old Persian: Grammar, Texts, Lexicon*, 2nd edn, New Haven, 1953.

Kerenyi, C., *Dionysos: Archetypal Image of Indestructible Life*, tr. R. Mannheim, London, 1976.

Kern, O., *Orphicorum fragmenta*, Berlin, 1922.

Kerschensteiner, J., *Platon und der Orient*, Stuttgart, 1945.

Kieckhefer, R., *Magic in the Middle Ages*, Cambridge, 1989.

Kingsley, P., 'The Greek Origin of the Sixth-Century Dating of Zoroaster', *BSOAS*, 53, 2 (1990), pp. 245–65.

—*Ancient Philosophy, Mystery and Magic: Empedocles and Pythagorean Tradition*, Oxford, 1995.

Klaniczay, G., *The Uses of Supernatural Power*, Cambridge, 1990.

Klein, W., *Die Argumentation in den griechisch-christlichen Antimanichaica*, Wiesbaden, 1991.

Klijn, A. F. and G. J. Reinink, *Patristic Evidence for Jewish-Christian Sects*, Leiden, 1973.

Klima, O., *Manis Zeit und Leben*, Prague, 1962.

Klimkeit, H. J., 'Vairocana und das Lichtkreuz. Manichäische Elemente in der Kunst von Alchi (West Tibet)', *Zentralasiatische Studien*, 13 (1979), pp. 357–98.

—'Hindu deities in Manichaean art', *Zentralasiatische Studien*, 14 (1980), pp. 179–99.

—'Christians, Buddhists and Manichaeans in Central Asia', in *Buddhist-Christian Studies*, 1 (1981), pp. 46–50.

Klimkeit, H.-J. and G. Wiessner (eds), *Manichaean Art and Calligraphy*, Leiden, 1982.

—*Studia Manichaica. II. Internationaler Kongress zum Manichäismus*, Wiesbaden, 1992.

Kluger, R. S., *Satan in the Old Testament*, tr. H. Nagel, Evanston, 1967.

Knibb, M., *The Ethiopic Book of Enoch*, 2 vols, Oxford, 1978.

Koenen, L. and C. Römer (eds) *Der Kölner Mani-Kodex*, Opladen, 1988.

Krause, M. (ed.), *Essays on the Nag Hammadi Texts: In Honour of Pahor Labib*, Leiden, 1975.

Kreyenbroek, P., 'Mithra and Ahreman, Binyāmin and Malak Tāwūs: Traces of an Ancient Myth in the Cosmogonies of two Modern Sects', *Recurrent Patterns in Iranian Religions: From Mazdaism to Sufism*, ed. P. Cignoux, Paris, 1992, pp. 57–79.

—'On Spenta Mainyu's Role in the Zoroastrian Cosmogony', in C. Altman

Bromberg (ed.), *BAI 7: Iranian Studies in Honor of A. D. H. Bivar*, 1993, pp. 97–103.

— 'Mithra and Ahreman in Iranian Cosmogonies', in Hinnels, J. R. (ed.), *Studies in Mithraism*, Rome, 1994, pp. 173–82.

— *Yezidism – its Background, Observances and Textual Tradition*, Lewiston, 1995.

Krstić, D., *Dushan's Code. The XIV Century Code of Serbian Tsar Stephan Dushan*, 2nd edn, Belgrade, 1989.

Kruglikova, I. T. (ed.), *Drevniaia Baktriia*, 2 vols, Moscow, 1976–9.

Krumbachet, K., *Geschichte der byzantinischen Literatur*, 2nd edn, Munich, 1897.

Kuhrt, A. and S. Sherwin-White (eds), *Hellenism in the East*, Berkeley, 1987.

—H. Sancisi-Weerdenburg, *et al.* (eds), *Achaemenid History*, 7 vols, Leiden, 1987–91.

Kuntzmann, R., *Le symbolisme des jumeaux au Proche-Orient ancien*, Paris, 1983.

Kuzhetzova, V. S., 'Dualisticheskie legendi o sotvorenii mira v vostochnosla-vianskoi fol'klornoi traditsii', PhD dissertation, Russian Academy of Science, A. M. Gor'ki Institute of World Literature, Moscow, 1995.

Kvaerne, P., 'Dualism in Tibetan Cosmogonic Myths and the Question of Iranian Influence', in C. I. Beckwith (ed.), *Silver on Lapis, Tibetan Literary Culture and History*, Bloomington, 1987, pp. 163–75.

Kvanvig, H., *Roots of Apocalyptic*, Neukirchen and Vluyn, 1988.

Lacau, P. *Sarcophages antérieurs au nouvel Empire*, Cairo, 1902.

Lambert, M., *Medieval Heresy: Popular Religious Movements from the Gregorian Reform to the Reformation*, 2nd edn, Oxford, 1992.

— *The Cathars*, Oxford and Malden, Mass., 1998.

Landes, R., *Relics, Apocalypse and the Deceits of History, Adémar of Chabannes, 989–1034*, Cambridge, Mass., 1995.

Lang, D. M., *The Bulgarians*, London, 1976.

Lansing, C., *Power and Purity, Cathar Heresy in Medieval Italy*, New York, 1998.

Làszló, K., *Egyptomi és antik csillaghit*, Budapest, 1978.

Laurent, J., *L'Arménie entre Byzance et l'Islam*, Paris, 1919.

Lavrent'evskaia letopis (Die Nestor-Chronik), ed. D. Tschizewskij, Wiesbaden, 1969.

Layton, B., (ed.), *The Rediscovery of Gnosticism: Proceedings of the International conference on Gnosticism at Yale, New Haven, Connecticut (March 28–31, 1978)*, vol. 1, *The School of Valentinus*, Leiden, 1980; vol. 2, *Sethian Gnosticism*, Leiden, 1981.

Le Goff, J, (ed.), *Hérésies et sociétés dans l'Europe pré-industrielle, 11e–18e siècle*, Paris, 1961.

Le Roy Ladurie, E., *Montaillou: village occitan de 1294 à 1324*, Paris, 1978.

Lea, H. C., *A History of the Inquisition of the Middle Ages*, 3 vols, New York and London, 1888.

Leff, G., *Heresy in the Later Middle Ages*, Manchester, 1967.

Léger, J., *Histoire générale des églises évangéliques vaudoises des vallées de Piemon:*

SELECT BIBLIOGRAPHY

Ou Vaudoises, Leiden, 1669.

Legge, F., *Forerunners and Rivals of Christianity*, 2 vols, Cambridge, 1915.

Leitz, C., *Studien zur ägyptischen astronomie*, 2nd edn, Wiesbaden, 1991.

Lemerle, P., 'L'Histoire des Pauliciens d'Asie Mineure d'après les sources grecques', *T&M*, 5 (1973), pp. 1–137.

Levack, B. P., *The Witch-hunt in Early Modern Europe*, London, 1987.

Lévi-Strauss, C., *Le structures élémentaires de la parenté*, Paris, 1949.

—'Les organisations dualistes, existent-elles?', *Bijdragen tot de Taal-Land-en Volkenkunde*, 112 (1956), pp. 99–128.

—*Anthropologie structurale*, Paris, 1958.

—*La pensée sauvage*, Paris, 1962.

Lexa, F., *La magie dans l'Égypte antique, de l'ancien empire jusqu'à l'époque copte*, 3 vols, Paris 1925.

Libistros and Rhodamne, ed. J. A. Lambert, Amsterdam, 1935.

Lichtheim, M. (tr.), *Ancient Egyptian Literature, A Book of Readings*, vol. 1, *The Old and Middle Kingdoms*, Los Angeles, 1973.

Lieu, S. N. C., *The Religion of Light: An Introduction to the History of Manichaeism in China*, Hong Kong, 1979.

—*Manichaeism in the Later Roman Empire and Medieval China*, 2nd rev. edn, Tübingen, 1992.

—*Manichaeism in Mesopotamia and the Roman East*, Leiden, 1994.

Life of St. Leo of Catania, A. A. Longo (ed.), 'La vita di s.Leone vescovo di Catania e gli incantesimi del mago Eliodoro', *Rivista di studi bizantini e neoellenici* 26 (1989), pp. 3–98.

Lindt, P. V., *The Names of Manichaean Mythological Figures, A Comparative Study on Terminology in the Coptic Sources*, Wiesbaden, 1992.

Ling, T., *The Significance of Satan*, London, 1961.

Lintforth, I. M., *The Arts of Orpheus*, Berkeley, 1941.

Lloyd, C. E. R., *Polarity and Analogy: Two Types of Argumentation in Early Greek Thought*, Cambridge, 1966.

Logan, A. H. B. and A. J. M. Wedderburn (eds), *The New Testament and Gnosis, Essays in Honour of R. McL. Wilson*, Edinburgh, 1983.

—*Gnostic Truth and Christian Heresy: A Study in the History of Gnosticism*, Edinburgh, 1996.

Löhr, W. A., *Basilides und seine Schule*, Tübingen, 1996.

Loorits, O., *Grundzüge des estonischen Volksglauben*, Uppsala and Lund, 1949.

Loos, M., *Dualist Heresy in the Middle Ages*, Prague, 1974.

Lossky, V., *The Mystical Theology of the Eastern Church*, Cambridge, 1957.

Lotman, Iu. M. and B. A Uspenskij, *The Semiotics of Russian Culture*, ed. A. Shukman, Ann Arbor, 1984.

Lourdaux, W. and D. Verhelst (eds), *The Concept of Heresy in the Middle Ages*, Leuven and The Hague, 1976.

Luckenbill, D. D., *Ancient Records of Assyria and Babylonia*, 2 vols, Chicago, 1926–7.

Lukonin, V. G., *Drevnii i rannesrednovekovii Iran. Ocherki istorii kul'tury*, Moscow, 1987.

Luttikhuizen, G. P., *The Revelation of Elchasai, Investigation into the Evidence of a Mesopotamian Jewish Apocalypse of the Second Century and its Reception by a Judaeo-Christian Propagandist*, Tübingen, 1985.

McGinn, B., *The Foundation of Mysticism*, New York, 1991.

MacMullen, R., *Enemies of the Roman Order*, Cambridge, Mass., 1966.

Maisell, C. K., *Early Civilizations of the Old World, The Formative Histories of Egypt, the Levant, Mesopotamia, India and China*, London and New York, 1999.

Maisonneuve, H., *Études sur les origines de l'inquisition*, Paris, 1942.

Malandra, W., *An Introduction to Ancient Iranian Religion*, Minneapolis, 1983.

Malinowski, B., *Magic, Science and Religion*, Boston, 1948.

Mandić, D., *Bogomilska crkva bosanskih krstjana*, Chicago, 1962.

Mango, C., *Byzantium: The Empire of New Rome*, London, 1980.

Manselli, R., 'Il manicheismo medievale', *Ricerche religiose*, 20 (1949), pp. 65–94.

— 'Per la storia dell'eresia catara nella Firenze del tempo di Dante', *Bolletino dell'instituto storico italiano per il Medio Evo e archivio Muratoriano*, 62 (1950), pp. 123–38.

— *L'eresia del male*, Naples, 1961.

— *Testi per lo studio della Eresia Catara*, Turin, 1964.

— 'Evangelisme et mythe dans la foi cathare', *Heresis*, 5 (1985), pp. 5–17.

— 'La fin du Catharisme en Italie', *Effacement du Catharisme? (XIIIe-XIVe siècles)*, CF, vol. 20, 1985, pp. 101–18.

Mansi, J. D., *Sacrorum conciliorum nova et amplissima collectio*, 54 vols, reprint of 1901–27 edn, Graz, 1960–1.

Marianu, Fl., *Insectele în limiba credinţele şi obiceiuvile Românilor*, Bucharest, 1903.

Markschies, C., *Valentinus Gnosticus?: Untersuchungen zur valentinianischen Gnosis; mit einem Kommentar zu den Fragmenten Valentins*, Tübingen, 1992.

Marquart, J., *Osteuropäische und ostasiatische Streifzüge*, Leipzig, 1903.

Martene, E. and E. Durand, *Veterum scriptorum et monumentorum historicum, dogmaticarum, moralium amplissima collectio*, 9 vols, Paris, 1724–33.

Martin, E., *A History of the Iconoclastic Controversy*, London, 1930.

Matthew of Paris, *Chronica majora*, ed. H. R. Luard, Rolls Series, no. 57, 7 vols, London, 1872–83.

— *Historia Anglorum*, ed. F. Madden, 3 vols, London, 1868–91.

Maybury-Lewis, D. and U. Almagor (eds), *The Attraction of Opposites: Thought and Society in the Dualistic Mode*, Ann Arbor, 1989.

Mercer, S. A. B., *The Religion of Ancient Egypt*, London, 1949.

Merkelbach, R., *Isisfeste in Griechisch-römischer Zeit*, Meisenheim-am-Glan, 1963.
— *Mithras*, Königstein, 1984.
Merlo, G. G., 'Eretici nel mondo communale italiano', repr. in *Eretici ed eresie medievale*, Bologna, 1989, pp. 233–59.
— (ed.), *Storia ereticale e antiereticale del medioevo*, Torre Pellice, 1997.
Messina, G., *Der Ursprung der Magier und die zarathustrische Religion*, Rome, 1930.
Meyendorff, J., *A Study of Gregory Palamas*, New York, 1964.
— *St Gregory Palamas and Orthodox Spirituality*, New York, 1974.
Meyer, C. H. (ed.), *Fontes historiae religionis slavicae*, Berlin, 1931.
Meyer, E., *Set-Typhon, Eine religionsgeschichtliche Studien*, Leipzig, 1875.
Meyer, M. W. (ed. and tr.), *The 'Mithras Liturgy'*, Missoula, 1976.
Midant-Reynes, B., *The Prehistory of Egypt*, tr. I. Shaw, Oxford, 2000.
Miletich, L., 'Nashite pavlikiani', *SBNU*, 19 (1903), pp. 1–369; 21 (1905), pp. 1–155.
Milik, J. and M. Black, *The Books of Enoch*, Oxford, 1976.
Miller, W., *The Balkans*, New York and London, 1896.
Mills, L. H. (tr.), *Zend Avesta*: Part 3, *The Yasna, Visparad, Afrinagan, Gahs and Miscellaneous Fragments*, SBE, vol. 31, Oxford, 1887, repr. Delhi, 1965.
Minns, E. H., *Scythians and Greeks*, Cambridge, 1913.
Mirecki, P. and J. BeDuhn (eds), *Emerging from Darkness: Studies in the Recovery of Manichaean Sources*, Leiden, 1997.
Mirecki, P. and M. Meyer (eds), *Ancient Magic and Ritual Power*, Leiden, 1995.
Mitchell, C. W. *et al.* (eds), *S. Ephraim's Prose Refutations of Mani, Marcion and Bardaisan*, 2 vols, London, 1912–21.
Molé, M., *Culte, mythe et cosmologie dans l'Iran ancien*, Paris, 1963.
— *La légende de Zoroaster selon les textes pehlevis*, Paris, 1967.
Momigliano, A., *Alien Wisdom*, Cambridge, 1975.
Moneta of Cremona, *Adversus Catharos and Valdenses libri quinque*, ed. T. A. Ricchini, Rome, 1743.
Monumenta Serbica spectantia historiam Serbiae, Bosnae, Ragusii, ed. F. Miklosich, Vienna, 1858.
Moore, R. I., *The Birth of Popular Heresy*, London, 1975.
— *The Origins of European Dissent*, Oxford, 1977; 2nd edn 1985.
— *The Formation of Persecuting Society*, Oxford, 1987.
Morenz, S., *Egyptian Religion*, tr. A. E. Keep, London, 1973.
Morghen, R., *Medioevo cristiano*, Bologna, 1968.
Morray-Jones, C. R. A., 'Merkabah Mysticism and Talmudic Tradition', PhD dissertation, University of Cambridge, 1988.
— 'Transformational Mysticism in the Apocalyptic-Merkabah Tradition', *JJS*, 43/1 (1992) pp. 1–31.

Moulton, J. H., *Early Zoroastrianism*, London, 1913.

— *The Treasure of the Magi*, Oxford, 1917.

Mundy, J. H., *The Repression of Catharism at Toulouse, The Royal Diploma of 1279*, Toulouse, 1985.

— *Men and Women at Toulouse in the Age of the Cathars*, Toronto, 1990.

Munro, R., *Rambles and Studies in Bosnia-Herzegovina and Dalmatia: with an account of the Proceedings of the Congress of Archaelogists and Anthropologists held in Sarajevo, August 1894*, Edinburgh, 1895.

Muratori, L. A., 'Dissertatio LX, Quaenam haereses saeculis rudibus Italiam divexarint,' *Antquitates Italicae Medii Aevi*, Milan, 1741, V, pp. 79–153.

al-Nadim, *The Fihristi of al-Nadim*, tr. B. Dodge, 2 vols, New York, 1970.

Natain, A. K., *The Indo-Greeks*, Oxford, 1957.

Needham, R. (ed.), *Right and Left: Essays on Dual Symbolic Classification*, London, 1973.

— *Symbolic Classification*, Santa Monica, Calif., 1979.

— *Counterpoints*, London, 1987.

Nelli, R., *Le Phénomène cathare*, Paris, 1964.

— (tr.), *Écritures cathares*, Paris, 1968.

— *La Philosophie du catharisme*, Paris, 1975.

Neusner, J. (ed.), *Judaism, Christianity and Other Graeco-Roman Cults: Studies Dedicated to Morton Smith*, Leiden, 1975.

Neusner, J., E. S. Frerichs and P. V. M. Flesher (eds), *Religion, Science and Magic in Concert and in Conflict*, Oxford, 1989.

Newberry, P. E., 'The Set Rebellion of the IInd Dynasty', *Ancient Egypt*, 1922, pp. 40–6.

Nicetas Choniates, *De Manuele Comneno*, in *Historia*, ed. I Bekker, *CSHB*, 1835.

Nicholas Eymeric, *Directorium inquisitorum*, Rome, 1587.

Nicholson, H., *Templars, Hospitallers and Teutonic Knights: Images of the Military Orders, 1128–1291*, Leicester, 1993.

Niel, F., *Montségur: Temple et fortresse des cathares d'Occitanie*, Grenoble, 1967.

Nilsson, M. P., *A History of Greek Religion*, tr. F. J. Fielden, Oxford, 1925.

— 'Early Orphism and Kindred Religious Movements', *HTR*, 28 (1935), pp. 181–230.

— *The Dionysiac Mysteries of the Hellenistic and Roman Age*, Lund, 1957.

Nock, A. D., *Essays on Religion and the Ancient World* (sel. and ed. Z. Stewart), 2 vols, Oxford, 1972.

Nordh, K., *Aspects of Ancient Egyptian Curses and Blessings, Conceptual Background and Transmission*, Uppsala, 1996.

Norelli, E., *et al.* (eds), *Ascensio Isaiae: Commentarius*, Turnhout, 1995.

— *Ascensio Isaiae: Textus*, Turnhout, 1995.

Nyberg, H. S., *Die Religionen des alten Iran*, tr. H. Schaeder, Leipzig, 1938.

Oates, J., *Babylon*, London, rev. edn, 1986.

Obolensky, D., *The Bogomils: A Study in Balkan Neo-Manichaeism*, Cambridge, 1948.

— *The Byzantine Commonwealth: Eastern Europe 500–1453*, London, 1971.

Odeberg, H., *3 Enoch or the Hebrew Book of Enoch*, New York, 1973.

Oeder, J. L., *Dissertatio inauguralis prodromum historiae Bogomilorum criticae exhibens*, Gottingae, 1734.

Oinas, F. J., 'Heretics as Vampires and Demons in Russia', in *Essays on Russian Folklore and Mythology*, Columbus, Ohio, 1985, pp. 121–30.

Olmstead, A. T., *History of the Persian Empire*, Chicago, 1948.

Olschki, L., 'Manichaeism, Buddhism and Christianity in Marco Polo's China', *Zeitschrift der schweizerischen Gesellschaft für Asienkunde*, 5 (1951), pp. 1–21.

Orbe, A., *Estudios valentinianos*, 4 vols, Rome, 1955–61.

Ort, J. van, *Jerusalem and Babylon, a Study into Augustine's 'City of God' and the Sources of his Doctrines of the Two Cities*, Leiden, 1991

Ort, L. J. R., *Mani: A Religio-historical Description of his Personality*, Leiden, 1967.

Osten-Sacken, P. von der, *Gott und Belial: Traditionsgeschichtliche Untersuchungen zum Dualismus in den Texten aus Qumran*, Göttingen, 1969.

Otto, R., *Reich Gottes und Menschensohn*, Munich, 1934.

Otto, W. F., *Dionysos: Mythos und Kultus*, Frankfurt-am-Main, 1933.

Pagels, E., *The Gnostic Gospels*, London and New York, 1979.

— *The Origins of Satan*, New York, 1995.

Pales-Gobilliard, A., *L'Inquisiteur Geoffroy d'Ablis et les cathares du Comté de Foix*, Paris, 1984.

Panaino, A., *Tištrya*, Part 1, *The Avestan Hymn to Sirius*, Rome, 1990; Part 2, *The Iranian Myth of the Star Sirius*, Rome, 1995.

Paolini, L., *L'eresia catara alla fine del duecento*, vol. 1, *L'eresia a Bologna fra XIII e XIV secolo*, Rome, 1975.

— *Eretici del Medioevo: L'albero selvatico*, Bologna, 1989.

Paolini, L. and R. Orioli, *Acta Sancti Officii Bononie ab a. 1291 usque ad 1310*, Rome, 1982.

Pavry, J. D. C. (ed.), *Oriental Studies in Honour of C. E. Pavry*, Oxford, 1933.

Pearson, B. A., *Gnosticism, Judaism, and Egyptian Christianity*, Minneapolis, 1990.

Pedersen, N. E., *Studies in the Sermon on the Great War*, Aarhus, 1993.

Peretto, E., *Movimenti spirituali laicali del medioevo: Tra ortodossia ed eresia*, Rome, 1985.

Perkins, P., *Gnosticism and the New Testament*, Minneapolis, 1993.

Perrin, J., *Histoire des Vaudois et des Albigeois*, Geneva, 1618.

La Pérsecution du Catharisme XIIᵉᵐᵉ–XIVᵉᵐᵉ siècles, Collection Heresis, VI, Arques, 1996.

Peter of Vaux-de-Cernay, *Historia albigensis*, ed. P. Guébin and E. Lyon, *Petri Vallium Sarnii monachi Historia albigensis*, 3 vols, Paris, 1926–39.

Peters, E., *The Magician, the Witch and the Law*, Hassocks, 1978.
— *Inquisition*, New York, 1988.
Petersen, S., '*Zerstört die Werke der Weiblichkeit, Maria Magdalena, Salome und andere Jüngerinnen Jesu in christlich-gnostischen Shriften*, Leiden, 1999.
Petranović, B., *Bogumili, Crkva bosanska i krstjani*, Zadar, 1867.
Pétrement, S., *Le Dualisme dans l'histoire de la philosophie et des religions*, Paris, 1946.
— *Essai sur le dualisme chez Platon, les Gnostiques et les Manichéens*, Paris, 1947.
Petrović, L., *Kršćane bosanske crkve*, Sarajevo, 1953.
Petrović, M. M., *Kudugeri-bogomili u vizantijskim i srpskami izvorima i 'crkva bosanska'*, Belgrade, 1998.
Petrukhin, V. *et al* (eds), *Ot Bytiia k Iskhodu. Otrazhenie bibleiskikh siuzhetov v slavianskoi i evreiskoi narodnoi kul'ture*, Moscow, 1998.
Petrus Higumenos, *Precis*, ed. C. Astruc *et al.*, *T&M*, 4 (1970), pp. 69–97.
Petrus Siculus, *Historia Manichaeorum qui et Paulicani dicuntur*, *PG*, vol. 104, cols. 1239–305; ed. C. Astruc *et al.*, *T&M*, 4 (1970), pp. 3–67.
Pettazzoni, R., *Essays on the History of Religions*, tr. J. H. Rose, Leiden, 1954.
Photius, *Contra Manichaeos*, *PG*, vol. 102, cols 15–265; ed. C. Astruc *et al.*, *T & M*, 4 (1970), pp. 99–183.
Piankoff, A. (tr. and intr.), *Mythological Papyri*, vol. 1, *Texts*, New York, 1957.
Pinch, G., *Magic in Ancient Egypt*, Austin, 1994.
Piotrovskii, B. B. (ed.), *Istoriia narodov severnogo Kavkaza s drevneishikh vremen do kontsa XVIIIv*, Moscow, 1988.
Pisani, V., *Le religioni dei celti e dei Balto-Slavi nell'Europa precristiana*, Milan, 1940.
Pletneva, S. A., *Ot Kochevi k gorodam*, Moscow, 1967.
— *Khazary*, Moscow, 1976.
Pocs, E., *Fairies and Witches at the Boundary of South-Eastern and Central Europe*, Helsinki, 1989.
Polotsky, H. J. (ed. and tr.), *Manichäische Homilien*, Stuttgart, 1934.
Polotsky, H. J. and A. Böhlig (trs and eds), *Kephalaia*, vol. 1, Stuttgart, 1940.
Popruzhenko, M. G. (ed.), *Sinodik tsaria Borila*, Sofia, 1928.
Primov, B. *et al.* (eds), *Dokumenti za katolicheskata deinost v Bŭlgariia prez XVII vek*, Sofia, 1993.
Pritchard, J. B., *Ancient Near Eastern Texts Relating to the Old Testament*, 3rd edn with supplement, Princeton, NJ, 1969.
Pritsak, O., 'The Origin of Rus', An inaugural lecture, Harvard Ukranian Research Institute, Occasional Papers, Cambridge, Mass., 1975.
— 'The Khazars Kingdom's Conversion to Judaism', *Harvard Ukranian Studies*, 2 (1978), pp. 261–81.
— *The Origin of Rus*: vol. 1, *Old Scandinavian Sources other than the Sagas*, Cambridge, Mass., 1981.

Pseudo-Psellus, *Dialogus de daemonum operatione (De Daemonibus)*, *PG*, vol. 122, cols 819–76; ed. P. Gautier, 'Le *De Daemonibus* du Pseudo-Psellus', *REB*, 38 (1980), pp. 105–94.

Puech, H.-C., *Le manichéisme: son fondateur, sa doctrine*, Paris, 1949.

Puech, H.-C. and A. Vaillant (eds and trs), *Le Traité contre les Bogomiles de Cosmas le prêtre*, Paris, 1945.

Quaife, G. P., *Godly Zeal and Furious Rage*, New York, 1987.

Quandt, G., *Orphei Hymni*, Berlin, 1941.

Quispel, G., *Gnosis als Weltreligion*, Zürich, 1951.

— *Gnostic Studies*, 2 vols, Leiden, 1974–5.

Rački, F., *Bogomili i patareni, Borba Juznih Slovena za drzavnu neodvisnost*, Belgrade, 1931, pp. 337–599 (1st edn in the *Rad Jugoslav. Akad. Znanosti i Umjetnosti*, VII, VIII, X, 1869–70).

Radchenko, K., *Religioznoe i literaturnoe dvizhenie v Bolgarii v epokhu pered turetskim zavoevaniem*, Moscow, 1896.

Radermacher, L., *Grechische Quellen zur Faustsage*, Vienna, 1927.

Radin, P., 'The Basic Myths of the North American Indians', *Eranos-Jahrbuch*, Zurich, (17) 1949, pp. 359–419.

— *The Trickster. A Study in American Mythology*, London, 1956.

Raevskii, D. S., *Model mira skifskoi kul'tury: problemy mirovozzreniia iranoiazy-chnykh narodov evraziiskikh stepei I tysiacheletiia do n.e.*, Moscow, 1985.

Rainerius Sacconi, *Summa de Catharis et Pauperibus de Lugduno*, ed. A. Dondaine, in *Un Traité néo-manichéen du XIIIe siècle*, Rome, 1939, pp. 64–78.

Rak, I. V., *Mify drevnego i rannesrednevekovogo Irana*, St Petersburg and Moscow, 1998.

Ralph of Coggeshall, *Radulphi de Coggeshall Chronicon Anglicanum*, ed. J. Stephenson, London, 1875.

Ralph the Bald, *Raoul Glaber: Les cinq livres de ses histoires [900–1044]*, ed. M. Prou, Paris, 1886.

Reeves, J. C., *Jewish Lore in Manichaean Cosmogony*, Cincinnati, 1992.

—(ed.), *Tracing the Threads: Studies in the Vitality of Jewish Pseudepigrapha*, Atlanta, Ga, 1994.

Regino of Prum, *Libri duo de Synodalibus causis et disciplinis Ecclesiasticis*, ed. F. G. A. Wasserschleben, Leipzig, 1840.

Reinach, S., *Antiquités du Bosphore cïmmérien*, Paris, 1892.

— *Cultes, Mythes et Religions*, 2 vols, Paris, 1905–6.

Reitzenstein, R., *Die Vorgeschichte der christlichen Taufe*, Leipzig and Berlin, 1929.

— *Hellenistic Mystery-Religions*, tr. J. Steely, Pittsburgh, 1978.

Reitzenstein, R. and H. H. Schaeder, *Studien zum antiken Syncretismus aus Iran und Griechenland*, Leipzig and Berlin, 1926.

Revard, S. P., *The War in Heaven: Paradise Lost and the Tradition of Satan's Rebellion*, New York, 1980.

Rhalles, G. and M. Potles (eds), *Syntagma ton theion kai hieron kanonon*, Athens, 1852–9.

Rhie, M. M., *Early Buddhist Art of China and Central Asia*, vol. 1, Leiden, 1999.

Rice, M., *Egypt's Making*, London and New York, 1990.

—*Egypt's Legacy: The Archetypes of Western Civilization 3000–30BC*, London, 1997.

Richter, S. G., *Die Aufstiegspsalmen des Herakleides: Untersuchungen zum Seelenaufstieg und zur Seelenmesse bei den Manichäern*, Wiesbaden, 1997.

Ricoeur, P., *The Symbolism of Evil*, Boston, 1967.

Ries, J. (ed.), *Gnosticisme et monde hellénistique*, Louvain, 1982.

—*Les études manichéennes. Des controverses de la Réforme aux découvertes du XXe siècle*, Louvaine-la-Neuve, 1988.

Rigo, A., *Monasi esicasti e monasi bogomili*, Florence, 1989.

—'Messalianismo=Bogomilismo: un equazione dell'ereseologia medievale bizantina', *OCP*, 56 (1990), pp. 53–82.

—'Il processo del Bogomilo Basilio (1099 ca.): una riconsiderazione', *OCP*, 58 (1992), pp. 185–212.

—*Eretici, dissidenti, musulmani ed ebrei a Bisanzio, Una raccolta eresiologica del xii secolo*, Venice, 1993.

—'Il patriarca Germano II (1223–1240) e i Bogomili', *REB*, 51 (1993), pp. 91–110.

Ritner, R. B., *The Mechanics of Ancient Egyptian Magical Practice*, Chicago, 1993.

Robert of Auxerre, *Roberti canonici S. Mariani Autissiodorensis Chronicon*, ed. O. Holder-Egger, *MGH SS*, vol. 26, pp. 219–87.

Robinson, J. T. *et al.* (eds), *The Nag Hammadi Library*, Leiden, 1973.

—(ed.), *The Nag Hammadi Library in English*, Leiden, 1977, 4th edn, Leiden, 1996.

Roche, D., *Études manichéennes et cathares*, Arques, 1952.

Rohde, E., *Psyche: The Cult of Souls and Belief in Immortality among the Greeks*, tr. (from the 8th edn) W. B. Hillis, London, 1925.

Romaios, C. A., *Cultes populaires de la Thrace*, Athens, 1949.

Roquebert, M., *L'Épopée cathare, I. 1198–1212: L 'invasion. II. 1213–1216 Muret ou la dépossession. III. 1216–1229. Le lys et la croix. IV. Mourir á Montségur*, Toulouse, 1971–89.

Rose, E., *Die Manichäische Christologie*, Wiesbaden, 1979.

Rosenfield, J. M., *The Dynastic Art of the Kushans*, Berkeley, 1967.

Rostovtzeff, M. I., *Iranians and Greeks in South Russia*, Oxford, 1922.

—*Skifia i Bospor*, Leningrad, 1925.

Rottenwöhrer, Gerhard, *Der Katharismus*, Bad Honnef, 1982–93. Bd. I, vol. 1, *Quellen zum Katharismus*, vol. 2, *Anmerkungen*, Bad Honnef, 1982; Bd. II, *Der Kult, die Religiöse Praxis, die Kritik am Kult und Sakramenten der Katholischen Kirche*, vol. 1, *Der Kult*, vol. 2, *Die Religiöse Praxis, die Kritik am Kult und Sakramenten der Katholischen Kirche*, Bad Honnef, 1982; Bd. III, *Die Herkunft der Katharer nach Theologie und Geschichte*, Bad Honnef, 1990; Bd. IV, *Glaube und Theologie der Katharer*, 3 vols, 1993.

Rousseau, H., *Le Dieu du mal*, Paris, 1963.

Rubinkiewicz, R., *L'Apocalypse d'Abraham*, Lublin, 1987.

Rudolph, K., *Die Mandäer I*, *Prolegomena: das Mandäerproblem*; II, *Der Kult*, Göttingen, 1960–1.

— *Gnosis*, ed. and tr. R. McL. Wilson, Edinburgh, 1983.

— *Gnosis und spätantike Religionsgeschichte*, Leiden, 1996.

Runciman, S., *A History of the First Bulgarian Empire*, London, 1930.

— *The Medieval Manichee: A Study of the Christian Dualist Heresy*, Cambridge, 1946.

— *The Eastern Schism*, London, 1955.

Russell, D. S., *The Method and Message of Jewish Apocalyptic*, Philadelphia, 1964.

Russell, J. B., *Dissent and Reform in the Early Middle Ages*, Berkeley, 1965.

— *The Devil: Perceptions of Evil from Antiquity to Primitive Christianity*, New York, 1977.

— *Satan: The Early Christian Tradition*, New York, 1981.

— *Lucifer: The Devil in the Middle Ages*, New York, 1985.

— *Dissent and Order in the Middle Ages. The Search for Legitimate Authority*, New York, 1994.

Russell, J. R., *Zoroastrianism in Armenia*, Harvard Iranian Series v, Cambridge, Mass., 1987.

Ryan, W. F., 'Witchcraft Hysteria in Early Modern Europe: Was Russia an Exception?', *SEER*, 76, 1 (1998), pp. 1–36.

— *The Bathhouse at Midnight, Magic in Russia*, Stroud, 1999.

Ryazanovskii, T. A., *Demolonolgiiya v drevnerusskoi literature*, Moscow, 1915.

St Bernard of Clairvaux, *Epistolae*, 241, 242, *PL*, vol. 182, cols 434–7.

— *Sermones super Cantica canticorum*, in J. Leclercq, C. H. Talbot and H. M. Rochais (eds), *Sancti Bernardi Opera*, 2 vols, Rome, 1957–8.

Sanjek, F., *Les Chrétiens bosniaques et le mouvement cathare XIIeme – XVeme siècles*, Paris, 1976.

Santos Otero, A. de, *Die handschriftliche Überlieferung der altslavischen Apocryphen*, 2 vols, Berlin and New York, 1978–81.

Scharff, A., *Die Ausbreitung des Osiriskultes in der Frühzeit und während des Alten Reiches*, *SBAW*, Munich, 1947.

Schlerath, B. (ed.), *Zarathustra: Wege der Forschung*, Darmstadt, 1970.

Schmidt, C., *Histoire et doctrine de la secte des Cathares on Albigeois*, 2 vols, Paris and Geneva, 1849.

Schmidt, W., *Der Ursprung der Gottesidee*, 12 vols, Münster, 1929–55.

Schmidt-Glintzer, H., *Chinesische Manichaica, Mit textcritischen Anmerkungen und einem Glossar*, Wiesbaden, 1987.

Schmithals, W., *Neues Testament und Gnosis*, Darmstadt, 1984.

Schmitz-Vackenberg, G., *Grundlehren katharischer Sekten des 13. Jahrhunderts*,

Eine theologische Untersuchung mit besonderer Berücksichtigung von 'Adversus Catharos et Valdenses' des Moneta von Cremona, Munich, 1971.

Scholem, G., *Jewish Gnosticism, Merkabah Mysticism and Talmudic Tradition*, New York, 1960.

— *Major Trends in Jewish Mysticism*, 3rd edn, New York, 1961.

— *The Messianic Idea in Judaism*, London, 1971.

— *Origins of the Kabbalah*, tr. A. Arkush, Princeton, N.J., 1987.

Schott, S., *Mythe und Mythenbildung im alten Ägypten, UGÄ*, 5, Leipzig, 1945.

— *Bemerkungen zum ägyptischen Pyramidenkult, BÄBA*, 5, Cairo, 1950.

Schwartz, M., 'Coded Sound Patterns, Acrostics, and Anagrams in Zoroaster's Oral Poetry', in R. Schmitt and P. O. Skiærvø, *Studia Grammatica Iranica: Festschrift für Helmut Humbach*, Munich, 1986, pp. 327–93.

Scylitzes, Joannes, *Synopsis historiarum*, ed. H. Thurn, Berlin and New York, 1973.

Sedlar, J. W., *India and the Greek World*, Totowa, N.J., 1980.

Segal, A., *Two Powers in Heaven*, Leiden, 1977.

Sethe, K., *Amun und die acht Urgötter von Hermopolis, Eine Untersuchung über Ursprung und Wesen des ägyptischen Götterkönigs, APAW*, 4, Berlin, 1929.

— *Urgeschichte und älteste Religion der Ägypter*, Leipzig, 1930.

— *Übersetzung und komentar zu den altägyptischen pyramidentexten*, Glükstadt and Hamburg, 4 vols, 1935–39.

Severin, M., *Le dossier baptismal séthien: Etudes sur la sacramentaire gnostique*, Québec, 1986.

Shafer, B. E. (ed.), *Religion in Ancient Egypt: Gods, Myths and Personal Practice*, London, 1991.

Shaked, S., 'Esoteric Trends in Zoroastrianism', *The Israel Academy of Sciences and Humanities, Proceedings*, (Jerusalem), 3 : 7 (1969), pp. 175–221.

— 'Qumran and Iran: further considerations', *IOS*, 2 (1972), pp. 433–46.

— (tr.), *The Wisdom of the Sasanian Sages (Denkard VI)*, Boulder, Colorado, 1979.

— (ed.), *Irano-Judaica*, 2 vols, Jerusalem, 1982–90.

— *Dualism in Transformation: Varieties of Religion in Sasanian Iran*, London, 1994.

— *From Zoroastrian Iran to Islam*, Aldershot, 1995.

Sharenkoff, V. N., *A Study of Manichaeism in Bulgaria with Special Reference to the Bogomils*, New York, 1927.

Sharf, A., *Byzantine Jewry*, London, 1971.

Sharpe, E. and J. Hinnells (eds), *Man and His Salvation: Studies in Memory of S. G. F. Brandon*, Manchester, 1973.

Sinor, D., *Introduction à l'étude de l'Eurasie Centrale*, Wiesbaden, 1963.

— *Inner Asia and its Contacts with Medieval Europe*, London, 1977.

— (ed.), *The Cambridge History of Early Inner Asia*, Cambridge, 1990.

Smirnov, K. F., *Savromaty*, Moscow, 1964.

Smith, C. E., *Innocent III: Church Defender*, Baton Rouge, 1951.

Smith, J., *Map is not Territory. Studies in the History of Religions*, Leiden, 1978.

Smith, S., *Babylonian Historical Texts Relating to the Capture and Downfall of Babylon*, London, 1924.

—*Isaiah Chapters XL–LV: Literary Criticism and History*, London, 1944.

Söderberg, H., *La Religion des Cathares: Étude sur le gnosticisme de la basse antiquité et du moyen âge*, Uppsala, 1949.

Sokolov, M., *Materialy i zametki po starinnoi slavianskoi literature*, 1, Moscow, 1888.

—*Slavianskaia kniga Enokha pravednago*, Moscow, 1910.

Spencer, A. J., *Early Egypt. The Rise of Civilization in the Nile Valley*, London, 1993.

Spiedel, M. P., *Mithras-Orion: Greek Hero and Roman Army God*, Leiden, 1980.

Spinka, M., *A History of Christianity in the Balkans*, Chicago, 1933.

Sponberg, A. and H. Hardacre (eds), *Maitreya, the Future Buddha*, Cambridge, 1988.

Staats, R., *Gregor von Nysa und die Messalianer*, Berlin, 1968.

Starr, J., 'An Eastern Christian Sect: The Athinganoi', *HTR*, 2 (1936), pp. 93–106.

Staviskii, B., *La Bactriane sous les Kushans*, tr. P. Bernard, M. Burda, F. Grenet and P. Leriche, Paris, 1986.

Stein, R. A., *Tibetan Civilization*, tr. J. E. S. Driver, London, 1972.

Stevenson, J., *A New Eusebius*, London, 1968.

Stock, B., *The Implications of Literacy: Language and Models of Interpretation in the Eleventh and Twelfth Centuries*, Princeton, NJ, 1983.

Stone, M. E. (ed.), *Jewish Writing of the Second Temple Period*, Philadelphia, 1984.

Stoodt, H. C., *Katharismus in Untergrund, Die Reorganisation durch Petrus Auterii*, Tübingen, 1996.

Strayer, J. R., *The Albigensian Crusade*, New York, 1971.

Stroumsa, G. A. G., *Another Seed: Studies in Gnostic Mythology*, Leiden, 1984.

—*Savoir et salut*, Paris, 1992.

—*Hidden Wisdom: Esoteric Traditions and the Roots of Christian Mysticism*, Leiden, 1996.

Stroumsa, G. A. G. and A. Kofsky, *Sharing the Sacred: Religious Contacts and Conflicts in the Holy Land. First-Fifteenth Centuries CE*, Jerusalem, 1998.

Stuckenbruck, L. T., *The Book of Giants from Qumran, Text, Translation, and Commentary*, Tübingen, 1997.

Sulimirski, T., *The Sarmatians*, London, 1970.

Sumpton, J., *The Albigensian Crusade*, London, 1978.

Sunderman, W., *Mittelpersische und parthische kosmogonische und Parabeltexte der Manichäer*, Berlin, 1973.

—*Mitteliranische manichäische Texte kirchengeschichtlichen Inhalts*, Berlin, 1981.

Suzuki, B. L., *Mahayana Buddhism*, 4th edn, London, 1981.

Symeon of Thessalonica, *Symeonis Thessalonicensis archiepiscopi, Adversus omnes haeresis*, *PG*, vol. 155, cols 33–176.

Tacheva-Hitova, M., *The Oriental Cults in Moesia Inferior and Thracia*, Leiden, 1983.

Tajadod, N., *Mani le Bouddha de Lumière. Catéchisme manichéen chinois*, Paris, 1990.

Tambiah, S. J., *Culture, Thought and Social Action. An Anthropological Perspective*, Cambridge, Mass., 1985.

— *Magic, Science, Religion and the Scope of Rationality*, Cambridge, 1990.

Tardieu, M., *Le Manichèisme*, Paris, 1981.

Tarn, W. W., *The Greeks in Bactria and India*, 2nd edn, Cambridge, 1951.

— *Hellenistic Civilization*, 3rd edn, London, 1952.

Tasis, A. M. A. i, and P. C. i Roca, *Càtars i Catarismea a Catalunya*, Barcelona, 1996.

Tcherikover, V., *Hellenistic Civilization and the Jews*, Philadelphia, 1959.

Teixidor, J., *The Pagan God*, Princeton, NJ, 1977.

Ter Mkrttschian, K., *Die Paulikianer im byzantinischen Kaiserreiche und verwandte ketzerische Erscheinungen in Armenien*, Leipzig, 1893.

Testuz, M., *Les Idées religieuses du livre des Jubilés*, Paris, 1960.

Theiner, A., *Vetera monumenta historica Hungariam sacram illustrantia*, 2 vols, Rome, 1859–60.

— *Vetera monumenta Slavorum Meridionalium historiam illustrantia*, Rome, 1863.

Theophanes, *Chronographia*, ed. C. de Boor, Leipzig, 2 vols, 1883–5.

Theophanes Continuatus, *Chronographia*, ed. I. Bekker, *CSHB*, 1838.

Theophylact Lecapenus, *Epistula*, ed. I. Duichev, 'L'epistola sui Bogomili del patriarca constantinopolitano Teofilatto', *Mélanges E. Tisserant II*, Vatican City, 1964, pp. 89–91.

Thillo, J., *Codex apocryphus Novi Testamenti*, Leipzig, 1832.

Thomas, K., *Religion and the Decline of Magic*, New York, 1971.

Thouzellier, C., *Un Traité cathare inédit du début du XIIIe siècle d'après le 'Liber contra manicheos' de Durand de Huesca*, Louvain, 1961.

— *Catharisme et valdéisme en Languedoc à la fin du XIIe et au début du XIIIe siècle, Politique pontificale-controverses*, rev. edn, Paris, 1969.

— *Hérésie et hérétiques: Vaudois, cathares, patarins, albigeois*, Rome, 1969.

Tikhonravov, N., *Pamiatniki otrechennoi russkoi literatury*, 2 vols, Moscow, 1863.

Todorova, M., *Imagining the Balkans*, New York, 1997.

Tongerloo, A. van and S. Giversen (eds), *Manichaica Selecta. Studies Presented to Prof. J. Ries on the Occasion of his Seventieth Birthday*, Louvain, 1991.

Tongerloo, A. van and J. van Ort, *The Manichaean ΝΟΥΣ, Proceedings of the International Symposium Organized in Louvain from 31 July to 3 August 1991*, Louvain, 1995.

Torchia, N. J., *Creatio ex nihilo and the Theology of St Augustine: the Anti-*

Manichaean Polemic and Beyond, New York, 1999.

Toynbee, A., *A Study of History*, 10 vols, London, 1934–54.

— *Constantine Porphyrogenitus and His World*, London, 1973.

Trachtenberg, J., *The Devil and the Jews*, New Haven, 1943.

Trigger, B. G. *et al.* (eds), *Ancient Egypt: a Social History*, Cambridge, 1983.

Tritton, A., *The Caliphs and their Non-Muslim Subjects*, London, 1930.

Tröger, K.-W. (ed.), *Gnosis und Neues Testament, Studien aus Religionswissenschaft und Theologie*, Berlin, 1973.

— (ed.), *Altes Testament-Frühjudentum-Gnosis, Neues Studien zu Gnosis und Bible*, Berlin, 1980.

Trombey, F. R., *Hellenic Religion and Christianization c. 370–529*, Leiden, 1993.

Tsukhlev, D., *Istoriia na bŭlgarskata tsŭrkva*, vol. 1, Sofia, 1910.

Tucci, G., *The Religions of Tibet*, tr. G. Samuel, London and Berkeley, 1980.

Turberville, A., *Medieval Heresy and the Inquisition*, London, 1920.

Turcan, R., *Mithras Platonicus*, Leiden, 1975.

— *The Cults of the Roman Empire*, tr. A. Nevill, Oxford, 1996.

Turdeanu, E., 'Apocryphes bogomiles et apocryphes pseudo-bogomiles', *RHR*, 138 (1950), 1, pp. 22–52, II 176–218.

— *Apocryphes Slaves et Roumains de l'Ancien Testament*, Leiden, 1981.

Turner, H. J. M., 'St. Symeon the New Theologian and Dualist Heresies – Comparisons and Contrasts', *St. Vladimir's Theological Quarterly*, 32, 4 (1988), pp. 359–66.

— *Symeon the New Theologian and Spiritual Fatherhood*, Leiden, 1990.

Turner, J. D. and A. McGuire (eds), *The Nag Hammadi Library after Fifty Years, Proceedings of the 1995 Society of Biblical Literature Commemoration*, Leiden, 1997.

Ulansey, D., *The Origins of the Mithraic Mysteries, Cosmology and Salvation in the Ancient World*, Oxford, 1989.

Urbach, E. E., *The Sages, Their Concepts and Beliefs*, 2 vols, Jerusalem, 1975.

Ustinova, Y., *The Supreme Gods of the Bosporan Kingdom: Celestial Aphrodite and the Most High God*, Leiden, 1999.

Vaillant, A., *Le Livre des secrets d'Hènoch: Texte slave et traduction français*, Paris, 1952.

Vaklinov, S., *Formirane na staro-bŭlgarskata kultura 6–9 vek*, Sofía, 1977.

Valeev, F. H., *Drevnee i srednevekovoe iskusstvo srednego povolzia*, Joshkar Ola, 1975.

Van Cleve, J. C., *The Emperor Frederick II of Hohenstaufen: Immutator Mundi*, Oxford, 1972.

Vanderkam, J., *Enoch and the Growth of the Apocalyptic Tradition*, Washington, D C., 1984.

Vanderkam, J. and W. Adler (eds), *The Jewish Apocalyptic Heritage in Early Christianity*, Assen, 1996.

Vassiliev, A. V., *Anecdota graeco-byzantina*, Moscow, 1893.

Velde, H. Te, *Seth, God of Confusion*, Leiden, 1967.

Vermaseren, M. J., *Corpus inscriptionum et monumentum religionis mithraice*, 2 vols, The Hague, 1956–60.

—*Mithras the Secret God*, tr. T. and V. Megaw, London and Toronto, 1963.

Vermes, G., *The Dead Sea Scrolls in English*, 3rd edn, Harmondsworth, 1987.

Vicaire, M. H., *Saint Dominic and His Times*, tr. K. Pond, New York, 1965.

Vilinskii, S. G., *Zhitie sv. Vasillia Novago v russkoi literature*, Odessa, 1913.

Volpe, G., *Movimenti religiosi e sette ereticali nella società medievale italiana* (*secoli XI–XIV*), 2nd edn, Florence, 1926.

Wagh, S. L. and P. D. Diehl (eds), *Christendom and its Discontents*, Cambridge, 1996.

Wakefield, W., *Heresy, Crusade and Inquisition in Southern France*, London, 1974.

Wakefield, W. and A. Evans (eds and trs), *Heresies of the High Middle Ages*, New York, 1969.

Walter Map, *De nugis curialium*, ed. M. R. James, Oxford, 1914; rev. edn 1983.

Warner, H. J., *The Albigensian Heresy*, 2 vols, London, 1922–8.

Watterson, B., *The House of Horus at Edfu: Ritual in an Ancient Egyptian Temple*, Stroud, 1998.

West, E. W. (tr.), *The Bundahis, Selections of Zad-sparam, Bahman Yast, and Shayast la-shayast*, in: *Pahlavi Texts*, Part I, *SBE*, vol. 5, Oxford, 1880, repr. Delhi, 1965.

—(tr.), *The Dadistan-i Dinik and the Epistles of Manuskihar*, in: *Pahlavi Texts*, Part 2, *SBE*, vol. 18, Oxford, 1882, repr. Delhi, 1965.

—(tr.), *Dina-i Mainög-i Khirad, Sikand-Gümanik Vigar, Sar Dar*, in: *Pahlavi Texts*, Part 3, *SBE*, vol. 24, Oxford, 1885, repr. Delhi, 1965.

—(tr.), *Dinkard*, Books VIII and IX, in: *Pahlavi Texts*, Part 4, *Contents of the Nasks, SBE*, vol. 37, Oxford, 1892, repr. Delhi, 1965.

—(tr.), *Dinkard*, Books VII and V, *Selections of Zad-sparam* in: *Pahlavi Texts*, Part 5, *Marvels of Zoroastrianism, SBE*, vol. 47, Oxford, 1897, repr. Delhi, 1965.

West, M. L., *Early Greek Philosophy and the Orient*, Oxford, 1971.

— *The Orphic Poems*, Oxford, 1983.

Widengren, G., *The Great Vohu Manu and the Apostle of God, Studies in Iranian and Manichaean Religion*, Uppsala and Leipzig, 1945.

—*Iranisch-Semitische Kulturbegegnung in partischer Zeit*, Cologne and Opladen, 1960.

—*Mani and Manichaeism*, London, 1965.

— *Les Religions de l'Iran*, Paris, 1968.

—(ed.), *Der Manichäismus*, Darmstadt, 1977.

Widengren, G., A. Hultgård and M. Philonenko, *Apocalyptique Iranienne et Dualisme Qoumrânien*, Paris, 1995.

Wiessner, G. (ed.), *Festschrift für Wilhelm Eilers*, Wiesbaden, 1967.

Wikander, G., *Études sur les mystères de Mithras*, Lund, 1950.

Wild, G., *Bogomilen und Katharer in ihrer Symbolik I*, Wiesbaden, 1970.

Wilkinson, T. A. H., *Early Dynastic Egypt*, London and New York, 1999.

William of Auvergne, *Guilelmi Alverni . . . Opera Omnia*, 2 vols, Paris, 1674.

Williams, M. A. (ed.), *Innovation in Religious Traditions*, Berlin, 1992.

— *Rethinking Gnosticism: An Argument for Dismantling a Dubious Category*, Princeton, NJ, 1996.

Wilson, R. McL., *The Gnostic Problem*, London, 1958.

— *Gnosis and the New Testament*, Oxford, 1968.

Winston, D., 'The Iranian Component in the Bible, Apocrypha and Qumran: A Review of the Evidence', *HR*, 5 (1966), pp. 183–216.

Wislocki, H., *Märchen und Sagen Transsylvanische Zigeuner*, Berlin, 1892.

Witt, R. E., *Isis in the Greco-Roman World*, London, 1971.

Wolf, J., *Historia Bogomilorum*, Vitembergae, 1712.

Wolff, Christian, *Psychologia rationalis*, Frankfurt, 1734.

Worp, K. A. (ed.), *Greek Papyri from Kellis, I*, Oxford, 1995.

Woschitz, K. M. *et al.*, *Das manichäische Urdrama des Lichtes*, Vienna, 1989.

Yadin, Y., *The Scroll of the War of the Sons of Light against the Sons of Darkness*, Oxford, 1962.

Yamauchi, E., *Pre-Christian Gnosticism*, London, 1973.

Yates, F., *Giordano Bruno and the Hermetic Tradition*, London, 1978.

Zaba, Z., *L'orientation astronomique dans l'ancienne Égypte et la précession de l'axe du monde*, Prague, 1953.

Zaehner, R. C., *Zurvan: A Zoroastrian Dilemma*, Oxford, 1955.

— *Teachings of the Magi*, London, 1956.

— *The Dawn and Twilight of Zoroastrianism*, London, 1961.

Zakonik Stefana Dushana, cara Srpskog, ed. S. Novaković, Belgrade, 1898.

Zanella, G., 'L'eresia catara fra XIII e XIV secolo: in margine al disagio di una storigrafia', *BISIAM*, 88 (1979), pp. 239–58.

— *Itinerari ereticali: patari e catari tra Rimini e Verona*, Rome, 1986.

— *Hereticalia: Temi e discussioni*, Spoleto, 1995.

Zhukovskaia, N. L., *Lamaism i rannie formy religii*, Moscow, 1977.

Zieme, P., *Manichäisch-türkische Texte*, Berlin, 1975.

Zigabenus, Euthymius, *Panoplia Dogmatica*, *PG*, vol. 130; vol. 131, cols 39–48.

— *De haeresi Bogomilorum narratio*, ed. G. Ficker, *Die Phundagiagiten*, Leipzig, 1908, pp. 89–111.

Zlatarski, V. (ed.), *Zhtite i zhizn prepodobnago otsa nashego Teodosiia*, Sofia, 1904.

Zolotarev, A. M., *Perezhitki totemizma v narodov Sibiri*, Moscow, 1934.

— *Rodovoi stroi i pervobytnaia mifologiia*, Moscow, 1964.

Zonaras, Ioannes, *Annales Epitome Historiarum*, ed. M. Pinder, T. Büttner-Wobst, 3 vols, *CSHB*, 1841–1897.

Zotović, L., *Mitraizam na tlu Jugoslavije*, Belgrade, 1973.

Index

Aaron, brother of Samuel, 167
Aaronids, 168
Abakan Tartars, 132–3
Abbasids, 115, 126, 156
Abd ar-Rahman III, Caliph of
  Cordoba, 155
Abel, son of Adam, 88, 89, 91, 94, 110,
  267
Abraham, 60, 91, 94, 110, 156
Abrasax, 91
Achaemenids, Achaemenid Empire,
  18, 35–9, 43–4, 45, 49, 50, 54–5, 64,
  65, 66, 70, 77, 97
Adam, 41, 60, 88–9, 94, 110, 124, 156,
  171, 266–7, 271, 285
Adamas, 92
Adonis, 74
Adoptionists, 127
Adriannopolis, 202
Aeschylus, 30, 32
Aetna, 19
Agave, 31, 70
Agen, 190, 196, 200, 212, 214, 215
Agobard of Lyons, 282
Ahab, 57
Ahriman, 26, 33–4, 38–43, 58, 63, 65,
  74, 78, 80, 81–2, 96, 100–1, 108,
  163, 273, 281; see also Angra Mainyu
Ahura Mazda, 24–5, 26–7, 28, 34, 36,
  37, 38–9, 71, 77, 97, 126; see also
  Ohrmazd

ahuras, 23, 24
Aimery, Arnold, 205, 207
Aion, 81
Akhenaten, 6
Akkad, 50
Alan de Lille, 234
Alans, 67, 140, 141, 142
Albanenses, 199, 276; see also
  Desenzano
Albania, 167
Albania, Caucasian, 100
Albi, 190, 192, 194, 195, 196, 215, 219
Albigensian Crusade, 200, 203,
  204–9, 217, 292
Albigensians, 192, 199–200, 277–8; see
  also Cathars
Alexander IV, Pope, 237
Alexander V, Pope, 238
Alexander the Great, 21, 36, 64, 65–6,
  76, 97, 156
Alexandria, 147
Alexius I Comnenus, Emperor, 174,
  176–9, 204, 244, 264
Alfred the Great, 157
Alphonse of Poitiers, 218
Altai, 134, 139; Altaian Turkic
  cosmogonic legends, 134
Amaury de Montfort, 207–8
Amesha Spentas, 24–5
Amestris, 37
Ammianus Marcellinus, 97

Ephesus, Council of (431), 99
Epiphanius, 88, 89, 103, 121
Epirus, 202
Ereshkigal, 42
Erlik Khan, 134, 135
Ermessinda, 215
Esagila, 35–6, 48, 50
Esaldaios, 92
Esau, 83, 89
Esclarmonda, 192
Euchites, 162, 172–3, 229–30, 232,
    246, 247; *see also* Massalians
Eudemus of Rhodes, 42
Eugenius IV, Pope, 238
Euphrates, river, 71, 151, 154
Eurasia, 71, 139–40; 'Eurasian
    dualism', 138
Euripides, 30, 71
Eusebius, 20, 122
Eustratius of Nicaea, 174
Euthymius, Patriarch, 232
Euthymius of Peribleptos (Acmonia),
    169–71, 172, 177, 178, 243–5
Euthymius Zigabenus, 178, 244–5,
    259, 260, 263, 284
Evans, Arthur, 256, 289, 290, 291
Eve, 41, 60, 88, 91, 92, 110, 266–7,
    271, 277
Ezekiel, 276

Faivre, A., 292–3
Fars, 126
Fathers of the Church, 85, 86, 169
Fatima, 156
Fatimids, 156, 157, 167
Ficino, Marsilio, 22
Finno-Ugrians, 132–3, 139–40, 141
Foix, 213, 219
France, 183–9, 190–3, 205–9, 210–16,
    220
Franciscans, 224, 227, 232, 236

Franks, 144, 145, 152, 155, 157
Frederick I Barbarossa, Emperor, 194,
    236
Frederick II, Emperor, 210, 211,
    212–13, 214, 219–20, 236, 237
Frederico III, King of Sicily, 221
Freemasonry, 75
Fukien, 117, 118, 119

Gabriel, archangel, 55
Gabriel-Radomir, Tsar of Bulgaria,
    167, 168
Gandhara, 73
Gaul, 144, 145
Gayomart, 40
Geb, 9
Gennadius Scholarius, Patriarch of
    Constantinople, 250, 253
Genoa, 190
George the Athonite, St, 242
Georgia, 99, 106
Geralda of Lavaur, 206
Gerbert of Aurillac, *see* Sylvester II,
    Pope
Germanus II, Patriarch of
    Constantinople (at Nicaea), 216,
    248
Germany, 191, 210
Getae, 28
Ghibellines, 219–20
Gilgamesh, 79
Glycas, Michael, 181
Gnosticism, 18, 74, 82, 87–95, 102,
    105, 107, 124, 125, 130, 162, 247,
    264, 279, 281
Goethe, Johann Wolfgang von, 288
Goths, 140
Gratian, 235, 237
Great Bear, 12, 14–15, 41
Greece, 20, 28, 31, 34, 35, 37, 43, 65–8,
    130, 167

Philadelphia, 190, 197
Philaster, 121
Philip Augustus, King of France, 204, 207, 208
Philippa, Countess of Foix, 192
Philippopolis, 162, 166, 175
Philistines, 55
Phoenecia, 33, 43
Photius, Patriarch of Constantinople, 239
Phrygia, 76, 86, 121, 150, 168, 241
Phudul, 232
Phundagiagites, 171, 243, 244, 245
Piedmont, 225, 228
Pindar, 29
'Piphli', 190
Piropul, 232
Pistis Sophia, 90, 279
Pius II, Pope, 225
Plato, 18, 21, 22, 31, 33, 80, 176
Platonism, 20, 33, 78, 80
Plotinus, 174
Plutarch, 8, 47, 66, 74–5, 77, 81
Polo, Marco, 118
Pompey, 77
Porphyry, 79, 82
Prajapati, 135, 137
Priscillian, 123
Proclus, 174
Procopius of Caesarea, 115, 130
Provence, 190, 207
Psellus, Michael, 164, 172, 250
Ptah, 9, 20
Ptahil, 124
Ptolemies, 18, 19, 66, 68
Punjab, 36, 67
Pyrenees, 188, 203, 221
Pythagoras, Pythagoreanism, 18, 22, 30, 31, 33

Qarmatians, 156

Qumran sect, 61–3, 272

Rabanus Maurus, 233
Rachel, 285
Rački, F., 207
Raheas, 171
Rainerius Sacchoni, 197, 201, 215, 216, 263
Ralph the Bald, 187
Rameses II, 16–17
Raphael, archangel, 55
Raymond IV, Count of Toulouse, 191
Raymond V, Count of Toulouse, 193
Raymond VI, Count of Toulouse, 192, 193, 204, 205–7, 208
Raymond VII, Count of Toulouse, 207, 210, 211–12, 214, 218
Raymond Aghuiller, 214
Raymond-Roger, Count of Foix, 191, 207
Raymond of Alfaro, 213
Raymond of Pereille, 213, 214
Raymond-Roger Trencavel, Viscount of Béziers, 206
Raymond Trencavel, 208, 209, 211–12, 213
Razés, 209, 212
Re, 6, 14, 16, 20
Reformation, 2
Renan, Ernest, 76
Rhea-Demeter, 30
Rheims, 234
Rhineland, 188, 190, 191
Robert the Bulgar, 210
Robert the Pious, King of France, 185
Roger-Bernard II of Foix, 215
Roger Trencavel II, Viscount of Béziers, 192, 194
Rohde, Erwin, 28
Roman Empire, 70–1, 72, 74–7,